SPANISH
BORDERLANDS
SOURCEBOOKS

Presenting Over Four Hundred and Fifty Scholarly Articles and Source
Materials Documenting Interactions Between Native Americans and
Europeans from California to Florida

Each Volume Edited with an Introduction by a Major Scholar

General Editor
David Hurst Thomas
American Museum of Natural History

A GARLAND SERIES

27

HISPANIC URBAN

PLANNING IN

NORTH AMERICA

Edited with an Introduction by
Daniel J. Garr

GARLAND PUBLISHING, INC.
NEW YORK & LONDON, 1991

Introduction © 1991 Daniel J. Garr

Hispanic urban planning in North America / edited with an introduction by Daniel J. Garr.

p. cm. — (The Spanish borderlands sourcebooks ; 27)

Includes bibliographical references.

ISBN 0-8240-2425-7 (alk. paper)

1. City planning—Southwest, New—History. 2. City planning—Mexican-American Border Region—History. 3. Cities and towns—Southwest, New—History. 4. Cities and towns—Mexican-American Border Region—History. 5. Missions—Southwest, New—History. 6. Missions—Mexican-American Border Region—History. I. Garr, Daniel J. II. Series.

HT167.5.S68H57 1991

307.1'216'0979—dc20
90-22359

Printed on acid-free, 250-year-life paper.
Manufactured in the United States of America

CONTENTS

SOURCES

ALMARÁZ, FÉLIX D., JR.

1987   San Antonio's Old Franciscan Missions: Material Decline and Secular Avarice in the Transition from Hispanic to Mexican Control. *The Americas* 44(1):1–22. Reprinted by permission of the Academy of American Franciscan History.

ARCHIBALD, ROBERT

1976   The Economy of the Alta California Mission, 1803–1821. *Southern California Quarterly* 58(2):227–240. Reprinted by permission of the Historical Society of Southern California.

BOLTON, HERBERT E.

1917   The Mission as a Frontier Institution in the Spanish-American Colonies. *The American Historical Review* 23(1):42–61.

CROUCH, DORA P.

1982   Santa Fe. In *Spanish City Planning in North America*. Dora P. Crouch, Daniel J. Garr, and Axel I. Mundigo. Pp. 69–115. Cambridge, Mass.: The MIT Press. Reprinted by permission.

GARR, DANIEL J.

1972   Planning, Plunder and Politics: The Missions and Indian Pueblos of Hispanic California. *Southern California Quarterly* 54(4):291–312. Reprinted by permission of the Historical Society of Southern California.

1975   A Rare and Desolate Land: Population and Race in Hispanic California. *Western Historical Quarterly* 6(2):133–148. Reprinted by permission of the Western History Association.

1976   A Frontier Settlement: San José de Guadalupe, 1777–1850. *San Jose Studies* 2(3):93–105. Reprinted by permission.

1978   Villa de Branciforte: Innovation and Adaptation on the Frontier. *The Americas* 35(1):95–109. Reprinted by permission of the Academy of American Franciscan History.

1978/79   Power and Priorities: Church-State Boundary Disputes in Spanish California. *California History* 57(4):364–375. Reprinted by permission of the California Historical Society.

1979   Los Angeles and the Challenge of Growth, 1835–1849. *Southern California Quarterly* 61(2):147–158. Reprinted by permission of the Historical Society of Southern California.

1982   Monterey: Planless Capital. In *Spanish City Planning in North America*, Dora P. Crouch, Daniel J. Garr, and Axel I. Mundigo. Pp. 215–236. Cambridge, Mass.: The MIT Press. Reprinted by permission.

KELSEY, HARRY

1987   The Mission Buildings of San Juan Capistrano: A Tentative Chronology. *Southern California Quarterly* 69(1):1–32. Reprinted by permission of the Historical Society of Southern California.

MOORHEAD, MAX L.

1975   The Civilian Settlement. In his *The Presidio: Bastion of the Spanish Borderlands*. Pp. 222–242. Norman: University of Oklahoma Press. Copyright © University of Oklahoma Press. Reprinted by permission.

MUNDIGO, AXEL I. AND ANNA MERCEDES MUNDIGO, TRANSLATORS
1990   *Ordinances for the Discovery, New Settlement and Pacification of the Indies*, issued by Philip II on 13 July 1573. Seville: General Archive of the Indies (Indifferente General, Legajo 427, Libro XXIX). Original translation.

REPS, JOHN W.
1979   Spanish Towns of the Texas Frontier. In his *Cities of the American West: A History of Frontier Urban Planning*. Pp. 57–84. Princeton: Princeton University Press. Reprinted by permission.

SIMMONS, MARC
1969   Settlement Patterns and Village Plans in Colonial New Mexico. *Journal of the West* 8(1):7–21. Reprinted by permission of Sunflower University Press.

1980   Governor Cuervo and the Beginnings of Albuquerque, Another Look. *New Mexico Historical Review* 55(3):189–207. Reprinted by permission.

SPELL, LOTA M., EDITOR AND TRANSLATOR
1962   The Grant and First Survey of the City of San Antonio. *The Southwestern Historical Quarterly* 66(1):73–89. Reprinted by permission of the Texas State Historical Association.

WHITEHEAD, RICHARD S.
1983   Alta California's Four Fortresses. *Southern California Quarterly* 65(1):67–94. Reprinted by permission of the Historical Society of Southern California.

WILLIAMS, JAMES C.
1978   Cultural Tension: The Origins of American Santa Barbara. *Southern California Quarterly* 60(4):349–377. Reprinted by permission of the Historical Society of Southern California.

INTRODUCTION

The Spanish overseas empire was the first of the modern era, unrivaled in its extent until the zenith of British imperialism during the nineteenth century. Despite the vicissitudes of international struggles for dominion in Europe and abroad, for nearly 300 years Spain engaged in the energetic endeavor of colonization, a process spanning three continents and comprehending heroic feats of human endurance. The Spanish Borderlands of North America were the venue for many of these legendary efforts. Extending from Florida to Texas and on both sides of the Mexican border to the Pacific Ocean further north than San Francisco, the Borderlands comprise a vast and heterogeneous terrain more recognizable as modern parlance—Pacific Rim, Oil Patch, Sunbelt—than as historical artifacts such as Gran Quivira, the Cities of Cibola, and the more mundane designation of Provincias Internas.

As remote as they might seem and as timeless as the overland journeys they required, the Borderlands were no mere afterthought of a well-ensconced colonial administration in Mexico City. Within twenty-five years of Hernando Cortés's improbable conquest of the Aztec Empire in 1521 Baja California had been discovered, Cabeza de Vaca had explored much of the territory between Florida and the modern Mexican state of Sinaloa on that nation's northwest coast, an expedition led by Francisco de Coronado reached eastern Kansas and although Hernando de Soto failed to locate the Fountain of Youth, his expedition trekked as far as the Mississippi River. Finally, though not as overtly spectacular a feat, the superb anchorage at San Diego Bay was navigated by Juan Cabrillo. As the seventeenth century dawned, the Rio Grande Valley had been settled, and the founding of Santa Fe, nearly 700 miles from Mexico City, was underway.

Even as these remarkable events were unfolding, the Spanish colonial administration had been churning out legislation designed to regulate uniformly the vast territories and populations who were, consciously or not, subject to its sovereignty. If the period which preceded the reign of Philip II (1556–1598) was characterized by the fabulous exploits of the conquistadors and the aggressive imperialism led by the warrior-king Charles V, then the years following bear the ineradicable stamp of Philip, the consummate bureaucrat, the first "professional ruler" (Elliott 1966:249)

Town planning directives were among the first to emanate from the Spanish court. As early as 1501, instructions for urban site selection were issued and although such criteria were refined over the years, it should not be inferred that colonial city planning legislation arose solely from haphazard experimentation. An ample body of planning literature pre-dates the Spanish Age of Discovery and includes most notably the work of the first-century architect Vitruvius as well as the fifteenth-century Italian, Leone Battista Alberti, best remembered as the author of the first printed book on architecture and as a popularizer of classical Roman aesthetics, which were heartily embraced during the Renaissance (Alberti 1955; Pollio 1960).

Combining both classical theory of urban form and the on-site observations of those who founded towns in the rapidly expanding zones of Spanish settlement were the *Ordenanzas*, the first systematic regulations dealing with town planning. These were promulgated by Philip II in 1573 and are believed to be the work of Juan de Ovando, president of the Council of the Indies from 1569 to 1573 (Manzano 1950 I:229). These *Ordenanzas* may be viewed as a response to the numerous and complex problems posed by Spanish colonization (*Ordenanzas* [1573] 1864–1884:31: 13–25). While prior statutes may have proven adequate to meet the needs of the often simultaneous processes of discovery and conquest, the complex problems posed by the incremental process of colonization demanded far more sophisticated approaches.

During the mid-sixteenth century a great debate raged concerning counterposing solutions to the exigencies of colonization. Addressed by the most illustrious jurists and theologians of the epoch, the central issue was the manner in which Spaniards were to establish themselves in the Americas. The extremes in opposition were the hard-line juridical approach of Juan López de Palacios Rubios and the humanitarian, pro-Indian views of the churchmen, most notably the Dominican friar Bartolomé de las Casas.

The middle ground between these views is set forth in the 1573 *Ordenanzas* wherein neither military force nor exclusive evangelical actions would predominate. Instead, the carefully considered policy of *pacificación* is enunciated so that military force can be utilized if indigenous peoples refuse to cooperate with an evangelical approach. Thus, the *Ordenanzas* circumscribe the founding of new towns with questions of preserving the integrity and inviolability of Native American interests. Nevertheless, while Spanish colonial law was the most humane and well intentioned of all colonial legislation, it was frequently not enforced and even ignored entirely; hence, the well-known *modus operandi* of the colonial official, many hundreds of miles from a higher authority, "obedezco pero no cumplo" (I obey, but I do not comply).

It is logical, then, to begin this volume with the Spanish-English transliterations of these 1573 *Ordenanzas*. They should be viewed within the context of a legislative middle ground between conquest by force of arms on the one hand and the higher and more abstract appeal offered by the missionaries. Of course, no legal system can guarantee perfection in the society to which it applies. But as revealed in the other articles in this collection, the 1573 *Ordenanzas* and their successors made a profound impact on many generations of colonizers over a span of nearly two and a half centuries. Further, once Mexican independence was achieved, Spanish colonial law continued to persist as suggested by this statement found in the preface to an 1829 Mexican edition of a collection of decrees and orders of the 1813 Spanish *Cortes:*

Although the obligation of dependence on Spain is forever broken, these laws which regulate the obligations and rights of those who compose the new community, cannot and ought not to lose their force. . . . Thus, all . . . laws which had emanated from the kings of Spain and the sovereign authority . . . are acknowledged and respected. (Rockwell, I, p. 18)

Since relations between Spaniards and Indians are the essential focal point for the 1573 *Ordenanzas*, let us now proceed to the question of missions as urban communities, for it is there that the interaction of these groups was most intense. This is the case for two reasons. First, the process of evangelization and what the Spanish preferred to think of as "civilization" occurred in that setting. Second, the establishment of urban settlements for Spaniards, presidios and pueblos, occurred in a context that was to be separated from and mutually exclusive of missions. If the mission system were to be successful, it must produce able citizens who could be productively integrated into secular society, thereby increasing population and adding to the pool of useful skills. The readings in this volume's section on missions will explore to what degree the system was successful and how colonial legislation fared in achieving its goal, the separate but parallel prosperity of Native Americans and the adjacent secular society.

Without question, one of the most influential articles ever published on the Spanish Borderlands was written by Herbert E. Bolton in 1917 (this volume). "The Mission as a Frontier Institution in the Spanish-American Colonies" places the mission in its historical and theoretical context. As the replacement for the institution of *encomienda,* the mission emphasized discipline, instruction, agricultural productivity, and evangelization. In order to fulfill these objectives, a fixed place of residence was required as many Indians sought to flee, perhaps an understandable reaction. Under *encomienda*, Indians were "commended" to a Spaniard who, in exchange for their labor and some commodity tribute, would provide them with the material and spiritual necessities of life. Invariably, however, despite the assurance of compliance with which the *encomendero* sought to appease the Crown, it was a short and direct step from *encomienda* to slavery, and the missionary orders were able to seize the initiative to serve the needs of both the state and the Indian, or so they claimed. Additionally, as Spanish influence penetrated further from earlier colonial bases, the duties of the *encomendero* grew more onerous. Not only were the Indians less concentrated in number, but they were more belligerent and would have little to do with whatever enticements a Spaniard were to offer.

Bolton establishes the mission not only as the successor to *encomienda* but also as an urban institution whose status was transitory in spiritual matters but permanent in the civic structure of colonial affairs. This polarity between temporal and spiritual worlds is a crucial observation on Bolton's part, since it epitomizes the uneasy symbiosis between church and state, a prominent theme in the uneasy history of the Borderlands.

Initially, missions operated on funds received from private bequests as well as on support provided by the state. Much of the latter went for stipends for the friars and military escorts from nearby presidios. But given the political ends achieved by the missions such as the establishment of Spanish presence to discourage foreign interlopers, exploration conducted by the missionaries, and the diplomacy engaged in by the missionaries insofar as potentially hostile tribes and European circumnavigators were concerned, their efforts provided a just return to secular interests.

Just what was the physical plant of the mission like? While many may have an image of the facade of the Alamo, the most well known mission vista in Texas, and perhaps in the entire United States, the dimensions of the mission as a working urban-agrarian institution may be less known. Harry Kelsey's (1987 this volume) chronology of the development of structures at Mission San Juan Capistrano is of interest since it shows the incremental growth achieved by missionary and Indian labor and resources over an extended period.

The wealth that mission principals created was the focal point of Bolton's observation of the polarity between church and state concerning the mission system. In the first two decades of the nineteenth century, the wealth amassed by the California missions attracted the envious eyes of their secular neighbors, particularly after 1810 when contact with Mexico was virtually terminated by her struggle for independence. It was at this time that secular interests began to suggest that the already lengthy period of missionary tutelage was sufficient to allow the Indians to govern themselves. Not surprisingly, some suggested that the missionaries were exploiting their economic position at the expense of the Indian souls and that this was being accomplished to the detriment of the California colony. Robert Archibald (1976 this volume) provides insights into this situation which had ominous overtones for the missions' future.

Another manifestation of the church-state polarity with regard to the mission system is discussed in Daniel Garr's (1978–1979 this volume) exploration of colonial legislation as it relates to locational conflicts between civil settlements and missions. Although this examination of colonial law is based on the *Recopilación de Leyes de Los Reynos de las Indias* (1791), a later codification that includes materials from the 1573 *Ordenanzas*, it provides an interesting testing ground for the protection of Native American interests in light of important secular objectives. The issue here is church-state boundary disputes, the rule of law, and whether secular authorities are bound to comply with such rules. The intuitive reader may have already formulated some suspicions on this question.

What is remarkable about these boundary disputes is that each side went to great lengths to support its position with an alacrity that would be admirable in any contemporary courtroom. The first confrontation involved the Mission of Santa Clara (California) and subsequent intrusions by the neighboring pueblo of San José, now better known as the hub of the Silicon Valley. This case established a precedent for the behavior of secular authorities fifteen years later when the Mission of Santa Cruz sought to remedy encroachments by its neighbor, the Villa de Branciforte. In each case, the needs of the state prevailed even though its legal position was by far the weaker of the two. However, considerations of agricultural self-sufficiency for Alta California (San José vs. Santa Clara) and for the defense of the colony (Branciforte vs. Santa Cruz) ultimately gained the upper hand, thus supporting the desire of the colonial official to obey the law without having to comply with it.

If these bouts of litigation foretold an ominous future for California missions, that outcome was already unfolding in Texas, where pressures on the land and on mission wealth were less severe than those that were to ultimately prevail in California. The discussion of mission secularization by Félix D. Almaráz, Jr. (1987 this volume) highlights the pressures and tensions that were nevertheless brought to bear by an impatient secular world. Sadly, the Indians had virtually disappeared from these establishments or had become absorbed into the local *mestizo* subculture, thus providing a grim commentary on the efficacy of the missionary's stewardship. Instead, we have only a description of the physical state of the missions and of the bureaucratic process of land distribution by diligent town councils. This in itself is no small feat, for as Almaráz points out, the alternative would have been "a rampage of malfeasance and destruction."

A similar outcome awaited the secularization of the Franciscan missions in California, albeit without the restraints present in Texas. As a result, the downward spiral in the California missions was a precipitous one, shocking even an inspector dispatched by the United States government in 1852 about fifteen years after secularization took place (Wilson 1952). While this plundering marked a tragic terminus of the history of California's Franciscan missions, much can be learned concerning their status as urban settlements, not only in light of colonial legislation but also in terms of improvements and modifications which colonial officials sought to effect in California. While Daniel Garr (1972 this volume) notes that plunder was the ultimate fate of the missions, some interesting planning concepts and political innovations were also offered by colonial officials in the years before secularization became an issue.

Just as the mission system required the agglomeration of Indians into an urban settlement where labor could be organized and instruction administered in both the temporal and spiritual realms, Spanish colonization legislation also specified compact civilian urban settlements replete with municipal institutions as well as an agrarian orientation to insure self-sustenance. These directives were designed to maintain the collective welfare of the colonizing population, especially with regard to defense. However, as demonstrated by Marc Simmons (1969 this volume) settlement patterns in colonial New Mexico responded to other imperatives. The Spanish administration was resigned to the fact that since there was no mineral wealth to attract large numbers of settlers, it would have to accept an agricultural economy based on land ownership as the glue which held the colony together. Consequently, despite efforts to regulate settlement, an urban pattern of any substance was impossible to achieve, and economic self-sufficiency was an even more elusive goal.

If flexibility dictated by circumstance often compromised legislative goals in the Borderlands, the founding of Albuquerque lends emphasis to this imperative. Again, Marc Simmons (1980 this volume) delves into the New Mexico past to examine the frayed fabric of Borderlands urbanism and finds that doubts had been cast on the veracity of accounts relevant to that city's founding in 1706. When United States jurists scrutinized Albuquerque's legal claim as the descendent of the original eighteenth-century lawful Spanish municipality, missing documentation jeopardized the city's claim to the traditional four square leagues of territory (17.2 square miles) implied in a Spanish municipal grant. Also adversely affected were water rights that Albuquerque claimed as the rightful heir to its Spanish legacy. Simmons concludes that circumstantial evidence underlies Albuquerque's legitimacy, though this rather loose and informal status may be more appropriate in remote and sparsely populated colonial New Mexico than in the labyrinthine scrutiny of pettyfogging American jurisprudence.

Of course, Albuquerque was not the only city to be a courtroom wallflower while Anglo attorneys attempted to waltz with obscure remnants from Spanish archives. In doing so, they cast the initial survey of San Antonio in a most interesting light, not to mention the initial process of the founding and planning of a Spanish colonial settlement. The latter exercise is clearly described in Lota M. Spell's (1962 this volume) translation of an obscure document relating to San Antonio that was discovered in a Guadalajara library. As such, it is an exemplary instance of a process undertaken hundreds of times in the course of three centuries of Spanish colonization in the Americas.

However, in addition to its value as an urban artifact, Spell's contribution solves an intriguing mystery in Borderlands urban history. The riddle involves the discrepancy between the original grid-and-plaza plan of San Antonio which is also familiar as a generic statement of Spanish colonial urban form and the rather perplexing triangular survey of 1731 which is echoed by a rather similar American document of 1852. The reader will recall the church-state boundary disputes between Alta California missions and their adjoining secular towns which were noted above in this essay. In those cases, the needs of the state prevailed despite the compelling legal arguments marshalled by the missionaries. However, in Texas the pressures on urban settlement were not so great nor were the distractions posed by potentially hostile foreign powers. As a result, the expansion of San Antonio acknowledged the rights of a preexisting mission to the east without so much as a grumble, while in California two prolonged legal tussles arose out of identical circumstances but different imperatives.

Although Alta California's pueblo of San José de Guadalupe stood on an infinitely more solid legal foundation than did Albuquerque, their development patterns had much in common. Daniel Garr's (1976 this volume) essay emphasizes the urban versus agrarian tension that accompanied San José's development as California's first civilian settlement. Perhaps a victim of the Spaniards' uncanny ability to choose superb sites for their pueblos, San José progressed far less well as a city than as the seat of a pastoral economy. Similarly, Simmons (1969 this volume) observes that the population of Albuquerque made a weekly pilgrimage to their town, but the majority of their time was spent in the pursuit of their agricultural holdings and livestock. While coastal California and its maritime-oriented presidios became focal points of activity, an inland pueblo such as San José might have more in common with the isolated settlements of New Mexico than with its coastal neighbors, today no more than an hour's drive distant.

While San José was clearly eclipsed by the seat of government and customs house of Monterey, not to mention by the growing world emporium that was to flourish on the west shore of San Francisco Bay, California's other urban-agrarian settlement, Los Angeles, came of age in a far more precocious manner. Without another regional rival, the City of Angels quickly asserted its dominance and by 1830 sought to seize control of the territorial capital from Monterey. This early ignition of the sometimes bitter north-south rivalry in California signaled a sense of urgent municipal enterprise rarely associated with Borderlands urban settlement in the colonial era.

The challenge of growth to which Los Angeles responded in the 1830s and 1840s is a convincing refutation of the oft-encountered disparaging remarks of Anglo sojourners who spared little tolerance in their evaluation of another culture's endeavors. As Daniel Garr (1979 this volume) observes, Los Angeles' civic leaders had much in common with their ambitious contemporaries in frontier towns such as Pittsburgh, Cincinnati, and St. Louis.

Even though Los Angeles entertained great dreams for the future during the first decades of the nineteenth century, the growth and sustenance of most of Spanish and Mexican California was threatened by a serious lack of industrious inhabitants. The problem of how to populate California was dealt with in various ways, some controversial, some rather novel, but all part of a venerable Spanish tradition which is preoccupied with matters of "purity of blood." Such stratification was rendered quite pointless, Daniel Garr (1975 this volume) observes, by the Yankee-led seaborne inundation of California in the 1840s. The newcomers held the caste-conscious Californians in contempt just as they had scorned the despised Indians and others of darker skin who were the product of centuries of Spanish, Afro-American, and Indian miscegenation.

In contrast to the well-ordered world of statute that regulated missions and civilian pueblos, it is surprising that the presidio, a settlement extension of the regimented world of the military, would be without any legislative guidelines to shape its future development. As Max Moorhead (1975 this volume) emphasizes, the expense of maintaining a presidial garrison plus the eternal potential for peace with hostile neighbors limited the presidio to a temporary and transitional function. However, its very existence signaled an opportunity for civilian settlements to develop, and many communities in the Borderlands can trace their origins to this source. Moorhead provides an interesting overview of the emergence of the presidio as a settlement form in the Borderlands.

An opportunity to examine the characteristics of the California presidio is provided by Richard S. Whitehead's (1983 this volume) research. Drawings of these installations both during and subsequent to their military function illustrate their gradual transition to civilian life. However, sometimes this transition occurred all at once. There were settlements that combined the qualities of two or more distinct institutions in order to meet the demands of extraordinary circumstances. In the case of the Villa de Branciforte, the qualities of the civilian pueblo and the presidio were joined in what was a venerable tradition in the Borderlands. Daniel Garr's (1978 this volume) research discusses the innovative aspects of a flexible approach to the role of presidios in California during the 1790s. Although the settlement itself ultimately foundered, its legislative background and relations with the nearby Santa Cruz Mission provide additional insights into presidial urban development.

Because no legislative guidelines were provided for the eventuality of presidial urbanization, considerable confusion arose not only in matters of land use planning for a system of rational streets and legally valid property titles but also in how the transition from military to civilian rule was to be accomplished. The work of James C. Williams (1978 this volume) and Daniel Garr (1982 this volume) with respect to Santa Barbara and Monterey addresses these vexing problems.

The case of Santa Fe is an amalgamation of the above-noted concerns. First, it is described as a presidio with an enclosed quadrangle-type configuration, but at the same time it carried the title of "Villa," though without the detailed legislative pedigrees of Branciforte. This is understandable, for Dora Crouch's (1982 this volume) article stresses the isolation and sparse population resources that one might expect at the time of the founding of this New Mexico town in 1610. Nevertheless, its civilian component and martial bearing render it a hybrid of sorts even though it is measured by the urban standards set forth in the 1573 legislation. Second, the transition to American rule and culture posed many of the same problems encountered in Monterey and Santa Barbara with respect to future urban growth, albeit without the urgency experienced in coastal California.

Finally, the Spanish presence in Texas is discussed by John W. Reps (1979 this volume) whose exhaustive contributions to urban planning history have animated and enlivened the work of countless scholars of the present as well as of future generations. Portraying the Spanish effort in Texas as a century-long chess game, Reps not only chronicles the numerous blocks and parries of Franco-Spanish geopolitics but has also uncovered a remarkable collection of rich and imaginative plans that nearly reached the threshold of permanence.

In conclusion, Spanish colonization in the Borderlands employed three basic forms of urban settlement. Missions and presidios had long served as agents of conquest, pacification, and civilization, while the founding of pueblos was a secondary response to the occupation of this vast and isolated terrain. The circumstances associated with the planning of urban communities in the Borderlands suggest an initial dutiful adherence to colonial legislation that was later compromised by the vast distances separating the region from centers of political authority. However, the return to orderly planning that characterized the late 1840s and early 1850s reflected the integrity of the settlements' original plans in addition to the desire of American authorities to maintain confidence in their municipal institutions and to stimulate economic development. The security of land titles was a basic premise of this attitude.

Even though urban settlements throughout the Borderlands were to be overwhelmed by a largely Yankee group of immigrants, their legal status was tied to their original Spanish pedigree. This is demonstrated by the litigation from Albuquerque and San Antonio noted in this collection. However, these are only two examples of an endless parade of Spanish titles that were later opened to American legal scrutiny.

The abrupt transition in northern California from pastoral Mexican backwater to booming American commercial emporium and mining frontier produced a transformation as dramatic as it was transfiguring. Elsewhere, particularly in New Mexico, it was not sudden death for the Spanish legacy which persisted throughout the rest of the nineteenth century and well into the twentieth. At first the object of scorn, then of nostalgic romanticism, the Hispanic heritage of the Borderlands is today less real than imagined; the gold-seekers, the railroad builders, and the land speculators neglected to give it even a hasty backward glance.

SUGGESTIONS FOR FURTHER READING

There is certainly nothing resembling an abundance of material on Spanish city planning in the Borderlands outside the articles reprinted here and their sources. However, Mattie Alice Austin's "The Municipal Government of San Fernando de Béxar, 1730–1800," *Texas State Historical Association Quarterly* 8 (April 1905), 277–352, complements information on that town's urban development. Similarly, *Spanish Institutions of the Southwest* (Baltimore: John Hopkins, 1891) is a venerable source that is still of relevance.

Two more recent classics that serve well as intellectual gateways to the Borderlands are François Chevaliers's *Land and Society in Colonial Mexico* (Berkeley & Los Angeles: University of California Press, 1963) and Robert Ricard's *The Spiritual Conquest of Mexico* (Berkeley & Los Angeles: University of California Press, 1966). Other works of a general nature that are of value are C. Alan Hutchinson, *Frontier Settlement in Mexican California: The Híjar-Padrés Colony and its Origins, 1769–1835* (New Haven: Yale University Press, 1969); William Carey Jones, *Report on the Subject of Land Titles in California* (Washington, D.C., 1850); Richard Morse, "Latin American Cities: Aspects of Function and Structure," *Comparative Studies in Society and History* 4 (July 1962), 473–493 and the same author's "Some Characteristics of Latin American Urban History," *American Historical Review* 67 (January 1969), 317–338.

Of course, the major cities of Spanish origin in the Borderlands are in California. For Los Angeles, Robert M. Fogelson's *The Fragmented Metropolis: Los Angeles, 1850–1930* (Cambridge, Mass.: Harvard University Press, 1967) has some interesting information for the latter years of the colonial period. For San Francisco, John W. Dwinelle's *The Colonial History of the City of San Francisco*, 3rd ed. (San Francisco, 1866), Bernard Moses's *The Establishment of Municipal Government in San Francisco* (Baltimore: Johns Hopkins, 1889), and Gunther Barth's *Instant Cities: Urbanization and the Rise of San Francisco and Denver* (New York: Oxford University Press, 1975) all are noteworthy.

Other Borderlands cities were of lesser importance during the nineteenth century, but the best study of these secondary centers is Richard F. Pourade's multi-volume *History of San Diego*, 5 vols. (San Diego: San Diego Union, 1960–1965). A volume which is more disappointing than useful, given its title and the concerns of this anthology, is Henry Dobyns' *Spanish Colonial Tucson* (Tucson: University of Arizona Press, 1976). In making note of it, the intention is to suggest that ample opportunity awaits the individual to continue the work of John Reps and others who were inspired by his intellectual alacrity and leadership. There are many more frontiers in Borderlands urban development that remain to be explored.

Daniel J. Garr

REFERENCES

ALBERTI, LEONE BATTISTA
1955   *Ten Books on Architecture*, James Leoni, trans., Joseph Rykwert, ed. London: Alec Tiranti.

ALMARÁZ, FÉLIX D., JR.
1987   San Antonio's Old Franciscan Missions: Material Decline and Secular Avarice in the Transition from Hispanic to Mexican Control. *The Americas* 44:1–22.

ELLIOTT, J.H.
1966   *Imperial Spain, 1469–1716.* New York: Mentor Books.

MANZANO, JUAN MANZANO
1950–1956 *Historia de las Recopilaciones de Indias,* 2 vols. Madrid.

1864–1884 Ordenanzas sobre descubrimento nuevo y poblacion (Segovia, July 13, 1573). *In Colección de documentos inéditos relativos al descubrimento, conquista y organización de las antiguas posesiones españolas de América y Oceania sacados de los Archivos del Reino,* 42 vols. Madrid.

POLLIO, MARCUS VITRUVIUS
1960   *The Ten Books on Architecture,* Morris Hickey Morgan, trans. New York: Dover Books.

Recopilación de leyes de los Reynos de las Indias, 4th ed., 3 vols. Madrid.

ROCKWELL, JOHN A.
1851   *A Compilation of Spanish and Mexican Law in Relation to Mines, and Titles to Real Estate, in Force in California, Texas and New Mexico,* 2 vols. New York.

WILSON, BENJAMIN DAVIS
1952   *The Indians of Southern California in 1852,* John Walton Caughey, ed. San Marino, California: Huntington Library.

LEGISLATIVE FOUNDATIONS OF SPANISH COLONIAL SETTLEMENT

Translation of the *Ordinances for the Discovery, New Settlement and Pacification of the Indies*, issued by Philip II, on 13 July 1573, in the Segovia Woods, based on the original that is kept in the General Archive of the Indies (*Indiferente General, Legajo 427, Libro XXIX*), in Seville, Spain.

Prepared by Axel I. Mundigo, Ph.D.
and Anna Mercedes Mundigo

The order that must be
adhered to in discovery and settlement.

Don Phelipe [Philip II], etc - To the Viceroys, presidents of the Courts [*Audiencias*], and governors of our Indies of the ocean sea, and to all other persons to whom the hereafter mentioned be of interest and appertain in any way, be it known that for the discoveries, new settlements and pacifications of the lands and provinces to be discovered, populated and pacified in the Indies, to be carried out with greater facility and in a manner appropriate to the service of God and of ourselves, and for the wellbeing of the natives, among other things, we have prepared the following ordinances:

1

No person, regardless of state or condition, should on his own authority make a new discovery by sea or land, or enter a new settlement or hamlet in areas already discovered. If he were found without our license and approval or by those who had our power to give it, he would face a death penalty and loss of all his possessions to our coffers. And, we order all our viceroys, courts [*audiencias*], and governors and other justices of the Indies, that they give no license to make new discoveries without previous consultation with us and only after having obtained our permission; but we do consent that in areas already discovered, they can give license to build towns as necessary, adhering to the order that in so doing they must keep to the laws of this book regarding settlements in discovered lands, [and] then they should send us a description.

2

Those who are in charge of governing the Indies, whether spiritually or temporally, should inform themselves diligently whether within their districts, including lands and provinces bordering them, there is something to be discovered and pacified, of the wealth and quality, [and] of the peoples and nations who inhabit there; but do this without sending to them war personnel nor persons who can cause scandal. They [the governors] should inform themselves by the best means available; and likewise, they should obtain information on the persons who are best suited to carry out discoveries - and with those who are best fit for this purpose, they [the governors] should confer and make arrangements, offering them the honors and advantages that justly, without injury to the natives, can be given them - and - before carrying out what has been arranged or has been learned, give narratives to the viceroy and the courts [*audiencias*] and also send them to the Council, which, after looking at the case, will issue a license to proceed with the discovery, which should be carried out in the following order:

3

Having made, within the confines of the province, a discovery by land, pacified it, [and] subjected it to our obedience, find an appropriate site to be settled by Spaniards - if there is a disposition towards it - and if not, it should be of vassal Indians so that they be secure.

4

Setting out from the populated town in the confines [of the province], by way of commerce and trade go with vassal Indians and interpreters to discover those lands, and with churchmen and Spaniards, carrying trade [items] and offerings and peace, try to learn about the place, the contents and quality of the land, the nation(s) to which the people there belong, who governs them, and carefully take note of all you can learn and understand and always send account thereof to the governor so he can send it to the Council [*Consejo de las Indias*].

5

Look carefully at the places and ports where it might be possible to build Spanish settlements without damage to the Indian population.

6

As to discoveries that might be done by sea, the following instructions should be adhered to: He who with our licence or provision, or who by us has been so entrusted, should resolve to go and make a discovery by sea, be obligated to take at least two small ships, caravels or vessels, no larger than sixty tons, that can go far into the sea and follow the coastline, without danger of shoals.

7

That said ships always go in pairs because the one can assist the other, and if one should be in distress, the persons on it can be brought over to the one remaining.

8

In each of the ships of said size, there should be thirty persons, between sailors and discoverers, and no more, so they can be well provisioned, nor less, so they can be well ruled.

9

That in each of said ships go two pilots, if available, and two priests or religious men, so they can be in charge of conversions.

10

That these [ships] bear provisions for at least twelve months from the day they leave, well provided with sails, anchors and cables, and other riggings and tackle necessary for navigation, with a double set of rudders.

11

To trade and barter with the Indians and the people of the territories that they reach, each ship should carry goods of little value, such as scissors, combs, axes and knives, fishing hooks, colored bonnets, mirrors, rattles, glass beads and other items of this nature.

12

The pilots and sailors on said ships should mark the ship's location, and carefully observing the navigational charts, the currents, tides, winds, flood tides and areas that contain fresh water supplies and the time of the year; and with a depth finder in hand make a note of the shoals and reefs they strike below water level; [also] the islands, land masses, rivers, harbors, coves, inlets and bays that they encounter; and in the book that each ship carries log the latitude and points at which these are found, one ship consulting the other - as often as possible and time permitting - so that should differences exist, these be made to agree and the most accurate ascertained, and if not, it should remain as first recorded.

13

Persons who would go on discoveries, whether by land or by sea, should take possession, in our name, of all lands of the provinces [crossed out: "lands that they might discover"], they might reach and, upon setting foot onto land, perform the necessary ceremonies and writs, of which they should bear public evidence and faithful testimony.

14

Once the discoverers arrive at newly discovered provinces or lands, together with the officials, they should name each land, each province, and the mountains and principal rivers they might encounter as well as the settlements and towns they might find or that they may found.

15

They should endeavour to take along some Indians to communicate in the language of the places where they might arrive, from wherever it might seem most appropriate - the same should be done in the provinces that might be discovered while going from one place to another - giving them good treatment and by means of said languages or as best they can, speak with the natives, beginning talks and converse with them, seeking to understand their customs, conditions, and way of life of the people of the land and of their neighbours; obtaining information about their religion, the idols worshipped, what sacrifices and forms of worship, and whether they have a doctrine and form of writing; how they are ruled and governed, if they have kings and whether elected or designated by blood descendance, or if they are governed by commonwealth or by lineage; what taxes and tributes are given or paid or in what manner and to whom; and what things are most precious to them. And what is in the land, and what is brought in that they esteem from other places; if the territory has metals and of what quality; if there are spices or some sort of drugs or aromatic products for which purpose take along samples of our own spices such as pepper, cloves, cinnamon, ginger, nutmeg and other such things, so they can be shown, and ask the natives whether they know them; and likewise find out if there are any precious stones or things of the type valued in our kingdom; and also learn about the nature of domestic and wild animals, the types of trees and plants - cultivated and non-cultivated - that might exist on the land and of their utilization; and finally of all the things comprised under the heading of such descriptions.

16

To inform themselves of the foods and victuals that exist in the territories; and of those of good quality, they should provision themselves for their journeys.

17

If it is observed that the people are gentle and that it would be safe for a man of religion to stay among them - and there should happen to be one so disposed to indoctrinate them and establish peace - he should stay with the promise of returning for him within one year or earlier if possible.

18

The discoverers should not linger in the territory, nor should they in any way or for any reason wait for their provisions to be finished during their voyage, but having used up half of the provisions that they departed with, should return to inform of what they found, discovered and learnt, both of the people that they entered into contact with as well as others from neighbouring territories they might have learnt about.

19

If upon undertaking discoveries by sea, additional ships of a larger size than those prescribed should be included, great care be exercised while skirting the coast to search for a safe harbor in which to leave these larger vessels in safe shelter while the smaller ships and vessels continue along the coast, searching and using depth finders until another safe harbor is found and, from there, return to the larger ships, navigating these through the secure route toward the next harbor and in this manner successively continue moving ahead.

20

The discoverers traveling by land or sea should in no way become entangled in wars or conquests, nor help Indians in fights against others, nor be involved in problems or disputes with the inhabitants of the land, no matter what the cause or reason; nor do them any harm or injury, nor take their property against their will, unless it is in exchange or has been given away in good will.

21

Having completed the discovery and voyage, the discoverers should return to give account to the courts [audiencias] and governors responsible for sending them out.

22

Discoverers going by land or sea should write a chronicle or keep a daily record of everything they encounter, find or happens to them in the lands they discover; and everything should be entered in a book and once written down it should be publicly read every day to those who participate in the discovery so that more is found out about what happened, and the truth may be ascertained of every occurrence, the most notable among them signing the book, which shall be kept with great care, so that upon their return it be brought out and presented before the court [audiencia] that endorsed their departure.

23

Persons who have made a discovery by sea or by land should return to give account to the courts [audiencias] of what they have discovered and done during their discoveries; of which, detailed and lengthy account must be sent to our Council of the Indies so that, on this basis, decisions be made as to what pertains to the service of God our Lord, and to ourselves. The discoverer should be charged with the settling of that which has been discovered - having the necessary endowment for this - or be given the compensation he merits for his services and expenditures; or if a contract existed, that it be kept to, he having met his own obligations.

24

Those who make discoveries by sea or by land cannot and should not bring any Indians from the lands they discover even though they might be told that they can be bought as slaves or they might want to come along with them; nor in any other way, under penalty of death, except for three or four persons for language purposes, treating them well and paying them for their work.

25

Although it is our zeal and desire that everything there is to be discovered in the Indies be discovered so that the Holy Gospel can be made known and that the natives learn about our Holy Catholic Faith; and aware that for such a saintly endeavor all that we can spend from our royal exchequer would not suffice; but mindful that experience has shown that many discoveries and navigations *made on our behalf are undertaken at a great cost, and with little care and diligence, by persons departing with the purpose of taking advantage of the royal exchequer* [italics in Spanish text] rather than of achieving the intended objective; we order that no new discovery, navigation or settlement be undertaken at the cost of our exchequer, nor those in charge of governing should be allowed to spend any of it - even though they may have our authorization and instructions to carry out discoveries and navigations - unless they have special authorization to do so at our expense.

26

If there be priests and religious men from those orders that are permitted to travel to the Indies, who with the desire to be employed in the service of our Lord would wish to go and discover lands, and make known the Holy Gospel, that they, rather than others, be put in charge of discoveries and be given license to this effect, and be supported and provided at our cost with everything necessary for such holy and good endeavor.

27

Persons to whom new discoveries are entrusted should be selected for their piety and good conscience, for their zeal in honoring God and our service, for being peace loving and desirous of converting Indians so that we can be fully satisfied that no wrongdoing nor harm be done them, and that by means of their virtue and kindness they might satisfy our wishes and the obligation that we have to secure that this is undertaken with great devotion and temperance.

28

Discoveries cannot be entrusted to persons foreign to our Kingdom nor to those who are forbidden to travel to the Indies, nor can the persons asked to undertake these [discoveries] take them along.

29

Discoveries should not be made in the name of conquest or for the sake of it but should be conducted - as we have wished it - with extreme peace and benevolence, and they should not provide opportunity nor pretext for using force or offending the Indians.

30

Discoverers should adhere to the Ordinances of this book, especially to those intended to protect the Indians, and to the specific instructions that are given to this effect; and these should be implemented in a manner suitable to the condition of the province and territory that they might embark to.

31

No discoverer nor settler can go to discover or settle in lands entrusted to others or that others have discovered earlier; and in the case that there might be doubts or differences about the boundaries, for this given reason the ones and the others should cease to discover or settle in the part or parts over which there might be doubts or disputes. And they should inform the court [audiencia] of the district under which the land falls; and if the doubts and disputes should concern different courts, these should be so informed, as well as the Council of the Indies [Consejo de las Indias]; and until an agreement has been reached in those courts or in the Council and a settlement decreed, they should not go ahead with discoveries or the settling of populations, and should

9

adhere to what is determined by the Council or by the courts under penalty of death and loss of property.

New Settlements

32

Before discoveries are granted, no new population settlements are permitted, whether in the discovered areas or in those still to be discovered; but in those parts which are already discovered, pacified, and subject to our mandate, population settlements of both Spaniards and Indians, be ordered and where settled, agreements and perpetuity be given to both commonwealths, as specified in the fourth and fifth books [of the Laws of the Indies], especially in those parts dealing with population settlements and with land allotments.

33

Having populated and settled the newly discovered area, pacified it, and subjected it to our mandate, efforts should be made to discover and populate adjacent areas, and then set forth again to discover.

34

In order to populate those areas that are already discovered, pacified, and under our mandate, as well as areas that might be discovered and pacified in the course of time, the following sequence should be adhered to: choose the province, country, and place that will be settled, taking into consideration the health of the area, which will be known from the abundance of old men or of young men of good complexion, natural fitness and color, and without illness; and in the abundance of healthy animals of sufficient size, and of healthy fruits and fields where no toxic and noxious things are grown; but that it be of good climate, the sky clear and benign, the wind pure and soft, without impediment or alterations; and of good temperature, without excessive heat or cold, and having to choose, it is better that it be cold.

35

And they should be in fertile areas with an abundance of fruits and eatables, of good land to plant and harvest, of grasslands to raise livestock, of mountains and forests for wood and building materials for homes and buildings, and of good and plentiful water supply for drinking and irrigation.

36

And that they should be populated by Indians and natives to whom we can preach the gospels since this is the principal objective for which we mandate that these discoveries and settlements be made.

37

And they [the populated areas] should have good access and outlets by sea and by land, [and also] good roads and waterways, so that one can enter and leave easily to do commerce, govern, succour and defend.

38

Once the region, province, country, and land are decided upon by the discoverers, experts should select the site to establish head towns [cabecera: English aproximation: county seat] , and hold it, without harm to the Indians because these did not occupy it, or because they agree to it of their own free will.

39

The site and position of the towns should be selected in places where water is nearby and where it would be possible to deflect it to better make use of it in the town and nearby cultivated lands; and that the materials that are needed for the buildings be close by, and [also] the lands for farming and cultivation, and those for pasturage, so as to avoid the excessive work and cost, that any of these things would entail if distant.

40

Do not select sites that are too high up because these are affected by winds, and access and service to these are difficult; nor in lowlands, which tend to be unhealthy; choose places of medium elevation that enjoy good winds, especially from the north and south, and if there were to be mountains or hills, these should be in the [crossed out: "north"] west and [or] in the east; and if there should be a need to build in high places, be it in areas not subjected to fogs; take note of the terrain and its accidental features and in case that there should be a need to build on the banks of a river, it should be on the eastern bank, so that when the sun rises it strikes the town first, then the water.

41

Do not select sites for towns in maritime locations because of the danger that exists of pirates and because they are not very healthy, and also because in these [locations] people are not so inclined to work and cultivate the land, nor do they form habits in these [places] as well, unless the site is in an area where there are good and important harbors; and of these, select for settlement only those that are necessary for passage, commerce and for the defense of the land.

42

Having selected the site for population settlements, the head town be selected in the territory. The sites that there might be for population settlements [be] subject to and within the jurisdiction of the head town, [as well as] cattle farms, vegetable farms, and granges, without detriment to Indians or natives.

11

43

Having selected the area, province, and site where the new settlement is to be built, and having established the existing opportunities for development, the governor in whose district [the site] is, or borders upon, should decide whether the site that is to be populated should become a city, town, or village settlement. And according to his decision, a council [or] commonwealth [república] be set up, and its corresponding officers and members - in accordance to what is stipulated in the Book of the Republic [crossed out: "and officers and members"] of Spaniards [Libro de la República de Españoles]. Thus were it to become a metropolitan city, it should have a judge with title and name of governor [adelantado: title given to a person who will undertake a discovery and who has been granted prior authorization to be the governor of those lands], or governor, or principal mayor or magistrate [corregidor] or ordinary mayor, who would have jurisdiction jointly and separately with the body of aldermen [regimiento]; the administration of the commonwealth should have three officers of the Royal Exchequer [Hacienda Real], twelve aldermen [regidores], two executors, two jurors for each parish, one general procurator, one steward, one scribe for the council, and two public scribes: one for mines, another for the register; one chief town-crier, one broker for commercial transactions, two ushers, and if diocesan or suffragan, [then] eight aldermen [regidores] and the rest of said officers. Permanent, for the towns and villages [there should be]: an ordinary mayor, four aldermen, one constable, one scribe for the council and for the public, and a steward.

44

Having constituted and instructed the council and commonwealth of the people of what is to be done, one of the cities, towns or village settlements within its governance be appointed to constitute a commonwealth through colonization.

45

Place the justice and its [the town's] body of aldermen in charge so that the people interested in going to a new settlement be registered before a Council's clerk; admitting all those who are married or are sons or descendants of the inhabitants of the city from which the colonizers will start out; and who have no house lots nor pasture nor arable lands, and those who already have these should not be admitted in order not to depopulate areas that are already settled.

46

Having attained the [proper] number of people to go to the new settlement, they should select from amongst them those most apt for the justice and for the body of aldermen; and the justice and aldermen thus elected should order that each person register the assets they have for use in the new settlement.

47

In accordance with the assets that each person possesses, in the same proportion he should be given building lots [solares], pasture and arable lands, and Indians, and other farm-hands that he can support and provide with supplies to settle, cultivate and breed animals.

48

Craftsmen necessary for the work of the commonwealth should receive public salaries.

49

Farm-hands should be taken by the nobles at their expense, with the obligation of maintaining and providing them with lands for cultivation and cattle breeding, for which they in return should give them part of their yield.

50

As farm-hands and craftsmen for the new settlements Indians can go along at their free will, as long as they are not already settled and have houses and land - in order not to depopulate what is settled - nor Indians already alloted to lands [repartimiento] so as to avoid offending the encomenderos [who by royal consent had Indians granted to them] excepting those who are left over from a repartimiento because there was nothing in them to cultivate, and who would wish to go with the approval of the encomendero.

51

There not existing a city or other place inhabited by Spaniards in the Indies that can offer settlers for additional colonization, and there existing another place convenient to begin a new settlement, the Council should give orders on how to obtain [settlers] from another city among the main ones in Spain or from one of its provinces.

52

There not existing a city in the Indies nor in these Kingdoms of Spain that readily can offer groups of settlers for a new settlement,
arrangements be made with private persons who can be charged with going and starting the new settlements for the designated places, and [these be] given the title of governor [adelantado], or principal mayor, or of magistrate [corregidor] or ordinary mayor.

53

The governor [adelantado] consents to an agreement by which he is obligated, within a specified time, to set up, found, build and populate at least three cities: one provincial and two suffragans.

54

The principal mayor [*alcalde mayor*], consents to an agreement by which he is obligated, within a specified time, to set up, found, and populate at least three cities: one diocesan and two suffragans.

55

The magistrate [*corregidor*], consents to an agreement by which he is obligated, within a specified time, to set up, found and populate one suffragan city, and the places under his jurisdiction that would suffice for the farming and animal raising in the lands of said city.

56

The governor [*adelantado*] who fulfills the obligations regarding the new discoveries, the settling and pacification thereof, be granted the following: title of governor [*adelantado*] and of governor and captain general [*gobernador* and *capitán general*] for life and for one of his sons or designated heir.

57

To him or to his son or heir for the full time that he remains as governor, captain general, or chief of justice [*justicia mayor*], he be given a suitable salary each year from the royal exchequer belonging to us in that province.

58

Vagrant Indians can be granted to them and [also] those who wander about in the districts of the cities of the Spaniards, which have already been settled [Unreadable in original manuscript]-[Between lines: "Two"] for twenty years and in those to be settled, for thirty years, leaving ports and head towns to us.

59

The principal *alguazilasgo* [the office of an "*alguacil*"] of the entire governorate should be granted to him and to one son or heir; and the power to designate and remove the marshalls [*alguaciles*] of settled places and those to be settled.

60

He [the *adelantado*] or his son or heir can build three fortresses and having built them and supplied them, be given title to them and to his successors in perpetuity; and with it a suitable salary should be given from our treasury, and the yields from the land that in that province belongs to us.

61

He [the *adelantado*] can choose for himself, for twenty years, an allotment of Indians [*repartimiento*] from the district of each town of Spaniards that already is settled or about to be settled; and having thus chosen, he can improve his situation by leaving one and taking another; the one being vacated can then be given and distributed to his legitimate or natural children, [also] building lots, lands [*caballerías de tierras*] and cattle farms. The allotment of Indians that he might have taken for himself, leave them to his elder son or distribute them between this son and the other legitimate children - or among the natural children, if there be no legitimate ones - provided that each allotment [*repartimiento*] remain as a whole for the son so designated, without subdivision [There is here an unreadable crossing-out and between lines is added "*dividirse*".] and leaving a legitimate wife, the law of succession be respected.

62

He [the *adelantado*] can keep the Indians that might have been granted [*encomendados*] to him in another province, or that are to be granted to him, by placing amongst them a squire who will keep good relations for him and who cannot be removed.

63

He [the *adelantado*] and his son or heir or successor in the governorate can engrave markers and stamps, and place them in the towns of the Spaniards that are settled, or to be settled, with which to mark the metals.

64

Not having officials of the royal treasury, he [the *adelantado*] can name them, and supply them, while waiting for us to do so, or until those we provide arrive.

65

He [the *adelantado*] and his son, principal heir or successor, with the agreement of the officials of the royal exchequer, or a majority, can draw from our treasury what is deemed necessary to control any revolt.

66

He [the *adelantado*] can issue ordinances for the governance of the territory and for the work in the mines; provided they are not against the established laws and what by us has been decreed, and that these undergo confirmation within two years [but] be observed in the meantime.

67

They can divide the province into districts of principal mayoralties [*alcaldías mayores*] and magistratures [*corregimientos*] and ordinary mayoralties; and install principal mayors and magistrates [a part is unreadable in original manuscript] and designate their salaries based on the yields of the land; and confirm the appointment of ordinary mayors elected by the councils.

68

He [the *adelantado*] and his son or successor, heir in government, should have civil and criminal jurisdiction over the type of appeals made by the lieutenant-governor, and of the principal mayors, magistrates and ordinary mayors, so there be no need to appear before the councils.

69

He [the *adelantado*] and his son or successor, heir in government and jurisdiction, should report directly to the Council of the Indies so that none of the Viceroys nor local courts [*audiencias*] can interfere in the affairs of his sphere of authority, neither by special requests, nor by means of appeal, nor provide commissioned judges.

70*

The Council of the Indies can be informed about matters of government by means of official letters or by special request or by means of appeal and in cases of dispute between parties it should be informed, by way of appeal about civil suits involving six thousand pesos or above; and in criminal suits, those in which sentences include the death penalty or mutilation of limbs.

70*

Judges that were provided to the province before we granted it to a governor [*adelantado*], once he arrives and provides new ones, [the former judges] should no longer exercise their office and should leave it unencumbered, departing from the territory unless - once they have left their office - they should desire to reside in the territory and stay in it as settlers.

---

* It is possible that the first of these two
ordinances, both numbered "70", is part of 69 -
see original manuscript.

71

They can grant common lands, watering holes, roads and paths to those towns that are newly settled [Between lines: "if not already designated by us], together with the municipal councils [*cabildos*].

72

They can name aldermen [*regidores*] and other public officials in towns that are newly settled, if not already designated by us, as long as within a period of four years, those so-named receive our confirmation and provision.

73

They should be given warrants so they can enlist people in any of these parts of our Kingdoms of the Crown of Castile and of Leon, for settlement and pacification, and name captains to this effect who can raise flags and beat drums and announce the expedition, without asking anything of them or those that might go along.

74

The magistrates [*corregidores*] of said cities, towns and places - where the captains might enlist said people - should neither hinder nor obstruct but rather should help to render it possible for them to undertake these recruitments; and [also] the people, who agree to go along; and that no fee be charged them for this.

75

Those who have agreed to go on the expedition and to the new settlements being undertaken by the governor [*adelantado*] should obey him; and they should not deviate course, nor withdraw their allegiance, nor undertake another expedition without his approval, under penalty of death.

76

Warrants should be given to them so that the justices of neighboring territories - of those from where they might depart for the expedition - and of those areas through which they must pass, facilitate their safe passage; and help rather than hinder them, and give them the provisions and supplies that they might need, charging just and moderate prices. And if they must start out from these Kingdoms of Castile, these warrants should be given for the House of Trade [*Casa de Contratación*] officials at Seville, so that they can be appropriately furnished and supplied, and thus facilitate their voyage; and they should not be asked for information concerning the people they might take along, in accordance with the agreement, but he must make an attempt to take people of integrity, and not of those prohibited by these ordinances.

77

And also warrants should be given him so that officials of the neighboring territories do not impede the passage of cattle, necessary for the population of his province, and which he may be required to take for his settlement and [according to his] agreement; and so that the officials do not bother those who may want to go along - be they Indians or Spaniards - even though they may have committed an offence, but not existing a legal suit, they cannot be punished for these.

17

78

They can take slaves in compliance with the agreement, who are free of all duties, for which a warrant should be given.

79

He can take every year two ships with arms and provisions for the land and for the work of the mines, free of any duties [almojarifazgo] that may have to be paid in the Indies, as long as they are ready to leave with the fleets that from this Kingdom depart to the continent or to New Spain or when to this effect authorized.

80

The governor [adelantado] and his son or an heir who is the first to succeed him in the governorate, and the settlers, should not pay duties exceeding a tenth of the metals and precious stones, for a period of ten years.

81

Neither should they pay excise taxes [alcabala] for a period of twenty years.

82

Nor should they pay the duty [almojarifazgo] that is paid in the Indies for all those things they take for furnishing their homes - for a period of ten years - and the governor and his son or first successor in the governorate shall not pay this for a period of twenty years.

83

When the governor [adelantado] takes up residence, consideration should be given to the quality of his services, in order to assess whether he should be suspended from that jurisdiction or whether to leave him there for the entire period of his residency.

84

For the governor [adelantado] who has completed successfully his expedition and fulfilled successfully his agreement, we will ensure that he is given vassals in perpetuity, and the title of marquis or another.

85

Likewise, we plan to give countenance and bestow our kindness on the new discoverers, settlers, and pacificators - and to their children and descendants - giving them building lots, lands for pasturage and cultivation, and for cattle raising, and the wherewithal; and to those to whom these gifts were granted, and who have settled and resided in their lands for a period of five years, they should then be entitled to them in perpetuity. To those who have set up and settled sugar plantations and administered and maintained them well, they should not be subjected to seizure thereof, nor of their slaves, nor of their tools and equipment used for cultivation; and we order that they retain all exemptions, privileges, and concessions that we have stipulated in the books of the Spanish commonwealth.

86

The discoveries, settlements and pacifications with the title of governor [*adelantado*] can only be granted and bestowed from those provinces that are not adjacent to districts of provinces already under [the jurisdiction of] a Viceroy or Royal Court; from where it is convenient to govern and undertake the discovery, new settlement, and pacification; and from where it is possible to have recourse in the form of appeals or grievances.

87

Discovery, settlement, and pacification of a province or provinces - that are adjacent or form part of provinces already under [the jurisdiction of] a Viceroy or Royal Court, should be granted and bestowed with the title of principal municipality [*alcaldía mayor*] or magistrature [*corregimiento*] - [if] by way of colonization from some city of the Indies, or of these Kingdoms; or [if] by way of an agreement, with the title of principal municipality [*alcaldía mayor*], magistrature [*corregimiento*], and principal mayor [*alcalde mayor*] or magistrate [*corregidor*]; and his son or heir or the person by him so designated, should be granted the same - as already has been stated - that is granted to the governor [*adelantado*] or his son inheritor, or person so designated by him; except that, as to its governance, they are subordinate to the Viceroy or Royal Court in whose district it be included or with whose district it borders. And, in what respects the administration of justice, by its means of appeals and petitions, recourse should be made to the court of justice, as it is done with the other principal mayors and magistrates; and residence be given him, and a salary paid, in conformity with other principal mayors and magistrates.

88

If there not exist a provision for a new settlement, it should be undertaken through colonization, or from the settlement of a governorate, principal mayoralty, or magistrature; and if there should exist such a provision to populate a town - with the counsel of ordinary mayors [*alcaldes ordinarios*], and aldermen [*regidores*], and yearly [appointed] officials - and if a person exists who would wish to enter into an agreement to settle it, he should be taken with the following stipulations:

89

The person who is placed in charge of populating a town with Spaniards should see to it that within the lands specified in the agreement, there be at least thirty settlers, and each one with his own house, ten pregnant cows, four oxen or two oxen and two steer and a pregnant mare, five pregnant pigs, six chickens and one rooster, [and] twenty pregnant sheep from Castile; and there should [also] be a clergyman who can administer the sacraments; and he [the person in charge] shall provide the ornaments to the church as well as the necessary artifacts for the divine service - and he will pledge to accomplish it within the given time; if not he should lose everything already built, cultivated and harvested; and it shall be ours; and in addition he will incur a fine of a thousand gold pesos. He [also] should be given four *leguas* [a *legua* equals three and a half miles] of land and territory - either square or rectangular - according to how the quality of the land happens to be, [between lines: "to be"] so that in whatever way the boundaries be set it turns out to be four square *leguas*, provided the boundaries of said territory are at least five *leguas* from any city, town or place inhabited by Spaniards that was previously settled and where it may not result in prejudice to any of the towns inhabited by Spaniards, or by Indians, that were already settled nor to any person in particular.

90

The aforesaid lands and territory should be divided as follows:
Separate first the land that is needed for building lots [*solares*] of the town, then [allocate] sufficient common land and grounds for pasture where, the cattle the settlers are expected to bring with them, can obtain abundant feed, plus another portion for the natives of the area. The rest of the said lands and territory should be divided into four parts: one is for the person in charge of building the town; the other three should be subdivided into thirty lots for the thirty settlers of the town.

91

[*Note:* This Ordinance is skipped in the original manuscript creating a different number sequence than appears in other versions. It seems that No. 91 may in fact be a part of Ordinance No. 90. *See also* note Ordinance 99]

92

Territory and lands [*término*: lands under the jurisdiction of an *ayuntamiento*] for a new settlement cannot be granted nor seized in sea harbors nor in areas that at some point might redound to the detriment of our Royal Crown nor to the commonwealth, therefore we want those to be reserved for us.

93

We declare that the son or daughter or children of a new settler, or his relatives within or outside the fourth degree, who have separate homes and families of their own, and are married, and each having his own household be considered resident citizens.

94

If due to some unanticipated circumstance the settlers are not able to complete the said settlement [crossed-out: "the said settlement"] according to the terms contained in the agreement [*asiento*], they should not give for lost nor loose what they have already spent or built, nor incur the penalty. He who governs the lands can extend the terms according to the particular circumstances of the case.

95

The pastures of said lands should be common - once harvested - except those set aside for cattle raising and for the council.

96

He who has bound himself to undertake the said settlement should have civil and criminal jurisdiction in the first instance for the rest of his life and his son or heir, and he can name ordinary mayors, aldermen, and the other officials of the town council of said town. And [according to] degree of appeals, the lawsuits be sent before the principal mayor or to the law courts in whose district said settlement comes under.

97

He who has fulfilled his agreement and established said settlement in accordance with what was stipulated, we give him license and authority to set up an entailed estate, or entailed estates, of what he has built up and of that part of the lands granted to him and in which he has planted and built.

98

Likewise, we grant the gold and silver mines and other mines thereof, and salt mines, and pearl fisheries that are in the said extension of land; as long as of the gold, silver and pearls and everything else that they might extract from the said metals and mines, the said settler and the inhabitants of the said town - or any other person - must give and pay to us and to our successors one-fifth of everything that they extract, especially in gold. [This refers to the famous "Royal Fifth" which the Spanish kings charged on all that was extracted, found or produced].

99

Likewise, we grant to the said settler, and to the other citizens of the town, that of all the [things] they take for their homes and sustenance in the first voyage they undertake should [Between lines: "not"] pay us the duties [almojarifazgo] nor any other fees that we are entitled to receive.

[Translators Note: In the previous translation the following two Ordinances - 100 to 101 - were numbered 99 and 100 respectively, due to the fact that a previous Spanish transcription did not account for the missing number 91 in the original.]

21

100

Those who have bound themselves to undertake the said settlement, and have populated it and carried out their agreement, to honor them and their descendants and so that a laudable memory of them as founders remains, *we pronounce them illustrious men [hijosdalgo] of ancestry known to them* [italics in Spanish text] and to their legitimate descendants so that in the place that they have settled and in any other parts of the Indies, they will be *hijosdalgo* and persons of noble lineage and known ancestry and as such should they be known and considered, and enjoy all honor and privilege, and [they] can do all the things that all the *hijosdalgo* men and gentlemen of the Kingdoms of Castile pursue: the statutes, laws and customs of Spain, they can and should make and enjoy.

101

And those who should want to be bound to undertake a new settlement, in the form and manner already prescribed, be it of more than 30 citizens or of less - provided that it not be of less than ten - he be granted the corresponding lands and territory, and with the same conditions.

102

There not existing persons to make an agreement and to be bound to begin a new town, but having an abundance of married men who would agree to carry out the founding of a new town in whatever place already designated - provided there are no less than ten married men - they can proceed; and they should be given land grants and territory in accordance with what is stipulated; and they can select amongst them an ordinary mayor and yearly council officials.

103

Having taken up an agreement for [the settlement of] a new town - be it by way of colony, governorship [*adelantamiento*], principal municipality, magistrature [*corregimiento*], town or land grant - the Council [of the Indies] and those in charge of the governance of the Indies should not be content with having taken and made said agreement, but should continue to govern and direct how such settlement is to be administered, and keeping track of what is being done.

104

The governor having made an agreement for a new town by way of townspeople, *adelantado*, principal mayor or magistrate [*corregidor*] for the town; the town or persons with whom the said agreement was established must likewise make an agreement with each person who has registered or who comes to register for the new settlement as a private individual; to which agreement, the person under whose charge the said new town is, will be obligated to give to the person who with him wants to settle the designated town [the following]: building-lots for houses, and land for pasture and cultivation in an amount of *peonias* and *caballerias* [see 105 and 106 below], in which each settler undertakes to build, but not exceeding nor giving each more than five *peonias*, or more than three *caballerias* to those receiving the latter.

105

A *peonia* is: a building lot of fifty feet in width and one hundred in length; one hundred *hanegas* [also known as *fanega*, an agrarian measurement] of land for the cultivation of wheat and barley, ten for corn, two *huebras* [tract of land that can be plowed in a day] of land for an orchard, and eight for planting other trees for dry lands; [also] pasture land for fifty pregnant sows, twenty cows, five mares, one hundred sheep and twenty goats.

106

One *caballeria* is: a building lot for a house, measuring one hundred feet in width and two hundred in length; and of all the rest, as about five *peonias*, that would be five hundred *hanegas* for cultivating wheat for bread or barley, fifty for corn, ten *huebras* of land for orchards, forty for planting other trees for dry lands, [also] pasture land for fifty pregnant sows and one hundred cows, twenty mares, five hundred sheep and one hundred goats.

107

The *caballerias*, whether for building lots or for pasture or land for cultivation, should be given surveyed and with marked boundaries, in an enclosure; and the *peonias*, building lots and lands for cultivation and planting, should be given surveyed and divided [but] those for pastures should be common lands.

108

Those who accept the agreement to reside in the *caballerias* and *peonias*, take upon themselves the obligation to: have the building lots built up and the house inhabited; the lands and the labor for its cultivation distributed, and [that] these be tilled and planted, and cattle raised in those for pasture; this should be done within the given time and by the terms set, and stating what in each of the terms is to be done, under penalty of losing the allocation [*repartimiento*] of building lots and lands, plus the paying of a fine in *maravedis* [old Spanish currency] to the state, and he must post a public bond secured with an honest and guaranteed credit.

109

Those who have undertaken an agreement and have committed themselves to build, cultivate and graze their land [*caballeria*], can make and should make agreements with laborers to assist them to build and cultivate and graze, in accordance to how they agreed [to these], committing themselves the ones with the others, in order that with greater facility the land may be settled, cultivated and grazed.

110

The governor who has authorized the new settlement and the justices of the town that is being resettled, by means of written communication or by petition, should ascertain that the commitments to settle a new town be fulfilled. This should be done with great diligence and care. And the aldermen and the procurators of the Council should initiate due process against the settlers who, bound by a specified term, have not complied with it and should make them meet the terms. And those who might have left should be prosecuted, seized, and brought back to the town in order that they comply with the terms of settlement, and if they were in another jurisdiction, a requisitioning order should be issued in order that justice be done, the penalty being withdrawal of our favor.

111*

Having made the discovery, selected the province, county, and area that is to be settled, and the site of the lands where the new towns are to be built, and having taken possession of it, those placed in charge of its execution are to do it in the following manner: On arriving at the place where the new settlement is to be founded - which according to our will and disposition shall be one that is vacant and that can be occupied without doing harm to the Indians and natives or with their free consent - a plan for the site is to be made, dividing it into squares, streets, and building lots, using cord and ruler, beginning with the main square from which streets are to run to the gates and principal roads and leaving sufficient open space so that even if the town grows, it can always spread in the same manner. Having thus agreed upon the site and place selected to be populated, a layout should be made in the following way:

111*

Having made the selection of the site where the town is to be built, it must, as already stated, be in an elevated location, where it is healthy [and] invigorating; [have] fertile soil and with plenty of land for farming and pasturage; have fuel, timber, and resources; [have] fresh water, a native population, ease of transport, access and exit; [and be] open to the north wind; and, if on the coast, due consideration should be paid to the quality of the harbor and that the sea does not lie to the south or west; and if possible not near lagoons or marshes in which poisonous animals and polluted air and water breed.

---

* See translators note at the end of the text.

112

The main *plaza* is to be the starting point for the town; if the town is situated on the sea coast, it should be located at the landing-place of the port; but inland [crossed-out: "sea coast"] it should be at the centre of the town. The *plaza* should be rectangular, being in length at least one and a half its width because this shape is best for celebrations [*fiestas*] in which horses are used and for any other *fiestas* that should be held.

113

The size of the ˉplaza shall be proportioned to the number of inhabitants, taking into consideration the fact that in Indian towns, inasmuch as they are new, the intention is that they will increase, and thus the plaza should be decided upon taking into consideration the growth the town may experience. [The plaza] shall be not less than two hundred feet wide and three hundred feet long, nor larger than eight hundred feet long and five hundred and thirty feet wide. A good proportion is six hundred feet long and four hundred wide.

114

From the plaza shall begin four principal streets: One [shall be] from the middle of each side, and two streets from each corner of the plaza; the four corners of the plaza shall face the four principal winds, because in this manner, the streets running from the plaza will not be exposed to the four principal winds, which would cause much inconvenience.

115

Around the plaza as well as along the four principal streets which head from it, there shall be porticoes [portales], for these are of considerable convenience to the merchants who generally gather there; the eight streets running from the plaza at the four corners shall open on the plaza without encountering these porticoes [portales], which shall be kept back in order that there may be sidewalks even with the streets and plaza.

116

In cold places the streets shall be wide and in hot places narrow; but for purposes of defense, in areas where there are horses, it would be better if they are wide.

117

The streets shall run from the main plaza in such manner that even if the town increases considerably in size, it will not result in some inconvenience that will make ugly what needs to be rebuilt, or endanger its defense or comfort.

118

Here and there in the town, smaller plazas of good proportion shall be laid out, where the temples associated with the principal church, the parish churches, and the monasteries, can be built, [in] such [manner] that everything may be distributed in a good proportion for the instruction of religion.

119

For the temple of the principal church, parish, or monastery, there shall be assigned specific lots; the first after the streets and plazas [have been laid out], and these shall be a complete block so as to avoid having other buildings nearby, unless it were for practical or ornamental reasons.

120

The temple of the principal church - when the town is situated on the coast - shall be built in such place that it may be seen on going out to sea and its frame should serve in part as the defenses of the port itself.

121

Next, a site and lot shall be assigned for the royal council [*casa real*], counsel house [*casa de consejo*] and municipal council [*cabildo*] as well as for the custom house and arsenal [*atarazana*], near the same temple and port, [located] in such a manner that in times of need the one may aid the other. The hospital for the poor and those sick of noncontagious diseases shall be built next to the temple as its cloister; and the hospital for the sick with contagious diseases shall be built in such a way that no harmful wind blowing through it may cause harm to the rest of the town; and if it be built in an elevated place, so much the better.

122

The site and building lots for slaughter houses, fisheries, tanneries, and other business which produce filth shall be so placed that the filth can easily be disposed of.

123

It shall be of considerable convenience if those towns that are laid out away from seaports, inland, be built if possible on the shore of a navigable river; and attempts should be made to place the town on the side from which the cold north wind blows; and that buildings that cause filth be placed on the downriver part of the town.

124

The temple in inland places shall not be situated on the *plaza* but at a distance from it; and in a place that is separate, and the nearest building should not be adjoining; and [the temple] ought to be seen from all sides so that it can be embellished better, thus acquiring more authority; efforts should be made that it be somewhat raised from ground level in order that it be entered by a series of steps; and that near it be approached the main *plaza* and erected the royal council, and *cabildo*, and customs houses; and these shall be built in a manner that would not diminish the temple but add to its prestige. The hospital for the poor who are not affected by contagious diseases shall be built next to the temple and as its cloister, and the [hospital] for contagious diseases shall be built in an area away from the cold north wind, but arranged in such a way that it may enjoy the south wind.

125

The same plan shall be observed in any inland place without [river] shores, taking considerable care to ascertain the availability of those conveniences that may be required.

126

In the *plaza*, no lots shall be assigned to private individuals; instead, they shall be used for the buildings of the church, the royal houses and those for the city; and shops and houses for the merchants should be built first, to which all the settlers of the town shall contribute, and a moderate tax shall be imposed on goods so that these buildings may be built.

127

The other building lots shall be distributed by lottery to the settlers, continuing with the lots closer to the main *plaza*, and the lots that are left shall be held by us for assignment to those who shall later become settlers, or for the use that we may wish to make of them, and so that this may be ascertained better, the town shall maintain a plan of what is being built.

128

Having made the plan of the town and having distributed building lots, each of the settlers shall set up his tent on his plot if he should have one. For this purpose the captains should persuade settlers to carry them, and those who did not bring one should make their huts of easily available local materials, so that they may have shelter, and everyone as soon as possible shall make a palisade or ditch encircling the *plaza* so that they may not be harmed by the native Indians.

129

Within the town, a commons shall be delimited, large enough so that even if the population may experience a rapid expansion, there will always be sufficient space where the people may go to for recreation and take their cattle to pasture without them doing any damage.

130

Adjoining the commons there shall be assigned pasture ground for the work oxen and for the horses as well as for the cattle for slaughter and for the usual number of cattle that the settlers must have according to these Ordinances; and a good number more so they can be used as pastures for the purposes of the Council; and the rest shall be assigned as farm lands, which will be distributed by lottery in such a number as is available so that [farm lots] would be as many in number as the lots in the town; and if there should be irrigated lands, lots shall be cast for them and they shall be distributed in the same proportion to the first settlers according to their lots; the rest shall remain for ourselves so that we may assign it to those who later may become settlers.

131

In the farmlands that may be distributed, the settlers should immediately plant the seeds they brought with them and those they might have obtained at the site; to this effect it is convenient that they go well provided; and in the designated pasture lands, all the cattle they brought with them and that they might have gathered so that they may soon begin to breed and multiply.

132

Having planted their seeds and made [the necessary] arrangements for the cattle - in such numbers and with such good diligence that they expect to obtain an abundance of food - they [the settlers] shall begin with great care and efficiency to establish their houses and to build them with good foundations and walls; to this effect they shall go provided with molds or planks, and all the other tools needed for building quickly and at small cost.

133

They shall arrange the building lots [*solares*] and the edifices placed thereon in such a way that when living in them they may enjoy the winds of the south and north as these are the best; throughout the town arrange the structures of the houses in such a way, generally that they might serve as a defense or barrier against those who may try to disturb or invade the town; and each individual thing be so built that they may keep therein [in the *solar*] their horses and work animals, and shall have *patios* and corrals, and as large as possible for health and cleanliness.

134

They shall try as much as possible to have the buildings all of one type for the sake of the beauty of the town.

135

The loyal executors and builders as well as the persons who may have been deputed for this purpose by the governor shall be most careful in overseeing that the above [ordinances] be executed; and they shall make haste in their labor and building so that the town may be completed in a short time.

136

If the natives should resolve to take a defensive position toward the [new] settlement, they should be made aware of how we intend to settle, not to do damage to them nor to take away their lands but to gain instead their friendship and teach them how to live civilly; and also to teach them to know our God so they learn His law through which they will be saved. This will be done by religious, clerics, and other persons designated for this purpose by the governor and through good interpreters, taking care by the best means available that the town settlement is carried out peacefully and with their consent, but if they [the natives] still do not want to agree - after having been so requested repeatedly through various means - the settlers should build their town without taking what belongs to the Indians and without doing them more harm than it were necessary for the protection of the town, in order that the settlers be not disturbed.

137

While the town is being completed, the settlers should try, inasmuch as this is possible, to avoid communication and traffic with the Indians, nor going to their towns, nor go off the main roads, nor scatter over the land; nor [should the settlers] allow the Indians to enter within the confines of the town until it is built and its defenses ready; and the houses built so that when the Indians see them they will be struck with admiration and will understand that the Spaniards are there to settle permanently and not temporarily. They [the Spaniards] should be so feared that they [the Indians] will not dare offend them, but they will respect them and desire their friendship. At the beginning of the building of a town, the governor shall assign a person who will occupy himself with the sowing and cultivation of the land, for bread and vegetables so that the settlers can soon be provisioned for their maintenance. And the cattle that they brought shall be put out to pasture in a safe area where they will not damage cultivated land nor Indian property, so that from the aforesaid cattle and its offspring the town may be serviced, provisioned and sustained.

138

Having completed the erection of the town and its buildings - and not before this is done - the governor and settlers, with great care and holy zeal, should attempt to bring in peace to the fraternity of the Holy Church and to our obedience, all the natives of the province and its surrounding areas, by the best means they know and can understand, and for the following:

139

Obtain information of the diversity of nations, languages, sects, and prejudices of the natives within the province, and about the lords they may pledge obedience to, and by means of commerce and exchange, [the Spaniards] should try to establish friendship with them [the Indians], showing great love and treating them lovingly and also giving them things in barter that will attract their interest, and not showing greediness for their things. [The Spaniards] should establish friendship and alliances with the principal lords and head men who would be most useful in the pacification of the land.

140

Having made peace and alliance with [the Indian lords] and with their commonwealths, try to get together; and [then] those who preach, with utmost solemnity and much clarity, should attempt to persuade them that they [the Indians] do desire to understand the matters pertaining to the Holy Catholic Faith. Then shall begin the teaching [efforts] with great care and discretion, and in the order stipulated in the first book of the Holy

Catholic Faith, utilizing the mildest approach so as to entice the Indians to want to learn about it. Thus they will not start by reprimanding their vices or their idolatry, nor taking away their women nor their idols, because they should not be scandalized or develop an enmity against the Christian doctrine. Instead, they should be taught first, and after they have been instructed, they should be persuaded that of their own will they should abandon all that runs contrary to our Holy Catholic Faith and evangelical doctrine.

141

We should make clear to them the position that God has placed us in and the power given us and our solicitude to serve Him, and bring into his Holy Catholic Faith all the natives of the Western Indies; and the fleets and squadrons that we have sent and continue to send, and the many nations and provinces that are subject to our obedience, and the great benefit and advantages that from this have accrued to them; and, especially, that we have sent them someone who will teach them the Christian doctrine and the faith in their salvation; and having received it in all the provinces under our control, we keep them under the rule of justice, so that no one can harm another, and we maintain them in peace so that they do not kill nor eat each other, nor perform sacrifices as it was done in some parts; and thus are able to go about safely on the roads, dealing and making contracts and trading; and having taught them propriety, they now wear clothes and shoes and have many other goods previously forbidden to them, and having removed their burdens and servitude, having brought to them the use of bread, wine and oil and many other things for their livelihood - cloth, silk, linen, horses, cattle, tools, arms, and all sorts of things brought from Spain - and also taught them trades and craftsmanship with which they can live well; and that all these benefits will be enjoyed by those who come to know our Holy Catholic Faith and have submitted to our obedience.

142

Although those who preach the Faith hope to be, and might be received peacefully, also their doctrine, when visiting towns they should exercise great caution [and] prudence, and ensure their safety so that even though they [the natives] might behave insolently towards them, irreverence not be done those who preach the Faith because of a lack of respect - and because of irreverence, force punishment on the culprits, as this would be a great impediment to the furtherance of pacification and conversion; and although they might have to heed this warning to preach and spread the doctrine, it should be done with such care so that they [the natives] do not perceive a mistrust as they should not be scared. This can be achieved by first bringing to the Spanish settlement the children of chieftains and high ranking persons and leaving them there as hostages, under the pretext of teaching them how to wear clothes, and making presents to them or by other appropriate means - thus they should proceed with the preaching through all the Indian villages and communities that would wish to receive them in peace.

143

In those areas and places where the Christian doctrine of peace is not wanted, the following procedure could be followed in order to preach it: Be in concert with the most important local person who is at peace and who has warring neighbors, that these come to his lands to amuse themselves or for any other reason that might attract them; and by then those who preach the Faith should be there concealed - together with some Spaniards and friendly Indians to ensure their safety - and when the time is propitious they should appear and together with the others, through their intepreters and using their languages, should begin to teach the Christian doctrine; and in order that they may be accorded greater respect and admiration they should be wearing at least white vestments, or surplices and stoles, and with the Cross in their hands; and once they are seen, the Christians [present] should listen to them with great humility and veneration, so that the infidels imitate them and become interested in being taught and, should they wish to generate greater admiration and attention among the infidels - and if available - they might use music, by way of singers and high and bass wind instruments, in order to entice the Indians to join them - and to use other means available that they might think suitable to subdue and pacify belligerent Indians; and even if it may seem that they have become peaceful, and those who preach are asked to go to their lands, this should be undertaken with the same caution and the same protective measures as already stated by us, asking them for their sons - under the guise of teaching them - while retaining them as hostages in the land of their friends, and thus amuse them; and persuade them that they should first erect churches where they might be taught, until such time as they [the churchmen] feel safe; and through these means and others that may appear more appropriate they should continue pacifying and indoctrinating the natives without in any way, or by any means, causing them harm because all that we wish is their well-being and conversion.

144

Having pacified the land, and its local chiefs and natives submitted to our authority, the governor with their assent should endeavor to distribute the land among the settlers in order that each settler take responsibility for the Indians of his allotment [repartimiento] to defend and assist them, and provide them with a clergyman to teach them the Christian doctrine and to administer to them the sacraments; and teach them propriety, and do with them everything else that the encomenderos are required to do with the Indians in their repartimiento in accordance to what is said in the terms that deal with this matter.

145

Those Indians who have been submitted to our authority and have been allotted, should be persuaded that in recognition of the universal power and jurisdiction that we exercise over the Indies, they should come to us with a tribute of modest amounts from the fruits of the land, in accordance with what is stipulated under the terms dealing with tributes; and that tributes thus obtained be given to the Spaniards to whom the Indians are entrusted [encomendados] and who in turn must comply with their obligations, reserving for us the principal towns and sea ports; and, from those to be distributed, ensure the amount necessary to pay the salaries of those in charge of governing and defending the district and administering our treasury.

146

If to better achieve the pacification of the natives it might be necessary to give them immunity from paying tribute for a certain period, this should be granted as well as other privileges and exemptions, and what is promised to them should be respected.

147

In those parts where there are enough [churchmen] to preach the Gospel in order to pacify the Indians, and convert them and make them peace loving, no other persons should be allowed to go there who might interfere with their conversion and pacification.

148

The Spaniards, to whom Indians are entrusted [*encomendados*], should seek with great care that the assigned Indians be settled into towns, and that, within these, churches be built so that the Indians can be instructed in Christian doctrine and live with propriety.

Because we order you to see to it that these Ordinances, as presented above, be incorporated, complied with, and executed, and that you make what in them is contained be complied with and executed, and never take action or move against them, nor consent that others take action or move against either their content or form, the penalty being withdrawal of our favor. Dated in the Woods of Segovia, the thirteenth of July, in the year fifteen hundred and seventy-three. I the King; countersigned by Antonio de Erasso, [and] conveyed by the gentlemen: President Juan de Ovando, Licenciados Castro, Don Gomez, Zapata, Botello, Maldonado, Otalaza, ...

Translators note:

The translation of the "Ordenanzas de descubrimiento, nueva poblacion y pacificacion de las Indias, dadas por Felipe II en 1573" published in Crouch, Dora P., Garr, Daniel J., and Axel I. Mundigo, *Spanish City Planning in North America* (Cambridge, Mass., The MIT Press, 1982) has been completely revised and edited, as well as enlarged, in the present version. The earlier translation was prepared for a book dealing primarily with the planning of towns. Therefore, certain aspects of the material, particularly those that address the organization of the discovery, preparation of expeditions, bringing the natives into order and peace, and structure of local, provincial and territorial government, did not seem directly relevant to the purpose of that book. Additionally, the length of the ordinances - 148 of them, also prevented including all of them in that book. Since that time a facsimile edition, reproducing the original manuscript kept in the Archivo General de Indias of Seville, Spain, and issued by the Housing Ministry and the Institute of Hispanic Culture (Deposito Legal: M-29.920-1973) has become available. This version not only includes the original manuscript but a complete and literal transcription of the old Spanish text which exactly reflects the original. This has permitted a revision of the earlier translation, which had used other, edited modern Spanish versions of the original text, and correct minor errors. It has also made it possible to complete some ordinances which were only partially translated, e.g. 89, 100. The present text also corrects some problems with the numbering of the ordinances - there are two in the present transcription numbered 70, one of which may be a part of 69, and two numbered 111, which affects numbers 109 and 110 in the previous translation (109 becomes 110 and 110 the first 111). The actual manuscript has a correction in the second 111 indicating that it can also be read as 109. Be as it may it was decided to keep two ordinances numbered 70 and two 111. In fact several ordinances have their numbers corrected in the original - when and who did these corrections is not known. In revising the translation and adding the missing ordinances to complete it, every effort has been made to keep both the flavor of the original language and accuracy. Despite this effort, and particularly because the transcription does not have any punctuation or breaks to separate logical statements, it is always possible that a slight misinterpretation may crop in. The punctuation that appears in the English translation has been added by the translators in an effort to make this material more readable and accessible to English-speaking scholars and interested laymen. Some words, e.g. *Adelantado, Alguacil, Audiencias,* etc., are shown both in Spanish and in English in the text in order to avoid possible doubts by readers as to what is meant since there is often no exact English translation for them yet they are crucial to an understanding of the text and its message.

PUEBLOS

SETTLEMENT PATTERNS AND VILLAGE PLANS IN COLONIAL NEW MEXICO

By Marc Simmons

Visiting Assistant Professor of History,
University of New Mexico, Albuquerque

P ATTERNS OF SETTLEMENT IN NEW MEXICO fluctuated during the two and one-quarter centuries of Spanish rule. Expansion and contraction of the European population was determined by availability of arable land, territorial requirements of the Pueblo Indians and pressures of hostile nomadic tribes. Study of the influences which shaped settlement patterns in New Mexico and review of attempts by government officials and others to regulate the settling of new lands and towns offer insights into some of the economic and social problems of colonial times.

When the Spaniards reached the Southwest in 1540, they found the largest concentration of Pueblo Indians along the upper Río Grande and its tributaries with outlying nuclei of settlement to the west at Acoma, Zuñi and Hopi and to the east at Pecos Pueblo and the villages beyond the Manzano Mountains. The Río Grande drainage offered suitable home sites for the Pueblo people with sufficient land to meet their agricultural needs. The Spanish colonists as well, found the environment attractive, so they fixed their earliest farms, ranches and towns on lands adjacent to the Pueblos. To the present day heavy population clusters occur in this same area.

Extensive exploration in the early colonial period quickly dashed hopes that New Mexico would yield treasure in gold, silver or other profitable minerals. The fading of prospects for a mining boom meant that population growth and economic development would lack the spectacular quality which attended the colonization of some of the other frontier provinces. New Mexico, in fact, to the end of the colonial era remained thinly populated and dependent upon royal subsidies to meet her expenses. Land served as the principal source of what little wealth she possessed.

THE LEGAL BASIS OF SETTLEMENT

The ultimate proprietorship of all lands in New Mexico belonged to the Spanish sovereign. By royal concession, private individuals or groups of persons might apply for lands, and after fulfilling certain legal

7

requirements, receive a grant called a *gracia* or *merced real*.[1] All properties not conveyed in an official grant remained in the possession of the crown and were known as *tierras realengas y baldías* (royal and vacant lands). These served as a kind of reservoir from which new grants were made and to which lands whose grantees could not acquire final title, were returned.[2]

Land grants in New Mexico were generally of three categories: (1) municipal concessions made by the crown to an individual *(poblador principal)* or to a group of settlers who wished to found a new community;[3] (2) private grants to farmers, stockraisers and others who agreed to develop rural property; and (3) Pueblo Indian grants which awarded title and guaranteed full possession to the Indians of all lands they occupied or used.[4]

The laws regarding the laying out of new towns throughout the Spanish realm were extensive and precise. Municipal planning was to follow the grid-system, which required straight parallel streets with rectangular blocks and one or more rectangular plazas, the principal one to be designated as the *plaza mayor*.[5] Lots were distributed to the citizens *(vecinos)* or were reserved for government and church buildings. Lands on the fringe of the municipality were set aside as commons *(ejidos)*, pasture lands *(dehesas)* and municipal lands *(propios)*, revenues from which helped defray community expenses.[6] Carefully composed ordinances provided that town sites be selected after consideration had been given to matters of health, climate and defense. With regard to the last of these, settlers were instructed to erect jointly and with the greatest possible haste some kind of palisade or dig a ditch around the main plaza so that Indians could not harm them. In addition, they were encouraged to fortify their own houses.[7]

The royal regulations regarding conditions for the fulfillment of terms for private grants were somewhat less specific, since local conditions often determined particular requirements. A concession of land, however, was sure to include a demand that the recipient place it under cultivation and reside on it for a specified number of years. Restrictions ordinarily included the following: no grant could be made which was prejudicial to the rights of the Indians or which caused injury to a third party; a grant of land conveyed no judicial powers; and mineral rights were retained by the crown.[8]

New Mexico Land and Settlement Procedures

The colonial governors possessed broad powers with regard to the founding of new towns and the assignment of lands and water rights. The contract awarded to New Mexico's founder, Juan de Oñate, set forth in explicit terms his prerogatives in this area. It is apparent that the Ordinances of 1573 concerning the laying out of towns and other laws of the time served as the basis for the authority assigned to him. In

8

addition to determining the location and boundaries of new communities, Oñate was empowered to decide whether the settlement should be designated a *ciudad*, *villa*, or *pueblo* and to organize the municipal government.[9]

Instructions to Don Pedro de Peralta, who assumed the governorship of New Mexico in 1609, provided for the establishment of the villa of Santa Fé, and the terms contained therein also seem to be in conformity with the current legislation.[10] The conduct of succeeding governors furnishes evidence that they were fully cognizant of the laws of the Indies which pertained to the establishment of towns and the distribution of lands.[11] Upon founding the villa of Albuquerque, Governor Francisco Cuervo y Váldez certified that he acted in accordance with royal regulations contained in title seven, book four of the *Recopilación*.[12]

Unfortunately in practically all instances the official records of the actual founding of New Mexico colonial towns are missing. The *instrumentos de la fundación* which conveyed legal status to a new community often contained the petition of the person or persons seeking to establish a settlement, the authorization of the governor, and an account of the formal proceedings whereby the petitioners were placed in possession.[13] Were these instruments available today, doubtless they would shed much light on the motives of Spaniards who participated in expanding New Mexico's frontier and would also aid in solving certain legal problems of modern towns whose foundations date back to Spanish colonial times.[14]

In viewing Spain's land grant policy and the influence it had on settlement patterns, it is important to keep in mind that ultimate title to all lands was retained by the king. Grants were made for occupation and use, the subject taking the rents and profits.[15] If an individual failed to meet the requirements of his grant, or if a grant was abandoned because of the Indian menace, as was often the case, the lands reverted to the crown. Even lands designated as belonging to municipalities remained subject to close royal supervision. This may be noted particularly for town lots or outlying lands which the town corporation failed to assign to citizens.[16] Occasionally after lots had been assigned, the government found it necessary to reclaim them for official use. Such a case occurred in the villa of Santa Fé in 1788 when construction work and expansion of the presidio necessitated the retaking of the lots and houses of three citizens, who were compensated for their loss out of the *tierras realengas y baldías*.[17]

The Seventeenth-Century Pattern

The statements above provide necessary background for an understanding of the introduction and spread of settlement in colonial New Mexico. The initial attempt to found a Spanish community was made by Oñate at San Gabriel near San Juan Pueblo. By the spring of 1610,

9.

however, the effort at this site had been given up, and under viceregal orders the colonists moved southward to establish the villa of Santa Fe.[18] Governor Pedro de Peralta, who was entrusted with carrying out the transfer to the new location, received instructions on the creation of a municipal government and the manner in which lands were to be distributed to citizens. Settlers who received lots in the new villa were required to live upon them for ten years, and if they should absent themselves for three months continuously without permission of the municipal authorities, they were to forfeit all property and rights of citizenship.[19]

Down to the Pueblo revolt of 1680, Santa Fé remained the only formally organized community in the province, as the old San Gabriel settlement was totally abandoned.[20] During this period a trend was established which was carried over and reinforced in the following century: the tendency for the majority of the population to become dispersed throughout the rural areas in isolated farms, ranches and hamlets.

By tradition the Spaniard was a town dweller, accustomed to residing in communities welded into a unit by the practical necessity of defense and the common need to produce an adequate food supply. In New Mexico, as in other remote districts of northern New Spain, the municipal tradition or "sense of community" was greatly weakened and in some cases broke down altogether. This occurred, paradoxically, when the needs of defense and economic cöoperation appeared the greatest.

During the seventeenth century, the small European population labored to sustain and defend the missionary friars and to extract what meager rewards it could from the province's limited resources. Land grants were made to a number of Spanish families, the more affluent of which founded fairly prosperous haciendas. In other cases simple farmsteads strung along river or stream courses were developed by the rural folk. The principal areas of occupation were the valleys north of Santa Fé and the middle Río Grande flood-plain from the Santo Domingo plains southward through the Albuquerque and Belen Valleys. The Spaniards favored these regions because the best agricultural lands were situated here as were the heaviest concentrations of the Pueblo Indian population.

The native towns were distributed in *encomienda* to the leading colonists, who received from them an annual tribute, principally in maize and cotton mantas. Of greater economic significance to the majority of the settlers was Indian labor required on farms and ranches. The going wage was half a *real* a day until 1659, at which time it was increased to a full *real* a day by Governor López de Mendizábal.[21] There is abundant evidence, however, that even this nominal sum was not always maintained, the colonists preferring to squeeze labor out of the Indians while neglecting to compensate them.

10

The Spaniards sought to locate themselves close to exploitable labor and within easy range of their *encomienda* grants. During the first two-thirds of the seventeenth century, the ratio of Spaniard to Indian was such that the number of potential workers probably exceeded the labor demands of the colonists. After 1665, however, famine, pestilence and raids by nomadic tribes on the Pueblo people so depleted their numbers that the village Indians were hard-pressed to meet the labor requirements of the colonists. In fact, one of their chief complaints at the time of the Pueblo revolt was that the Spaniards so burdened them with tasks, that they had little time left to care for their own fields.

The more prosperous ranches might have developed in New Mexico a settlement pattern similar to that which soon appeared in the neighboring province of Nueva Vizcaya, with widely-scattered large properties supported by the labor of dependent Indians or poor mestizos. The Pueblo revolt of 1680, however, extinguished the Spanish settlement clusters in the upper Río Grande Valley and forced a withdrawal of surviving colonists to the El Paso district down-river. When colonization was resumed some twelve years later, new patterns emerged.[22]

NEW TRENDS OF THE EIGHTEENTH CENTURY

In the years following the Pueblo revolt and the reconquest of New Mexico by the Spaniards, the character of settlement underwent a significant change. From 1700 to the end of the Spanish period, loose agglomerations of small farmsteads termed *ranchos* became the typical unit of colonization, in marked contrast to the seventeenth century during which the *hacienda* had predominated. In considerable measure, this shift from large land holdings to farms of more modest size may be attributed to the decrease in Pueblo Indian population, which greatly reduced the labor supply, and to the increase in the numbers of Spanish colonists, whose arrival created a heavy demand for farmlands in the old core area of the Río Grande Valley.[23]

By 1695 Diego de Vargas had reclaimed New Mexico for the Spanish crown, missions had been reëstablished, the villa of Santa Fé had been put in some order and a large number of colonists concentrated there in anticipation of the reöccupation of outlying areas. A survey shortly was made of abandoned farms and ranches, and lands were distributed to both new and old settlers. In some cases it was discovered that Indians had built pueblos on the foundations of former Spanish settlements. Tano people, for example, had moved into such a location in the valley of the Santa Cruz River. As recolonization proceeded they were evicted and the new villa of Santa Cruz de la Cañada was created on the site.[24]

Governor Vargas was eager to found new towns, although orders from the superior government instructed him to keep the settlers together for better defense.[25] Within a brief time, new communities ap-

11

peared and advances were begun into regions which had not previously known European settlement. Since the population expanded far beyond previous limits, it becomes possible to place in sharper focus the distribution patterns for the later colonial years.

DESCRIPTION OF LIFE

New Mexico was essentially a rural province dominated by a rural population living in dozens of small communities. Even in the several villas there is little evidence of true urbanism since the people did not group their houses compactly but scattered them over the neighboring countryside to be near their fields. An examination of the several categories of "village types" which can be defined for the late colonial period will serve to illustrate the direction and character which the pattern of settlement assumed. New Mexican communities may be categorized as *villas* and *poblaciones* or *plazas* for the European population, and for the Indians, *pueblos* and *reducciones*.

The Villas

No New Mexican municipality ever attained the rank of *ciudad*. The formal villas, however, numbered four and included Santa Fé, Albuquerque, Santa Cruz de la Cañada, and El Paso del Norte. All were poorly organized and had populations of probably under 2,500, conditions which elicited the following terse comment from Fray Francisco Domínguez in 1776. Regarding Santa Fé, he declared, "Its appearance, design, arrangement, and plan do not correspond to its status as a *villa*." And he observed that in New Spain there were *pueblos* (a less pretentious title than *villa*) which had far more to recommend them than Santa Fé, a town that "in the final analysis lacked everything."[26]

According to George Kubler, the original plan of Santa Fé had embodied the royal regulations of 1573 for the laying out of new towns, so that this *villa* "of all Hispanic cities in the New World is a paradigm of these ordinances."[27] This statement, however, represents something of an exaggeration. There may have been more regularity to the *villa* in the seventeenth century than in the period after the Pueblo revolt, but at no time did it conform in more than a rudimentary way to the grid-system or to the requirement that adequate fortifications be provided. True, there was a *plaza mayor* fronting on the governor's residence and offices, and perhaps a secondary plaza existed to the west of San Miguel Church, but as to carefully marked streets required by the grid-pattern there were none.[28] Domínguez reported only the semblance of a single street for the entire *villa* in 1776.[29]

This lack of order in the municipal plan developed, not because of the negligence of local government officials, but through the willful determination of Santa Fé citizens to place their residences close to their fields, which were spread along the narrow valley of the Santa Fé River.

12

They desired not only convenient access to farm plots, but wished to keep a constant surveillance over them to prevent the loss of crops to thieves and wild animals. As a result of this scattering, the limits of the *villa* measured about three leagues in circumference by the third quarter of the eighteenth century.[30]

Apparently the formlessness of the community of Santa Fé was repeated in the remaining *villas*. Bishop Tamarón in 1760 reported that at Santa Cruz de la Cañada there was no true town, the settlers being distributed over a wide area.[31] The people of El Paso preferred to live near their vineyards located several leagues above and below the *villa*,[32] while at Albuquerque only twenty-four houses were situated in the vicinity of the church, the rest being scattered for a league upstream.[33] Each *villa* did possess a plaza adjacent to the main church with "town houses" of prominent families and perhaps a government building or two on the square or nearby. Otherwise, homes and small businesses were randomly placed according to the needs of their owners, and in defiance of colonial legislation which demanded adherence to an orderly plan of municipal development.

Poblaciones and Plazas

In New Mexico the loosely-grouped Spanish *ranchos* were generally referred to as *poblaciones*, or if the population consolidated for mutual defense, as *plazas*. The term "plaza," and its derivative "placita," thus were employed in this province to mean a town or village. A very small place was sometimes called merely a *lugar*.[34]

A *rancho* consisted of one or more Spanish households located adjacent to farm and orchard lands. The agricultural plots were small and generally long and narrow as a result of the Spanish custom of subdividing among all the heirs.[35] Land grants were usually apportioned along ditch or stream frontage — those made to Ojo Caliente settlers in 1793 were 150 *varas* wide — with the strip extending sometimes as much as one mile back from the water.[36]

In frontier zones *ranchos* were often established informally, that is, without government sanction, by poor family heads who owned no lands in the more settled central regions and who simply did not wish to abide by the proper legal forms. In 1772, Governor Mendinueta suggested that perhaps the majority of those living on *ranchos* were "intrusive owners of their lands or voluntary holdings."[37] If the farms prospered and survived Indian attack, the original settler or his descendants later might apply for a formal grant.

Scattered *ranchos* or "houses of the field," as they were occasionally termed, were the most characteristic units of rural New Mexico.[38] Even when the farmsteads were dispersed over several leagues, however, a church built by the settlers served as a focal point for community activity. Under pressure of severe Indian raids in the later eighteenth cen-

13

tury, rural people increasingly forsook their isolated *ranchos* and congregated in small fortified towns or *plazas*. In such instances, permission was usually sought from the governor through a formal petition, and regulations regarding construction of fortifications were received and executed.

Walled towns were no novelty to the Spaniard. Fortified villages were a common feature on the Moorish frontier in Spain, and at least one authority asserts that the fortifications for the military camp of Santa Fé de Granada constructed by Ferdinand and Isabella served as the fore-runner of defensive establishments in the New World.[39] Cities protected by walls arose in the Antilles and in those districts of New Spain subject to enemy attack. The villa of Santa Fé had an eight-foot wall with parapets, portions of which survived well into the nineteenth century. And as a defensive measure, the lieutenant-governor at El Paso in 1780 proposed that a wall be constructed around that town, though it seems nothing was done.[40]

On the New Mexico frontier, the settlers usually preferred not to construct a separate wall to shield communities from Indian assault; rather the common practice was to place houses contiguously about a central plaza. The outer walls were left devoid of windows, livestock could be corralled in the square during attack and the single gate barred. Often there were towers or *torreones* constructed in a circular or polygonal fashion. Defensive *plazas* of this kind were known at Chimayo, Truchas, Las Trampas, Taos, Ojo Caliente, Cebolleta and elsewhere.[41]

The type of *plaza* just described was comparatively large, was composed of a number of families, and possessed the aspect of a true town. Similar to it was the "restricted plaza" or fortified dwelling of a single extended family. Such residential clusters of kin were often known by the lineage surname, and those of more imposing nature were designated as haciendas.[42] The hacienda or *casa grande* frequently had extensive walls, towers, parapets and other defensive features similar to those found on the wealthy estates of northern New Spain.[43]

Fortified *plazas* and haciendas in varying degrees conformed to the royal ordinances which laid down measures to be taken for defense. As indicated, the same could not be said for the individual *ranchos* which were located haphazardly according to no particular plan. In certain instances, however, it seems the owners of these humble farmsteads did give some attention to the protection of their families and property. The result was a unique arrangement known as the *casa-corral* unit. As described by Conway it consisted of

> ... a dwelling — usually the conventional one-story adobe structure — with a corral or yard for holding livestock adjoining it in the rear. The walls of the corral were frequently as high as the walls of the house and of one piece with them. A door led directly from the dwelling into the corral ... and the general impression was of a small fortress with stout, high walls, few openings and a compact, economical design.[44]

14

This kind of family unit clearly was derived from the Ordinances of 1573 which required "houses to be constructed so that horses and household animals can be kept therein, the courtyards and stockyards being as large as possible to insure health and cleanliness, ... and to be planned so they can serve as ... a fortress."[45] Admittedly however, as a defensive structure, the New Mexican *casa-corral* unit was far less ambitious than the original laws intended.

Settlers on the edges of the province in the late eighteenth and early nineteenth centuries frequently petitioned the superior authorities for license to desert their homes and retreat to relative safety in the Río Grande Valley. In almost every case, their petitions were denied. Many left the frontier anyway, unmindful of threats of dire penalties. Cases of this kind were common in the Ojo Caliente-Chama district and at other points.[46] In 1805, for example, settlers at Cebolleta beyond the Río Puerco abandoned their community because of Navajo incursions, but they soon were ordered to return by Commandant General Nemesio Salcedo, who promised to send troops to punish the Indians.[47]

Indian Towns

These were of three kinds: (1) those of the Pueblo Indians, (2) the settlements of *genízaros*, and (3) the *reducciones* for members of nomadic tribes. As suggested, the colonial era saw a general reduction in the area occupied by the Pueblo peoples. This trend, which had begun as early as 1300 A. D., was greatly accelerated after the Spanish conquest, so that the Pueblo population and number of villages steadily declined. Remaining Indians concentrated into ever larger communities which were closely integrated and carefully organized for defense.[48]

The strategic value and secure shelter afforded by the pueblos was obvious, even to the Spaniard. Governor Mendinueta in 1772 urged a law with teeth in it which would require settlers to live in compact towns like the Indians.[49] The colonists, however, appear to have been less perturbed by enemy raids than were the Pueblo people; at least they could be induced to take defensive measures only under the most severe pressure.

Many settlers in the Taos valley, one of the areas most vulnerable to Comanche and Ute attack, spent a great deal of time in the eighteenth century living inside Taos Pueblo.[50] A *plaza* and fortified houses of their own had proven inadequate, so they took up more secure homes with the Indians. Father Domínguez in 1776 said of the pueblo, "Its plan resembles that of those walled cities with bastions and towers that are described to us in the Bible."[51] And he mentions heavy gates, fortified towers, a very high wall and solid blocks of houses. While all the pueblos were not as well-defended as this one, nevertheless, they served as a far more effective refuge for their people than did the loose communities of the Spaniards.

15

The settlements of *genízaros* represent a special case, and as a village type they may be classed as a variant of the Indian pueblo. Originally the *genízaros* were Indian captives or slaves of nomadic tribes who were ransomed by the Spanish government. Parceled out among the colonists, they became domestic servants or laborers. As neophytes they were given Christian names and religious instruction. Unfortunately many were mistreated by their Spanish masters and became apostates. Others, however, with the support of Franciscan missionaries petitioned for permission to found their own settlements on the frontier. Believing in the justice of the *genízaro* complaints, the Governor of New Mexico ordered that all who were abused might apply to him for relief and receive assignment to a new town. One of the earliest of such communities was created at the Cerro de Tomé south of Albuquerque.[52] Other *genízaros* later were placed at Abiquiú and the Pecos River towns of San José and San Miguel del Bado.

Since most of these people were of nomadic ancestry, they proved useful to the Spaniards as scouts, spies and auxiliary soldiers. More significant for the discussion here, their towns, located on the fringes of European settlement, constituted an important barrier between the Spanish farmers and the hostile tribes on the frontier.

During colonial times repeated efforts were made to reduce the nomadic native people to community life under supervision of proper religious and civil authority. The *reducción*, an instrument of Spain's Indian policy from the days of earliest settlement in the New World, aimed at nothing short of full social and cultural reörientation of native ways. In many parts of Spanish America, congregation of wandering Indians into a community had been achieved through the use of force. But in New Mexico the several tribes of nomads remained unsubjugated, so that establishment of *reducciones* or formal settlements for them depended upon their voluntary submission. At various times in the eighteenth century, the Spaniards responded to pleas from Navajos, Apaches and Comanches for aid in establishing their own towns, but in the end the Indians returned to a roving life. Since the experimental *reducciones* were situated on the far frontiers, had they succeeded, the jurisdiction of the New Mexican government would have been appreciably expanded and new areas might have been made safe for Spanish colonization.

ATTEMPTS TO REGULATE SETTLEMENT PATTERNS

A recurrent theme in official reports of the colonial years centered upon the problems raised by dispersal of the New Mexican population and the need to consolidate for defense. As early as 1609, the people of New Mexico were described as being "scattered over [that country] so that they are destitute of administration because very few reside in each place . . . ." As a result, orders were issued to gather the colonists

16

46

together so they could stand united against the Indian menace.[53] No significant action was taken, however, and consequently the Spaniards suffered heavy casualties in the 1680 revolt — the isolation of individual families or small settlement clusters permitting the Indian forces to sweep the countryside.

In spite of this tragic experience, the same patterns of dispersal appeared on an even grander scale in the eighteenth century. The case was clearly put by Antonio de Bonilla, who, in 1776, remarked that in New Mexico,

> The settlements of the Spaniards are scattered and badly defended . . . and quite exposed to entire ruin. Because the greater number of them are scattered ranches, among which the force of the settlers is divided, they can neither protect themselves nor contribute to the general defense of the country. This, in consequence, results in the abandonment of their weak homes and the terror of seeing themselves incessantly beset by the enemy.[54]

Of course, the government was concerned at the loss of life and the extra expense entailed in trying to protect an area in which patterns of settlement lacked regularity. But from a long view, of even more fundamental importance was the fact that erratic colonizing practices resulted in loss of entire blocks of territory to enemy raiders and a shrinking rather than an expansion of the frontier at various places. At least one historian has called attention to the Miera y Pacheco map of 1779, which shows there were more abandoned towns in New Mexico than there were occupied towns.[55]

The scattering of *ranchos* and settlements was, in part, an outgrowth of the region's peculiar agricultural requirements — in a country where plowland was scarce, farms, as pointed out, were ribboned along stream valleys, and the people insisted on living near their fields, considerations of defense aside. Critics of the dispersal pattern claimed that the obstinacy and inertia of the colonists were the principal barriers to fulfillment of numerous government orders regarding establishment of organized communities. The issue was stated most forcefully by Father Juan de Morfi writing sometime in the 1780's, who declared that the settlers like to live apart so that, far from the prying eyes of neighbors and the restraining influence of the authorities, they could commit with impunity all manner of immoral and criminal acts. He reported that some isolated colonists "were not ashamed to go about nude so that lewdness was seen here more than in the brutes, and the peaceful Indians were scandalized."[56] While moral looseness does seem to have been common in colonial society — decrees were issued with frequency condemning concubinage, indecent dances and excessive gambling — other causes, as already noted, were chiefly responsible for population dispersal.

This problem, which Bonilla and others regarded as of considerable magnitude, was finally met head-on by the Spanish government. Ac-

17

tion came, nevertheless, only when it was realized that consolidation of the settlers was essential to the defense of the province, and that it was less costly to issue orders to that effect than to accede to repeated requests for additional presidios to supply protection.

Governor Mendinueta in a report of 1772 to Viceroy Bucareli advocated compelling "settlers of each region who live ... dispersed, to join and form their pueblos in plazas or streets so that a few men could be able to defend themselves."[57] The viceroy was in full agreement, but some delay arose before orders could be issued and the task of concentrating the New Mexican settlers begun.[58]

On July 4, 1778, a council was held in Chihuahua which recommended prompt measures for the unification of the New Mexico population. Commandant General Teodoro de Croix then issued orders to Governor Juan Bautista de Anza calling upon him to "regularize" the settlements of his province by collecting scattered families and obliging them to dwell in compact units.[59] By 1779 the villas, except Santa Fé, were reduced to some order, and in the following year considerable success was achieved in concentrating the rural folk.[60] It was in this period of activity that many of the fortified or walled towns on the frontier had their beginnings.

The problem of concentrating the residents of the provincial capital remained unresolved for sometime. The authorities, aware of "the churlish nature of Santa Fé's inhabitants" and of "the perfect freedom in which they always lived," decided to tread slowly and to seek alternative ways to strengthen defenses of the villa.[61] A formal presidio was begun adjacent to the governor's residence on the *plaza mayor* and was brought to completion in the early 1790's. Its purpose was to provide quarters near the center of town for officers and men of the garrison. Heretofore, some of the soldiers had lived as much as a league away from the plaza, and often it required several hours merely to assemble the troops. It is not certain what other measures may have been employed at this time to pull in the limits of the capital and congregate the residents, but in the long view it is doubtful if any fundamental change in the established pattern was achieved.

CONCLUSION

As may be seen from the foregoing, informality and a general lack of planning characterized New Mexican settlements through much of the colonial period. Economic necessity, a strong spirit of frontier individualism, a sense of fatalism about the Indian danger and perhaps a wish to escape the paternal eye of civil government and the Church — these all influenced the settler and nourished in him the desire to build and farm on land of his own choosing, disregarding laws which were aimed at maintaining the collective welfare of the populace.

18

Of all causes contributing to the dispersal pattern, that which required the small farmer to live near his fields to give them proper care and protection was of uppermost importance. In this regard, it is interesting to note that the closely integrated villages of the Pueblo Indians began to break up as soon as the hostile nomads were subdued by the United States Government in the second one-half of the nineteenth century. With that event, it became safe for individual farmers and their families to reside permanently near more distant fields, returning to the main pueblo only on ceremonial occasions.[62] Thus, it appears that only the threat of enemy raiders had prevented the Pueblo people from scattering as the colonial New Mexicans had always done.

Overall, then, it may be said that settlement patterns in this province during the period of Spanish rule were shaped primarily by economic needs of the rural folk and only secondarily by considerations of defense. The strong tendency toward dispersion of the population was probably characteristic of most of northern New Spain, but may well have been more pronounced in New Mexico owing to greater isolation and looser enforcement of governmental decrees.

NOTES

1. J. M. Ots Capdequí, *El estado Español en las Indias* (4th ed.; Mexico, 1965), p. 34.
2. *Ibid.*, p. 36; and Julio Jiménez Rueda, *Historia de la cultura en México, El vierreinato* (Mexico, 1951), p. 42.
3. Professor Clark S. Knowlton sharply distinguishes the "proprietary grant" (that of a *poblador principal*) from a community grant (one extended to a petitioning group of at least ten families seeking to establish a community). "Land Grant Problems Among the State's Spanish Americans." *New Mexico Business*, Vol. XX (1967), p. 2.
4. The existence of actual grants for the Pueblos must be inferred, since no original title papers are known today. The "Cruzate Grants" for the Pueblos have been proven to be largely fraudulent. See Myra Ellen Jenkins, "The Baltasar Baca 'Grant': History of an Encroachment," reprinted from *El Palacio*, Vol. LXVIII (1961), pp. 51-52.
5. See Dan Stanislawski, "The Origin and Spread of the Grid-Pattern Town," *The Geographic Review*, Vol. XXXVI (1946), pp. 105-120; and by the same author, "Early Spanish Town Planning in the New World," *ibid.*, Vol. XXXVII (1947), pp. 94-105.
6. O. Garfield Jones, "Local Government in the Spanish Colonies as Provided by the *Recopilación de Leyes de los Reynos de las Indias,*" *The Southwestern Historical Quarterly*, Vol. XIX (1916), p. 68. Municipal plans which might show the *ejidos, propios* and *dehesas* for New Mexico communities are generally lacking. A colonial plan of the villa of San Fernando de Béxar in Texas, however, clearly manifests these features. Reproduced in Herbert Eugene Bolton, TEXAS IN THE MIDDLE EIGHTEENTH CENTURY (new ed.; New York, 1962), p. 6.
7. Zelia Nuttall (trans.), "Royal Ordinances Concerning the Laying Out of New Towns," *Hispanic American Historical Review*, Vol. V (1922), p. 252.
8. Ots Capdequí, *El estado Español en las Indias*, p. 35; and Agustín Cue Cánovas, *Historia social y económica de México, 1521-1854* (Mexico, 1963), pp. 114-16.
9. George P. Hammond and Agapito Rey, DON JUAN DE ONATE, *Colonizer of New Mexico, 1595-1628* (2 vols.; Albuquerque, 1953), Vol. II, p. 599. The classification of a municipality as *ciudad, villa* or *pueblo* (city, town or village) was more than a mere formality since these terms implied definite ranking according to prestige and importance. Also the number of municipal magistrates and councilmen allowed by law depended upon the status of the community. See especially Ralph Emerson Twitchell, "Spanish Colonization and the Founding of *Ciudades* and *Villas* in the Time of Oñate," New Mexico Bar Association Minutes, 32nd Annual Session, Albuquerque, August, 1918, pp. 27-43.
10. "Ynstrucción a Peralta por vi-rey" *New Mexico Historical Review*, Vol. IV (1929), pp. 178-80.
11. See, for example, the remarks of Pedro Fermín de Mendinueta in Alfred B. Thomas,

19

"Governor Mendinueta's Proposals for the Defense of New Mexico, 1772-1778," *New Mexico Historical Review*, Vol. VI (1931), p. 33.

12. Charles Wilson Hackett, HISTORICAL DOCUMENT RELATING TO NEW MEXICO, NUEVA VIZCAYA, AND APPROACHES THERETO, TO 1773 (3 vols.; Washington, 1937), Vol. III, p. 379.

13. Lansing B. Bloom (ed.), "Albuquerque and Galisteo, Certificate of Their Founding, 1706," *New Mexico Historical Review*, Vol. X (1935), pp. 49-50.

14. Richard E. Greenleaf, "The Foundation of Albuquerque, 1706: An Historical Legal Problem," *New Mexico Historical Review*, Vol. XXXIX (1964), pp. 1-15.

15. Frank W. Blackmar, SPANISH INSTITUTIONS OF THE SOUTHWEST (Baltimore, 1891), p. 319.

16. The general theory of Castilian law on the subject indicates that citizens received allotments for their use and enjoyment, "but the domain itself remained in the person of the sovereign." Ralph E. Twitchell, "Spanish Colonization in New Mexico in the Oñate and De Vargas Periods," Historical Society of New Mexico, *Publications*, No. 22, p. 9.

17. Jacobo Ugarte y Loyola to Fernando de la Concha, Chihuahua, July 22, 1788, Archivo General de la Nación, México, Provincias Internas, Vol. 161, pt. 4. (From a photocopy in the Coronado Room, University of New Mexico Library, Albuquerque. Archivo General de la Nación hereinafter cited as AGN.)

18. Lansing B. Bloom, "When Was Santa Fé Founded?" *New Mexico Historical Review*, Vol. IV (1920), p. 194.

19. "Ynstrucción a Peralta," *New Mexico Historical Review*, Vol. IV (1929), p. 180.

20. France V. Scholes, "Civil Government and Society in New Mexico in the Seventeenth Century," *New Mexico Historical Review*, Vol. X (1935), p. 94.

21. France V. Scholes, *Troublous Times in New Mexico, 1659-1670*, Historical Society of New Mexico, *Publications in History*, Vol. XI (1942), p. 25.

22. Wilfred D. Kelley, "Settlement of the Middle Río Grande Valley," *The Journal of Geography*, Vol. LIV (1955), p. 393.

23. Pueblo population in 1600 has been estimated at 35,000. According to Hubert Howe Bancroft, by 1660 it had dropped to about 20,000, and in 1760 it was down to some 9,000. HISTORY OF ARIZONA AND NEW MEXICO (new ed.; Albuquerque, 1962), pp. 172, 279.

24. J. Manuel Espinosa, CRUSADERS OF THE RIO GRANDE (Chicago, 1942), pp. 221-25.

25. *Ibid.*, p. 227.

26. Fr. Francisco Atanasio Domínguez, THE MISSIONS OF NEW MEXICO, trans. by Eleanor B. Adams and Fr. Angélico Chávez (Albuquerque, 1956), p. 39.

27. THE RELIGIOUS ARCHITECTURE OF NEW MEXICO (Colorado Springs, 1940), p. 18.

28. Vargas mentions two *plazas* for Santa Fé in 1695 (Espinosa, *Crusaders of the Río Grande*, p. 225), and the Urrutía map of ca. 1766-68 shows an open space in front of San Miguel Church in the Indian *barrio* of Analco. Mr. Bruce Ellis of the Museum of New Mexico suggests that the present plaza was the *plaza mayor* or *plaza de armas* of the colonial documents, and that the secondary *plaza* may have existed immediately to the east in front of the parish church.

29. Domínguez, *The Missions of New Mexico*, p. 40.

30. Fernando de la Concha to Jacobo Ugarte y Loyola, Santa Fe, November 10, 1787, AGN, Prov. Int., 161.

31. Eleanor B. Adams (ed.), BISHOP TAMARON'S VISITATION OF NEW MEXICO, *1760*, Historical Society of New Mexico, *Publications in History*, Vol. XV (1954), p. 63.

32. Petition of Residents of El Paso, April 13, 1780, Spanish Archives of New Mexico, State Records Center and Archives, Santa Fé. (Spanish Archives of New Mexico hereinafter cited as SANM).

33. Domínguez, *The Missions of New Mexico*, p. 151.

34. The designation of "pueblo" for a Spanish community was usually avoided in New Mexico since the village Indians from a very early time were called Pueblos. The term "rancho" should be translated as small farm rather than ranch. For a definition of this word as it was used in colonial New Spain see Roberto Mac-Lean y Estenós, *Indios de América* (Mexico, 1962), pp. 79-80.

35. Kelley, "Settlement of the Middle Río Grande Valley," *The Journal of Geography*, Vol. LIV (1955), p. 394.

36. E. Boyd, "Troubles at Ojo Caliente, A Frontier Post," *El Palacio*, Vol. LXIV (1957), pp. 349, 359.

37. Thomas, "Governor Mendinueta's Proposals," *New Mexico Historical Review*, Vol. VI (1931), p. 33.

38. *Ibid.*, p. 27

39. Robert C. Smith, "Colonial Towns of Spanish and Portuguese America," *Journal of the Society of Architectural Historians*, Vol. XIV (1955), p. 4. It is curious to note that early documents and maps occasionally designate the capital of New Mexico as "Santa Fé de la Granada."

40. Petition, April 13, 1780, SANM.

20

41. Bainbridge Bunting and John P. Conron, "The Architecture of Northern New Mexico," *New Mexico Architecture*, Vol. VIII (1966), p. 16. There existed abundant precedent in New Spain for this type of community. For example, an early plan called for a *casa-muro*, or wall of houses, to be built in Mexico City soon after the conquest. George Kubler, MEXICAN ARCHITECTURE OF THE SIXTEENTH CENTURY (2 vols., New Haven, 1948), Vol. I, p. 78. Also, fortified towns had been common on the Chichimec frontier. Philip Wayne Powell, SOLDIERS, INDIANS AND SILVER (Berkeley, 1952), pp. 153-55.
42. Hugh and Evelyn Burnet, "Madrid Plaza," *Colorado Magazine*, Vol. XLII (1965), p. 224. This article includes the sketch of a "restricted plaza" of the nineteenth century.
43. For a description of the *casa grande* of Pablo de Villapando near Taos, see the legend on the Miera y Pacheco map, translated by Adams and Chávez in Domínguez, *Missions of New Mexico*, p. 4.
44. A. W. Conway, "Southwestern Colonial Farms," *Landscape, Human Geography of the Southwest*, Vol. I (1961), p. 6. According to the author, the *casa corral* unit was distributed throughout the Southwest and the north Mexican provinces.
45. Nuttall, "Royal Ordinances Concerning the Laying Out of New Towns, *Hispanic American Historical Review*, Vol. V, (1922), p. 252.
46. Boyd "Troubles at Ojo Caliente," *El Palacio*, Vol. LXIV (1957), *passim*. Regarding a petition of Chamita settlers to leave their residences, and a refusal of permission by Governor Vélez Cachupín see Ralph Emerson Twitchell, THE LEADING FACTS OF NEW MEXICAN HISTORY (2 vols.; Albuquerque, 1963), Vol. II, p. 317n.
47. Salcedo to Chacón, Chihuahua, January 11, 1805, SANM.
48. Fred Wendorf, "Some Distributions of Settlement Patterns in the Pueblo Southwest," in Gordon R. Willey (ed.), *Pre-historic Settlement Patterns in the New World*, Viking Fund Publications in Anthropology, No. 23 (New York, 1956), pp. 21-22.
49. Bancroft, *History of Arizona and New Mexico*, p. 259.
50. Myra Ellen Jenkins, "Taos Pueblo and Its Neighbors, 1540-1847," *New Mexico Historical Review*, Vol. XLI (1966), pp. 98-99.
51. Domínguez, *The Missions of New Mexico*, p. 110.
52. Declaration of Fr. Miguel de Menchero, Santa Bárbara, May 10, 1744, in Hackett, *Historical Documents*, Vol. III, pp. 401-2.
53. "Ynstrucción a Peralta," *New Mexico Historical Review*, Vol. IV (1929), p. 184.
54. Alfred B. Thomas (ed. and trans.), "Antonio de Bonilla and Spanish Plans for the Defense of New Mexico, 1777-1778," in NEW SPAIN AND THE WEST (2 vols.; Lancaster, Pa., 1932), Vol. I, p. 196.
55. Cleve Hallenbeck, LAND OF THE CONQUISTADORES (Caldwell, Idaho, 1950), p. 243.
56. Fr. Juan Agustín de Morfi, Desórdenes que se advierten en el Nuevo Mexico, AGN, Historia, 25.
57. Thomas, "Governor Mendinueta's Proposals," *New Mexico Historical Review*, Vol. VI (1931), p. 29.
58. Luís Navarro García, *Don José de Gálvez y la comandancia general de las Provincias Internas del Norte de Nueva España* (Sevilla, 1964). p. 244; and Thomas. "Bonilla and Spanish Plans for the Defense of New Mexico," *New Spain and the West*, Vol. I, p. 201.
59. Concha to Ugarte, Santa Fe, June 20, 1788, AGN, Prov. Int., 161.
60. *Ibid.*; and Alfred B. Thomas, FORGOTTEN FRONTIERS: *A Study of the Spanish-Indian Policy of Don Juan Bautista de Anza* (Norman, 1932); pp. 94; 101.
61. Concha to Ugarte, Santa Fe, June 20, 1788, AGN, Prov. Int., 161.
62. Wendorf. "Some Distributions of Settlement Patterns," in Willey (ed.), *Pre-historic Settlement Patterns*, p. 22.

21

Repostero of the eighth Duke of Alburquerque, Don Francisco Fernández de la Cueva, twenty-second Viceroy of Mexico, 1653-1660. Courtesy of T. M. Pearce.

GOVERNOR CUERVO AND THE BEGINNINGS
OF ALBUQUERQUE: ANOTHER LOOK

MARC SIMMONS

On APRIL 23, 1706, some seventy years before the American
Revolution, Governor Francisco Cuervo y Valdés of New Mexico
sat at a writing table in the dimly lit halls of his mud palace on the
Santa Fe plaza. He was composing a formal document to his
sovereign in Spain and to the viceroy in Mexico City, attesting to
the creation of a new town. Deftly he wrote, "I certify to the king,
our lord, and to the most excellent señor viceroy . . . That I
founded a villa on the banks and in the valley of the Río del Norte
in a good place as regards land, water, pasture, and firewood . . .
I gave it as patron titular saint the glorious apostle of the Indies,
Señor Francisco Xavier, and called and named it the villa of
Alburquerque."[1]

With a hint of pride in his words, Governor Cuervo went on to
relate the progress that had been made to date. Thirty-five families, he asserted, had already taken up residence in the town, comprising 252 adults and children. A spacious church had been completed, and a house for the priest was well underway. A start had
been made on the *casas reales*, that is the government buildings for
local officials. The settlers had finished their houses, which were
provided with corrals for livestock. Irrigation ditches were open
and running. Crops were sown. The town was now in good order,
well-arranged, and all had been achieved without any expense to
the Royal Treasury. This last implied that the people themselves
had borne the entire costs for the town's founding.

The governor wished to emphasize the legality of his actions.
Therefore, he declared that he had followed the procedures prescribed for the establishment of new municipalities as set forth in
the royal laws contained in the *Recopilación*, the law book that

0028-6206/80/0700-0188 $2.00/0

governed the conduct of colonial officials. Having said that, and having added a note attesting to the refounding of the Pueblo of Galisteo, which had been abandoned during the turbulence of the Pueblo revolt and reconquest, Francisco Cuervo y Valdés affixed his signature to the paper, had it witnessed by his secretary, and sealed it with an impression of his coat of arms.[2]

The governor's words contained in this formal document of certification are straightforward and clear enough: he founded the villa of Albuquerque in 1706, he provided his superiors certain details about the number of settlers and the buildings then under construction or already completed, and he stated that the project had been carried out in strict conformity with the law. The legal code, which he referred to as the *Recopilación*, was the celebrated *Recopilación de las Leyes de Indias*, Spain's monumental compilation of laws covering practically all aspects of colonial government and public life. One section dealt specifically with the procedures and requirements for creation of new towns.

According to that code, a minimum of thirty family heads was necessary to charter a villa. The site chosen should have good water, arable land, and some timber, if possible. The town received four square leagues of land, measured with a cord. At its center, space was to be marked off for a plaza, a church, and government buildings. As soon as streets were laid out, each family should be given a lot for a house and assigned farm plots in severalty. After living upon the lots and improving the farmland for a specified number of years, residents obtained final title. Portions of the town grant, not distributed to citizens, were reserved as commons *(ejidos)* available to all for pasturing, wood gathering, or rock quarrying. Further, a villa was to have an elected council *(cabildo)* with jurisdiction over executive and judicial affairs of the municipality.[3] These major provisions, and other minor ones, were all designed to provide Spanish colonial towns with an orderly form of government.

Three days after certifying to the founding of Albuquerque, Governor Cuervo wrote a letter to the Viceroy, Francisco Fernández de la Cueva, Duke of Alburquerque.[4] In it he provided background information about the new villa which had not been included in the earlier notice of certification. Motivated by a desire to see New Mexico expand and prosper, Governor Cuervo said that he had issued orders for the placing of a villa on the river below Bernalillo and Alameda. In advance of actual settlement, he had sent one of his subordinates, General Juan de Ulibarrí, to scout the area and find a suitable site. The spot Ulibarrí selected possessed the necessary tillable land, water, pasture, and firewood, as the law required. It had other natural advantages, too, which though left unmentioned by Cuervo in his letter to the viceroy, could scarcely have escaped notice. For one, the center of the proposed villa was situated on ground slightly elevated above the surrounding bottom lands affording some protection from periodic flooding by the Rio Grande, or Rio del Norte as the governor called it. For another, the geographical position of the town appeared ideal as far as the practical needs of the future settlers were concerned. It lay astride the Camino Real, a good ford on the river existed nearby to the west, and a dozen miles due eastward yawned the mouth of the Cañon de Carnué (Tijeras Canyon), a pass giving access to the plains beyond the Sandia Mountains.

Once the site had been chosen, Cuervo explained that he made a public announcement throughout the province inviting citizens to join in creating the new community. Many families responded, he told the viceroy, bringing with them herds of cattle and flocks of sheep. For security, he detached a squad of ten soldiers from the Santa Fe presidio and sent it to escort the settlers while on the road and then to take up permanent guard duty at the villa. The troops, accompanied by their families, were led by Captain Martín Hurtado. Their presence played an important part in attracting participants to the endeavor, because, as the governor himself noted gravely, the country south of Bernalillo was alive with hostile Apaches. Even as few as ten soldiers stationed in the villa could offer considerable comfort to the Spanish colonists.

Thus far Governor Cuervo had provided the viceroy with simple information, but now he could not resist the temptation to make an optimistic forecast about his municipal creation. "I do not doubt, very excellent lord, that in a short time this will be the most prosperous Villa for its growth of cattle and abundance of grain, because of its great fertility and for [my] having given it, in spiritual and temporal things, the patron saints that I have chosen, namely the ever glorious apostle of the Indies, San Francisco Xavier, and Your Excellency, with whose names the town has been entitled Villa de Alburquerque de San Francisco Xavier del Bosque."⁵ Clearly the governor was bucking for favor when he gave the viceroy's name to the new town.

In conclusion, Cuervo declared, "The Villa was sworn, taking into account the things ordered by his Majesty in his royal laws."⁶ By the word "sworn," he meant that the heads of households had taken an oath as charter citizens to live upon and improve lands allotted to them as a requirement for gaining final title of possession.

From the foregoing statements, it is clear Governor Cuervo intended to show that, through his own efforts, he had assembled a respectable number of colonists and chartered the new villa of Albuquerque; that he had ordered delineation of the outer boundaries of the community as well as the marking of a site for a plaza; and that he had caused a church and government offices to be built. Unfortunately, other evidence indicates that the ambitious governor, in his claims, strayed several degrees from the truth. Indeed, as a subsequent review of other documents will show, he uttered numerous half-truths and several outright falsehoods. Some doubt is, therefore, cast upon the traditional belief that Albuquerque was founded as a lawful Spanish municipality.

The subject is of more than academic interest. As child and heir of the Spanish colonial villa, the modern city of Albuquerque has on occasion asserted claim to land and water rights in the courts by reference to Hispanic law governing the community at its founding. Such a stand has always been predicated upon the position that Governor Cuervo, true to his word to the king and viceroy, conducted the formal proceedings and followed the steps as stipulated by the *Recopilación* which were needed to establish Albuquerque as a legal entity.

In 1881, at the beginning of the boom occasioned by arrival of the railroad, the city of Albuquerque placed a petition before the state Surveyor General asking that he survey a tract of four square leagues (roughly 17.2 square miles), centering upon the Old Town plaza, and then recommend to Congress that it place Albuquerque in possession. The claim was based solely upon the old Spanish practice of granting four square leagues to each new villa. Although Governor Cuervo had never referred in existing documents to such a grant, it has always been supposed that one was made, owing to his sweeping assertion that he had hewed to the letter of the law as spelled out in the *Recopilación*.

The Surveyor General of New Mexico evidently assumed as much, for he acted favorably upon Albuquerque's petition, surveyed the "imagined" four square leagues, and recommended it for confirmation by Congress. He was careful to explain to Washington, however, that, "No original documents constituting or creating the grant hereby are known to exist, and therefore no such document can be filed herewith."[7] What he supposed, as have most lawyers and historians since, was that the original grant papers, which Cuervo must have drawn up, had become lost over the years, but that unfortunate circumstance notwithstanding, Albuquerque was still entitled to its four leagues of land. The tough-minded Congressmen, though, were not swayed by such an argument, and eventually the city's claim was disallowed.

The issue came up again in 1959, but this time in relation to water rights. The city became involved in a dispute with the state over use of waters in the surrounding Rio Grande basin. It claimed that under Spanish law the villa of Albuquerque was conceded all the water necessary for its growth and development and that since the modern city was the legal heir of the villa, its right in this regard remained unimpaired. The New Mexico Supreme Court finally decided against the city on the basis of other legal points. Yet what is significant here is that much of Albuquerque's stand rested upon the popular assumption that in the year 1706 Governor Francisco Cuervo y Valdés officially established a valid community according to the laws of Spain.[8]

It is now possible to clarify, in some measure, the incidents attendant upon Albuquerque's beginnings, particularly the actions of Governor Cuervo. But since serious gaps still exist in the documentary record, our picture, though revised and brought into sharper focus, remains disappointingly fuzzy around the edges. Keeping that fact in mind, we can begin by taking a close look at what was going on in New Mexico, and especially in the Middle Rio Grande Valley, during the years immediately prior to 1706.

When Governor Diego de Vargas died at Bernalillo in April 1704, his second in command Juan Paéz Hurtado, a native of Andalucia and a staunch soldier, took charge of the province. At once he notified the viceroy, the Duke of Alburquerque, of Vargas's passing, and then he set about holding things together until a replacement could be named.

Paéz Hurtado had no easy task, for New Mexico was in a state of extraordinary disarray. Predatory bands of Apache and Navajo stalked the small Spanish settlements and ranches, and nothing the few score soldiers were able to do seemed to stem their constant attacks. Those same soldiers, in whose hands defense of the frontier lay, suffered from lack of provisions, a shortage of horses, inadequate pay, and low morale. Compounding the Indian problem, some of the western Pueblos still refused to submit to Spanish rule. The Zuni, after first pledging loyalty, had changed their minds and abandoning their pueblo fled to a neighboring mesa top where they remained until a Spanish priest talked them down in 1705. The Hopi, still farther west, continued defiant and, indeed, would persist as a thorn in the side of Spanish governors throughout the remainder of the colonial period.

The settler folk who had come with Vargas in 1693 and others who arrived in a thin but steady trickle in succeeding years had not fared well. Government support in the form of provisions and tools sustained them initially, while they commenced to rebuild the province, but such aid was drastically curtailed in 1698 when officials of the royal treasury in Mexico City arbitrarily decided that New Mexicans should have made enough headway by then to go it alone. The loss of material backing unluckily coincided with the beginning of a severe drought which stretched without relief from 1698 to 1704. Streams evaporated, scorched pastureland was grazed over and became ankle-deep in dust. Crops withered and produced at harvest scarcely enough seed for the next planting. Livestock wasted away. And hunger became a grim spectre stalking the colonists. The stars, it seemed, were aligned against them.[*]

The miserable economic conditions led inevitably to social discord. Petty controversies split the populace into squabbling factions and produced so much poisoned air that many embittered persons threatened to pull stakes and return to El Paso.

It was this atmosphere of despair and gloom which Francisco Cuervo y Valdés found when he arrived at Santa Fe on March 10, 1705, to take over the reins of government. He had received his appointment to office directly from the viceroy, on condition that the king approve. But since such approval might be months in coming, owing to the slowness of trans-Atlantic mail service, Cuervo had hastened on to New Mexico to begin at once putting affairs there in order. Until confirmed in office, he would be merely the provisional governor. That temporary status perhaps explains his strenuous efforts to make a good showing during the first months after his arrival.[10]

Cuervo was well fitted by background and experience to follow in the footsteps of the lamented Governor Vargas. A native of Santa María de Grado in the province of Asturias, northern Spain, his family was evidently of the nobility, for noble lineage was one of the requirements for membership in the military order of Santiago, to which Cuervo was elected sometime after 1698.[11]

He arrived in the New World in the year 1678 and proceeded to Sonora (which included much of present-day southern Arizona) where he took up duties as an infantry captain. Three years later, he became lieutenant-governor of the province. Thereafter, he served in succession as the military governor of the provinces of Nuevo León and Coahuila, which lay immediately to the south of Texas. It was his skillful performance in the handling of those offices and his wide knowledge of frontier affairs that led the Duke of Alburquerque to name him to the governorship of New Mexico late in 1704.

Once in Santa Fe, Cuervo made a hasty survey of local conditions and discovered excellent grounds for apprehension. The depth of his dismay is evident in words he addressed to the king. "I have never seen so much want, misery, and backwardness in my life," he wrote His Majesty. "I suspect this land was better off before the Spaniards came."[12] Such a candid admission indicates that the new governor was something of a realist.

Since military defense was one of his prime concerns, Cuervo undertook a quick inspection of the one hundred regular troops attached to the Santa Fe presidio. Then he called for a general muster of the citizens' militia. Because of the constant danger from hostile Indians, all able-bodied men were enrolled in militia companies. Under orders of the governor, those from the towns of Santa Cruz de la Cañada and Bernalillo marched to the capital for a review and inspection. The Bernalillo contingent, the military records note, was led by three captains: Fernando de Chávez, Diego de Montoya, and Manuel Baca. All were destined to play a prominent role in the early history of Albuquerque.[13]

With a coldly professional eye, Governor Cuervo tallied up his forces, both regular and volunteer, and determined that their number was far too small to defend his broad domain. He fired off a letter to Mexico City asking for reinforcements, but as he may well have anticipated, the economy-minded viceroy simply pigeonholed the request. No more soldiers were to be forthcoming.

The governor's next move was to take the troops already quartered in Santa Fe and spread them out on the frontier. He hoped that by patrolling the danger zones with small squads, the Apaches and other tribes could be stopped from running rough-shod over the New Mexican settlements. To that end, temporary detachments were stationed at the pueblos of Santa Clara, Cochiti, Jemez, Laguna, Acoma, and Zuni.

As part of a broad policy to gain cooperation of the Pueblo Indians, Cuervo toured their villages, spoke to the leaders in conciliatory terms, and obtained promises of aid in the continuing war against the Apache. From those meetings, he drew a high opinion of the Pueblo people, referring to them as handsome in appearance and industrious by nature.[14] The Indians, for their part, responded favorably to the governor's overtures. Indeed, they came to regard him as something of a savior, or so he tried to convince the king. By letter, Cuervo declared immodestly that Pueblo spokesmen who gathered at Santa Fe in January 1706 voluntarily composed a document urging that "Don Francisco Cuervo y Valdés be continued and maintained in this administration for such time as is His Majesty's will. . . ."[15]

The implication is plain. Worried over his pending confirmation, the governor had contrived an endorsement from the Indians in a bid to polish his image and win approval from the crown. Something of the same motive, in part, was behind Cuervo's move to create a new villa in the Bosque de Doña Luisa. Certainly, he exaggerated on paper the dimensions of the project and his role in its initiation, as we shall see shortly.

Actually, interest in founding a villa somewhere in the Middle Valley of the Rio Grande had existed long before Cuervo y Valdés assumed the governorship. The idea first surfaced in 1662 when Governor Peñalosa made an unsuccessful attempt to promote a town in that area. The matter came up again after the revolt and reconquest. The municipal council of Santa Fe in 1698 called upon the governor to establish a villa in the Rio Abajo, but once more, nothing was done.[16]

While officialdom may have been guilty of heel dragging with regard to organizing a formal villa, the same could not be said for individual Spanish colonists who were eager to develop the potentially rich agricultural lands of the Middle Valley. Some of them, as mentioned earlier, had peeled off from Vargas's returning column in 1693 and reoccupied portions of the valley, especially the Bernalillo district. Over the next several years, Governor Vargas made a number of land grants to persons who desired farms in the country between Alameda and the swamps of Mejía. One of those grants, issued in the summer of 1704, went to Luís García, who reclaimed the estate of his grandfather, the former lieutenant-governor, Alonso García.[17]

The pueblo of Alameda itself, which had been burned by the Spaniards in the aftermath of the Pueblo Revolt, remained untenanted until 1702 when missionaries gathered about fifty stray Tiwas and rebuilt the village. This population, however, was evidently too small to maintain a viable community, and six years later, the Indians moved downstream and joined Isleta Pueblo.[18] That left the abundant and fertile farmland, stretching south from Bernalillo, available to Spanish citizens who might wish to apply for grants.

One nucleus of settlement, predating the founding of Albuquerque, was the village of Atrisco, located on the west bank of the river and facing the site of the future villa. At least by 1703, the place was recognized as a community even though in form it was no more than a collection of farms. Lacking any municipal organization, Atrisco was attached for administrative purposes first to Bernalillo and, then after 1706, to Albuquerque. Throughout the remainder of the colonial period, the village was a satellite of its larger neighbor, and in fact was often spoken of as "Atrisco de Albuquerque."[19]

Tenth Duke of Alburquerque. During his term as Viceroy of New Spain the Villa de Alburquerque was founded. Courtesy of T. M. Pearce.

One thing is clear then: a number of Spanish property holdings existed on both sides of the Rio Grande well before Governor Cuervo certified to the king and viceroy in the spring of 1706 that he had founded the Villa of Alburquerque. But in spite of that start, there had been no great rush of settlers from elsewhere in New Mexico to claim a share of the plentiful cropland and pasture available in the region. The vulnerability of the valley to Indian attack offered the major stumbling block to expansion of settlement. That problem, Cuervo hoped to alleviate by stationing the detachment of ten soldiers at the new villa. Their presence plainly proved to be a key factor in luring colonists to Albuquerque.

Information surrounding the actual formation of the villa, including the ceremonial taking of possession and distribution of lands to residents, is very thin. Most writers have tried to reconstruct a picture of the event by reference to procedures set down in Spanish law and to ceremonies, described at a later date, for the founding of other New Mexico towns.[20] There would seem to be justification for such guessing because Governor Cuervo, as noted, did give the king flat assurance that in establishing Albuquerque he followed the laws as set down in the *Recopilación*.

In a remote area, such as New Mexico, however, some flexibility in application of the laws seems to have been permitted. General Vargas, for example, upon creating the villa of Santa Cruz in 1695, placed it under an appointed alcalde mayor, who also had the title of militia captain, rather than under the usual elective municipal council, or cabildo. As he pointed out, he gave the town "this style and form of government because of its being on the frontier."[21] In addition, he specifically decreed that Santa Fe, the first villa of the province, should alone have the privilege of operating under a municipal council. The precedent established by that order as well as Albuquerque's status as a frontier community, perhaps explain why Governor Cuervo in chartering his new villa in 1706 provided it with an alcalde mayor rather than a cabildo.

A native born New Mexican, forty-six year old Captain Martín Hurtado, was the man Governor Cuervo selected to serve as the first alcalde mayor of the Villa of Alburquerque, as well as the commander of the ten man military squad to be garrisoned there.

To Hurtado must go credit for partitioning lands among charter members of the villa, which he did during January 1706, and for conducting the founding ceremony on the following February 7. We would like to believe that the assembled populace gathered at the spot selected for a plaza, participated in the marking off of streets and town lots, and helped designate the sites for a church and soldiers' quarters. They would also have followed behind Captain Hurtado while the town's lawful four square leagues were measured and marked. In conformity with ancient Spanish custom, they would have pulled up grass, thrown rocks in the air, and shouted, "long live the king!", symbolic acts associated with the taking possession of new lands. Later, some of the colonists recorded that they had sworn an oath, which confirms that some kind of formal proceedings took place. But whether the four leagues were actually surveyed and whether plaza, streets, lots, and commons were marked is open to question.[22]

Further uncertainty surrounds the actual number of charter citizens. The governor's own declaration that there were thirty-five families with 252 people has generally been accepted by scholars. But Juan Candelaria, recollecting seventy years after the fact, stated that the villa got its start when twelve families from Bernalillo moved to the site, accompanied by the soldier escort which Governor Cuervo had assigned to them.[23]

A wholly different picture emerges from the records of an investigation into the governor's activities which was conducted in 1712, after he had left office and returned to Mexico. At that time the king's ministers, while reviewing documents in their archive, discovered discrepencies in some of the claims put forth by former governor Cuervo y Valdés of New Mexico. As a result, they prevailed upon the crown to issue a royal *cédula*, or decree, directing the current governor of the province, Juan Igancio Flores Mogollon, to open an official inquiry. Specifically, they wanted to know whether Albuquerque had been legally founded and whether the charter families had numbered thirty-five, as Cuervo maintained. They also asked that his claims to having created another villa north of Santa Fe, called Santa María de Grado, and having refounded the abandoned pueblos of Galisteo and Pojoaque with displaced Indians be examined.

At Santa Fe, Governor Flores Mogollon, upon receiving the king's cédula, appointed Vargas's old friend and subordinate, General Juan Paéz Hurtado, to carry out the investigation. The general spent several months traveling about the province taking depositions from citizens, and his findings, particularly as they relate to the beginnings of Albuquerque, are most illuminating.

Opening the judicial inquiry at the Villa of Alburquerque on October 21, 1712, Paéz Hurtado summoned witnesses and received their testimony "under the sign of the cross," that is, under oath. Here is the statement of Pedro Azencio López:

Question: Was he one of the founding citizens of the villa which was settled by order of Don Francisco Cuervo?

López: That was true. He had joined with his father, Pedro López, when the governor founded it.

Question: How many persons were in his family?

López: Five.

Question: Did he know the total number of founding families?

López: There were nineteen original families, plus the ten soldiers, with their women and children, who served as guard for the vicinity. The nineteen families at the time comprised 103 people, not counting dependents of the soldiers. Now they totaled 129 people.

Question: Had the said Don Francisco Cuervo provided them any government aid (*ayuda de costa*) at the founding?

López: He knew of none.

Question: Had the villa been established in proper form with streets and a plaza?

López: He and the other settlers had moved into the houses abandoned by the Spaniards in 1680, occupying the same estancias and farms. What was called the villa stretched for more than two and a half miles (one league) from the first house to the last.

Question: Were there now any families here beyond those settled by Don Francisco Cuervo?

López: Yes. Seven additional families with twenty-two people.

Pedro López then declared that he knew no more about the matter and was dismissed. A succession of other witnesses gave similar testimony, in each case verifying López's population figures. From their statements, a few supplementary details can be gleaned. For example, Captain Fernando Durán y Chávez, long one of the leading men of the valley, was asked if Albuquerque had been lawfully formed with streets and a plaza, as His Majesty required. He responded that from the day of its founding, the villa had the same layout as it did then, with the residents living in homes built before 1680. They were scattered for a league from the first house of Baltasar Romero on the north [at modern Ranchos de Albuquerque] to the last house on the south, that of Pedro López [below Central Avenue]. All of this area, he noted, was heavily wooded (*en mucha alameda*). And, he reports that it was by the authority of Governor Cuervo that the pre-revolt estancias and farms were allotted to the new citizenry.

From these declarations, it can be seen that the governor's original account to the king and viceroy in 1706 varied rather widely from that of the witnesses interviewed by General Paéz Hurtado. Not only that, the general learned in his continuing investigation that Cuervo had fraudulently claimed to have created a new villa above Santa Fe, naming it after his birthplace in Spain, Santa María de Grado. No such town, in fact, had been founded. Further, while the governor had actually resettled the pueblos of Galisteo and Pojoaque in the north, he grossly inflated the number of Indians involved. All this, Paéz Hurtado entered into the formal record of his inquiry.[24]

As already indicated, Governor Cuervo y Valdéz seemed to have been intent upon currying favor among his superiors. No doubt, it was that simple motive which led him to color the truth. To the Spanish mind, the founding of a villa carried immense prestige, and the governor beyond question wished to add that accolade to his name. An eighteenth century friar-scholar, Silvestre Vélez de Escalante, who composed a history of early New Mexico, wrote with biting sarcasm that Governor Cuervo, "eager to accumulate merits, falsified his reports."[25] It is difficult to disagree with that judgment.

But where does that leave us with regard to the status and early history of Albuquerque? Must all of Cuervo's utterances on its founding be dismissed, or did he mix truth with fiction? Is it possible to draw any satisfactory conclusions on the matter at this late date?

Assimilating all currently available information, this much seems evident. Governor Cuervo, in writing to his superiors, portrayed himself as the architect of the new and glorious villa of Albuquerque. He erroneously claimed a founding population of thirty-five families, when in fact there were little more than half that number. Perhaps the governor pumped up the figure so that it would surpass, by a comfortable margin, the minimum requirement of thirty families as specified in the *Recopilación*. Very few of the other stipulations pertaining to new villas seem to have been met. Whatever was done, must have been performed in the most casual, haphazard manner. At the time of the judicial inquiry of 1712, none of the witnesses indicated that even the elementary task of designating a plaza and streets had been carried out. Nor did they make reference to the building of a church, although other contemporary documents affirm that one was in progress during the villa's first years. Certainly, Governor Cuervo's solemn assertion to the king in 1706 that a church was already completed must be viewed with skepticism.

What appears to have occurred is this: Upon learning that ten soldiers were to be stationed in the area, nineteen families migrated to the Albuquerque valley, probably coming in piecemeal fashion, that is, not in a body, and, upon arrival they were assigned individual land grants. Many of those, especially the twelve families Juan Candelaria mentions as coming from Bernalillo, were actually reclaiming properties that had belonged to their ancestors before the revolt of 1680. All households, so far as we can tell, received private grants of farm and ranch land. There is no evidence that any family was enrolled as a member of the four square league community grant alleged to have been made to the Villa of Alburquerque. As the settlers in 1712 made plain, Albuquerque was not the usual compact urban town one thought of in connection with the rank and title of a villa. Rather it was a mere collection of farms spread along the Rio Grande. From all reports, this pattern of dispersal continued throughout much of the century.

General Pedro de Rivera, for instance, while on a military inspection tour of New Mexico in 1726, passed through Albuquerque and observed that the majority of its population, made up of Spaniards, mestizos and mulattos, lived on scattered farms. In 1754, Father Manuel Trigo, traveling upriver from Isleta spoke of reaching the villa, "or I might say the site of the villa of Albuquerque, for the settlers, who inhabit it on Sunday, do not live there. They must stay on their farms to keep watch over their cornfields, which are planted at a very pretty place three leagues distant, called La Alameda." And finally as late as 1776, another priest, Fray Francisco Domínguez, spoke of the villa itself as consisting of only twenty-four houses located near the mission. "The rest of what is called Albuquerque," he wrote, "extends upstream to the north, and all of it is a settlement of farms on the meadows of the said river for the distance of a league."[26] It bears mentioning that throughout the colonial years, New Mexico's other villas, Santa Fe and El Paso del Norte, and especially Santa Cruz de la Cañada, all showed similar characteristics of population dispersal and lack of genuine urbanism.

After a church was up and functioning, the Albuquerque citizenry evidently erected second homes, or "Sunday residences," on or near today's Old Town Plaza. Thereafter, for at least the first three quarters of the eighteenth century, the community retained this loose and informal aspect. Only gradually in later years did a body of permanent residents take root around an emerging plaza. But notwithstanding its uncharacteristic and extra-legal design, the town was known from 1706 onward as the Villa de Alburquerque, and no one appears to have challenged its right to use the prestigious title of "villa."

NOTES

1. Charles Wilson Hackett, ed., *Historical Documents Relating to New Mexico, Nueva Vizcaya, and Approaches Thereto, to 1773*, 3 vols. (Washington, D.C.: Carnegie Institution, 1923-1937), 3:379.

2. A Spanish facsimile of the original document of certification, together with an English translation, is provided by Lansing B. Bloom, ed., "Albuquerque and Galisteo, Certificate of Their Founding, 1706," *New Mexico Historical Review* (NMHR) X (January 1935): 48-50.

3. *Recopilación de Leyes de los Reynos de las Indias*, 4 vols. (1681; reprint ed., Madrid: Ediciones Cultura Hispanica, 1973), book IV, title V, law 6; and book

IV, title VII, laws 1-12. The requirement of thirty families to found a villa was not a rigid one. San Antonio, Texas, was organized as a villa in 1731 with only sixteen families—Canary Islanders enlisted by the king to colonize New Spain's frontier. The enterprise was carefully superintended by the viceroy, and his instructions to the governor of Texas gave precise details as to the manner of forming a plaza, streets, residential lots, and commons. The viceroy also provided a map, *plano de la población*, to serve as a guide for forming the new villa. Lota M. Spell, ed. and trans., "The Grant and First Survey of the City of San Antonio," *Southwestern Historical Quarterly* 66 (July 1962):73-89.

4. The Spanish use of an extra "r" in Albuquerque was dropped, through Anglo American usage during the first half of the nineteenth century. An article in the *Rio Abajo Weekly Press*, July 7, 1863, contending that Albuquerque with a single "r" was the correct spelling in Spain, is erroneous.

5. Archivo General de la Nación, Mexico, Provincias Internas, legajo 38, expediente 8 (AGN); and Richard E. Greenleaf, "The Founding of Albuquerque, 1706: An Historical-Legal Problem," NMHR 39 (January 1964):9-10.

6. Greenleaf, "The Founding of Albuquerque," p. 10.

7. Petition, March 8, 1892, Records of the Court of Private Land Claims, Microfilm Roll 34, State Records Center and Archives, Santa Fe (SRCA). In this file see also the Plat of the City of Albuquerque Grant, showing the "imagined four square leagues."

8. Greenleaf, "The Founding of Albuquerque," pp. 1-15; and Applicant's Brief, no. 70800, District Court Records of Bernalillo County, Albuquerque.

9. Hubert Howe Bancroft, *History of Arizona and New Mexico, 1530-1888* (1889, reprint ed., Albuquerque: Horn and Wallace Publishers, 1962), p. 221; and Ovidio Casado, "Don Francisco Cuerbo y Valdes, Governor of New Mexico: 1705-1707, His Career and Personality" (Master's thesis, University of New Mexico, 1965), p. 24. The alternate spellings, "Cuervo" and "Cuerbo," are both used in the contemporary documents.

10. Prior to the reconquest, New Mexico governors were appointed by the viceroy. But beginning with the term of Vargas, they received their appointments directly from the king. The viceroy then could make only provisional, or interim, appointments when a governor died in office or resigned. Ted J. Warner, "Don Félix Martínez and the Santa Fe Presidio, 1693-1730," NMHR 45 (October 1970):271.

11. "Méritos de Cuervo, con memorial y suplico. . . ." Mexico, October 6, 1712, in Archivo General de las Indias (AGI), Guadalajara, leg. 116, part 2. See also, Casado, "Don Francisco Cuerbo y Valdes," pp. 1-4.

12. Casado, "Don Francisco Cuerbo y Valdes," p. 26

13. Ralph Twitchell, *Spanish Archives of New Mexico* (SANM), 2 vols. (Cedar Rapids, Iowa: The Torch Press, 1914), 2: doc. 110; *Autos* and muster roll, Santa Fe, April 1705, SRCA.

14. Casado, "Don Francisco Cuerbo y Valdes," p. 42.

15. John L. Kessell, *Kiva, Cross, and Crown* (Washington, D.C.: National Park Service, 1979), p. 303.

16. "Certification of the Santa Fe Cabildo," February 23, 1706, AGI, Guadalajara, leg. 116, part 2.

17. "Inventory of the Archives of the Cabildo of Santa Fe, 1715," SANM, I: doc. 1136. This grant and similar ones in the Middle Valley were probably not occupied until late 1705 or 1706.

18. Hackett, *Historical Documents*, 3:375; Isidro Armijo, trans., "Information Communicated by Juan Candelaria, Resident of This Villa de San Francisco Xavier de Alburquerque Born 1692—Age 84," *NMHR* 4 (July 1929):276.

19. Richard E. Greenleaf, "Atrisco and Las Ciruelas, 1722-1769," NMHR 42 (January 1967):6.

20. See, for example, Peter Gallagher, "The Founding of Albuquerque," *Rio Grande History* 7 (1977):2-5; and Fray Angelico Chavez, "The Albuquerque Story," *New Mexico Magazine* 34 (January 1956):18-19.

21. Ralph E. Twitchell, *Spanish Colonization in New Mexico in the Oñate and De Vargas Periods* (Santa Fe: Historical Society of New Mexico, 1919), p. 21.

22. That Captain Martín Hurtado, rather than Governor Cuervo, carried out the actual founding of Albuquerque is confirmed by a land grant document of March 9, 1707, addressed to Hurtado as alcalde mayor of the villa. It reads: "Lorenzo de Carabajal, a resident of this town of Albuquerque and San Javier, appears before you and asking that all privileges allowed by law be given him, says that . . . on the seventeenth day of the past year of 1706, the alcalde mayor assigned to me and gave me possession of the ruins of an old house which had belonged to my father [before the revolt], and you were also pleased to set off to me a small piece of farm land on the day that you made the partition of the lands of this villa to the citizens and new settlers by virtue of the royal authority which was given you for that purpose and for other purposes. . . ." Signed: Lorenzo de Carabajal. SANM, I: doc. 156, SRCA.

The founding date of February 7 is given by Juan Candelaria. However, the reliability of this and other statements of his concerning early Albuquerque has been questioned by Chavez, "The Albuquerque Story," p. 51. Candelaria also claimed that the villa occupied four leagues of land. Armijo, "Information Communicated by Juan Candelaria," p. 275. An undated document directed to Governor Cuervo by the soldiers at Albuquerque declares that the new villa was "certified" on February 23. Cited by Gallagher, "The Founding of Albuquerque," p. 3.

Fernando Durán y Chaves and Baltazar Romero, in a petition of 1708, referred to having left their homes at Bernalillo in 1706 and having gone to the new villa of Albuquerque where they were "impelled to take an oath and settle said villa." SANM, I: doc. 1205, SRCA.

23. Armijo, "Information Communicated by Juan Candelaria," p. 274. Names of the families are provided.

24. All of the preceding testimony, together with a copy of the king's original cédula and a viceregal order, are found in "Testimonio de unas diligencias," Santa Fe, 1712, Misc. SANM, Microfilm Roll 33, SRCA.

25. *Documentos Para Servir a la Historía del Nuevo México, 1538-1778* (Madrid: Ediciones José Porrua Turanzas, 1962), p. 434.

26. Vito Alessio Robles, ed., *Diarlo y Derrotero de Brigadier Pedro de Rivera* (Mexico: Taller Autografico, 1946), p. 51; Hackett, *Historical Documents*, III: p. 464. Eleanor B. Adams and Fray Angelico Chavez, eds. and trans., *The Missions of New Mexico, 1776: A Description by Fray Francisco Atanasio Domínguez with other Contemporary Documents* (Albuquerque: University of New Mexico Press, 1956), p. 151. Spanish law recognized the right of the citizens of a municipality to operate farms and ranches in the adjacent countryside. But it is clear that their main residence was to be in the town and not on such properties. *Recopilación*, book IV, title VIII, law 11.

The Grant and First Survey of the City of San Antonio

Translated and Edited by LOTA M. SPELL

THE PECULIAR SHAPE OF THE CITY OF SAN ANTONIO as presented in the 1849 survey by the first city engineer has never been satisfactorily accounted for. During the nineteenth century, the congress of the republic and the legislature, district courts, and the supreme court of the state, as well as many individuals, puzzled over the original boundary line of this—the first city established in Texas. The mystery is solved by the report of the execution in 1731 of orders issued by the king of Spain and the viceroy of Mexico for the establishment of the villa of San Fernando de Bexar.[1] The document not only clears up the boundary problems but gives many interesting details of the arrival and settlement on the west bank of the San Antonio River of the sixteen families of Canary Islanders who made up the first group of settlers.

As early as 1723 the king of Spain, in his desire to prevent the encroachment of the French in the territory presently included in the state of Texas, issued orders for the transportation of four hundred families from the Canary Islands and other points, but this order seems never to have been carried out. A similar order, issued in 1729, resulted in the transportation of a group of Canary Islanders to the port of Veracruz, from which point the party traveled overland by way of Mexico City to Cuauhtitlan, where a halt was made before the long journey northward was begun.

From the minute description of each member of the party, made by order of the viceroy during the halt at Cuauhtitlan, it is possible to picture the first settlers of San Antonio. The first family

---

[1]The original of this grant and survey was found among the heaps of manuscripts in the Public Library of Guadalajara by its Director, Luis M. Rivera. Realizing its historical importance, he called it to the attention of the editor of the *Gaceta Municipal* of that city, who published it in Vol. IV, No. 11 (December 15, 1920). This translation of the transcription was made shortly afterward, but was mislaid among other papers and only lately came to light.

consisted of Juan Leal Goras, fifty-four years old, tall, long faced, blind in the left eye, with thick black beard and hair, dark complexion, sharp nose, and light gray eyes; and his sons, Vicente, eighteen years old and Bernardo, thirteen. The second family was that of Juan Curbelo, fifty years old, tall, broad-shouldered, rather bald, full-faced with a fair complexion, gray beard and hair, light gray eyes, black eyebrows, and a sharp nose; with his wife, aged forty-six; two sons, José and Juan, twenty-five and nine years old respectively; and María, a daughter, aged thirteen. The third family was that of Juan Leal, Jr., son of Juan Leal of the first family, with his wife, four sons and one daughter, María, aged six. The fourth family consisted of Antonio Santos, approximately fifty years old, medium height, broad-shouldered, with a round face, dark complexion, large nose, black eyes, thin beard, black hair, and black eyebrows; Isabel, his wife, one son and three daughters. In the fifth family were Joseph Padrón and his wife, each about twenty-two years old. The sixth was that of Manuel de Niz and his wife Sebastiana de la Peña; Vicente Alvarez Travieso and his wife, María Ana Curbelo, made up the seventh family. Salvador Rodríguez, with his wife and fifteen-year-old son, Patricio, constituted the eighth. Francisco de Arocha with his fourteen-year-old wife, Juana Curbelo, were accounted the ninth family. Antonio Rodríguez, eighteen years old, with his wife, nineteen years old, who was described as having a long face pitted with smallpox, black eyes, hair and eyebrows, a thin nose, and a dark complexion, made up the tenth family. Another son of Juan Leal, Sr., with a wife, Ana Santos, aged fifteen; Juan Delgado, with his wife Catherine, aged sixteen; and Joseph Cabrera with a son aged thirteen and a daughter aged six, were reckoned the next three families. The fourteenth consisted of a widow, María Rodríguez Provayno, with three sons and three daughters. The fifteenth family was made up of another widow, a son aged sixteen, another aged two, and a daughter aged four. The sixteenth family consisted of four unmarried men, the three Pérez brothers, and Martín Lorenzo de Armas. These sixteen families constituted the group who first settled, by royal decree, the city of San Antonio.

In return for settling in such a remote spot as Texas, these families were furnished their transportation to their new home and subsistence for one year at the king's expense. This included equipping them with the necessary animals for traveling and for cultivating the land after the settlement was made. After a two months' halt at Cuauhtitlan, all was made ready for the advance into Texas by way of Saltillo, where supplies and animals were to be furnished the travelers. Among the supplies issued to them were eighty-eight horses; seventy-seven mules, twenty-seven of which were required to carry the stock of biscuits, meat, and other food; four mules to carry implements for farming, such as plows, axes, and pickaxes; household goods including a *metate* for each family; and sixteen yoke of oxen.

On November 30, 1730, the date on which the Islanders set out for Texas, the viceroy issued the following:

Order for the Establishment of San Antonio

Don Juan de Acuna, etc. ... I now command the governor of the province [of Texas] Don Juan Antonio Bustillo y Bustamante, or in the case of his absence, his failure to act, or of any impediment, the captain of the presidio of San Antonio to go, as soon as the families shall arrive, taking such persons of intelligence as may be available, to examine the site a gunshot's distance to the western side of the presidio, where there is a slight elevation forming a plateau suitable for founding a very fine settlement. Because of its location it will have the purest air, and the freshest water flowing from two springs or natural fountains situated on a small hill a short distance northeast from the presidio of Bexar. From these are formed, on the east, the San Antonio River, and, on the west, the small river called the Arroyo which flows to the south. These two rivers unite eight or nine leagues from their sources, and before joining the Medina River. Between the two streams the presidio is built. East of the river is the mission of San Antonio; while to the west of it is the mission of San José from which one can go to the presidio without crossing the river; and since there is a church there which they can visit for that purpose until a church is built for them, these families may attend the mass and other Catholic services without the trouble of crossing the river.

The governor, having examined the elevation and the plateau, shall survey the land, lay off the streets, the town blocks, the main plaza, and the site for the church, the priest's house, the public hall, and the other buildings shown in the map which is sent with these instructions, to the end that, observing the measurements in feet and varas indicated in each direction for each block and street, and for the plaza, church, and public hall, he shall mark out these with a cord. In addition he shall make a furrow with a plow, and to distinguish every block from every other block, he shall place stakes in the four corners; and to mark the center of each block he shall dig a hole for the church, the public hall, and the plaza, taking care to make the streets straight and exact as shown on the map.

As soon as the fifteen families arrive, he shall give a block to each of them in order that each family may build its house thereon, indicating to them the limits marked out by the stakes so that they may not go beyond them. He shall assign the blocks facing the plaza to the principal families, giving to each of them possession and title to the corresponding block or lot, and he shall see that the tent which each family carries, or the awning, or the hut of twigs, be placed in the center of its block.

Likewise he shall go with intelligent persons to examine the land suitable for cultivation adjoining the lands assigned as blocks for the settlement. These are to the north and south of the presidio. Having reserved as much as he may think necessary for these families and for those who may come later, he shall set apart a sufficient amount for commons, so that if the population increases, the people will have ample recreation grounds, and room for the stock to graze without doing any damage.

In addition to these commons, he shall lay off sufficient lands for pastures, on which to keep the work oxen, the horses, the stock for the slaughter-houses that may be built, and for the other stock which by law the settlers are required to keep.

Coterminous with the pasture lands, he shall set apart others as the property of the city council which is to be formed from these families and those who may join them.

In addition to the pasture lands, he shall mark off the farm lands making just as many tracks as there are lots in the town. From the irrigable lands he shall make divisions and distribute them in just proportion to the first settlers. The remainder shall be unappropriated lands to be given to others later. From the farm lands he shall reserve the amount he may think proper as public lands; so that from these public arable lands and from the pasture lands, which shall together compose the lands of the town, it may be possible to secure from the yield or rent the salaries of the councilmen and the expenses connected with the public duties.

Details of the Survey

In order that the division of lots, commons, pastures, and farm lands may be made with such exactness that it will be possible to apportion the lands destined for the inner town, as well as the irrigable, the non-irrigable, and the pasture lands; and in order that the settlers may have an equal share in each class, the governor, using the map on which there are marked out from the door of the church four exact squares—the laterals not being marked off (and these are sufficient for the families who are now here and for those who may come soon), shall measure from the door of the church, passing over the four squares above mentioned, 1,093 usual varas containing 3,280 geometric feet in a straight line from the church door in one direction, making up twelve blocks. From the door of the church, including the church itself, he shall measure 1,093 varas in the opposite direction in which there shall be included twelve other squares and streets. From the same door, on the other side, he shall measure 1,093 varas in which shall be 12 other blocks and streets—all of the same size, each block containing 240 feet square—each geometric foot equal to a third of a usual vara—and each street between the blocks 40 feet wide. Having thus formed a cross with the church as a center, he shall make a square on the four sides of the whole area or plan with a cord 1,093 varas long, and shall place at each of the four corners of the square a large stone in a hole which he shall have dug, in order that the plan destined for the present and future town may be laid out. He shall make a furrow with a plow along the four sides of the square marked by the cord, in order that willows and other trees may be planted to mark out the four sides of the area of the inner town. They will serve not only to beautify it, but as soon as they grow to the height of a man their branches will furnish shade to the settlers.

In order that the dwellings may be beautiful they shall be of the same size and similar to each other with patios and corrals in which the horses and other work animals of the owners may be kept. The houses shall be adapted for defense, for cleanliness, and for the health of the inmates, and shall be built so that, as indicated on the map, the four winds, north, south, east, and west, may enter the four angles or corners of the town and of each of the houses, making them more healthful.

When this measurement has been made in the form and manner prescribed, the governor, using the usual vara of three tercias, shall measure 1,093 varas from each of the furrows, which he has made at right angles to each other on the northeast, southeast, northwest, and southwest in forming the square about the above mentioned plan, making this measurement in the same direction, and placing large stones in the corners to mark the boundaries of the commons.

From these boundaries he shall begin another measurement, and lay off 2,186 varas—that is twice the 1,093 varas in the same directions, placing stones in holes in the corners of the squares to mark the boundaries of the territory containing the land destined for pastures. He shall set apart a fifth of this for *propios*. From the boundaries of this square he shall begin another measurement, and mark off 2,186 varas in each direction above mentioned. All the land within this square he shall set apart for farms; and, having reserved 1/5 for town lands, he shall give the remainder to the fifteen families, assigning to each the tract which it should have for its farm.

The lands remaining after this measurement has been made, the governor shall declare unappropriated lands, so that from them grants may be made to the families who in the future may decide to settle at that town.

To each of these fifteen families he shall give possession of the tract of land assigned it, and title to the enjoyment of the possession of the same in the name of his Majesty, and by virtue of this order, and *ley* iv, *tit.* xii, book v of the *Recopilación de Indias*, charging each family to plant trees on the boundaries of its tract of land, and to make use of the waters of the above mentioned Arroyo and of the San Antonio River. The governor must remember that, in this division, he shall apportion the tracts of land and the water equally among the families, and that if, in any of the directions he cannot make any one or any number of squares, on account of the land being occupied, he shall make them in the other directions. He is likewise reminded that this order must be kept in the strong box of the city council, so that what should be done in the future may always be evident.

At eleven o'clock on the morning of March 9, 1731, after more than three months of overland travel, the Islanders arrived at the site of the presidio of Bexar, near which their future homes were to be established. The presidio consisted of quarters sufficient to house about fifty men who, in reality, lived with their families in huts scattered about the post. With the families of the soldiers lived some few settlers who, without authority to make a settlement, had come from Coahuila as early as 1715. These persons had selected some of the most fertile spots along the river for their fields, the possession of which remained undisputed until the appearance of the *Isleños* upon the scene. The only other settlements near the site of the prospective villa were those connected with the missions, San Antonio Valero (the Alamo) just to the east across the San Antonio River, and Concepción and San José to the south. Lands had been granted to the missions before arrangements were made for the coming of the Islanders, and they were cautioned by the viceroy to refrain from infringing upon territory already held by the missions. The result of this condition is made clear by the report of the presidio captain, Juan Antonio Pérez de Almazán, who, in the absence of the governor, was authorized to carry out the instructions of the viceroy.

PLANO DE LA POBLACION

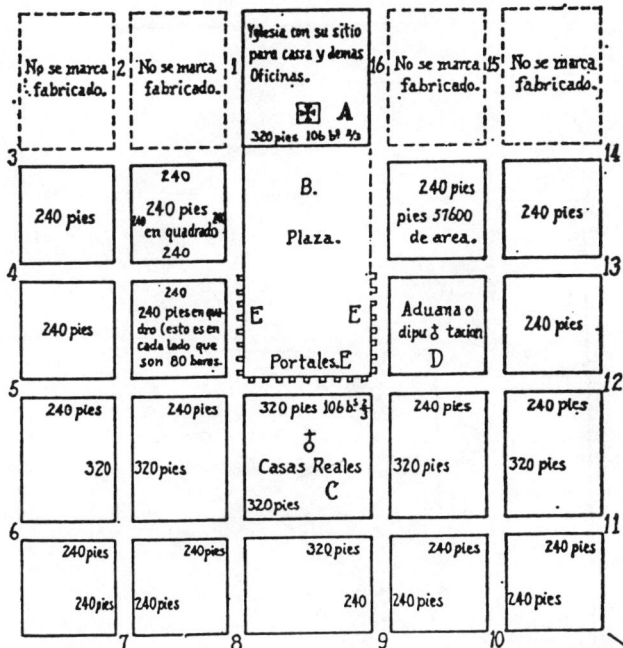

No se marca fabricado.	2 No se marca fabricado.	1 Yglesia con su sitio para cassa y demas Oficinas. ⊞ A 320 pies 106 b³ ⅔	16 No se marca fabricado.	15 No se marca fabricado.

3 — 14

| 240 pies | 240 240 pies en quadrado 240 | B. Plaza. | 240 pies pies 57600 de area. | 240 pies |

4 — 13

| 240 pies | 240 240 pies en quadro (esto es en cada lado que son 80 baras.) | E   E Portales.E | Aduana o dipuᵗ taxion D | 240 pies |

5 — 12

| 240 pies 320 | 240pies 320pies | 320 pies 106 b³ ⅔ ♄ Casas Reales C 320pies | 240 pies 320pies | 240 pies 320pies |

6 — 11

| 240pies 240pies | 240pies 240pies | 320pies 240 | 240 pies 240 pies | 240 pies 240 pies |

7   8   9   10

Las Calles han de tener de ancho 40 pies que son .13 baras ⅓

Mapa de plano, y perfil de la Poblacion que se ha de hacer la qual esta arreglada á las leyes Reales de Indias en la qual consta la plaza de Seiscientas baras de largo y quatro cientas de ancho y las calles tienen quatrocientas baras de claro con todo lo demas que expresa: siendo la letra, A, el Templo con su sitio, la B. la plaza de la poblacion, la C. las Casas Reales, la D. la Duana ó alᵗ hondiga, la E. los Portales Y los numeros del contorno las bocas de las Calles.

Componese este plano y su sitio de diez y seis quadros de vecindario las menores sinquenta y siete mill y seis cientos pies Geometricos de area, y las mayores de Ciento dos mill y quatrocientos; cuyas quadras se reputan por familias fundadoras para que las lebanten en quadro y gozen su resinto los decendientes.

D. Joseph de Villaseñor fecit.

Escala de seiscientos pies Geometricos

Plan of San Antonio if the original order had been followed

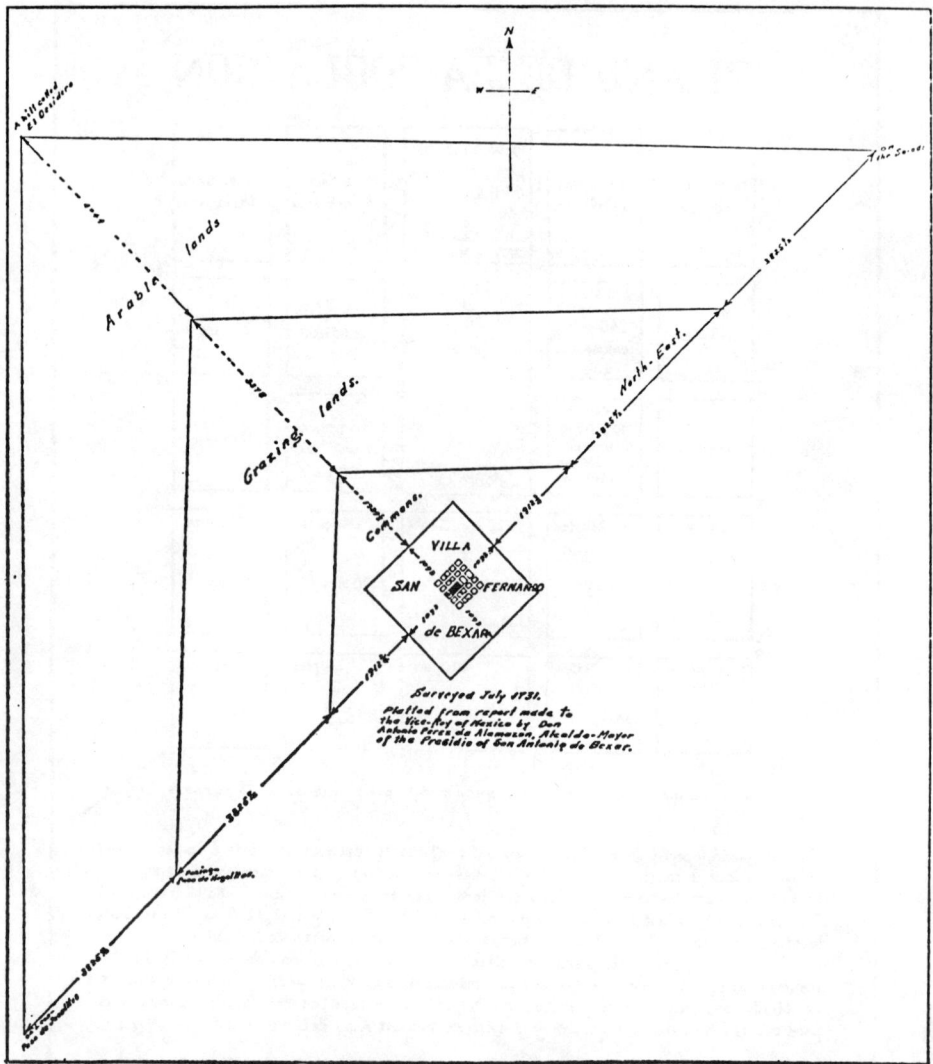

San Antonio as actually surveyed in July, 1731, by Juan Antonio Pérez de Almazán

PLAT
OF THE
CITY TRACT
OF
SAN ANTONIO DE BEXAR
as surveyed and divided
1852

In the royal presidio of San Antonio de Bexar, March 9, 1731, I, Don Juan Antonio Pérez de Almazán, captain of the said presidio, do declare that I have received the preceding eight page order, issued on the day named by the Marquis of Casafuerte, viceroy, governor, and captain-general of New Spain, and that, being informed of its tenor and form, I order that it be punctually and exactly fulfilled. In order that it may become a matter of record, I sign it with two attesting witnesses due to the lack of a notary in this place. ... Juan Antonio Pérez de Almazán. Sevastián de Monarriz. Antonio de Espronceda. ...

In compliance with the said superior order, I, the said judge, immediately thereafter took under consideration the conditions existing at this time and the impediments which prevented the immediate selection, examination, measurements, construction, and other things ordered to be done in connection with the establishment of the Villa de San Fernando for the families of the Islanders at the spot and location named and designated in the said superior order. These are: 1st, the land to the west of the presidio, the spot designated for the location of the said villa, has no facilities for irrigation, and to provide them for these families would take time and money—though it can be done; 2nd, the present season is the time of year for preparing the ground for planting corn—and this is absolutely necessary for the maintenance of the families; and 3rd, I have arranged and ordered that the said Islanders and their families be accommodated in the homes of the soldiers and citizens of this presidio where, for the present, they are as comfortable as could be expected.

The following sections of the report are signed by Pérez de Almazán. Writing on March 12, he told of his investigation of the head of the Arroyo (San Pedro Springs), and of the decision reached with the heads of the most important families to apportion the land suitable for cultivation at once, and to postpone the survey and permanent distribution of the land until more time was available for that task. Three days later he wrote again recounting the examination of the lands between the San Pedro and the San Antonio River which were suitable for irrigation, and the manner in which these lands were temporarily distributed by drawing lots. While still without title to the plots assigned, the families were charged to plow the lands which were clear, to clear other portions, and to set about the planting of a crop with the greatest speed possible.

On June 30, 1731, the presidio captain reported to the viceroy that as a result of his appeal to the sixteen families to exert themselves to the fullest in planting crops, they have succeeded in planting 22 fanegas [about 22 bushels] of corn and smaller quantities of beans, barley, cotton, peppers, melons, watermelons, and pumpkins, as well as a quantity of such fruits as they were able to bring. The most remarkable thing of all is that they brought some grape cuttings from Coahuila, and they have taken root and borne this year. The crops, in spite of the scarcity of rain, are not suffering much at the present time.

As soon as the field work was sufficiently advanced to insure sufficient food for the settlers, Almazán turned his attention to the orders of the viceroy regarding a survey of the town and the distribution of lands to the settlers. The viceregal order directed him to go west from the presidio, which then occupied the space between the still existent Military Plaza and the San Pedro, a distance of a gunshot, and on the spot later occupied by the Market House to locate the center of the proposed city. As Almazán had said in his letter of March 9, however, he did not consider that spot suitable for the center of the settlement because of the difficulties which attended the securing of water and because no money was available for improving the facilities. As time had also become a consideration, he decided to place the settlement in a more advantageous spot. Accordingly he directed his attention to a spot a gunshot's distance to the east of the presidio and there proceeded to attempt to execute the other instructions of the viceroy.

The map which accompanied the order indicated the plan by which it was intended that the town should be laid out. A few moments study of this shows that had Almazán followed the directions accompanying the map, the church should have faced west. Measuring from the spot he selected for the door of the church, had he proceeded west the necessary distance for the prescribed length of the plaza, Almazán would have run into the presidio almost immediately. He was forced, then, either to put some of his blocks west of the presidio, which was not in conformity with his instructions, or to relocate the town. This he did by turning the whole plan in the opposite direction—thus making the church face east instead of west, as do most of the mission churches.

In the presidio, jurisdiction of the province of Texas and Nuevas Philipinas, on the second day of July, 1731, I, Don Juan Antonio Pérez de Almazán, . . . declare that, as the time has come when the 16 families of Islanders are relieved of their crops so that they can proceed to the selection and location of the plot for the villa of San Fernando, ordered founded and erected by the superior order of the viceroy of New Spain which is at the beginning of these records, I therefore in conformity therewith commanded that the said families present themselves to me—as they did—at the plateau and spot designated in the said order for the said establishment bringing two cart loads of large stones and ten stakes for each of the families. With all of these, I went in person with the most intelligent persons that could be found in these regions to the plateau and spot mentioned in the said superior order which was found to be a gunshot's distance to the east from this presidio and from the Arroyo which washes the walls of the presidio and which is to form the boundary of the location of the villa of San Fernando to the west. And arriving at the said plateau and location, with a sundial and a cord of fifty common Spanish varas in length, I located the southwest and northwest points of the compass, and began measuring from the place marked as the square which was to serve as the location of the church. Starting from the middle of the point designated as the door of the church, I ran the cord to the northeast and measured 200 varas which are equal to 600 geometric feet, as is ordered in the said superior order and as is shown on the map as the length of the plaza. And having finished this measurement, I laid off a square facing the church, designating it for the *casa real*. This square and that for the church are equal, each of them being the width of the plaza. To mark this quadrilateral both in length and breadth, I ordered that there be placed in the center of the plaza and in the corners and openings of the streets tall thick stakes, and large stones, and that its outline be marked with a plow, so that a plaza two hundred varas in length and 133 and 1/3 varas in breadth was marked out, there being included in this last the width of the streets, which measured 13 and 1/3 varas each. . . .

On the following day four blocks intended as homes for the settlers were laid out, two on the northern side of the plaza and two on the southern. Each contained eighty square varas. Three streets were to issue from the plaza on each side. The northeastern square was reserved as the *aduana* or grain market; the others were assigned to the principal families. In this respect the assignment of land for homes did not conform with the Spanish laws which stipulated that all such grants should be made without respect to individuals. To insure this protection to all concerned, land should have been assigned by the drawing of lots.

On July 4, the presidio captain, in company with the leading settlers, laid off thirteen other blocks which were destined as homes for the remaining thirteen families. These blocks formed a square about the three sides of the plaza; the square for the church occupied the western side.

Almazán on the following day recorded that:

In the said presidio, on the fifth day of the month of July, 1731, I ... declare that for the execution and fulfillment of the measures provided for in the order at the beginning of these proceedings, that, in company with the families of the Islanders, I repaired to the spot designated for the plaza and that, having reached that place, from the spot designated as the door of the church and over the four squares in the direction of the northeast, I ordered a measurement of 1,093 varas made with a cord of 50 common varas and where the last measurement fell, I ordered a hole dug and a large stone placed in it to serve as a marker and designation of the square. From thence, I returned to the church door and in the opposite direction, that is, to the southwest, I ordered another 1,093 varas laid off and where the last measurement fell, I ordered another marker placed as before. From this point I returned to the center of the church door and to the northwest I ordered 1,093 varas laid off, and when I had finished I ordered a marker of large stones put in place as before. And having returned from this place to the center of the church door for the purpose of completing the quadrilateral commanded laid off for the settlement, I ordered another 1,093 varas in the opposite direction to the southeast, and on the spot at which the last measurement ended I ordered a marker made of a large stone as before. Thus there was formed a cross with the church door for the center, there being included therein in each direction twelve squares and streets. To square this plan I ordered measurements made from the four extremes with the same cord to the amount of 1,093 varas for each side of the area or plan, this quadrilateral being a perfect square of 2,186 varas on each of the four sides, because the measurement was taken from the extremes of the first measurement of the cross 1,093 varas and in the same amount in the opposite direction, thus forming the quadrilateral I mentioned. In order that it might be recognized as in this form, I ordered that large stones be placed in each corner to serve as perpetual markers and likewise that a furrow be made with a plow in the form mentioned. ...

Immediately thereafter I ... repaired to the location of the new settlement and standing at the corner of the extreme of the quadrilateral, I ordered a measurement made to the northeast with the cord of 50 common varas 1,912¾ varas, and when the last measurement had been made, I ordered that a large stone be placed to serve as a perpetual marker for the commons; and from this point I returned to the extreme of the end of the cross forming the plan which looked to the northwest and in this direction with the same cord, I measured 1,639½ varas. When I had finished the last measurement, I ordered a hole dug and a large stone placed therein to serve as the marker for the corner of the said commons. From this point I went to the third extreme of the cross laid off for the first plan of the settlement and to the southwest, I measured 1,912¾ varas. Markers and bounds were placed as ordered by the superior dispatch. This increase was made necessary in the three lines because it was not possible to lay off lands for commons to the southeast of the town, for with the first measurement of the plan for the town the banks of the San Antonio River were reached, and this is to serve as the division and boundary between this settlement and the missions—especially that of San Antonio [the Alamo] which is separated from the presidio only by the river. Therefore the three lines were increased so as to make the measurement with the equality and justice ordered in the said dispatch.

In the said presidio on the 6th day of July, 1731, I ... declare that, in conformity with what has been commanded by the superior dispatch ... and for the exact fulfillment and execution of the third measurement ordered made outside of the commons and to be used as pastures and grazing lands for all kinds of stock, said lands being required to have in each direction from the point where the commons ended 2,186 varas, and as I had not been able to form the quadrilateral to the southeast, I ordered the full amount laid off in the three remaining directions as required by the order dividing among them the amount lacking. This division was made with all possible care for the making of exact records, measuring first to the northeast from where the commons ended 3,825½ varas. When the last measurement was made, I ordered a marker of large stones to serve as a perpetual boundary for the pasture lands of the settlement. I then went to the opposite extreme of the lands laid off for the commons and to the southwest I measured another 3,825½ varas. There I also placed a marker of stones. This was immediately facing Paso de Nogalitos on the Arroyo lying in this settlement. This finished I went to the third extreme of the lands measured off for the commons and to the northwest I had 3,378 varas laid off for pastures. When the final measurement had been made, I ordered a marker of large stones to serve as a perpetual boundary, having thus completed the measurement of the whole amount of land according to the conditions prescribed for the laying off of the pasture and grazing lands. ... The lands mentioned in this order were within the following boundaries: on the northeast, from the head of the principal spring at the head of the San Antonio River in a straight line to the spot called Arroyo de Norillo; from this point along the quadrilateral west to a point called the Real de Nicolas Hernández which is slightly to the north-west; turning south along the quadrilateral crossing the Llano de Leon and spot called the Real de la Escaramuza to the place called the Real de la Lagunilla which is to the right of the point called Jacalitos; thence northeast straight to the Paso de Nogalitos where the final point falls. To the east of these lands lie the farming lands and the San Antonio River which runs from north to south.

Immediately thereafter I ... made the division and apportionment of the fifth part of all the lands measured off for pasture and grazing lands as is evident from the preceding record. These were set apart and designated from this time forward for all time as town lands for this new settlement so that when they produce through cultivation these funds may be used for the purposes and ends that His Majesty ... had ordered by his royal decree. These lands are marked off and set apart to the south of this settlement from the outside boundaries of the lands marked off for commons to Paso de Nogalitos and from this point to the southwest to the place called the Lagunilla where lies the corner of these lands marked off and designated as town lands for the settlement. From this point, to the north, crossing the Llano de Leon, the Escaramuza, to the point called the Real de Nicolas Hernández where another of the corners of these lands lies; thence to the east where measurement of these lands coincides with the boundaries of those which have been marked off and designated as commons for this settlement. For the present these are to remain separate until the time comes to join them to the fifth part of the irrigable lands and the principal spring of the settlement, which as His Excellency orders, shall also be separated and set apart for the same purpose.

In the presidio ... on the 7th of July, 1731, I declare that, for the purpose of completing these measurements ordered by the viceroy, I repaired to the boundary and marker placed for the pasture lands, in the direction of the northeast, and, for the purpose of making the fourth and final measurement for this settlement, I had 3,825½ varas laid off in this same direction, the last measurement falling upon the Arroyo Salado. And although it was so definite and well known a boundary, I ordered a pile of stones placed to serve as a perpetual marker. To continue this measurement, I returned to the northwest corner of the third measurement, i.e., that of the pasture lands, and in this direction, there was counted off and measured 4,044 common varas which reached to a hill called the Divisadero, where I ordered a marker of stones placed. And having returned to the third corner of the said pasture lands previously laid off, i.e., to the southwest, I measured off 3,825½ common varas, the point falling upon the Leon and the Paso de los Jacalitos, where I ordered a marker of stones placed. This measurement was made in conformity with the orders mentioned with the difference in varas indicated for the reason that to the southeast it was impossible to lay off lands in a quadrilateral for the reasons above mentioned—that the middle of the San Antonio River had been reached and this is the dividing line and boundary between the lands of this settlement and those of the mission. Therefore, the amount lacking in this direction was added to the three remaining measurements. This quadrilateral, although an imperfect one, was laid off with all possible care; the lands measured off for the town proper, those for the commons, as well as those for the pasture lands, and those of the final measurement [arable lands] lay between the following boundaries: to the east, the San Antonio River; to the west, the Arroyo de Leon; to the south, the lands of the mission San José, through the Paso de Nogalitos; and to the north, the Arroyo Salado. . . .

On July 11, Almazán distributed the plots of land which could be irrigated to the heads of the sixteen families by lots. That included in the "Potrero," the land enclosed on three sides by the San Antonio River, was reserved to the city, but the lands below, extending from the San Pedro to the San Antonio River, were apportioned to the settlers.

From these reports several facts of interest connected with the original grant of land to the city of San Antonio are revealed. Of perhaps the greatest interest is the establishment of the eastern limits of the city—that boundary being the San Antonio River. In the course of many arguments concerning the grant for the establishment of the city presented in various courts before the supreme court ruled on the boundary of the city of San Antonio, this was never brought out. It was the previous grant of lands to the mission located east of the San Antonio River which caused Almazán to resort to enlarging his measurements in three directions, and thus prevented San Antonio from having the square shape prescribed for all Spanish settlements. In the light of this document, some of the statements in the decision of the supreme court are curious: one judge having declared that San Antonio must have been a square because Spanish law called for a square.

While the loss of this document at the time the city limits were in litigation caused some of the original settlers' heirs to lose lands rightfully theirs, San Antonio gained all the lands east of the San Antonio River within the city limits in the nineteenth century.

In an attempt to produce this document the Bexar Archives were searched in vain; the records of Mexico City and the Spanish archives were appealed to without results; and the courts finally ruled that the document was hopelessly lost. In its place the memories of the oldest settlers were relied on to establish the boundary lines of the city as founded in 1731.

A Frontier Agrarian Settlement:

San José de Guadalupe, 1777–1850

Daniel J. Garr

A LTHOUGH the founding of well-planned, compact urban settlements was the essential intent of Spanish colonization, other considerations sometimes produced an outcome at variance with the urban centrality favored by the framers of colonial legislation. The failure to nucleate, although stemming from a variety of underlying causes, was mainly the result of both the lax political control characteristic of frontier environments and the agrarian orientation which inevitably superseded urban pretensions. Such was the case with California's first civilian settlement, the pueblo (town) of San José de Guadalupe, now a metropolitan center of more than 500,000 inhabitants located at the southern end of San Francisco Bay.

It was survival rather than strategic or developmental considerations which provided the primary motivation for the founding of pueblos in California. Seaborne shipments of supplies from the Gulf of California port of San Blas were costly, aud the journey around Baja California and up the Pacific Coast was perilous. The Franciscan missionary, Francisco Palou, tells us that the establishment of towns was one of Felipe de Neve's primary objectives upon becoming Governor of the Spanish province of California in 1774:

> From the very moment when Governor Don Felipe [de] Neve entered Monterey he was seized with anxiety as to how to support the inhabitants of the new establishments. He thought in the beginning that by increasing agriculture in the missions. ... they could assist the three presidios with the surplus. But, being informed that this could not be done at once, for as the crops increase the consumers also increase, because of the new Christians who are being secured, he agreed to

93

found a pueblo in a good place, made up entirely of Spaniards and castes, to be employed in the raising of every kind of grain and crops, so that all the presidios might be provided from them, especially when barks should not come or if they should suffer some disaster.[1]

In June, 1776, de Neve proposed to Viceroy Antonio Maria de Bucareli that experimental sowings be conducted to check the inevitable food shortages and to provide supplies at low cost.[2] But his intended solution involved plans on a larger scale, and he sought the Viceroy's endorsement for an ambitious and sweeping measure which would insure agricultural self-sufficiency for California. Once this approval was received, it was possible for de Neve to implement his design. During his 1777 provincial tour of inspection, he selected two particularly well-suited river locations where such cultivation could be instituted — one in northern California and the other in the south. Later on in that year, de Neve proceeded to found the northern pueblo of San José de Guadalupe. "The settlers," wrote Palou, "set out from the presidio of San Francisco on the 7th day of November, 1777, accompanied to the site by . . . lieutenant [José Joaquin Moraga]."[3] The friar chronicled the founding as follows:

> Arrived there, he [Moraga] gave them possession in the name of his Majesty, marking out for them the plaza for the houses and distributing the houselots among them. He measured off for each one a piece of land for planting a *fanega* of corn, and for beans. They also proceeded to build a dam to take the water from the Guadelupe River, which is the one from which it must be drawn in ditches to irrigate the fields.[4]

In reporting his undertaking to Viceroy Bucareli, de Neve stressed San José's agrarian orientation. He wrote, "Considering the importance of said works . . . I have resolved to transfer nine soldiers, experienced in farming, from the small garrison of this [Monterey] Presidio and that of San Francisco." He related that the colonists numbered fourteen, "who with their families consist of sixty-six souls."[5] Bucareli heartily endorsed de Neve's actions and praised the selection of a "spacious plain which permits the distribution of lands to the present settlers and to new ones who will settle and give to the Town all the extensions filled with groves that are intended as *Ejidos* and *Dehesas*."[6] He also predicted that "within two years . . . there will be sufficient harvests to maintain not only this Presidio [Monterey] but also that of San Francisco which will result in the sufficient saving to the Royal Treasury for the population of these establishments and for the extension of the Catholic Religion to the numerous Gentiles who live in these lands."[7]

Unfortunately, circumstances did not bear out the Viceroy's optimism. The first sowing was almost completely lost in unseasonable flooding which occurred in July, 1778. A year later, inundations left San José submerged under more than three feet of water.[8] De Neve attempted to remedy the

94

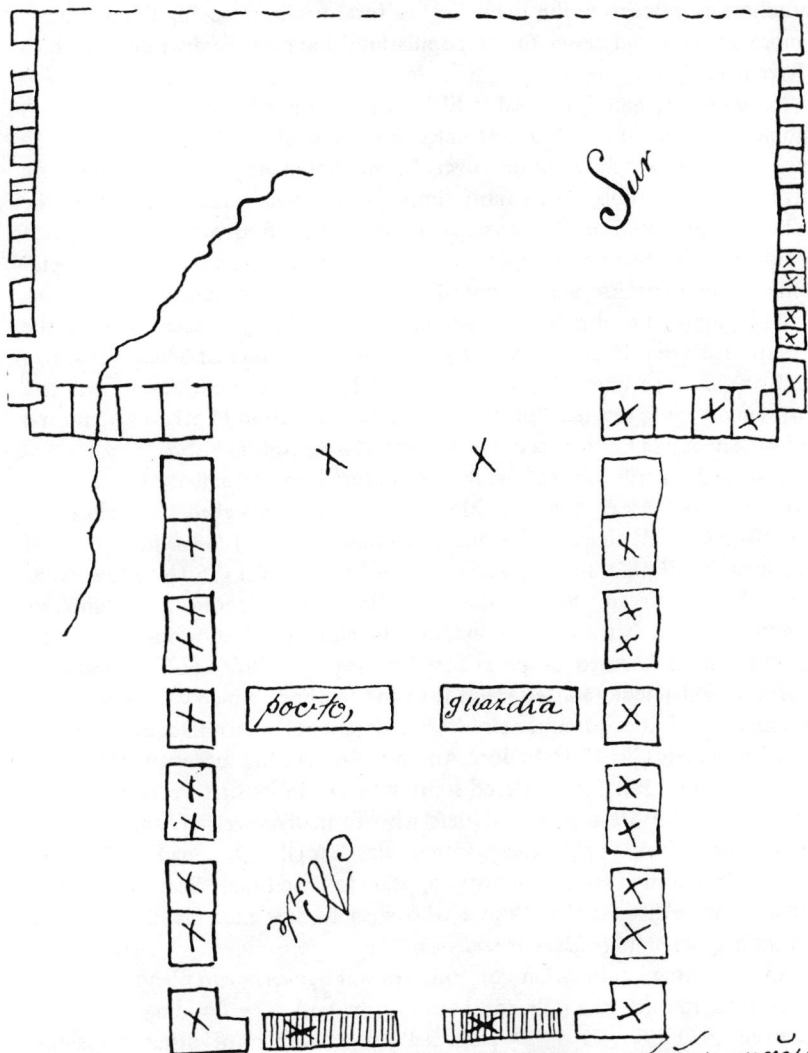

Plan of the Pueblo of San José, probably before 1780. This unsigned, undated plan could be the work of José Joaquin Moraga. Reprinted through the courtesy of Western Title Insurance Company, San José, California.

situation by relocating the town's agricultural lands, removing them to a site "more suitable and closer to the population, changing the distribution which I have made."[9]

Nevertheless, San José's early difficulties continued unabated. An order, probably dating from 1780, instructed the corporal of the escort assigned to the town to watch carefully over its development and progress.[10] An inventory of tools and farm implements was called for and the militarily-appointed *alcalde* was instructed to audit frequently the supply of tools "in order to punish anyone who sells them or ruins them by neglect." Similar instructions were applied to livestock, weapons and horses; card-playing was prohibited.[11] Such surveillance does not speak well for the government's confidence in the early colonists, and Bancroft believes that San José was an experimental venture until 1781, and, apparently, one with less than encouraging results. But the Spanish determination to attain agricultural self-sufficiency in California compelled the town's continuation.

A formal distribution of lands was ordered in December, 1782, and a month later José Joaquin Moraga officially assigned houselots *en propriedad*.[12] Municipal government commenced in 1783 when the first elections for *alcalde* and *regidores* were held. But by 1786 Governor Pedro Fages had observed that "abuses have been experienced in its interior government and little activity in [the fulfillment of] its obligations." He therefore commissioned Corporal José Dominguez to "root out promptly the abuses in said pueblo and establish it in the methods which were advised for the success of the establishment."[13] This situation is reflected in one of Fages' comments in 1791 to José Antonio Romeu, his successor. He wrote, "The pueblo of San José suffered some setbacks in its first years due to . . . maldirection."[14] Of the nine settlers who formally received land grants in 1783, one left in 1785 and another was expelled for bad conduct.[15] Nevertheless, a modicum of industry appears to have finally been achieved by 1786. Fages indicated that "those who wish to sow more lands than they possess may do so in *baldios* or *realengas*."[16]

However, the cultivation of this vacant government land was not undertaken to add to an already bountiful harvest. The flooding which had occurred in 1778 and 1779 persisted on a number of other occasions, probably because the town and its agricultural lands were still on too low a site and were prone to the climatic excesses of the rainy season.[17] It was first suggested in early 1785 that the only effective means to avoid these disasters would be to move the town to a higher elevation, but Moraga hesitated to initiate such drastic action partially because of boundary disputes that inevitably arose between the Santa Clara Mission and the pueblo, as well as the logistical problem of moving. The sentiment of the settlers, however, was in favor of relocation, and in August Fages wrote to Jacobo Ugarte y Loyola, Commandant General of the *Provincias Internas* requesting permission to move the town to a *lomita poco distente*. The change of site would not have represented a major dislocation for the settlers since at the time their houses

96

were only palisade structures with earthen roofs.[18] Ugarte approved the idea "as it would be more useful and advantageous," but warned that it must be done "without altering or varying . . . the limits and boundaries of the lands or districts assigned to said Town."

Yet, despite the decade or so of contemplation, the move was not undertaken until 1797. In January of that year, Marcos Chavoya, the *alcalde*, officially requested that the town be transferred, "recognizing the deplorable situation in which the Pueblo has found itself owing to the flooding of the *arroyos* which surround it."[19]

Although agricultural lands had been distributed formally in 1783, by 1794 the pattern of ownership bore no resemblance to its original state. This irregularity was noted by Governor José de Arrillaga in a report to Diego de Borica, his successor:

> In my last visit to the pueblo of San José I was told that the settlers attached to it did not own tillage lands and said lands were loaned by a Commissioner of Realengas; this arrangement impeded their working of those lands *con amor* as each time during the following year he would give those lands to someone else. I advised him that he should distribute four *suertes* to each settler under penalty of fines from the government and that these lands may not be transferred or sold without the consent of the Governor.[20]

But even under such conditions a surplus was achieved in 1796 which permitted the sale of two-hundred *fanegas* of maize to the Carmel Mission and six-hundred to that of San Francisco. An additional eight hundred were exported from the province. In 1790 only fifty-six *fanegas* of maize had been produced, thirty of which were surplus, and twenty-six were allocated to defray the expenses of municipal government.[21] The distribution of property suggested by de Arrillaga was contrary to all legislation and might have been the first in a series of incidents which provoked a stern warning from Mexico in 1805.[22] However, it may also reflect the uncertain conditions which were precipitated by the periodic inundations.

The second formal concession of land at San José took place in June, 1798 on the new town site.[23] Governor Fages noted that "it is proper to carry out the formalities requisite to confer possession of lands to the settlers of the Pueblo of San José de Guadelupe in order that they may live in uniform peace and quiet."[24] In distributing the lands, a space of ten *varas* between houselots was allocated for "the boundary for a division or street."[25] After the *solares* and *suertes* were allocated, the remaining territory was to be divided among *propios* and *realengas*.[26] The absence of *ejidos*, common lands, must have been the product of either confused terminology or of official indifference. The former is not likely since the governor of California was previously known to have possessed a copy of the *Recopilación*. Given the isolation and lack of development in California, it would appear plausible

97

that all the stipulations for municipal land tenure provided in the *Recopilación* were simply not taken seriously.

With respect to population, San José's original complement of nine households in 1777 had grown to eighteen in 1790; the total population was eighty, all of whom were natives of Mexico with the majority coming from Durango and Sonora.[27] By 1800 this number had more than doubled to 165.[28] Bancroft reported that it declined to about 125 in 1810, the reduction attributed to a mustering of troops in 1805-1806, which was dictated by colonial adjustments to the Napoleonic Wars. The presidial forces at Monterey and San Francisco were accordingly bolstered by some sixty men, half of them from San José, a fact substantiated by a report by Governor José de Arrillaga which indicated that there were very few able-bodied colonists remaining at San José.[29] Had such circumstances not intervened, the population of San José would have numbered about 250 in 1810.[30]

The 1820's witnessed a succession of foreign visitors who were more adventurous than those earlier who paid calls only at trade-oriented coastal presidios. Otto von Kotzebue's second visit to California brought him to San José which, in the fall of 1824, he described as a veritable Arcadia:

> This Pueblo lies in a beautiful spot. The houses are pleasant, built of stone, and stand in the midst of orchards, and hedges of vines bearing luxuriant clusters of the richest grapes. The inhabitants came to meet us, and with much courteousness, blended with the ceremonious politeness of the Spaniards, invited us to enter their simple but cleanly dwellings. All their countenances bespoke health and contentment, and they have good cause to rejoice in their lot. Unburthened by taxes of any kind, and in possession of as much land as they choose to cultivate, they live free from care on the rich produce of their fields and herds.[31]

Duhaut-Cilly saw things in a somewhat harsher light in July, 1827. He was impressed with the great fertility of the Santa Clara Valley, but found that "the natural laziness of these creoles . . . has arrested the development and led to the decadence of the establishment."[32] He estimated the population at 800, including about 150 Indian domestics.[33] But these figures seem to be exaggerated in light of his count of only eighty dwellings. A few months earlier, Beechey guessed the population to be about 500. By that time, the well-known tree-shaded *alameda* that led from the Santa Clara Mission to San José was completed; Beechey was the first to mention it and wrote that the town consisted of "mudhouses miserably provided for in every respect."[34] And those who lived in them were wont to "style themselves *Génte de Razon*, to distinguish them from the Indians, whose intellectual qualities are frequent subjects of animadversion amongst these enlightened communities."[35] An 1828 census revealed all previous guesses to be inflated; the population was 415, rising to 524 three years later.[36] Alfred Robinson, in

98

the spring of 1829, observed that San José had grown to about 100 houses and possessed the basic complement of public buildings typical of an Hispanic town: a church, a town hall, and jail. Unfortunately, he made no remarks concerning the appearance of the plaza or the plan of the town. His comments with respect to the inhabitants elaborated on those of Duhaut-Cilly:

> The men are generally indolent, and addicted to many vices, caring little for the welfare of their children, who, like themselves, grow up unworthy members of society. Yet, with vices so prevalent amongst the men, the female portion of the community . . . do not seem to have felt its influence, and perhaps there are few places in the world where . . . can be found more chastity, industrious habits and correct deportment than among the women of this place.[37]

By the mid-1830's San José was the largest town in northern California. Faxon Atherton first arrived in May of 1836 and was impressed with the rich and extensively-cultivated lands.[38] He returned the following November and remarked that it was "beautifully situated for a large town," but there his enchantment ended. The people were "a most villainous set of scoundrels, their chief pride being to see who can cheat a foreigner the most."[39] He must have had a series of unfortunate experiences in San José because upon his return in August, 1837, he wrote, "It would in my opinion be dangerous for me to stop (in) this vile place over a week as I am sure I should shoot myself the second. A mere sight of the place give me the blues for a week."[40]

The agrarian character of San José was quite pronounced during this period. Wilkes found it almost deserted when he passed through in 1841.[41] It had developed a prosperous agricultural economy, and Belden wrote that those "who had any wealth, had it in cattle, at their ranches in the vicinity."[42] Contrary to Kotzebue's recollections, he asserted that the town possessed only a few adobe houses; the rest were *pala parada*, consisting of "posts standing upright in the ground, and then filled in with mud, and with a thatch of straw over the roof." Belden offered these further comments on housing:

> The people lived in a primitive rude state. Although they had large houses, they were only partially floored; they usually contained one large room in the middle, for a kind of hall or general room, and at the end a kind of shed for the kitchen and cooking. Except in some of the best families, they did not generally have any table set in their rooms. They would commonly go into the kitchen and have the food taken from the kettles, and passed around in plates.[43]

Even by the necessarily limited standards of a native Californian, San José "was in a condition of greater backwardness than those of the other points on the map . . . and still more so in its fiestas and amusements."[44] As late as

99

1846, it was still a "straggling village . . . hardly worth describing."[45] And in the spring of 1847, General Sherman reported it to be "a string of low adobe houses festooned with red peppers and garlic."[46]

The first real indication of the urban form of San José dates from 1846, and, apparently, it differed little from the laissez-faire arrangement of other California towns. Bryant wrote that "the streets are irregular, every man having erected his house in a position most convenient to him."[47] The plaza was the area for the frolicking of "hundreds, perhaps thousands of squirrels, whose abodes are under ground."[48] It is not known which buildings faced on the plaza; the church was located "near the centre of the town [and] exteriorly resembled a huge Dutch barn." The other buildings, by then mostly adobe, lacked "even the smallest pretensions to architectural taste or beauty."[49]

The first survey of San José was carried out in February, 1847. Prior to that time there was no regular arrangement of streets nor, as elsewhere, did most settlers possess written titles to their land.[50] The *ayuntamiento* directed William Campbell to survey a plot of land measuring one mile square and to divide it into streets and building lots, the latter measuring fifty square *varas*. Upon completion of the survey, those owning land within its limits were instructed to present their claims so that written titles could be registered.[51] Another survey by Campbell and his brother was conducted in May, 1847 from which additional lot grants were made, all of which were sustained in subsequent litigation. The extent to which these surveys differed is not known, and it is doubtful whether they still survive. In July, 1847, J.D. Hutton was commissioned to undertake a survey of outlying lands, dividing them into lots of 500 acres (2,000 square *varas*), a measurement which was intended to correspond to *suertes;* as if to emphasize the validity of the survey, the tracts were to be distributed by lot. However, these subdivisions were later annulled. Since a *suerte* measured 200 square *varas* and, according to prior practice, an individual was normally granted four, it is not surprising that this irregularity caused the survey not to be confirmed. In January, 1848 the *alcalde* complained that Hutton had defrauded the citizens; his 500 acre lots were found to measure from 200 to 300 acres at most.[52] Still another survey was conducted in 1847 by C. S. Lyman, a Yale professor and United States surveyor; this effort served as the basis for the municipal grant to which the town was entitled.[53] In appearance, the Lyman survey bore little resemblance to the original Spanish plan. Only in its directional orientation is there evidence of Hispanic planning. The corners of the plaza are roughly in correspondence to the so-called cardinal points of the compass. Thus, the streets would not be exposed to the winds which the Spanish archaically believed to originate from those four directions.

At the close of the Mexican era, San José was predominantly a Hispanic-Californian town with a population of about 700.[54] Shortly after, it was selected as the capital of California which "gave to it an impetus, and

100

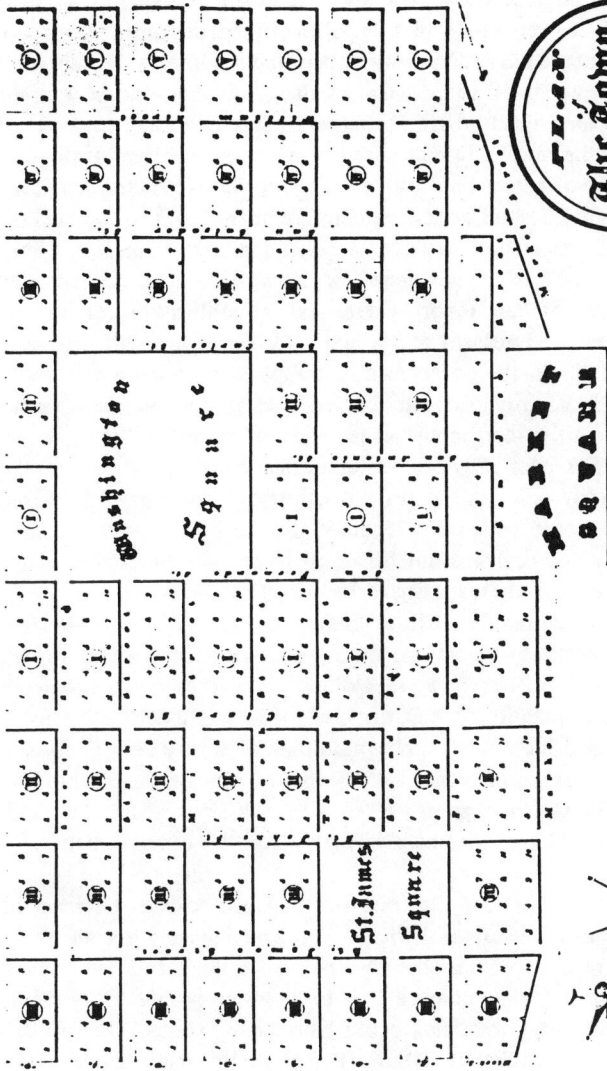

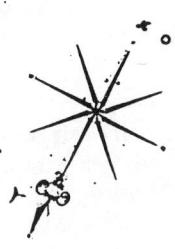

Plan of the Town of St. Joseph, 1847. Drawn by C. S. Lyman. Reprinted with the permission of Mrs. Helen Kennedy, Stockton, California.

brought it at once into notice"; but this status was short-lived.[55] When Bayard Taylor passed through in 1849, San José "was mainly a collection of adobe houses, with tents and few clapboard dwellings, of the season's growth, scattered over a square half mile."[56]

It is clear that San José was not a town of much consequence prior to American rule. There were none of the political intrigues which made Los Angeles a hotbed of activity. There was little or no commerce to compete with that of Monterey, the perennial seat of the customs house, or with the fabulous growth experienced at San Francisco. It was a pastoral town, as had been conceived at the outset. Bryant noted that "the population of the place is composed chiefly of native Californian land-proprietors. Their *ranchos* are in the valley, but their residences and gardens are in the town."[57] As was the case with many towns in northern Mexico, San José was delineated by the forces of dispersal. Certainly, there were few, if any, resources concentrated in the development of the town. There was no obligation for *vecinos* (citizens) to maintain a house in town, and only twice in California, both times prior to 1800, did the government attempt to encourage such urban centrality. In 1773, Viceroy Bucareli ordered that those who were granted lands "according to their merit and means of labor" must live "in town and not dispersed."[58] Later, in 1797, Governor Borica sought to compel retired soldiers to settle in towns instead of at their countryside *ranchos*.[59] However, the threat of militia duty which was tendered did not precipitate the desired change. Government control was not sufficient to enforce the whims of the Madrid bureaucracy when these designs lacked practical incentive.

With no political activity and little commerce, San José possessed few magnetic attractions. Its chief asset was the Santa Clara Valley, which, Bryant observed, "if properly cultivated, would alone produce breadstuffs enough to supply millions of population."[60] Duflot de Mofras was indeed uncanny in his prediction of a South Bay metropolis more than a century before it was to flourish: "It is without doubt that . . . the population of the Pueblo will grow, and the space which separates it from Santa Clara will be filled with houses, the location being extremely favorable for the establishment of a great city."[61]

The early years of San José illustrate the inherent conflict between its agrarian rationale and its urban heritage, an irreconcilable set of cross-purposes which permitted neither objective to be adequately fulfilled prior to 1800. If it's agricultural pre-eminence had been given proper recognition, perhaps the problem of poor siting could have been avoided. These difficulties symbolize the inability of California's colonial officials to merge the Hispanic urban tradition with the exigencies of topography. By the time an equilibrium could be reached, it was the agrarian and pastoral impulses which prevailed over considerations of urban form and the lesser corollary objectives of economic and social cohesion.

102

Footnotes

1 Francisco Palou, *Noticias de la Neuva California*, ed. & trans. Herbert E. Bolton (4 vols; New York: Russell & Russell, 1966), IV, 166.

2 Hubert Howe Bancroft, *History of California* (7 vols; San Francisco: A. L. Bancroft & Co., 1884-1890), I, 311.

3 Palou, IV, 167-168.

4 Ibid.

5 De Neve to Bucareli, Monterey, April 15, 1778, California Archives, Bancroft Library (CA), *Provincial Records*, I, 9.

6 Bucareli to de Neve, Mexico, July 22, 1778, CA, *State Papers. Missions and Colonization*, I, 29-30. Charles III acknowledged and approved the founding on March 6, 1779; it was communicated to de Neve on July 19, 1779 (Teodoro de Croix to de Neve, Nombre de Dios, July 17, 1779, CA, *Provincial State Papers*, I, 334). In addition, much of the detail is re-stated in Bucareli's report to the King (Bucareli to Charles III, Mexico, July 27, 1778, Romulo Velasco Ceballos, ed., *La Administración de D. Frey Antonio Maria de Bucareli y Ursua* [2 vols; Mexico: Publicaciones del Archivo General de la Nación, 1936]), I, 436-437.

7 Ibid.

8 Maynard J. Geiger, O.F.M. *The Life and Times of Fray Junípero Serra* (2 vols; Washington, D.C.: Academy of American Franciscan History, 1959), II, 200.

9 De Neve to Croix, Monterey, August 11, 1778, CA, *Provincial Records*, I, 92.

10 Anonymous, n.pl., n.d. [c. 1780], CA, *Provincial Records*, I, 339-341.

11 Ibid.

12 Moraga to Governor Pedro Fages, San Francisco, January 4, 1783, CA, *State Papers. Missions*, II, 31-33.

13 Fages to Teodoro de Croix, Monterey, February 1, 1785, CA, *Provincial Records*, I, 188. Bancroft attributed the difficulties to conflict among the *alcalde* and *regidores*, (I, 478).

14 Fages to Romeu, "Informes Particulares al Gobr Romeu," Monterey, February 26, 1791, CA, *Provincial State Papers*, VI, 154.

15 Bancroft, I, 477.

16 Fages to Ignacio Vallejo, Monterey, November 1. 1785, *Departmental State Papers, San José*, I, 15.

17 Bancroft, I, 479.

18 Ibid.

19 Chavoya to Gov. Diego de Borica, San José, January 10, 1797, CA, *Provincial State Papers*, IX, 25-26.

20 Arrillaga to Borica, n.pl., n.d., 1794, CA, *Provincial State Papers*, VII, 189.

21 Santiago Arguello to Fages, San José, December 31, 1790, CA, *Provincial State Papers*, V, 225-226. (Borica to San José *comisionado*, Monterey, November 30, 1796, CA, *Departmental State Papers. San José* I, 73).

22 Conde del Valle de Orizaba, Mexico, December 20, 1805, CA, *Provincial State Papers*, XII, 15.

103

[23] Fages, Monterey, June 12, 1798. CA. *State Papers, Missions and Colonization,* I, 241-268.

[24] Ibid., p. 241.

[25] Ibid., p. 249.

[26] Ibid., p. 268.

[27] Census, October 5, 1790, CA, *State Papers. Missions,* I, 61-64.

[28] Census, December 31, 1800, CA, *Provincial State Papers,* XI, 181-183.

[29] Cited in Bancroft, II, 133.

[30] Ibid.

[31] Otto von Kotzebue, *A New Voyage Round the World in the Years 1823-1826* (2 vols; London: Henry Colburn and Richard Bentley, 1830), II, 100-101.

[32] Auguste Duhaut-Cilly, *Voyage Autour du Monde* (2 vols; Paris: Arthus Bertrand, 1834-35), II, 91.

[33] Ibid.

[34] Frederic W. Beechey, *Narrative of a Voyage to the Pacific and Beering's Strait* (2 vols; London: Henry, Colburn and Richard Bentley, 1831), II, 47.

[35] Ibid., pp. 47-48.

[36] Census, September 30, 1828, CA, *Departmental State Papers,* I, 249; H. S. Foote, ed. *Pen Pictures from the Garden of the World or Santa Clara County, California* (Chicago: Lewis Publishing Co., 1888), p. 36.

[37] Alfred Robinson, *Life in California* (Oakland: Biobooks, 1947), p. 47.

[38] Faxon Dean Atherton, *California Diary, 1836-1839,* ed. Doyce B. Nunis, Jr. (San Francisco, & Los Angeles: California Historical Society, 1964), p. 7.

[39] Ibid., p. 36.

[40] Ibid., p. 60.

[41] Charles Wilkes, *Narrative of the United States Exploring Expedition during the Years 1838, 1839, 1840, 1841, 1842,* (5 vols; Philadelphia: Lea & Blanchard, 1845), V, 208.

[42] Josiah Belden, *Memoir and Early Letters,* ed. Doyce B. Nunis, Jr. (Georgetown, Cal: Talisman Press, 1962), p. 47. The location of Belden's San José dwelling is now marked by a sign on North First Street.

[43] Ibid., pp. 47-48.

[44] José Arnaz, *Recuerdos* (Bancroft Library MS, 1878), p. 48.

[45] Joseph Warren Revere, *A Tour of Duty in California* (New York & Boston: C.S. & J.H. Francis, 1849), p. 54.

[46] William Tecumseh Sherman, *Recollections of California, 1846-1861* (Oakland: Biobooks, 1945), p. 21.

[47] Edwin Bryant, *What I Saw in California ... in the Years 1846, 1847* (Minneapolis: Ross & Haines, 1967), p. 316.

[48] Ibid.

[49] Ibid.

[50] Of the few land grants made in 1846, only one was subsequently confirmed in the United States courts (Bancroft, V, 664).

104

51 Foote, p. 81.

52 Bancroft, V.665.

53 Foote, p. 82

54 Bancroft, VI, 4.

55 John Russell Bartlett, *Personal Narrative of Explorations and Incidents in Texas, New Mexico, California, Sonora, and Chihuahua* (2 vols; New York: D. Appleton & Co., 1854), I, 68.

56 Bayard Taylor, *Eldorado, or Adventures in the Path of Empire* (2 vols;New York: G. Putnam's Sons, 1850), I, 68.

57 Bryant, p. 316.

58 Bucareli, "Instrucción que debe observar el Commandante nombrado para los Establecimientos de San Diego y Monterey," Mexico, August 17, 1773, CA, *State Papers. Missions and Colonization*, I, 324-328.

59 Borica to Presidio Commandants, Monterey, October 15, 1797, CA, *Provincial Records*, II, 435-436.

60 Bryant, p. 316.

61 Eugène Duflot de Mofras, *Exploration du Territoire de l'Orégon, des Californies, et de la Mer Vermeille* (2 vols; Paris: Arthus Bertrand, 1844), I, 416.

105

Los Angeles and the Challenge of Growth, 1835-1849

BY DANIEL J. GARR

Los Angeles came of age long before it was throttled in the iron grip of transportation technology. Half a century before the arrival of the transcontinental railroad in the early 1880s, it was, to quote an apt phrase, "overwhelmed by its imaginary present greatness and its debt to the future."[1] Accordingly, the leading citizens of Los Angeles entertained aspirations for their community which were as lofty as those cherished in the bustling Anglo-American towns straddling the rivers of the transmontane urban frontier. Like Pittsburgh, Cincinnati and St. Louis, Los Angeles wrestled with the dilemmas of growth posed by the existing pattern of improvised remedies while simultaneously attempting to create an environment conducive to the implementation of orderly urban development. Its civic leaders demonstrated a sense of the growing responsibilities of municipal endeavor and this furnished the arena for a still grander vision of the town's future prospects.[2] By 1830 emergent Los Angeles had established its regional dominance and sought to extend its sphere by wresting control of the California provincial capital, that biggest of all prizes in a growing territory.

Maritime Monterey had been the seat of territorial government since its founding in 1770, one year after the settling of Alta California. Site of the customs house, Monterey was indispensable for commerce and further doubled as an administrative center. Thirty miles inland, Los Angeles could not hope to usurp the function of a reliable port of entry; San Pedro's deep water port was still decades away. However, it could enjoy the perquisites of the hub of other government activities. The inspiration for this ambition was hardly remote. From 1825 to 1831, Governor José María de Echeandía succeeded in shifting both capital (informally) and customs house (legally) to San

[147]

Diego, thereby triggering the venerable north-south rivalry which has continued to define this state's internal relations. Citing reasons of health and Monterey's cool, damp climate, Echeandía set a precedent which Los Angeles sought to repeat.

Alexander Forbes, the British consul at Tepic, astutely observed in the early 1830s that efforts were afoot to remove the seat of government from Monterey to Los Angeles. This seemed to be a ploy lacking in innocence but strong in tradition "as the Spaniards have in their colonies always chosen an inland situation for their capital towns."[3] José Carrillo, a native son and California's congressional delegate to Mexico City, was responsible for this turn of events. By May of 1835 this master of political intrigue had succeeded in drawing more blood in the perennial struggle between the state's northern and southern factions.

When informed of Carrillo's handiwork, all Monterey was outraged. William Hartnell and Francisco Pacheco drew up a document of protest which stated without restraint the case of the eclipsed seat of government:

> Monterey has been the capital for more than 70 years; both Californians and foreigners have learned to regard it as the capital; interests have been developed which should not be ignored; and a change would engender serious rivalries. The capital of a maritime country should be a port, and not an inland place. Monterey is a secure, well-known, and frequented port, well provided with wood, water, and provisions. . . . Monterey has a larger population than Los Angeles; the people are moral and cultured; and the prospects are superior. Monterey has decent buildings for government uses, which to build at Los Angeles will cost $30,000; and some documents may be lost in moving the archives. Monterey has a strategic location, mild climate, fertile soil, advanced agriculture; here women, plants, and useful animals are very productive![4]

Although the valid Monterey protest was not without its latino flair, Los Angeles did in fact lack not only the proper buildings for a capital, but also the public spirit sufficient to furnish a rent-free structure suitable for the governor's residence. One man offered to rent a hall for $400 and contribute $75 of that sum, but that is as close as anyone came to demonstrating the necessary civic concern conducive to the maintenance of the flagship city.' Thus, the *Angelenos* were unable to capitalize on the master-ful political stroke perpetrated by one of their number. With the passing of a year eroding the coup, Governor Juan Alvarado was able to proclaim in 1836 that the capital would be restored to his native Monterey, though not without making political concessions to placate the southern Californians.

This flirtation with pre-eminence precipitated Los Angeles' first real estate boom. The events of 1835 created a brisk demand for lots, but there were no maps from which grants could be made. The confusion which resulted from this unprecedented interest in urban land and the vague status of all existing grants prompted the *ayuntamiento* (town council) to appoint a commission to give the matter further study. It was unanimously agreed that a uni-form procedure for the acquisition of land had to be established. An *alcalde* (councilman) remarked in January 1836 that "ques-tions frequently arise with respect to the ownership of houselots and agricultural lands because of the lack of titles."' The com-mission reported its findings on March 8 of that year:

> We consulted some of the founders and old *Alcaldes,* and found that since the founding of the *pueblo* (town) of Los Angeles, the concessions of *solares* (houselots) and *tierras de labor* (land for cultivation) had been made, first by *comisionados* (military constables) and later by the *Ayuntamiento verbally* and without other formality than indicating to the grantees the site and extent that they were to occupy.
>
> In order to make this report more complete the commission examined an instruction signed by el Señor Don José Francisco de Ortega made at San Gabriel, the second day of February 1782, and noted articles 3, 4, and 17 . . . required that the Government provide the grantees with written titles . . . but there is not a single proprietor who has a written title to his possessions.'

Thus, the vagueness over land titles merged with that of imprecise lot boundaries and both contributed to the ensuing confusion concerning the town's public rights of way.

Accordingly, another commission was also appointed in 1836. Its assignment was to study the problems which resulted from the arrangement of streets, alleys and plazas and "to report a plan for repairing the monstrous irregularity of the streets brought about by ceding houselots and erecting houses in this city."' The

[149]

commission recommended the drawing of "a topographical plan of the city as it actually exists, on which shall be marked the names of the streets, alleys, and plazas; also the house lots and common lands of the pueblo."⁹ But no competent surveyor could be found and the matter was dropped although the commission declared itself "amazed, seeing the disorder and manner how the streets run, more particularly the street which leads to the cemetery whose width is out of proportion to its length, and whose aspects offend the sense of the beautiful which should prevail in the city."¹⁰

Even though this initial effort to restore the orderly intents of the original plan did not succeed, there are indications that some progress was soon made in the direction. In October 1840 Santiago Arguëllo granted fifty square *varas* (Spanish yards) to Antonio Alvitre and stressed the importance of "keeping the order and harmony necessary in the formation of alleys."¹¹ The following year some steps were taken to mark off the town's four square leagues of land which constituted the limits of Los Angeles' pueblo grant. Bancroft believed that nothing was accomplished initially in this matter, but in January 1842, Arguëllo ruled that grants "may not be situated outside the City, and interested parties must solicit houselots within the limits."¹²

Continuing prosperity relentlessly pressured the civic authorities to come to terms with growth and the concomitant problem of maintaining the integrity of real estate. The Hudson Bay Company's Sir George Simpson observed that Los Angeles was situated "in one of the loveliest and most fertile districts of California; and being, therefore, one of the best marts in the province for hides and tallow, it induces vessels to brave all the inconveniences and dangers of the open and exposed bay of San Pedro."¹³ The waterfront drew an international clientele, among whom was Richard Henry Dana of Boston, whose *Two Years Before the Mast* remains the best popular account of Mexican California and of that trade in bovine raw materials.¹⁴ Overland commerce also favored Los Angeles as the terminus of caravans from New Mexico bringing woolen goods. Blankets and *serapes* were exchanged for mules and horses from the surrounding range land at the prevailing rate of two blankets for each animal.¹⁵

[150]

A further challenge to the municipal authorities was posed by the sizeable Indian population whose lives were characterized by misery and squalor. Most of this landless group had arrived in the early 1830s following the secularization of the southern Franciscan missions. As early as 1833 Fr. Narciso Durán called attention to their plight:

I have seen . . . that in and about said town there are two or three hundred Indian squatters. Beyond comparison they live far more wretched and oppressed lives than those in the missions. There is not one who has a garden of his own, or a yoke of oxen, a horse, or a house fit for a rational being. . . . All in reality are *slaves,* or servants of white men who know well the manner of of securing their services by binding them for a whole year for an advanced trifle.[16]

Conditions had improved only marginally by 1841. In that year Duflot de Mofras commented:

All the Pueblo's cultivation is done by the Indians who live in a little village planted at the brink of a rivulet at the edge of the houses of the town. These unfortunates are often badly mistreated, and do not always receive exactly the price of a day's work which is fixed at one *real* in silver and one in merchandise.[17]

The *ayuntamiento* decided to take action against these Indian squatters in March 1847. It cited the "frequent complaints which have been made against the huts of Indians situated in the pueblo, and principally the scandalous reunions which occur every Saturday." Therefore, it required all individuals with Indian servants to house them within the limits of their property, "keeping them subject and sleeping in the house in which they serve in order to check their excesses." Those Indians who were not regularly employed were to be granted lots on the edge of the city "where they will be given ownership with their respective titles and separate houselots in such a manner as to avoid scandalous meetings."[18]

Despite its size, Los Angeles was not an ethnically-diverse community. Hastings estimated its population in 1843 at 1,500 consisting chiefly of Mexicans and Indians. He wrote that "although this town is the largest found in the country, yet from the fact of its being situated in the interior, it is of much less im-

[151]

portance."[19] Consequently, the foreign merchant community was quite small and Los Angeles exuded its distinct Hispanic character. In appearance, Hastings noted, its few hundred buildings were "small, and otherwise inferior, the walls of which are generally constructed of 'adobies' which are large dried brick, and the roofs chiefly of tiles; they are but one story high, though many of them are very convenient."[20]

Unlike the civic lassitude of a decade earlier, the mid-1840s were characterized by a heretofore unknown brand of municipal vigor and public spirit which, if not efficacious, was at least infectious. The venerable problem of land titles was again broached. In March 1844 the *ayuntamiento* declared that all agricultural lands must be cultivated each year or else forfeited by their owners; and in keeping with the precedents of Spanish law, these *suertes* (agricultural land) could not be alienated.[21] In May the *sindico* (city attorney) proposed that all those who possessed houselots, developed or not, and those who claimed *tierras de labor* or who had harvested on communal lands were to present themselves within fifteen days in order to solicit the necessary documents for proper title to that real estate. It was also stipulated, hereafter, that no land may be occupied without an appropriate written description.[22] The movement towards rationalization continued in November 1844; the *ayuntamiento* resolved that the city should be divided into districts of 500 voters. However, this action proved to be premature as the elections scheduled for the following December 16 were not held because of insufficient voter registration.[23] Tentative action was also begun at this time concerning the formation, closing and straightening of streets.[24] A commission for such matters was proposed in July 1845 and a year later it numbered among the town's four permanent ones which included those of police, water and vacant lands.[25]

Having laid the groundwork for the legal integrity of municipal growth, the civic conscience next turned its eye to the visual realm. The first "city beautiful" movement in California was launched virtually singlehandedly by *regidor* (alderman) Leonardo Cota in April 1845. In a dramatic address before the *ayuntamiento* he argued:

It appears that the time has come in which the City of Los Angeles has begun to figure in the political sphere of things . . .

[152]

and with appreciable elements of progress; what is now required in order to finish the work? Although this small city is beginning to show its astral magnificence and brilliance in a manner that when a traveler comes to the City of Los Angeles . . . everybody tells him that it will be the Mexican paradise; but not as it finds itself today, with the majority of buildings presenting an appearance so melancholy, somber, sad, and dreadful that the hecatombs of ancient Rome made a better impression than the buildings of a free people.[26]

Inspired accordingly, the *ayuntamiento* passed five ordinances which were drafted by Pío Pico and Juan Bandini.[27] First, it was ruled that owners of houses must shingle and whitewash their dwellings within three months or sustain a fine of from five to fifteen pesos. Secondly, owners of buildings under construction on main streets who failed to complete them would be fined according to the value of what had been built and the land would then be subject to confiscation.[28] Thirdly, lots on which only ruined walls stood would be confiscated after two months following the ordinance's publication if they continued in the same abandoned condition. Fourth, those persons, who because of poverty, illness or other circumstances could not comply with the preceding, were allowed to present their cases to the *ayuntamiento* for consideration. And fifth, revenue from fines would be applied to the municipal fund for purposes of improving and beautifying the city.

The task of delimiting the pueblo boundaries was recommenced in May 1846. The document in question contains the notation, "the order was given for the measuring *ejidos* (commons) taking two leagues for each wind of the four cardinal points. Said measurement was suspended and now is recommenced."[29] If two leagues had been measured in each direction, the area encompassed by Los Angeles would have been sixteen square leagues, four times that to which it was entitled. This confused notion concerning the extent of pueblo lands in California seems to have plagued the *angelenos* to a greater extent than others. Later, the situation was to become even more chaotic as Yankee immigrants failed to distinguish between leagues and miles. The surveyor of two years hence, Edward O. C. Ord, was to share in this confusion.

[153]

By 1847 Los Angeles was the largest town in California and also the focus of Hispanic population and wealth.[30] But apparently little progress had been made in attaining the regulation and realignment of previous disorderly development. In January of that year Edwin Bryant reported:

> Its streets are laid out without any regard to regularity. The buildings are generally constructed of adobes one and two stories high, with flat roofs. The public buildings are a church, quartel, and government house. Some of the dwelling-houses are frames, and large. Few of them, interiorly or exteriorly, have any pretensions to architectural taste, finish, or convenience of plan or arrangement.[31]

Apparently, agriculture had received much greater attention. General Sherman remarked, "Every house had its inclosure of vineyard, which resembled a miniature orchard, the vines being very old, ranged in rows trimmed very close, with irrigating ditches so arranged that a stream of water could be diverted between each row of vines."[32]

Meanwhile, after two years of deliberation, the Commission on the Arrangement of Streets tendered its report during July 1847. It found that the streets were too wide and did not "present the vista required for the beauty of the city."[33] The Commission determined that each street should be fifteen *varas* (Spanish yards) wide, based on a provision in the *Recopilación*.[34] However, on a more comprehensive level, it recommended, "we must proceed effectively in order to avoid the disorder which we have had with respect to this matter," and more specifically, it resolved to narrow the streets and eliminate alleys.[35]

However, the municipal authorities once again failed to initiate action on a previously approved policy. In this instance it is presumed that the political turmoil prior to the assertion of American sovereignty precluded any concerted effort directed at correcting the chaos which resulted from past indifference to matters of urban form. Of major importance was the long-standing absence of a competent surveyor, a situation which was soon remedied by the presence of the American army. Although the introduction of order was one of the primary tasks of the American authorities, the prevailing urban chaos in Los Angeles was of minor importance. Rather, the prime concern was a map which accurately identified land holdings. It was recognized that "the permanent prosperity of any new country is identified with the perfect security of its land titles" and a competent blueprint for future land distribution and prior land ownership was prerequisite.³⁶ Thus, Edward O. C. Ord was chosen to conduct a survey and draw what amounted to an expansion plan for Los Angeles. His task was to

> . . . determine the four points of the compass and taking the Parish Church for a center, measure two leagues in each cardinal direction. These lines will bisect the four sides of a square within which the lands of this Municipality will be contained, the area being sixteen square leagues and each side of the square measuring four leagues.³⁷

Either the *Ayuntamiento* specifically planned to expropriate a pueblo grant far in excess of the traditional four square leagues (i.e., one in each cardinal direction), or it misunderstood the legislation in question. In any case this municipal grant was later to cause complications in the confirmation of Los Angeles' title by the United States Land Commission. With reference to the dimensions for the new map, Ord was instructed to "lay out streets and blocks where there are no buildings, . . . the streets to the southwest of 75 feet in width, and to each one [block] 212 yards, and the streets which run from the vineyards to the hills of 60 feet width and to each one [block] 200 yards."³⁸

A land auction was held in December 1849 in order to raise $3,000 for Ord's fee; that sum had initially been advanced to him by local merchants "after a good deal of haggling."³⁹ Fifty-four lots measuring 40 x 56 *varas* were sold for a total of $2,490 and subsequent sales were to follow until the full amount had been secured.⁴⁰ Although the Los Angeles lots were perhaps half the size of similar parcels auctioned in San Francisco, land in the latter town fetched prices of upwards of ten times as much per unit of land and frequently much more than that.

A few months after the completion of the survey, Ord described Los Angeles as consisting of "an old adobe church, and about a hundred adobe houses scattered around a dusty plaza and along three or four broad streets leading thereto."⁴¹ The

[155]

immediate effects of his survey are not known. Perhaps his description indicates that some streets were straightened but not narrowed. A gradual process of "beautification" was apparently underway for Ord observed in 1850 that Los Angeles "has improved in appearance though not in morals."[42]

The discovery of gold brought with it a wave of prosperity that entrepreneurial *angelenos* were quick to exploit; the supplying of beef to the forty-niners was their main activity. As a result, Los Angeles "enjoyed the unique distinction of having an organized town life situated far enough away from the north and its rough-hewn inconveniences, and yet close enough to siphon off the real wealth that was dredged from the Sierra."[43]

Amidst this plenty, perhaps the challenge of growth appears less formidable. Further, we are confronted with an unflattering portrait of Hispanics drawn by judgmental Anglo travelers. Simpson, for example, wrote that Los Angeles was "a den of thieves [and] the noted abode of the lowest drunkards and gamblers of the country."[44] Nevertheless, the catalog of concerns which motivated the civic conscience is an impressive one: a map on which land grants would be registered (a practice previously superfluous in the Spanish borderlands); a re-alignment of streets and other rights-of-way to conform to a prior plan; the proper demarcation of municipal limits (twice attempted); the regulation of the Indian population; the compulsory development of house lots and agricultural lands with forfeiture as a penalty in some instances, fines in others; the attempt to organize election districts of five hundred voters; the establishment of four permanent civic commissions; the emergence of a city beautiful movement replete with a system of development incentives; and the completion of the official municipal survey by Lt. Ord. Thus, however inflated its imagined greatness in the 1840s, Mexican Los Angeles did not lack the effort necessary for its attainment. As for its debt to the future, it would appear small indeed to later generations of American settlers who lost little time converting the rhetoric of their predecessors to the bond issues that built a metropolis.

NOTES

[1] Daniel J. Boorstin, *The Americans: The National Experience* (New York, 1965), p. 113.

[2] Richard C. Wade, *The Urban Frontier* (Chicago, 1959), Ch. 9.

[3] Alexander Forbes, *A History of Upper and Lower California* (San Francisco, 1937), p. 130. This also recalls IV:7:4 of the *Recopilación*, which warned against establishing major towns in maritime locations. *Recopilación de leyes de los Reynos de las Indias*, 4th ed., 3 vols. [Madrid, 1791], II, 20.

[4] Quoted in Susanna Bryant Dakin, *The Lives of William Hartnell* (Stanford, 1949), p. 208.

[5] Hubert Howe Bancroft, *History of California*, 7 vols. (San Francisco, 1884-1889), III, 416-417.

[6] Manuel Requeña to Nicolás Gutiérrez, Los Angeles, January 26, 1836, California Archives, Legislative Records, III, 3, Bancroft Library, University of California, Berkeley.

[7] Los Angeles Comisión de Policía, March 8, 1836, Los Angeles City Archives, I, 77-78; Requeña to Gefe Politico, Los Angeles, April 22, 1836, Legislative Records, III, 4. The only written title granted in Los Angeles before 1836 was conceded on June 22, 1821, Los Angeles City Archives, I, 2. All other titles were, or should have been, written entries in the *libro de población*.

[8] Quoted in J. M. Guinn, "From Pueblo to Ciudad, the Municipal and Territorial Expansion of Los Angeles," *Publications of the Historical Society of Southern California*, 7 (1908), 218.

[9] *Ibid.*, pp. 218-219: Los Angeles *Ayuntamiento*, session of January 28, 1837, Ayuntamiento Records, I, 395, Los Angeles City Archives.

[10] Guinn, "From Pueblo to Cuidad," p. 218. With reference to this matter, IV:7:10 of the *Recopilación* was recalled which stipulated that in cold climates streets were to be wide and in warm climates narrow (II, 21).

[11] Argüello to Alvitre, Los Angeles, October 3, 1840, Ayuntamiento Records, II, 477, Los Angeles City Archives.

[12] Bancroft, IV, 635-636; Argüello to Casiano Carrion, Los Angeles, January 31, 1842, Los Angeles City Archives II, p. 144.

[13] Sir George Simpson, *Narrative of a Journey Round the World During the Years 1841 and 1842*, 2 vols. (London, 1847), I, 420.

[14] Richard Henry Dana, *Two Years Before the Mast* (New York, 1909).

[15] Eleanor Lawrence, "Mexican Trade Between Santa Fe and Los Angeles, 1830-1848," *California Historical Society Quarterly*, 10 (March 1931), 27-39. The caravan which arrived in November 1841 included sixty Americans, forty of whom departed for San José, presumably to settle. Eugene Duflot de Mofras, *Exploration du Territoire de l'Orégon, des Californies, et de la Mer Vermeille*, 2 vols. [Paris, 1844], I, 354-355.

[16] Durán to Gov. José Figueroa, San Diego, July 3, 1833, quoted in Zephyrin Engelhardt, O.F.M., *The Missions and Missionaries of California*, 4 vols. (San Francisco, 1908-1915), III, 477-478.

[17] Duflot de Mofras, *Exploration*, I, 356.

[18] Los Angeles *Ayuntamiento*, session of March 13, 1847, Ayuntamiento Records, II, 430-431, Los Angeles City Archives.

[19] Lansford W. Hastings, *The Emigrants' Guide to Oregon and California*, (Cincinnati, 1845), p. 108.

[20] *Ibid.*

[157]

[21] Los Angeles *Ayuntamiento*, session of March 8, 1844, Ayuntamiento Records, II, 127-130, Los Angeles City Archives.

[22] Los Angeles *Ayuntamiento*, session of May 11, 1844, *Ibid.*, pp. 131-133.

[23] Bancroft, *California*, IV, 633.

[24] *Ibid.*, p. 628.

[25] Los Angeles *Ayuntamiento*, session of July 26, 1845, Ayuntamiento Records, II, 281, Los Angeles City Archives; Bancroft, *California*, IV, 367-385.

[26] Cota, Los Angeles, April 19, 1845, Ayuntamiento Records, II, 298-300, Los Angeles City Archives. A similar, but less eloquent proposal was set forth two days later by Juan Sepúlveda. Departmental State Papers, Benicia, II, 348-349, Bancroft Library.

[27] Pico and Bandini, Los Angeles, April 23, 1845, Departmental State Papers, Angeles, III, 111-112, Bancroft Library.

[28] An unidentified individual objected to this ordinance, apparently with success. He argued that there was a shortage of building materials, difficulty in finding construction help, and that work was extremely difficult during the rainy season. Los Angeles *Ayuntamiento*, session of July 3, 1847, Ayuntamiento Records, II, 435-436, Los Angeles City Archives.

[29] Jose Sepúlveda to Secretario de Gobierno, Los Angeles, May 29, 1846, Departmental State Papers, Benicia, Perfecturas y Juzgados, p. 414.

[30] William R. Emory, *Notes of a Military Reconnaissance, from Fort Leavenworth, in Missouri to San Diego, in California* (New York, 1848), p. 161.

[31] Edwin Bryant, *What I Saw in California . . . in the Years 1846, 1847* Reprint ed.; (Minneapolis, 1967), p. 405.

[32] William Tecumseh Sherman, *Recollections of California, 1846-1861* (Oakland, 1945), p. 18.

[33] Los Angeles *Ayuntamiento*, session of July 22, 1847, Ayuntamiento Records, II, 437-438, Los Angeles City Archives.

[34] See *note* 10 *ante*.

[35] Los Angeles Ayuntamiento, session of July 22, 1847, Ayuntamiento Records, II, 437-438, Los Angeles City Archives.

[36] Secretary of State James Buchanan to William V. Voorhies, Washington, D.C., October 7, 1848, quoted in John A. Rockwell, *A Compilation of Spanish and Mexican Law in Relation to Mines, and Titles to Real Estate, in force in California, Texas, and New Mexico*, 2 vols. (New York, 1851), I, 421.

[37] Los Angeles *Ayuntamiento*, session of July 18, 1849, in William W. Robinson, ed., "The Story of Ord's Survey as Disclosed by the Los Angeles Archives," *Historical Society of Southern California Quarterly*, 19 (September-December 1937), 123.

[38] Ord's contract with the Los Angeles *Ayuntamiento*, July 22, 1849, *Ibid.*, pp. 124-125.

[39] William Rich Hutton, *Glances at California, 1847-1853*, ed. Willard O. Waters (San Marino, 1942), p. 20.

[40] Los Angeles *Ayuntamiento*, sessions of November 6 and December 24, 1849, quoted in Robinson, "The Story of Ord's Survey," pp. 126-127.

[41] Ord to Gen. Bennet Riley, Monterey, December 30, 1849, quoted in Philip T. Tyson, *Geology and Industrial Resources of California* (Baltimore, 1851), p. 126.

[42] Ord, "Diary, 1850-1856," MS, p. 39, Bancroft Library.

[43] Leonard Pitt, *The Decline of the Californios: A Social History of the Spanish-Speaking Californians, 1846-1890* (Berkeley and Los Angeles, 1966), p. 127.

[44] Simpson, *Narrative*, I, 420.

[158]

A Rare and Desolate Land:
Population and Race in Hispanic California

Daniel J. Garr

The settlement of California was an effort crippled by the logistic difficulties inherent in a remote frontier and by the steadily declining resources and determination of the Spanish and Mexican colonizers. They were unable to populate a land which in many cases offered the colonist little incentive. Hispanic settlement efforts contrast with the covetous and timely enterprise of the Anglo-American frontiersmen drawn across the Great Divide by mineral riches, fertile and sparsely populated territories, and the magnet of the Pacific. In practice, Hispanic population policy in California was primarily one of channeling a reluctant and frequently unstable population to secure the distant hinterland while simultaneously purging the Mexican heartland of those whose presence was deemed undesirable. In sharp contrast, we find the Spanish juristic mandate that respectable and industrious soldiers and settlers, accompanied by their families, should populate the frontier provinces. The fact that the program of expedience embodied the extraofficial goals of both viceregal and, later, national governments was ignored, though hardly overlooked. As so often occurred in the annals of Spain overseas, the best designs of those who formulated policy were thwarted and compromised by circumstances beyond their ken and control. Also woven into this coarse fabric was the characteristic Latin American preoccupation with matters pertaining to socioracial stratification. This is a key variable in frontier population policy as well as in official attitudes concerning unstable social conditions.

The earliest California settlers were soldiers, followed by civilians recruited from northern Mexico after the decision had been made the estab-

This essay by Daniel J. Garr, assistant professor of urban and regional planning at San José State University, San José, California, is the winner of the Herbert E. Bolton Award in Spanish Borderlands History, 1974. The award is sponsored through the *WHQ* by Lawrence Kinnaird, professor emeritus, University of California, Berkeley.

lish the pueblos of San José and Los Angeles. The presence of a military contingent posed two related problems: first, the social composition of the frontier population; second, and more crucial, the characteristic absence of women in a military environment. The latter was indeed a factor remiss in the desired augmentation of the non-Indian population, especially since the missionaries were faced with the unenviable task of segregating indigenous women from theoretically celibate soldiers. These unyielding circumstances affecting the coexistence of missionaries and military were further exacerbated by the nature of the frontier army's troops. Ideally, enlistment was voluntary and limited to men of sturdy character and physique. It was not, however, unusual for authorities to resort to the conscription of "recycled" deserters, vagabonds, drunkards, and assorted criminals, all of whom were invariably drawn from the scorned lower strata of a racially mixed society.[1] Thus, the men of the Army of New Spain were frequently other than what Teodoro de Croix specified in his instructions for the recruitment of soldiers for the California presidios. Like the settlers, each was to be "healthy, robust, and without known vice or defect that would make him prejudicial," in addition to possessing "greater strength and endurance for the hardships of frontier service."[2]

The inherent difficulty with the frontier army was that it provided a convenient outlet for the expulsion of undesirables from Mexico. As early as 1773, Padre Junípero Serra entreated the government "not to look upon Monterey and its missions as the *China* or *Ceuta* of exile for the soldier. . . . Being sent to our missions should not be a form of banishment, nor should our missions be filled with worthless people who serve no purpose but to commit evil deeds."[3] Although Viceroy Antonio María de Bucareli saw to it that Serra's wishes were accommodated, subsequent administrations were not inclined to give high priority to missionary preferences. By the mid-1820s, the estate of California had fallen so low in

[1] Lyle N. McAlister, "The Army of New Spain, 1760–1800" (Ph.D. dissertation, University of California, Berkeley, 1950), 194–95.

[2] Teodoro de Croix, "Instrucción que debe observar el Capitán D. Fernando Rivera y Moncada para la recluta y habilitación de familias, pobladores y tropa . . . para el resguardo, beneficio y conservación de los nuevos y antiguos establecimientos de aquella Península," Arispe, December 27, 1779, quoted in Historical Society of Southern California, *Annual Publication Commemorating the One Hundred and Fiftieth Anniversary of the Founding of Los Angeles, September 4, 1781* (Los Angeles, 1931), 192.

[3] Padre Junípero Serra to Viceroy Antonio María de Bucareli, Mexico, June 11, 1773, Junípero Serra, *Writings,* ed. Antonine Tibesar, O. F. M., 4 vols. (Washington, D. C., 1955–1966), I, 383.

Mexico that in 1826 it was proposed without further pretense that the army be purged of its dead wood by recruiting virtuous citizens for its ranks and exiling all the jetsam and flotsam to the distant dependency. This policy was described by Alexander Forbes, British vice-consul at the port of Tepic:

Whatever soldiers are sent to California are the refuse of the Mexican army, and most frequently are deserters, mutineers, or men guilty of military crimes. Those presidios are also appropriated as receptacles for transported felons; so that California is the Botany Bay of Mexico.[4]

The situation apparently continued to deteriorate until the era of American rule. For example, in 1845, Belden observed that the soldiers "committed all sorts of outrages and were very apt to commit violence with their knives, . . . and were a bad lot generally, . . . very disagreeable with the native population, overbearing and insolent."[5]

The implications for frontier settlement are both obvious and ominous. Since each mission required a protective military escort, the friars were presented with a trying problem—the security implicit in the soldiers' presence was often outweighed by their importunity. The first decade of California colonization saw the formation of military and missionary settlements exclusively; the acrid basis for subsequent discord was quickly established between hapless secular and embattled religious authorities. Neither side would reap much consolation from the fact that it was always difficult to attract a stable and balanced population to a frontier environment, but particularly for the defensive settlement of a remote colony.

The troublesome qualities of the initial contingent of soldier/colonists were immediately apparent during California's early years, especially between 1769 and 1779. One of the reasons for the relocation of the San Diego Mission was the missionaries' desire to avoid proximity to the soldiers at the presidio.[6] The military was well aware that California posed a difficult situation for the friars since, as even the anticlerical Teodoro de Croix acknowledged, not only did the priests require protection but

[4] Alexander Forbes, *A History of Upper and Lower California* (San Francisco, 1937), 128.

[5] Josiah Belden, *Memoirs and Early Letters,* ed. Doyce B. Nunis, Jr. (Georgetown, California, 1962), 66–67.

[6] Richard F. Pourade, *The History of San Diego,* 5 vols. (San Diego, 1960–1965), II, 19–20.

they also had to shield their charges, "who are docile and without malice, like all Indians, to the first impressions of good or bad example set by the Spanish who settle among them." [7] Missionary accounts of insubordination and immorality were numerous, with emphasis on the latter. In 1773, for example, Serra confided to Bucareli:

Then, too, the presence of so many women . . . it would be a great miracle, yes a whole series of miracles, if it did not provoke so many men of such low character to disorders which we have to lament in all our missions; they occur every day; it is as though a plague of immorality had broken out. [8]

Although the missionary viewpoint may seem to belabor the obvious, it nevertheless delimits the full extent of the problem, and with it the shortsightedness of the secular authorities. Shortly after, dismayed but undaunted, Serra again informed the viceroy that "the soldiers, clever as they are at lassoing cows and mules, would catch an Indian woman with their lassos to become prey for their unbridled lust." [9] However easily diagnosed were the symptoms of the problem, the cure required measures as arduous as they were evident. It was no mean task to lure single women to a distant environment barren of cultural and other societal amenities. Yet, a year later, as much without warning as without permanence, the long awaited remedy materialized. Serra's witty acknowledgment hardly concealed his relief:

Don Rafael, the warehouse keeper at San Diego, brought his wife with him. So now the number of families is increasing. And the people here will now be rid of their belief that the Spaniards are the offspring of mules, a notion they previously had, seeing that mules were the only members of the female gender they saw among us. [10]

Not until 1795 was active government concern with women manifested as both a factor in population growth and as an agent of societal stability. At that late date, Governor Diego de Borica noted the small number of settlers in California and the enusing, if not dire, necessity of encouraging population growth for reasons of both security and sociability; unmarried soldiers were singled out as the chief, however unwill-

[7] Teodoro de Croix, "Instrucción," 192.

[8] Serra to Bucareli, Mexico, April 22, 1773, Serra, *Writings,* I, 341.

[9] Serra to Bucareli, Mexico, May 21, 1773, Serra, *Writings,* I, 363.

[10] Serra to Melchor de Peramas, Monterey, June 14, 1774, Serra, *Writings,* II, 67.

ing, culprits remiss in this situation. He called upon the four presidio commandants to promote marriage by all honorable means, and offered a bonus of forty *pesos* to any soldier who took upon himself the bonds of matrimony.[11] When the viceregal government concurrently adopted the policy of sending convicts to California, Borica requested equal numbers of *mujeres blancas*. He also cited the need to supplement the small number of "women of quality . . . since many would forcefully resist emigration rather than consent to these unions; their guardians can procure suitors of correct habits, and as there are few here, it appears to me that few marriages of this kind will take place." [12] Therefore, he continued, if women of social pretensions were unavailable, it would be advantageous to furnish ones of lesser status with the trappings of respectability, such as a serge petticoat, a serviceable shawl, and a linen jacket.[13] Although the viceroy, the Marqués de Branciforte, concurred and indicated that he would send women to California at government expense, it appears that his efforts were not productive.[14] A similar project, which was never followed through, brought nineteen female orphans to California in 1800. They were distributed among presidial families, and two girls had found husbands by the year's end.[15]

The only specific and sustained government program for populating California consisted of periodic shipments of vagabonds and convicts from the streets and jails of New Spain. The practice had a venerable past. In response to the startling growth of mestizo and mulatto vagrancy in the sixteenth century, Philip II advised his viceroys that "some men are incorrigible, inobedient, or harmful and are to be expelled from the land and sent to Chile, the Philippines, or other parts." [16] The populating of frontier areas certainly provided a convenient solution to the problem of idle urban masses. In eighteenth-century Mexico, trouble with the lower classes was chronic, particularly in the economically unstable mining

[11] Borica to presidio commandants, Monterey, April 13, 1795, California Archives (CA), Bancroft Library, Provincial Records, 5 vols., II, 405–6.

[12] Borica to Viceroy Miguel de la Grúa Talamanca y Branciforte, Monterey, September 17, 1797, CA, Provincial Records, III, 379–80.

[13] Borica to Branciforte, Monterey, September 17, 1797, CA, Provincial Records, III, 379–80.

[14] Branciforte to Borica, Orizaba, January 25, 1798, CA, Provincial Records, VI, 55–56. Hubert Howe Bancroft, *History of California*, 7 vols. (San Francisco, 1884–1890), I, 605.

[15] Bancroft, *History of California*, I, 606.

[16] *Recopilación*, II, Libro VII Título 4 Ley 2, 359.

regions. Visitor-General José de Gálvez was instructed that he and the viceroy, the Marqués de Cruillas, were to "confer on the matter of forming settlements in the provinces in suitable places with the idle, undesirable people who are in Mexico and other large towns." [17] However, Gálvez ordered that no vagabonds were to be sent to California. He sought to insulate the new colony against the time-tested methods of social purgation which were soon to prevail.[18] Later, in 1787, Governor Pedro Fages, yielding to the urgent need for more people, proposed that those imprisoned in Mexico, particularly craftsmen, be exiled to California in lieu of completing their sentences if they agreed to remain there as settlers.[19] In 1791, three *presidarios* arrived, and in the same year there is a report of a convict blacksmith instructing the Indians of the San Francisco Mission in his trade.[20]

The impact of the policy of populating California with convicts was felt within a short time. San José appears to have been the primary victim of the emigration. By the fall of 1800, several complaints of robberies, disputes, and other disorders had been recorded. An official report stated that there were many vagabonds without useful employment "who have caused the *regidores* and *alcaldes* to patrol at night from eleven to one and from one to three." [21] Apparently, many of these were squatters who had named their own interim *Alcalde de Campo!*[22]

The initial attempt to deal with the problem resulted in a proposal to distribute the *presidarios* among "honest *vecinos*." But Governor José de Arrillaga subsequently argued that such a plan was not feasible because "the settlers are committing frequent scandals and are insolent, vicious, buffoons, and immoral; it is asked that the transportation of other new ones be suspended." [23] Fray Fermín de Lasuén, in rare but predictable unison, echoed the governor's sentiments:

[17] Julián de Arriaga to José de Gálvez, Madrid, March 26, 1765, quoted in Herbert I. Priestley, *José de Gálvez: Visitor-General of New Spain, 1765–1771* (Berkeley, 1916), 413.

[18] Priestley, *José de Gálvez*, 259.

[19] Bancroft, *History of California*, I, 605.

[20] Bancroft, *History of California*, I, 605.

[21] Macario de Castro to Hermenegildo Sal, San José, September 30, 1800, CA, Provincial State Papers, XI, 6–7. Sal to Governor José de Arrillaga, Monterey, October 2, 1800, CA, Provincial State Papers, XI, 5–6.

[22] Sal to Arrillaga, CA, Provincial State Papers, XI, 6.

[23] Arrillaga to Viceroy Félix Berenguer de Marquina, Loreto, April 29, 1801, CA, Provincial State Papers, Indices, 67–68.

I have never known of anyone whatever of the convicts in question who has the character, ability, skill, or trade which is needed here. I do hear of crimes and scandals in connection with them; and I see them in the presidios, ranches and pueblos almost like tramps. . . . It seems to me that sending convicts to these parts to serve as colonists holds out no prospect of good, and has many disadvantages for the service of God, the King, and of the common good.[24]

It had been hoped initially that errant artisans in particular would be rehabilitated in California if given the opportunity to practice their trade and to impart their skills to mission Indians. However, the result of the policy, as noted above, made a mockery of whatever aspirations the government had entertained.

The viceregal administration in Mexico City was made well aware of the difficulties caused by its exported felons, and it appears that no more were sent during the remaining two decades of Spanish rule. In 1805, the policy of convict immigration was roundly criticized by the Conde del Valle de Orizaba. He reiterated that "the first need of this colony is the increase of its population. The precedent of minor criminals destined for this objective should not be construed as a solution." [25] He recommended instead that families with children be sent to the frontiers and that, in contrast to the previous settlers, legitimate tradesmen be included among them.[26]

When, in 1825, republican Mexico reinstituted the policy of utilizing California as a penal colony, local opposition flared once again and the issue became a persistent source of rancor between the central government and its distant dependency.[27] Governor José María de Echeandía accused the Mexico City authorities of "ignoring that in the peninsula there exist decent families of education," and asserted that this program of exile con-

---

[24] Fermín Francisco de Lasuén to Arrillaga, Mission San Francisco, December 27, 1801, Lasuén, *Writings*, ed. and trans. Finbar Kenneally, O. F. M. 2 vols. (Washington, D. C., 1965), II, 285–86.

[25] Conde del Valle de Orizaba to Felipe de Goycoechea, Mexico, December 20, 1805, CA, Provincial State Papers, XII, 17–18.

[26] Del Valle de Orizaba to de Goycoechea, Provincial State Papers XII, 17–18.

[27] A decree issued by President Anastasio Bustamente in 1830 provided that the government would pay for the transportation of convicts and their families. Said convicts would be employed in public works projects and would be eligible for grants of land and subsistence for one year upon the expiration of their terms. Anastasio Bustamente, Mexico, April 16, 1830, cited in John A. Rockwell, *A Compilation of Spanish and Mexican Law in relation in Mines, and Titles to Real Estate, in force in California, Texas and New Mexico*, 2 vols. (New York, 1851), I, 621.

stituted a grave danger to California's prosperity and stability.[28] But by 1829, the force of this opposition dwindled to a mere request that only "useful" convicts be sent since California had no jails and the government could not be held responsible for the exiles.[29] However, Echeandía's protest was ignored; shipments continued, and one even deposited its reluctant emigrés on Santa Cruz Island where they were left to fend for themselves with only a supply of cattle and fishhooks.[30]

The Californians believed, Vallejo recalled, "that Mexico had no right to infest its growing towns with subjects who had a hatred for morality, who preferred lies to the truth, idleness to industry, murder to a peaceful life, and whose presence was a constant menace, terrible for the peace and tranquillity of honorable families." [31] Juan Alvarado opposed "this absurd project," and vowed that he would take "all necessary means to abort this plan of thieves." [32] However, this did not dissuade the central government. By 1835, Governor José Figueroa had authorized *alcaldes* to establish special tribunals for vagabonds so that speedy and efficient justice might be dispensed.[33]

However, it should be pointed out that not all the exiles were of the same parcel of rogues, nor did they all live up to the notoriety which had preceded their arrival in California. Many were banished to California for so-called political crimes. For example, an 1828 statute forbade secret meetings, and made the third offense punishable by four years' exile in California.[34] A native Californian and diarist, Mrs. Angustias de la Guerra Ord, recounted that in 1829 a shipload of about eighty convicts arrived at Santa Barbara. The men, "most of them naked," were exiled for "very grave offenses." She continued, "I am compelled to relate this episode by the desire to record that these unfortunate Mexicans never afterwards gave cause for complaint, but always conducted themselves well." [35] Vallejo,

---

[28] Marian\> G. Vallejo, Recuerdos Históricos y Personales tocante á la Alta California, 5 vols. (Bancroft Library MS, 1875), II, 70.

[29] Bancroft, *History of California*, III, 48.

[30] Bancroft, *History of California*, III, 48.

[31] Vallejo, Recuerdos, II, 71–72.

[32] Juan B. Alvarado, Historia de California, 5 vols. (Bancroft Library MS, 1876), IV, 9–10.

[33] Figueroa, Monterey, May 18, 1835, CA, Santa Cruz Archives, 1 vol., 80.

[34] Theodore H. Hittell, *History of California*, 4 vols. (San Francisco, 1897), II, 89.

[35] Angustias de la Guerra Ord, *Occurrences in Hispanic California*, trans. and ed. Francis Price and William H. Ellison (Washington, D. C., 1956), 15.

despite his opposition to the government's use of California as a penal colony, nevertheless claimed success in his efforts to assimilate convicts into his Sonoma community. "From 1834 until the arrival of Commodore Stockton [in 1846]," he recalled, ". . . the Sonoma frontier was the Ceuta of Alta California; it was customary to send all unruly and rebellious spirits here and with pleasure I can assure that without the use of severe measures I succeeded in converting all my involuntary guests!" [36]

Perhaps at times the plague of convicts was more imagined than real. Alvarado conceded that, since the perpetrator was "the government of a Republic of new creation, it was not easy to regulate all manner of those who were discontented in the territory."[37] Although there were more than a few incorrigibles included among all the convicts, many went on to live productive lives in California. Nevertheless, the situation does not speak well of the Mexican program to secure and develop the province.

The state of affairs in California brought forth additional proposals designed not only to increase its population, but also to improve its quality. As early as 1775, Serra advocated sending "soldiers from respectable stock, taking care that in their number would be some . . . families . . . , that two such families be placed in each mission, so that the wives of these soldiers should devote themselves to instructing the women of the missions." [38] This idea was echoed by Viceroy Revillagigedo in 1793, although circumstances compelled him to admit that finding families—and especially stable and industrious families—would be difficult.[39] The intent of this scheme was to relieve the presidios of the burden of supplying escorts for the missions while simultaneously promoting population growth and industry. It was also again suggested that artisans be sent to California in order to "instruct the Indians in the arts necessary to society . . . for there is no better way then to introduce families among them who are industrious and useful." [40] Although twenty artisans were sent to California, chiefly

[36] Vallejo, Recuerdos, III, 293.

[37] Alvarado, Historia, II, 120.

[38] Serra to Bucareli, Monterey, January 8, 1775, Serra, Writings, II, 203.

[39] Revillagigedo, "Carta de 1793," cited in Bancroft, History of California, I, 602.

[40] Miguel Costansó, "Informe de Don Miguel Costansó al Virrey, Marqués de Branciforte, sobre el Proyecto de Fortificar los Presidios de la Nueva California," Noticias y Documentos acerca de las Californias, 1764–1795 (Madrid, 1959), 231. Alvarado, Historia, I, 81.

in 1792 and 1795, most returned to Mexico before 1800 upon the expiration of their contracts.[41]

Collaterally, a rather crude effort was made to upgrade the quality of the indigenous population. Viceroy Revillagigedo lamented in 1794 that there were no European immigrants "who might have improved the Indian race in many ways." [42] In that same year Miguel Costansó recommended that families of Spaniards, or of *individuos de castas mixtas*, be settled in the California missions, believing that intermarriage would benefit the Indians, who

when reduced to a civil life, procreate much less, and the mixture with the Spaniards or as we say with white people in general produces by the second or third generation individuals who scarcely retain the least defect of Indians inasmuch as having bred among Spaniards, their language, habits and customs hardly differ from ours.[43]

But the desired level of integration was not achieved since it was thought more important to bolster the population of the pueblos. As for eugenic modifications of the Indian population, Lasuén reported in 1801 that only twenty-four colonists had married California Indian women during the preceding three decades.[44]

Costansó's statement is particularly interesting since it shows that, even in an isolated frontier colony such as California, the characteristic Latin American preoccupation with matters of "purity of blood," or the lack thereof, was an essential feature of a stratified society. This standard enjoyed legal sanction until the end of the colonial period, but the aversion to miscegenation persisted beyond that time as a cultural practice.[45]

The state of racial affairs in California is best reflected in the socioracial census enumerations.[46] Mörner has observed that "the disdain of both Spaniards and criollos for mestizos and other 'castas' was as good

[41] Bancroft, *History of California*, I, 615.

[42] Quoted in Bancroft, *History of California*, I, 57.

[43] Costansó, "Informe," 233.

[44] Lasuén, Mission San Carlos, June 19, 1801, Lasuén, *Writings*, II, 212.

[45] As late as 1806, the Council of the Indies endorsed the idea of a hierarchical, multiracial colonial society. See Magnus Mörner, *Race Mixture in the History of Latin America* (Boston, 1967), 75.

[46] See, for example, CA, Provincial State Papers, VIII, 90 (San José, December 31, 1794); CA, State Papers: Missions, I, 5–10 (Santa Barbara, December 31, 1785), 61–64 (San José, October 5, 1790), 85–91 (San Francisco, October 2, 1970), 103–4 (Los Angeles, December 31, 1792); CA, State Papers: Missions and Colonization, II, 98–99 (Los Angeles, November 19, 1781).

as boundless," and this was reflected in the highly evolved socioracial terminology of the eighteenth century.[47] Such nomenclature, derived from New Spain, was used in several censuses of the 1780s and 1790s in California, and indicates the widespread importance attached to precision in racial distinction. The complexity of the various systems of ethnic classification indicates that they were "completely absurd, especially in dealing with people who more often than not were illegitimate." [48] Admittedly, few of the terms used in California went beyond the basic classifications and their derivatives which were drawn chiefly from physical appearance. But it is interesting that they were used and that some were even drawn from Peruvian nomenclature.[49]

Spanish colonization efforts—whether viewed in terms of quantity or quality of settlers, or by whatever standard population policy may be measured—failed to make a significant impact in California. In December 1793, Vancouver observed that "the mode originally adopted and since constantly pursued, in settling this country is by no means calculated to produce any great increase of white inhabitants." [50] Such a consideration had attained primary importance by 1795 as a result of the Nootka Sound controversy. Costansó stressed the importance of populating California if only for strategic reasons, since without additional colonists the province would not only be a liability but also an easy prey for an ambitious foreign power.[51]

It had always been recognized in California that military personnel represented the most economical source of manpower for colonization. The utilization of sailors who wished to settle on shore was especially advantageous since no transportation expenses were involved in their immigration. In 1785, Felipe de Goycoechea recommended that mariners be permitted to settle permanently—although twelve years earlier Serra had argued successfully, but without tangible results, a similar position

---

[47] Mörner, *Race Mixture*, 57.

[48] Mörner, *Race Mixture*, 59.

[49] See Mörner, *Race Mixture*, 58–59, for a listing of terms from both Mexico and Peru. In addition to the standard classifications of Spaniard, Indian, mestizo, and mulatto, the terms lobo, coyote, pardo, negro, and chino appear in California, as does the designation "de color quebrado," the latter in the San José census of December 1794.

[50] George Vancouver, *Voyage of Discovery to the North Pacific Ocean and Round the World*, 3 vols. (London, 1798), II, 496.

[51] Costansó, "Informe," 230.

before Viceroy Bucareli.[52] Later, in 1790, Viceroy Revillagigedo wrote that "it is a good, useful, and industrious custom for sailors to remain in the labor and founding of new missions." [53] Governor Pedro Fages recommended to José Antonio Romeu, his successor, that presidial and other soldiers be settled in pueblos.[54] And, in 1794, Costansó urged Viceroy Branciforte to permit sailors of the Manila Galleon to settle in Monterey if they so desired. This suggestion was thwarted by the crew's insistence that the ship make directly for Acapulco without further delay.[55]

Yet, despite the futility of government programs, the colonial era's sole private proposal to colonize California was not well received. An apparently advantageous proposition was made in 1802 by Lieutenant Luis Pérez de Tagle of Manila. He requested permission to bring a colony from the Philippines to California. In his petition to the king, Tagle stated that he had spent time in California and was familiar with the country's condition. The program which he proposed centered on the development of trade to counteract the English commercial influence in the Pacific. But the plan vanished in the maze of viceregal bureaucracy, and Bancroft speculated that it died a premature death because of Tagle's "modest demand" that he be placed in command of Monterey and the coast.[56] Not surprisingly, recommendations continued that the population be augmented by industrious persons who could flourish in the benign climate of California.[57] The failure to obtain even a modest number of desirable immigrants led not only to internal problems, but also to the eventual inundation of the country by ambitious foreign elements, particularly American.

The supreme irony of the population debacle was the rejection of precisely those measures so ardently awaited in earlier years. The persistent requests for skilled artisans and their families found belated fruition in the Híjar-Padrés Colony of 1834-35. Planned and organized by Mexi-

[52] Goycoechea to Governor Don Pedro Fages, Santa Barbara, August 9, 1785, CA, Provincial State Papers, III, 165. Serra to Bucareli, Monterey, August 24, 1774, Serra, *Writings*, II, 151.

[53] Revillagigedo to Fages, Monterey, December 14, 1790, CA, Provincial State Papers, V, 243.

[54] Fages, "Papel de varios puntos concernientes al Gobierno de la Península de California é Inspección de Tropas . . . ," Monterey, February 26, 1791, Provincial State Papers, VI, 152–53.

[55] Costansó, "Informe," 234–35.

[56] Bancroft, *History of California*, II, 4.

[57] Conde del Valle de Orizaba to Goycoechea, Mexico, December 20, 1805, CA, Provincial State Papers, XII, 20.

can vice-president Valentín Gómez Farías, the colony was dispersed after it arrived in California. Predictably, this occurred because the colony threatened the dominion of decayed local interests which no longer were able to discern the difference between the welfare of their country and their own shortsighted objectives. Although traditionally viewed within the context of Mexican efforts to take advantage of the Californians, the dissolution of the colony by Governor José Figueroa only paved the way for the Yankee usurpation of California within the decade. Given the pervasive atmosphere of distrust sown by the policies set in Mexico City, the endemic political instability and intrigue afoot in California, and the basic fear that the colony would preempt secularized mission lands long coveted by the Californians, contemporary public opinion favored Figueroa's measures, although hindsight would lead us to question their sagacity.

The alternative of last resort, the promotion of settlement by non-Spanish colonists, quite naturally had long been discouraged by Spanish law and colonial policy.[58] Yet, as early as 1793, Vancouver recognized that Spain's own resources and those of her empire would not be sufficient to populate California. "Progress towards civilization seems to have been remarkably slow; and it is not likely to become more rapid, until the impolicy of excluding foreign visitors shall be laid aside," he commented.[59] On this issue, Mexican ideas differed sharply from those of Spain. Just prior to independence, Mexico City's first impulse was to work within the framework of Spanish law. Viceroy del Venadito wrote that the *Recopilación* allowed settlement by foreigners who "profess useful arts and trades," but no program to attract settlers was formulated.[60] In 1824 the Mexican Congress passed the first of a handful of colonization laws which gave liberal, albeit only rhetorical, encouragement to foreign settlement.[61] A similar enactment dating from 1830 provided not only transportation costs for both Mexican and foreign families, but also authorized that up

---

[58] For a detailed statement of official thought on the problem, see Libro IX Título 27 of the *Recopilación* (III, 326–35). Only one statute is even mildly favorable with respect to foreign settlement (III, Libro IX Título 27 Ley 13, 329).

[59] Vancouver, *Voyage of Discovery*, II, 498.

[60] Viceroy del Venadito to Gov. Pablo Vicente de Solá, Mexico, October 20, 1819, CA, Departmental State Papers: Juzgados; Naturalization, 174. He probably was referring to Libro IX Título 27 Ley 13 of the *Recopilación*.

[61] "Decreto del Congreso Mejicano sobre Colonización," Mexico, August 18, 1824, cited in Bancroft, *History of California*, II, 516.

to one hundred thousand *pesos* be allocated to sponsor foreign immigrants. However, this bill never got beyond the Senate.[62]

Nevertheless, a great many foreigners settled in California on their own initiative and soon managed to dominate the hitherto straitened commercial affairs of the province. Fernandez dates the beginning of this period from the year 1822.[63] By 1841, the Anglo-American commercial conquest was complete, and in trade-oriented northern California the foreigners had also gained political ascendancy. "By their monopoly of trade and their command of resources, to say nothing of their superior energy and intelligence," Simpson wrote of the mercantile community, "they already possess vastly more than their numerical proportion of political influence."[64]

It is therefore not surprising that xenophobic forces emerged in California by the late 1830s. In Los Angeles foreigners were forbidden to acquire land even if they chose to follow the secular and sacred legal dictates by becoming naturalized citizens.[65] Duflot de Mofras related two incidents in which foreigners were murdered — one of them a fellow Frenchman — without any attempt by the authorities to bring the culprits to justice.[66] But the days of Hispanic preponderance were numbered. Hastings heralded "a new era in the affairs of California, ... about to rise ... bursting forth in a day, as it were, into brilliant intelligence, commendable activity, and unbounded enterprise."[67] Two months later the imminent

[62] C Alan Hutchinson, *Frontier Settlement in Mexican California: The Hijar-Padrés Colony and its Origins, 1769–1835* (New Haven, 1969), 172.

[63] José Fernandez, Cosas de California (Bancroft Library MS, 1874), 33. He also related an amusing incident on the subject:

"The majority of those who established commercial houses in Alta California were citizens of the state of Massachuseet [*sic*] and when the Indians asked them from where they had come, they replied that they were from Boston; the Indians, whose knowledge of geography was very limited, believed that all white men came from a single place, and for this reason whenever they saw an Englishman, or a German, or an American, they would exclaim, 'There goes a Boston!' "
Fernandez, 33–34.

[64] Sir George Simpson, *Narrative of a Journey Round the World during the Years 1841 and 1842*, 2 vols. (London, 1847), I, 293.

[65] Tiburcio Tapia to Los Angeles Ayuntamiento, Los Angeles, July 19, 1839, CA, Departmental State Papers: Angeles, II, 44. Los Angeles Ayuntamiento to Tapia, Los Angeles, July 25, 1839, CA, Departmental State Papers: Angeles, II, 57.

[66] Eugène Duflot de Mofras, *Exploration du Territoire de l'Orégon, des Californies, et de la Mer Vermeille*, 2 vols. (Paris, 1844), I, 232.

[67] Lansford W. Hastings to Larkin, New Helvetia, March 3, 1846, Larkin. *Larkin Papers*, IV, 221.

arrival of two thousand American families was announced by Vallejo, and like Texas twelve years earlier, California was virtually annexed to the United States by the abdication of an underpopulated and underfinanced Mexican nation.[68] Governor Pio Pico's reaction to the news was typical of many Californians. In a speech before the Departmental Assembly, he warned:

We find ourselves threatened by hordes of Yankee immigrants who have already begun to flock into our country, and whose progress we cannot arrest. Already have the wagons of that perfidious people scaled the almost inaccessible summits of the Sierra Nevada, . . . and penetrated the fruitful valley of the Sacramento. What that astonishing people will next undertake, I cannot say; but in whatever enterprise they embark they will sure to be successful. Already these adventurous voyagers . . . are cultivating farms, establishing vineyards, erecting mills, sawing up lumber, and doing a thousand other things which seem natural to them.[69]

Pico's apprehensions were more than justified. The coming of the Yankees created a new social order. Despite the Americans' narrow values and denigration of Latin culture, they merely replaced, in a qualitative sense, Mexican California's well delineated hierarchical social structure. Writing of Monterey society in 1840, Arnaz found that it was "organized on the basis of separate classes, with gaiety and perfect order prevailing in its diversions."[70] Dana was struck by the efforts of the Californians to maintain their hierarchical society which was dominated by those families claiming "pure" Spanish blood. There were only a few of these families, he observed, and they vigorously defended their status

. . . intermarrying, and keeping up an exclusive system in every respect. They can also be told by their complexions, dress, manner, and also by their speech; for, calling themselves Castilians, they are very ambitious of speaking the pure Castilian language which is spoken in a somewhat corrupted dialect, by the lower classes. From this upper class, they go down by regular shades, growing more and more dark and muddy, until you come to the pure Indian, who runs about with nothing upon him but a small piece of cloth.[71]

[68] Mariano Vallejo to Manuel Castro, Sonoma, May 25, 1846, Departmental State Papers, V, 59.

[69] Quoted in Frederic Hall, *The History of San Jose and Surroundings* (San Francisco, 1871), 143.

[70] José Arnaz, Recuerdos (Bancroft Library MS, 1878), 38.

[71] Richard Henry Dana, *Two Years Before the Mast* (New York, 1909), 79.

But this societal configuration was to be short-lived as California was settled by overwhelming numbers of Yankee emigrants, persons who were to hold the caste-conscious Californians in contempt, much as they had despised the Indians and *castas*. Hastings deprecated his hosts' "dorment [*sic*] intelligence, inert energy, and dead and buried enterprise." [72] Indeed, the clash of basic values, antagonisms of religion and race, and the Anglos' catalog "of the venial and cardinal sins practiced in the province" underscored the divisions between the two groups.[73] Pitt has written that "judgmental is the word for Anglo-Saxon spirit in California in this period."[74] Perhaps this heavy-handed search for justification could not be avoided. The spoilation wrought by the gold hysteria rendered the bucolic past even more valuable than the ephemeral glitter of precious metal, for no amount of panning would produce even the smallest nugget of an irretrievable and fragile era. One of Mexican California's shrewdest Yankee traders, Thomas O. Larkin, wrote in 1856, "I begin to yearn after the times prior to July, 1846 and all their beautiful pleasures, flesh-pots of those days — halcyon days they were. We shall not enjoy the same again."[75]

The abrupt transition from pastoral Mexican backwater to booming American commercial emporium and mining frontier produced a social transformation in northern California as dramatic as it was transfiguring. Elsewhere, particularly in the south, the gold rush did not mark sudden death for the Hispanic culture. Los Angeles, Santa Barbara, and even Monterey maintained their cultural links with the past well into the final quarter of the nineteenth century. The shattered Hispanic heritage of California was at first the object of scorn and derision, and then of nostalgic, if overblown domanticism. Still visible in mission ruins, ersatz architecture, and place names enveloped by suburban sprawl, it is today less real than imagined. The gold seekers, the railroad builders, and the land speculators, ruthlessly pursuing their notions of progress, failed to cast even a hasty backward glance.

[72] Hastings to Larkin, New Helvetia, March 3, 1846, Larkin, *Larkin Papers*, IV, 221.

[73] Leonard Pitt, *The Decline of the Californios: A Social History of the Spanish-Speaking Californians, 1846–1890* (Berkeley, 1966), 14.

[74] Pitt, *Decline of the Californios*, 14–15.

[75] Larkin to Abel Stearns, San Francisco, April 24, 1856, Larkin, *Larkin Papers*, X, 263.

MISSIONS

THE MISSION AS A FRONTIER INSTITUTION IN THE SPANISH–AMERICAN COLONIES

Of the missions in Spanish America, particularly those in California, much has been written. But most of what has been produced consists of chronicles of the deeds of the Fathers, polemic discussions by sectarian partizans, or sentimental effusions with literary, edifying, or financial intent. They deal with the heroic exploits of individuals, with mooted questions of belief and practice, or with the romance that hovers round the mission ruins. All this is very well, and not to be ridiculed, but it is none the less true that little has been said of these missions in their relation to the general Spanish colonial policy, of which they were an integral and a most important part. Father Engelhardt's learned books are a notable exception, but his view is confined closely to California, whereas the mission, in the Spanish colonies, was an almost universal establishment.

One of the marvels in the history of the modern world is the way in which that little Iberian nation, Spain, when most of her blood and treasure were absorbed in European wars, with a handful of men took possession of the Caribbean archipelago, and by rapid yet steady advance spread her culture, her religion, her law, and her language over more than half of the two-American continents, where they still are dominant and still are secure—in South America, Central America, and a large fraction of North America, for fifty million people in America to-day are tinged with Spanish blood, still speak the Spanish language, still worship at the altar set up by the Catholic kings, still live under laws essentially Spanish, and still possess a culture largely inherited from Spain.

These results are an index of the vigor and the virility of Spain's frontier forces; they should give pause to those who glibly speak of Spain's failure as a colonizing nation; and they suggest the importance of a thoughtful study of Spain's frontier institutions and methods. Professor Turner has devoted his life to a study of the Anglo-American frontier, and rich has been his reward. Scarcely less conspicuous in the history of the Western world than the advance of the Anglo-American frontier has been the spread of Spanish culture and for him who interprets, with Turner's insight, the methods

(42)

134

and the significance of the Spanish-American frontier, there awaits
a recognition not less marked or less deserved.

Whoever essays this task, whoever undertakes to interpret the
forces by which Spain extended her rule, her language, her law,
and her traditions, over the frontiers of her vast American possessions, must give close attention to the missions, for in that work
they constituted a primary agency. Each of the colonizing nations
in America had its peculiar frontier institutions and classes. In the
French colonies the pioneers of pioneers were the fur-trader and
the missionary. Penetrating the innermost wilds of the continent,
one in search of the beaver, the other in quest of souls to save,
together they extended the French domains, and brought the savage
tribes into friendly relations with the French government, and into
profitable relations with the French outposts. In the English
colonies the fur-trader blazed the way and opened new trails, but it
was the backwoods settler who hewed down the forest, and step
by step drove back the Indian with whom he did not readily
mingle. In the Spanish colonies the men to whom fell the task of
extending and holding the frontiers were the *conquistador,* the
presidial soldier, and the missionary.

All of these agents were important; but in my study of frontier
institutions in general, and in my endeavor in particular to understand the methods and forces by which Spain's frontiers were extended, held, and developed, I have been more and more impressed
with the importance of the mission as a pioneering agency. Taking for granted for the moment its very obvious religious aspects, I
shall here devote my attention more especially to the mission's political
and social meaning. My point of view embraces all of New Spain
—all of the Spanish colonies, indeed—but more particularly the
northern provinces, from Sinaloa to Texas, from Florida to California. My conclusions are based on the study of documents,
unprinted for the most part, which have been gathered mainly
from the archives of Mexico and Spain.

The functions of the mission, from the political standpoint, will
be better understood if it is considered in its historical relations.
The central interest around which the mission was built was the
Indian. In respect to the native, the Spanish sovereigns, from the
outset, had three fundamental purposes. They desired to convert
him, to civilize him, and to exploit him. To serve these three purposes, there was devised, out of the experience of the early conquerors, the *encomienda* system. It was soon found that if the
savage were to be converted, or disciplined, or exploited, he must

be put under control. To provide such control, the land and the
people were distributed among Spaniards, who held them in trust,
or in *encomienda*. The trustee, or *encomendero,* as he was called,
was strictly charged by the sovereign, as a condition of his grant,
to provide for the protection, the conversion, and the civilization of
the aborigines. In return he was empowered to exploit their labor,
sharing the profits with the king. To provide the spiritual instruction and to conduct schools for the natives—for Indian schools were
actually prescribed and maintained—the *encomenderos* were required to support the necessary friars, by whom the instruction
was given. Thus great monasteries were established in the conquered districts.

But the native had his own notions, especially about being exploited, and he sometimes fled to the woods. It was soon discovered, therefore, that in order properly to convert, instruct, and
exploit the Indian, he must be kept in a fixed place of residence.
This need was early reported to the sovereigns by *encomenderos*
and friars alike, and it soon became a law that Indians must be
congregated in pueblos, and made to stay there, by force if necessary. The pueblos were modelled on the Spanish towns, and were
designed not alone as a means of control, but as schools in self-
control as well.

Thus, during the early years of the conquest, the natives were
largely in the hands of the *encomenderos,* mainly secular land-
holders. The friars, and afterward the Jesuit priests, came in great
numbers, to preach and teach, but they lacked the authority of later
days. In 1574 there were in the conquered districts of Spanish
America nearly nine thousand Indian towns, containing about one
and a half million adult males, representing some five million people, subject to tribute. These nine thousand towns were *encomiendas* of the king and some four thousand *encomenderos.*

The *encomienda* system then, by intention, was benevolent. It
was designed for the conversion and the civilization of the native,
as well as for the exploitation of his labor. But the flesh is weak,
and the system was abused. The obligations to protect, convert,
and civilize were forgotten, and the right to exploit was perverted into
license. Practical slavery soon resulted, and the *encomienda* system became the black spot in the Spanish-American code. Philanthropists, led by Las Casas, begged for reform; abuses were
checked, and *encomiendas* were gradually, though slowly, abolished.

This improvement was made easier by the decreasing attractiveness of *encomiendas,* as the conquest proceeded to the outlying dis-

tricts. The semi-civilized Indians of central Mexico and Peru had been fairly docile, had had a steady food supply and fixed homes, were accustomed to labor, and were worth exploiting. The wilder tribes encountered later—the Chichimecos, as they were called—were hostile, had few crops, were unused to labor, had no fixed villages, would not stand still to be exploited, and were hardly worth the candle. Colonists were no longer so eager for *encomiendas,* and were willing to escape the obligation to protect and civilize the wild tribes, which were as uncomfortable burdens, sometimes, as cub-tigers in a sack. Moreover, the sovereigns, with increasing emphasis, forbade the old-time abuses of exploitation, but as strongly as before adhered to the ideal of conversion and civilization. Here, then, was a larger opening for the missionary, and to him was entrusted, or upon him was thrust, consciously or unconsciously, not only the old work of conversion, but a larger and larger element of responsibility and control. On the northern frontier, therefore, among the roving tribes, the place of the discredited *encomendero* was largely taken by the missionary, and that of the *encomienda* by the mission, the design being to check the evils of exploitation, and at the same time to realize the ideal of conversion, protection, and civilization.

These missionaries became a veritable corps of Indian agents, serving both Church and State. The double capacity in which they served was made easier and more natural by the close union between Church and State in Spanish America, where the king exercised the *real patronato,* and where the viceroys were sometimes archbishops as well.

Under these conditions, in the seventeenth and eighteenth centuries, on the expanding frontiers of Spanish America, missions became well-nigh universal. In South America the outstanding examples were the Jesuit missions in Paraguay. Conspicuous in North America were the great Franciscan establishments in Alta California, the last of Spain's conquests. Not here alone, however, but everywhere on the northern frontier they played their part—in Sinaloa, Sonora, and Lower California; in Chihuahua, Coahuila, Nuevo León, and Nuevo Santander; in Florida, New Mexico, Texas, and Arizona. If there were twenty-one missions in California, there were as many in Texas, more in Florida, and twice as many in New Mexico. At one time the California missions had over thirty thousand Indians under instruction; but a century and a half earlier the missions of Florida and New Mexico each had an equal number.

The missionary work on the northern frontier of New Spain was conducted chiefly by Franciscans, Jesuits, and Dominicans. The northeastern field fell chiefly to the Franciscans, who entered Coahuila, Nuevo León, Nuevo Santander, New Mexico, Texas, and Florida. To the Northwest came the Jesuits, who, after withdrawing from Florida, worked especially in Sinaloa, Sonora, Chihuahua, Lower California, and Arizona. In 1767 the Jesuits were expelled from all Spanish America, and their places taken by the other orders. To Lower California came the Dominicans, to Alta California the Franciscans of the College of San Fernando, in the City of Mexico.

The missions, then, like the presidios, or garrisons, were characteristically and designedly frontier institutions, and it is as pioneer agencies that they must be studied. This is true whether they be conside ed from the religious, the political, or the social standpoint. As relig ious institutions they were designed to introduce the Faith among t'ie heathen. Having done this, their function was to cease. Being d signed for the frontier, they were intended to be temporary. As soon as his work was finished on one frontier, the missionary was expected to move on to another. In the theory of the law, wi hin ten years each mission must be turned over to the secular clergy, and the common mission lands distributed among the Indians. But this law had been based on experience with the more advanced tribes of Mexico, Central America, and Peru. On the northern frontier, among the barbarian tribes, a longer period. of tutelage was always found necessary.

The result, almost without fail, was a struggle over secularization, such as occurred in California. So long as the Indians were under the missionaries, their lands were secure from the land-grabber. The land-grabber always, therefore, urged the fulfillment of the ten-year law, just as the " squatters ", the " sooners ", and the " boomers " have always urged the opening of our Indian reservations. But the missionaries always knew the danger, and they always resisted secularization until their work was finished. Sooner or later, however, with the disappearance of frontier conditions, the missionary was expected to move on. His religious task was beside the soldier, *entre infieles,* in the outposts of civilization.

But the missionaries were not alone religious agents. Designedly in part, and incidentally in part, they were political and civilizing agents of a very positive sort, and as such they constituted a vital feature of Spain's pioneering-system. From the standpoint of the Church, and as viewed by themselves, their principal work was to spread the Faith, first, last, and always. To doubt this is to confess complete and disqualifying ignorance of the great mass of existing missionary correspondence, printed and unprinted, so fraught with unmistakable proofs of the religious zeal and devotion of the vast majority of the missionaries. It is quite true, as Engelhardt says, that they "came not as scientists, as geographers, as school-masters, nor as philanthropists, eager to uplift the people in a worldly sense, to the exclusion or neglect of the religious duties pointed out by Christ". But it is equally true, and greatly to their credit, that, incidentally from their own standpoint and designedly from that of the government, they were all these and more, and that to all these and other services they frequently and justly made claim, when they asked for government aid.

The missions, then, were agencies of the State as well as of the Church. They served not alone to Christianize the frontier, but also to aid in extending, holding, and civilizing it. Since Christianity was the basic element of European civilization, and since it was the acknowledged duty of the State to extend the Faith, the first task of the missionary, from the standpoint of both State and Church, was to convert the heathen. But neither the State nor the Church—nor the missionary himself—in Spanish dominions, considered the work of the mission as ending here. If the Indian were to become either a worthy Christian or a desirable subject, he must be disciplined in the rudiments of civilized life. The task of giving the discipline was likewise turned over to the missionary. Hence, the missions were designed to be not only Christian seminaries, but in addition were outposts for the control and training schools for the civilizing of the frontier.

Since they served the State, the missions were supported by the State. It is a patent fact, and scarcely needs demonstrating, that they were maintained to a very considerable extent by the royal treasury. The Franciscan missions of New Spain in the eighteenth century had four principal means of support. The annual stipends of the missionaries (the *sínodos*) were usually paid by the government. These *sínodos* varied in amount according to the remoteness of the missions, and on the northernmost frontier were usually $450 for each missionary. In 1758, for example, the treasury of New Spain was annually paying *sínodos* for twelve Querétaran friars in Coahuila and Texas, six Jaliscans in Coahuila, eleven Zacatecans in Texas, ten Fernandinos in the Sierra Gorda, six Jaliscans in Nayarit, twenty-two Zacatecans in Nuevo León and Nueva Vizcaya, seventeen Zacatecans in Nuevo Santander, five

San Diegans in Sierra Gorda, and thirty-four friars of the Provincia del Santo Evangelio in New Mexico, or, in all, 123 friars, at an average of about 350 *pesos* each. This report did not include the Provincia de Campeche or the Yslas de Barlovento, for which separate reports had been asked. Other appropriations were made for missionaries in the Marianas and the Philippine Islands, dependencies of New Spain.

Besides the *sinodos,* the government regularly furnished the missionaries with military protection, by detaching from the near-by presidios from two to half a dozen or more soldiers for each mission. In addition, the royal treasury usually made an initial grant (*ayuda de costa*) of $1000 to each mission, to pay for bells, vestments, tools, and other expenses of the founding, and in cases of emergency it frequently made special grants for building or other purposes.

These government subsidies did not preclude private gifts, or alms, which were often sought and secured. In the founding of new missions the older establishments were expected to give aid, and if able they did respond in liberal measure. And then there were endowments. The classic examples of private endowments on the northern frontier were the gifts of Don Pedro de Terreros, later Conde de Regla, who offered $150,000 to found Apache missions in Coahuila and Texas, and the Jesuit Fondo Piadoso, or Pious Fund, of California. This latter fund, begun in 1697, grew by a variety of gifts to such an amount that the missions of Lower California were largely supported by the increase alone. With the expulsion of the Jesuits in 1767 the fund was taken over by the government, and became the principal means of support of the new Franciscan missions of Alta California, besides being devoted in part to secular purposes. Even in Alta California, however, the royal treasury paid the wages (*sueldos*) of the mission guards, and gave other financial aid.

Finally, the Indians of the missions were expected soon to become self-supporting, and, indeed, in many cases they did acquire large wealth through stock-raising and agricultural pursuits. But not a penny of this belonged to the missionaries, and the annual *sinodos,* or salaries, continued to be paid from other sources, from the Pious Fund in California, and from the royal treasury generally elsewhere.

While it is thus true that the missions were supported to a very considerable degree by the royal treasury, it is just as plain that the amount of government aid, and the ease with which it was secured, depended largely upon the extent to which political ends could be combined with religious purposes.

The importance of political necessity in loosening the royal purse-strings is seen at every turn in the history of Spanish North America. Knowing the strength of a political appeal, the friars always made use of it in their requests for permission and aid. While the monarchs ever used pious phrases, and praised the work of the padres—without hypocrisy no doubt—the royal pocket-book was not readily opened to found new missions unless there was an important political as well as a religious object to be gained.

Striking examples of this fact are found in the histories of Texas and California. The missionaries of the northern frontier had long had their eyes on the "Kingdom of the Texas" as a promising field of labor, and had even appealed to the government for aid in cultivating it. But in vain, till La Salle planted a French colony at Matagorda Bay. Then the royal treasury was opened, and funds were provided for missions in eastern Texas. The French danger passed for the moment, and the missions were withdrawn. Then for another decade Father Hidalgo appealed in vain for funds and permission to re-establish the missions. But when St. Denis, agent of the French governor of Louisiana, intruded himself into Coahuila, the Spanish government at once gave liberal support for the refounding of the missions, to aid in restraining the French.

The case was the same for California. Since the time of Vizcaíno the missionaries had clamored for aid and for permission to found missions at San Diego and Monterey. In 1620 Father Ascensión, who had been with Vizcaíno eighteen years before, wrote, "I do not know what security His Majesty can have in his conscience for delaying so long to send ministers of the Gospel to this realm of California", and, during the next century and a half, a hundred others echoed this admonition. But all to no purpose till the Russian Bear began to amble or to threaten to amble down the Pacific Coast. Then money was forthcoming—partly from the confiscated Pious Fund, it is true—and then missionaries were sent to help hold the country for the crown. On this point Father Engelhardt correctly remarks:

The missionaries, who generally offered to undergo any hardships in order to convert the Indians, appear to have been enlisted merely for the purpose of securing the territory for the Spanish king . . . [and] the Spanish government would not have sent ships and troops to the northwest if the Russians had not crept down the Pacific coast. . . .

The men who presumed to guide the destinies of Spain then, and, as a rule ever since, cared not for the success of Religion or the welfare of its ministers except in so far as both could be used to promote political schemes.

In this last, I think, Father Engelhardt is too hard on the Spanish monarchs. Their pious professions were not pure hypocrisy. They were truly desirous of spreading the Faith. But they were terribly "hard up", and they had little means to support religious projects unless they served both political and religious ends.

The value of the missionaries as frontier agents was thus clearly recognized, and their services were thus consciously utilized by the government. In the first place, they were often the most useful of explorers and diplomatic agents. The unattended missionary could sometimes go unmolested, and without arousing suspicion and hostility, into districts where the soldier was not welcome, while by their education and their trained habits of thought they were the class best fitted to record what they saw and to report what should be done. For this reason they were often sent alone to explore new frontiers, or as peace emissaries to hostile tribes, or as chroniclers of expeditions led by others. Hence it is that the best of the diaries of early exploration in the Southwest—and, indeed, in most of America—were written by the missionaries.

As illustrations of this kind of frontier service on the part of the missionaries we have but to recall the example of Friar Marcos, who was sent by Viceroy Mendoza to seek the rumored "Seven Cities" in New Mexico; the rediscovery of that province, under the viceroy's patronage, by the party led by Fray Agustín Rodríguez; the expeditions of Father Larios, unattended, into Coahuila; the forty or more journeys of Father Kino across the deserts of Sonora, and his demonstration that California was a peninsula, not an island, as most men had thought; the part played by Kino in pacifying the revolt of the Pimas in 1695, and in making the frontier safe for settlers; the diplomatic errands of Fathers Calahorra and Ramírez, sent by the governors of Texas to the hostile northern tribes; the lone travels of Father Garcés, of two thousand miles or more, over the untrod trails, in Arizona, California, and New Mexico, seeking a better route to California; and the expedition of Fathers Domínguez and Escalante, pathfinders for an equal distance in and about the Great Basin between the Rockies and the Sierras.

· The missions served also as a means of defense to the king's dominions. This explains why the government was more willing to support missions when the frontier needed defending than at other times, as in the cases, already cited, of Texas and California. It is significant, too, in this connection, that the Real Hacienda, or Royal Fisc, charged the expenses for presidios and missions both to the same account, the Ramo de Guerra, or "War Fund". In a report for New Spain made in 1758 a treasury official casually remarked,

Presidios are erected and missions founded in *tierra firme* whenever it is necessary to defend conquered districts from the hostilities and invasions of warlike, barbarian tribes, and to plant and extend our Holy Faith, for which purposes *juntas de guerra y hacienda* are held.

It is indeed true that appropriations for missions were usually made and that permission to found missions was usually given in councils of war and finance.

The missionaries counteracted foreign influence among their neophytes, deterred them from molesting the interior settlements, and secured their aid in holding back more distant tribes. Nearly every army that was led from San Antonio, Texas, in the eighteenth century, against the hostile Apaches and Comanches, contained a strong contingent of mission Indians, who fought side by side with the Spaniards. Father Kino was relied upon by the military leaders of Sonora to obtain the aid of the Pimas, his beloved neophytes, in defense of the Sonora settlements. When he was assigned to California, in company with Salvatierra, the authorities of Sonora protested, on the ground that, through his influence over the natives, he was a better means of protection to the province than a whole company of soldiers. When a Spanish expedition was organized to attack the Apaches, Kino was sent ahead to arouse and enlist the Pima allies. When the Pimas put the Apaches to flight, it was Kino to whom they sent the count of the enemy's dead, recorded by notches on a pole; on the same occasion it was Kino who received the thanks of citizens and officials of the province; and, when doubt was expressed as to what the Pimas had accomplished, it was Kino who rode a hundred miles or more to count the scalps of the vanquished foe, as evidence with which to vindicate his Pima friends.

The very mission plants were even built and often served as fortresses, not alone for padres and neophytes, but for near-by settlers, too. Every well-built mission was ranged round a great court or patio, protected on all sides by the buildings, whose walls were sometimes eight feet thick. In hostile countries these buildings were themselves enclosed within massive protecting walls. In 1740 President Santa Ana wrote that Mission Valero, at San Antonio, Texas, was better able to withstand a siege than any of the three presidios of the province. This of course was only a relative excellence. Twenty-two years later the same mission was surrounded by a wall, and over the gate was a tower, equipped with muskets, ammunition, and three cannon. At the same time the mission of San José (Texas) was called "a castle" which more than once had been proof against the Apaches.

Not only were the missionaries consciously utilized as political agents to hold the frontier but they often served, on their own motion, or with the co-operation of the secular authority, as "promoters" of the unoccupied districts. They sent home reports of the outlying tribes, of the advantages of obtaining their friendship, of the danger of foreign incursions, of the wealth and attractions of the country, and of the opportunities to extend the king's dominion. Frequently, indeed, they were called to Mexico, or even to Spain, to sit in the royal councils, where their expert opinions often furnished the primary basis of a decision to occupy a new outpost. As examples of this, near at home, we have but to recall Escobar, Benavides, and Ayeta of New Mexico, Massanet, Hidalgo, and Santa Ana of Texas, Kino of Lower California, and Serra of Alta California. Thus consciously or unconsciously, directly or indirectly, with or without secular initiative, the missionaries served as most active promoters, one might even call them "boosters", of the frontier.

But the missionaries helped not only to extend and hold and promote the frontier; more significantly still, they helped to civilize it. And this is the keynote of my theme. Spain possessed high ideals, but she had peculiar difficulties to contend with. She laid claim to the lion's share of the two Americas, but her population was small and little of it could be spared to people the New World. On the other hand, her colonial policy, equalled in humanitarian principles by that of no other country, perhaps, looked to the preservation of the natives, and to their elevation to at least a limited citizenship. Lacking Spaniards to colonize the frontier, she would colonize it with the aborigines. Such an ideal called not only for the subjugation and control of the natives, but for their civilization as well. To bring this end about the rulers of Spain again made use of the religious and humanitarian zeal of the missionaries, choosing them to be to the Indians not only preachers, but also teachers and disciplinarians. To the extent that this work succeeded it became possible to people the frontier with civilized natives, and thus to supply the lack of colonists. This desire was quite in harmony with the religious aims of the friars, who found temporal discipline indispensable to the best work of Christianization.

Hence it is that in the Spanish system—as distinguished from the French, for example—the essence of the mission was the *discipline,* religious, moral, social, and industrial, which it afforded. The very physical arrangement of the mission was determined with a view to discipline. The central feature of every successful mission was the Indian village, or pueblo. The settled tribes, such as the Pueblo Indians of New Mexico, or the Pimas of Arizona, could be instructed in their native towns, but wandering and scattered tribes must be assembled and established in pueblos, and kept there, by force if necessary. The reason why the missions of eastern Texas failed was that the Indians refused to settle in pueblos, and without more soldiers than were available it was impossible to control them. It was on this question that Father Serra split with Governor Neve regarding the Santa Barbara Indians in California. To save expense for soldiers, Neve urged that the friars should minister to the Indians in their native rancherías. But the missionaries protested that by this arrangement the Indians could not be disciplined. The plan was given up therefore, and instead the Indians were congregated in great pueblos at San Buenaventura and Santa Barbara. Thus, the pueblo was essential to the mission, as it had been to the *encomienda.*

Discipline called for control, and this was placed largely in the hands of the missionaries. The rule was two friars for each mission, but in many instances there was only one. The need of more was often urged.

As a symbol of force, and to afford protection for missionaries and mission Indians, as well as to hold the frontier against savages and foreigners, presidios, or garrisons, were established near by. And thus, across the continent, from San Agustín to San Francisco, stretched a long and slender line of presidios—San Agustín, Apalache, Pensacola, Los Adaes, La Bahía, San Antonio, San Juan Bautista, Rio Grande, San Sabá, El Paso, Santa Fé, Janos, Fronteras, Terrenate, Tubac, Altár, San Diego, Santa Barbara, Monterey, and San Francisco—a line more than twice as long as the Rhine-Danube frontier held by the Romans, from whom Spain learned her lesson in frontier defense.

To assist the missionaries in their work of disciplining and instructing the neophytes, each mission was usually provided with two or more soldiers from the nearest presidio. To help in recovering runaways—for the Indians frequently did abscond—special detachments of soldiers were furnished. The impression is often given that the missionaries objected to the presence of soldiers at the mis-

sions, but as a rule the case was quite the contrary. What they did
object to was unsuitable soldiers, and outside interference in the
selection and control of the guard. It is true, indeed, that immoral
or insubordinate soldiers were deemed a nuisance, and that since the
presidials were largely half-breeds—mestizoes or mulattoes—and
often jailbirds at that, this type was all too common. But in general military aid was demanded, and complaint of its inadequacy was
constantly made. On this point the testimony of Fray Romualdo
Cartagena, guardian of the College of Santa Cruz de Querétaro, is
valid. In a report made in 1772, still in manuscript, he wrote,

What gives these missions their permanency is the aid which they
receive from the Catholic arms. Without them pueblos are frequently
abandoned, and ministers are murdered by the barbarians. It is seen
every day that in missions where there are no soldiers there is no success, for the Indians, being children of fear, are more strongly appealed
to by the glistening of the sword than by the voice of five missionaries.
Soldiers are necessary to defend the Indians from the enemy, and to
keep an eye on the mission Indians, now to encourage them, now to
carry news to the nearest presidio in case of trouble. For the spiritual
and temporal progress of the missions two soldiers are needed, for the
Indians cannot be trusted, especially in new conversions.

This is the testimony of missionaries themselves. That protection was indeed necessary is shown by the martyrdom of missionaries on nearly every frontier—of Father Segura and his entire
band of Jesuits in Virginia in 1570; of Father Saeta in Sonora; of
Fathers Ganzábal, Silva, Terreros, and Santiesteban in Texas; of
Fathers Carranco and Tamaral in Lower California; of Father
Luis Jayme at San Diego (Alta California); of Father Garcés and
his three companions at Yuma, on the Colorado; and of the twenty-
one Franciscans in the single uprising in New Mexico in 1680.
But these martyrdoms were only occasional, and the principal business of the soldiers was to assist the missionaries in disciplining and
civilizing the savages.

As teachers, and as an example to new converts, it was the
custom to place in each new mission three Indian families from the
older missions. After a time the families might return to their
homes. As Father Romualdo remarked: "It is all the better if
these families be related to the new, for this insures the permanence of the latter in the missions, while if they do flee it is easier to
recover them by means of their relatives than through strangers."

Notable among the Indians utilized as teachers and colonists in
the northern missions were the Tlascaltecans, of Tlascala, the native
city of Mexico made famous by Prescott. Having been subdued

146

by Cortés, the Tlascaltecans became the most trusted supporters of the Spaniards, as they had been the most obstinate foes of the "Triple Alliance", and, after playing an important part in the conquest of the Valley of Mexico, they became a regular factor in the extension of Spanish rule over the north country. Thus, when San Luis Potosí had been conquered, colonies of Tlascaltecans were set to teach the more barbarous natives of that district both loyalty to the Spaniards and the elements of civilization. In Saltillo a large colony of Tlascaltecans was established by Urdiñola at the end of the sixteenth century, and became the mother colony from which numerous offshoots were planted at the new missions and villages further north. At one time a hundred families of Tlascaltecans were ordered sent to Pensacola; in 1755 they figured in the plans for a missionary colony on the Trinity River, in Texas; two years later a little band of them were sent to the San Sabá mission in western Texas to assist in civilizing the Apaches; and twenty years afterward it was suggested that a settlement, with these people as a nucleus, be established far to the north, on the upper Red River, among the Wichita Indians of Texas and Oklahoma. To help in civilizing the mission Indians of Jalisco, Sinaloa, and Sonora, the Tarascans of Michoacán were utilized; further north, the Opatas, of southern Sonora, were sent into Arizona as teachers of the Pimas; to help in civilizing the Indians of California, Serra brought mission Indians from the Peninsula.

Discipline and the elements of European civilization were imparted at the missions through religious instruction, through industrial training, and, among more advanced natives, by means of rudimentary teaching in arts and letters.

Every mission was, in the first place, a Christian seminary, designed to give religious discipline. Religious instruction, of the elementary sort suited to the occasion, was imparted by a definite routine, based on long experience, and administered with much practical sense and regard for local conditions.

Aside from the fundamental cultural concepts involved in Christianity, this religious instruction in itself involved a most important means of assimilation. By the laws of the Indies the missionaries were enjoined to instruct the neophytes in their native tongues, and in the colleges and seminaries professorships were established to teach them. But it was found that, just as the natives lacked the concepts, the Indian languages lacked the terms in which properly to convey the meaning of the Christian doctrine. Moreover, on some frontiers there were so many dialects that it was impossible for the friars to learn them. This was pre-eminently true of the lower Rio Grande region, where there were over two hundred dialects, more than twenty of which were quite distinct. On this point Father Ortiz wrote in 1745:

> The ministers who have learned some language of the Indians of these missions assert that it is impossible to compose a catechism in their idiom, because of the lack of terms in which to explain matters of Faith, and the best informed interpreters say the same. There are as many languages as there are tribes, which in these missions aggregate more than two hundred. . . . Although they mingle and understand each other to some extent, there are twenty languages used commonly by the greater number of the tribes. And since they are new to us, and there are no schools in which to learn them, and since the Fathers are occupied with ministering to the spiritual and temporal needs of the Indians, and in recovering those who flee, the Fathers can hardly be held blameworthy for not learning the native languages.

For these reasons, on the northern frontier instruction was usually given in Spanish, through interpreters at first, and directly as soon as the Indians learned the language of the friars. In the case of children, who were the chief consideration, this was quickly done. And thus incidentally a long step toward assimilation was accomplished, for we all know the importance of language in the fusing of races and cultures. The firmness of the hold of the Spanish language upon any land touched by Spain, however lightly, has often been noted. It was partly, or even largely, due to this teaching of the native children at the missions.

The routine of religious discipline established by the Franciscans in the missions taken over from the Jesuits in Sonora, in 1767, was typical of all the Franciscan missions, and was not essentially different from that of the other orders. It was described by Father Reyes, later Bishop Reyes, as follows:

> Every day at sunrise the bells call the Indians to Mass. An old Indian, commonly called *mador*, and two *fiscales*, go through the whole pueblo, requiring all children and unmarried persons to go to the church, to take part in the devotion and silence of the Mass. This over, they repeat in concert, in Spanish, with the minister, the prayers and the Creed. At sunset this exercise is repeated at the door of the church, and is concluded with saying the rosary and chanting the *salve* or the *alavado*. The *mador* and the *fiscales* are charged, on Sundays and feast days, to take care to require all men, women, and children to be present at Mass, with their poor clothes clean, and all washed and combed.

The very act of going to church, then, involved a lesson in the amenities of civilization. There was virtue then as now in putting on one's "Sunday clothes".

> On these days [Father Reyes continues] Mass is chanted with harps, violins [all played by the natives], and a choir of from four to six [native] men and women. In Lent all have been required to go to Mass daily. . . .

148

On Palm Sunday, at the head missions (*cabeceras*), that feast is observed with an image and processions. After Easter, censuses are made to ascertain what ones have complied with the Church. In the first years it seemed impossible to us missionaries to vanquish the rudeness of the Indians, and the difficulties of making them confess, and of administering communion. But lately all the young men and some of the old have confessed. In the principal pueblos, where the missionaries reside, many attend the sacraments on feast days. On the Day of Santa María the rosary is sung through the pueblo. On other occasions they are permitted to have balls, diversions, and innocent games. But because they have attempted to prohibit superstitious balls and the scalp dance, the missionaries have encountered strong opposition from the [secular] superiors of the province, who desire to let the Indians continue these excesses.

They contributed, no doubt, to the war spirit, and thus to the defense of the province against the Apaches.

If the mission was a Christian seminary, it was scarcely less an industrial training school. Father Engelhardt writes:

It must be remembered that the friars came to California as messengers of Christ. They were not farmers, mechanics, or stock breeders. Those who, perhaps, had been engaged in such pursuits, had abandoned them for the higher occupation of the priest of God, and they had no desire to be further entangled in worldly business. In California, however [and he might have added, quite generally] the messengers of the Gospel had to introduce, teach, and supervise those very arts, trades, and occupations, before they could expect to make any headway with the truths of salvation. . . . As an absolutely necessary means to win the souls of the savages, these unworldly men accepted the disagreeable task of conducting huge farms, teaching and supervising various mechanical trades, having an eye on the livestock and herders, and making ends meet generally.

The civilizing function of the typical Spanish mission, where the missionaries had charge of the temporalities as well as of the spiritualities, was evident from the very nature of the mission plant. While the church was ever the centre of the establishment, and the particular object of the minister's pride and care, it was by no means the larger part. Each fully developed mission was a great industrial school, of which the largest, as in California, sometimes managed more than 2000 Indians. There were weaving rooms, blacksmith shop, tannery, wine-press, and warehouses; there were irrigating ditches, vegetable gardens, and grain fields; and on the ranges roamed thousands of horses, cattle, sheep, and goats. Training in the care of fields and stock not only made the neophytes self-supporting, but afforded the discipline necessary for the rudiments of civilized life. The women were taught to cook, sew, spin, and weave; the men to fell the forest, build, run the forge, tan leather, make ditches, tend cattle, and shear sheep.

Even in New Mexico, where the missionaries were not in charge of the temporalities—that is, of the economic interests of the Indians—and where the Indians had a well-established native agriculture, the friars were charged with their instruction in the arts and crafts, as well as with their religious education. And when the custodian, Father Benavides—later Bishop of Goa—wrote in 1630, after three decades of effort by the friars in that province, he was able to report fourteen monasteries, serving fifty-odd pueblos, each with its school, where the Indians were all taught not only to sing, play musical instruments, read, and write, but, as Benavides puts it, "all the trades and polite deportment", all imparted by "the great industry of the Religious who converted them".

In controlling, supervising, and teaching the Indians, the friars were assisted by the soldier guards, who served as *mayor domos* of the fields, of the cattle and horse herds, of the sheep and goat ranches, and of the shops. In the older missions, even among the most backward tribes, it sometimes became possible to dispense with this service, as at San Antonio, Texas, where, it was reported in 1772, the Indians, once naked savages who lived on cactus apples and cotton-tail rabbits, had become so skilled and trustworthy that "without the aid of the Spaniards they harvest, from irrigated fields, maize, beans, and cotton in plenty, and Castilian corn for sugar. There are cattle, sheep, and goats in abundance", all being the product of the care and labor of the natives.

The results of this industrial training at the missions were to be seen in the imposing structures that were built, the fertile farms that were tilled, and the great stock ranches that were tended, by erstwhile barbarians, civilized under the patient discipline of the missionaries, assisted by soldier guards and imported Indian teachers, not in our Southwest alone, but on nearly every frontier of Spanish America.

The missionaries transplanted to the frontiers and made known to the natives almost every conceivable domestic plant and animal of Europe. By requiring the Indians to work three days a week at community tasks, the Jesuits in Pimería Alta—to give a particular illustration—established at all the missions flourishing ranches of horses, cattle, sheep, and goats, and opened fields and gardens for the cultivation of a vast variety of food plants. Kino wrote in 1710 of the Jesuit missions of Sonora and Arizona,

There are already thrifty and abundant fields . . . of wheat, maize, frijoles, chickpeas, beans, lentils, bastard chickpeas (*garabanzos*), etc. There are orchards, and in them vineyards for wine for the Masses; and fields of sweet cane for syrup and panocha, and with the favor of Heaven, before long, for sugar. There are many Castilian fruit trees, such as figs, quinces, oranges, pomegranates, peaches, apricots, pears, apples, mulberries, etc., and all sorts of garden stuff, such as cabbage, lettuce, onions, garlic, anise, pepper, mustard, mint, etc.

Other temporal means [he continues] are the plentiful ranches, which are already stocked with cattle, sheep, and goats, many droves of mares, horses, and pack animals, mules as well as horses, for transportation and commerce, and very fat sheep, producing much tallow, suet, and soap, which is already manufactured in abundance.

An illustration of some of the more moderate material results is to be had in the following description of the four Querétaran missions in Texas, based on an official report made in 1762.

Besides the church, each mission had its *convento,* or monastery, including cells for the friars, porter's lodge, refectory, kitchen, offices, workshops, and granary, usually all under a common roof and ranged round a *patio.* At San Antonio de Valero the *convento* was a two-story structure fifty *varas* square with two *patios* and with arched cloisters above and below. The others were similar.

An important part of each mission was the workshop, for here the neophytes not only helped to supply their economic needs, but got an important part of their training for civilized life. At each of these four missions the Indians manufactured *mantas, terlingas, sayales, rebozos, frezadas,* and other common fabrics of wool and cotton. At Mission San Antonio the workshop contained four looms, and two store-rooms with cotton, wool, cards, spindles, etc. At Concepción and San Francisco there were three looms each.

The neophytes of each mission lived in an Indian village, or pueblo, closely connected with the church and monastery. Of those of the four Querétaran missions we have the fullest description of the pueblo at Mission San Antonio de Valero. It consisted of seven rows of houses built of stone, with arched porticoes, doors, and windows. There was a plaza through which ran a water-ditch, grown with willows and fruit trees. Within the plaza was a curbed well, to supply water in case of a siege by the enemy. The pueblo was surrounded by a wall, and over the gate was a tower, with embrasures, and equipped with three cannon, firearms, and ammunition. The houses were furnished with high beds, chests, metates, pots, kettles, and other domestic utensils. The pueblo of San Antonio was typical of all.

Agricultural and stock-raising activities had increased since 1745. At the four Querétaran missions there were now grazing 4897 head of cattle, 12,000 sheep and goats, and about 1600 horses, and each mission had from thirty-seven to fifty yoke of working oxen. Of the four missions San Francisco raised the most stock, having 2262 head of cattle and 4000 sheep and goats. Each mission had its ranch, some distance away, where the stock was kept, with one or more stone houses, occupied by the families of the overseers; the necessary corrals, farming implements, and carts; and tools for carpentry, masonry, and blacksmithing. Each mission had well-tilled fields, fenced in and watered by good irrigating ditches, with stone dams. In these fields maize, chile, beans, and cotton were raised in abundance, and in the *huertas* a large variety of garden truck.

This picture of the Texas missions is interesting, but in magnitude the establishments described are not to be compared with those in Paraguay or even in California, where, in 1834, on the eve of the destruction of the missions, 31,000 mission Indians at twenty-one missions herded 396,000 cattle, 62,000 horses, and 321,000 hogs, sheep, and goats, and harvested 123,000 bushels of grain, and where corresponding skill and industry were shown by the neophytes in orchard, garden, wine-press, loom, shop, and forge.

The laws of the Indies even prescribed and the missions provided a school for self-government, elementary and limited, it is true, but germane and potential nevertheless. This was effected by organizing the Indians of the missions into a pueblo, with civil and military officers, modelled upon the Spanish administration. When the mission was founded the secular head of the district—governor, captain, or alcalde—as representative of the king, formally organized the pueblo, appointed the native officers, and gave title to the four-league grant of land. In constituting the native government, wisdom dictated that use should be made of the existing Indian organization, natives of prestige being given the important offices. Thereafter the civil officers were chosen by a form of native election, under the supervision of the missionary, and approved by the secular head of the jurisdiction.

The civil officers were usually a governor, captain, alcaldes, and alguacil, who by law constituted a cabildo, or council. The military officers were a captain or a *teniente,* and subalterns, and were appointed by the secular head, or by a native captain-general subject to approval by the secular head. The military officers had their own insignia, and, to give them prestige, separate benches were placed in the churches for the governor, alcalde, and council. In Sonora there was a *topil,* whose duty was to care for the community houses —a sort of free hostelry, open to all travellers, which seems to have been of native rather than of Spanish origin. The Indians had their own jail, and inflicted minor punishments, prescribed by the minister. Indian overseers kept the laborers at their work and, indeed, much of the task of controlling the Indians was effected through Indian officers themselves. Of course it was the directing force of the padres and the restraining force of the near-by presidio which furnished the ultimate pressure.

This pueblo government was established among the more advanced tribes everywhere, and it succeeded in varying degrees. It was often a cause for conflict of jurisdiction, and in California, where the natives were of the most barbarous, it was strongly opposed by the missionaries. It has been called a farce, but it certainly was not so intended. It was not self-government any more than is student government in a primary school. But it was a means of control, and was a step toward self-government. It is one of the things, moreover, which help to explain how two missionaries and three or four soldiers could make an orderly town out of two or three thousand savages recently assembled from divers and sometimes mutually hostile tribes. So deeply was it impressed upon the Indians of New Mexico that some of them yet maintain their Spanish pueblo organization, and by it still govern themselves, extra-legally. And, I am told, in some places even in California, the descendants of the mission Indians still keep up the pueblo organization as a sort of fraternity, or secret society.

In these ways, then, did the missions serve as frontier agencies of Spain. As their first and primary task, the missionaries spread the Faith. But in addition, designedly or incidentally, they explored the frontiers, promoted their occupation, defended them and the interior settlements, taught the Indians the Spanish language, and disciplined them in good manners, in the rudiments of European crafts, of agriculture, and even of self-government. Moreover, the missions were a force which made for the preservation of the Indians, as opposed to their destruction, so characteristic of the Anglo-American frontier. In the English colonies the only good Indians were dead Indians. In the Spanish colonies it was thought worth while to improve the natives for this life as well as for the next. Perhaps the missions did not, in every respect, represent a twentieth-century ideal. Sometimes, and to some degree, they failed, as has every human institution. Nevertheless, it must not be forgotten that of the millions of half-castes living south of us, the grandparents, in a large proportion of cases, at some generation removed, on one side or the other, were once mission Indians, and as such learned the elements of Spanish civilization. For these reasons, as well as for unfeigned religious motives, the missions received the royal support. They were a conspicuous feature of Spain's frontiering genius.

HERBERT E. BOLTON.

The Mission Buildings of San Juan Capistrano: A Tentative Chronology

by Harry Kelsey

I F THE FRANCISCANS FRIARS ever drew formal plans for the buildings at San Juan Capistrano, these have disappeared. None are known today, nor are there any plats made during the mission period that show the evolution of the permanent structures in the mission quadrangle. The surviving record consists largely of vague descriptions of mission buildngs in the reports and correspondence of the missionaries. But it is possible to use these documents in conjunction with other historical and archaeological evidence in order to arrive at a reasonable approximation of the look of the mission in the early years.

Building construction at Mission San Juan Capistrano properly begins in 1778, when the present site was occupied. But there were earlier structures on an earlier site, and these have some bearing on the buildings erected later.

The mission was founded near the end of October 1775, at a place in the San Juan Creek basin called Arroyo de la Quema, or the Burned Arroyo. The mission cross was erected immediately, and after a week of work a spacious corral had been enclosed, timber cut for temporary buildings, and holes dug for the upright poles. But suddenly news arrived of a disastrous raid at Mission San Diego. Consequently, the bells were buried, and the whole party beat a hasty retreat.[1]

Work began again within a few months, and some basic structures were ready for occupancy by fall.[2] The formal dedication took place on 1 November 1776, the Feast of All Saints, probably in a temporary church built of timber and

1

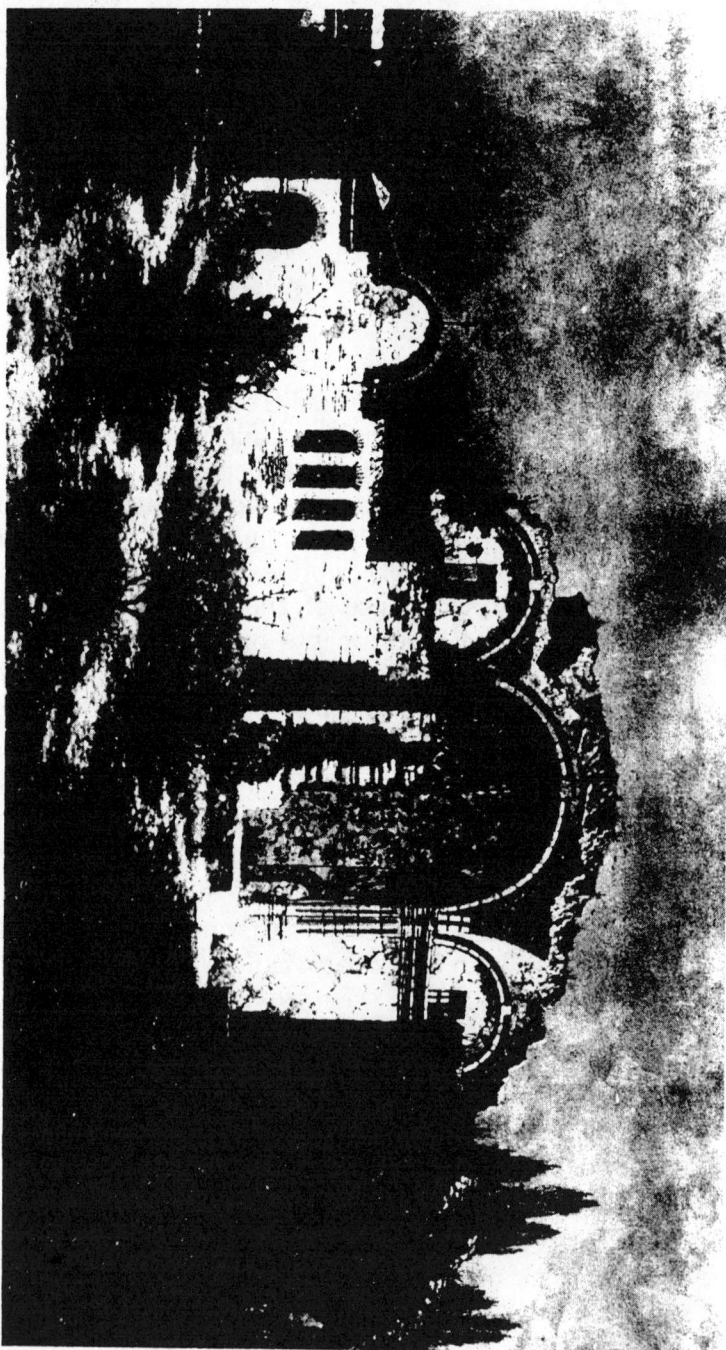

Oil painting by Edwin Deakin based on sketches made at the mission between 1897 and 1899.

brush.[3] At any rate the church was in use by 19 December 1776, when the first baptism in the mission was recorded as having taken place "in the church."[4] Seemingly, the missionaries had second thoughts about calling this structure a church, and for the next eleven months they refrained from using this phrase.

These early months at Capistrano were not auspicious. Water was in short supply at La Quema, crops did not flourish, and the soldiers who had been assigned to erect the new mission buildings mutinied, simply refusing to perform the work. Despite these problems, a more substantial church building was ready for occupancy by 2 December 1777, when for the first time in months the missionary could write in his record book that a baptism was solemnly performed "in the church of this mission."[5]

By this time it was clear that the Arroyo de la Quema was not a good location for the mission, and plans were made to move to the present site. This was accomplished on 4 October 1778.[6] There are no exact records of construction for the earliest buildings, but it is possible to locate and identify surviving structures. Some are known with certainty, others only by approximation.

In their official reports, the missionaries listed building dimensions in *varas,* a unit of measurement equalling about 33 inches, and *cuartas,* a standard measure equalling a forth of a vara. Their measurements were approximations, sometimes changing in successive years or even in the same report. Conversion of these figures to feet or meters results in fractional readings that are deceptive in their seeming precision. Keeping in mind that a vara is about a yard, it is easy to imagine the size of a building measured in varas.[7]

It seems likely that a number of buildings at the new site were ready for occupancy before the move was made. One of these was the church, a structure about 20 x 4 varas in size and located perhaps where the present brick building housing the gift shop now stands.[8] The church was an adobe building with a flat roof, a very temporary structure with walls only half an adobe in thickness. This description of the wall was a standard description used by the padres, and it means simply that the

157

3

long dimension of the bricks paralleled the walls of the building.[9]

The first church on the present site is actually the third church at Mission San Juan Capistrano. The obvious plan was to use this structure for a few years while a larger, more substantial church was being built. Since it was temporary, the church was located outside the area planned as the mission courtyard. Other temporary structures, housing soldiers, Indian neophytes, and mission staff members, were probably located here as well. The temporary wood and brush structures were seldom mentioned in the annual reports, except perhaps when permanent adobe buildings replaced them.[10]

One other permanent building was ready for occupancy before the mission was moved. It was a three-room adobe, 16 x 5 varas in size, with walls an adobe and a half in thickness. The flat roof was covered with *jacal* as added protection from the elements.[11] Two of the rooms were used as a temporary residence for the missionaries. The third was the kitchen. This structure still stands, the oldest building on the site, and perhaps the oldest building in the state of California.

Two buildings were added in 1779. The first was a permanent residence for the priests, a four room adobe building, 25 x 5.5 varas in size, with walls an adobe and a half in thickness. The flat roof had an extra covering of brush to protect the place from heavy rains. A second building, 6 x 5 varas in size, was added to the west end of the 1778 structure to serve as a dormitory for the unmarried girls of the mission.[12]

No report is available for 1780, but some of the building activity can be inferred from later records. Two small adobe structures were added to the west side of the dormitory, one to serve as a storeroom, and the other to serve as a chicken coop and dovecot. These had simple flat roofs without the added covering of tule or brush.[13]

One warehouse was also probably built by 1780. This was a building 25 x 6 varas in size, with walls a single adobe in thickness (measured as though the short dimension ran parallel with the walls). The flat roof had a brush cover for added protection.[14]

4

N

San Juan Capistrano
1778

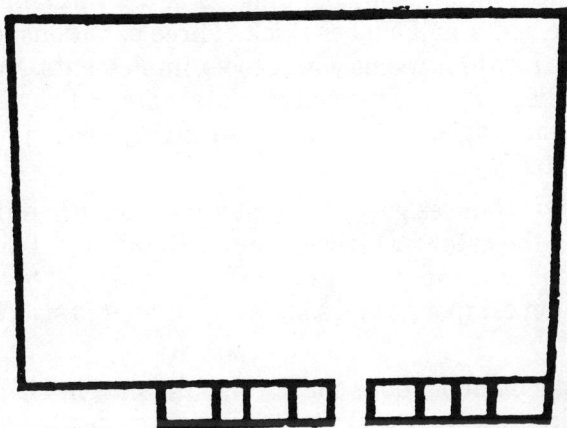

1779

5

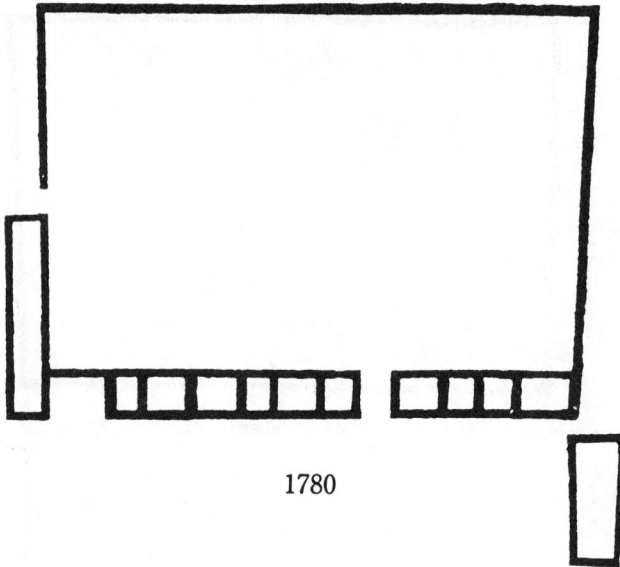

1780

In 1781 a second warehouse was built, and very likely construction was started on a new church. The warehouse was probably erected at the north end of the one completed in 1780. It was a substantial adobe building, 22 x 5.5 varas in size, with walls one and a half adobes thick. Three partitions divided the structure into four rooms where tools, implements, and supplies could be kept. Both of the warehouses were on the western side of the quadrangle, the wing in which the mission museum is now located.[15]

The warehouses gave the west wing a length of fifty varas, including the gateway between the two buildings. This gateway became the entrance to a "pasture" or corral built to the west of the mission compound and somewhat smaller in size, fifty varas square.[16]

The permanent adobe church was finished in 1782, so far as anyone knows, for the first description comes from the 1782 annual report. It was a building 25 x 7 varas in size, with a sacristy 6 x 7 varas. The walls were two adobes thick. The main entrance faced the patio, with another entrance at the south end of the building, leaving a wide, open space between the church

6

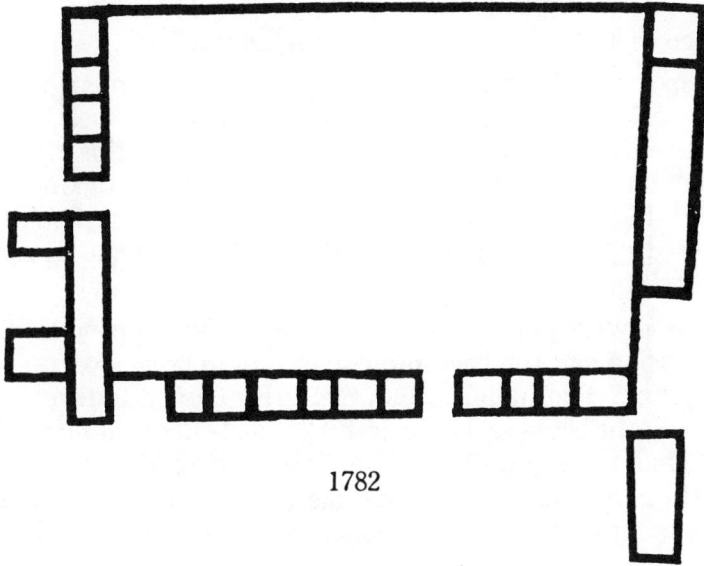

1782

building and the padre's quarters. The flat roof was also covered with jacal to help make the roof waterproof.[17]

A shop 6 x 5 varas in size probably joined the north end of the west wing, where the two warehouses were located. It soon became a *quesero* or cheese factory.[18] A wooden calf barn built in 1779 was replaced by an adobe structure 8 x 3 varas in size. This building and another (6 x 3 varas) for the storage of agricultural implements were added in 1782. These were very likely built adjoining the west side of the 1780 warehouse, but most certainly inside the corral. An adobe wall three varas high ran across the north end of the compound and in the open spaces at each end of the south wing. The only adobe building outside the main quadrangle was the original church, which was probably being converted for use as a military barracks.[19]

In 1783 the livestock pens, originally built of adobe and brush, were rebuilt entirely in adobe and expanded to accommodate the growing mission herds, and moved a decent distance from the mission. The corral used for cattle was sixty varas square, with a smaller bullpen, 20 x 12 varas, walled off within the enclosure. The sheep corral was fifty varas square, including a main corral as well as a few smaller pens for lambs and

7

ewes. About this same time the agricultural storage building erected in 1780 was converted to use as a winery.[20]

Reports for 1784 and 1785 are missing, so we must guess at what took place during those years. It may very well be that some work was done on the water system, as this was the subject of correspondence with the military commander in 1783.[21] Permanent barracks for the troops were doubtless provided at this time, probably in the building that had served as a church in 1777.[22]

These were years of great increases in Indian population at the mission and the beginning of growth in crop and livestock production. The Indian population grew by nearly three hundred percent between 1782 and 1792. Cattle herds multiplied to more than ten times their original size during the same period, and sheep multiplied at an even faster rate.[23] In fact, efforts to improve agricultural performance were so successful that in

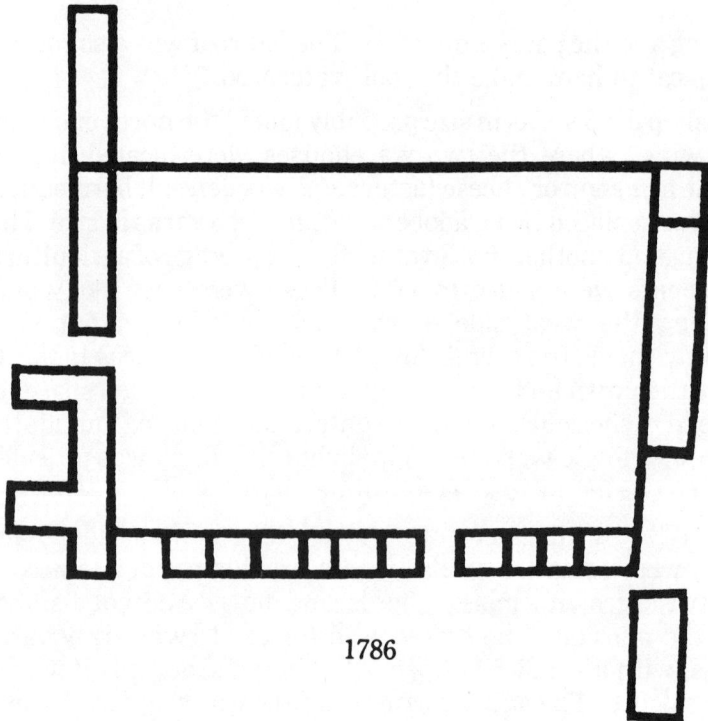

1786

1786 a new granary was built, probably at the north end of the west wing. This was an adobe structure, 25 x 5.5 varas, with walls one and a half adobes in thickness and a roof of jacal. A new corral was also constructed, partly of adobe, and partly of palisades, to accommodate the growing herds of farm animals.[24]

There was no construction reported in 1787, but this must have been the year when furnaces were built some distance from the mission for firing brick and tile. Since protection of storage buildings was such a critical matter, the 1780 warehouse was probably reroofed immediately, as the original tule roof would not have lasted much longer than six or seven years. By 1788 production was far enough advanced that the 1781 warehouse could be reroofed with tile, still leaving a sufficient stock on hand to replace the roofs on other buildings.[25]

The two original structures in the south wing received a tile roof in 1789, probably with the addition of a roof over the central gateway, which was doubtless not covered when the buildings had flat roofs. Before the new roof was added, the kitchen was rebuilt with the conical ceiling and brick lattice chimney it has today. A new adobe extension, 15 x 5 varas in size, was added to the west end of the south wing in 1789, with a tile roof to match the new roof on the main part of the wing. A portal was constructed on the patio side, with brick pillars and a tile roof, though perhaps not with the arches now seen there.[26]

The cattle herds continued to grow at a rapid rate. A new adobe corral sixty varas square was enclosed in 1789 in an attempt to accommodate these huge herds of cattle.[27]

Since the roof on the church was ready for replacement in 1790, it was removed, the walls were raised five cuartas, the building was enlarged (though the report fails to mention this), probably by removing the wall between the church and the sacristy, and another sacristy of twenty varas in length was added at the north end of the building. New roof timbers were then installed, and the entire structure was covered with tile.[28]

The 1786 warehouse in the west wing was also reroofed with tile in 1790, and two small rooms were built, probably the wing just to the east of the newly reconstructed church. One of the rooms may have been used as a baptistry, though this is not

9

certain. Two colonnades with tile roofs and pillars of brick and mortar were built along the patio side of the church and along the south side of the south wing.[29]

A new barracks was built in 1791, opposite the original church. Because the ground here slopes away, the foundations were placed somewhat out of line with the rest of the mission quadrangle. The main portion of the new structure was 10 x 5.5 varas, with an adjacent room 5 x 5 varas, both roofed with tile. The main building had its own tile-roofed portico in front, though the smaller room did not, perhaps because the walls were too thin to support the weight.[30]

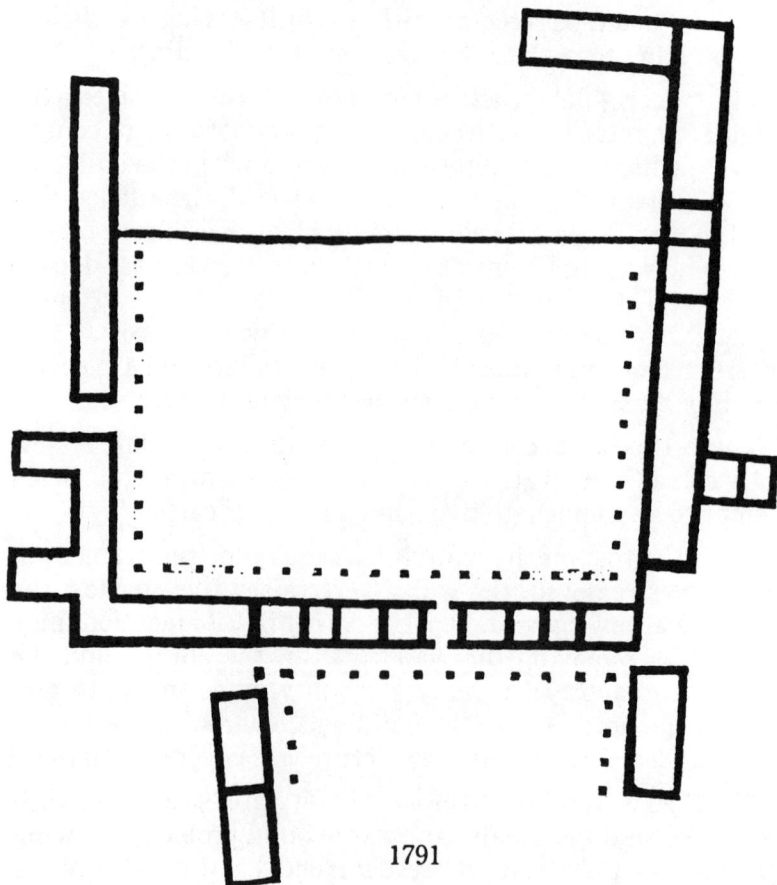

1791

10

View to the east from the southwest corner of the mission quadrangle. Note the westward extension of the ruined adobe walls in the foreground, the kitchen in the center of the picture, and the military barracks to the right.

Taken about 1874, this view shows the military barracks and the south wing, with the rest of the quadrangle obscured by the ruins of the great stone church.

The old cuartel, which was very likely the original church, was redesigned as a lodging for the craftsmen who supervised construction and maintenance at the mission. Perhaps it was at this time that the building was faced with fired brick. Both the refurbished church-cuartel and the brick-pillared portico were reroofed with tile.[31]

Since the old dormitory for the young unmarried women was just adjacent to the new cuartel, a new dormitory was built, probably at the north end of the church. Two other rooms were added at this time to provide permanent quarters for the majordomo and his family. The size of the dormitory is not given in the report, but it was probably about 10 x 7 varas, while the family of the mayordomo had rooms 6 x 7 and 4 x 7 varas in size.[32]

Another new granary was added in 1791, extending westward from the north end of this wing. The structure was 36 varas long and 6 wide. This building was extended to the west the following year, creating an entire new wing north of the wall that had formed the north end of the quadrangle.[33]

The adobe wall that originally enclosed this end of the

View to the south from the ruins of the little tower surmounting the gate in the north wing. This photograph was taken in 1895 during the restoration of the buildings by the Landmarks Club.

The rubble pile cutting across the quadrangle in the lower part of the picture may be the remains of the stone foundation of the wall that was the northern edge of the quadrangle until its removal in 1792.

quadrangle had come to serve as the facade for a number of temporary buildings, but it had deteriorated to such an extent that in 1792 when the new north wing was completed, these flimsy structures were demolished.[34]

The new range of warehouses and shops included a storage building 26 varas long, a weaving room 18 varas in length, and a small tower over an arched gateway that cut through the center of the buildings. On each side of this tower were small rooms 7 and 14 varas in length to be used for storage and shop purposes.[35]

The dyeing vats in the northwest corner of the west wing may have been added at this time, for the master weaver Antonio Domingo Henríquez came to the mission that year to build spinning and weaving machinery and instruct the Indians in the use of the narrow loom.[36] In any case, the vats were certainly in place by the spring of 1796, when another weaving

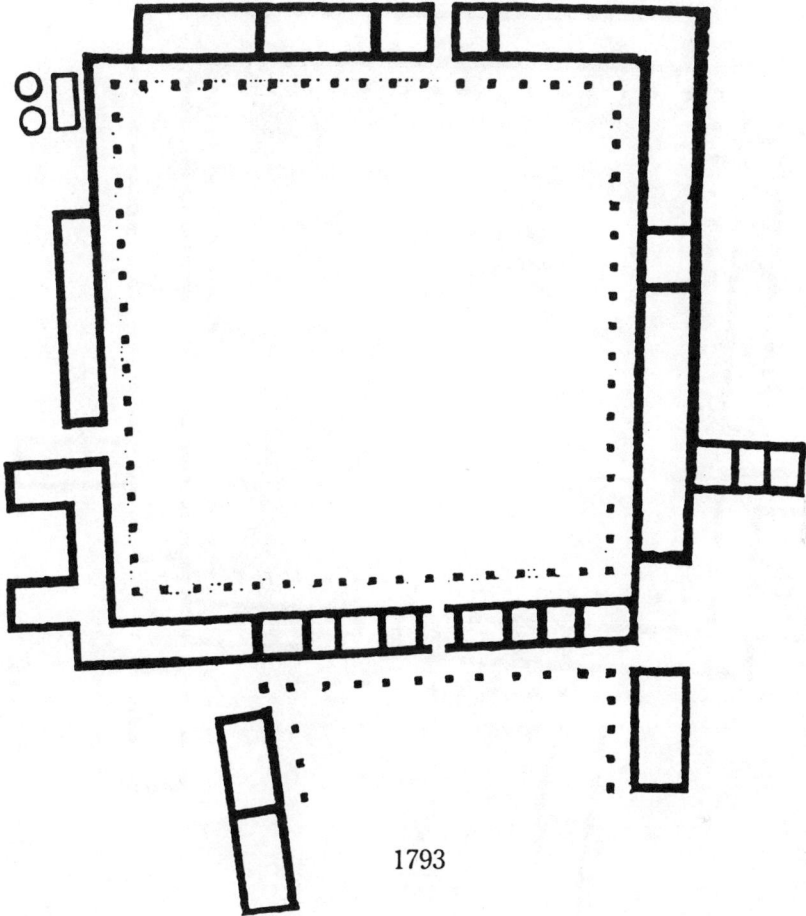

1793

instructor attempted to improve the dyeing techniques used by the Indian weavers.[37] Cattle herds were also very large, and the nearby tallow rendering works may also have been added at the same time.[38]

The buildings at the mission were becoming more sophisticated in design, and the mission craftsmen were more skilled. Perhaps as practice for a great new church, the priests decided to give the north wing a roof of brick and mortar. This was a tremendous weight to rest on adobe walls, and the building is one of those that has disappeared. No trace of it remains today.

15

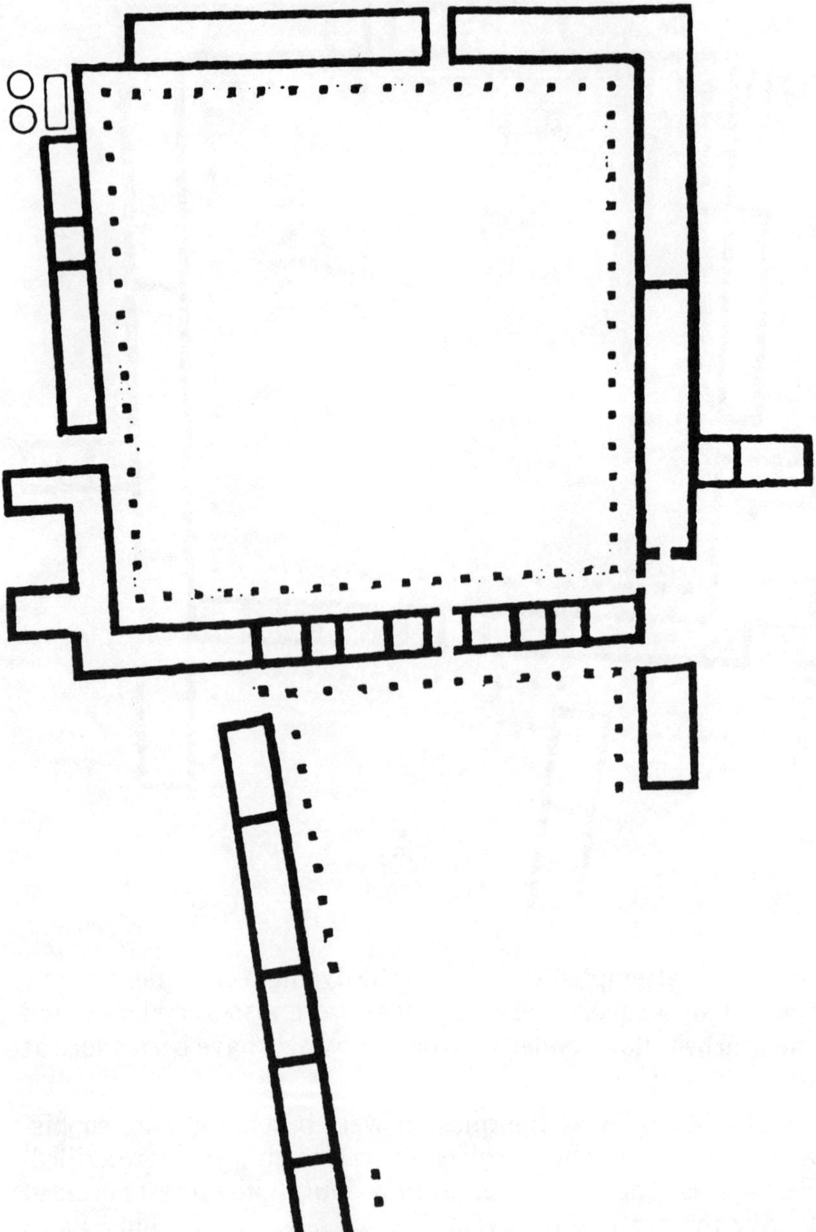

1796

The south front of this wing was faced with a graceful new colonnade with brick pillars and a tile roof. Another new colonnade was built on the east front of the west wing, where a less permanent portico had been built some years earlier.[39]

A building added in 1793 was probably constructed outside the main quadrangle, for it does not fit the specifications of any known building at the mission. This structure was 30 varas long and 6.75 varas wide, with walls 5 varas high. No purpose was mentioned in the report, but this may have been intended for use as a hospital, which was surely needed by that time.[40]

A small room was added to the wing that extended eastward from the church. The garden was enclosed with a permanent adobe wall one hundred varas square, and another adobe enclosure sixty varas square was built as an additional corral.[41]

Two other warehouses were built in 1794, one 34 x 5.5 varas in size and the other 20 x 5.5 varas. The walls were 5 varas high, and the roofs were tile. It is not possible to say where they were located, but they may simply have been renovations of the two oldest warehouses in the west wing.[42]

The Indians at the mission, who had been living in their traditional tule huts, finally had permanent housing in 1794. Forty small adobes were built south of the quadrangle for this purpose, some with tule roofs and some with tile.[43]

In 1795 another garden was enclosed with an adobe wall, perhaps the garden east of the church. No other major construction was completed that year, though major repairs were made to many of the oider buildings at the mission.[44]

Another extension was added to the cuartel in 1796, plus several adobe houses for the soldiers, all with tile roofs. One building was given a roof of brick and mortar, perhaps the blacksmith shop in the center of the west wing, since the report for 1796 lists a shipment of "everything necessary for a forge."[45]

By this time, the missionaries were planning to build a great new church. Diego de Borica, newly appointed governor of California, had determined to see the mission system enlarged so that all the California Indians might be converted. Moreover, he found a congenial counterpart in Padre Fermin Francisco de

17

Lasuén, father president of the missions, who shared Borica's zeal for expansion of the mission system. On 2 March 1797, the first stone was laid for the new church. This was to be an imposing brick and stone structure 53 varas in length, 10 varas wide, with a transept, a tower and baptistry, and a sacristy 10 x 7 varas in size.[44]

In order to make room for this massive edifice, a few structures, probably temporary, had to be removed. Two temporary shelters were built in 1798 for shops and for the storage of building materials. One was 7 x 4 varas in size; the other shelter was 5 x 4. Two additional temporary structures built the following year were of such flimsy construction that dimensions were not given in that report.[47]

No significant work has been done on the priest's quarters in nearly a decade. Consequently, one of these rooms was thoroughly renovated in 1798, and a new reception room was added at the east end, 11 x 6 varas in size. This building is now occupied by one of the mission shops.[48]

The major work in 1799 was church construction, although time was taken to remove the roof from one of the oldest buildings and replace the timbers and tiles.[49] This was doubtless the warehouse building of 1780-1782, which had been converted to use as a winery in about 1784. Winemaking at Mission San Juan Capistrano was first mentioned in the annual report of 1799, which doubtless means that production had reached a respectable level by that year.[50]

A small earthquake shook the walls of the new church in 1800, cracking them badly enough that extensive repairs were needed. Even so, the vaulting proceeded smoothly, so that it was possible to install the main altar that year, an "elegant" piece "and very much to the liking of the missionaries."[51]

In 1801 while work on the church proceeded, two of the colonnades were rebuilt. The oldest one, on the north side of the padre's quarters, perhaps became an arcade at this time, if it was not already built that way.[52]

During this same year one of the buildings used as a storage place for tallow and grain was destroyed by fire. It was rebuilt in

18

View to the north, across the mission quadrangle. Note the ruined walls of the little tower surmounting the north gate.

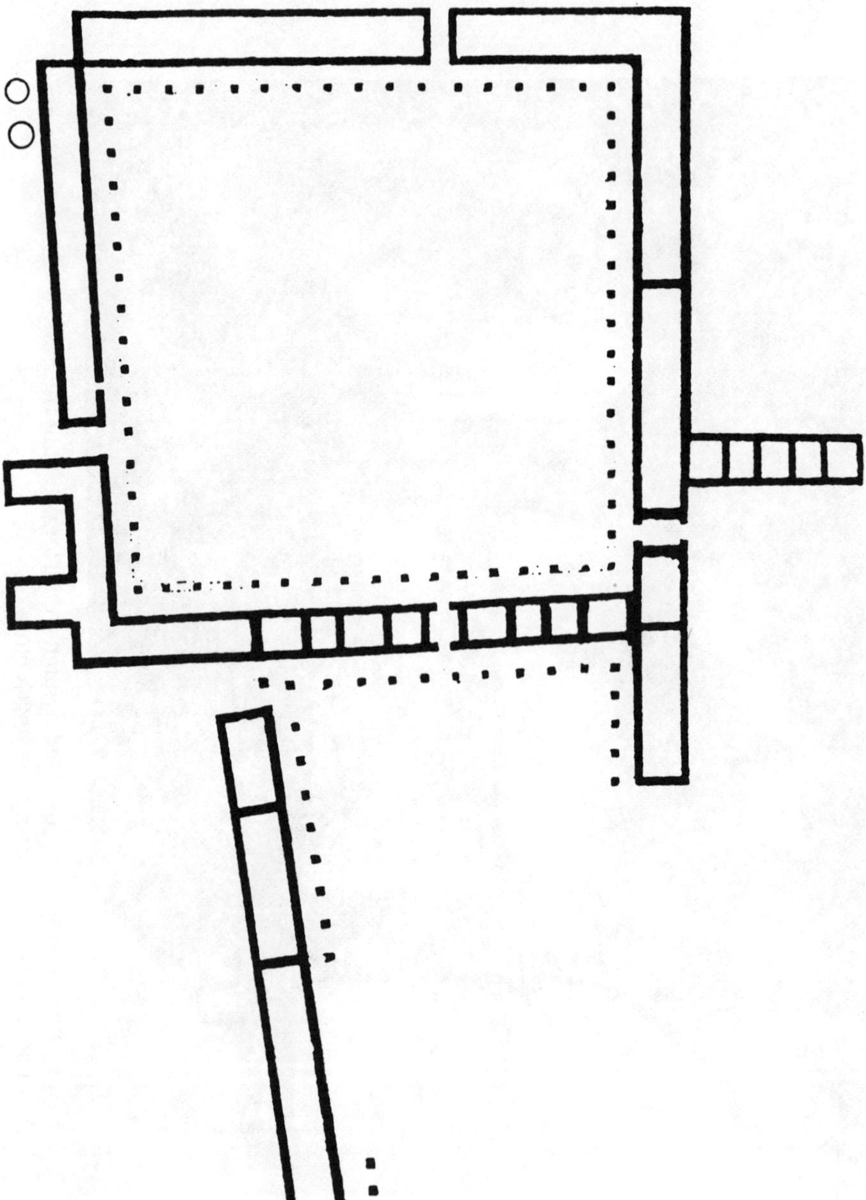

1798

1802, other buildings were renovated, and the colonnade along the north side was reconstructed as an arched walkway.[53]

Work on the church stopped temporarily in 1803, when the master mason died. He was a difficult man to replace, but work began again after a long delay, and by 1805 five of the vaults in the main structure were finished. The whole church was completed in 1806, when it was blessed and dedicated.[54]

From this time forward information about the buildings is even more fragmentary than the information available for the earlier years. Thirty-four adobe houses were built in 1807 for the use of the Indians at the mission.[55] Alfred Robinson, who saw the huts two decades later, said they were built of whitewashed adobe, "forming five or six blocks, or streets, in front of the mission, and they seemed "neat and comfortable."[56]

A major part of the stone church collapsed in the massive earthquakes that shook California late in 1812.[57] The tower fell into the main aisle of the church, crushing the Indians who had gathered for Holy Mass.[58] The death toll was so great that the entire mission program was halted for a time. As if this were not enough, severe floods that year caused additional damage, and it was all the padres could do to keep the place in one piece.[59]

Probably as a temporary measure at first, the church was moved back to the adobe quadrangle, occupying the building where Father Serra had confirmed a group of Indian converts in 1783. One of the rooms east of the church was converted for use as a baptistry, just where it is today. It was ready for use in March 1813, when the first baptismal ceremony was performed there.[60] The report of 1815 reported that the church at Capistrano, destroyed in the earthquake of 1812, was being rebuilt. If so, the work was soon abandoned, perhaps because the Indian population in the area was beginning to decline.[61]

Disease, always a problem in the California missions, began to exact a tragic toll among the Indian population. The most common ailments were dysentery and syphilis, which were serious enough among the general population but real killers for the Indians.[62] Conditions were so bad that a new hospital was constructed in 1814 just to deal with these endemic afflictions.[63]

21

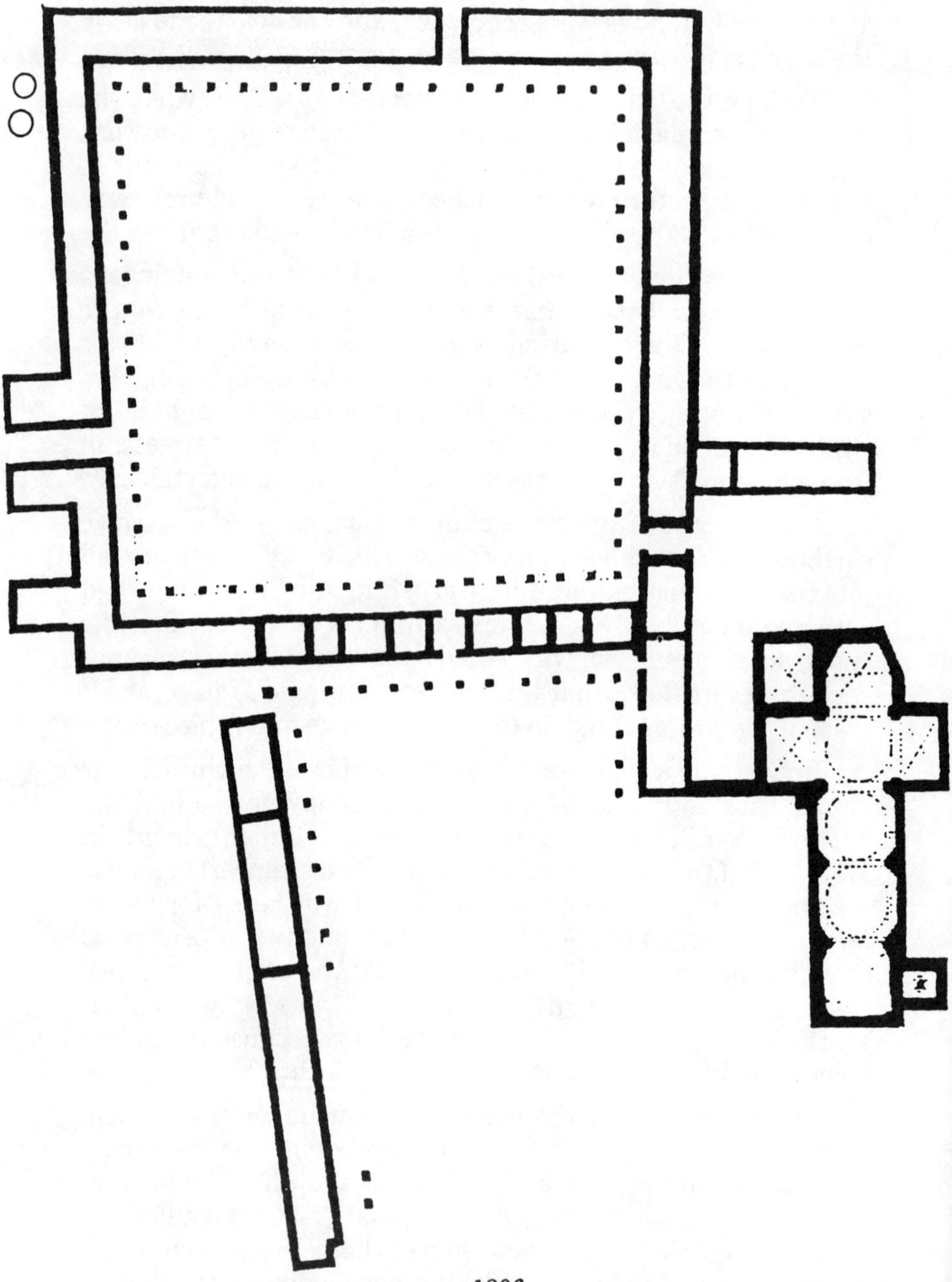

1806

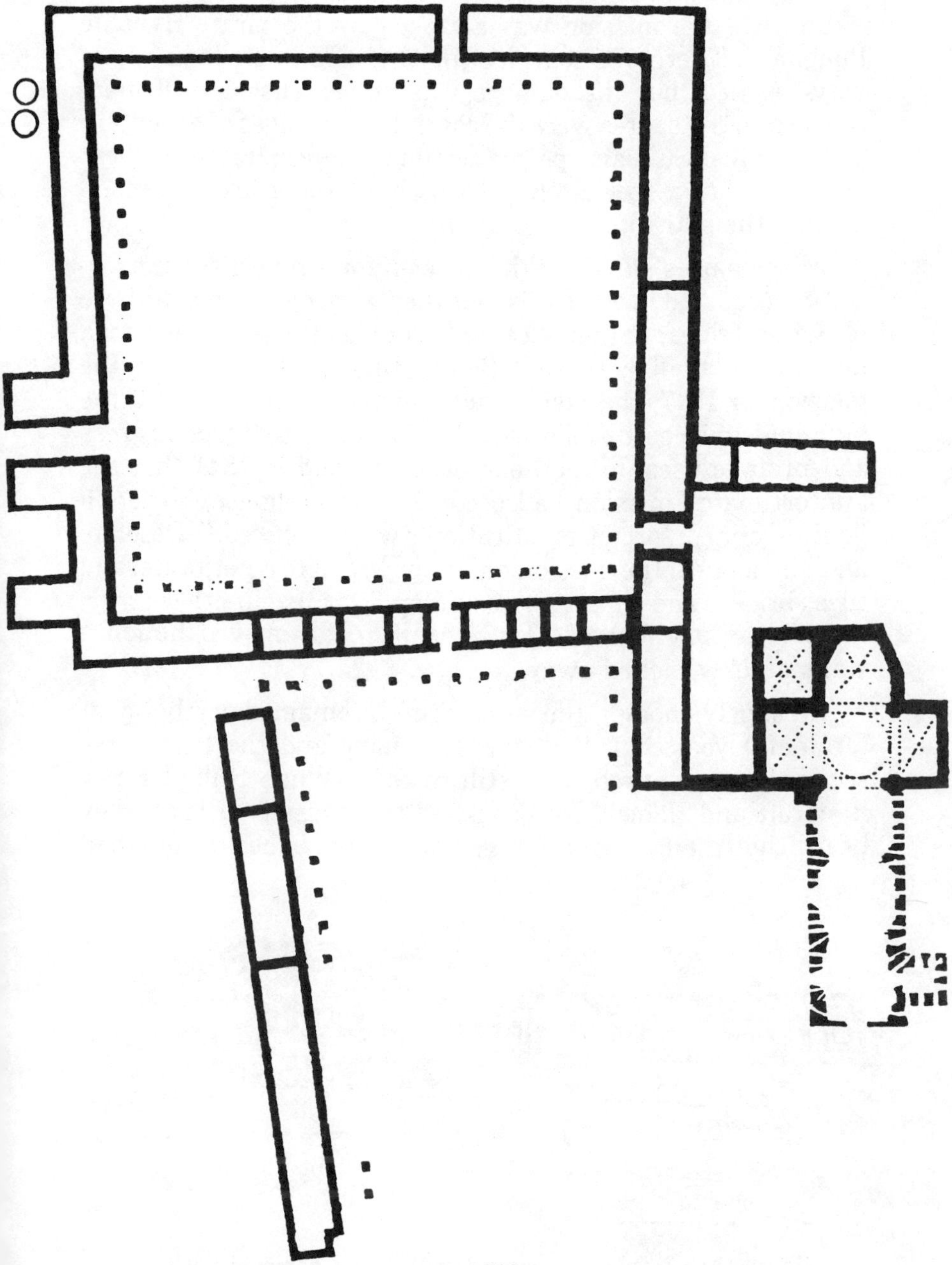

1812

In 1818 the mission was attacked by the pirate Hypolite Bouchard. There was some looting, and a few tule Indian huts were burned, but the damage was not extensive.[64] Of more concern to the padres were the continuing ravages of dysentery and syphilis. So many people were in the hospital with these ailments that a special chapel was built there just to accommodate the patients.[65]

Missionaries stayed at the mission for a time after secularization occurred in the 1830s, but they were deprived of full use of the buildings. Father Vicente Oliva was the last Franciscan missionary to live there.[66] Before this good priest left the mission in 1847, the civilian administrators had allowed the buildings to be occupied by people who converted them to gross and profane uses. In fact, one observer said in 1841 that the "unfortunate" mission had become a "whorehouse," where a "quite refined sort of prostitution" was practiced.[67] Desolate and abandoned, the mission buildings began to deteriorate, and tiles, bricks, and timbers were pilfered for use in other structures in the neighborhood. With the tile roofs removed the adobe walls quickly melted away.

Strangely enough, the stone church remained partly intact for many years. In 1850 the sanctuary and the transverse section of the church were still roofed.[68] When Hubert Howe Bancroft and Henry L. Oak visited the mission in 1874, they heard that the lantern and two domes above the transept had

The entire transept was still roofed and adorned with a lantern when H.M.T. Powell saw the ruins in 1850.

24

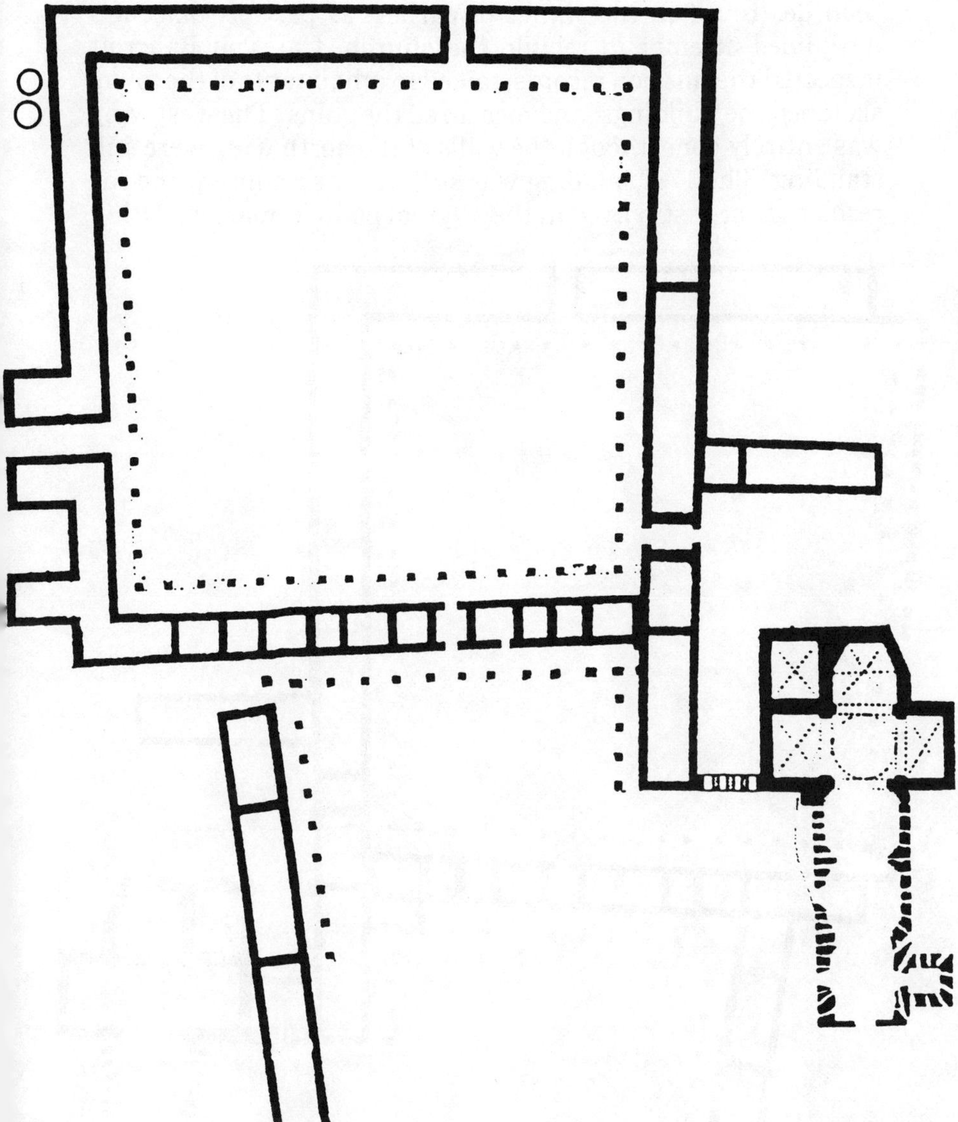

1815

been destroyed in the sixties or earlier, as part of someone's misguided attempt to rebuild the church. Oak and Bancroft inspected the mission records, talked to inhabitants of the town, sketched the buildings, and measured the ruins. The west wing was entirely gone, though the walls of the north wing were still standing. The 1782 building was still used as a church, and the resident pastor still lived in the original padre's quarters. Other

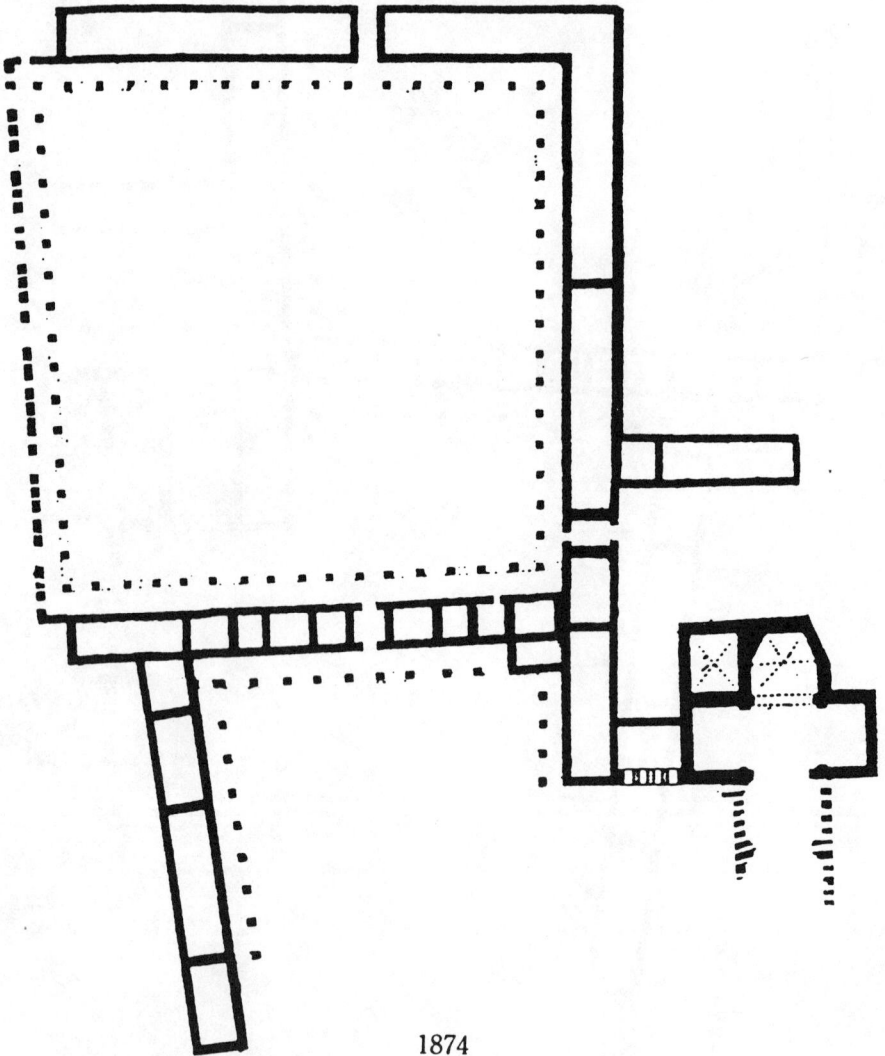

1874

buildings in the quadrangle were used as stables or sheds, and one or two were dwellings. The existing arcade roofs were no longer covered with tile but with tule.[69]

Before the turn of the century, when the Landmarks Club began stabilizing the structures, more than half the buildings had disappeared. Everything in the north wing was gone. The entire west side of the quadrangle had collapsed. The north end of the east wing, where the adobe church was located, had been unroofed, and the walls were fast melting away. The padre's

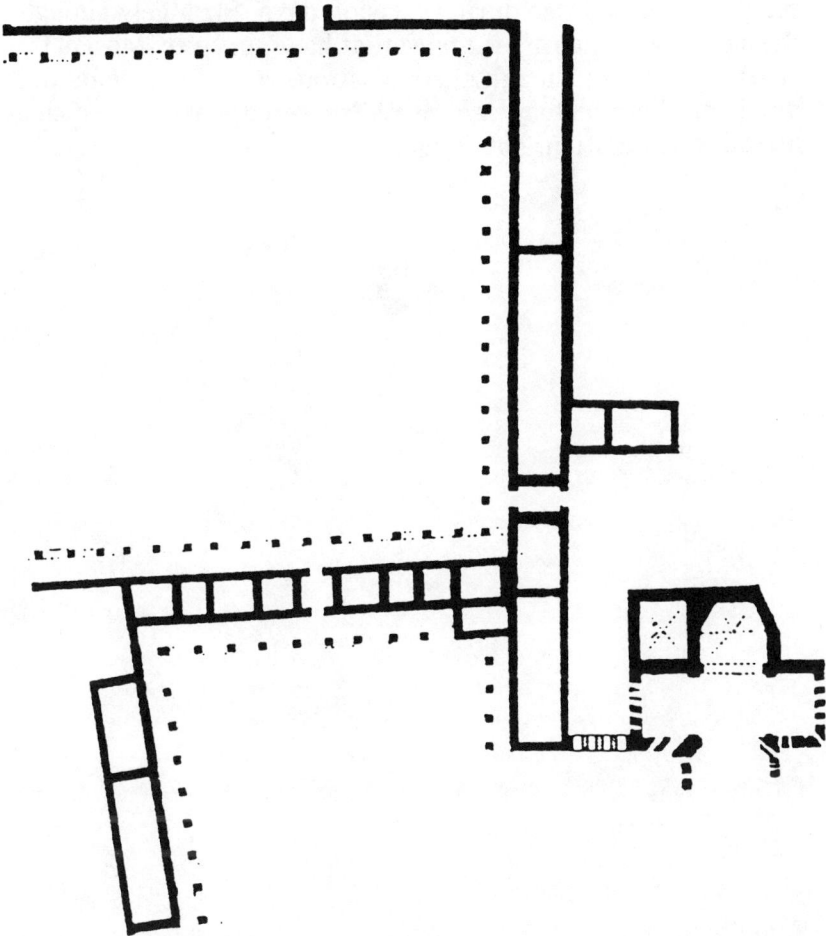

1890

27

quarters had been remodeled by the addition of a second story. The adobe church had been abandoned, and the brick building had been converted to use as a chapel, with part of the south arcade walled in to serve as a sacristy. Most interesting of all, a rounded pediment had been added on the south facade of the brick building, making this the first mission and perhaps the first building in California to have a Mission Revival facade.[70]

Since that time various buildings have been stabilized, remodeled, reconstructed, and rebuilt. But that is another story. Here we are concerned only with the original buildings and their construction and use during mission days. Strangely enough, the oldest buildings are the ones that have survived. Most of the others are gone, though their locations and dimensions and much of their history can be rediscovered through archaeological investigation, now under way.

NOTES

Acknowledgment. Illustrations are published by courtesy Bancroft Library, University of California, Berkeley, for the H.M.T. Powell drawing; all the others are courtesy Seaver Center for Western History Research, Los Angeles County Museum of Natural History.

[1] Fermín Francisco de Lasuén to Juan Prestamero, 28 January 1776, in Finbar Kenneally, trans. and ed., *Writings of Fermín Francisco de Lasuén*, 2 vols. (Washington: Academy of American Franciscan History, 1965), 1:60.

[2] *Writings of Lasuén*, 1:69.

[3] Annual report, 31 December 1783, Misiones de la Alta California, 2a serie, tomo 2, no. 14, Archivo General de la Nación, typescript copy Santa Barbara Mission Archives. Hereafter annual report, 1783, no. 14, SBMA.

[4] See the photographic copy of the entry in Zephyrin Engelhardt, *San Juan Capistrano Mission* (Los Angeles: Zephyrin Engelhardt, 1922), 172.

[5] See the photographic copy of the entry in Engelhardt, *San Juan Capistrano*, 17.

[6] Annual report, 1782, no. 32, SBMA. Note that the reports are not numbere din chronological order.

[7] Real Academia Española, *Diccionario de la lengua Castellana* (4th ed.; Madrid: Viuda de Don Joaquin Ibarra, 1803), 703, 874.

[8] Pablo de Mugartegui to Junípero Serra, 18 April 1779, quoted in Edith Buckland Webb, *Indian Life at the Old Missions* (Los Angeles: Warren F. Lewis, 1952), 95. Annual report, 1782, no. 32, SBMA. Father William Krekelberg, archivist for the Roman Catholic Diocese of Orange, considers it more likely that the early adobe church was built on the site later occupied by the stone church. My reasons for preferring the gift shop site appear later in the text.

[9] See the plan of the Real Presidio de Sta. Barbara, 16 September 1788, which seems to imply that "three *quartas* in width" and "an adobe and a half in width" are the same measurement. Copy signed by Pedro Fages in Richman Collection, uncataloged manuscripts, Ayer Collection, Newberry Library. If this is correct, then a standard adobe at that time would have been a forth of a vara wide and half a vara long.

[10] Ibid. One such temporary structure was a calf barn made before April 1779. Mugartegui to Serra, 18 April 1779, quoted in Webb, *Indian Life at the Old Missions*, 95.

[11] Ibid.

[12] Annual report, 1779, no. 3, SBMA. Annual report, 1782, no. 32, SBMA. The 1782 report specifies that these buildings are in the same wing, and they can be identified by their measurements.

[13] Annual report, 1782, no. 32, SBMA.

[14] Ibid.

[15] Annual report, 1781, no. 26, SBMA.

[16] Ibid. Several factors support this argument. First, the two warehouses formed one side of a fifty vara square corral, which would be possible only if the buildings were located end to end and separated by a three vara gateway. Secondly, the buildings and gateway match ruins recently uncovered at the mission. Nicholas M. Magalousis and Dolores Schiffert, *The Ongoing Search: Archaeological Research at Mission San Juan Capistrano*, Joint Archaeological Research Project, Chapman College, February, 1986, pages 1, 8. Finally, the width of the buildngs in this wing corresponds to the building widths given in the ground plan prepared by Richard Egan about 1900, though the lengths do not, as the structures were extensively remodeled in later years. A copy of the Egan plan is filed in the San Juan Capistrano Mission Archives.

[17] Annual report, 1782, no. 32, SBMA.

[18] Ibid. This location is conjectural. It is also possible that the building was located in the south wing, along with the other small rooms built there.

29

[19]Ibid. As will be noted later, the "agricultural" building became the winery, when the vines, planted in 1779, began to produce grapes in sufficient quantity. See Mugartegui to Serra, 15 March 1779, quoted in Webb, *Indian Life at the Old Missions*, 95.

[20]Annual report, 1783, no. 14, SBMA. Francisco Palóu, *Relación historica de la vida y apostolicas tareas del venerable Padre Fray Junipero Serra* (México: Imprenta de Don Felipe de Zuñiga y Ontiveros, 1787), 199, is authority for the statement that the winery was in operation by 1785. The vines can scarcely have been productive in 1783, when the report mentioned only that there were "some grape vines" in the garden. For more information on the wine vats in this building, see Magalousis and Schiffert, *The Ongoing Search*, 1, 8, and 9.

[21]Ibid. See also Francisco Palou, "Noticia succinta de las 9 Miss. i 3 Presidos de la Nueva California," Documentos para historia de Mexico, ser. II, tomo XV, fol. 262, MS, Archivo General de la Nacion, Mexico City.

[22]Ibid. If it seems strange that quarters for the troops were not provided earlier, recall that the troops had mutinied, rahter than assist in the construction of quarters for the missionaries. Then it is easy to understand why the friars found it difficult to fit the barracks project into their construction schedule.

[23]Annual report, 1782, no. 32, SBMA. Annual report, 7 January 1793, no. 133, SBMA. Robert Archibald, *The Economic Aspects of the California Missions* (Washington: Academy of American Franciscan History, 1978), 174-175. Engelhardt, *San Juan Capistrano*, 175, 182, 184. There are no accurate population statistics for the missions. The figures listed in annual reports and mission registers need to be approached with a great deal of caution. There is no modern mission population study based on careful, critical research in the original sources. For more on this point, see Harry Kelsey, "European Impact on the California Indians, 1530-1830," *The Americas*, 41 (April 1985) 508-511.

[24]Annual report, 1786, no. 49, SBMA.

[25]Annual report, 1788, no. 90, SBMA. Only one warehouse is listed as having been reroofed, and it can be identified by its measurements.

[26]Annual report, 1 January 1790, no. 103, SBMA. The report says "a wing sixty varas long was roofed with tile." The south wing is the only structure fitting that description. The new room also fits well into the open space at the west end of this wing, although the annual report does not actually say that it was built there. Contrary to most current representations, the area at the west end of the south wing was not an open space, but was a building site. This fact was partially confirmed by archaeological investigation in 1980-1981. See Magalousis and Schiffert, *The Ongoing Search*, pages 4 and 8. It is also confirmed by early plats of the mission site, including the oldest, the survey done by John G. Cleal in September 1854, Survey Plats Submitted by Bishop Alemany, Map Drawer F, SBMA. I am indebted to Father William Krekelberg for calling this to my attention. The map is reproduced, without date, in Engelhardt, *San Juan Capistrano*, 167. Dr. Norman Neuerburg kindly provided me with information about the addition of the chimney in the kitchen.

[27]Ibid.

[28]Annual report, 14 February 1791, no. 148, SBMA.

[29]Ibid. while the location of the newly-roofed warehouse is not specified in the report, the 1786 warehouse had a roof of jacal, exactly the kind mentioned in the report of 14 February 1791.

[30]Annual report, 31 December 1791, no. 126, SBMA.

[31]Ibid.

[32]Ibid. The location of these structures is conjectural, based largely on the supposition that (1) they would not be located in the shop or warehouse wings; (2) they would be located close to the church and garden; and (3) they would be as far removed as possible from the military barracks.

[33]Ibid.

30

[34]Annual report, 7 January 1793, no. 133, SBMA. It is difficult to make much sense out of the brief description given of these operations. Father Maynard Geiger thought the passage in question meant that "an entire wing of earlier buildings was torn down because it was in a deteriorated condition" and that "a small tower was constructed in the middle of the quadrangle." See his "New Data on Mission San Juan Capistrano," *Southern California Quarterly*, 49 (March 1967), 43. The interpretation depends on the meaning of *lienzo*, which I assume to be a "wall" and not "wing"; and *quadro*, which I assume to be a "wing," as in the 1789 annual report, rather than the entire "quadrangle," as Father Maynard has it. The apparent remains of the stone foundation of this wall can be seen in some of the early photographs of the mission quadrangle. A notched stone in the face of pillar number 10 on the east side of the quadrangle makes it seem that the padres originally planned to build an arcade from east to west at this point.

[35]Ibid. Annual report, 7 January 1793, no. 133, SBMA. The location of the weaving room in this wing partly confirms the accuracy of the site plan prepared by Capistrano resident Richard Egan in the 1890s. Copy in the Capistrano Mission Archives. Judge Egan led the movement to save the mission and performed much of the Landmarks Club restoration work at Capistrano by himself. See "The Landmarks Club," *Land of Sunshine*, 4 (May 1896), 285. It ought to be noted that there were several looms in operation at the mission in 1790, before the new weaving building was finished. Annual report, 14 February 1791, no. 110, SBMA.

[36]Lasuén to José Joaquín de Arrillaga, 21 December 1792, in *Writings of Lasuén*, 1:263-264. Webb thinks these structures are wine presses, which seems unlikely. See her *Indian Life at the Old Missions*, 200. The area was probably roofed with tule but otherwise open. Nicholas Magalousis correctly calls them multi-purpose industrial vats, part of a mission tanning system. See the site drawing in Nicholas M. Magalousis and Scott MacLeod, *A Reassessment of the Interpretation of Two Structures at Mission San Juan Capistrano*, Joint Archaeological Research Project, Chapman College, Special Subject Publication, June 1982.

[37]Hubert Howe Bancroft, *History of California*, 7 vols. (San Francisco: The History Co., 1886), 1:658. See also the letters from Vicente Fuster and Norberto de Santiago to Governor Borica, 17 April 1797, and from Fuster to Borica, 31 May 1797, in Engelhardt, *San Juan Capistrano*, 33-36.

[38]Nicholas Magalousis has shown that these structures could have served several purposes, including the smelting of iron for use in the mission. See Magalousis and MacLeod, *A Reassessment of the Interpretation of Two Structures at Mission San Juan Capistrano*.

[39]Annual report, 7 January 1793, no. 133, SBMA.

[40]Annual report, 31 December 1793, no. 148, SBMA.

[41]Ibid.

[42]Annual report, 9 January 1795, no. 165, SBMA.

[43]Ibid.

[44]Annual report, 31 December 1795, no. 177, SBMA.

[45]Annual report, 31 December 1796, no. 159, SBMA. For information about excavation in the smithy see Magalousis and Schiffert, *The Ongoing Search*, pages, 2, 8, and 12.

[46]California Mission Documents, no. 471, 31 December 1797, SBMA. Engelhardt, citing baptismal entry number 2723, says the project started on 2 February 1797. See his *San Juan Capistrano*, 41. Dr. Iris Engstrand reminded me of Borica's important role during this period of mission expansion. For more information see Theodore H. Hittell, *History of California*, 4 vols. (San Francisco: Pacific Press Publishing House, 1885), 1:474-489.

[47]California Mission Documents, no. 471, December 1798, SBMA.

[48]California Mission Documents, no. 471, December 1798, SBMA.

[49]California Mission Documents, no. 471, 31 December 1799, SBMA.

31

[50]Noticia de las misiones de la Nueva California, 20 February 1799, photocopy, SBMA.

[51]Noticia de las misiones de la Nueva California, 5 February 1801, SBMA. Engelhardt, *San Juan Capistrano*, 39. I am indebted to Dr. Norman Neuerburg for information about the use of *colateral maior* to describe the main altar of a church.

[52]Engelhardt, *San Juan Capistrano*, 39.

[53]Ibid., 40.

[54]Noticia de las misiones de la Nueva California, 21 February 1803, 21 February 1805, 13 March 1807, SBMA. Engelhardt, *San Juan Capistrano*, 41-43. After studying the poor quality of the stone work in the final portion of the church, Dr. Neuerburg concluded that the master mason was not replaced, but that the work was continued without supervision by a competent craftsman. This poor workmanship was quite possibly a factor in the collapse of the roof in the nave of the church during the earthquake of 1812.

[55]Engelhardt, *San Juan Capistrano*, 44.

[56]Alfred Robinson, *Life in California during a Residence of Several Years in That Territory* (New York: Wiley & Putnam, 1846), 20.

[57]Noticia de las misiones de la Nueva California, 9 April 1813, SBMA.

[58]Bancroft, who interviewed inhabitants of the town in 1874, thought the tower collapsed on the church. See his comments in his *History of California*, 2:200. Henry L. Oak also makes the same statement. See Ruth Frey Axe, Edwin H. Carpenter, and Norman Neuerburg, eds., *A Visit to the Missions of Southern California in February and March 1874 by Henry L. Oak* (Los Angeles: Southwest Museum, 1981), 46. Father St. John O'Sullivan, pastor for many years, investigated the matter thoroughly and was convinced that the tower fell away from the church; the roof fell in because it was cracked by the earthquake. See his comments in "Devastation by Earthquake, 1812," *The Jewel of the Missions: A Documentary History of San Juan Capistrano*, comp. and ed. by Francis J. Weber (Los Angeles: n.p., 1976), 29. The official report is ambiguous on this point. See the translation in Engelhardt, *San Juan Capistrano*, 53-54.

[59]Engelhardt, *San Juan Capistrano*, 57.

[60]*Ibid.*, 180.

[61]Noticia de las misiones de la Nueva California, May 1815, SBMA.

[62]Noticia de las misiones de la Nueva California, 4 May 1819, SBMA.

[63]Engelhardt, *San Juan Capistrano*, 57.

[64]Noticia de las misiones de la Nueva California, 4 May 1819, SBMA. Bancroft, *History of California*, 2:240-241.

[65]Bancroft, *History of California*, 2:348. Possibly the present bell wall was built at this time.

[66]Engelhardt, *San Juan Capistrano*, 200.

[67]Santiago Argüello to José Antonio de la Guerra y Noriega, 1841, De la Guerra Papers, SBMA.

[68]See the drawing made 13 March 1850 by H.M.T. Powell, *The Santa Fe Trail to California, 1849-1852; The Journal and Drawings of H.M.T. Powell*, ed. by Douglas S. Watson (San Francisco: Book Club of California, 1931), opp. 206.

[69]Axe, Carpenter, and Neuerburg, *A Visit to the Missions of Southern California*, 41-46.

[70]See the brief report of the reconstruction work at San Juan Capistrano in "The Landmarks Club," *The Land of Sunshine*, 5 (November 1896), 244; and *The Landmarks Club and Its Work* (Los Angeles: Out West Co., 1903), 24 pp. A very close approximation of the same information is in "Thus Far - And Much Farther," *Out West*, 19 (July 1903): 5-24, which also has interesting photographs of the work. The west wing may have disappeared by 1874, as it is not shown in Henry Oak's sketch of that year. Axe, Carpenter and Neuerburg, *A Visit to the Missions*, 44.

32

The Economy of the Alta California Mission, 1803-1821

BY ROBERT ARCHIBALD

On June 26, 1803, Father President Fermín Francisco de Lasuén died. The following day he was solemnly buried at the foot of the altar in the chapel of Mission San Carlos near his missionary companions, Juan Crespí and Junípero Serra. Lasuén and Serra, opposites in personality, had firmly planted Spain upon the soil of Alta California. The affable and yet firm Lasuén had inaugurated the "golden age" of the California missions. Staple crop production had reached limits undreamed of by the pioneers of Serra's day. During Lasuén's tenure as Father-President nine new missions were begun, bringing the total to eighteen. Under the firm prodding of the gentle Basque priest, older missions implemented systems of irrigation, orchards were planted and buildings were improved. Technicians were imported from New Spain who taught the secrets of their crafts to Indian neophytes. By Lasuén's death in 1803, the mission chain was well supplied with competent weavers, masons, carpenters, blacksmiths, leather workers and even ribbon-makers. Some experiments had faltered; notably hemp culture and a fur-trade monopoly. Serra, the founding pioneer, had laid the basis for the missions and Lasuén, gentle and conciliatory, had brought them to their peak of development.

The years from 1803 to 1821 witnessed turmoil, revolution and bloodshed throughout Hispanic America as disgruntled Creoles took advantage of the discomfiture of the Spanish monarchy at the hands of Napoleon, and the consequent turmoil in Spain. California had no Hidalgo, Bolívar or San Martín. It was little affected by the ideology of revolution, although the revolution itself profoundly affected the area. The decline of Spain's power since the halcyon days of Charles III had little by little opened the gates to foreign intruders. The years from 1803-1821 were to see what had been a trickle become a flood. The process was given much impetus when normal trade channels were interrupted by revolution signaled by the "Grito de Dolores" of Father Hidalgo

[227]

in 1810. Foreigners became an increasingly familiar sight along the California coast. The interruption of pay and supplies for the presidios made them dependent upon the food surpluses and manufactured items which only the missions could supply. The missions became the economic mainstays of California.

The relative wealth of the missions in this time of scarcity eventually led to attacks upon them and growing demands for their secularization. The presidial soldiers and even commandants who were deprived of food, clothing and pay by the interruption of the San Blas trade, were embittered by the apparant unwillingness of the missions to share the bounty which was theirs.

Without a doubt the most difficult area of the mission economy to assess during the period from 1803 to 1821 is the impact of smuggling operations. This trade, which was blatantly illegal, finds slight mention for obvious reasons in mission reports. The problem of smuggling was common to all of Spain's colonies in the New World during the period. The trade, although illegal, was profitable to both parties. Spanish mercantile restrictions gave the missions no legal outlet for excess trade items. The problem had been recognized and a solution proposed by Naval Lieutenant Don Francisco de Paula Tamariz. Tamariz, in an 1814 memorial to the king, proposed that California might be open to trade with other Spanish possessions since it could supply much food.[1] He reminded the king of the largess of the California missions which had no legal outlet. He noted that weekly the missions butchered, for the maintenance of the neophytes, 350 or 400 cows. In one year the missions slaughtered close to 19,000 head of cattle. An equal number of hides were available for export, in addition to 26 or 30 thousand *arrobas* of tallow and fat.[2] The hides were discarded since they lacked a market and the tallow and fat was worth 4 to 6 *reales* of silver per *arroba*. Tamariz noted the smuggling which was already prevalent. Some 2,500 to 3,000 furs came into the hands of the missions annually.[3] Few of them were remitted to San Blas because China-bound "Boston Men" appeared each year to purchase the furs. The missionaries, he added, had no scruples about engaging in this nefarious business. In spite of the lieutenant's entreaties, a faltering Spain was unable to take advantage of the production which California had to offer.[4]

[228]

After 1800 the connection with San Blas ceased to be an adequate outlet for the burgeoning mission economies. California furs, which were carried to China via San Blas, followed a laborious and expensive route. The San Blas vessels took skins from California to San Blas where they were loaded on mules and sent off to Mexico City. From there they were returned to Acapulco where the Manila Galleon loaded and transhipped them to the Philippines where the Chinese completed the last leg by taking them to the mainland.[5] Obviously the extent of the trade was severely limited by cargo space and profits were limited by what could at best have been astronomical expenses.

The problem of insufficient supplies and a limited market was a recurrent theme. In 1806 Father José Señán at Mission San Buenaventura complained that during the year 132 skins of tallow weighing 741 *arrobas*, 200 dressed cowhides and 64 sheepskins had been consigned to an agent in Mexico, but that the agent had not settled the mission account in two years.[6] In 1808 Señán claimed that mission production had been so great that it was impossible to ship at a profit. San Buenaventura had that year produced 200 skins of tallow weighing 1,428 *arrobas* which were sold to an unnamed purchaser in Mexico who was to pay the Syndic at Tepic. The same purchaser also contracted for fifty skins of lard weighing 321 *arrobas*. The lard and tallow had brought the mission 1,956 *pesos*, 2 *reales*.[7] The core of the problem preventing the marketing of mission surpluses was transportation. Shipments from each mission were accepted on a prorated basis. This was due to the limited cargo space of the San Blas supply vessels and the fact that ships officers tended to speculate on the tallow trade on their own and hence take up valuable space. Even hemp, which was produced by order of the king to supply cordage for ships, ran into the problem of inadequate transportation. By 1810 Señán complained that 450 animal skins remained unsold at Mission San Buenaventura. These pelts would have yielded 3,000-4,000 *pesos*. Further, he argued, hemp was produced for the king's account, yet its export was limited by the capacity of the San Blas vessels.[8]

An inadequate market for mission products was compounded by the uncertainty of payment which made illicit trade with its immediate and certain rewards more attractive. The missions

[229]

were frequently called upon to contribute surpluses to the presidios, and in return they received a credit entry in the account book of the *habilitado.*⁹ When the balances mounted up a draft was issued on Mexico City. At best two years passed before the profit on grain sold to the presidios could be realized. Since a bill of credit was of no use in California, it was left to the Procurator of the College of San Fernando in New Spain to purchase with it items of utility to the missions. Added to the fact that the presidios paid low prices in the first place were the transportation charges on goods shipped to California.¹⁰ This was in contradiction to the suggestion by former governor Felipe de Neve that grain should be paid for in the form of merchandise needed by the missions at Mexico City prices.¹¹ Even though furs were shipped to San Blas it was done reluctantly since risks incumbent in shipping and storage were borne entirely by the missionaries. Fray Martín Landaeta at San Francisco complained that a shipment of furs remained in the hands of the Comisario because they had not been registered. What doubly disturbed him was the possibility that they would be treated poorly while in storage.¹²

The restrictions placed upon the missions by the prevailing system of mercantilism, the low prices, uncertainty of payment and hazards of shipment combined to make illicit trading attractive to California missionaries. The official attitude of the Spanish government between 1800 and 1810 was one of benign neglect. Possibly due to a lack of money and manpower, laws relating to illegal trading in California were never strictly enforced.¹³ California became a smuggler's paradise and the missions benefited.

In 1803 Fray Landaeta warned his superior of the attractiveness of trade with Americans. He explained that he was remitting four sea otter pelts but that three Americans ships had cast anchor in the course of the summer and that they were willing to pay 8 to 10 *pesos* per pelt. Discreetly, he added that "even if they had paid much more, I would not have engaged in smuggling."¹⁴ Despite the holy father's protestations, Americans found the pious Franciscans very willing to barter on the side.

William Shaler, a true Connecticut Yankee, found the missionaries to be willing accessories in smuggling. From 1803 to 1805 he was a frequent, although clandestine visitor to the missions. In his journal of 1804 he gave welcome advice to all who would follow:

[230]

For several years American trading ships have frequented this coast in search of furs and they have left annually in the country about $25,000 in specie and merchandise. The missionaries are the principle monopolizers of the fur trade. Anyone acquainted with the coast can easily obtain abundant provisions.[15]

Shaler was able to find provisions for his vessel, the *Lelia Byrd*, with remarkable ease. By the time he finished canvassing the missions, some twenty, or at least one half of the pious padres owed him money. Of these, only four had honored their notes, proving to be no more prompt in bill paying than the Spanish government which they criticized.[16]

Although in contravention of the Nootka Sound Convention, Shaler was not the only trespasser on the Spanish domain.[17] By 1810 the Yankees became bolder as the interruption of regular supplies increased demand for clandestine trade. For example, in 1812 George Eayrs was trading with the padre at San Luis Obispo. In return for 58 otter skins, grain and meat, the mission received $1,384 worth of goods.[18]

The eruption of the Mexican Independence movement in 1810 inaugurated more than a decade of turmoil which was resolved only by absolute independence from Spain. Although peripheral to the struggle, the balance of power in California was altered. The missions found themselves in the seemingly enviable position of having a virtual monopoly on technical skills and the food supply. Smuggling now became a necessity of life. Presidial soldiers whose families were improperly clothed and poorly fed were embittered by the missionaries who supplied them meagerly and reluctantly.

The supply shortage forced the missionaries to begin production of such items as clerical habits, sandals and a host of other items which had previously come from Mexico.[19] In addition, attempts were made to increase food production to meet presidial demands. To supply items for trade, more encouragement was given to Indian neophytes to hunt otter.[20] Inevitably the padres began to depend more heavily upon illicit trade for those items which they could not produce. Adelbert von Chamisso, the naturalist aboard the Russian ship *Rurik*, noted that only the smuggling trade, which Governor Pablo Vicente de Solá attempted to suppress, had been able to supply indispensable articles.[21] Trade was carried

[231]

on with Russians, Americans and Peruvians. The *Flora* and *Tagle* from Peru brought cloth and articles to barter. Trade was carried on with Fort Ross and in 1813 amounted to $14,000 worth of goods.[22] Father-President Señán complained in 1819 that the province no longer enjoyed its former connections which once supplied necessities. He bemoaned the reliance on foreign supplies because of the outrageous prices which they extorted. The Peruvians had raised the premium which they charged on goods from 15 to 50 per cent.[23] Althought the Franciscans nostalgically longed for the "good old days" the impact of the Mexican independence movement had few poor effects, and may even have bolstered the mission economy.

With the passage of time the quarrel over presidial supplies assumed ominous proportions and contributed to the propaganda urging mission secularization. The ability of the missions to sustain their military counterparts testifies to their economic strength. At times the presidios served as middlemen who exacted a profit from the trade carried on between missions and foreign merchants. In 1815 Governor Solá demanded that Mission San Juan Bautista deliver 150 *arrobas* of flour along with some wool and tallow. The merchandise was sold to a Spanish corvette and in return the mission obtained some plowshares, pickaxes, crowbars, iron and copper kettles.[24]

The supplies of food and other items requisitioned by the presidios from the missions brought little benefit to the missions. In exchange for goods delivered, the missions received from the *habilitados* drafts on the treasury in Mexico City. Although padres and military officials squabbled over prices, the arguments were academic since few of the drafts were ever honored. As early as 1811 some $14,000 worth of mission drafts had accumulated with no money in the Royal Treasury with which to redeem them.[25] Six years later, in 1817, outstanding *habilitado's* drafts in favor of the missions had reached the staggering sum of $400,000.[26] The missions pleaded poverty, but the evidence suggests that they were far from poor.

The variety of items supplied to the presidios provides an idea of the ability of the mission economies to diversify and prosper. In 1815, among other items, San Carlos supplied serapes.[27] San Buenaventura contributed mules and leather bags.[28] In 1816 Mission San Buenaventura supplied sombreros, tallow drippings (*manteca*), soap, blankets and cloth.[29] Other missions supplied shoes, hides, saddles, mules, knapsacks, muskets, leather shields, cartridge pouches, garters and lances. Obviously some of these articles, such as muskets, were not made at the missions but most were. In 1815 Governor Solá decided to outfit the four presidios with lances and the missions were called upon to furnish the iron, steel and even the blacksmiths and tools. The missions supplied the necessary articles and in return received worthless drafts on Mexico.[30] In addition to the manufactured items, the usual food supplies, cattle, horses and mules were furnished.[31]

The contribution which aggravated the Franciscans the most was cash. This was understandable since in what was essentially a barter economy, cash was a precious commodity and was badly needed for trade. For the most part the only source of cash was foreign trade. Generally the governor would present the demand for cash to the Father-President who would then apportion it among the missions on the basis of their cash reserves and general prosperity. In 1814 Mission La Purísima contributed $800 in cash to the *habilitado* of Santa Barbara by order of Governor José Argüello.[32] One of the largest assessments came in 1821 when the missions donated $3,000 for an arsenal at Monterey. Each mission contributed from $25 to $200. Mission cash reserves were relatively large. A conservative estimate was given by Father Mariano Payéras in 1821 in a protest against Governor Solá's interference in the temporalities of the missions. Most missions, he said, had from $100 to $1,000 in cash and a few $3,000 to $4,000.[33] Despite protests, the missions had the only cash in Alta California.

While the outside world suffered the violence of revolution, the missions of California were able to further increase and diversify mission production. The extent of the production of the mission workshops is difficult to estimate because no reports were required. It is certain, however, that this type of production increased in importance as it became essential to have items with which to barter for necessities from passing foreigners. A critic of the missions, Tamariz, went so far as to claim that the missions were so involved in commercial production that they ignored the needs of the Indians.[34]

[233]

Wine production assumed significant proportions between 1803 and 1821, although the basis had been laid as early as 1780. At one time or another grapes were grown at all of the missions, but because of the variable factors of climate and soil, leadership in wine production went to San Gabriel, San Fernando, San Buenaventura and San José. Techniques of grape growing and wine harvesting were archaic. The land was poorly cultivated. Visitors and missionaries disagreed over the quality of mission wine and the disagreement itself proves that it was simply a matter of personal preference. Of all mission wines San Gabriel was commonly agreed to have the best.[35] Don Francisco de Paula Tamariz observed in 1814 that the mission vines had multiplied fruitfully and that they were of the best quality.[36]

After a faltering start in the late eighteenth century, hemp production began to be increased for use as an item of trade. In 1801 hemp production was inaugurated with official encouragement. In that year Joaquín Sánchez, sergeant of marines and an expert in the manufacture of hemp was sent from Mexico. In 1804 he distributed seed to Missions San Luis Obispo, Purísima, Santa Ines and San José. Hemp was sown in April and harvested in August. The government agreed to pay $4.00 per arroba. The industry seemed to flourish, especially in the south. Bancroft claims that the industry declined after 1810 with the severing of the connection with San Blas and the lack of money to pay for the hemp.[37] Evidence suggests that while hemp production may have declined somewhat, it was traded to foreign vessels for other items.

Hide production was a function of increased presidial demands for shields, saddlery and shoes in addition to the demands of foreign traders. Boston men in particular demanded hides for the developing leather industries of New England. The Spanish were generally unfamiliar with the finer points of tanning and as a result the mission product was suitable only for crude shoes, rough saddles and saddle pads. Hides were poorly scraped and placed into a vat of tanning liquor where they remained until cured.[38] Tallow, another by-product of the cattle industry had been shipped to Mexico but the slack in the trade was eagerly taken up by Americans after 1810. Tallow was also used at the missions to produce soap for local consumption. Tallow and leather production stimulated the construction of brick vats for tanning and the making of soap, while Indian neophytes provided a cheap labor source.[39]

Generally the period from 1803-1821 was a time of elaboration and expansion within the mission system. New buildings were constructed, granaries and houses for neophytes were built. Indians made blankets, coarse cloth and their own clothing with wool shorn from rapidly increasing flocks. Langsdorff observed, that the neophytes cleaned and combed the wool in addition to spinning and weaving. The implements and looms were of moderate quality, and the process of fulling was poorly understood. The product was a cloth of ordinary quality.[40] The missionaries refused to wear the products of their own looms until the exigencies of short supply forced them to. Father Señán made a plea in 1812 for clothing for the missionaries lest it become necessary to make them out of the domestically produced sackcloth. He admitted the shortcomings of the mission cloth which he said at times turned out light gray and sometimes whitish or dark. Because of the lack of combs and fulling equipment, the cloth was flimsy and lacked durability.[41]

Masonry and tiles were used to construct aqueducts and reservoirs to supply water for irrigation. Forges became common sights throughout the mission chain. Rude tools were made at the missions, while more sophisticated tools such as molds, saws, files and chisels were purchased from foreigners. In one letter, Señán complained that a diamond point for glass was missing from a recent shipment. This and the fact that glass windows were coming into use point to the development of glass manufacture.[42] Storage buildings were constructed for tallow, corn, peas, soap, butter, salt, wool and hides. Workshops for making tallow, for all types of smiths work and for cabinet makers and carpenters appeared. For most of the goods produced, the mission was the only source in Alta California.[43]

The production of agricultural staples remained relatively stable from 1803-1821. The pressure for secularization, although increasing, had not yet forced the missionaries into either falsifying annual reports or ignoring agriculture. The fact that agricultural production remained static reflects declining yields and backward technology. The Indian population remained relatively stable, but at the same time the demand from presidios for food

[235]

for the table and for provisions to trade for manufactured items decreased mission food supplies. This, it seems, would indicate a declining dietary standard for the mission residents.

In consistency with trends established in prior years the missionaries emphasized wheat at the expense of corn. In keeping with Spanish preferences, wheat production was always encouraged where ever it could successfully be grown. At Mission San Carlos wheat and corn harvests were both 200 fanegas in 1803. By 1821 720 *fanegas* of wheat were harvested and only 80 of corn.[44] The phenomenon was repeated at San Buenaventura where during the same period wheat increased from 1000 to 4500 *fanegas* while corn decreased from 450 to 366 *fanegas*.[45] San Diego, which had always had problems retaining agricultural self-sufficiency saw a gradual increase in the production of both wheat and corn.[46] With few exceptions the same process is evident at all of the missions.

Severe droughts hit the missions in 1807, 1809, 1817 and 1820.[47] Naturally the southern missions suffered most. In the early days of California such events would have caused extreme suffering and Indian neophytes would have been released to fend for themselves as best they could. The missions of 1810 were much more highly developed institutions than those of 1775. By this time several alternative measures had been developed to insure survival in case of crop failure. The increase in the number of missions decreased the chances that all would simultaneously have a food shortage. The general productivity of missions like San Juan Capistrano and San Gabriel insured that surpluses would be available to aid institutions like San Diego which suffered chronic food shortages. Systems of irrigation also proved to be hedges against drought. Earlier droughts had taught bitter lessons. At San Diego, after the droughts of 1801 and 1803, an extensive system of irrigation works was constructed. This included a dam with an aqueduct which carried water to the mission and fields. The aqueduct was constructed of tiles resting on cobblestones in cement and was approximately one foot deep and two feet wide.[48] The third expedient which could be relied upon in lean years was the storage of surpluses from years of plenty. In 1806 Von Landsgdorff noted that Mission San José had granaries which held 2000 *fanegas* of wheat and a proportionate quantity of maize, barley, peas, beans and other grain. At Mission San Francisco, he observed magazines for storing tallow, soap, and ox hides, in addition to facilities for the storage of corn, peas, and beans. While crop failures were indeed serious, the devastation which they caused was not comparable to that of earlier years.[49]

The productivity of the mission gardens continued although no exact statistics were kept. The usual garden herbs and vegetables which had been common since the early days were still grown. Fruit trees had by this time matured and were producing fruit, although success varied from mission to mission depending on climate. At San Francisco, for example, fruit often failed to ripen properly because of the fog.[50]

The period after 1810 began a time of precipitous rise in the death rate caused, among other things, by an alarming infant mortality. In 1818, out of a total of 64,000 neophytes baptized, some 41,000 died.[51] This total includes baptisms for both adults and children and suggests high mortality for both groups. At San Buenaventura the number of deaths exceeded the total number of Indians resident at the mission for the first time in 1809.[52] The same point was reached at Mission Purísima Concepción in 1808, while it was reached as early as 1790 at San Carlos.[53] In 1809 deaths exceeded the total population at San Juan Bautista and continued thereafter.[54] Surprisingly, because of a rapidly increasing number of baptisms, the total population of the missions declined only gradually throughout the period. The signs of future decline were clear. As soon as the rate of baptisms began to decline, so would neophyte populations and with them the mission as a viable institution.

The reasons for the rapid increase in the death rate appear to be variations on those familiar throughout the New World. The Indian was exposed to various alien European diseases for which he had developed little or no tolerance. The first of these was measles whose devastating effect was felt time and time again by the natives of the Western Hemisphere. Langsdorff noted in 1806 that measles had killed thousands of Indians and he went on to add that almost all pregnant Indian women who contracted measles, miscarried as a result.[55] The gathering of Indians at missions simply magnified any epidemic because of the rapid

[237]

spread of contagious disease among people living in close quarters. A high incidence of inherited venereal disease also took its toll. Several other factors must have aggravated the accelerating death rate. According to William Shaler in 1804, the padres did not seem to know even the rudiments of medicine.[56] Added to this, as mentioned previously, the diet of the mission Indians probably decreased in nutritive value. While the missions still enjoyed an outward appearance of prosperity, the germ of future decline was present.

The mission period in Alta California extending from 1803 to 1821 is unique. In this compressed period of time, the California mission closely approximated the ideal of "the mission as a frontier institution," while in the same two decades those forces which would eventually undermine and destroy the system were gathering. From the outside liberal forces were gaining force in Spain and Mexico and would soon find the mission system incompatible with liberal ideals of equality, liberty and justice. No one could foresee that the California Indian, ill-equipped to compete in western culture would be destroyed by those very ideals.

The Franciscan padres of California unwittingly participated in the destruction of the very system to which they were so devoted. The mission as an institution was a part of the old regime and its life depended on the absolutism and paternalism of the Spanish monarchy. Mercantilist economic restrictions were an integral part of this scheme. The free trade which the missionaries espoused in their dealings with foreigners was a part of the new liberalism given force by the French Revolution. Free trade would ultimately lessen the economic ties with Spain and eventually break those with Mexico.

NOTES

¹ "Memoria que presenta al Rey N.S. el teniente de navío D. Francisco de Paula Tamariz, sobre mejorar el sistema de gobierno de la Alta California," as printed in *Colección De Documentos Historicos*, Tomo II, *Las Missiones de la Alta California* (México, 1914), p. 92.

² An *arroba* was a measure expressed in terms of weight. In Spain and her colonies it was generally accepted as being slightly over twenty-five pounds.

³ "Memoria que presenta al Rey N.S. el teniente de navio D. Francisco Tamariz," p. 100.

⁴ *Ibid.*

⁵ John Polich, "Intrusions on Spain's Pacific Coast 1786-1810" (Unpublished dissertation, University of New Mexico, 1968), p. 42.

⁶ Señán to Father José Viñals, San Buenaventura, November 3, 1808, as trans. by Paul Nathan and ed. by Lesley Byrd Simpson, *The Letters of José Señán*, O.F.M. (San Francisco, 1962), p. 35.

⁷ *Ibid.* The position of syndic derived from the Franciscan vow of poverty which prevented members of the order from handling financial transactions. The syndic was a layman who handled purchases of mission supplies.

⁸ Señán to Fray José Guilez, San Buenaventura, November 6, 1810. *Ibid.*, p. 49.

⁹ This was the presidial supply officer elected by his comrades. The presidial accounts were his responsibility.

¹⁰ Señán to the Marquis de Branciforte, May 14, 1796, *The Letters of Señán*, p. 4. The Procurator resided in Mexico City and received drafts on the military and requests for provisions from the missions. This office was usually held by a missionary who had seen some service in the Alta California Missions.

¹¹ *Ibid.*, p. 5.

¹² Fray Martín Landaeta to Fray Tomás de la Peña, July 20, 1805, as printed in *Biblioteca Historica Mexicana de Obras Ineditas*, Vol. 22, *Noticias Acerca del Puerto de San Francisco* (Mexico, 1949), p. 53. The *Comisario* was a government official in residence at Tepic or San Blas who was responsible for overseeing all shipments to California.

¹³ Polich, "Intrusions on Spain's Pacific Coast," p. 154.

¹⁴ Fray Martín Landaeta to Fray Tomás de la Peña, August 30, 1803, *Noticias Acerca del Puerto de San Francisco*, p. 49.

¹⁵ William Shaler, *Journal of a Voyage Between China and the Northwest Coast of America Made in 1804 by William Shaler* (Claremont, Calif., 1935), p. 59.

¹⁶ Roy F. Nichols, *Advance Agents of American Destiny* (Philadelphia, 1956), p. 80.

¹⁷ The Nootka Convention of 1790 prohibited foreign vessels from hunting or trading along any part of the California coast occupied by Spain. For a detailed study of the Nootka Controversy see Warren L. Cook, *Flood Tide of Empire: Spain and the Pacific Northwest. 1543-1819* (New Haven, Conn., 1973).

¹⁸ Adele Ogden, *The California Sea Otter Trade, 1784-1848* (Berkeley, 1941), p. 67. Captain George Washington Eayrs commanded the *Mercury* which was owned partly by Benjamin Lamb of Boston.

¹⁹ Zephyrin Engelhardt, *Mission San Diego* (San Francisco, 1920), p. 187.

²⁰ Ogden, *The California Sea Otter Trade*, p. 43.

²¹ August Mahr, *The Visit of the Rurik to San Francisco in 1816* (Palo Alto, Calif., 1932), p. 35. This ship had left Unalaska on September 14 for California in quest of fresh supplies with which to continue her explorations.

²² Hubert H. Bancroft, *Bancroft's Works*, Vol. XIX, *History of California* (San Francisco, 1886), p. 202.

²³ Señán to Governor Pablo Vicente de Solá, San Buenaventura, January 4, 1819, *The Letters of Señán*, p. 35.

[24] Zephyrin Engelhardt, *Mission San Juan Bautista* (Santa Barbara, 1931), p. 27.

[25] Bancroft, *Works*, XIX, 199.

[26] *Ibid.*, p. 259.

[27] Zephyrin Engelhardt, *Mission San Carlos Borromeo* (Santa Barbara, 1934), p. 180.

[28] Señán to Governor Solá, San Buenaventura, January 28, 1817, *The Letters of Señán*, p. 101.

[29] Zepyhrin Engelhardt, *San Buenaventura, The Mission by the Sea* (Santa Barbara, 1930), p. 54.

[30] *Ibid.*

[31] Zephyrin Engelhardt, *San Luis Rey Mission* (San Francisco, 1921), p. 48.

[32] Zephyrin Engelhardt, *Mission La Concepción Purísima* (Santa Barbara, 1932), p. 46.

[33] Zephyrin Engelhardt, *The Franciscans in California* (Harbor Springs, Mich., 1897), p. 154.

[34] "Parecer formado por el Padre Domingo Rivas a petición de D. Joaquín Cortina, en repulsa del informe dado S.M. sobre mejoras de la Neuva California," as printed in *Colección De Documentos Historicos*, Tomo II, *Las Misiones de la Alta California*, p. 176. The critic was Don Francisco de Paula Tamariz, who presented a memorial to the King in 1814. He was a naval lieutenant out of San Blas who at the time of his memorial had visited California in 1805 and 1807. Domingo Rivas was a secular priest who had visited California and approved of the missions.

[35] Irving McKee, "The Beginnings of California Winegrowing," *Quarterly of the Historical Society of Southern California*, 29 (1947), 60-62.

[36] "Memoria que presenta al Rey N.S. el teniente de navío D. Francisco Tamariz," *Documentos Historicos*, p. 100.

[37] Bancroft, *Works*, XIX, 178-179.

[38] Patricia M. Bauer, "The Beginnings of Tanning in California," *California Historical Society*, 23 (1954), 61. The source of tanning in California was the Tanbark Oak.

[39] G. H. Von Langsdorff, *Voyages and Travels in Various Parts of the World During the Years, 1803, 1804, 1805, 1806, and 1807* (London, 1814), Part II, 160-169.

[40] Von Landsdorff, *Voyages*, p. 159.

[41] Señán to Father Pedro Martínez, San Buenaventura, December 3, 1812, *The Letters of Señán*, p. 70.

[42] Señán to Father Guilez, San Buenaventura, April 15, 1810, *The Letters of Señán*, p. 70.

[43] Von Langsdorff, *Voyages*, pp. 160-161.

[44] Engelhardt, *Mission San Carlos*, p. 245.

[45] Engelhardt, *Mission San Buenaventura*, pp. 112-113.

[46] Engelhardt, *Mission San Diego*, p. 294.

[47] Bancroft, *Works*, XIX, 89. Also see Señán to Fray Baldomero Lopéz, San Buenaventura, April 21, 1820, *Letters of Señán*, p. 121.

[48] Engelhardt, *Mission San Diego*, p. 154.

[49] Von Langsdorff, *Voyages*, pp. 161, 193.

[50] *Ibid.*

[51] Bancroft, *Works*, XIX, 250.

[52] Engelhardt, *San Buenaventura*, p. 110.

[53] Engelhardt, *Mission San Carlos*, p. 243.

[54] Engelhardt, *Mission San Juan Bautista*, p. 125.

[55] Von Langsdorff, *Voyages*, p. 210.

[56] Shaler, *Journal of a Voyage*, pp. 57-59.

SAN ANTONIO'S OLD FRANCISCAN MISSIONS:
MATERIAL DECLINE AND SECULAR AVARICE IN THE TRANSITION FROM HISPANIC TO MEXICAN CONTROL

In the twilight years of the eighteenth century, Spanish authorities of church and state resolved that the original Franciscan missions of Texas had achieved the goal of their early foundation, namely conversion of indigenous cultures to an Hispano-European lifestyle. Cognizant that the mission as a frontier agency had gained souls for the Catholic faith and citizens for the empire, Hispanic officials initiated secularization of the Texas establishments with the longest tenure, beginning with the missions along the upper San Antonio River.[1] Less than a generation later, in the

* A version of this paper was presented at a joint session of The Texas Catholic Historical Society and The Texas State Historical Association in 1979. The author gratefully acknowledges the generous support provided by the UTSA Research Center for the Arts and Humanities, The San Antonio Project, an educational experiment funded by The National Endowment for the Humanities, and The Bexar County Historical Commission.

[1] Carlos E. Castañeda, *Our Catholic Heritage in Texas, 1519-1936* (7 vols.; Austin: Von Boeckmann-Jones Company, 1936-1958), V, 40. The history of the missions along the San Antonio River originated in 1718 when friars of the Apostolic College of Santa Cruz de Querétaro founded San Antonio de Valero with the assistance of soldiers who subsequently established Presidio San Antonio de Béxar in the immediate vicinity. Next, in 1731, the fledgling frontier community received vital reinforcement with the arrival of settlers from the Canary Islands (who promptly inaugurated a civil town and government) and the transfer of three Queretaran missions from the pine forests of east Texas to the Río San Antonio. Depending on circumstances and personalities, throughout the entire colonial period the proximity of church and state institutions in a riparian environment contributed to an atmosphere of cooperation and conflict. The benchmark year of 1772 was a pivotal juncture in church-state relations in the borderlands. First, the friars of Querétaro voluntarily relinquished administration of their Texas missions to Franciscans of the College of Zacatecas. Secondly, in response to an invitation from the viceregal government, the Querétaro friars assumed responsibility of former Jesuit missions in Sinaloa, Sonora, and Arizona. Thirdly, in the wake of the Marqués de Rubí's comprehensive inspection of military fortifications in the north, Hispanic Bourbon reformers designated San Antonio de Béxar as the provincial capital of Texas. The designation simultaneously enhanced the geopolitical importance of the region and accelerated human demands upon available resources, but the presence of the provincial governor was a moderating influence that safeguarded the missions. Consult Benedict Leutenegger [trans.] Marion A. Habig and Barnabas Diekemper [eds.], "Memorial of Father Benito Fernández Concerning the Canary Islanders, 1741," *Southwestern Historical Quarterly*, 82 [January 1979], 265-296; Castañeda, *Our Catholic Heritage*, IV, 266-267; Félix D. Almaráz, Jr., *Crossroad of Empire: The Church and State in the Río Grande Frontier of Coahuila and Texas, 1700-1821* [San Antonio:

transition from Spanish dominion to Mexican rule in the nineteenth century, the Franciscan institutions, woefully in a condition of material neglect, engendered widespread secular avarice as numerous applicants with political contact in municipal government energetically competed to obtain land grants among the former mission temporalities.

Secularization in Texas, a process by which the missions changed status from transitory ecclesiastical centers to permanent civil pueblos and parishes, commenced in April 1793, with the inventory and distribution of temporal properties to the native Christians of San Antonio de Valero.[2] The process continued in the summer of 1794 with secularization of the adjacent riverside missions: San Francisco de la Espada (July 11), San Juan Capistrano (July 14), San José y San Miguel de Aguayo (July 16), and Nuestra Señora de la Purísima Concepción de Acuña (July 31).[3]

After the implementation of the secularization decree, missionaries of the Aposotlic College of Nuestra Señora de Guadalupe de Zacatecas, who since 1772 had administered all Texas missions, willingly remained in San Antonio at the four riverfront pueblos to instruct the new parishioners in their civil responsibilities "to become citizens and to exercise the right of suffrage."[4] In effect, the uninterrupted work of the Franciscan friars signified only partial secularization of the missions. In the final years of Spanish rule, as the Franciscans attended the spiritual needs of the faithful, occasionally, owing to shortages of missionary personnel, one friar assumed the heavy burden of caring for all four missions, such as in 1813 during the ministry of Father Bernardino Vallejo of San José. Friar Vallejo's successors observed the custom as late as the inauguration of Mexican independence.[5] In 1823, Mexico's national government issued a mandate requiring

University of Texas at San Antonio Center for Archaeilogical Research, 1979], p. 29; Walter Prescott Webb, H. Bailey Carroll, and Eldon S. Branda [eds.], *The Handbook of Texas* [3 vols.; Austin: Texas State Historical Association, 1952-1976],II, 542.

[2] Walter Flavius M'Caleb, "Some Obscure Points in the Mission Period of Texas History," *Southwestern Historical Quarterly*, 1 (January 1898), 227; Edwin P. Arneson, "The Early Art of Terrestrial Measurement and its Practice in Texas," *Southwestern Historical Quarterly*, 29 (October 1925), 85.

[3] Castañeda, *Our Catholic Heritage*, V, 40-64.

Exempted from the 1794 secularization decree were three missions near the Gulf coast — Nuestra Señora del Espíritu Santo, Nuestra Señora del Rosario, and Nuestra Señora del Refugio (Paul H. Walters, "Secularization of the La Bahía Missions," *Southwestern Historical Quarterly*, 54 [January 1951], 387).

[4] Castañeda, *Our Catholic Heritage*, V, 115-116.

[5] Marion A. Habig, *The Alamo Chain of Missions: A History* of San Antonio's five Old Missions (Chicago: Franciscan Herald Press, 1968), pp. 220-221. In the last quarter of the 18th and the beginning of the 19th century, authorities of church and state introduced changes that affected the province of Texas. In the political-military realm, Bourbon reformers experimented with a defensive measure called

Early San Antonio Missions and Irrigation System

the Commandancy General of the Interior Provinces. Originally instituted in 1776 to control native aggression and foreign encroachment in the northern borderlands, the Commandancy General in the initial phase encompassed the territory from Texas to the Californias. In the second phase, the harsh realities of maintaining frontier security convinced Spanish officials to modify the administrative structure to a more manageable level, with the Texas gubernatorial office operating as a subordinate unit of the Commandancy General.

Meanwhile, in ecclesiastical affairs, in 1777 the Vatican, in consort with the Spanish monarchy, authorized the creation of the Diocese of Monterrey in New Spain, comprising the provinces of Nuevo León, Nuevo Santander, Coahuila, and Texas. After assuming office as the fourth bishop of Monterrey, Marín de Porras in 1805 became the first episcopal leader to inspect the principal towns in Texas in anticipation of assigning diocesan priests to parish chruches. Notwithstanding Bishop Marín de Porras' inspection and intention, as late as 1809 he lamented being unable to staff all parishes. The significance of these developments is that in spite of partial secularization, Texas, with an aggregate population of 6,400 (most of whom resided in San Antonio), remained under the spiritual care of a few itinerant Franciscan missionaries. Consult Marc Simmons, *Spanish Government in New Mexico* [Albuquerque: University of New Mexico Press, 1968], pp. 25-32; Félix D. Almaráz, Jr., *Tragic Cavalier: Governor Manuel Salcedo of Texas, 1808-1813* [Austin: University of Texas Press, 1971], p. 14; José Bravo Ugarte, *Diócesis y Obispos de la Iglesia Mexicana (1519-1965)* [Mexico: Editorial Jus, 1965], p. 65; Nettie Lee Benson, ''Bishop Marín de Porras and Texas,'' *Southwestern Historical Quarterly*, 51 [July 1947], 37; Carlos E. Castañ[rteda ans.], ''Statistical Report on Texas by Juan N. Almonte,'' *Southwestern Historical Quarterly*, 28 [January 1925], 186.

"full and complete secularization." The last friar to work in Texas, José Antonio Díaz de León, in compliance with the decree, transferred spiritual and administrative supervision of the former missions to the pastor of San Fernando Church. In February 1824, the missions of San Antonio officially ended.[6]

[6] Habig, *Alamo Chain of Missions*, pp. 220-221.

When Mexico's federal constitution downgraded the political status of Texas to a department, San Antonio's former missions, devoid of spiritual guidance and temporal conservation, declined materially due to the avarice of townspeople and the zeal of the municipal council to fulfill a national objective. Although in the last two decades of Spanish rule settlers in Béxar sporadically petitioned the city government for parcels of mission properties,[7] the heaviest impact of widespread land distribution occured at the advent of Mexican nationhood.

On the eve of Mexican independence, the presidio, the town council (*ayuntamiento*), and the missions symbolized loyal bastions of the colonial heritage. Illustrative of the cooperation between church and state in the throes of revolutionary upheaval was the governorship of Antonio Martínez. In the summer of 1819, writing to Commandant General Joaquín de Arredondo, the governor politely inquired about the delicate matter of the semi-secularized missions;

> Since the missions were secularized at an earlier date I have searched these archives for the document authorizing this measure in order to inform myself of the conditions on which it was based, but not having found anything which has given me the least explanation of the matter it is necessary to ask you please to tell me whether the conservation and care of the property of said missions, including the sacred vessels and other ornaments in their churches, is left solely to their respective ministers and [college] president or whether the governor of the province shall intervene so that in such cases I may try to give due recognition to the problem (with the proper respect) and overcome whatever objection their aforesaid ministers may raise; also, please tell me if the latter can be absent from their offices and retire to their convent or college by consulting only with their deputies and guardians instead of the government and unless others come to relieve them of the discharge of their services; if I am cognizant of these matters, I can refrain from entering into discussions on the special status of these ministers.[8]

In a candid letter to Viceroy Juan Ruiz de Apodaca, the Texas executive described conditions at the missions and alluded to their material assets that undoubtedly attracted the attention of town residents:

> Before the [Hidalgo] revolution this province had nine missions and only

[7] For example, see Petition for Land by Manuel Sarcho, 1806; Grant of Land and Granary of Mission Concepción to José Antonio Huízar, 1806; Petition for Land by Ygnacio Calvillo, 1809; Petition for Land by Subdeacon Juan Manuel Zambrano, 1809; Grant of Land and House to José Antonio Huízar, 1815; Grant of Land at Mission San José to José Julián Reyes, 1818; Mission Records 29-37, 62-70, and 71-74, Archives of the County Clerk, Bexar County Courthouse, San Antonio, Texas. [Mission records hereinafter referred to as MR.]

[8] Antonio Martínez to Joaquín de Arredondo, June 6, 1819, Letter No. 505, in Virginia H. Taylor (trans. and ed.), *The Letters of Antonio Martínez: Last Spanish Governor of Texas, 1817-1822* (Austin: Texas State Library, 1957), pp. 234-235.

four are left, one in the jurisdiction of the Presidio of La Bahía and three in this capital, but they cannot be considered as such since each one has only from eight to ten inhabitants, most of whom are too old and poor to provide for their own maintenance (not even so little as a gun for defense). . . .

Among said abandoned missions Nuestra Señora de la Concepción is the principal one because of the excellence of its land and its extensive irrigation system, also because it has the advantage of being near this capital; it also protects and gives aid to the others, San José, La Espada, and San Juan Capistrano, all forming a chain. Although I have made the greatest effort to have them occupied again, I have not been successful because the few able citizens in this capital are also in a miserable condition. . . .[9]

When Father Refugio de la Garza assumed charge of the parish of San Fernando just prior to Mexican independence, Governor Martínez deplored the ruinous appearance of the parochial church. Casting covetous glances at Mission San José as a source of relief, the governor carefully observed the sensitive issue of protocol.

Therefore, [Martínez informed the viceroy] I made a formal petition to the present Minister of the Mission of San José [Fr. Miguel Muro], asking him to tell me whether that Mission had any ornaments, sacred vessels, and other useful items that did not belong to it, such as those which were delivered there from the Mission of Nuestra Señora de la Concepción when it was abandoned . . . and in his reply, said Royal Minister tells me that in order to grant my petition, which seems just, he must apply to the prelates of the College [Zacatecas] on which he depends; for this reason, and because things of this nature occur frequently, . . . and also being perplexed about the proper procedure to follow, I must ask Your Excellency to dispel this uncertainty of mine; although I know there is a difference between the military and political state and the ecclesiastical, I also know that the ornaments with which the missions are adorned belong to the King, Our Lord, and I consider myself a faithful administrator of his royal interests in this province in which he has been pleased to place me.[10]

Manifesting secular optimism about the region and its natural resources, the ayuntamiento of San Antonio evaluated the mission properties in a detailed memorandum to the Provincial Deputation that advised Commandant General Arredondo. Commenting on each mission separately, Juan Antonio Padilla, author of the report, described both deficiences and attributes. In order of geographic descent away from San Antonio, he began with Concepción.

---

[9] Martínez to Viceroy Juan Ruiz de Apodaca, June 7, 1819, Letter No. 103, in *Letters from Gov. Antonio Martínez to the Viceroy Juan Ruiz de Apodaca*, trans. by Virginia H. Taylor and ed. by Félix D. Almaráz, Jr. (San Antonio: The University of Texas at San Antonio Research Center for the Arts and Humanities, 1983), p. 33.

[10] Martínez to Apodaca, February 16, 1820, Letter No. 137, in *Ibid.*, 41.

That of Concepción [he wrote], distant one league from Bexar, has a church of hewn stone carefully constructed with arches, although it is [in] bad condition because of damage by time. It has deteriorated considerably because of the absence of priests and natives. The buildings of the convent and other offices are in the worst condition. Of other buildings, there remain only heaps of rubbish. This mission has a large irrigating ditch, although not in use now. With it they irrigated a considerable piece of land from which they gathered crops of all kinds. For three years some citizens of Bexar have been planting these *labores* [farm lands], but without irrigation since their poverty will not permit the expense of rebuilding the dam and cleaning the ditch. But, because that land is so rich, they have not lost their labor.[11]

Concerning San José, Padilla indirectly criticized the resident friar for not coordinating the mission's human and natural assets toward the goal of common improvement.

> The mission of San José . . . has a chapel which is well built of hewn stone although it is damaged by time through lack of repair. It owns rich ornaments, sacred vases, and much silver set with jewels and ornaments. All these show its former splendor and riches. The convent has a portion which is threatened with ruin. As for the rest [of the structures], some have fallen down and others are poorly repaired by certain *vecinos agregados* [squatters]. There are also some casts [sic] among descendants of the Indians who formerly inhabited it. It has a large irrigating ditch and a considerable quantity of farming land which is cultivated with great success by these citizens. In this mission there is no lack of priests, for it has usually been the residence of the president of all the missions.[12]

Less critical of San Juan Capistrano, probably because of the obvious contrast to San José, Señor Padilla limited his commentary to a terse record of activities.

> Many *vecinos agregados* have lived in it for many years. The church is unfinished, although it has a chapel in which mass is said. Its buildings are almost demolished, and the best of them are in poor repair. It has an irrigating ditch and farm land of which the settlers avail themselves.[13]

About Mission San Francisco de la Espada, Padilla was more concise yet cautiously optimistic.

> At an equal distance [of a league from San Juan] is the mission of Sn. Francisco de la Espada, settled by a small number of persons, as in the former cases. Its buildings are in a similar state. Although it is eleven years since the death of Fr. Pedro Noreño, the last priest it had, the water for irrigation is still abundant and the farm land conciderable [sic] in quantity and rich in quality.[14]

Summarizing the material and social environment of the mission communities, Padilla recommended a resettlement program that incorporated distribution of land, riparian rights, and other concessions.

> These four missions are in a state of decadence [sic] for lack of repair of the buildings. Each of them, at small cost, would support a settlement of Spaniards if the lands, water, and ruined buildings were divided among those who

---

[11] Mattie Austin Hatcher (trans.), "Texas in 1820 [by Juan Antonio Padilla]," *Southwestern Historical Quarterly*, 23 (July 1919), 59.

[12] *Ibid.*, 59-60.

[13] *Ibid.*, 60.

[14] *Ibid.*

would voluntarily present themselves as the first settlers. None of them have any Indian settlers, the principal objective of their establishment. If there are any [native converts], they are but few in number and changed into casts [sic] by mixture with the settlers of Bexar. Those who are there [at the missions] have lived in the character of *arrimados* so that his Majesty has had to pay the stipends of the priests without securing the execution of his royal will which is the conversion of the Indians.[15]

[15] *Ibid.*

In the euphoria of Mexican independence, the union of church and state continued during Agustín Iturbide's short-lived empire, but not with the strict observance of propriety as in the Spanish period. Following the collapse of Mexico's first imperial rule in 1823, the national government adopted a federalist experiment that resulted in major adjustments in the borderlands. As a prelude of imminent modification of the administrative structure for Texas, the federalists eliminated the governor's office and replaced it with an innovative *jefe político*. Moreover, in creating the dual state of Coahuila y Texas, they demoted the latter's status to a Department of Béxar, with leadership shared by the jefe político and the town council. Subsequently, in October 1823, the Mexican government issued a mandate requiring total secularization of the Texas missions. The municipal ayuntamiento of San Antonio therefore assumed the dominant role in the distribution of land and other tangible assets of the Franciscan missions.[16]

Reserving only the church buildings as the patrimony of the diocesan bishop, the main thrust of the council's disposal of mission properties occurred in the autumn and winter of 1823, continuing into 1824. Among the first applicants was Francisco Herrera who, acknowledging the proximity of La Purísima Concepción, changed his petition in favor of land and water rights near Mission San José. Jefe Político José Antonio Saucedo specified the conditions of Herrera's grant.

> . . . in recognition of the services rendered by the petitioner Francisco Herrera, . . . I hereby grant in the name of the Mexican Nation one dula of water in the conduit of the Mission San José with its corresponding land, . . . for his own advantages, and that of his children, or descendants with the tax of five pesos to be paid annually for the said dula granted for the period of four years in accordance with the decree of the . . . [national] Deputation [Congress], after which time he may enjoy it free of all encumbrance, . . . [17]

While Herrera deliberated the location of his desired grant, other applicants filed petitions with the city council for the lands of abandoned Mission Concepción. Typical of the industrious applicants was Juan Montes who requested irrigated farmland and two *dulas* of water. The ayuntamiento, reviewing Montes' petition, recommended to Jefe Político Saucedo the award of only one dula and a plot of land as "an equitable distribution." Saucedo considered the merits of the case, and, apparently impressed with Montes' conduct and dedication to farming, decided in favor of the peti-

[16] Félix D. Almaráz, Jr., "Aspects of Mexican Texas: A Focal Point in Southwest History," *Red River Valley Historical Review*, 2 (Fall 1975), p. 370; Walters, "Secularization of the La Bahía Missions," *SHQ*, 54: 291.

[17] Francisco de Herrera, Petition for Land and Water, October 24, 1823; Decree of José Antonio Saucedo and the Ayuntamiento of San Fernando de Béxar, December 4, 1823 (quotation); MR 29-37.

tioner. On December 6, 1823, the jefe político led a delegation of council members, public witnesses, grantees of land, and interested spectators to Mission Concepción to perform the traditional act of possession. Regarding the grant of Juan Montes, Saucedo defined the boundaries, affirming that he

> . . . measured two *suertes* [plots of land], each of 100 varas frontage and 800 varas depth, that are bound on the east by the Camino of San Juan; on the west by the old Camino of Concepción; on the south by lands granted to Don Francisco Rivas; and on the north by lands granted to Don Erasmo Seguín . . . .

The formal *acto de posesión* was replete with high drama for the jefe político and the recipient. Saucedo documented the event in the following words:

> Of these suertes and their corresponding water, I placed the petitioner, Don Juan Montes, in real and physical possession, declaring in a loud and distinctly audible voice: 'In the name of the Mexican Nation and by virtue of the order of the High Executive Power which I find in my possession concerning the distribution of the Mission lands, I place you in possession of this *labor* of land for yourself, your children, heirs, and successors.'

Montes discharged the visible responsibilities of a grantee by shouting, pulling weeds, casting stones, placing boundary markers, and performing "all the other customary ceremonies." The recipient gave assurances that he understood the terms of the grant and the obligation to pay municipal fees for water.[18]

In the course of processing applications, Jefe Político Saucedo received an unusual request from a leading citizen, Juan Martín de Beramendi. Alluding to services rendered to the cause of Mexican independence in Texas, Beramendi reminded the city givernment that he "provided in money, implements and cattle an amount of 1,469 pesos reales for the troops of your garrison." As evidence of the claim he offered to submit "receipts and tickets for such loans made from the commissioners and troop leaders."

---

[18] Juan Montes, Petition for Land and Water, October 26, 1823; Ayuntamiento to Saucedo, November 10, 1823; Decree of Saucedo, December 4, 1823; Saucedo, Ylario de la Garza, and Victoriano Zepeda, December 6, 1823 (quotations); MR 29-37.

Other individuals who received land around Mission Concepción in the initial post-independence period included José Farías (1 suerte and 1 dula), Baltazar Calvo (1 suerte and 1 dula), Manuel Yturri Castillo (3 suertes of wooded land and 3 dulas), and Tiburcio Ruiz (2 suertes and 2 dulas) nd Grant to José Farías from the Mexican Government, 1823; Grant of Land and Water to Baltazar Calvo, 1823; Grant of Land and Water to Manuel Yturri Castillo, 1823; MR 29-37; and Donation of Land and Water to Tiburcio Ruiz, 1823; MR-76-85].

For an analysis of the *dula* and its relationship to frontier society, see Thomas F. Glick, *The Old World Background of the Irrigation System of San Antonio, Texas* (El Paso: Texas Western Press, 1972).

Notwithstanding noble gestures of patriotism, when royalist forces reconquered Texas in 1813, Commandant General Arredondo confiscated Beramendi's property, including sizable herds of cattle and mules, and flocks of goats. For losses suffered in the struggle for Mexican independence, Beramendi asked for compensatory ranch land in the Río Guadalupe watershed near San Marcos. In addition, he requested six contiguous farm lots with irrigation rights at Mission Concepción and two houses for himself and his workers. Failing to receive satisfaction on his original petition, Beramendi filed a second application, confining the request only to property at Concepción. He displayed remarkable perception concerning the mission's temporalities.

> I have heard [Beramendi acknowledged] that the buildings of the four missions are going to be distributed among the resident, . . . There are some difficulties as to this distribution because the convents seem to have been built for only one family; therefore, they cannot be divided among several individuals. These convents will most probably collapse soon, leaving only ruins.

Hence, for use by his family, Beramendi asked Jefe Político Saucedo that he "be granted the monasterial buildings of Mission Concepción along with all its furniture." Furthermore, he applied for six suertes of land with appropriate dulas of water. In the event the number of petitions exceeded the limits of distributive property available at Concepción, Beramendi of his own accord agreed to transfer the scope of his request to Mission San José. Aware of the extent of the application, and plausibly to motivate the city council into unprecedented agility, Beramendi offered "as a sign of gratitude" to pay 1,200 pesos in bills and coins from his account in the newly chartered National Bank of Texas.[19]

Apparently a rift developed between the jefe político and the city council over the matter of Beramendi's petitions. After carefully examining the complete file, the ayuntamiento (Manuel Yturri Castillo, José Antonio de la Garza, José María Cárdenas, Vicente Fortari, Gaspar Flores, and Ygnacio Villaseñor) unanimously approved three dulas of water and analogous land at San José. In view of the monetary proposal, the council also awarded to Beramendi the monasteries, but it restricted the number of suertes of land to five, cautioning that "they will not be discounted from the sum he offers."

---

[19] Juan Martín de Beramendi to Señor Gefe Político, February 5, 1822 (quotation); Beramendi to Gefe Político, November 1, 1823; MR 76-85. [Hereinafter, due to the frequency of the citation to Señor Gefe Político, the abbreviation SGP is used.]

For details of early banking operations in Mexican Texas, see Carlos E. Castañeda, "The First Chartered Bank West of the Mississippi: Banco Nacional de Texas," *Bulletin of Business Historical Society [Business History Review]*, 25 (December 1951), 242-256.

The ayuntamiento then endeavored to terminate the issue with a curt pronouncement to the effect it had nothing more to say on the matter.[20] Saucedo reminded the council that the land cession was independent of Beramendi's offer to pay 1,200 pesos for the mission buildings, and that it was their responsibility to decide whether they would approve the grant. In turn, the council replied that the jefe político had contradicted himself, first in considering Beramendi's generous offer "as a gift to this city," and then by attempting to exempt him from paying for the land. Assuredly the council irritated Saucedo's sense of civic pride when it returned the problem to him with the recommendation that the "only solution . . . is to grant the monasteries requested but no payment for them accepted."[21] Obviously piqued by the ayuntamiento's action, Saucedo dropped the matter of the buildings and concentrated only on land distribution, reducing the size of Beramendi's grant at San José to four suertes of land adjacent to the San Antonio River with a corresponding number of dulas of water for irrigation.

> We went to the land I granted to Juan Martín de Beramendi [reported Saucedo]. I measured four suertes of land with 150 varas in frontage. It is bound on the west by the old San Juan Road, on the north by lands of the citizen José María Escalera, on the south by lands that are to be distributed, and on the east by the San Antonio River.[22]

The distribution of land at San José presented an interesting panorama of contrasts, ranging from applications submitted by disadvantaged widows, orphaned adolescents, and veteran militia officers in Béxar to unpretentious requests by area residents at the mission proper. The inhabitants of San José, some of whom traced their lineage to early settlers, competed with townspeople for the patrimony they considered rightfully their own. Miguel Menchaca, for instance, assured Jefe Político Saucedo that farming was the only occupation by which he supported his family. Accordingly, he asked for one suerte of land of sufficient capacity to cultivate a fanega of corn (approximately 8.8 acres), water rights, and a house within the mission compound. The town council approved the grant, after which Saucedo placed Menchaca in possession of

> . . . a suerte of land of 100 varas on each side; . . . bound on the East by the [San Antonio] on the North by land of José María Escalera; on the West by the Acequia Madre and on the South by the lands to be granted.[23]

[20] Manuel Yturri Castillo [Hereinafter MYC.]et al. to SGP, November 10, 1823; MR 76-85.

[21] Saucedo to the Ayuntamiento of San Antonio, December 1, 1823; MYC et al. to SGP, December 1, 1823 (quotation); MR 76-85.

[22] Decree of José Antonio Saucedo, december 4, 1823; Saucedo, Land Grant to Beramendi, December 6, 1823 (quotation); MR 76-85.

[23] Miguel Menchaca to SGP, November 8, 1823; Vicente Gortari et al. to SGP, December 1, 1823; Saucedo et al., Grant of Land and Water to Menchaca, December 6, 1823; MR 71-75.

Another resident, Eustaguio Sierra, alleged he had lived at Mission San José for fifteen years and occupied "a little house" that he constructed at his own expense. Upon learning that the mission lands were to be distributed, Sierra humbly implored the jefe político to award to him formal possession of the house he had built, as well as an arable suerte upon which "to grow half a fanega of corn, with one dula of water." In agreement with the city council, Saucedo donated to Sierra the land he requested, with a half dula of water, at the main gate of Mission San José.[24]

Felipe Casillas, cognizant of the government decree that mandated the granting of secularized mission estates with priority to area residents, applied for a modest suerte of farmland. The grant he received measured 100 varas of frontage, with riparian privileges from two acequias which bordered his land.[25] Antonio García, claiming the house his family occupied as a gift from Father Bernardino Vallejo, entreated Jefe Político Saucedo to regularize the property and "the tract of land adjoining it." The city council recommended approval since the applicant was "a native of Mission San José." Saucedo assigned to García a plot of land described as a half-suerte, measuring 300 varas in frontage and 300 varas in depth. García's grant extended north and east to the property of Antonio Huízar, on the south to the central acequia, and on the west to unoccupied woodlands.[26]

Along similar vein, José María Ruiz informed the jefe político that he descended from "the first Spanish settlers" of the mission. To render the fields productive, Ruiz declared it was common knowledge that he had "cleared the lands of brush." He beseeched Saucedo to give to him the same suerte that he currently cultivated with concomitant irrigation rights. Concerning the dwelling in which Ruiz' family resided, the applicant asked for solemn retention that could be satisfied either with payment or "in any manner" that Saucedo deemed appropriate. Evidently the jefe político approved the request for the house, because he apportioned one half-suerte, with a frontage of 50 varas, near a familiar landmark at the mission called *Rincón del Burro*. Then Saucedo reserved another half-suerte for Ruiz, with a frontage of 250 varas and a depth of 450 varas. Although dimensions varied, the limits of both properties ended at the acequia on the west.[27]

[24] Eustaquio Sierra to SGP, November 14, 1823; Saucedo to the Ayuntamiento, December 1, 1823; Grant of Land and Water to Sierra, December 6, 1823; MR 86-96.

[25] Felipe Casillas to SGP, December 1, 1823; MYC to SGP, December 1, 1823; Decree of Saucedo, December 4, 1823; Donation of Land and Water to Casillas, December 6, 1823; MR 76-85.

[26] Antonio García to SGP, November 15, 1823; MYC to [SGP], December 1, 1823; Decree of Saucedo, December 4, 1823; Donation of Land and Water to Garcí, December 6, 1823; MR 76-85.

[27] José María Ruiz to SGP, December 1, 1823; MYC to [SGP], December 1, 1823; Donation of Land and Water to Ruiz, December 6, 1823; MR 76-85.

Another descendant of "original settlers" at the mission, José Padilla de Luna, maintained that upon the death of his parents he inherited a *solar* known as *El Jardín* adjacent to a strip of farmland. Within the mission wall he occupied a house with a kitchen that he believed was his legal possession. In fact, convinced of the legality of the tenancy, Padilla had conveyed the house to a fellow resident, Eustaquio Sierra, and now he appealed to the jefe político to validate the transaction by acknowledging him as prior owner. Saucedo referred the matter to the city council for guidance. In turn, the ayuntamiento decided to concede the request "without prejudice to a third party." The land Padilla received was a half-suerte that measured 100 varas square.[28]

As an indication of the equality of Mexican law, based on Hispanic jurisprudence, María de Jesús Treviño, in the absence of her husband, José Eusebio Anzures, appeared before Jefe Político Saucedo and declared that they were residents of Mission San José. Moreover, she reminded Saucedo that her husband as militiaman always had answered the government's call to arms. In compensation for faithful service, Doña María de Jesús petitioned the jefe for a dula of water and proportional land at Mission San José, preferably the house in which they lived. The city council, acknowledging the merits of the solicitation, advised Saucedo land was unavailable in the immediate area. As an alternative it recommended a comparable grant of a half-dula located elsewhere in the vicinity. On December 6, 1823, in behalf of her absent husband, Doña María acquired legal possession of a half-suerte near the acequia, measuring 170 varas of frontage and 300 varas of depth. In strict observance of the law, Doña María executed all rituals "necessary to make her a lawful owner."[29]

In notable contrast to mission residents at San José, some citizens of San Antonio de Béxar filed ambitious petitions with the ayuntamiento. For instance, José de la Garza requested two suertes of arable land, a site within the mission wall to construct a house and to cultivate a vegetable garden, four *sitios* (approximately 17,696 acres) to establish a cattle ranch, and a house pasture in the upper section of the old mission called *El Pasto*. In view of numerous appeals submitted for review, the town council advised Saucedo to limit De La Garza's award to two suertes of farmland, with a half-day of irrigation privileges, and two sitios to raise beef cattle. Without

[28] José Padilla de Luna to SGP, December 3, 1823; Saucedo to Yltre. Ayuntamiento, December 3, 1823; José Antonio de la Garza *et al.* to SGP, December 4, 1823; Grant of Land and Water to Padilla de Luna, December 6, 1823; MR 86-93.

[29] María de Jesús Treviño to SGP, December 22, 1823; Vicente Gortari *et al.* to SGP, January 22, 1824; Grant of Land to José Eusebio Anzures, December 6, 1823; MR 86-93.

reference to pastoral enterprise, Saucedo placed De la Garza in actual possession of only a half-suerte of 50 square varas.[30]

Doña María de la Trinidad, a widow with three sons and two daughters, applied for a land grant at Mission San José. She informed Jefe Político Saucedo that when Indian agressors killed her husband, José Adanto Ximénez, she had no visible means of support other than her children. The eldest son, she said, was capable of farming, with assistance of his two brothers, a yoke of oxen, and a few implements. Hence, Doña María requested a dula of water with sufficient land for her sons to cultivate a fanega of corn (8.8 acres) and the house next to the residence of the mission alcalde. The council recommended approval, and Saucedo, in addition to the house, assigned to her a suerte of 50 varas south of the grant given to José de la Garza.[31]

Fulgencio Bueno, an orphan representing his elder brother, Juan Francisco, beseeched the jefe político for a plot of land. Declaring that Juan Francisco had sole responsibility for three minor siblings, Fulgencio, assisted by Juan Martín de Beramendi, asked for a merciful grant of land and a dula of water, pledging: "We believe we can cultivate it and with its profits sustain ourselves." Apparently in sympathy with young Bueno, the ayuntamiento counseled Saucedo to bestow the dula of water and farmland. The benvolent jefe accorded to Juan Francisco a suerte of 150 varas of frontage adjacent to Beramendi's extensive property, which Fulgencio gratefully accepted.[32]

Another minor who begged Saucedo for land at the "Queen of the Texas Missions" was José María Ureña, who although "not yet a full adult," avowed he was responsible for the support of his mother and two sisters. He ended the application with a dramatic appeal: "I beseech Your Highness, please, to listen to my petition, so I may receive justice and grace." Ureña requested two dulas of water, but the town council recommended to Saucedo that a half-dula with proportional farmland would be sufficient for the young man's subsistence. Taking into consideration the applicant's good

[30] José Eligio de Alvarado for José de la Garza [to the Ayuntamiento of San Antonio], November 6, 1823; Vicente Gortari *et al.* to SGP, December 1, 1823; Grant of Land and Water to De la Garza, December 6, 1823; MR 71-75.

[31] María de la Trinidad Guerrero to SGP, November 8, 1823; MYC to SGP, December 1, 1823; Decree of Saucedo, December 4, 1823; Donation of Land and Water to Guerrero, December 6, 1823; MR 76-85.

[32] Juan Martín de Beramendi for Fulgencio Bueno, [November 11, 1823]; MYC [to Saucedo], December 1, 1823; Donation of Land and Water to Juan Francisco Bueno, December 6, 1823; MR 76-85.

conduct and professed interest in agriculture, the jefe político approved the recommendation and ordered a survey of one-half suerte of land with 50 varas of frontage on the river adjacent to Miguel Menchaca's grant.[33]

A local applicant whose family identified closely with the cause of Mexican independence in Texas was José Antonio Navarro. Within two days after Saucedo posted an announcement concerning imminent distribution of mission lands, Navarro submitted a plea in behalf of his brother, Militia Captain José Ángel Navarro, for one and a half dulas of water and adjoining land, one house, and an additional tract of land next to Mission San José. Navarro affirmed that José Ángel was "strong and energetic," capable of performing "all types of jobs." Furthermore, if the militia captain had "some land of his own," then he could earn a comfortable livelihood, including cattle raising, which would enable him to aid their widowed mother. In the process of filing an application for his brother, José Antonio took advantage of the opportunity to present a joint proposal. After evaluating the Navarros' solicitation, the city council advised Saucedo to finalize legal proceedings. The land grant Saucedo awarded to José Antonio measured 450 varas in frontage and 523 varas in depth. Coterminous with the first property was another suerte of 170 varas in frontage and 300 varas in depth, extending "all the way up to the river." Together, the brothers Navarro received a fairly large estate from an appreciative city government.[34]

In 1824, of various land grants the ayuntamiento authorized for distribution at Mission San Juan Capistrano, the most generous went to a diocesan priest, Francisco Maynes, and to the jefe político, José Antonio Saucedo. In the years before the outbreak of the Hidalgo rebellion, Father Maynes (who preferred the title of *Bachiller* to denote university training) served as parish priest at Villa de Salcedo on the east bank of the Trinity River. Maynes then moved to San Antonio where he became chaplain of the presidial soldiers. In 1822, when Father Refugio de la Garza, curate of San Fernando, took temporary leave of absence to represent Texas in the national constituent congress in Mexico City, Maynes assumed duty as acting pastor. Keenly aware of the implications of the secularization decree, Maynes appealed to

---

[33] José María Ureña to SGP, November 11, 1823 (quotation); MYC [to Saucedo], December 1, 1823; Donation of Land and Water to Ureña, December 6, 1823; MR 76-85.

[34] José Antonio Navarro to SGP, November 11, 1823; MYC to SGP, December 1, 1823; Donation of land and Water to José Antonio Navarro, December 6, 1823; MR 76-85.

For details of Navarro's involvement with the movement for Mexican independence in Texas, see Anastacio Bueno, Jr., "In Storms of Fortune: José Antonio Navarro of Texas, 1821-1846" (M.S. Thesis, University of Texas at San Antonio, 1978), pp.22-51.

Saucedo to confer to him land and riparian rights, and either to sell or to rent two or three abandoned single-room houses that formed part of the mission convent. The town council rendered a collective opinion that although Maynes should receive only one dula, the jefe undoubtedly would determine whatever was expedient. Predictably, Saucedo decided to award the bachiller two suertes of land of 200 varas frontage,[35] thus establishing precedent for a systematic process by which the military chaplain ultimately acquired ample land holdings in the region south of San Antonio.

In an administrative action that unquestionably was a conflict of interest, José Antonio Saucedo the private citizen applied to the institutional office of jefe político for an extensive tract encompassing several well-known terrestrial points of reference — El Rincón del Tulillo, El Nogal, and La Arena — plus a labor for dry farming. Observing all formalities, the jefe, in addition, asked for water from the Río San Antonio to irrigate a section of the grant suitable for agriculture, while reserving the rest of the area for open grazing. Ramón Músquiz, as first secretary of the ayuntamiento, accepted Saucedo's petition and presented it to the municipal corporation. In the meantime, Saucedo's tenure in office expired, and he temporarily retired from public service. After giving the matter a thorough examination, the council in early March 1824 instructed Secretary Músquiz to proceed with the task of giving "lawful possession" of land and irrigation water to Saucedo. In turn, Músquiz assigned the duty of actual transfer of possession to the Barón de Bastrop. On March 8, Bastrop, assisted by official witnesses (Manuel Granados and José María de Cárdenas) accompanied Saucedo and other grantees to Mission San Juan Capistrano for the ritual of ownership.[36]

At the southernmost mission in the chain, San Francisco de la Espada, area residents energetically competed with townspeople for legal landholder rights, irrigation privileges, and housing. In contrast to the other missions, probably due to the remote isolation, the distribution of property at Espada was more equitable. Among the senior applicants of long tenure at the mission were Nicolás Páez y Colomo and Rafael Casillas. A local alcalde with thirty-five years in residence, Don Nicolás Páez asked for the house he had occupied for nearly a quarter century and a tract of farmland immediately

---

[35] Almaráz, Tragic Cavalier, pp. 53-54; Habig, Alamo Chain of Missions, pp. 108-109, 146; Bachiller Francisco Maynes to SGP, November 3, 1823; Gaspar Flores et al. to SGP, January 10, 1824; Grant of Land and Irrigation Water to Maynes, February 7, 1824; MR 4-10.

[36] José Antonio Saucedo to His Excellency [the Office of Jefe Político], November 15, 1823; Ramón Músquiz et al. to the Ayuntamiento, January 8, 1824; Gaspar Flores et al., January 10, 1824; Miguel Arciniega et al., March 6, 1824; El Barón de Bastrop et al., March 8, 1834; MR 4-10.

outside of the north wall (known as *El Potrero*) with special permission for unrestricted irrigation. The town council, comparing the amount of resources available for distribution against the number of applications, recommended that Páez be assigned a half dula. In February 1824, José Antonio Saucedo, acting in the capacity of jefe político pro tempore while his own case awaited final resolution, directed surveyors to designate a small plot of arable land with access to water for Don Nicolás, the mission alcalde.[37]

Even more senior to the alcalde in terms of residency was Rafael Casillas, who, at the time of applying for a grant, had lived at Mission Espada forty-five years. Regarding temporal property to be distributed, Casillas manifested considerable discretion when he asked merely for a fanega of farmland, preferably the area he had cultivated in earnest, and irrigation rights for 48 hours per month. Don Rafael also requested a house within the mission pueblo, but if this were not possible then he would be content with another location where he could construct living quarters for his large

[37] Josef Nicolás Páez y Colomo to the Very Excellent Deputation [the Ayuntamiento], October 30, 1823; Gaspar Flores *et al.* to SGP, January 10, 1824; Grant of Land and Water to Páez y Colomo, February 6, 1824; MR 48-54.

family. The city council routinely processed Casillas' application with a favorable recommendation. On the day of actual distribution, Saucedo measured a suerte of 150 by 500 varas near the main entrance of the mission plaza and assigned it to Casillas with full formality.[38]

Unlike the mission's two senior residents, Juan Cortina associated himself with both the City of San Antonio de Béxar and San Francisco de la Espada. According to Cortina's own testimony, shortly after the celebration of Mexican independence in Texas, he moved into a house situated midway between the Río San Antonio and Mission Espada where he cultivated a cornfield. Aside from making the land productive "by the sweat of my brow," Cortina asserted he had cleaned his share of the principal acequia. During the brief interlude of Agustín Iturbide's empire, Cortina appealed to Governor José Félix Trespalacios for title to the riverside land. Admitting he lacked specific authority to act on this request, Trespalacios allowed Don Juan to continue cultivating the land with the explicit understanding that in the event mission properties were secularized, preference would be given to the prior occupant. In view of this understanding among gentlemen, Cortina filed claim on the property. With consent of the ayuntamiento, Saucedo awarded to Don Juan two separate sections of land "with sowing capacity of one-half fanega of corn," both of which shared the irrigation canal as a common boundary.[39]

Serving as an indication of material property Mexican citizens of San Antonio received at Mission Espada, on the last day of 1824, the outgoing civil alcalde of Béxar, Gaspar Flores, prepared for his successor, Juan Martín de Beramendi, an inventory of eleven houses the city government had donated for nominal fees. Besides awards to Nicolás Páez, Rafael Casillas, and Juan Cortina, the list included the surnames of Casanova, Conti, Cuéllar, De la Garza, Hernández, Leal, and Rodríguez.[40]

With the inauguration of Mexican independence, the active missions of San Antonio, deprived of Franciscan zeal and tradition, soon passed into quiesant oblivion. Even so, the spiritual values inculcated by the missionaries remained fervent in the culture of resident families at the riverside

[38] Rafael Casillas to Excellent Deputation, October 30, 1823; Gaspar Flores et al. to SGP, January 10, 1824; Donation of Land and Water to Rafael Casillas, February 6, 1824; MR 38-47.

[39] Juan Cortina to SGP, October 31, 1823; Gaspar Flores et al., January 10, 1824; Donation of Land and Water to Cortina, February 6, 1824; MR 38-47.

[40] Index of Houses Sold in the Mission of San Francisco de la Espada by Gaspar Flores, 1823; MR 62-70.

pueblos. With varying degrees of practice and observance, the spiritual heritage outlasted the buildings' material decline caused by civil neglect and secular avarice.

The extent to which individuals, both men and women, applied for diversified properties at Concepción and San José partially testified to the Franciscans' success in an earlier century in transforming a rugged countryside into productive agricultural fields. While lands surrounding San Juan Capistrano and San Francisco de la Espada were comparably fruitful, their distance from San Antonio rendered them vulnerable to external danger. Plausibly the insecurity factor, coupled with an awareness of diminishing resources, motivated the jefe político and the city council to restrict the size of land grants to an average of two suertes. Moreover, the nearly equitable distribution gave to properties at the two downriver missions a certain compactness that offered a standard of protection.

The ayuntamiento of San Antono de Béxar, in its cumbersome administration of the secularized lands, conceivably prevented a rampage of malfeasance and destruction. Nonetheless, the city government's implementation of the national decree mandating the distribution of land, water, and housing at all four of the San Antonio missions in 1823 and 1824 unintentionally fostered material decline and secular avarice that gradually accelerated in the latter years of Mexican Texas and continued during the successor governments.

University of Texas at San Antonio
San Antonio, Texas   FÉLIX D. ALMARÁZ, JR.

Daniel J. Garr

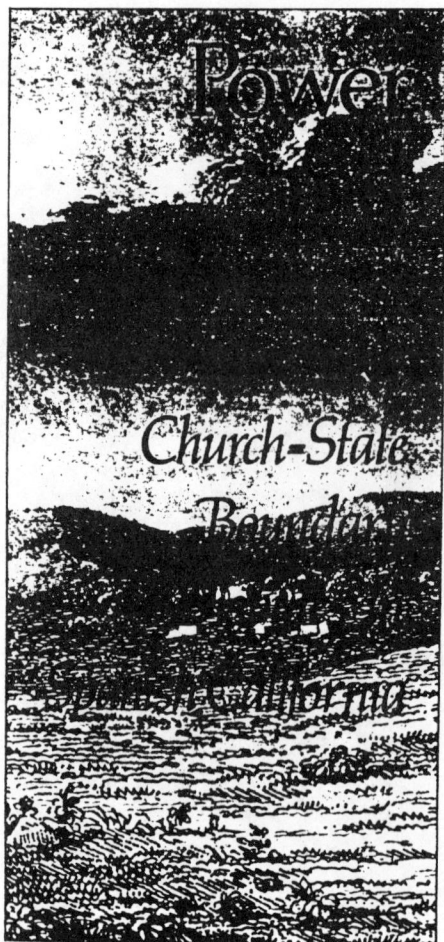

Few will dispute historian Lewis Hanke's observation that "no European nation . . . took her Christian duty toward native peoples so seriously as did Spain."[1] Despite this national commitment, however, Spanish colonial officials of Church and State found it difficult to agree as to how this broad consensus would be translated into policy on the local level. This was especially apparent in Spain's frontier territories where the guiding beacon of statutory orthodoxy was eclipsed by distance and compromised by the pragmatic considerations of the business of empire. Thus arose the classic blanket rejoinder of the theoretically culpable but nevertheless autonomous secular official, "Obedezco pero no cumplo" ("I obey but I do not comply"). The immunity effectively built into these local decisions frequently came at the expense of the missionary orders, particularly in the more remote areas of the sprawling American empire. Despite the central role played by the aspiring missionary church in the course of empire in the sixteenth century, the institution increasingly became a perennial thorn in the side of a resource- and revenue-hungry colonial government.

By the waning years of the colonial era, the vulnerable and impoverished Spanish empire could no longer afford the luxury of an ecclesiastical establishment which clung to the anachronistic mandate of paternalistic stewardship that it had secured nearly three centuries earlier. Monumental in their achievements under conditions which stretched the limits of human endurance, the missionary orders proved equally tenacious in their resistance to any perceived incursion into their hegemony. Although the nature of colonial society had undergone massive change by the eighteenth century, the missionaries remained intransigent in their determi-

Dr. Garr is an Associate Professor of Urban and Regional Planning at San Jose State University. His interests are California urban history, housing policy, and the quality of life of suburbia. In 1974, he was presented with the Herbert E. Bolton Award by the Western History Association. He was recently awarded a Fulbright-Hays Research Grant for the study of urbanization in the Netherlands.

364

nation to thwart adjustments in their equilibrium with the secular world. The formal expulsion of the Jesuits from the colonies in 1767 was only the most dramatic blow which the State finally leveled at the missionary orders; it reflected a situation of much greater cumulative enmity.

The eighteenth-century colonization of California provides a case in point of Spain's Church-State conflict. The specific issue around which larger antagonisms surfaced was the objection by missionaries to the choice of locations for the pueblo of San José de Guadalupe in 1777 and the Villa de Branciforte two decades later. This happened, in part, because the three forms of urban settlement in California—the mission, presidio, and pueblo—were distinct yet symbiotic entities. Missions were reconstituted Indian villages centered around a church and a strictly-supervised regimen of agriculture and crafts.² Their purpose was the introduction of Spanish civilization and the proselytization of the Catholic faith to Native Americans. Presidios, or forts, were to provide protection for mission communities as well as serve as coastal sentries and ports of entry; they were dependent on the missions for their sustenance. Pueblos or the more exalted villas (at least in title) were civilian agrarian settlements; their presence in California reflected the need to establish agricultural self-sufficiency in the province and to eliminate their dependence on the missions, as well as to increase the province's sparse Spanish population. From the beginning of the colonization effort, carefully drawn regulations prescribed where pueblos could be located with respect to Indian mission communities. In theory, this policy of separation of the mission from the secular world was to be vigorously enforced until such time as the mission completed its educational and evangelical tasks among the natives.

The mission-pueblo boundary disputes in late-eighteenth century Spanish California illustrate three dimensions of the Church-State problem. First, it becomes apparent that the acrimony of successive genera-

Despite the central role played in the course of empire by the aspiring missionary church, the institution became a perennial thorn in the side of a resource and revenue-hungry colonial government.

tions of conflict had made impossible harmonious dialogue between the clergy and secular interests, not only in matters of major impact (such as the timing of mission secularization), but also in rather minor if not wholly avoidable issues (such as boundary disputes). Second, it is revealed that secular interests chose to proceed with town foundings in a manner not only patently illegal, but also designed to tread heavily upon, if not humiliate, the Franciscan missionaries. Thirdly, it is evident that the California friars actively kindled the flames which were eventually to consume them by strenuously opposing the establishment of such secular communities from the very beginning. By turning a deaf ear on the needs of the State, the missionaries sowed the fateful seeds of exasperation and vindictiveness among their military and agrarian brethren.

It is therefore not surprising that tensions often ran high in the early years of the settlement of California. For example, following the midnight Indian uprising at the San Diego mission in November, 1775, Junípero Serra, father president of the missions, quarreled with Captain Fernando de Rivera y Moncada concerning measures to deal with rebellious and hostile Indians. Both parties had cause for anger because deteriorating relations between Rivera's soldiers and the mission community had led the missionaries to insist that the troops withdraw from the immediate area. This left the mission virtually defenseless against the surprise attack. Concurrently, the padres constantly bridled at the government-imposed prices at which their grain was to be sold to the military,

365

225

and they retaliated by withholding spiritual services from the troops; these services they regarded as voluntary charity, not a prescribed duty. The military, in turn, could counter by providing decreased protection to the missions, thus inviting the possibility of another tragedy like that at San Diego. Behind these squabbles was the difficulty of separating policies from the individuals empowered to carry them out. In these years personalities in conflict produced frequent disagreements which, according to historian Hubert Howe Bancroft, were "often petty in all their phases, and such as might easily have been avoided by slight mutual concessions and efforts to promote harmony."[3] For example, it required two years to resolve the seemingly trivial issue of State-sanctioning of the missionaries' power to administer the sacrament of confirmation. Father Serra and Governor Felipe de Neve battled from 1779 to 1781 on this issue alone.[4]

Although the role of individual personalities should not be minimized, the sources of the boundary conflict in California were as cumulative as they were circumstantial. In the sixteenth century, the Spanish monarchy realized that the secular clergy were more malleable than the religious orders whose primary ties were to Rome rather than to the Crown. Philip II thus sought to minimize the role of the regular clergy in the colonies, but he was never able to achieve this end due to the scarcity of secular priests. This perpetual condition insured the continued sway overseas of the regular clergy, a fact which sorely vexed successive sovereigns, particularly the eighteenth-century Bourbon monarchs.[5]

The overriding factor in Church-State discord was not abstract conflicts of authority and allegiance, but rather the control of territory and population. As early as 1530, royal governors were instructed to respect the integrity of Indian communities, their organization, and their customs, excepting what was deemed justifiable intervention in matters involving pagan customs or barbarous practices.[6] The implications of territorial integrity extended to other fronts as well. It was very early viewed as a necessity, writes historian J. Preston Moore, "to protect the Indians against legal injustices at the hands of the *encomenderos*, *caciques*, and pettifogging attorneys."[7] Through the centuries, the rationale for this almost too fiercely protective attitude remained remarkably consistent. An early spokesman, the Franciscan mystic Géronimo de Mendieta (1525-1604), similarly wrote:

The Indian with respect to the Spaniard is like a small dog in front of a mighty lion. The Spaniards have both the evil desire and the strength to destroy all the Indians in New Spain, if they were ever given the chance. The Indian is so phlegmatic and meek, that he would not harm a fly. Consequently, one must always assume in case of doubt that the Spaniard is the offender and the Indian is the victim.[8]

Considerably later, at the virtual end of the colonial era, Father President Fermín Francisco de Lasuén reiterated the separatist attitude long fostered by missionary rule. Articulating much the same fears as did Mendieta, Lasuén brought the matter still closer to the outright proprietary paternalism to which the friars had so accustomed themselves. "If in some missions, or in all of them," he wrote,

certain Indian men and women are sometimes denied permission to associate with certain individual people *de razón*, it is for precisely the same reasons as those for which every good father of a family in every civilized nation should forbid his children to go with bad companions.[9]

The specifics which may be read into this attitude extended to include actions of vigorous resistance to any and all perceived incursions of the secular society into the broadly-defined sphere of interest which the missionaries took as their mandate. These included opposition to institutional changes relevant to internal mission organization such as governance and land uses. Although attempts to manipulate mission internal affairs were

loudly contested by the friars, it was a relatively simple matter for them first to resist and then to put on a show of compliance, while absorbing only a minimum of change. Thus, in 1778 when Governor Felipe de Neve ordered that mission Indians commence electing their own *alcaldes*, or mayors, and *regidores*, or councilmen, Lasuén countered with narrow objections based on technicalities, then quietly yielded. However, in the end, he cleverly dodged de Neve's directive by lengthening the interval between elections and then by eliminating them entirely, substituting municipal officers appointed by missionaries.[10]

But not all threats to the missionary realm could be quite so easily parried. Supreme in a land where they dominated both resources and population, the friars were content to maintain the *status quo*. But the larger objectives of empire, specifically the populating of the province and the encouragement of agrarian endeavor, dictated a change in this hegemony. Felipe de Neve realized that the introduction of civil agricultural settlements was essential to California's security, if not survival,

and his term as governor was to witness the founding of two pueblos, San José de Guadalupe in 1777 and Nuestra Señora de Los Angeles de Porciúncula in 1781. It was with the establishment of San José that a new tale of acrimony began.

Father Junípero Serra was outspoken in his opposition to the introduction of secular establishments in California. The presidios he acknowledged as a necessary evil; but as for "pueblos composed of Spaniards, or of people of mixed blood," he had "never been able to see or recognize any advantage in it whatever, either on the temporal or spiritual side."[11] Serra believed that establishing more missions offered a better means of attaining agricultural self-sufficiency, for not only would they "be the means of supplying foodstuffs for themselves and for the Royal Presidios," but they would "accomplish this far more efficiently than these pueblos without priests."[12] However, the problem of populating the country remained, and Serra's ideas drew de Neve's sarcasm: "He forgets," wrote the governor, "that this would not people the land with Spanish subjects."[13]

367

Pragmatically, therefore, Serra could not easily dismiss the idea of civil towns in California. Not surprisingly, however, he relegated their advent to a date far in the future when "the gentiles that are spread throughout these lands have become Christian, and when they are settled in their various reservations or missions, . . . then will be the proper time for introducing towns of Spaniards." He warned, too, that the people must "be of good conduct and blameless life."[14]

If San José's colonists did not meet Serra's rigorous standards, then far less could be said for the site selected for California's first civilian settlement. In both 1778 and 1779 unseasonable flooding had inundated the pueblo, and in the latter year it languished under three feet of water. In his efforts to correct the situation, de Neve relocated the town's agricultural lands, relating that he had found a site "more suitable and closer to the population, changing the distribution which I have made."[15] However, this action failed to remedy the immediate circumstances and instead initiated a prolonged round of acerbic sparring with the clerics which was to endure for twenty years.

The bitter controversy with the nearby mission at Santa Clara began to flare in earnest by the early summer of 1778. De Neve observed, "Said pueblo has not only encountered difficulties with the sowings, but also with the bad arrangement in which its lands were distributed, all in the direction in which the Mission of Santa Clara is situated."[16] In June, 1778, Father Serra reiterated his vehement opposition to civil settlement to Viceroy Antonio María de Bucareli. Serra once again asserted that increasing the number of missions would provide a satisfactory solution to the problem of agricultural supply and suggested, "The settlers who can suitably fit into such a scheme—and at present their numbers are

few—should be distributed until more promising times among the missions."[17]

Serra took a necessary precaution in preparing the missionaries for the anticipated struggle with the secular authorities. In August, 1779, he wrote to his superior, the Guardian of the College of San Fernando, requesting that

... the *Recopilación de Leyes de Indias* (Code of Laws) [be] brought at the expense of all the missions and placed at this mission, where the President has his residence. The gentleman [Governor de Neve] has a copy, and he is outmatching us with his quotations. Although I remember quite an amount from the time I read these laws, I have also forgotten a great deal—especially the quotations. And so I would appreciate it if they came, and we can let him know he is not dealing with ignorant men.

The truth is that he will always get the better of us because of the knack he seems to have of getting around any law.[18]

Serra's fears notwithstanding, however, the body of laws enabled the missionaries to argue their case from an unassailable position, and their eventual defeat stemmed not from the intrinsic merits of the issue, but from the uncompromising and stubborn determination of the secular authorities to win their case.

The missionaries' "brief" may be divided into two distinct sections. One pertained to the rights of Indians and the prerogatives of Indian settlements, and the other consisted of statutes which limited the location of Spanish towns. In summary, the case presented by the religious observed that all royal officials were charged with the duty to protect and defend the rights of Indians and to punish transgressors vigorously, while the ecclesiastics' function was to insure that the privileges and prerogatives of the Indians in their jurisdictions were not jeopardized in any way.[19] Consequently, Indian settlements were to have sufficient lands and water, as well as a commons of one league in length where cattle could be pastured without interference from herds belonging to Spaniards.[20] Once Indians were reduced to a settlement, they were to remain on that land for at least

368

228

five years in order to learn to cultivate it and profit thereby, and so they would learn the proper mode of government.[21]

With respect to limiting the settlement activities of Spaniards, the missionaries probably inadvertently omitted from their case key statutes which prohibited the founding of towns on sites that were not vacant or that were prejudicial to the interests of Indians.[22] But equally appropriate was their citation of a prohibition against distributing land in newly-founded towns which adversely affected Indian holdings.[23] Infractions involving livestock were items of particular rancor with the missionaries, who invoked legislation which stipulated that ranches and other lands granted to Spaniards must not be in opposition to the interests of Indians, and if granted, such lands must be returned to their rightful owners.[24] More specific, however, was the stipulation that cattle ranches must not be situated within one and one-half leagues of older Indian settlements or within three leagues of new ones; otherwise, severe penalties for violations were to be exacted.[25] The presence of a pueblo adjacent to an Indian settlement constituted a far greater threat, or at least annoyance, than an *estancia*, or ranch, they continued. The missionaries' contentions, as it turned out, were all valid, and none were offered in rebuttal by the secular authorities.

Despite Father Serra's undisputable position, however, nothing was done to remedy what he considered to be an unjust state of affairs. Of Governor de Neve, Serra wrote, "Common sense, laws, and precedents mean nothing to him."[26] Further, although de Neve surely realized the sound basis on which the religious grievances rested, he

went ahead with his project, even though he often changed the plans and details of its development, and even the people who lived there. But it remained on the same site. . . . On one occasion the gentleman in question [de Neve] went so far as to admit that everything had been . . . carried out contrary to the laws. But he excused himself by saying that his

A change of site in 1785 would not have represented a major dislocation for the settlers, because their houses were only palisade structures with earthen roofs.

instructions had not been obeyed, that his wishes were that it should be in a different town. He even went so far as to hint that it would be changed.[27]

Serra continued that neither de Neve nor any other official had ever made the effort to set a boundary between the mission and pueblo because "justifiable complaints would be made and lawsuits started."[28] Such complaints were lodged by the missionaries at Santa Clara in 1782. They wrote to Pedro Fages, de Neve's recent successor as governor:

When we recall how short a distance there is between the two, we can see how much annoyance and damage will be caused to our poor convert Christians, and what a source of constant friction it will be to them. . . . It is contrary to His Majesty's laws that any land should be owned by citizens of the said pueblo. . . . This is clear from the measures Your Lordship might order to be made and also when you compare your findings with the laws contained in *La Nueva Recopilación de Indias*.[29]

Serra, however, realized that righteous anger in an isolated province such as California would not convince the secular authorities in Spain to change the location of the town. Accordingly, he wrote to his superiors in frankness, "If the laws dealing with such matters, and they are very specific, are of no account, then everything else is to no avail."[30]

Unhappily, the civilian authorities were equally frustrated in their intents. Flooding continued to plague San José despite the considerable efforts and tribulations which earlier difficulties had exacted from the settlers. In early 1785 it was first suggested that it would again be

369

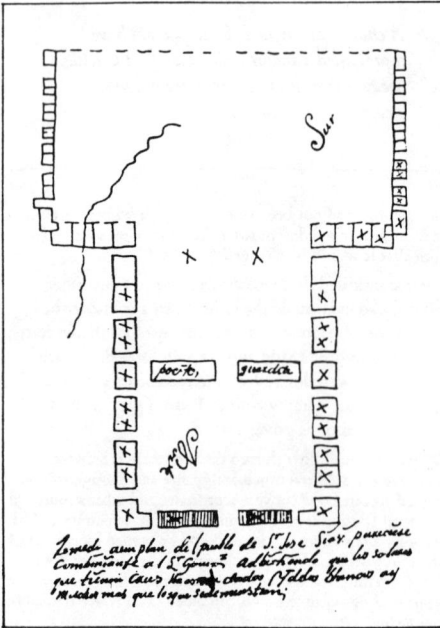

necessary to move the town to a higher elevation, but *Comisionado* José Moraga hesitated to initiate such drastic action. However, the sentiment of the settlers was in favor of relocation, and in August, Governor Fages wrote to Jacobo Ugarte y Loyola, commandant general of the *Provincias Internas*, requesting permission to move the town to a small nearby hill. The change of site would not have represented a major dislocation for the settlers, because at the time their houses were only palisade structures with earthen roofs.[31] Ugarte approved the idea "as it would be more useful and advantageous," but warned that it must be done "without altering or vary-

ing . . . the limits and boundaries of the lands or districts assigned to said Town or to the contiguous Mission of Santa Clara since there is no just reason for it to claim said site."[32] In other words, Ugarte stressed that the transfer of land uses must not jeopardize in any way the uneasy *modus vivendi* with the mission. Furthermore, while he intended to give the missionaries no satisfaction in their dispute of past years, he believed it was important for the location of San José to stay within the area, presumably four square leagues, which it had been assigned.

Despite the decade or so of contemplation, the move was not undertaken until 1797. In January of that year, *Alcalde* Marcos Chavoya officially requested that the town be transferred, "recognizing the deplorable situation in which the Pueblo has found itself owing to the flooding of the arroyos which surround it."[33] Governor Diego de Borica assented, but he wrote in the margin of the document, "Determination of the matter reserved until the engineer Alberto de Córdoba returns from San Diego to examine the terrain and informs me of what he has seen."[34] However, even before Córdoba's arrival, the Santa Clara missionaries were protesting that the change would adversely affect their interests and prerogatives.[35]

When Córdoba arrived he was ordered to "reconnoiter carefully the environs of San José and indicate within its boundaries the site which is most proper for its transfer which is close to its tillage lands, and require the settlers to mark it off with stakes."[36] After Córdoba's work had been completed, Governor Borica attempted to mollify the missionaries by explaining to them how the determination had been made. Córdoba, after taking testimony from both sides "on their reciprocal claims," then proceeded to set the official boundary "not far from the lands which it today occupies, because these have been determined by the higher authorities." It was within these limits that "the settlers of said pueblo must immediately locate themselves."[37] The *pobladores*, or settlers, were then instructed to "go to construct their houses on the other side of the river in case of flooding."[38]

Despite their earlier defeat, the missionaries seized the opportunity to press their case once again. They wrote to Governor Borica, citing Libro VI, Título 3, Ley 9 of the *Recopilación*, "which prevents and prohibits Indians from leaving the lands which they had previously possessed."[39] At that time the friars claimed that the mission had 1,434 Indian neophytes, with 4,000 more living in surrounding *rancherías*, and thus, much more land would be required by the mission. They also argued that livestock from San José would stray from the pueblo's commons and destroy the mission's pastures.[40] Additionally, the validity of Córdoba's boundary determination was questioned.[41] Complaints concerning trespassing by San José livestock had only recently been registered, which the missionaries believed to be in violation of "various royal *cédulas* (statutes) and the law," and they threatened to take their case to a superior court of appeal.[42] But despite their apparent legal justification, even the viceroy did not see fit to take action and the matter was not broached again.[43]

The two decades of sustained acrimony experienced in the Santa Clara Valley provided a hard-earned lesson in tactics to the secular authorities. Accordingly, in their plans of 1796–97 to found the Villa de Branciforte on the northern rim of Monterey Bay, the subterfuge of a *fait accompli* was embraced. Although there is no indication of any overt effort to conceal the plans to establish Branciforte, it must nevertheless have been a well-kept secret. The missionaries, in fact, learned of the proposed founding only two weeks before the first colonists were scheduled to arrive. Accordingly, Lasuén wrote to the president of his missionary college that the villa was "the greatest misfortune that has ever befallen

mission lands. . . . This is a flagrant violation of all law. If any remedy can be found, it would be wrong not to apply it."[44] A few days later Lasuén wrote Governor Diego de Borica, politely suggesting his disapproval of the matter. Lasuén argued:

The King knew the situation quite well, and so did his Excellency the Viceroy, and Mission Santa Cruz had already been founded with royal approval. Hence it appears to me impossible that his Majesty should wish, ordain, or approve of a villa or pueblo in the immediate neighborhood, or that his Excellency should attempt it.[45]

The College of San Fernando lodged its formal protest with the office of the viceroy in August, 1797.[46] As with the case of San José, the missionaries substantiated their case with appropriate citations from the *Recopilación*, and in light of the similar circumstances underlying the two conflicts, it is perhaps worthwhile to make some comparisons. Again the friars' argument may be divided in two parts, one relevant to the protection of the rights of Indians, the other limiting the sites where towns of Spaniards might be established. In this instance the latter approach was not stressed to the viceroy, possibly because "the explanation given suffices to convince us that Your Excellency was not informed with the sincerity and truth, which the matter required, as to the site or location on which the new pueblo is projected against the express intent of such grand and equitable laws."[47] More conciliatory than before, the missionaries emphasized:

The College regards the project itself with favor as something useful. Nor does it venture to make representation in order to hamper or embarrass your Excellence. It merely desires to see the plan executed in accordance with the laws. Otherwise there will arise disputes, disorders and delays.[48]

Three statutes from the *Recopilación* were cited in the Villa de Branciforte dispute which were not cited previously by the missionaries in the course of the San José–Santa Clara boundary squabble. (A second treatment of those statutes mentioned in both is unnecessary,

371

as they are discussed above.) The first of these—Libro IV, Título 21, Ley 8—was obviously an error;[49] the law which precedes it, No. 7, appropriately forbade the founding of new towns in areas which were already populated or which were in situations contrary to the interests of existing inhabitants.[50] Ley 12 safeguarded territory assigned to Indians from cattle pastures used by Spaniards.[51] It should be emphasized that the villa and the Santa Cruz Mission were separated by the narrow San Lorenzo River and were "scarcely a stone's throw away" from each other.[52] Libro VI, Título 3, Ley 6 was another error, and probably the missionaries meant to refer to Ley 8, which provided for each mission "a location which has the convenience of water, arable lands . . . and a commons of one league in every direction."[53]

The missionaries' protest, however, was unfortunately timed, and in light of international tensions and the viceroy's resolution to found a town bearing his name, it is unlikely that there was any possibility of a significant change in the situation. But the protest did cause a delay and compel Borica to defend his actions. He argued in rebuttal that the mission had sufficient land for its declining Indian population and further suggested that the villa would be able to purchase whatever surplus the mission produced.[54] However, it was not until December, 1800, a hiatus of nearly three years, that the objections were laid to rest; finally, in March of 1801 the cost of the project was given final approval by the *Junta Superior de Real Hacienda* (Royal Treasury).[55]

W̲hat is the explanation for the circumstances which precipitated these conflicts? In 1778 Viceroy Bucareli had reported the founding of San José to Charles III. One of the items in the report which both men must have noticed was the specific indication that the new

town was but three-quarters of a league from a mission, a rather suspicious proximity.[56] Nevertheless, the purposes for which the town had been established received unquestioned precedence, and it is doubtful that the king would have seen fit to intervene in a dispute over a minor provincial settlement. Governor de Neve was the real culprit, because his unilateral decision to locate San José near the mission was ill-advised and contrary to law. Indeed, he had the entire Santa Clara Valley at his disposal for a site. Nevertheless, the decision was subject to higher approval, and if it had been reversed, San José would not have been the first Spanish colonial town to have been relocated during its early years. It was upon Viceroy Bucareli that the responsibility ultimately devolved, and although in him "Serra did not have a better friend," Bucareli did not see fit to take action with respect to San José.[57] Teodoro de Croix, commandant general of the *Provincias Internas*, was directly responsible for affairs in California. Though a religious man, Croix was not an ally of the missionaries. For these reasons the decision stood to maintain San José near its original site, and there existed no further avenue for appeal for the clergy.

Similarly, a feared confrontation with England, which led to the founding of the Villa de Branciforte,[58] dictated a course of action oblivious to the niceties of statutory orthodoxy as well as to the costs of internecine squabbling. Indeed, the California boundary disputes demonstrated that missionary (and presumably Indian) interests were of such low priority that even modest accommodations were spurned in favor of wholly uncompromised attainment of secular goals. This in turn reflects the continuing intransigence of the missionaries' attitudes concerning Indian stewardship and their chronic inability to define the well-being of the mission Indian in a context any broader than the societal isolation of the mission community. It was the increase of the Spanish population and the founding of Spanish towns, regardless of prior intents, that had become the only

372

Controversy over agricultural lands flared between San José and Mission Santa Clara. This 1842 sketch of the mission was made by G. M. Waseurtz af Sandels, who noted that it contained 1500 Indians and "one good flock of cattle."

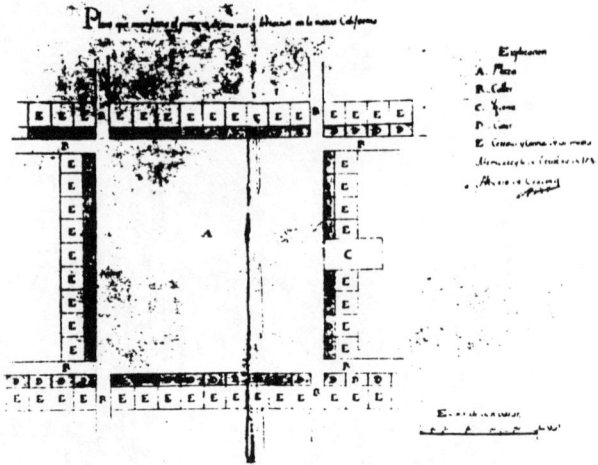

This 1796 plan of Branciforte, drawn and signed by Alberto de Córdoba, shows the layout of the projected new town. "A, plaza; B, streets; C, church; D, houses; and E, yards and kitchens of the same."

real goals of the California colonization. The missionaries and Indians may have been quite indispensable to the maintenance of California in the latter three decades of the eighteenth century, but their voices were rarely heard or heeded beyond the pale. For all their illusory power based on the domination of population and agricultural resources, the missionaries could never, or more correctly, would never establish their credibility as interpreters of the general welfare.

The drawing of Duran is from M. Duflot de Mofras, *Exploration de Territoire de l'Oregon, des Californies . . .* (Paris, 1844). The plan of Branciforte is from Lesley Byrne Simpson, *An Early Ghost Town of California, Branciforte* (San Francisco, 1935); that of Pueblo San José is from the files of the Western Title Insurance Company, San Jose. The sketch of Mission Santa Clara is from the CHS Library.

Notes

1. Lewis Hanke, *The Spanish Struggle for Justice in the Conquest of America* (Boston, 1965), p. 175.
2. See Herbert E. Bolton, "The Mission as a Frontier Institution in the Spanish-American Colonies," *American Historical Review*, 23 (October, 1917): 42-61.
3. Hubert Howe Bancroft, *History of California* (7 vols.: San Francisco, 1884-1890), I: 407.
   Occasionally, however, aberrant behavior transcended personal disharmony. The contentious existence of Fernando de Rivera y Moncada in California was apparently due to pathological causes. Fr. Pedro Font observed "he does not like to take suggestions from anybody about anything" (Pedro Font, *Diary of an Expedition to Monterey by Way of the Colorado River, 1775-1776*, ed. & trans. Herbert E. Bolton [Berkeley, 1933], p. 226). While attending to the distress of the San Diego Mission following the Indian uprising of 1775, Rivera's extreme course of action in dealing with one of the culprits caused Frs. Fuster, Lasuén, and Amurrio to excommunicate him (Bancroft, I: 266-267). Even Moncada's relations with his military colleagues were tempestuous. An observer of his interaction with the highly respected Juan Bautista de Anza believed that Rivera was mad; José Moraga shared this opinion (Bancroft, I: 270-271). Bancroft's assessment was perhaps more charitable: "Rivera was evidently a weak man. Whether insane, or influenced solely by a spirit of childish jealousy . . . is a question." (Bancroft I: 272).
4. Edwin A. Beilharz, *Felipe de Neve: First Governor of California*. (San Francisco, 1971), pp. 55-61.
5. Frederick B. Pike, *The Conflict Between Church and State in Latin America* (New York, 1964), p. 6.
6. J. H. Parry, *The Audiencia in Nueva Galicia in the Sixteenth Century: A Study in Spanish Colonial Government* (Cambridge, England, 1948), pp. 59-60.
7. J. Preston Moore, *The Cabildo in Peru Under the Hapsburgs, 1530-1700* (Durham N.C., 1954), p. 234.
8. Quoted in John Leddy Phelan, *The Millennial Kingdom of the Franciscans in the New World* (Berkeley, 1956), p. 61.
9. Lasuén, Mission San Carlos, June 19, 1801, Fermín Francisco de Lasuén, *Writings*, ed. & trans. Finbar Kenneally, O. F. M. (2 vols.; Washington D.C., 1965), II: 212.
10. For a discussion of this point, see Daniel J. Garr, "Planning, Politics and Plunder: The Missions and Indian Pueblos of Hispanic California," *Southern California Quarterly*, 54 (Winter, 1972): p. 296.
11. Serra to Teodoro de Croix, Monterey, August 22, 1778, Junípero Serra, *Writings*, ed. Antonine Tibesar, O. F. M. (4 vols.: Washington, D.C., 1955-1966), III: 263.
12. Ibid., 255.

374

13. Quoted in Bancroft, I: 314. See also Daniel J. Garr, "A Rare and Desolate Land: Population and Race in Hispanic California," *Western Historical Quarterly*, 6 (April, 1975): 133-148.
14. Serra, III: 255.
15. Felipe de Neve to Teodoro de Croix, Monterey, August 11, 1778, California Archives, Bancroft Library (CA), Provincial Records (5 vols.), I: 92.
16. Ibid., 9. The mission had been founded ten months earlier in January, 1777.
17. Serra to Bucareli, Monterey, June 30, 1778, *Serra Writings* III: 199.
18. Serra to Fr. Rafael Verger, Monterey, August 15, 1779, *Serra Writings* III: 133.
19. *Recopilación de leyes de los Reynos de las Indias*, 4th ed. (3 vol.: Madrid, 1791), II: Libro IV, Título 4, Ley 5, 13; II: Libro VI, Título 1, Ley 1, 189-190.
20. Ibid., II: Libro VI, Título 3, Ley 8, 209. An ordinance promulgated by Philip V in 1713 was also listed. It differed from the preceding in that the commons had to consist of one league in every direction; this regulation is not listed in the annotations in the *Recopilación* to the ley cited above (ordinance cited in Maynard J. Geiger, O. F. M., *The Life and Times of Fray Junípero Serra* (2 vols.; Washington, D. C., 1959), II: 196.
21. Ibid., II: Libro VI, Título 1, Ley 20, 194; II: Libro VI, Título 3, Ley 8, 209.
22. Ibid., II: Libro IV, Título 5, Ley 6, 16; II: Libro IV, Título 7, Ley 1, 19.
23. Ibid., II: Libro IV, Título 12, Ley 7, 41.
24. Ibid., II: Libro IV, Título 12, Ley 9, 41.
25. Ibid., II: Libro IV, Título 3, Ley 20, 211-212.
26. Serra to Fr. Francisco Pangua and the Discretorium, Monterey, December 8, 1782, *Serra Writings*, IV: 169.
27. Ibid.
28. Ibid., 169-171.
29. Frs. José Antonio Marquia and Tomás de la Peña to Governor Pedro Fages, Santa Clara, November 2, 1782, *Serra Writings*, IV: 397.
30. Serra to Pangua, *et al.*, *Serra Writings*, IV: 169.
31. Bancroft, I: 479.
32. Ugarte y Loyola to Fages, Arispe, June 21, 1787, CA, State Papers. Missions and Colonization (2 vols.), I: 271.
33. Chavoya to Governor Diego de Borica, San José, January 10, 1797, CA, Provincial State Papers (13 vols.), IX: 25-26.
34. Ibid.
35. Fr. Francisco Sánchez to Borica, Mission Santa Clara, April 30, 1797. CA, State Papers. Missions and Colonization, I: 269. There is a document from about 1790 which indicates that the land to the south of what is presumably Coyote Creek belongs to the pueblo and that on the north side to the mission. (Anonymous, n. pl., n. d. (c. 1790), CA, Departmental State Papers. San José (2 vols.) I: 45.

36. Borica to Córdoba, Monterey, May 11, 1797, CA, Provincial State Papers, Indices, 257.
37. Borica to Sánchez, Monterey, May 11, 1797, CA, State Papers. Missions and Colonization, I: 92-93.
38. Ignacio Vallejo to Borica, San José, September 26, 1797, CA, Provincial State Papers, VIII: 344. The move was to the east side of the Guadalupe River.
39. *Recopilación*, II: Livro VI, Título 3, Ley 9, 208.
40. The first of these documented incidents appears to have occurred in 1794 (José Pérez Fernandez to Borica, San Francisco, December 1, 1794, CA, Provincial State Papers, VII: 34).
41. Frs. Magín Catala and José Viader to Borica, Mission Santa Clara, August 6, 1797, CA, State Papers. Missions and Colonization, I: 276-280.
42. Frs. Isidoro Barcenilla to Ignacio Vallejo, San José, October 9, 1797, CA, Provincial State Papers, VIII: 351-352.
43. De la Peña to Viceroy Miguel José de Azanza, Mexico, Colegio de San Fernando, July 27, 1798, CA, State Papers. Missions and Colonization, I: 46-51.
44. Lasuén to Fr. Pedro Callejas, Mission San Carlos, May 1, 1797, Lasuén, II: 26.
45. Lasuén to Borica, Mission San Carlos, May 5, 1797, ibid., 27.
46. College of San Fernando to Viceroy Branciforte, Mexico, August 30, 1797, cited in Zephyrin Engelhardt, O. F. M., *The Missions and Missionaries of California* (4 vols.: San Francisco, 1908-1915), II: 517-519.
47. College to Viceroy, ibid.
48. College to Viceroy, ibid.
49. *Recopilación*, II: Libro IV, Título 12, Ley 8, 41.
50. Ibid., II: Libro IV, Título 12, Ley 7, 41.
51. Ibid., II: Libro IV, Título 12, Ley 12, 42.
52. College to Viceroy, Engelhardt, *Missions and Missionaries*, II: 517-519.
53. *Recopilación*, II: Libro VI, Título 3, Ley 8, 209.
54. Borica to Branciforte, Monterey, February 6, 1798, cited in Bancroft, I: 572.
55. Fiscal to Viceroy Felix Berenguer de Marquina, Mexico, December 11, 1800, cited in Florian F. Guest, O. F. M., "The Establishment of the Villa de Branciforte," *California Historical Society Quarterly*, 41 (March, 1962): p. 43.
56. Bucareli to Charles III, Mexico, July 27, 1778, *La Administración de D. Frey Antonio Maria de Bucareli y Ursua*, ed. Romulo Velasco Ceballos (2 vols.; Mexico, 1936), I: 436-437.
57. Quoted in *Serra Writings*, I: xvi.
58. For more information on the international pressures on Spain, see Guest, "Villa de Branciforte"; Daniel J. Garr, "Villa de Branciforte: Innovation and Adaptation on the Frontier," *The Americas*, Summer, 1978; and William Ray Manning, *The Nootka Sound Controversy* (1905).

375

Planning, Politics and Plunder:
The Missions and Indian Pueblos of
Hispanic California

by DANIEL GARR

Although the Franciscan missions ultimately made less of an impact in California than either the pueblos or the presidios, it should not be forgotten that the effort to colonize was initially and predominantly the work of a religious order. Missions were essentially frontier institutions and as such, their existence was a temporary one by definition.[1] In theory it was assumed that a mission community was to have completed its task of evangelization, education and civilization within a specified period of time, initially ten years, after which its spiritual affairs would be handed over to secular clergy, its lands distributed among the Indians, and its municipal government would function in the manner set forth in the *Recopilación*.[2] However, these assumptions were based upon experience with the Indians of Meso-America who had attained a significantly higher level of civilization than those on the frontiers where a much longer period of instruction and supervision was required.[3] As a result, it was inevitable that some form of conflict over secularization would arise whose aftermath was to witness the plundering of the religious domain.[4] Our concern with the California missions is in their urban organization and existence as towns in the years following their secularization.

The idea of congregating Indians into towns dates back to the first decade of the sixteenth century. In a 1503 *Instrucción* to Nicolás de Ovando, the Catholic monarchs suggested that "it is necessary that the Indians be gathered into towns in which they shall live together . . . and that each town shall have a Church and a Priest who will indoctrinate and instruct them in Our Holy Catholic Faith."[5] Said towns were to be planned "according to and like those of the people who live in Our realms."[6] Charles V encouraged the development of villages for Indians in 1523 and eleven years later he made suggestions, rather oversimplified, concerning methods of congregating the dispersed Indians of Michoacán

291

into a single town.[7] The Humanists, notably Juan de Zumárraga, Archbishop of Mexico from 1528 to 1548, believed that teaching Indians a trade and allowing them to live in villages planned "in the manner of Castilian towns," would alone be sufficient to raise their level of civilization within a short period of time and "quickly bring them riches."[8] Another consideration which favored urban settlement was the sheer physical inaccessibility of many Indian villages. This factor prompted Motolinía to write to Charles V in 1550 that if the Indians of New Spain were to be converted and civilized, it would be necessary to gather them into villages like those of the peasants of Spain.[9] And, perhaps most significantly, the establishment of Indian towns enabled the authorities to protectively enforce the policy of separation from Spaniards and *castas*.[10]

The *Recopilación* does not distinguish between missions and other Indian towns. In effect, they represent distinct and sequential stages in urban civilization. Bolton has written:

The central feature of every successful mission was the Indian village, or pueblo. The settled tribes . . . could be instructed in their native towns, but wandering and scattered tribes must be assembled and established in pueblos, and kept there, by force if necessary. . . . The essence of the mission was the *discipline*, religious, moral, social, and industrial, which it afforded.[11]

Whatever the era, the task of the missionaries was always the same: indoctrination, civilization and education. Perhaps when the Franciscans first entered the missionary field in Mexico in 1524 they lacked the understanding that was to come with experience. But their concern over the years remained a constant. Lasuén wrote in 1801:

Here then we have the greatest problem of the missionary: how to transform a savage race such as these into a society that is human, Christian, civil, and industrious. This can be accomplished only by "denaturalizing" them. It is easy to see what an arduous task this is, for it requires them to act against nature. But it is being done successfully by means of patience, and by an unrelenting effort to make them realize that they are men.[12]

As a political instrument of territorial conquest, the mission was the most appropriate mode of settlement to spearhead the Spanish thrust northward along the Pacific Coast. Whereas few colonists could be spared from underpopulated New Spain, there abounded in California an Indian population which was ripe for the proselytization activities of the Franciscan missionaries of the College of San Fernando. Missionary colonization was additionally advantageous in that the cost of the effort would be defrayed by the Pious Fund, a private endowment which had been administered by the Jesuits prior to their expulsion from the Spanish colonies in 1767. In Ricard's typology, the California missions were ones of "penetration," characterized by "the precarious establishment of sporadic houses in zones of difficult relief, unpleasant climate, and yet not pacified, or on the border of unsubjugated territories . . . [which] accompanied or preceded military conquest."[13] Serra's subsequently realized proposal to Viceroy Bucareli for a continuous chain of missions underscores the lifeline-like quality implicit in Ricard's approach:

If placed at proper intervals—say every twenty-five leagues, more or less, like the ones nearby—they would form from San Diego to here, stepping stones, so that every third day one might sleep in a village. With that, peace would be assured, and passage through all the country made easy; and a postal service might be established even though it operated every two months.[14]

The selection of mission sites and the planning of the settlements was to proceed along the same general lines as that for pueblos as specified in the *Recopilacion*.[15] These criteria were stressed continually during the colonial period in California.[16] Bucareli's 1773 *Instrucción* reiterated the necessity for abundant water, building materials and fertile land at all mission sites.[17] He emphasized, "All settlements have begun with few families and with time have grown to be large cities; and in those where defects were not immediately remedied, they grew with a lack of proportion and without symmetry."[18] Missions, he continued, "are to be cities in the future and care must be taken in their founding so that houses are built in a straight line with wide streets and good market squares." As a result, "In this harmony, not only will beauty be attained, but the Indians will be induced to stay and adopt the rational life."[19] Missions were to become secularized civil municipalities "when it becomes expedient" and at that time the nearest presidio commandant would be charged with reducing it "to the civil and economical government which, according to the laws, is observed in the other pueblos of this kingdom."[20] The timing of the change in status of the California missions was later to be the nexus of a controversy whose roots lay in the effectiveness of three centuries of missionary stewardship and the ideas on which it was based. The failure of the mission Indian to become "civilized" in the Spanish sense and thus live up to the expectations of the friars and the religious' ensuing chronic reluctance to move on to new areas of spiritual conquest placed the evangelical establishment on

293

a collision course with the secular authorities and the other interest groups mobilized in opposition to the missionaries.

There were attempts before long to modify the California mission system by both the religious and secular authorities. The latter's motives were conditioned by the desire to curb the missionaries' authority in a land where they dominated both resources and population. In some instances this autonomy exceeded the prescribed limits and became a matter of insubordination. The recalcitrance of the Dominican missionaries in Baja California moved Felipe de Neve to write in 1774:

Although the Illustrious Señor *Visitador General* [Gálvez] has ordered each mission now in the charge of the missionaries to mark off lands from which each respective pueblo must be formed, lands for planting, commons and others relative to its formal establishment, . . . since this measure is not in conformance with their ideas, notwithstanding that each Religious has been given that instruction, it remains in the archives of the Peninsula . . . and has nowhere been put into effect.[21]

Neve believed that the Franciscans in Alta California were adhering to the same pattern; his contentious relationship with Serra on all matters is well-known.

Modifications suggested by the clergy were the earliest set forth and are the most interesting. In 1772 it was proposed that Vasco de Quiroga's plan for establishing Indian towns in Michoacán be revived in California. But the Franciscans responded that the Indians were not sufficiently advanced in their state of civilization to make such an arrangement practicable.[22] In 1776 Antonio de los Reyes, Bishop of Sonora, recommended that Indians live in less-regimented reductions instead of in missions; however, this impractical plan was rejected by the Franciscan missionary colleges. Similarly, Manuel de la Vega, the Franciscan *Comisario-General,* suggested that "the Indians should retain their natural liberties without obligation to perform community labor or render personal service to the missionaries."[23] This plan received approval from both the Crown and the Council of the Indies, but it was never put into effect.[24]

Another departure from tradition was proposed in 1773 by Junípero Serra; he recommended that *gente de razón* who married Indians be permitted to remain at the mission of the spouse and, "as time goes on, he might be assigned a piece of land for his own personal use provided he has nothing else to fall back upon."[25] Apparently, a few Spaniards had married neophytes of the San Carlos mission and Serra was anxious

294

to incorporate them into the community.[26] As a result, Bucareli's 1773 *Instrucción* included an article which favored such an arrangement.[27] Serra greeted the legislation enthusiastically. In 1774 he wrote to Bucareli:

I myself am of the opinion that without this regulation that these men remain as settlers, . . . it will be utterly impossible for these missions and new establishments to make any progress. And thus, . . . these . . . families . . . form, as it were, the beginnings of a town. They . . . all live in houses so as to form two streets. They, . . . and the other buildings belonging to the mission establishment—they all together make up a square of their own. . . . I do all I can to encourage them, in order that by their diligence and work, and by their economy, they may serve as an example to the others.[28]

Unfortunately, there is no other information extant concerning the development of this racially-mixed mission town. Perhaps it was not an isolated occurrence.

It should not be assumed that this practice constituted serious competition with respect to recruitment for the pueblos. San Jose was not established until 1777, Los Angeles was founded four years later. Manuel Butrón, the recipient of the first mission grant, was later a *poblador* at San Jose.[29] Furthermore, in 1788 a statute was passed which provided that mission lands not cultivated by Spanish *vecinos* might be granted to Indians. Such grants were encouraged since their existence implied that the state of civilization of the neophytes permitted military escorts to return to the presidios and be available for other duties.[30] However, a measure of competition was suggested in 1794 when Miguel Costansó proposed to Viceroy Branciforte that craftsmen and others be introduced into mission communities in order to instruct the neophytes in their particular skills and, in time, Costansó theorized, exercise a healthy eugenic influence on the Indians. However, the defensive needs of California and the priority of the development of the civil towns effectively eliminated this attempt to accelerate the progress of the missions.[31]

When an Indian married a Spaniard and was removed from the mission, the friars reacted vigorously. They protested that Francisco Cayuelas, an *inválido,* was "preventing [his wife] from contributing the most minimal effort to the cultivation and utilization of those mission lands" and insisted that she continue her work "for the common good."[32] The missionaries were concerned that her removal would jeopardize her status when the mission lands were distributed among the neophytes

295

when each was able to manage his own affairs.[33] The protest received no satisfaction.

One of the primary secular tasks of the padres involved preparing the Indians for the day when they would be self-governing. In December 1778 Governor Felipe de Neve ordered that the Indians of each mission were to commence electing two *alcaldes* and two *regidores*.[34] Fr. Fermín Francisco de Lasuén, a vigorous defender of missionary prerogative, refused to implement the order, terming it "a notable innovation" that required the approval of the Father President, "without whose sanction we are not to introduce in the management of the missions any modification whatever in the system and method in which its missionaries have been trained."[35] He argued the technicality that, since parish priests were to supervise the elections, it would not be possible to comply with the order because, he explained:

We are apostolic missionaries bound by papal bulls to depart from the missions as soon as we recognize that the neophytes . . . are sufficiently instructed in the divine law, and sufficiently competent to care for the economic welfare of their families and for the political government of their pueblos. When that state is reached, they may then come under the jurisdiction of parish priests.[36]

But within a month Neve reported that municipal elections had been held and officers chosen at San Carlos, San Diego, San Antonio, San Luis Rey and San Gabriel, "according to the number of families that each one has."[37] Serra shared Lasuén's views on the matter. He wrote that the practice of conducting such elections was not productive and "this smashing up and breaking down simply wreaks havoc, and beyond repair, with the uniform organization of all the missions."[38] At San Luis Rey, for example, Serra related that "the *alcalde* took advantage of his office to indulge in numerous crimes;" while at San Carlos, the *alcalde* paraded in "strawberry-colored cotton drapes and knickers—and has made a fuss on account of it."[39]

The practice nevertheless continued sporadically and if elections were not held every year, the government allowed the padres to make appointments.[40] Later, the usual electoral abuses crept in, such as a candidate mobilizing his relatives to vote for him; but within the context of the institution, the *alcaldes* were reasonably effective.[41] Alvarado wrote that the Indian officers were in the confidence of the missionaries, who gave them careful instruction in their obligations and powers. Perhaps some pursued their vocation too vigorously, "occupying themselves in a constant observation and vigilance over the actions and discussions of

296

the other neophytes, denouncing and arresting all those who committed any crime, or who were remiss in the fulfillment of the obligations imposed by the work of the community."⁴² It is difficult to assess precisely the degree of exaggeration in this account. Alvarado's description leaves room to question his motives which were undoubtedly to demonstrate the success of the missions in the area of political instruction in order to justify their secularization. In any event, the selection of a few Indians of appropriate inclination and aptitude does not imply that such success was uniformly achieved on other levels or in other endeavors.

The secularization controversy was initiated by the liberal Spanish *Cortés* in September 1813. Encouraged by the success with which secularization had proceeded in Guiana, the *Cortes* passed a decree which ordered that all missions in the Americas which were in existence for more than ten years be secularized, "without excuse or pretext whatever, according to the laws."⁴³ The decree made its first appearance in California in January 1821 after what Bancroft terms "an unexplained delay."⁴⁴ But no such action was likely, or even possible. There were no secular priests available and provincial authorities were in no position to assume control of the missions. Instead, Governor Pablo Vicente de Solá proposed that "the most clever and useful Indians" be organized into two pueblos or distributed among the existing towns of *gente de razón*.⁴⁵ But the missionaries held firm in their resistance to change and they were aided by the government's dependence on the missions for supplies. This was understood by Solá and on at least one occasion his acknowledgement of this situation appeared in a Mexican official journal.⁴⁶

The needs of a newly-independent nation also played a role in secularization. Lucas Alamán reported to the Mexican Congress in November 1823, "It is necessary to consider other interests than those of the missionaries in the vast and fertile peninsula of the California," specifically those of economic development and defense. He argued:

If the mission system is that best suited to draw savages from barbarism, it can do no more than establish the first principles of society and cannot lead men to perfection. Nothing is better to accomplish this than to bind individuals to society by the powerful bond of property. The government believes, therefore, that the distribution of lands to the converted Indians, lending them from the mission fund the means for cultivation, . . . which . . . would give a great impetus to that important province.⁴⁷

However, the issue had other spokesmen closer to home. Vallejo questioned the pattern of land holdings; he asked, "is it just that

297

twenty-one mission establishments possess all the fertile lands of the peninsula and that more than a thousand families of *gente de razón* possess only that which has been benevolently given them by the missionaries?"[48] In 1828, José Bandini wrote:

The missions have extended their holdings from one end of the territory to the other and have had a way of bounding one piece of property to the next, always opposing private ownership of lands in between. They have unfeelingly appropriated the whole region, although . . . they do not need all they possess. It is to be hoped that the new system of enlightenment . . . will compel the government to take adequate measures to reconcile the interests of all.[49]

The attitude of the Spanish government had been quite different from that of Mexico on this matter. In 1794 Viceroy Branciforte wrote, "The Indians naturally appear to me to have the right to the most advantageous locations, even those which are outside the limited demarcation of four leagues." Although as future pueblos the missions were technically limited to that corporate area, they were allowed to appropriate far more than that. Branciforte believed that the missions were entitled to those lands because they were able to cultivate them and to "subsist by their own industry."[50] In 1796, Lasuén stated the Franciscans' position on the matter:

That, whereas the missionaries have no power to grant, deny, or hinder anyone from taking possession of lands, the fact that their opinion is sought regarding these matters must be due to the fact that, being charged with the conversion of the Indians, . . . it is their duty to procure for them a suitable and profitable way of making a living. . . . It is the wish of our Lord the King, therefore, that all the land which is necessary for this purpose should belong to the Indians.[51]

The secularization issue is perhaps summarized best by Beechey. On the one hand, as Governor Solá had acknowledged, "The missions have hitherto been of the highest importance to California, and the government cannot be too careful to promote their welfare, as the prosperity of the country in great measure is dependent upon them." But, on the other, "until settlers from the mother country can be induced to resort thither" the missions must not be harrassed.[52] This fact was recognized in a colonization law passed by the Mexican government in August 1824 which instructed that the missions be left undisturbed.

Governor José María de Echeandía's innocuous 1831 secularization decree is instructive if only for its instructions for the layout of ex-mission pueblos.[53] Houselots were to be seventy-five square *varas* and were to be arranged in blocks of four so as to form "beautiful and capa-

298

cious streets and plazas." *Suertes* were to be two hundred square *varas* and were to be distributed by lot or raffle. More than one *suerte* might be granted if the terrain permitted. All lands could be conceded in full ownership so that grantees could enjoy fully their benefits.[54] New settlers might be granted land after a residence of six months, for which purposes "a space of one-half league shall be left." Common lands were to be provided and single colonists would be granted only half a houselot and one *suerte* without the right of augmentation.[55]

It is difficult to assess the impact of traditional Spanish planning legislation in this situation. Firstly, the mission's physical plant and layout of buildings were suited to the organization of a mission community and it was within that context that the town was to be located.[56] Secondly, the main thrust behind the proposal was the transfer of mission land and property to secular control. Thus, the issue at hand was not the distribution of municipal land to the Indians within the assigned limit of four square leagues, but the disposition of the vast mission estates outside that boundary. Thirdly, the new town would not be one enfranchised with the necessary attributes of a municipal institution. It was to be governed by an administrator instead of by its own *ayuntamiento*. Clearly, the mission was not a town in the corporate sense, and physically, it existed by virtue of its prior organization.

In any event, secularization was inevitable. The Mexicans rightly believed that California's land and resources had to be developed in order to attain prosperity and thereby attract a large population for reasons of both security and economic advancement. While the Mexican government was concerned with the rights of the Indians to their native soil, the continuing existence of the missions on their fertile and far-flung estates was regarded as an absurd and unworkable situation. In 1833 Governor José Figueroa promulgated a secularization measure after consultation with Fr. Narciso Durán. It recognized the condition of the Indians and provided for a gradual and provisional change in their status. The incremental quality of the decree is indicated by Figueroa's proposal to leave the missions intact and instead, selecting those Indians who were deemed ready for emancipation, choose an appropriate site near the coast and establish a pueblo if there were a sufficient number of families. Lands would be granted and houses built "so as to form streets and plaza symmetrically as provided by ancient and modern law." The government for the town would be initially under the jurisdiction of the nearest municipality.[57]

But instead of forming one town, Figueroa later decided to gradually form a secularized settlement at each of the missions until all the Indians were emancipated, "for it cannot be done all at once without causing great disorder and harm."[58] The plan immediately encountered difficulties. Figueroa wrote to Mariano Vallejo:

I have made a beginning in emancipating some natives so that they may form separate towns and be given lands and some other possessions. But these unfortunates are so prejudiced and incapable of thinking that many of them refused to accept the favor.[59]

Bancroft commented, "The governor . . . made an earnest effort to give the Indians the civil liberty so little prized by them, but so valuable in the eyes of Mexican theorists."[60]

The immediate results of Figueroa's first efforts are as follows. At San Diego and San Luis Rey an insufficient number of families were willing to be emancipated in order to form a pueblo but they nonetheless received lands, managed their own property and became citizens. At San Juan Capistrano all the Indians appear to have been emancipated and lands were assigned to them. Later on, it appeared that a town would be formed at San Dieguito, located at a short distance from the San Diego mission, but little else is known.[61] In May 1834 Figueroa reported to the Territorial *Diputación* that he had established towns at Las Flores (north of San Luis Rey), San Juan Capistrano and San Dieguito.

All of them getting along quite well, and soon the great distance between emancipated Indians and the neophytes will be apparent. I dare to predict not only their elevation to the dignity of free men, but their better preservation away from the annihilation so evident in the missions.[62]

The development of each of the Indian towns will now be examined insofar as any information is available. It is fragmentary at best. Yet, it is worth examination if only for the reason that these towns represent the terminal stage of existence for many of the settlements which were of such primary importance in the Spanish colonization of California.

* * *

Las Flores

The pueblo of Las Flores was officially organized in 1833 and a year later Figueroa reported it to be flourishing. By 1836 its population was 196 and its government warranted an investigation which resulted in

300

the replacement of the *alcalde* and *regidores*. Elements of decline were evident by 1839 when William Hartnell observed that its population had decreased to 143. Additionally, within four years of the town's establishment, the Indian settlers had managed to dispose of half of their property and were warned that they would be returned to mission life if improvement was not demonstrated.[63] It proved to be an idle threat.

In April 1842 Pío Pico reported that "the lands marked off for the Pueblo of Las Flores are so restricted and scarce of water that the commodities required for the subsistence of the greater number of inhabitants who actually live there cannot even be borrowed."[64] However, a month later, Pico had obtained permission to settle there and was granted a houselot and agricultural lands.[65] Pico's impact on the struggling town was felt immediately. He required that all the Indians fence in their lands in order to keep out his cattle. Earlier, another petitioner had been refused a grant of 2,000 square *varas* because the pueblo's land would not support more people than were already there.[66] It soon became apparent why Pico, a former governor of California and member of an old Californian family, had taken an interest in the marginal Indian town. By means of a fraudulent grant issued in the name of an Indian, Pablo Apis, Pico acquired virtual control over the village, adding it to his family's already vast fiefdom.[67] By 1847, the establishment was in ruins and nothing more is known until a decade later.[68] In 1856 Las Flores was a *rancho* belonging to Andrés Pico. Benjamin Hayes observed that, two years earlier, many Indians remained but, "for some misconduct, their General, Manuchito [?] Cota, withdrew them into the interior—to Pala."[69]

San Francisco Dolores

The San Francisco mission was the first to have demonstrated interest in the planning of its future pueblo with respect to matters of form. Duhaut-Cilly observed in 1827 that although many of the buildings were in deteriorating condition, the houses of the Indians were regularly arranged in streets and that a fine stream flowed through the plaza.[70] Simpkinson noted in 1837 that a community had developed there, but with a striking division. "It is as miserable a place as can well be imagined," he wrote, "consisting of nothing more than a few rows of

301

wretched hovels for the Indians, and one row of whitewashed houses . . . for the people attached to the mission."[71]

In 1839 steps were taken to officially form a town. Juan Castro, Prefect at San Francisco, wrote, "I believe this project is of great public utility, particularly because those who are now scattered may be united in Society: thus, I will distribute houselots to those who wish to settle in this establishment."[72] Accordingly, grants were authorized and Castro specified "that in making the grants of house lots, they shall be in as good order and arrangement as possible, and as the situation of the place may require, in order that the streets and plazas which may be formed may have, from the beginning, proper uniformity and harmony."[73] However, from 1841 to 1845, only five houselots were distributed.[74]

Despite rhetoric to the contrary, a pueblo was never formally organized. In 1845 the residents petitioned so that they would be permitted to continue living in the ex-mission buildings, recalling an 1841 order of Governor Alvarado authorizing that a pueblo be established there. They argued that since there were no longer any Indians at the ex-mission, and since there was no room for livestock at Yerba Buena, they should be permitted to form "a frontier to the town of Yerba Buena, which is being formed entirely of foreigners."[75] Although the community was known as "Pueblo de Dolores," it actually had no municipal organization, and, according to Bernard Moses, it "occupied the same legal position as some of the smaller 'pueblos' of Mexico at the present time [1889]. It was embraced within a municipality of another name, to whose organization it was subordinated."[76]

San Juan Capistrano

It was decided to dissolve this mission community in May of 1841. A Prefect and *Juez de Paz* were appointed to assign lands provisionally to the Indians pending the issuance of permanent regulations; Agustín Olvera was appointed *comisionado* in June and was to distribute lands and see to it that the Indians were treated fairly. Still in residence at the mission were thirty-eight adult men; there are no statistics for women and children. They were told that the government was about to give them their liberty. One Julián was appointed captain and *alcalde* and was told that the Indians were to live as before until the proper documents arrived.[77] Prior to that time, Juan Bandini reported that a racially

302

integrated community lived there, apparently quite peacefully, on "lands abundant in pasturage and water."[78]

Olvera distributed thirty-eight grants in July 1841 and shortly after, a series of regulations arrived from Monterey.[79] They provided for the distribution of lands in the usual fashion as well as seeds and other materials. Lands would revert back to the town if they were abandoned and could be sold to another settler, but the original owner would be given preference should he again request permission to settle. An interesting feature of the regulations was their categorization of land according to its use. First, there was land and housing for the parish priest. Second, there were those lands which were granted to the indigenous families. And third, land was to be reserved for use by transients, primarily lodging, or for renting to non-Indians; the proceeds from these activities would accrue to the municipal treasury.[80] In theory, this represented a novel idea in land tenure. It is possible, in this instance, that the rights of Indians were to be protected by restricting, if not prohibiting, the ownership of land by non-Indians.

The establishment of the pueblo was not without conflict. A vote was taken on the matter which found a solid majority opposed to secularization. Juan Bandini wrote that Agustín Janssens, the *mayordomo*, opposed the change, "it being his object to continue with the *mayordomía*." He accused Janssens of inciting the Indians to oppose any change and ordered him to present himself with his "unintelligible accounts."[81] In his role as *mayordomo* Janssens claimed to have been responsible for many accomplishments, including the retrieving of refugees, building fences, repairing ditches, etc., "greatly to the joy of all concerned, though some of the neighbors ridiculed his zeal and predicted his efforts would go for nothing."[82] As an alternative to the formation of a pueblo, Janssens had applied, unsuccessfully, for a lease of six years in return for which he bound himself to return the property in improved condition.[83] Bancroft believes much of Janssens' story to be true but it is equally likely that he exaggerated the value of his services.[84]

Events took a turn for the worse by the beginning of 1842. Bandini reported that the pueblo was badly demoralized, "scoundrels having entered under pretence of being settlers, and vice and crime being prevalent."[85] Little else is known after that year. It was reported that six families of non-Indians and twenty or more ex-neophytes were living there quietly, "if not very prosperously."[86] In 1856 Benjamin Hayes

303

observed that some Indians were still at San Juan Capistrano cultivating their land. He wrote:

San Juan boasts a peaceful population. Sometimes they elect a couple of Justices of the peace and constables. The "elect" are not of an ambitious class: they have never taken the oath of office since 1851. How they settle their local controversies, I know not. They have few, I think. The last Justice of the peace made several concessions of "solares" . . . in what they call their "Pueblo"—and once it was a Pueblo. . . . In all there are 60 voters. *What there is* of San Juan is desirable to be owner of, for those who may wish to live here. . . . With or without township government, it gets along pretty well, in its own way—nobody knows how save the people themselves.[87]

San Luis Obispo

Events at San Luis Obispo indicate that, in contrast to the other missions, it was intended that a new town be established on a site close to the old mission. It marked quite a departure from the usual practice of continuing to utilize the decaying mission plant. Vicente Canet, the *mayordomo,* proposed that a new town be laid out on a site which was "most fitting to found a pueblo; its plan is one league square and can be watered from an arroyo and lagoon 2,000 *varas* distant from the Mission: the other lands are rough and without water." It is unlikely, however, that a *diseño* for this settlement was ever drawn.[88]

The full emancipation of all Indians was ordered by Governor Manuel Micheltorena in July 1844 and, as Canét indicated, the town was to be situated on the mission's vacant lands.[89] In December 1845 most of the buildings of the old mission were sold for 510 pesos.[90] A *bando de policia* dating from 1849 indicates that the San Luis Obispo pueblo continued to function as a corporate entity although no claim for pueblo lands was ever issued during the litigation before the United States Land Commission.[91] The *bando* dealt with the maintenance of clean and unobstructed streets, business hours of liquor stores, wage compensation for Indians, and the prohibition of dances and gatherings of Indians after 8 p.m.[92] William Rich Hutton was appointed the first surveyor of San Luis Obispo County in July 1850 and a month later he petitioned to make a map of the town. The survey was conducted, but reliable sources indicate that it is no longer in existence.[93]

*   *   *

304

The secularization of the missions immediately brought forth abuses which foretold the many difficulties which were to befall the new settlements. At San Francisco Solano, for example, described by Governor Manuel Victoria as "the most backward of the territory," the surrounding lands were insufficient to give each Indian the minimum amount to which he was entitled. Perhaps some of the claims by Californians concerning mission holdings were exaggerated. The situation was partly due to the fact that foreigners had secured large holdings, particularly in the north, in order to protect themselves from Indian attacks; many had returned to savagery after the missions were secularized. Victoria saw the imminent possibility of a land rush developing and stressed, "This is quite a delicate matter and it is important for the integrity of the nation."[94] He believed that land distribution resulting from secularization had to be carefully controlled; it was necessary to "reserve some *sitios* for officials and troops who may retire from the service . . . for now amidst such scarcity it is the only remuneration on which they can count and it is that for which they have always aspired."[95]

However, what was most to be feared was the ruthless plundering and preying upon Indians by whites. In 1835 William Hartnell wrote from the San Dieguito pueblo that Juan Osuña, the *alcalde* of San Diego, "had taken from [the Indians] the land which they had enclosed for their grain, and that he had left them nothing more than the salinous soil which did not produce enough for their maintenance."[96] A similar situation must have occurred at ex-mission San Buenaventura. Rafael Gonzáles wrote to Governor Alvarado that "it does not appear advantageous to allow *gente de razón* to establish themselves here as they will exploit the Indians and thus introduce demoralization and disorder."[97] At the San Pascual pueblo, the government at first was inclined to protect the grazing rights of Indian livestock and allowed the ex-neophytes to live quietly in their mud and grass shacks. But since no written titles were conceded, the arrangement did not last long. When the San Pascual Valley was opened for settlement the Indians were driven out and scattered to the interior.[98] It is significant that these Indians were never given the opportunity to put forth claims to their land or that they were never advised to do so.

Another abuse which eroded the mission towns was the unauthorized distribution of land there by *alcaldes*. In 1847, William Blackburn, the *alcalde* of Santa Cruz, issued and recorded several deeds to lands belonging to the ex-mission establishment. The practice was promptly

305

forbidden by Governor R. B. Mason;[99] he reprimanded Blackburn, informing him that:

Those Missions and Mission lands cannot be in any way incumbered or disposed of by any of the authorities in California. An *alcalde* cannot grant or dispose of lands, unless when a town has been authorized . . . by the proper authorities to be sold for the benefit and improvement of the place.[100]

In 1852 the United States government dispatched Benjamin Davis Wilson to report on the living conditions of the Indians in southern California. He wrote that only the most backward Indians were found to congregate around the old missions. There, he continued, they

. . . linger in their straggling huts of brush or tule, trying to get a meagre subsistence out of the small patches not yet taken up by the whites—ill clothed, in filth and wretchedness, without food half the year, save what is stolen. If there be savages among these southern Indians, a Mission is now the place to seek them, where riot and debauchery reign supreme.[101]

These Indian pueblos, he reported, "serve in no way to benefit their race, while there is too much danger that with all their bright promise, they may be drawn themselves in the vortex that swallows up the hopes of their brethren who hire out on the farms or crowd around the cities."[102] He proposed that the American authorities build towns for the Indians in a manner "which a people can determine after they have become settled." Wilson suggested that the towns be built "as compactly as health will admit of, and let the 'laws of the Indies' and some other Spanish laws suggest a part of the regulations, if better ones cannot be devised in these days of progress."[103]

The extinction of the California Indian was soon a matter of historical record. Their pueblos were but "feeble approximations to such towns of civilized and christianized natives as all the missions had been intended to become," Bancroft observed.[104] Elsewhere in Latin America the situation was not markedly better; there, too, governments systematically dismantled the collective ties which were the only legitimate cohesion which could be used to maintain the integrity of Indian settlements. In Mexico, even under a liberal regime, the situation of the Indian was not an enviable one. The Lerdo Law of 1856 broke up all collectively-held land, which specifically included that of the Indian communities. In that year, a progressive journalist wrote of such towns, " . . . the communism is opposed to liberty and civilization."[105] The Indian settlements of Peru were ordered by Bolivar in 1824 to distribute their

306

lands among individual households; he stipulated that they could not be alienated until 1850. But the measure was repealed and it was only a matter of time for merciless, obdurate *gente de razón* to divest the Indians of their rightful patrimony.[106] This situation also prevailed in Bolivia. Thus, despite the best of intentions, Spanish institutions of Indian acculturation and assimilation generally proved to be inadequate in terms of their political purpose; this situation was particularly acute in frontier environments where the protective force of centralized authority was at a minimum. The California Indian, even more so than his brother further to the south, could not survive in missions where he was accorded perpetual legal minority, nor in towns where misery and thralldom awaited him. Only in the biological phenomenon of race mixture is his presence occasionally remarked.

307

[1] The transitory existence of missions, external to their legal status, may be illustrated by the examples of Paraguay and California. The California missions consisted of twenty-one settlements containing at most 30,000 Indians; San Diego was the first to be founded (1769) and most were secularized in 1834. In Paraguay, the first mission was established in 1610 and by 1623 there were twenty-three with a population of 100,000. By the end of the eighteenth century this sizeable empire had crumbled; in California, following secularization, the decline was similarly precipitous. Stephen Neill, *A History of Christian Missions*, The Pelican History of the Church (6 vols., Harmondsworth and Baltimore, 1964), VI, 202–203. Both enterprises were characterized by the failure of the missionary orders, both Franciscan and Jesuit, to develop a sense of initiative and independence among their charges; neither did they develop a native clergy nor orders for women. The explanation invariably offered was the backwardness and inherent instability of character among the Indians which disqualified them from such responsibilities, e.g. the priesthood, let alone self-government. "This error," writes Ricard, "prevented the Church from striking deep roots in the [Mexican] nation, gave it the appearance of a foreign institution, and kept it strictly dependent on the mother country." Robert Ricard, *The Spiritual Conquest of Mexico*, trans. Lesley Byrd Simpson (Berkeley and Los Angeles, 1966), p. 235.

[2] *Recopilación de leyes de los Reynos de las Indias* (4th ed.; 3 vols., Madrid, 1791).

[3] Herbert E. Bolton, *The Mission as a Frontier Institution in the Spanish-American Colonies* (El Paso, 1962), pp. 5–6, reprinted from the *American Historical Review*, XXIII (October 1917), 42–61.

[4] *Ibid.*, p. 6.

[5] Reyes Católicos to Ovando, "Instrucción para el Gobernador é Oficiales, sobrel Gobierno de las Indias, é lo que en ello se deve observar," Cartagena, March 20–29, 1503, *Colección de Documentos Inéditos Relativos al Descubrimiento, Conquista y Organización de las Antiguas Posesiones Españolas de América y Oceanía sacados de los Archivos del Reino* (42 vols., Madrid, 1864–1884), XXXI, 156–174.

[6] *Ibid.*

[7] Ricard, *Spiritual Conquest*, p. 136.

[8] Quoted in François Chevalier, *Land and Society in Colonial Mexico*, trans. Alvin Eustis, ed. Lesley Byrd Simpson (Berkeley and Los Angeles, 1963), pp. 197–198.

[9] Ricard, *Spiritual Conquest*, p. 136.

[10] Recalling legislation that dates chiefly from the mid-sixteenth century, the *Recopilación* stipulates "that Indians are to be reduced to towns." *Recopilación*, VI, 3/1; II, 207–208. Also, that they should be segregated from non-Indians as per VI, 3/21–23, II, 212. Additionally, in 1686, shortly after the publication of the first edition of the *Recopilación*, a papal bull was published by Innocent XI directing that Indians be reduced to pueblos. Ordinances prohibiting vagrants from living among Indians date as early as 1536 as do statutes enforcing segregation. Magnus Mörner, *Race Mixture in the History of Latin America* (Boston, 1967), p. 46; *Recopilación*, VI, 3/23; II, 212.

[11] Bolton, *Mission as a Frontier Institution*, p. 13.

[12] Lasuén, Mission San Carlos, June 19, 1801, *Writings of Fermín Francisco de Lasuén*, ed. & trans. Finbar Kenneally, O.F.M. (2 vols., Washington, D.C., 1965), II, 202.

[13] Ricard, *Spiritual Conquest*, p. 78.

[14] Serra to Bucareli, Monterey, August 24, 1774, *Writings of Junípero Serra*, ed. Antonine Tibesar, O.F.M. (4 vols., Washington, D.C., 1955–1966), II, 143.

[15] *Recopilación*, IV, 7/1, 3, 9 and 10; II, 19–21.

[16] In 1779 Neve wrote to Teodoro de Croix that a mission site should be "abundant in water, firewood, and stone for building, with lands suitable for plantings and with the advantage of an accessible spring nearby so that the benefits of irrigation may be attained." Neve to Croix, Monterey, February 25, 1779; California Archives, Bancroft Library (hereafter referred to as CA), Provincial Records, I, 142. Later, in addition to the usual criteria, considerations of security came into prominence. In 1794 Governor Diego de Borica ordered that the site for Mission San Juan Bautista "be the most suitable, with a view towards a reconnoissance of its environs in order to free it from all surprises." Borica, "Instrucción para el Comandante de la Escolta destinada á la

308

fundación de la Mision San Juan Bautista," Monterey, May 18, 1797; CA, Provincial State Papers, X, 138–144.

¹⁷ Bucareli, "Instrucción que debe observar el Comandante nombrado para los Establecimientos de San Diego y Monterey," Mexico, August 17, 1773; CA, State Papers. Missions and Colonization, I, 324–328; Article 7.

¹⁸ *Ibid.*, Article 9.

¹⁹ *Ibid.*, Article 10.

²⁰ *Ibid.*, Article 15.

²¹ Felipe de Neve, Mexico, September 12, 1774, Ruth Lapham Butler, "A Statement by Phelipe de Neve," *Hispanic-American Historical Review*, XXII (May 1942), 358.

²² C. Alan Hutchinson, *Frontier Settlement in Mexican California: The Híjar-Padrés Colony and Its Origins, 1769–1835* (New Haven & London, 1969), p. 55. About 1524 Vasco de Quiroga, a judge of the Second Audiencia and later Bishop of Michoacán (1538–1565) established the "curious" settlement of Santa Fé—part hospital and part village for free Indian farmers; harvests were held in common as in More's *Utopia*. Chevalier, *Land and Society*, p. 54; see Ricard, *Spiritual Conquest*, pp. 159–160.

²³ Quoted in H. A. van Coenen Torchiana, *Story of the Mission Santa Cruz* (San Francisco, 1933), p. 98.

²⁴ Hutchinson, *Frontier Settlement*, p. 55. It is odd that this item has not received greater attention. It is significant because it is diametrically opposed to the mission system wherein the padre exercises complete control of the lives and labors of the Indians whose efforts are wholly on the behalf of the institution. Neve believed that missionaries hoarded produce and arranged that it be placed under the control of the viceroy so that the surpluses could be utilized more to the missions' benefit. *Ibid.*, pp. 54–55.

²⁵ Serra to Bucareli, "Representación," Item 30, Mexico, March 13, 1773, Serra, *Writings*, I, 325.

²⁶ This group apparently included three soldiers, two sailors, one blacksmith and one carpenter. In addition, three more soldiers who had married Indian women and three who were about to also wished to settle at San Carlos.

²⁷ Article 12 read:
With the desire to establish population more rapidly in the new establishments, I for the present . . . grant the power . . . to distribute lands in private to such Indians as may dedicate themselves to agriculture . . . for, having property of their own, the love of it will cause them to better establish themselves. . . . They must necessarily have their house in the town or mission where they have been established or settled.
Bucareli, "Instrucción que debe observar el Comandante . . .; CA, State Papers. Missions and Colonization, I, 324–328. Additionally, each Spanish settler was to receive a sailor's salary for two years and rations for both himself and spouse for five years. Serra to Bucareli, Monterey, August 24, 1774, Serra, *Writings*, II, 151. The compensation was substantially the equivalent to that of settlers in the civil towns. Neve, "Reglamento," Title 14, Article 2; CA, State Papers. Missions and Colonization, I, 104–105.

²⁸ Serra to Bucareli, "Representación," Item 30, Mexico, March 13, 1773, Serra, *Writings*, I, 325.

²⁹ Ignacio Vallejo, San Jose, n.d., 1796; CA, Provincial State Papers, III, 25.

³⁰ Nicolás Soler to Jacobo Ugarte y Loyola, Monterey, November 3, 1788. *Ibid.*, pp. 20–21.

³¹ Miguel Costansó, "Informe de Don Miguel Costansó al Virrey, Marqués de Branciforte, sobre el Proyecto de Fortificar los Presidios de la Nueva California," *Noticias y Documentos acerca de las Californias, 1764–1795* (Madrid, 1959), p. 232.

³² Gov. José de Arrillaga to Giribet, Monterey, June 13, 1790; CA, Provincial State Papers, V, 156–157. Lasuén to Pedro Fages, Mission San Antonio, July 26, 1790. *Ibid.* pp. 165–168.

³³ *Ibid.*

³⁴ The *Recopilación* contains the following statute which dates from 1618: "We order that in each pueblo, and Reduction there be one Indian *Alcalde* of the same Reduction;

309

and if there are more than eighty houses, two *Alcaldes* and two *Regidores*, also Indians." The term of office was to be one year, "as is the practice in Pueblos of Spaniards" and a parish priest was to supervise the election (VI, 3/15, II, 210–211).

³⁵ Lasuén to Neve, Mission San Diego, January 25, 1779, Lasuén, *Writings*, I, 75–76.

³⁶ *Ibid.* p. 76.

³⁷ Neve to Teodoro de Croix, Monterey, February 24, 1779, CA, Provincial Records, I, 121.

³⁸ Serra to Lasuén, Monterey, August 15, 1779, Serra, *Writings*, III, 365. In 1787 Lasuén was to write that "the institution of *alcaldes* and *regidores* . . . makes such persons independent of the missionaries as regards punishment and dismissal from office when they deserve it, and it makes those officials lazy and haughty, connivers at wrongdoing and partners in it." Lasuén to Ugarte y Loyola, Mission San Carlos, October 20, 1787, Lasuén, *Writings*, II, 168–169.

³⁹ Serra to Lasuén, Monterey, August 15, 1779, Serra, *Writings*, III, 365.

⁴⁰ James Culleton, *Indians and Pioneers of Old Monterey* (Fresno, 1950), p. 161.

⁴¹ Gov. José María de Echeandía to Monterey *alcalde,* Monterey, January 21, 1831; CA, Departmental State Papers. San Jose, I, 85.

⁴² Juan B. Alvarado, Historia de California (5 vols., Bancroft Library MS, 1876), I, 85.

⁴³ Quoted in Hubert Howe Bancroft, *History of California* (7 vols. San Francisco, 1884–1890), II, 339.

⁴⁴ *Ibid.* p. 431.

⁴⁵ Fr. Mariano Payeras, "Representación de Comisario Prefecto . . . sobre innovaciones del Sr Gobernador," Mission San Antonio, June 18, 1821, quoted in Zephyrin Engelhardt, O.F.M., *Missions and Missionaries of California* (4 vols., San Francisco, 1908–1915), III, 112.

⁴⁶ Bancroft, *History of California,* II, 437.

⁴⁷ Quoted in *Ibid.,* p. 488. In effect, this echoes Article 12 of Bucareli's 1773 *Instrucción*: the Indians, "having property of their own, the love of it will cause them to establish themselves." Bucareli, "Instrucción que debe observar . . . ;" CA, State Papers. Missions and Colonization, I, 324–328.

⁴⁸ Mariano G. Vallejo, Recuerdos Históricos y Personales tocante á la Alta California (5 vols. Bancroft Library MS, 1875), II, 107.

⁴⁹ José Bandini, *Descrision de l'Alta California en 1828,* trans. Doris Marian Wright (Berkeley, 1951), pp. 6–7.

⁵⁰ Branciforte to Borica, Mexico, August 25, 1794; CA, Provincial State Papers, VII, 46–48.

⁵¹ Lasuén, *Memoria,* Mission San Carlos, May 9, 1796, Lasuén, *Writings,* I, 377. However, such an attitude also invited abuse. In Nueva Galicia during the sixteenth century, for example, Indians would often send one or two men into deserted villages in order to create the semblance of an ongoing community and thus prevent the Spanish authorities from classifying the land as unoccupied or ownerless. In 1607, the viceroy, the Marqués de Montesclaros, reported that large areas were unoccupied because of this systematic opposition to Spanish grants; the Indians could always find missionaries to testify on their behalf in court (Chevalier, *Land and Society,* p. 206).

⁵² Frederick W. Beechey, *Narrative of a Voyage to the Pacific and Beering's Strait* (2 vols., London, 1831), II, 14.

⁵³ Echeandía, "Decreto de Secularización de Misiones," Monterey, January 6, 1831; CA, Departmental Records, IV, 66–78.

⁵⁴ *Ibid.,* Articles 6 and 7.

⁵⁵ *Ibid.,* Articles 9, 11 and 12; IV, 7/13 of the *Recopilación* does not specify a quantity of land for future increments of growth (II, 22).

⁵⁶ Alfred Robinson's description of San Luis Rey in 1828 gives a vivid picture of a mission with respect to layout and functional organization:

"The building occupies a large square, of at least eighty or ninety yards on each side, forming an extensive area, in the centre of which a fountain constantly supplies the

310

establishment with pure water. The front is protected by a long corridor, supported by thirty-two arches ornamented with latticed railings, which, together with the fine appearance of the Church on the right, presents an attractive view . . .; the interior is divided into apartments for the missionary and *mayordomos*, store-rooms, work-shops, hospitals, rooms for unmarried males and females, which near at hand is a range of buildings tenanted by the families of the superintendents. There is also a guard-house, where were stationed some ten or a dozen soldiers, and in the rear spacious granaries . . . also large enclosures for wagons, carts, and the implements of agriculture. In the interior of the square might be seen the various trades at work. . . . Adjoining are two large gardens, which supply the table with fruits and vegetables."

Alfred Robinson, *Life in California* (Oakland, 1947), pp. 16–17.

⁵⁷ Figueroa, "Prevenciones provisionales para la emancipación de Indios reducidos," San Diego, July 15, 1833, quoted in Engelhardt, *Missions and Missionaries*, III, 473–476.

⁵⁸ Figueroa to Vallejo, San Diego, August 6, 1833, quoted in Hutchinson, *Frontier Settlement*, p. 229.

⁵⁹ *Ibid.*

⁶⁰ Bancroft, *History of California*, III, 331.

⁶¹ *Ibid.*, pp. 331–332.

⁶² *Diputación*, session of May 1, 1834, quoted in Hutchinson, *Frontier Settlement*, pp. 229–230.

⁶³ Bancroft, *History of California*, III, p. 628.

⁶⁴ Pío Pico, Los Angeles, May 16, 1842; CA, Los Angeles Archives, II, 155–156.

⁶⁵ *Ibid.*

⁶⁶ Bancroft, *History of California*, IV, 628.

⁶⁷ At that time the Pico family owned 133,440 acres along the Pacific Coast, a twenty mile stretch from Oceanside to the Orange County line to San Clemente and extending eastward into the mountains. Richard F. Pourade, *The History of San Diego* (5 vols., San Diego, 1960–1965), III, 65.

⁶⁸ Juan Bandini, Historia de la Alta California, 1769–1845 (Bancroft Library MS, 1874), p. 28.

⁶⁹ Benjamin I. Hayes, Emigrant Notes (Bancroft Library MS), p. 126. He also confirms the transfer of Las Flores to the Pico family (p. 127).

⁷⁰ Auguste Duhaut-Cilly, *Voyage Autour du Monde* (2 vols., Paris, 1834–1835), I, 310.

⁷¹ Richard A. Pierce and John H. Winslow, eds., *H.M.S. Sulphur at California, 1837 and 1839* (San Francisco, 1969), p. 6. Francis Guillemard Simpkinson (1819–1906) was a midshipman with the *Sulphur* expedition.

⁷² Juan Castro to Monterey *Juez de Paz*, San Francisco, November 20, 1839; CA, Monterey County Archives. Miscellaneous Documents, p. 499.

⁷³ José Castro, San Francisco, April 23, 1841, quoted in Alfred Wheeler, *Land Titles in San Francisco* (San Francisco, 1852), p. 15.

⁷⁴ Bancroft, *History of California*, IV, 665–666.

⁷⁵ Quoted in *Ibid.*, V, 660. Evidently, as is indicated in the quotation, there was some ethnic animosity between the two towns. In June, 1845 a group of settlers from Dolores insulted those of Yerba Buena and stoned their houses (*Ibid.*, IV, 666).

⁷⁶ Bernard Moses, *The Establishment of Municipal Government in San Francisco*, Johns Hopkins University Studies in History and Political Science, 7th Series, Vols. II–III (Baltimore, 1889), p. 12.

⁷⁷ Bancroft, *History of California*, IV, 625–627.

⁷⁸ Juan Bandini, Historia de la Alta California, p. 30.

⁷⁹ Agustín Olvera, Los Angeles, July 12, 1841; CA, Departmental State Papers. Juzgados, Naturalization, pp. 137–138.

⁸⁰ Juan B. Alvarado, "Artículos que debe observar provisionalmente en el nuevo arreglo del Establecimiento de San Juan Capistrano," Monterey, July 29, 1841. *Ibid.*, pp. 142–145.

311

[81] Bandini to Alvarado, Los Angeles, October 12, 1841. *Ibid.*, pp. 145–146.

[82] Bancroft, *History of California*, IV, 625.

[83] This suggests the idea of *encomienda*.

[84] *Ibid.*

[85] Quoted in *Ibid.*, p. 627.

[86] *Ibid.*

[87] Hayes, Emigrant Notes, p. 123.

[88] Canet to Srio de Govt. Jimeno, San Luis Obispo, July 19, 1841; CA, State Papers. Missions, II, 255; the *mayordomo's* grandson, also named Vicente Canet, was still alive in 1971 but no information could be obtained from him.

[89] Bancroft, *History of California*, IV, 659.

[90] *Ibid.*

[91] *Ibid.*

[92] J. Mariano Bonilla, San Luis Obispo, October 20, 1849; CA, San Luis Obispo Archivo, pp. 20–21.

[93] William Rich Hutton, *Glances at California, 1847–1853*, ed. Willard O. Waters (San Marino, Calif., 1942), p. xvi.

[94] Victoria to Secretario de Relaciones, Monterey, May 6, 1831; CA, Departmental Records, IV, 126–130.

[95] *Ibid.*

[96] Quoted in Pourade, *History of San Diego*, III, 44.

[97] Gonzales to Alvarado, San Buenaventura, July 3, 1841; CA; State Papers. Missions, II, 228.

[98] Pourade, *History of San Diego*, III, 67; Frank W. Blackmar, *Spanish Institutions of the Southwest*, Johns Hopkins Studies in Historical and Political Science, Extra Vol. X (Baltimore, 1891), pp. 146–147.

[99] CA, Santa Cruz Archives, p. 108.

[100] Mason to Blackburn, Monterey, November 24, 1847, quoted in Torchiana, *Mission Santa Cruz*, p. 375.

[101] Benjamin Davis Wilson, *The Indians of Southern California in 1852*, ed. John Walton Caughey (San Marino, Calif., 1952), p. 25.

[102] *Ibid.*, p. 17.

[103] *Ibid.*, p. 53. In New Mexico, Indians lived in mission towns with an area of one square league. The land was held in common and a priest was maintained by and for the village. Other aspects were "conformable to the principles of the Spanish laws concerning the allotments of Indian villages." William Carey Jones, *Report on the Subject of Land Titles in California* (Washington, D.C., 1850), p. 10.

[104] Bancroft, *History of California*, III, 628.

[105] Quoted in Mörner, *Race Mixture*, p. 104.

[106] *Ibid.*

312

PRESIDIOS

IX

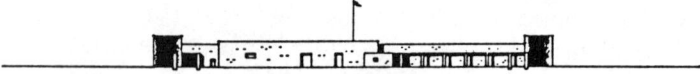

THE CIVILIAN SETTLEMENT

PERHAPS the most significant historical aspect of the frontier presidio was its role as a nucleus for civilian settlement, for many of the towns and cities of northern Mexico and southwestern United States emerged from presidial beginnings. At first the purely military character of the garrisons was altered by the arrival of the families of the soldiers. Some of these tilled the lands around the compound and some lived in huts outside the fortress walls. Eventually a number of purely civilian families came and settled at or near the presidio, drawn not only by the protection it afforded but also by the market it offered for their produce. Nor were these settlers officially discouraged. Rather, both the royal government and the military authorities promoted the growth of such establishments, for productive civilian communities simplified the problem of provisioning the remote garrisons.

Owing both to the immense cost of maintaining permanent garrisons on the northern frontier and to an anticipation of eventual peace with the hostile tribes, an opinion prevailed in high quarters during the seventeenth century that the presidio, like the mission, was only a temporary installation. José Francisco Marín, who inspected the garrisons of Nueva Vizcaya in 1693, was among those of this persuasion. He recommended that, gradually, as the Indian hostilities subsided, the number of presidios and the strength of their companies should be reduced and that,

222

eventually, the garrisons should be replaced by civilian towns. He felt that such settlements would be able to protect large areas of the province and that the productive labors of their inhabitants would enhance the royal revenues, whereas the expense of maintaining presidios had been a heavy drain on the royal treasury.[1]

Marín recommended that the sites of the abandoned presidios be occupied by the men of their disbanded companies. Since most of these had families, he felt they should be allotted land in the vicinity and provided at the outset with oxen, plows, and seed to cultivate it as well as Indian labor to assist them in the building of houses. He thought that each such community should have from sixty to seventy men capable of bearing arms, that the government should issue them harquebuses, ammunition, and horses, and that it should appoint a *capitán de guerra* in each town to see to its military readiness. Since the adult male population of each would have the obligations of militiamen, he felt that they should have all the prerogatives, exemptions, and enfranchisements of such. Should additional colonists be needed for these strategic towns, Marín preferred people from the Canary Islands, Galicia, and other realms of Spain rather than those from central Mexico. Finally, he recognized in the civilian community already formed near the presidio of Conchos a suitable pattern of government for those which might be established in the future.[2]

Marín's proposal to replace the presidios with towns defended by civilian militia, as Indian hostilities abated, seems to have been adopted, for in the 1760's civilian communities existed at several sites in Nueva Vizcaya which had formerly been occupied by presidios. Among these were

1 Marín to Viceroy Conde de Galve, Parral, September 30, 1693, in Hackett, *Historical Documents*, II, 384–409.

2 Marín's report of December 13, 1693, as summarized by the attorney for the royal treasury: Fiscal de la Real Hacienda, Respuesta, Madrid, April 1, 1698, in *ibid.*, II, 418–57.

223

El Gallo, Cerrogordo, Conchos, and Casas Grandes.[3] It should also be noted that later, when Croix established an entire system of civilian communities in that province as a second line of defense, he adopted many of the specifications which had appeared in Marín's proposals.

In addition to the formal towns that came to replace presidios, civilian settlements also developed where presidios continued to exist. By the 1760's all except one of the twenty-three garrisons in the several frontier provinces had significant civilian settlements. In eight of these there were, on the average, 37 civilian householders (*vecinos*) to each company of 50 officers and men.[4] According to available figures, there was an average of 5 persons in a household, which would have increased the ratio to approximately 185 civilians to each 50 soldiers in these eight communities. Actually, the non-military population was even larger if the families of the troops were included in this category. At the time, it was estimated that about ninety-five per cent of the presidials were married.[5]

There is some question as to how warmly the civilian families were received by the military as they gravitated to the protection of the presidios, at least before 1772, for the Reglamento of that year called attention to the point. It prohibited the commandants, or anyone else, from discouraging civilians of good reputation from gathering at the post, and stated the official intent to promote the growth of population at these centers. If necessary for the accommodation of a larger population at a presidio, one side of the

[3] Lafora, *Relación del viaje*, 61, 62, 67, and 113.

[4] Only El Pasaje with its company of thirty-six had no civilian settlers. Guajoquilla (seventy-six officers and men) had twenty-one *vecinos*, Janos (fifty-one) had fifty, Fronteras (fifty-one) had at least fifty, Terrenate (fifty) had about twenty, Tubac (fifty) had about forty, Altar (fifty) had about twenty-five, La Bahía (fifty) had about forty-six, and San Juan Bautista (thirty-three) had forty *vecinos. Ibid.*, 60, 65, 114, 121, 125, 127, 132, 190, 226, and 237–38.

[5] Rubi to Marqués de Croix, San Miguel, February 21, 1767 (enclosed with Rubí to Croix, No. 31, Tacubaya, April 10, 1768), AGI, Guad. 511.

224

compound was to be extended. Venders, artisans, and even transient laborers were to be admitted to the compound without prejudice. Farm land and town lots were to be distributed to the civilians who wished to settle at the presidios, and, in return, each settler was obligated to cultivate his land, to have in readiness a horse, weapons, and ammunition, and to join the troops on sorties against the hostiles whenever the commandant might order him to do so.[6]

A notable change in the relationship between military and civilian personnel occurred in 1777. In that year, Croix induced the crown to relax the regulations against officers marrying into frontier families without royal permission. Although Croix's purpose was primarily to reduce the scandalous conduct of some officers, he also expressed an interest in creating new families which would both increase the size of the frontier population and improve its quality.[7] He was shortly to see a close relationship between the productivity of the civilian settlers and the effectiveness of the presidial companies, an interdependence which the Reglamento of 1772 had already recognized.

According to that ordinance, the settlers were not to accompany the presidial troops when they were removed to new positions. Rather, they were to remain at the abandoned sites in civilian communities, and other colonists were to be encouraged to join them. Town lots, houses, and farm lands vacated by the soldiers were to be distributed to all who would undertake the military obligations of settlers. In Sonora, Spaniards who colonized such sites were to be provided with fire arms at original cost, and Opata Indians who settled there were to be furnished these weapons free of all charge.[8]

One of the fundamental weaknesses in the removal of

6 *Reglamento de 1772*, Title 11, Articles 1 and 2.

7 Croix to Gálvez, No. 8, Mexico, February 26, 1777, and Gálvez to Croix, Aranjuez, May 24, 1777, AGI, Guad. 516.

8 "Instrucción para la nueva colocación de presidios," Article 6, in *Reglamento de 1772*.

225

interior presidios to the northern line of defense, as ordered by the Reglamento, was that several of the new sites were so isolated from civilian settlements and in such barren terrain that their troops were often without sufficient food and other essential commodities to sustain themselves. Indeed, it was due in large part to this unfortunate circumstance that Croix withdrew several of the presidios of the Line and situated them in more populated areas. Croix realized that not only was a civilian population essential to the survival and strength of a presidio but that such a community had to be situated where there was adequate crop land, pasture, wood, and water. In general, these conditions were lacking in the remote latitude of the new Line.[9]

Croix also discovered that when the presidios were moved to those untenable positions, the towns and settlements from which they had been withdrawn had become so exposed to Indian raids that many were being abandoned. Especially beset were the civilian communities of Tubac and Fronteras in Sonora, of Valle de San Buenaventura in Nueva Vizcaya, and of Santa Rosa and Monclova in Coahuila. Meanwhile, in the barren terrain along the new Line, the troops and their families were suffering extremely from hunger. In several of their remote positions they lived for an entire year on tortillas and a small ration of beans. In a few of these presidios they had to go out like Indians to seek wild fruits, and in all of them the scanty supplies of food were brought in from afar at great risk and cost to the troops. It was for these reasons that Croix removed eight of the presidios of the Line to either their former positions or to sites where civilian settlements could be formed.[10]

[9] Croix to Gálvez, No. 458, Arizpe, January 23, 1780, paragraph 61, AGI, Guad. 278.

[10] Those repositioned were Terrenate (from Santa Cruz), Fronteras (from San Bernardino), San Buenaventura (from Velarde), El Príncipe (from Pilares), San Carlos (from the arroyo of that name), San Sabá (from San Vicente), Santa Rosa (from Aguaverde), and Monclova (from the Río Grande site of the same name). *Ibid.*, paragraphs 21, 22, 25, 27, 29, 33, and 34.

226

Croix's policy of promoting civilian communities at presidios can be examined in some detail in his instructions for the relocation of the companies of San Buenaventura in Nueva Vizcaya and Horcasitas in Sonora. Actually, the basic provisions for the founding of civilian towns were stipulated in the general Laws of the Indies,[11] but Croix modified and enlarged upon these stipulations to some extent in order to accommodate the peculiar local conditions.

In withdrawing the company of San Buenaventura from the Valley of Velarde to the more southerly site of Chavarría, some sixteen miles from the populated Valley of San Buenaventura, Croix chartered a civilian town which was to be situated under the shelter of the presidio. At Velarde, the presidio had been not only too far removed from the settled Valley of San Buenaventura to protect and to be provisioned by it, but it was also suffering from a most unhealthy situation. Only four years after its removal to that position an inspector reported that the creek which furnished its water had dried up, that drinking water could be found only in two large ponds nearby, and that this was polluted and so evil smelling that the chaplain of the company was loath to use it even for baptizing or celebrating Mass. Since the troops had experienced a great deal of sickness and the horses were losing weight from inadequate pastures, the inspector now recommended that the garrison be pulled back to the less remote site. Croix, believing that the land at Chavarría was fertile, open, and accessible to abundant wood, pasture, and water, approved the inspector's recommendations. On July 3, 1778, he ordered the withdrawal from Velarde and, three months later, drew up detailed instructions for the establishment of both a presidio and a *villa*, or chartered town, at the new site.[12]

[11] *Recopilación de leyes de los reynos de Indias* (originally published in 1681).

[12] Croix to Gálvez, No. 297, Chihuahua, October 23, 1778, AGI, Guad. 270.

227

It is largely from Croix's instructions to the presidio's commandant that the following details are drawn.[13] The new *villa* was to be settled by Indians as well as by what Croix euphemistically called Spaniards. There were to be from ten to fifteen families of Indians of proven loyalty, all recruited from those Tarahumara villages which could readily spare them, and there were to be from thirty-five to forty families of so-called Spaniards, all of whom were probably colonial-born and many of whom were undoubtedly of mixed ancestry. The Spanish families were to be recruited from the migrant or scattered population rather than from existing towns. It would appear that there were not enough Spaniards or even *mestizos* to populate the several new frontier towns which Croix was forming in Nueva Vizcaya and also that pacified Indians from such missionized villages as those of the Tarahumara were readily acceptable as colonists.

In keeping with new royal policy, there was no suggestion in the instructions that the Tarahumares were to be forcibly conscripted, either as settlers or laborers, or that they were to suffer any discrimination in the allotment of land. On the contrary, the instructions not only required that they be volunteers but also that they be granted land and issued rations on the same basis as the Spanish settlers.[14]

Both the Spaniards and the Indians were to make their way to Chavarría at their own expense, but from the day of their arrival onward, for the next twelve months, both were

[13] Croix to Captain Nicolás Gil, Instrucciones, Chihuahua, October 14, 1778, enclosed with *ibid*. In an attempt to avoid confusion between the new presidio and town, on the one hand, and the original town of Valle de San Buenaventura, on the other, Croix designated the new presidio site "La Princesa" and the new town "San Juan Nepomuceno," but neither of these names prevailed. Both the new presidio and the new town continued to be called San Buenaventura and the original town, Valle de San Buenaventura. In the nineteenth century the name of the latter was shortened to simply Buenaventura and that of the new town was changed to its present designation, Galeana.

[14] *Ibid.*, Articles 2–5, 10, and 27.

228

to be subsidized. An allowance for their food, calculated at a modest two *reales* (a quarter of a peso) per day for each family, was to be issued by the presidial paymaster in the same manner as the daily allowance for the troops; that is, the colonists were to be credited with the entire amount of the annual subsidy and then debited each day for the food they consumed, and the charge was to be no more than its original cost.[15]

According to plan, the first structure to be erected in the new community was the perimeter wall, then the houses, and lastly the church and the presidio's *casas reales* (guardhouse, storeroom, and quarters for the officers and chaplain).[16] The construction work was to be undertaken initially by the soldiers, who were to work without extra pay. As soon as possible, however, the troops were to be relieved by the arriving settlers, who were to receive only their modest food allowance, and by regular artisans, at the wages prevailing in the region. As soon as the perimeter wall was erected Croix would send convicts to assist in the construction, and these would receive only daily rations.[17] The work was to be allocated in such a manner that neither the soldiers nor the settlers would have to work extra shifts but so that the compound might be completed within one year. Working in rotating teams, the colonists were to serve alternately in the construction work, in cultivating the common field, and in reinforcing the troops who patrolled the environs, defended the town, and guarded the military horseherd.[18]

Crowbars, pickaxes, shovels, and other construction tools were to be purchased with monies borrowed from the presidial common fund (*fondo de gratificación*), whereas the oxen and mules needed for hauling materials for the *casas*

15 *Ibid.*, Articles 3, 20, and 21.
16 *Ibid.*, Article 15.
17 *Ibid.*, Articles 4, 23, 25, and 26.
18 *Ibid.*, Articles 7, 8, and 15.

229

reales had already been volunteered by the company's captain. He was to be reimbursed from the royal treasury. The other officers, the chaplain, and the soldiers had pledged a "voluntary" contribution amounting to 2,613 pesos in all for the construction of the presidio and the *casas reales*. According to Croix, they had willingly agreed to such deductions from their salaries over the next two years in order to live at a more hospitable and less remote site than before.[19]

Croix specified that the town lots, farm lands, and water rights were to be distributed equally among the families of the common soldiers and those of the Spanish and Indian settlers.[20] Although the jurisdiction of the *villa* was to extend over an immense square, measuring six leagues (almost sixteen miles) on each side, only the bottom land adjacent to the Santa María River was arable, and not all of the remainder was suitable even for grazing. The best lands were to be marked out as the town commons (*ejido*), and this was to be divided into tracts for specific uses. One quarter of it was to be reserved as the town's revenue-producing land (*propio*). During the first year this tract was to be farmed by convict labor, and all of the proceeds from that crop were ear-marked for reimbursing the presidial company for the money it had advanced the settlers for their seed and farm implements. After the first year the *propio* was to be cultivated by the settlers, each contributing a share of the labor, and its proceeds were then to provide the ordinary revenue of the community. One-eighth of the *ejido* was set aside during the first year for raising seed, and thereafter for allotments to future settlers. Another three-eighths was to be distributed in equal plots (*suertes*) among the soldiers, and the remaining quarter of the *ejido* was to be divided and assigned on the same basis to the Spanish and Indian settlers.

19 *Ibid.*, Articles 16–18. See also Croix to Gálvez, No. 458, January 23, 1780, paragraph 175.
20 Croix to Gil, Instrucciones, October 14, 1778, Article 4.

230

The only inequality permitted in the distribution of the uniformly sized parcels of land was that the captain of the presidio was to receive four *suertes*, each of the three subaltern officers and the chaplain was to receive three, and the two sergeants were each to receive two, whereas each of the sixty-three soldiers and approximately fifty civilian family heads was to be allotted only one. The precise size of a *suerte* was not specified beyond the requirement that it be adequate for the comfortable subsistence of one family.

After each family head had received his assigned *suerte*, he was obliged to delimit it by digging ditches, erecting markers, or enclosing it with fruit trees. Specific information as to its precise boundaries and ownership was then to be recorded in the town's official deed book (*libro de repartimiento*), which was also to contain a plat of the township. A separate copy of each deed was to be given to its owner as proof of his title to the land.[21]

It was presumed that the civilians would cultivate their own lands and that the paid servants of the commissioned officers and chaplain would work theirs. The noncommissioned officers and common soldiers were permitted to labor in their fields whenever they were off duty, and such of their kinsmen as might be living in the town could assist them at any time. A soldier without relatives could, if he wished, allow the captain to lease his land to a civilian settler, and under these circumstances the company paymaster would collect the rent and credit it to the soldier's account.

Some restrictions were placed on the ownership of individual parcels of land. Whereas the officers and men were to retain title to the land as long as they remained at the presidio, it would pass to their replacements if they gave up their residence or were transferred elsewhere. For such crops as they had left on the land, however, they would be compensated by the new owners. Likewise, if a sergeant or any other officer above that rank should retire from the

21 *Ibid.*, Articles 5–6, 10–11, 27.

231

service—even though he remained in the town as a settler—
he would have to surrender his land to his military replacement. On the other hand, if a common soldier retired and
stayed on as a civilian, he could retain possession of his land.
Finally, in the event the entire company was disbanded, the
soldiers were under obligation to remain as settlers while
the officers had the option of staying on in that capacity or
moving elsewhere.[22]

Neither a soldier nor a civilian resident—whether Spanish or Indian—was permitted to divide his parcel of land,
even among his legitimate heirs, nor was he permitted to sell
or bequeath it to the Church under any condition what-
soever. If he should die intestate, his land would revert to
the crown and be assigned to another resident of the town.
In no case was one settler or common soldier to come into
possession of more than one parcel. Rather, wherever there
were no heirs, the land of the deceased was to be assigned to
a new settler, a new member of the presidial company, or to
the younger son of a deceased settler who had left his property to his first-born son.

A civilian settler would be free to deed or sell his land,
but only after possessing it for a period of ten years. Even
then he could do so only with proper authorization and
within certain limitations. The recipient would have to be a
laborious and able person, preferably a member of one of
the original families, and never a member of the ecclesiastical profession. Special preference would be given to an established settler who had distinguished himself in civic
duty, especially in assisting in the repair of the community's
buildings and facilities. All such transfers would be duly
recorded in the town's deed book, and no such transaction
might infringe on either the rights of the king or the privileges of the town.

Since the newly created town was designated a *villa*, its
settlers were granted certain privileges and exemptions. For

[22] *Ibid.*, Articles 28–32.

the first ten years they would not have to pay the tithe (*diesmo*) on the produce of their lands, the excise tax (*alcabala*) on the sale or transfer of their goods, or the royal land dues (*enfiteusis*) on their acreage. For the same ten years the Indian settlers had an additional relief, from the annual head tax (*tributo*). Although the first settlers of this particular *villa* were accorded these special exemptions along with their food subsidy for the first year, they were not specifically granted the rank and privilege of *hidalgos,* as were the original settlers of some frontier *villas.* This omission may possibly have been due to the fact that so many of the first settlers at Chavarría were Indians and mixed bloods, who were not ordinarily eligible for even this minor rank in the social hierarchy of Spanish nobility.

The rights and privileges of the settlers were, of course, counterbalanced by a number of obligations. Specifically, all of the settlers, whether military or civilian, Spanish or Indian, had to maintain their residences in the *villa,* keep their houses in good repair, and cultivate their assigned lands. Failing in any of these obligations, they might lose their status as legal residents (*vecinos*) and be declared vagabonds. Under that penalty they would be liable for forced labor service elsewhere with no other compensation than daily rations.[23] Each resident had also to take his turn in repairing and maintaining the public buildings and utilities, such as the main irrigation ditch, and in cultivating the town's revenue land.[24] In keeping with the Reglamento of 1772, moreover, each *vecino* was under obligation to respond to the call of the presidio's captain in cases of military emergency, and in order to fulfill this duty, each was required to maintain in readiness a horse, firearms, and ammunition.

Although all of the adult male residents were required to contribute in person to the defense of the town and its

23 *Ibid.,* Articles 33–39.
24 *Ibid.,* Article 11.

233

271

environs, the inhabitants of the new *villa* were also required to support a formal militia unit. This was a squad of thirty Spaniards and ten Indians who were to be selected by the presidio's captain from among the brothers and other kinsmen of the soldiers and from those civilians who were most suited for military service. The corporal of the squad was to be selected from its membership by the commandant general, and was to be under the orders of the presidio's captain. That officer might call upon the militia to man the presidio's fortification, reinforce its horseherd guard, or protect its stores. The militia was to be armed in the same manner as the presidio's *tropa ligera*, that is, with only a short sword, a musket, and a brace of pistols. The uniform was to be that of other militia units in Nueva Vizcaya: a blue jacket with white buttons, red collar, and red cuffs; a pair of blue breeches; a blue cape; and a black hat.[25]

According to arrangements made in the following year for all such units in Nueva Vizcaya, the militiamen were to enjoy certain privileges over and above those of their fellow townsmen.[26] Specifically, for as long as they resided in town the militiamen were to be exempt from the labor draft (*repartimiento*) and from any other such burdensome duty (*oficio*), from involuntary guardianship (*tutela*) of their personal funds, and, except in urgent necessity, from impressment into the regular army or attachment of their horses and mules. They were also freed from having to pay feudal dues (*derechos de vasallaje*) or from having to quarter troops in their homes (*utensilos*). If a member of the militia were a minor, these same exemptions accrued to his parents. All militiamen were to be treated with the utmost equity whenever their estates and business transactions were evaluated for taxation.[27] In matters relating to their own and

25 *Ibid.*, Articles 40–46.
26 Croix to Commandant Inspector Antonio Bonilla, Chihuahua, February 8, 1779 (enclosed with Croix to Gálvez, No. 595, Arizpe, January 23, 1780), AGI, Guad. 281.
27 *Ibid.*, Articles 1–4.

234

their wives' hereditary estates and personal possessions, they were to enjoy the special military privilege (*fuero militar*) which gave immediate jurisdiction over such litigation to the captain of the presidio (and appellate authority to the commandant general) rather than to the civil or ecclesiastical courts. If faced with a criminal charge, the militiaman would enjoy the right to a military trial, and while on active duty both he and his wife had this privilege in civil as well as criminal cases. The militiamen were also to enjoy certain retirement privileges.[28]

For the political administration of the new *villa*, Croix authorized the captain of the presidio to act as municipal governor and to rule in accordance with the pertinent articles of the Reglamento of 1772, the most recently codified Laws of the Indies, and such supplemental orders as the commandant general himself might issue. However, the government was not to be exclusively military. Once the settlers were congregated and the town securely established, the *vecinos* were to elect the *alcaldes* and other municipal officials. Croix specified that his instructions for founding the *villa* were to be placed in the town's official deed book so that the articles would remain in force at all times and so that they would be observed as the permanent charter of the community.[29]

From the foregoing rather detailed specifications it becomes readily apparent that the privileges, exemptions, and guarantees of the civilian settlers living under the shelter of a presidio were inextricably linked to their obligations to assist in the military defense of the community, that they were mobilized not only for their own defense but also in order to support the presidio both militarily and economically. On the other hand, these particular instructions do not constitute sound evidence that the civilian settlers in presidial communities actually received the preferential

[28] *Ibid.*, Article 6 and following.
[29] Croix to Gil, Instrucciones, October 14, 1778, Article 50.

235

treatment which was prescribed. Rather, they merely specify the intentions of the king and the commandant general. As was the case with all Spanish policy and law, the actual enforcement of such articles seems often to have diminished in almost direct proportion to the distance of the situation from central authority. Since the new site for the presidio and *villa* of San Buenaventura was about 130 miles from Croix's headquarters at Chihuahua (and at least that far from his subsequent office at Arizpe), his detailed instructions were in fact largely ignored.

In October of 1779, fully twelve months after he had issued these instructions, Croix visited the new site and was appalled by what he found. Although a considerable portion of the funds for the project had been appropriated and spent, there had been no progress at all in erecting the presidial fortification or the municipal buildings. Moreover, the Tarahumara Indians, who were to have assisted with the construction work and stayed on as settlers, had quarreled with the superintendent over their remuneration and had gone back to their villages. Apparently the Spanish settlers had not even arrived, for none of the lands had been planted. At any rate, Croix felt that his instructions had not been observed in the least and that additional funds were now required. Finally, since the captain of the presidio had not carried out his orders for the completion of the new establishment, Croix now encharged the provincial governor with this responsibility.[30]

The presidial garrison itself was withdrawn from the Valley of Velarde at least as early as January of 1780, but sixty of its seventy-two soldiers were then residing with their families at Valle de San Buenaventura, some sixteen miles south of the new site.[31] Even as late as April of 1782, three and a half years after Croix had issued his instructions, the

---

[30] Croix to Gálvez, Informe General, July 29, 1781, paragraph 215, AGI, Guad. 279.

[31] Croix to Gálvez, No. 458, January 23, 1780, paragraphs 25 and 70.

236

fortification was still unfinished.[32] Sometime within the next four years the presidio was finally completed, but another two years passed without the *villa* having been formed.[33] Eventually, however, the *villa* was established, and (as the present small town of Galeana, in northwestern Chihuahua), it came to outlive the presidio itself.

At least one of Croix's presidial towns, El Pitic, was established in the interior, more than a hundred miles behind the frontier line. In 1780 the commandant general ordered the presidial company at Horcasitas to transfer to El Pitic, which had been its original site in Sonora, where a new *villa* was to be formed. The purpose of the removal was to provide better surveillance over the newly pacified Seri Indians, who had been congregated there. Since the instructions for founding the new community varied somewhat from those for San Buenaventura, having been drawn up by Croix's *auditor de guerra* rather than himself, they should be examined in some detail for a more complete description of the new civilian towns.[34]

For the construction of the presidio and *villa* of El Pitic, the commandant general was able to raise only 3,000 pesos at the outset. Even though the military governor of Sonora donated another 225 pesos for the project, it was necessary to induce merchants and other men of means to advance the settlers the funds they required to cultivate their new fields and to build their houses and some of the public facilities. Moreover, in order to encourage the Seris to remain on their new reservation, it was considered necessary to reserve for them the best lands available and to grant these in regular allotments (*suertes*) so that each Indian family might take pride in its ownership and also become self-sufficient by its

32 Croix to Gálvez, Informe General, April 23, 1782, paragraph 522, AGI, Guad. 279.

33 Rengel to Gálvez, No. 140, Chihuahua, March 2, 1786, AGI, Guad. 286; Ugarte to Flores, Valle de San Bartolomé, September 17, 1788, AGN, PI 127–4.

34 Pedro Galindo Navarro to Croix, Arizpe, December 22, 1782 (enclosed with Croix to Gálvez, No. 882, February 24, 1783), AGI, Guad. 284.

237

own labors. It was decided that, for the present, the Seris would be issued daily rations of food. However, since other, more loyal domestic tribes were becoming resentful of this preferential treatment, it was hoped that the rationing could be discontinued in the near future.[35]

The *villa* of El Pitic was to embrace a four-league square instead of one of six leagues, as in the case of San Buenaventura, and was to incorporate the existing Seri village on the southern bank of the San Miguel River. Although these Indian residents were to be under the jurisdiction of the new town, which was on the northern bank, they were to enjoy the same benefits as the white settlers and also the right to elect their own *alcaldes* and aldermen.

The Reglamento of 1772 had provided that the commandant of the garrison would exercise the governorship and administer ordinary civil and criminal justice in presidial communities, but Croix ruled that the status of the military company at El Pitic was that of a detachment, rather than a permanent garrison, and that, therefore, such jurisdiction would remain with the political governor of the province and the local officials he might appoint. In keeping with the Laws of the Indies, however, a town council (*cabildo* or *ayuntamiento*) was to be elected by the resident heads of households (*vecinos*) as soon as there were as many as thirty of these. This body was to consist of two municipal magistrates (*alcaldes ordinarios*), six aldermen (*regidores*), one public attorney (*procurador síndico*), and a city manager (*mayordomo de propios*), all of whom would be elected by the *vecinos* for the first one-year term and thereafter by the incumbent members of the council itself. The *alcaldes* would have original jurisdiction over local law suits, but appeals could be made to the *ayuntamiento* at large, to the provincial governor, and to the supreme court (*real audiencia*) of the realm.

Both the Spanish and the Indian residents were to enjoy

[35] *Ibid.*

238

in common the woods, pastures, waters, stone, fish, game, and fruits of the town's four-league-square *ejido* and also those of the uncultivated and royal lands (*tierras baldías y realengas*) which might exist beyond the township's boundaries.[36]

The plat for the *villa* was to be drawn by an army engineer, Manuel Agustín Máscaro, and all the streets and buildings were to be arranged in a rectilinear pattern, according to this plan. The size of the lots (*solares*) in the blocks formed by the streets was not prescribed, but the commissioner in charge of laying out the town was to assign an eighth, a fourth, a half, or an entire block (*manzana*) to each family according to its size and need. So as to avoid any complaints stemming from partiality, the particular lots of any one size were to be assigned by a public drawing.

Outside of the town itself was to be the commons (*ejido*), and a part of this was to be marked off for a pasture (*dehesa*). The most arable land was to be surveyed and marked off in *suertes* of equal size, four hundred *varas* in length and two hundred in width (about 1,110 by 555 feet, or a little over fourteen acres). Eight of the irrigated *suertes* were to be set aside as the town *propio*, or revenue land.

Unlike the situation at San Buenaventura, where each ordinary family was entitled to only one parcel of land, each at El Pitic might receive as many as three, if the number in the family merited it. As with the house sites in town, the parcels of farm land were to be distributed by the drawing of lots. The records of these grants were to be kept in the municipal archives, and each settler was to receive his own certificate of title.[37]

Permanent title to the town lots and farms were made conditional on the recipient's having taken possession and planted fruit trees along the boundaries within three months of the grant, having begun construction of his house

36 *Ibid.*, Articles 1–7.
37 *Ibid.*, Articles 8–17.

239

and cultivation of his field within two years, having resided in town with his family for at least four years without alienating or mortgaging the property, and having maintained weapons and horses for the local defense. Failure to comply with any of these conditions might result in forfeiture of either the town lot or farm land. As in all other towns, the property of the *vecinos* could never be sold or deeded to the Church or any of its agencies.[38]

The first public facility to be established was the irrigation system for the farm lands. Water from the river was to be diverted into a main canal (*acequia madre*) and thence into lesser ditches serving groups of individual tracts. An official selected each year by the town council would see that the water was distributed equitably and would supervise the cleaning and repairing of the ditches. All labor on the irrigation system would be performed by the *vecinos* as a civic obligation.

Two other officials were to be named by the *ayuntamiento* each year to see that the cattle belonging to any settler did not trample or otherwise damage the crop land of others while being driven to the pastures. They were to impound such animals and bring charges against their owners.

The *ayuntamiento* was to pass such municipal ordinances as might be required for the political and economic regulation of the community, but such acts would become valid only after approval by the commandant general.[39]

It was according to these requirements and guarantees that the Villa de San Pedro de la Conquista del Pitic was chartered late in 1782 under the shelter of the new presidio. In time this *villa* would become the present city of Hermosillo, capital of the state of Sonora.

Notwithstanding the special privileges of the military in Spanish society, the civilians seem to have gained more affluence than the soldiers in communities where both were

---

[38] *Ibid.*, Article 18.
[39] *Ibid.*, Articles 19–24.

240

formally established. Statistics are not available for such a comparison in the new presidial towns formed by Croix, but they do exist for some of the older *villas* where presidios existed. For instance, a rather detailed census for the presidio of San Antonio de Béjar and the Villa de San Fernando, which came to encircle it, was taken by the military governor of Texas in 1779.[40]

In that year there were 297 civilian families at San Antonio, the members and servants of which numbered 1,177 persons, while the military personnel included 80 non-commissioned officers and men, including inactives, whose families and retainers brought its total number to only 240 persons, or just under seventeen per cent of the entire community. While 51 of the civilian families (about 17.2 per cent of their total) owned houses and another 103 (34.7 per cent) owned huts (*jacales*), only 12 of the soldiers (15 per cent) possessed the former and 26 (32.5 per cent) the latter. Thus, the civilians were just slightly better off in housing. However, many of the soldiers, especially the bachelors, were adequately quartered in the barracks of the presidio. Whereas 71 of the *vecinos* (23.9 per cent) owned at least one allotment of dry farm land and 146 (49.2 per cent) held irrigated parcels, only 15 of the soldiers (18.75 per cent) possessed the former and 18 (22.4 per cent) the latter, which would indicate a somewhat larger degree of civilian affluence. As for livestock, 194 civilians (65.3 per cent) owned a total of 7,434 head as compared to 79 soldiers (98.8 per cent) with an aggregate total of only 1,067 animals. The large percentage of military owners of the comparatively small number of livestock was due, of course, to the military requirement that each of the soldiers possess six horses, one colt, and a mule. It should also be noted that a considerable

40 Domingo Cabello, Extracto General de la Tropa de dicho Presidio y Vezindario de la Villa de San Fernando en que se comprende el Padrón de sus Familias, Armamento, Ganados, y Vienes Raizes que cada una tiene, San Antonio de Béjar, July 6, 1779, AGI, Guad. 283.

241

number of the residents of the town who were classified as civilians were actually retired military personnel. In fact, the most affluent of all the *vecinos* at San Antonio was a sixty-year-old retired captain, Don Luis Menchaca. He owned two houses, two irrigated parcels of land, and 2,444 head of livestock.[41]

Whether or not the situation at San Antonio was typical of the relative prosperity of civilian settlers to military personnel in frontier communities would require further investigation. The same would be necessary to determine whether the original civilian families really benefited materially from the privileges, exemptions, and guarantees with which their presidial towns were chartered. However, the survival of many of these communities into the present time, long after the abandonment of the garrisons which justified their establishment in the first place, attests to the significance of the presidio as a civilizing influence on the Spanish frontier in North America. The presidio often became not only the nucleus for a community of Spanish, mixed-blood, and Indian settlers but also an internment center for hostile Indians and sometimes an agency and reservation for those tribesmen who agreed to make peace.

[41] *Ibid.*

242

280

Alta California's
Four Fortresses

BY RICHARD S. WHITEHEAD

Spain's plan for claiming and colonizing Upper California involved establishing a chain of missions to convert and civilize the heathen Indians under the care and guidance of Franciscan priests. The padres and their charges, in turn, were to be protected from attack by England, France and Russia as well as from other hostile Indians by four presidios, conveniently spaced to protect the missionary settlements. The dictionary translates the word "presidio" as "a garrison of soldiers, a fortress garrisoned by soldiers, a place destined for punishing criminals by hard labor, house of correction, penitentiary." Considering that under attack, occupants of a fortress are forcibly confined within its defensive walls, the double meaning is understandable. A Spanish-speaking person, however, might have some apprehensions about working or living in a presidio. In this article we are concerned only with the four presidios that protected Spanish settlements in Alta California from their enemies.

Actually there were five California presidios. Prior to August 29, 1804, Baja and Alta California were one Spanish province under one governor, the first being Don Gaspar de Portolá who, in 1769, led the expedition to explore the California coastline and rediscover the port of Monterey.[1] Portolá's initial headquarters were at the presidio at Loreto, capital city of the Californias, located on the east coast of the peninsula about 250 miles northwest of Cape San Lucas, the southerly tip of Baja California. Existence of this presidio explains why, in 1783, Diego Gonzales, commandant at the Monterey Presidio, received a directive to order five branding irons for the horses and mules of the presidios as follows:[2]

	Brand	Founding Date
Loreto	$\curlywedge$	October 1697
San Diego	2^A	July 16, 1769
Monterey	$A\atop 3$	June 3, 1770
San Francisco	$\triangle^A$	July 28, 1776
Santa Barbara	$A\atop 5$	April 21, 1782

The A above the number is presumed to be the feminine noun ending of the word *compania*, each presidio garrison being designated Company 1 through 5, corresponding to the chronological sequence of each presidio's founding.

Reliable documentary data for the presidios is generally much scarcer than for the missions. One might conclude that this is due to the fact that the priests were well educated and erudite while the soldiers were inclined to be more common individuals lacking education and even, in many cases, illiterate. Since the military has always had a reputation for its high volume of paperwork, this conclusion is faulty, but it does appear that much of the information we need is still hidden in the archives. There seems to be more information available for an authentic reconstruction of the Santa Barbara Presidio than for any of the other presidios, perhaps because more time and effort has been put into the research by the Santa Barbara Trust for Historic Preservation, the organization that is rebuilding that presidio.

One category of data which provides some information is the early plans of the San Francisco, Monterey and Santa Barbara presidios, together with limited descriptions of the buildings. A major breakthrough in this area only occurred early in 1982. Fr. Harry Morrison, a priest at St. Joseph's Catholic Church in Pinole, situated north of Berkeley, California, is also an avid history researcher who in his spare time delves into the archives of the Bancroft Library at Berkeley. Going through the papers of Edward Vischer (1808-1878), a talented artist who painted the California missions, he discovered a set of drawings of all four

Alta California presidios, dated 1820, Plates IV, VII, X and XI. Accompanying the plans was a request dated October 19, 1878, and signed by General Mariano G. Vallejo suggesting that the presidios were no less important than the missions, and that Vischer also paint them for posterity, using as a basis the 1820 plans.[3] Knowing of the interest and activity toward reconstructing the Santa Barbara Presidio, Fr. Morrison contacted the author of this article. Since both Vischer and Vallejo died soon after, the presidios were never painted at that time.

Who made the drawings, when and why, are questions so far unanswered. Since all four are dated the same year, it would seem logical that they resulted from an order, probably by the governor, who was also military commander. In 1820 Pablo Sola was governor. In 1818 he visited all four presidios and nineteen missions and reported his observations to the viceroy of New Spain (Mexico) by letter dated April 3, 1819.[4] No mention is made in this letter of plans of the presidios, but it is possible Sola ordered them drawn on this trip. It is also possible, since those sent Vischer are all on the same kind of blue-lined paper, that Vallejo had one of his staff make copies of the originals to send to Vischer, and the originals remain undiscoverd to date.

In addition to revealing the layout and state of the presidios after a period of some thirty to fifty years after their founding, during which earthquakes, fires and enemy attack occurred, the discovery of these drawings provided the first known plan of the San Diego Presidio. For nearly twenty years, archeologists had been probing the mounds on Presidio Hill above Old Town in San Diego and excavating the foundations of the Presidio Chapel without benefit of a plan to tell them what to look for. Comparing the 1820 plans with those of earlier dates and supplementing these data with various reports, the combined data provides us with some interesting sidelights on the history of these civil and military installations.

One must keep in mind that the presidios were not just forts, but fortified settlements, intended to house a garrison of soldiers with their families and with such amenities as were available to distant outposts during that period. Each presidio was located far enough back from the shoreline, generally 2,000 to

4,000 feet distant, that an enemy ship could not inflict much damage with cannonball ranges of that period. For protection of the harbor, each presidio had a fort, or *castillo*, a level esplanade of wood planking on which were emplaced several cannon behind an embankment of dirt or adobe and stone. This so-called battery was located on a hill overlooking the harbor and, in theory, prevented ships from attacking the presidio. Had a foreign power wished to invade the territory, however, they could easily have landed at a distance from the harbor and laid siege to the presidio.

All four presidios consisted of a quadrangle of buildings grouped around a parade ground and surrounded by a defense wall. In each case, the main gate faced toward the ocean and in some cases, the church was on the opposite side of the parade ground from the main gate. At San Diego, and probably in all of the initial or palisade construction, the defense wall also served as the back wall of the presidio buildings, thus saving the time and cost of building another wall. This design was also followed in the presidios, forming a cordon of earlier forts generally following the southerly boundary of the United States and protecting the northerly boundary of Mexico against the Apaches and other hostile Indians. In case of attack, the defending soldiers climbed on top of the roof of the buildings and fired over the defense wall, using it as a parapet.

The design that replaced it by the 1780s is illustrated by the Santa Barbara layout, Plate IX, in which the buildings are separate from the defense wall, providing a rear garden area for the houses and corrals for the horses. In the presidios of the Southwest where there were no corrals as part of the presidio and the horses were grazed outside the defensive wall, it was found that the fort could be immobilized when the Indians swooped down on the grazing herds, killed the handful of guards and stole the horses.

According to De Mofras, a visitor to the presidios in 1844, it was standard practice to construct a dry moat twelve feet wide and six feet deep around the outside of the defense wall. Excavated dirt formed an embankment along the outside of the ditch. Attacking Indians were first exposed to fire from the top

[70]

of the defense wall as they surmounted the embankment, then had to scale the ten-foot-high defense wall. If they were successful in climbing over the wall, they found themselves trapped in the back garden, exposed to fire from the rear windows and doors of the buildings. This design thus augmented the presidio defenses.

The earliest plan of the San Francisco Presidio (Plate I) is contained in a letter dated March 4, 1792, from Acting Commandant Hermenegildo Sal to Governor Antonio Romeu.[5] Sal gives the dimensions of the guardroom, barracks, jail cells, dry goods and provisions warehouses, commander's houses, church, casemate and sergeant's house, and shows the length of the north side as 319 feet and of the west side, 330 feet. Sal describes the deteriorated state of the structures, walls out of plumb, some walls wider at the top than at the bottom, stone walls cemented with mud, roofs of grass and reed, poor adobe and a shortage of timber. The plan shows that the entire east side of the quadrangle is completely gone, leaving the troops defenseless against an attack from that direction, although another document states that there was a post fence along that side. Sal states that the buildings shown on the plan represent the third construction since the founding sixteen years before, and attributes the bad state of the buildings to lack of intelligent workmen and supervision.

Plate II is a translated copy of a plan dated June 27, 1795, and signed by Governor Borica but prepared by Sal who submitted to the governor a detailed list of materials prepared by the stonemason Manuel Ruiz with the cost estimates by Sal.[6] Construction in accord with this plan was never accomplished, but Sal's warnings apparently led to the assignment of Engineer Captain Alberto de Córdoba to Alta California to make recommendations for improving its defenses. Plate III is a translated copy of Córdoba's plan for the San Francisco Presidio, but again it was not carried out, perhaps because Córdoba himself considered all the California presidios pretty much ineffective because of the fact that an enemy could land at a good many undefended points along the shoreline.[7] He recommended instead a greatly enlarged cavalry corps with mobility to repulse an attack anywhere along the coast, supplemented by mobile batteries on

[71]

PLATE I
LEGEND

Escala que demuestra las habitaciones que tiene el Presidio de San Francisco.

No. 1. Guardia de Prevension, tiene de largo 6¼ varas, de ancho 4½ y 3½ de alto.
2. Cuartel: de largo 16 varas, 3½ de alto, 2 de largo y 4½ de ancho.
3. y 4. Calabosos de 2 varas de alto, 2 de largo y 1½ de ancho.
5. Almacen de ropa, 18 varas largo, 4½ alto y 6 ancho.
6. Ydem de viveres, 18 varas largo, 4½ alto y 6 ancho.
7. y 8. Casas del Comandante, 37½ varas largo, 6 de ancho y 4½ de alto.
10. Yglesia 19 varas de largo, 8 de ancho y 4½ de alto.
11. Casa mata, 4 varas en cuadro y 2½ de alto.
9. Casa del Sargento
Habitaciones de la Tropa desde a hasta k.
(Es copia sacada del original)
Above north facade — Tiene este lienso 116 varas. Mira al Norte
Beside west facade — Tiene este lienza 120 varas. Mira al Poniente

TRANSLATION

Scaled drawing showing the rooms of the Presidio of San Francisco.

No. 1. Guard room, being 17.2 feet long, 12.4 feet wide and 9.6 feet high.
2. Soldier's barracks: 44 feet long, 9.6 feet high and 12.4 feet wide.
3. and 4. Jail cells 5.5 feet high, 5.5 feet long and 4.1 feet wide.
5. Clothing warehouse, 49.5 feet long, 12.4 feet high and 16.5 feet wide.
6. Provisions warehouse, same dimensions as clothing warehouse.
7. and 8. Commandant's dwelling, 103.1 feet long, 16.5 feet wide and 12.4 feet high.
10. Church, 52.2 feet long, 22 feet wide and 12.4 feet high.
11. Casemate, 11 feet square and 6.9 feet high.
9. Sergeant's quarters. From a to k, houses of the soldiers.
A copy taken from the original
Above north facade — This facade is 319 feet [long]. Looking to the north
Beside west facade — This facade is 330 feet [long]. Looking to the west

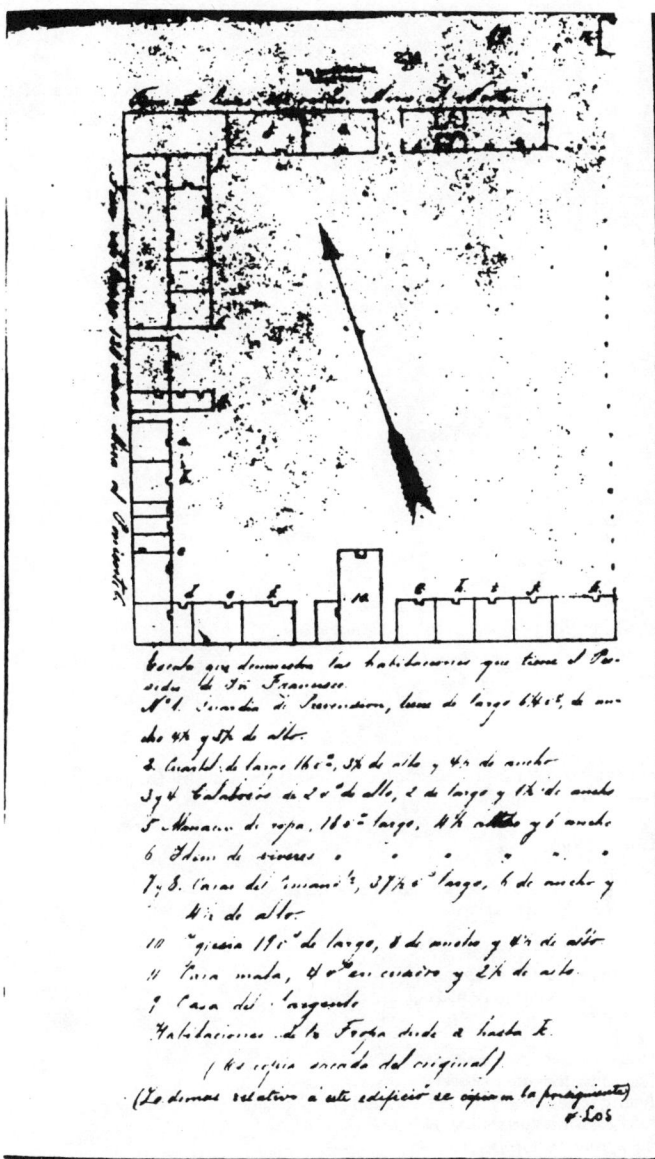

Plate I. The San Francisco Presidio. The drawing is a part of a letter dated March 4, 1792 at San Francisco from Heremenegildo Sal, acting commandant to Governor Antonio Romeu. California Archives 6, State Papers, XI: 234. Provincial. *Reproduced by permission of The Bancroft Library, University of California, Berkeley.*

[73]

PLATE II
LEGEND

Plan del Presidio que se propone para alojar la Compañia de Cavalleria del Puerto de San Francisco en la nueba California.

A. Puerta Principal
B. Cuerpo de Guardia
C. Calabozo
D. dos Almacenes para Sentenos y Viveres
E. Quarta para el Hato
F. Ydem para la sal
G. Casa del Abilitado
H. Idem del Capellan
I. Oficina para utencilios de Yglesia
J. Sacristia
K. Yglesia
L. Casa del Comandante
M. Ydem para Oficiales
N. 21 casas para la Tropa
O. Cozinas y corrales de Ydem
P. Carpinteria
Q. Herreria
R. Enfermería para Marinos
S. Callejones de los Rebellines
T. dos Rebellines
U. Casa del Sargento
X. Cozina para los Solteros
Y. Quartel
Z. dos Corrales para Cavalleria y Ganado

Monterey 27 de Junio de 1795
Diego de Borica

TRANSLATION

Plan of the Presidio that is proposed to house the Cavalry Company of the Port of San Francisco in New California.

A. Main gate
B. Guard room
C. Jail
D. Two warehouses for grains and provisions
E. Quarters for the cattle
F. The same for salt
G. House of the paymaster
H. The same for the chaplain
I. Workroom for the utensils of the church
J. Sacristy
K. Church
L. House of the commandant
M. The same for other officers
N. Twenty-one houses for the soldiers
O. Kitchens and corrals for the same
P. Carpenter's shop
Q. Blacksmith shop
R. Infirmary for seamen
S. Passageway to the bastions
T. Two bastions
U. House of the sergeant
X. Kitchens for the single soldiers
Y. Quarters for single soldiers
Z. Two corrals for horses and cattle

Monterey, June 27, 1795
Diego Borica

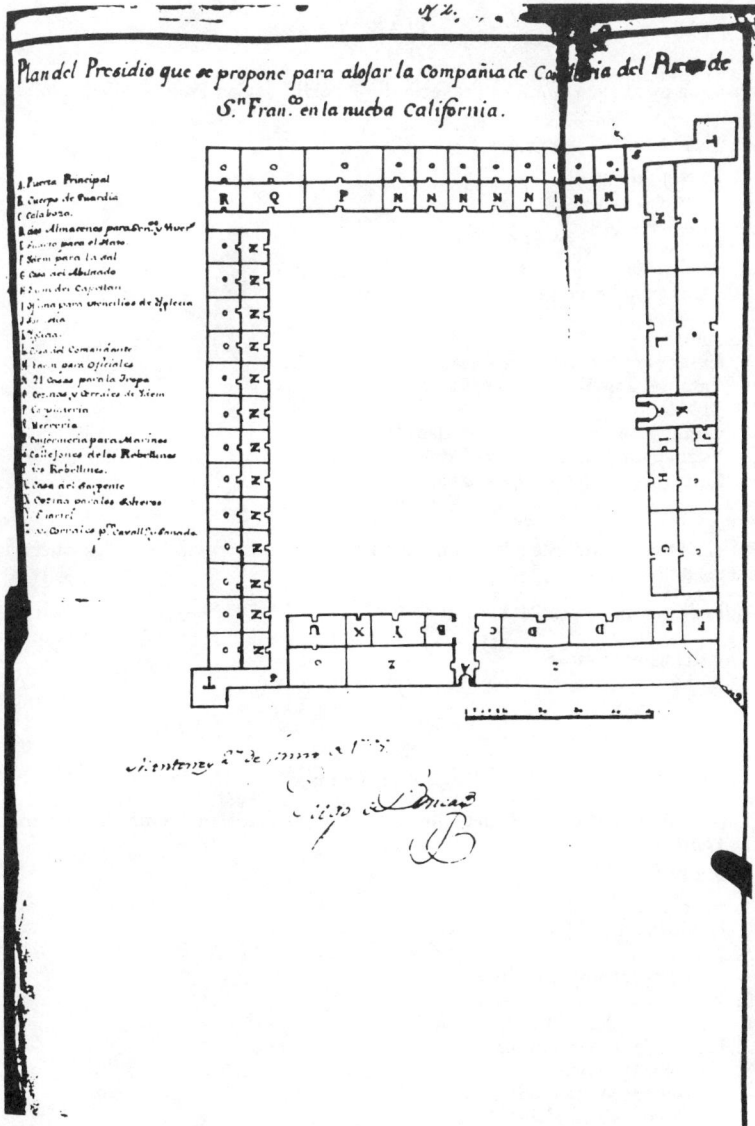

Plan del Presidio que se propone para alojar la Compañia de Ca...ria del Pue...de S.ⁿFran.ᶜᵒ en la nueba California.

Plate II. The San Francisco Presidio. This plan is incorporated in a report by Heremenegildo Sal, dated Monterey, June 26, 1795, to Governor Diego de Borcia which gives construction costs of the presidio from July 26, 1776 to November 1781. Provincias Internas, 216:217 (Tomo 216, Californias). *Courtesy Archivo General de la Nacion, Madrid; copy in The Bancroft Library.*

[75]

PLATE III
LEGEND

Plan que manifiesta el nuevo proyecto del Precidio de San Francisco para alojar las tropas de su Guarnicion.

Explicacion

1. Puerta principal
2. Cuerpo de Guardia
3. Calaboso
4. Quarteles
5. Almacenes
6. Casas para los Sargentos
7. Casas de los Oficiales
8. Almacen de Ropas
9. Casas para los Soldados Casados
10. Casa del Capellan
11. Yglesia
12. Corrales de los casas y Quarteles
13. Ydem para Ganado y Cavallada
14. Cerca y Baluartes para la defenza del Precidio

Nota

Por ser la escala de este Plano mui reducida, no se expresan en el las puertas y ventanas de las casas.

Precidio de San Francisco 24 de Julio de 1796

Alberto de Cordova

Escala de cincuenta varas

TRANSLATION

Plan that shows the new design of the Presidio of San Francisco for housing the troops of the Garrison.

Explanation

1. Main gate
2. Guardroom
3. Jail
4. Quarters for single soldiers
5. Warehouses
6. Houses for the sergeants
7. Houses for other officials
8. Clothing Warehouse
9. Houses for Married Soldiers
10. House of the Chaplain
11. Church
12. Corrals for the houses and quarters
13. Same for cattle and horses
14. Enclosure and Bastions for the defense of the presidio

Note: Because the scale of this plan is very small, the doors and windows of the houses have not been shown.

Presidio of San Francisco July 24, 1796

Albert Cordova

Scale of 50 varas

[76]

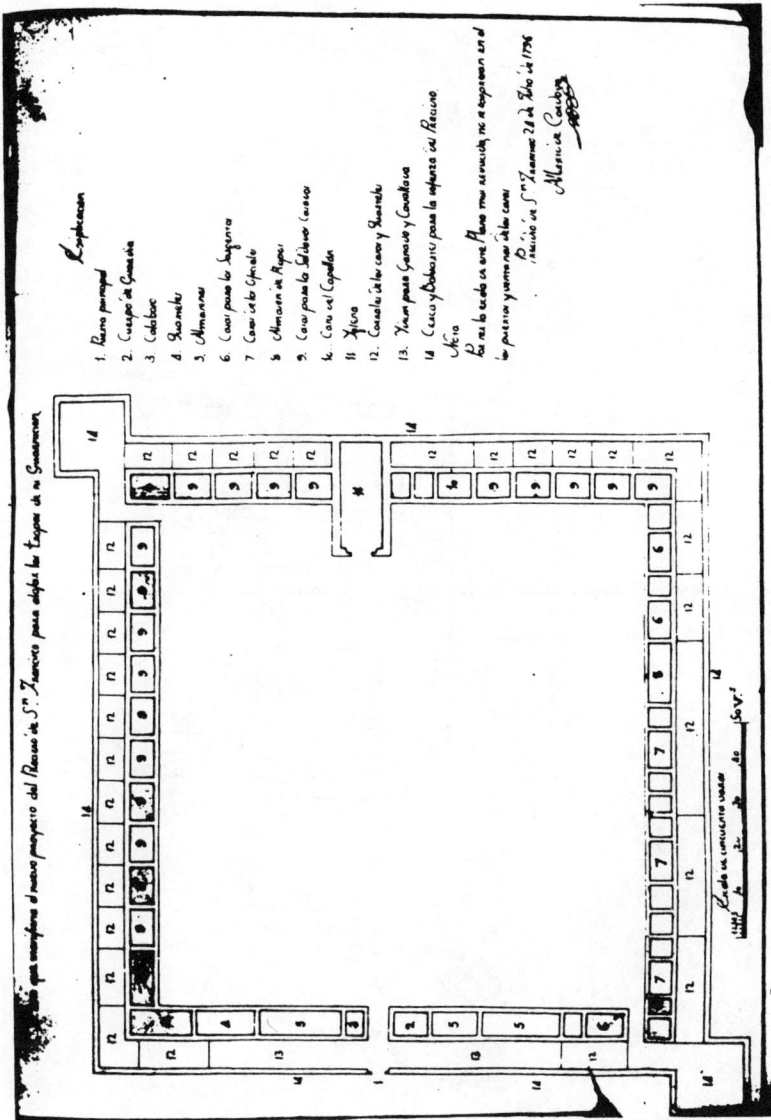

Plate III. The San Francisco Presidio. Plan by Alberto de Cordova, July 24, 1796. Provincias Internas, 216:245. *Courtesy Archivo General de la Nacion, Madrid; copy in The Bancroft Library.*

[77]

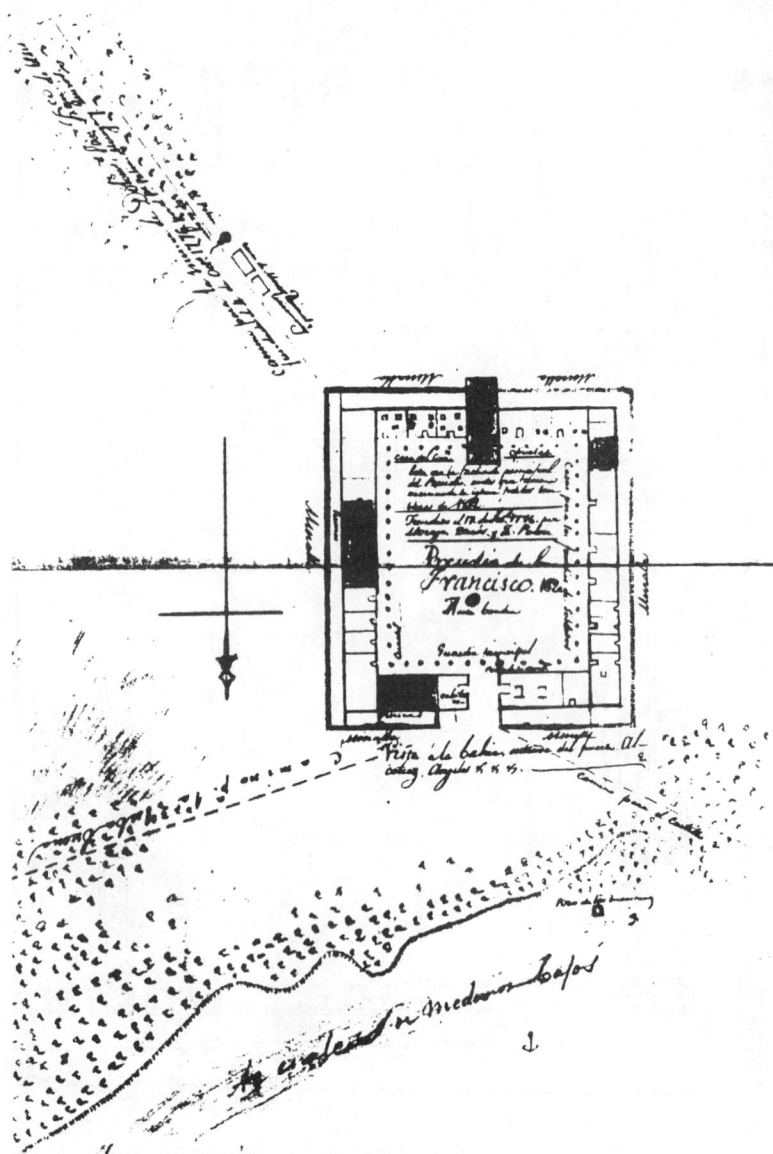

Plate IV. An 1820 map of the San Francisco Presidio found in the Edward Vischer Papers. *Reproduced by permission of The Bancroft Library.*

[78]

ships cruising along the coast. Perhaps because Córdoba's primary project while in California was to plan and found Branciforte, named after the viceroy and later to become the city of Santa Cruz, his recommendations were not acted upon.

Plate IV is the plan of the San Francisco Presidio found in the Vischer papers and dated 1820. This plan is quite similar to the 1792 plan prepared by Alférez Sal. It is also comparable to the plan for the Santa Barbara Presidio which could be considered the typical layout for all presidios after it was decided to separate the buildings from the surrounding defense wall.

Like the other three presidios, Monterey Presidio started out as a palisade structure, poles set close together in a trench and tied together with willows and reeds, called wattle construction, and the whole plastered with mud. Roofs were flat, covered with leaves and branches, grass and sod and then plastered with mud. Obviously such construction left much to be desired when winter came and the wet mud dripped down on the occupants, and adobe buildings were built as soon as the garrison could spend the time on them.

In 1967 the late Fr. Maynard Geiger, O.F.M., archivist at the Santa Barbara Mission Archive-Library, translated and edited for publication in the *Southern California Quarterly* an article entitled "A Description of California's Principal Presidio, Monterey, in 1773."[8] The article contains a translation of a report written by Captain Pedro Fages, commandant of that presidio but later governor of California.[9] Dated September 29, 1773, a little over two years after the presidio was founded, it describes the construction and design of the presidio. Details are given of the length, width and height of various buildings as well as the materials of construction and the uses of the various buildings. To illustrate the article, Fr. Maynard had historian Alan K. Brown make a drawing of the presidio utilizing measurements given in the report. In all probability, Dr. Brown was guided by a drawing of the Monterey Presidio attributed to Engineer Miguel Costansó made at Monterey prior to his departure for Mexico, July 9, 1770, never to return to California although he later wrote a report on California's defenses.[10] Costansó's drawing, merely a proposal, is shown in Plate V and Brown's drawing is

PLATE V
TRANSLATION OF LEGEND

Plan of the Royal Presidio of San Carlos of Monterey.

Interpretation

A. Present church
B. New church
C. Sacristy
D. Quarters for the Leather Jacket troops
E. Quarters for the Volunteer troops
F. Guardroom
G. Presidio warehouse
H. King's warehouse
Y. Mission Warehouse
J. Officer's dwelling
K. Dwelling of the reverend missionaries
L. Blacksmith shop and forge
M. Carpenter shop
N. Pack-train drivers' dwelling
O. Surgeon's dwelling
P. Infirmary
Q. Dwelling for visiting heathen
R. Hospital for new Christians
S. Dwelling for heathen women
T. Chicken yard
V. Pigpen
X. Common kitchen
I. Storage room for farm implements
Z. Privy
Vr. Embrasures

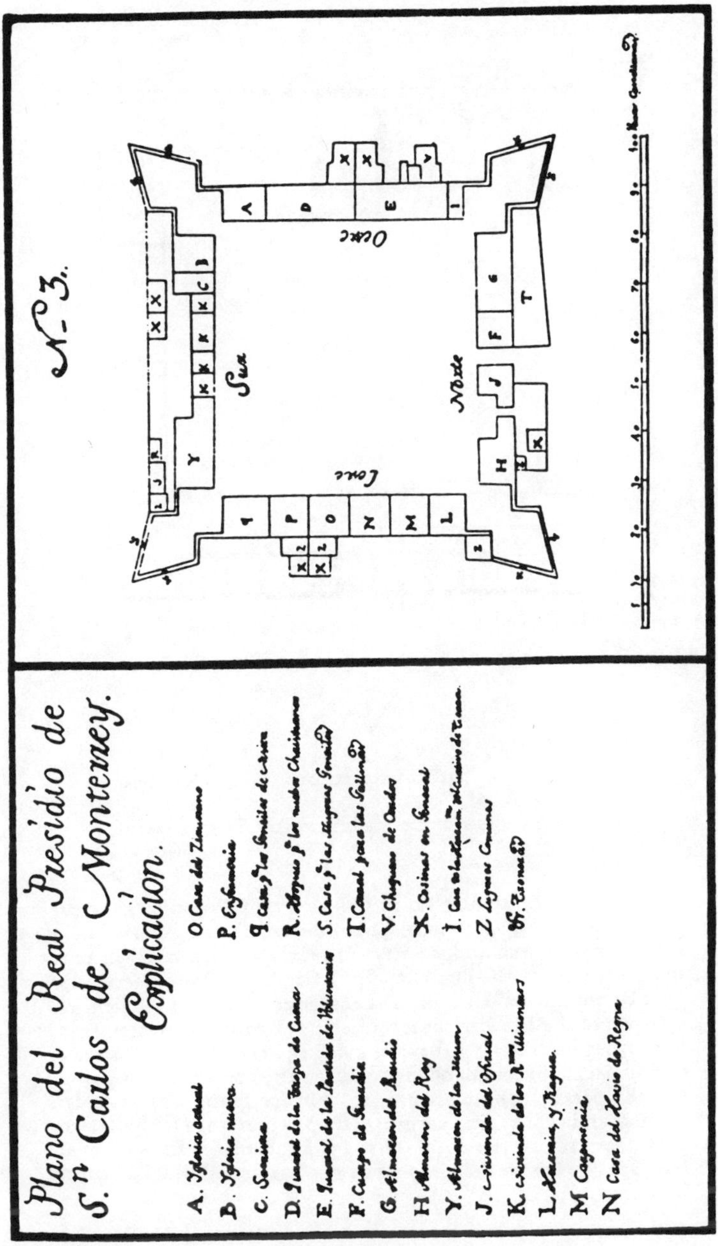
Plano del Real Presidio de
S.n Carlos de Monterrey.
Explicacion.

Plate V. The Monterey Presidio, c. 1771, prepared by Miguel Costanso, reproduced from Irving B. Richman, *California Under Spain and Mexico, 1535-1847* (Reprinted; New York, 1965), p. 338.

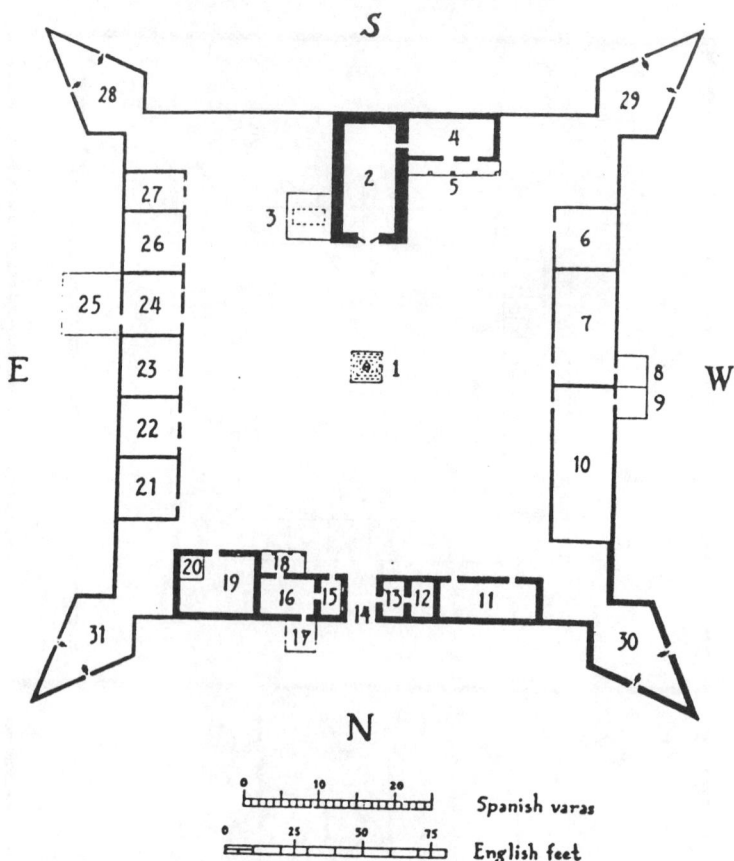

Location of various quarters in the Monterey Presidio: 1) central cross on pedestal; 2) church; 3) belltower; 4) missionaries' quarters, former church and sacristy; 5) porch; 6) dispensary or pharmacy—originally the first chapel; 7) Catalonian volunteers' quarters; 8) volunteers' kitchen; 9) Leatherjacket troop's kitchen; 10) quarters of the Leatherjacket soldiers; 11) government stores; 12) jail; 13) guardhouse; 14) main gate; 15) commandant's store or commissary; 16) commandant's quarters; 17) commandant's kitchen; 18) porch; 19) storehouse; 20) bin for grain; 21) postriders (mails) and smithy; 22) carpenter shop; 23) storage for muleteers' pack gear; 24) servants' quarters; 25) kitchen; 26) Indians' quarters; 27) storage for field implements; 28-31) ravelins with cannon in place.

Plate VI. The Monterey Presidio in 1773. Drawing by Alan K. Brown. Reproduced from the *Southern California Quarterly,* 49 (September 1969), 329.

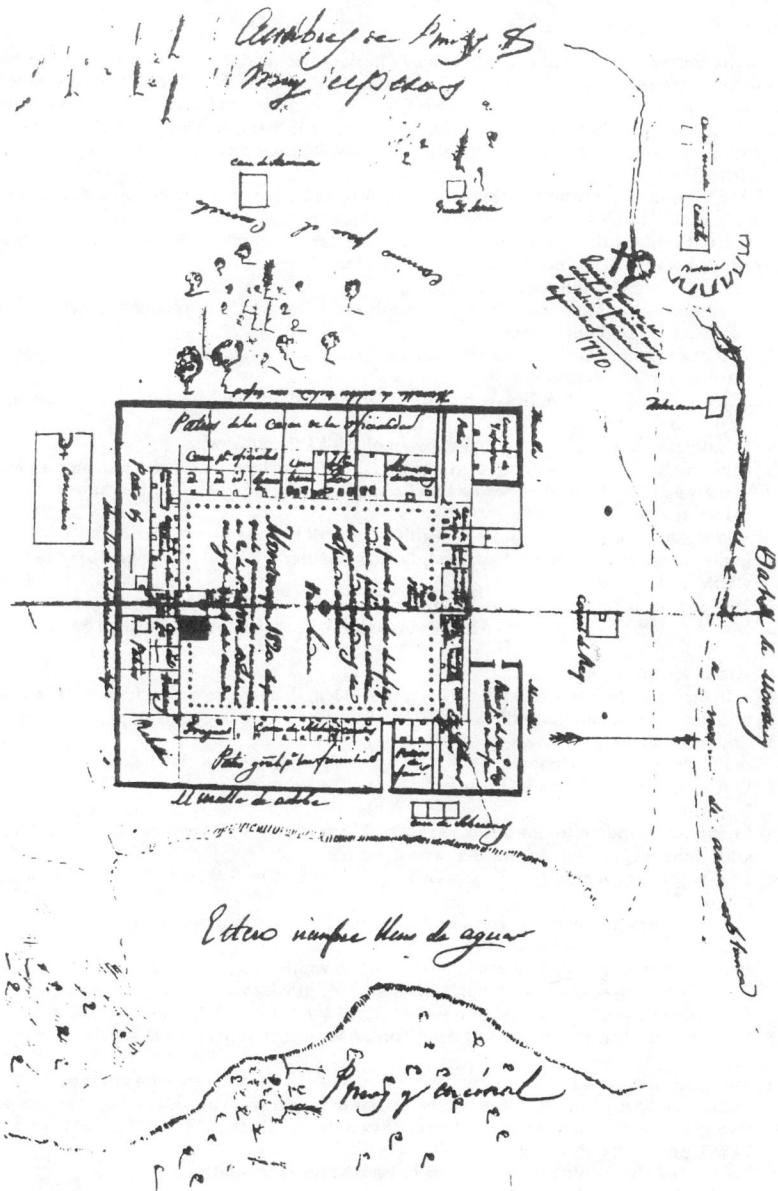

Plate VII. The Monterey Presidio in 1820 found in the Vischer Papers. *Reproduced by permission of The Bancroft Library.*

[83]

PLATE VIII
Tʀᴀɴsʟᴀᴛɪᴏɴ ᴏғ Lᴇɢᴇɴᴅ

Of the thirteen houses shown on the fourth front of the quadrangle, the walls are finished — three-quarters (of a vara) thick, and three varas high without the ridge of the roofs, which are to be the same as the other (houses) for the soldiers, and also the corresponding woodwork has been put into seven of them, and the little that is lacking for the rest is being brought, and more than four thousand tiles are made for their roofs. [Note: a *vara* = 33 in. or 2.75 ft.]

All of the outer wall shown in this plan is ready to be built, and it will be started beginning with the month of November, at which time the quadrangle will be completed.

The front walls of the first front are standing; they are one and a half adobe (bricks) thick, mortared, because of the poor quality of the soil for adobes.

1. Main gate with an opening of 4 varas.
2. A storehouse for supplies, 20 varas in length and 5½ in width, its roof of beams, finished boards, and good quality tile.
3. Two of the same, of the same size, for provisions and other effects, the roof of beams, wattles, and tile as above.
4. Thirteen houses for families — 8 varas in length and 5 in width — the roofs of rafters, wattles and good tile.
5. Private gate with an opening of 3 varas, roofed like the houses.
6. Church, 20 varas in length, 8 in width, and 7½ in height, lined with mortar and whitewashed — its roof of beams and finished boards and good tile, and adorned with painting.
7. Sacristy, 5 varas in length and 4 in width — its roof like the church.
8. Living-room of the second lieutenant, 8 varas in length, 5 in width — its roof of rafters, wattles, and good tile.
9. Two bedrooms for the above — 5 varas in the clear — the roof like the living-room.
10. Bedroom of the Comandante — 5 varas in the clear, its roof of beams, finished boards, and good tile.
11. House for the sentry.
12. A living-room for the Comandante, 11 varas in length and 5 in width, its roof of beams, finished boards, and good tile.
13. Entrance-hall of the above — 4 varas)
   in the clear — 4 in height (sic)) whitewashed on the inside,
14. Office for writing, 5½ varas in length,) 3½ varas in height.
   5 in width)
15. Living-room and bedroom of the chaplain, 11 varas in length for both rooms, and 5 in width, the roofs of rafters, wattles, and good tile.
16. Five houses for families — 8 varas in length, 5 in width — their roofs like that of the chaplain.
17. Fifteen houses on the fourth front for families — 9 varas in length and 5 in width, — their roof like those before-mentioned.
18. House of the sergeant, 15 varas in length, 5½ in width — its roof as above.
19. Barracks for the soldiers — 20 varas in length, 5½ in width — its roof as above.
20. Guard-house — 12 varas, and two small cells of 4 varas.
21. Kitchen and pantry of the second lieutenant, 6 varas in length and 4 in width, its roof as above.
22. Two yards for the second lieutenant's house — one of 14 varas and the other of 7.
23. Kitchen and pantry of the Comandante, 6 varas in length and 4 in width, roofed as above.
24. Two yards for the Comandante — one of 25 varas in length and 14 in width, and the other 14 in length and 8 in width.
25. Yard of the chaplain's house, 14 varas in length and 11 in width.
26. Bastion facing the west, of 6 varas.
27. The same, facing the east, of 6 varas.
28. Gates to two corrals for stock — 60 varas in length and 14 in width.
29. Gates or passage-ways to enter the bastions — 2½ varas in width.

Royal Presidio of Santa Barbara, September 16, 1783.
Pedro Fages
[Note: prepared by Felipe de Goycechea, but signed by Fages.]

[84]

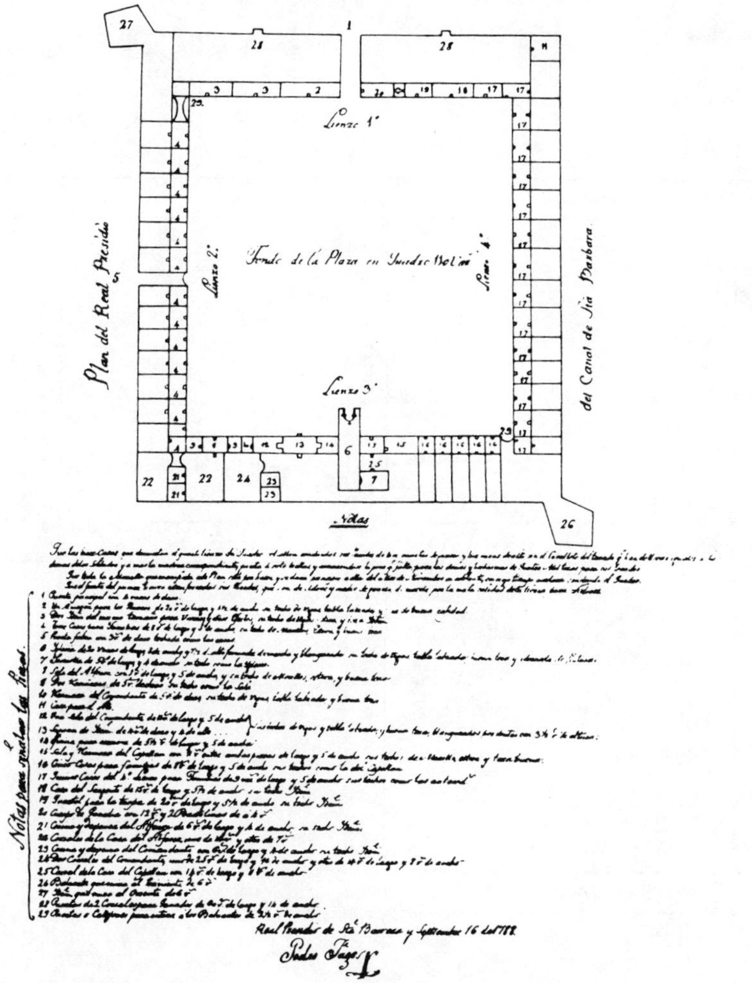
Plan del Real Presidio
del Canal de Sta Barbara
Lienzo 1°
Lienzo 2°
Lienzo 3°
Lienzo 4°
Notas

Plate VIII. The Santa Barbara Presidio in 1788 signed by Pedro Fages, although originally drawn and signed by Felipe de Goycoecha, the second commandant. *Reproduced by permission of The Bancroft Library.*

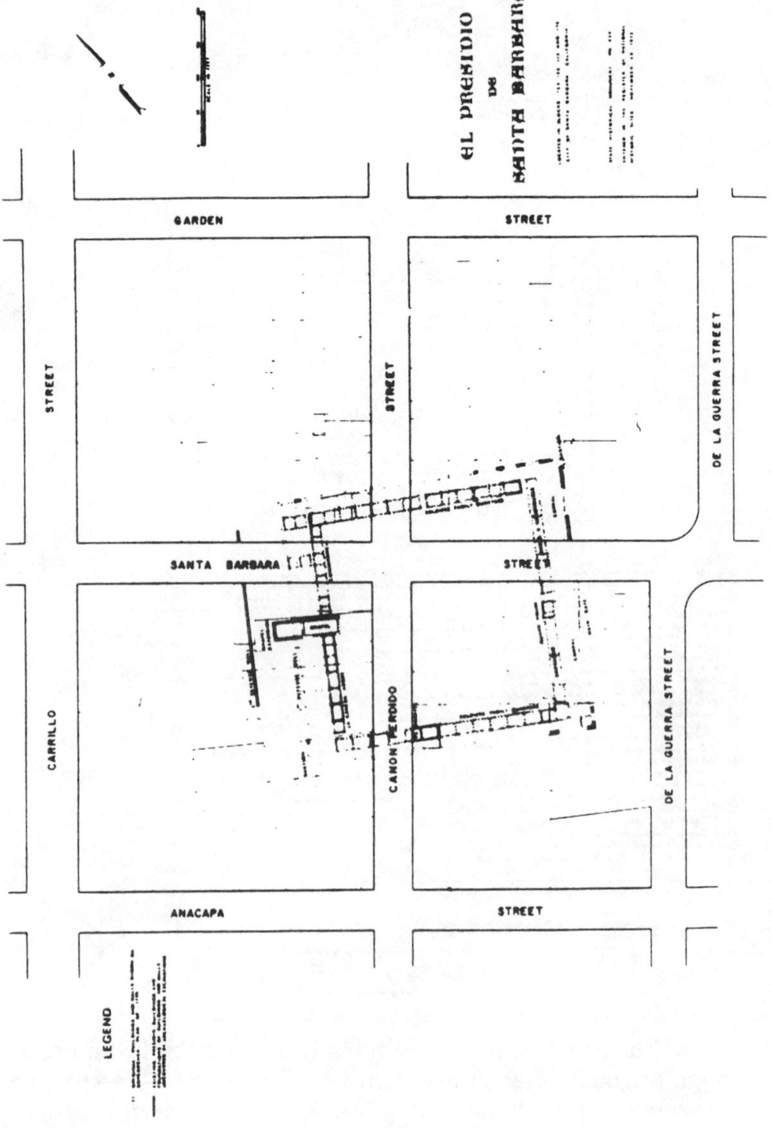
EL PRESIDIO
DE
SANTA BARBARA
GARDEN
STREET
STREET
STREET
DE LA GUERRA STREET
SANTA BARBARA
STREET
CARRILLO
CANON PERDIDO
DE LA GUERRA STREET
ANACAPA
STREET
LEGEND

Plate IX. The Santa Barbara Presidio superimposed on the present street and lot system. Drawing by Richard S. Whitehead.

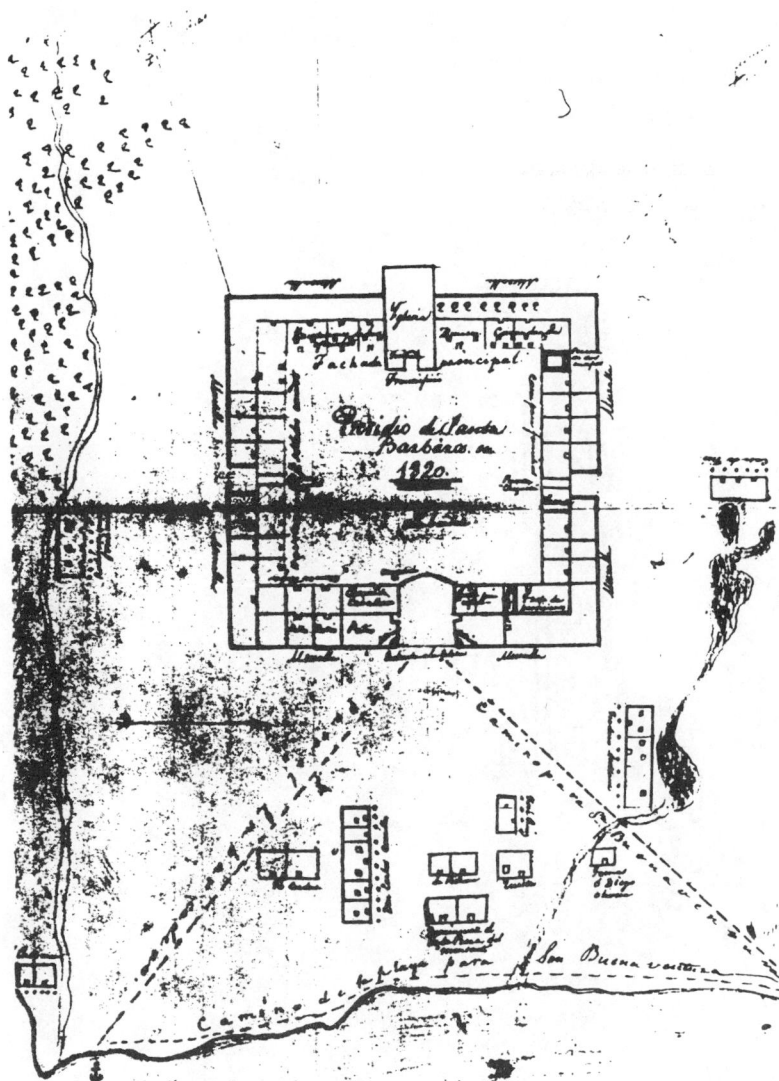

Plate X. The Santa Barbara Presidio in 1820 found in the Vischer Papers. *Reproduced by permission of The Bancroft Library.*

[87]

301

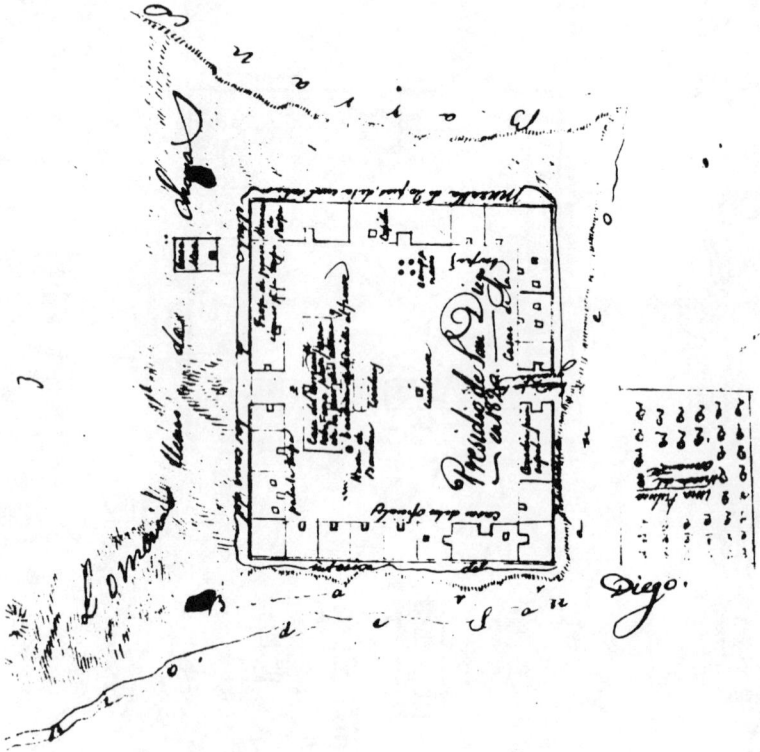

Plate XI. The San Diego Presidio in 1820 found in the Vischer Papers.
Reproduced by permission of The Bancroft Library.

[88]

reproduced in Plate VI which indicates that some of Costansó's features were not constructed.

A letter dated August 10, 1778, from then Governor Felipe de Neve to the commanding general at Arispe, Mexico, Teodoro de Croix, states that on July 3, 1778, the defense wall and bastions were completed, all constructed of stone.[11] The wall was 1,476 feet in circumference (approximately 369 feet on each side), 11 feet in height and 44 inches wide. It enclosed ten adobe houses, each having a frontage of nineteen feet and a depth of twenty-two feet, and the guardroom and soldiers' quarters with a frontage of 93 feet, a depth of 16½ feet and double wall of adobe, were under construction. These were the permanent structures to replace the temporary palisade buildings described in the 1773 article. Plate VII shows the 1820 plan preserved in the Vischer papers.

The first two years of the life of the Santa Barbara Presidio were under the command of Lieutenant José Francisco Ortega who was replaced by Lieutenant Felipe Antonio de Goycoechea in January 1784.[12] Although the record indicates that Ortega sent a plan of the Santa Barbara Presidio to the governor, no plan of such an early date has so far surfaced. It might have been a plan of Ortega's palisade construction or of a proposal for permanent construction. In any event, the earliest plan, representing permanent construction, is dated September 16, 1788, and is signed by Felipe de Goycoechea.[13] An identical plan, with the same notations and date, but with a few additional measurements and signed by then Governor Pedro Fages, is reproduced in Plate VIII.[14] Surveyed locations of buildings and structures in relation to city streets, based on archeological findings are depicted in Plate IX.

Utilizing deeds giving measurements tied to "the old church," the foundations of the presidio chapel were first uncovered in 1967. Since then, the foundations of buildings and structures in sixteen different locations in all four sides of the quadrangle have been uncovered and surveyed. One of the soldiers' family quarters in the southwest facade, now known as El Cuartel, survived the two hundred intervening years, although renovated, and another building reconstructed on the

foundations of one of the quarters for non-commissioned officers remains and is known as the Caneda Adobe. These, together with land totaling three quarters of the land within the
boundaries of the original presidio are now publicly owned by
the State Department of Parks and Recreation or by the city of
Santa Barbara in streets and the Federal government in the Post
Office property, plus land purchased by the non-profit Santa
Barbara Trust for Historic Preservation. The trust is conces-
sionaire for the State with responsibility for operating the Royal
Presidio of Santa Barbara State Historic Park and reconstructing
the presidio buildings. The Padre's Quarters, consisting of two
rooms, plus an adjoining non-commissioned officers' quarters
have been completely reconstructed on the original foundation
and the presidio chapel, a structure twenty feet high to the
eaves and over 100 feet long is currently (1982) under construction.

The reconstruction is as completely authentic as possible
within the requirements of the City Building Code. In preparation for this reconstruction, the Trust for Historic Preservation
researched and published in 1980 two reports written in the
1930s by Fred C. Hageman and Russell C. Ewing for the National Park Service, and edited by the author of this article. This
book, entitled *An Archeological and Restoration Study of Mission La
Purísima Concepción*, describes the history of that mission, its
original construction as revealed by the archeological excavations of the 1930s, its reconstruction by the Civilian Conservation Corps during the Great Depression, and its present status.
It is the most complete and detailed source of information available on mission-period construction. Features of the Padre's
Quarters and Chapel of the Santa Barbara Presidio not readily
duplicated from archeological excavations were reconstructed
using the original techniques and materials of construction discovered at Purísima Mission. Adobe blocks were handmade,
timbers were adzed and joined with rawhide, floor and roof tile
were handmade by an Indian tribe and hardware forged by a
Mexican blacksmith.

It is the intent of the Santa Barbara Trust for Historic Preservation to reconstruct the entire Santa Barbara Presidio in accord
with the 1788 plan updated by changes made up to 1800 as

[90]

recorded in archival documents. This will take years of work and considerable sums of money, but when completed, it will be the only reconstructed presidio of the eighteenth century in the West, and the only representation of the civil and military government institutions of the Mission period.

The earthquake of 1812 caused a considerable amount of damage to the Santa Barbara Presidio buildings, resulting in changes in the uses of structures reflected in the plan shown in Plate X, which is the 1820 plan found in the Vischer papers. This latter plan is useful not only in showing the earthquake damage and changes resulting therefrom, but also in verifying the location and use of structures shown in the 1788 plan.

Since 1965, the foundations of the chapel of the San Diego Presidio have been excavated archeologically by students of San Diego State College with cooperation from the San Diego Historical Society and the city of San Diego. Although no plan of the presidio was available until discovery of the 1820 plan in the Vischer papers in February 1982, the entire foundations of the presidio's most important building, the chapel, have been excavated along with the foundations of some adjacent structures. To what extent the 1820 plan shown in Plate XI will assist those involved in the excavation program depends on the future of the program. Because the presidio is in a city park devoted to recreational uses, the agreement by which the State College undertook its archeological program required backfilling and resodding after the excavation was completed, which has been done. It is hoped that at the very least, enough probing can be done to verify the accuracy of the 1820 plan and identify some of the mounds that outline the remains of presidio structures.

It cannot be emphasized too strongly that what remains undiscovered about the four California presidios, as well as the Loreto presidio, probably far exceeds what has already been discovered, both in documentary and archeological evidence. Virtually no work has been done to research the documents directly relating to the presidios in the Archivo General de Indias in Seville, Spain, and very little on documents in the Archivo General de la Nactón in Mexico City. Work is underway on a book on the Santa Barbara Presidio using as the primary source the California Archives at the Bancroft Library, Berkeley, California, and the archeological work at the Santa Barbara Presidio. Much of value would result from just a compilation of all the documentary information in the California Archives on the other three presidios permitting comparisons and filling in gaps in the knowledge of that period relating to the presidios. It is hoped this article will stimulate such research.

NOTES

[1] Don Gaspar de Portolá was a captain of dragoons in the Spanish army who had distinguished himself in Europe before migrating to Mexico in 1767. He was born in Catalonia about 1723. Visitor General José de Galvez assigned him the job of removing the Jesuit priests from their mission to be replaced by Franciscans in 1767. From November 1767 to July 1770 he was governor of the province of Alta and Baja California. He died about 1784.

[2] Nicolas Soler to Diego González, January 10, 1783. California Archives 15, Provincial State Papers, Benecia Military, Vol. V, machine page 166, Bancroft Library, University of California, Berkeley, Lt. Diego González was in command at Monterey from 1781 to 1785 and at San Francisco from 1785 to 1787. According to Bancroft's *History of California* (7 vols.; San Francisco, 1884-1890), III: 700, he was an incompetent officer who was dropped from the rolls in 1793. Soler was an inspector of presidio accounts.

[3] Mariano G. Vallejo to Edward Vischer, October 19, 1878, Call No. 77/37 c, Bancroft Library.

[4] Governor Sola to Viceroy, April 3, 1818, California Archives 25, Provincial Records Vol. IX, machine page 425. Don Pablo Vicente de Sola was a lieutenant-colonel of the provincial militia, born in Spain in 1761 and appointed governor of Alta California by the viceroy December 31, 1814. Promoted to colonel in 1819 because of his services against the pirate Bouchard, he served until November 10, 1822 as governor and died about 1826.

[5] Hermenegildo Sal to Governor Antonio Romeu, March 4, 1792, California Archives, 6, Provincial State Papers Vol. XI, machine pages 233-237, and Hermenegildo Sal to Governor José Joaquín Arrillaga, December 29, 1792, *Ibid.*, machine pages 237-242. Hermenegildo Sal came to California with the Anza expedition in 1776. He was appointed *guarda-almacen*, in charge of the warehouse at San Francisco from 1778 to 1782, became sergeant at Santa Barbara in May 1782, and three months later was commissioned *alférez* at Monterey. In 1795 he was commissioned a lieutenant. He was acting commandant at San Francisco from 1791 to 1794 and commandant at Monterey from 1785 to 1787 and 1796 to 1800.

[6] Governor Diego Borica, June 27, 1795. Provincias Internas, Vol. 216, pp. 215-220. Archivo General de la Nación, Mexico City, D.F.

[7] Alberto de Córdoba to Governor Diego Borica, July 24, 1796 and July 30, 1796. Provincias Internas, Vol. 216, pp. 242-245, Archivo General de la Nación, Mexico City, D.F. Córdoba was a member of the Royal Corps of Engineers along with the most famous engineer, Miguel Costansó. Arriving in California late in 1795, he spent three years there working on the defenses of all four presidios.

[8] *Southern California Quarterly*, 49 (September 1967), 327-336. The document is in Vol. XII, folios 177-183, Sección de Misiones, Archivo General de la Nación, Mexico City, D.F.

[9] Pedro Fages was governor of the Californias from July 12, 1782 to April 16, 1791. Born in Catalonia, Spain, in 1734, he arrived in Mexico in 1767, was military chief of the sea branch of the Sacred Expedition to explore and settle California in 1769, and accompanied Portolá on the trips north to Monterey in 1769 and 1770. Commissioned a captain in 1771. He was commandant of the California establishments from July 9, 1770 when Portolá left, until May 25, 1774, during which time he incurred the enmity of Fr. Junípero Serra who made a successful trip to Mexico City partly to have Fages removed as commandant.

[10] Miguel Costansó was the most famous and competent engineer of the mission period. He was born in 1741 in Barcelona, Spain, and was accepted into the Corps of Engineers in 1762. He was assigned to the command of José de Gálvez in 1768 and accompanied Portolá on the expedition to rediscover Monterey in 1769 and was with the party that discovered San Francisco Bay. Most of his service was in Mexico, and he died in Mexico City in 1814.

[11] Governor Felipe de Neve to Commanding General Teodoro de Croix, August 10, 1778. California Archives 22, Provincial Records Vol. I, machine page 90. Born in 1727 in Bailén, Spain, de Neve was commissioned a lieutenant in the army in 1749. Arriving in Mexico in 1765, he also was involved in the arrest and expulsion of the Jesuits in 1767. In 1775 he was appointed governor of the Californias with headquarters at the presidio at Loreto, Baja California, and in February 1777, he took up residence in Monterey when it was designated to replace Loreto as capital of the Californias. He was promoted to full colonel in 1778, wrote the *Reglamento* of 1781 and served as governor until July 1782, participating in the founding of the Santa Barbara Presidio just before his term ended. In 1783 he succeeded Teodoro de Croix as commanding general of the Frontier Provinces and died in November 1784.

[12] José Francisco de Ortega was born in 1734 in Zelaya, Guanajuato, Mexico. At the age of twenty-one, he enlisted in the army and rose to sergeant when he joined the Portolá expedition to Alta California in 1769, distinguishing himself as the point man of the cavalcade, traveling ahead of the main body to scout the best route for the next day's journey. He was with the party that discovered San Francisco Bay. In 1773 he was promoted to lieutenant. He was a favorite of Junípero Serra who unsuccessfully recommended him to succeed Fages as governor of the Californias. After eight years as commandant at the San Diego Presidio, he was appointed the first commandant of the presidio of Santa Barbara and built its palisade structures, but being a poor manager of financial affairs, he earned the displeasure of a critical inspector, Nicolas Soler, and was replaced in 1784 by Felipe de Goycoechea. He was nevertheless commandant at Monterey from 1787 to 1791 and at Loreto until 1795. He died in 1798 after having been granted the Rancho Nuestra Señora del Refugio up the coast from Santa Barbara.

Felipe de Goycoechea was born in 1747, probably at Alamos, Sonora, according to Bancroft's *History of California*, but his service record states that his *pais* (country) was Real de Cozolá, a town about fifty miles southeast of Culiacan in Sinaloa, Mexico. He was thirty-five when he became a cadet in June 1782, two months after the Santa Barbara Presidio was founded. Fifteen days later he was appointed an *alférez* and less than seven months later he was promoted to lieutenant. After a year and a half service in northern Mexico and Baja California, he was given command of the Santa Barbara Presidio, a heavy responsibility for a man with so little military experience, unless he had gained some prior to his appointment as a cadet about which information is lacking. His performance must have been adequate, since he was promoted to captain in June 1797.

All of the permanent construction at the Santa Barbara presidio was done under the supervision of Goycoechea. He was a bachelor who, however, had descendants. His tenure as commandant at Santa Barbara was without any particular distinction, except that when George Vancouver, the English sea captain, visited Santa Barbara in November 1793, he was well-received by Goycoechea and greatly impressed by the presidio, stating that it excelled all others in neatness, cleanliness and other smaller, though essential comforts. He described the settlement, which consisted primarily of the presidio and mission, as bearing the appearance of a far more civilized place than any other of the Spanish settlements, the buildings appearing to be regular and well constructed, the walls clean and white, and the roofs of the houses covered with a bright red tile. In August 1793, Governor Arrillaga reported to the viceroy that the presidio at Santa Barbara, although begun last, was the most complete of all owing to the activity of the commandant. Goycoechea remained in command until August 1802 when he was made *Habilitado General* in Mexico City. In 1805 he was appointed governor of Baja California, a position he held until his death in September 1814 at Loreto.

[13] Felipe de Goycoechea, September 16, 1788. California Archives 7, Provincial State papers Vol. XII, machine page 61. Since the plan signed by Fages, Plate VIII is almost identical and much clearer, the plan signed by Goycoechea is not reproduced herein.

[14] *Plan del Real Presidio del Canal de Santa Barbara* signed by Pedro Fages, September 16, 1788. Papers of Irving Berdine Richman, Ayer Collection, Newberry Library, Chicago, Illinois. (Copy of original on linen.)

[94]

VILLA DE BRANCIFORTE: INNOVATION AND ADAPTATION ON THE FRONTIER

CONCEIVED in trepidation, plagued by ineptitude, and ultimately relegated to obscurity, the Villa de Branciforte marked the last Spanish colonial town to be founded in California, or for that matter, in the Americas. A hybrid of civilian and military enterprise, Branciforte was envisioned as California's grandest town only to become instead an early casualty of incompetence and Madrid's depleted exchequer. Yet, despite its misfortunes, the Villa was within a venerable and generally successful tradition of frontier endeavor. In certain instances, the resources of Spain's distinct urban institutions of settlement and pacification—the presidio, pueblo and mission—were joined in varying combinations to meet the demands of extraordinary circumstance. If the Villa de Branciforte failed in its assignment, it was primarily for want of sagacity.

The amalgamation of two or more theoretically mutually-exclusive forms of urban settlement occurred only on the frontier in response to difficult conditions for which the resources of one mode were insufficient. During the late sixteenth century, for example, presidios which had been established on the Chichimeca frontier in the north of Mexico failed to provide the requisite peace and security for both Spanish silver mining operations at Zacatecas and the maintenance of communication with Mexico City. Military force alone could not further the ends later achieved by purchase, diplomacy and missionary evangelization.[1] Self-sufficient villas of soldier-settlers proved to be a far more effective and economically viable alternative. "Defensive Spanish towns," Powell writes, "[were] a fundamental and enduring consequence of the sixteenth century fight in the Gran Chichimeca."[2] These towns were loci of security, offering inducements of land to attract settlers. The Villa of León, established in 1576, required that *vecinos* furnish their own arms and horses in order to be eligible for grants.[3] Celaya, founded in 1570, was intended additionally to be a center for the settlement of local nomadic tribes sought as allies.[4]

Another example of innovative amalgamation was brought into exis-

---

[1] Philip Wayne Powell, *Soldiers, Indians and Silver: The Northward Advance of New Spain, 1550-1600* (Berkeley & Los Angeles, 1952), p. 149.

[2] *Ibid.*, p. 151.

[3] This standard condition reappeared in California in Felipe de Neve's *Reglamento*; see California Archives, Bancroft Library (CA), *State Papers. Missions and Colonization*, I, pp. 114-115. The Villa is a town of greater importance—real or imagined—than a pueblo.

[4] Powell, pp. 152-153.

95

tence by the failure of the Franciscan missions in Texas during the early eighteenth century. They were ineffectual in their religious and political task of congregating Indians in pueblos. Concurrently, the danger of French invasion from Louisiana was not sufficient to warrant the costly presence of a large military garrisoned in presidios. Thus, the number of soldiers in the area was reduced and most existing presidios were abandoned. The establishment of the Villa of San Fernando de Béxar in 1731 secured the settlement and occupation of Texas as well as discouraged the French. In this instance the amalgamation resulted from the adjacent situation of a presidio and a mission.[5]

Visitador-General José de Gálvez created a third form of mixed community in his effort to strengthen the Californias in the late 1760's. The site of Loreto, Baja California's oldest mission, was chosen to be rehabilitated as the capital of the peninsula because of its existing warehouse and presidio, central location, and serviceable port.[6] This settlement was to consist of two distinct but contiguous towns, one for Indians and one for Spaniards. Loreto's elevated status required substantial new construction; a church, arsenal, government buildings and maritime facilities all had to be built. The traditional grid-and-plaza plan was to govern the layout of both towns, although regional functions and their appropriate edifices were centered in the Spanish town. The Indian town, an expansion of the pre-existing mission, was to have its complement of government buildings as well. The chief formal difference between the two was the size of the plaza, a space which measured one hundred square *varas* in the Spanish town whereas the Indian settlement was centered about a smaller square, "a *plazuela* of fifty to sixty *varas* square, or more, if the precinct of the site permits."[7] The circumstances for this combination of forms were dictated by the existence of the mission, the qualities inherent in the location, and the presence of a large Indian labor force.

Gálvez was determined that no modifications be allowed to obstruct his program. All existing houses which interfered with the new physical plan were to be demolished and the owners compensated with new ones.[8] An unusual feature of this dual settlement was that houses were

[5]Mattie Alice Austin, "The Municipal Government of San Fernando de Bexar, 1730–1800," *Texas State Historical Association Quarterly*, VIII (April, 1905), pp. 287–301. The mission is the Alamo.

[6]Herbert I. Priestley, *José de Gálvez, Visitor-General of New Spain (1765–1771)* (Berkeley, 1916), p. 255; Hubert Howe Bancroft, *History of the North Mexican States* (2 vols. San Francisco, 1884–1889), I, p. 692.

[7]Gálvez, Loreto, April 29, 1769, Articles 4 and 5, CA, *Provincial State Papers*, I, pp. 54–59.

[8]*Ibid.*, Article 10.

to remain the property of the Crown; the settlers would pay only a nominal rental.[9] Additionally, the settlement was distinguished by unusually precise instructions for locations and dimensions of government buildings. Matters pertaining to grants of land at Loreto appear to have been set forth at an earlier date by Gálvez.[10] The only significant departure from previous practice was that *suertes* would be allocated on the basis of an individual's "quality and merit" to be determined by missionary and secular authorities.[11]

However, not all attempts to combine different modes of settlement met with success. About 1780 Teodoro de Croix had resolved to establish two towns on the arid Colorado-Gila frontier whose qualities combined the features of all three genres.[12] Settlers were to be granted lands in the usual manner while the soldiers garrisoned in each town provided protection. Missionaries were to act as pastors for the colonists but convert Indians would also receive grants of land in the Spanish town since there would be no separate mission community. Croix predicted, "I do not doubt that they will be happy, because the respectable union of the two pueblos of Spaniards offers the advantage of attracting docilely heathen Indians to reduction and vassalage, of protecting communication with New California, of assuring that with Sonora, and of attempting at an opportune time that with New Mexico."[13]

Croix's plan received a justifiably cool reception. Needless to say, the missionaries, still determined to nurture the Indians in isolation

---

[9]*Ibid.*

[10]*Ibid.*, Articles 5–9.

[11]Gálvez, Santa Anna, August 12, 1768, *ibid.*, pp. 60–67. The unique circumstances underlying the founding of Loreto suggest interesting possibilities for further research, not only for the events of its early years, but also for the events resulting from the elevation of Monterey to capital of Alta California in 1774 and for its pre-eminence over the entire peninsula three years later. Thus, the projects at Loreto were never carried out on the scale that Gálvez had envisioned.

[12]It should be pointed out that the quality of construction of a non-military settlement could alone enable it to function in a dual role. Some missions were effective bastions and were even better suited to that purpose than presidios. Mariano Vallejo wrote of the California missions:

> The larger part of those edifices called missions were . . . true fortifications, capable of resisting an assault as well as the presidios, and to be truthful, some of the missions were more suited to offer resistance than were some of the presidios; because they were built with great care and in their construction it was never forgotten that they could be exposed to regular assaults.

(Mariano G. Vallejo, *Recuerdos Históricos y Personales tocante á la Alta California* [5 vols.; Bancroft Library MS. 1875], I, pp. 174–175).

[13]Teodoro de Croix, "Report of 1781," Item 531, quoted in Alfred Barnaby Thomas, *Teodoro de Croix and the Northern Frontier of New Spain, 1776–1783* (Norman, Okla., 1941), p. 221.

from the rough and rowdy mestizo culture of the frontier, opposed the idea across the board. Fr. Francisco Palou sarcastically labeled Croix's proposal "a new method of conquest!"[14] Bancroft, in light of reports by Anza and other qualified sources, termed it "a criminally stupid blunder."[15] A contemporary writer objected to the ill-founded basis for the settlement, calling Croix to account for his ignorance, false notions of economy, and blind pride, all of which jeopardized the lives of more than fifty families.[16] Thomas, on the other hand, has attempted to exonerate Croix by asserting, however questionably, that the missionaries desired that the settlement be undertaken as a mixed enterprise and, as a result, there were insufficient resources to guarantee adequate protection for the two new towns.[17] Recriminations aside, the colonists did little to abet their cause with numerous acts which violated the rights of neighboring Indians. For example, their livestock destroyed large portions of traditional and valuable Indian agricultural land. The inevitable reaction culminated in a bloddy massacre by the Yuma tribe in July, 1781 and no further attempts were made to colonize the area. Further, the tragic fate shared by the towns provided the missionaries with an unimpeachable example of the inadvisability of challenging old methods of settlement.

The founding of California's third town, the Villa de Branciforte, occurred within this context of multifunctional settlement. As in earlier instances, the Spanish government was confronted with a situation which required an innovative approach within the constraints imposed by available resources. The events which underlie the Villa's establishment are to be found in Spanish efforts to secure the California coast in the years immediately following the resolution of the Nootka Sound crisis. The Marqués de Branciforte,[18] Viceroy of New Spain, was concerned that "perfidious Britain, changing her actual agreement with Spain, might direct her designs to the Sandwich Islands and the coast of India."[19]

---

[14] Francisco Palou, *Noticias de la Nueva California*, ed. & trans. Herbert E. Bolton (4 vols; New York, 1966), IV, p. 200.

[15] Hubert Howe Bancroft, *History of California* (7 vols: San Francisco, 1884–1890), I, p. 358.

[16] J. D. Arrivicita, *Crónica Seráfica y Apostólica* (Mexico, 1792), cited in *ibid.*

[17] Thomas, p. 59.

[18] Branciforte was a protege of the "supreme mountebank," Manual Godoy. The Viceroy possessed "an extraordinary gift for flattery" and was a "venal man, who came to the vice-royalty determined to feather his nest." He was replaced immediately when Charles IV "was forced by universal indignation and the insistence of the French to part with Godoy." (Justo Sierra, *The Political Evolution of the Mexican People*, trans. Charles Ramsdell [Austin & London, 1969], pp. 140–141).

[19] Branciforte to the Duque de la Alcudia, Mexico, August 29, 1794, quoted in Florian

It was the Viceroy's contention that the founding of a multifunctional town would best realize "the desire to combine defense, prosperity, and economy."[20] And if soldier-colonists were to populate the town, the Marqués continued, "they would cause the Royal treasury the same expenses in a time of serene peace as in that of cruel war." Branciforte justified his decision by invoking the glorious past. "It will be recalled," he noted, "that the old Spanish soldiers, even those who conquered the Americas . . . joined Military discipline with politic instruction in Agriculture, Trades & Arts; so that at the same time winning and defending their conquest, cultivating the earth, manufacturing important materials, and teaching the vanquished to look for sustenance and how to wear clothes."[21]

In the Fall of 1794, Branciforte instructed Governor Diego de Borica to provide him with information concerning a possible site for the new town. Borica relayed the communication to the commandants of the four presidios in January, 1795, directing them to:

> Formulate and send to me a detailed report of the inhabited places that are in your jurisdictional charge with an indication of the names of the owners, the class and number of goods which they have, the quality of the land and water for agriculture and . . . abundant land and water and good sites for the establishment of settlements of Spaniards of 25 or 30 settlers in the same manner as are found with those of San Jose and N Sra de los Angeles.[22]

The final responsibility for the selection of a site lay with Borica and Engineer Extraordinary Alberto de Córdoba. Its location was to serve the purpose of guarding the coast and minimizing the impact of a surprise attack, "making use of the rules of Military Fortification in which he [Córdoba] has been instructed."[23] The town was to be planned as provided by the *Recopilación*. Córdoba was to "designate lands with the conveniences of Rivers and Forests, proceeding to mark sites for Churches, government buildings, Plazas and Streets."[24] An additional provision reminiscent of de Croix's ideas, but apparently never put into practice, was Branciforte's notion that "between the officers' houses are to be incorporated sites in order that chieftains of *Rancherías* may

---

Guest, O.F.M., "The Establishment of the Villa de Branciforte," *California Historical Society Quarterly*, XLI (March, 1962), p. 30.

[20] Branciforte, "Informe del Real Tribunal y Audiencia de la Contaduría de Cuentas sobre Fundación de un Pueblo que llamara Branciforte," Mexico, November 18, 1795, CA, *Provincial State Papers*, VII, p. 400.

[21] *Ibid.*, p. 398.

[22] Borica to Presidio Commandants, Monterey, January 9, 1795, CA, *Provincial Records*, II, pp. 402–403.

[23] Branciforte, "Informe . . .," *op cit.*, pp. 400–401.

[24] *Ibid.*

be invited to live among Spaniards and thus assure the loyalty of their subjects."[25] Although the policy of racial separation inherent in the *República de españoles* and the *República de indios* was set forth in the *Recopilación*, it was soon undermined by miscegenation.[26] Only in frontier areas under missionary control could this segregation be enforced effectively[27] and this was recognized officially only as late as 1767.[28] Thus, if the Viceroy's idea had been implemented, it would have been a noteworthy development.

In the Summer of 1796, Governor Borica directed Córdoba and Pedro de Alberni, commander of the projected town's soldier-colonists, to select the best location for the settlement. The areas which were proposed were the Pájaro Valley (near Monterey), the vicinities of the Santa Cruz and San Francisco Missions, and what is now the site of Alameda. The latter two locations were immediately rejected because they lacked the minimum qualifications for a settlement and the Pájaro Valley was eliminated because a maritime location was required;[29] it was the Santa Cruz location which proved to be the best. Two decades earlier, Palou had described it as "fit not only for a town, but for a city, without wanting any of the things necessary."[30] Córdoba reported to Borica that the site would enable the town to be wholly self-supporting with

---

[25] *Ibid.*

[26] *Recopilación de leyes de los Reynos de las Indias,* 4th ed. (3 vols; Madrid, 1791), VI:3:21–23, II, p. 212.

[27] Spanish policy on this matter in California may be illustrated by an item from a series of instructions issued in 1786 by Viceroy Bernardo de Gálvez (a nephew of the former Visitor-General):

> You will charge the governor, Don Pedro de Fages, with the care of maintaining their innocence the Indians of the Santa Barbara Channel, in tranquility those of the missions of San Diego, San Gabriel, and San Francisco, and in the most just order, subordination, and discipline the troops who only serve in the present system to inspire respect, give a good example to the Indians, punish with prudence the excesses which they commit, and prohibit them the use and handling of the horse.

(Bernardo de Gálvez to Jacobo Ugarte y Loyola, Mexico, n.d., 1786, *Instructions for Governing the Internal Provinces of New Spain,* ed. & trans. Donald E. Worcester [Berkeley, 1951], Article 116, p. 59).

[28] Magnus Mörner, *Race Mixture in the History of Latin America* (Boston, 1967), p. 48.

[29] Engelhardt insisted that Pájaro site would have been the best for Branciforte even though the town would have been 15 miles inland. His understandable pro-missionary bias nevertheless ignored the basic defensive and maritime requirement stated by the Viceroy. (Zephyrin Engelhardt, O.F.M., *The Missions and Missionaries of California* [4 vols; San Francisco, 1908–1915], II, p. 520). Fr. José Señan claimed that about halfway between San Francisco and Santa Cruz there was an ideal site for the new town. It had ample fields and water, few Indians in the vicinity and a well-sheltered anchorage. Furthermore, both Monterey and San Francisco Bays were both visible from that point. However, a consensus of opinion agrees that there is no such location in the Bay Area. (José Señan, *Letters, 1796–1823,* trans. Paul D. Nathan, ed. Lesley Byrd Simpson [San Francisco, 1962], p. 7.

[30] Palou, III, p. 301.

two large markets nearby at San Francisco and Monterey if a means of transporting produce could be made available. Córdoba predicted, "The inhabitants will seek the proper mode of living and attempt to better themselves with energy and zeal, so that their descendants may prosper."[31]

Within six months Viceroy Branciforte approved the measures which were taken to found the new town and its establishment awaited the passing of the winter rains. The colonists were to be drawn from Alberni's regiment, the Catalonian Volunteers, landless families from San Jose and Los Angeles, and from Mexican vagrants and criminals who had been convicted of minor offenses.[32] Earlier, Córdoba had provided the Marqués with a plan for the new town but, oddly enough, it was found that sites were not designated for government buildings and the town hall. In his criticisms, the Viceroy cited IV:7:8 and I:4:2 of the *Recopilación*.[33] In all other respects he was satisfied that the provisions of Book IV, Title 7 of the *Recopilación* had been fulfilled.[34] He concluded, "This office approves the establishment of the new villa with the glorious name of Branciforte."[35]

However, the Viceroy was less than meticulous in his critique of Córdoba's plan. In addition to the absence of sites for government buildings, both the form of the plaza and the arrangement of streets failed to correspond to IV:7:8 of the *Recopilación*. Códoba's plaza was a perfect square, whereas the *Recopilación* specified that its length should exceed the width by half. Furthermore, one street should bisect each side of the plaza in addition to the eight streets which extend from the four corners.[36] In view of the close attention given the Villa's establishment, it is curious that one in as important a position as a viceroy should disregard the letter of the law. Nevertheless, it must be said that when one examines the plans of other Spanish colonial towns, the degree of compliance with the *Recopilación* does not differ materially with that of Branciforte in matters of plaza form and street arrangement.[37]

[31]Córdoba to Borica, San Francisco, July 2, 1796, quoted in E. L. Williams, *Santa Cruz: A Peep into the Past* (Bancroft Library MS), p. 55.

[32]Branciforte to Borica, Mexico, January 25, 1797, CA, *State Papers. Missions and Colonization*, I, pp. 79–83.

[33]*Recopilación*, IV:7:8, II, p. 21; I:4:2, I, p. 25. The latter provided for a hospital and is the first mention of such an institution in California. However, it was never built, let alone given serious thought.

[34]Branciforte to Borica, *op. cit. Recopilación*, II, pp. 19–25.

[35]Branciforte to Borica, *op. cit.*

[36]*Recopilación*, IV:7:8, II, p. 21.

[37]See *Planos de Ciudades Iberoaméricanas y Filipinas existentes en el Archivo de Indias* (2 vols; Madrid, 1951), vol. I.

The basis for the political government of Branciforte was provided by instructions which had been issued for the founding of the Villa of Pitic in 1789.[38] Hittell asserted that Borica enclosed a copy of the Pitic material in his orders to Córdoba and directed him to proceed as they specified except where otherwise noted.[39] The Villa of Pitic had been formed by transferring the Presidio of San Miguel de Orcasitas to the mission location of Pitic where Indians were encouraged to remain in the new settlement. The *Recopilación* was frequently cited in the text of the Pitic regulations reflecting the legalistic framework within which innovations were often justified.[40]

Although there is no indication of any effort to conceal the plans to establish the Villa de Branciforte, they must have been a well-kept secret; the missionaries learned of the founding only two weeks before the first colonists were scheduled to arrive. Lasuén wrote to the President of his missionary college that the Villa was "the greatest misfortune that has ever befallen mission lands. . . . This is a flagrant violation of all law. If any remedy can be found, it would be wrong not to apply it."[41] A few days later he wrote to Borica, politely suggesting his disapproval of the matter. He argued:

> The King knew the situation quite well, and so did his Excellency the Viceroy, and Mission Santa Cruz had already been founded with royal approval. Hence, it appears to me impossible that his Majesty should wish, ordain, or approve of a villa or pueblo in the immediate neighborhood, or that his Excellency should attempt it.[42]

The College of San Fernando lodged its formal protest with the office of the Viceroy in August, 1797, substantiating its case with some appropriate citations from the *Recopilación*.[43] The friars' argument may

---

[38]Today's Hermosillo, Sonora.

[39]Theodore H. Hittell, *History of California* (4 vols; San Francisco, 1897), I, p. 578. Thus, "while the plan was principally intended for Pitic, its authors contemplated that it should also furnish a general plan for the founding of pueblos throughout the *comandancia* of the Internal Provinces of the West." (*Ibid.*, p. 579).

[40]Juan Gascot y Miralles, "Instrucción aprobada por S.M. que se formo para el estableci-miento de la nueva Villa de Pitic en la Provincia de Sonora, y mandada adaptar a las demas nuevas poblaciones proyectadas," Chihuahua, November 14, 1789, CA, *Provincial State Papers*, V, pp. 54–77. The legislation also appears in CA, *State Papers. Missions and Colonization*, I, pp. 340–357. Therefore, it is quite likely that Borica provided a copy in his instructions pertaining to the founding of Branciforte.

[41]Fermin Francisco de Lasuén to Fr. Pedro Callejas, Mission San Carlos, May 1, 1797, Lasuén, *Writings*, ed. & trans. Finbar Kenneally, O.F.M. (2 vols; Washington, D.C., 1965), II, p. 26.

[42]Lasuén to Borica, Mission San Carlos, May 5, 1797, *ibid*, p. 27.

[43]College of San Fernando to Viceroy Branciforte, Mexico, August 30, 1797, cited in Engelhardt, II, pp. 517–519.

be divided in two parts, one relevant to the protection of the rights of Indians, the other limiting where towns of Spaniards may be established. However, in this instance the latter approach was not stressed before the Viceroy, possibly because "the explanation given suffices to convince us that Your Excellency was not informed with that sincerity and truth, which the matter required, as to the site or location on which the new pueblo is projected against the express intent of such grand and equitable laws."[44] The missionaries emphasized:

> The College regards the project itself with favor as something useful. Nor does it venture to make representation in order to hamper or embarras you Excellence. It merely desires to see the plan executed in accordance with the laws. Otherwise, there will arise disputes, disorders and delays.[45]

But they were particularly piqued that the Villa and the Santa Cruz Mission were separated by a river and were thus "scarcely a stone's throw away" from each other.[46] And, as we shall see, this proximity proved to be disadvantageous to both settlements. However, the protest was inopportunely timed and in light of the Viceroy's resolution to found a town which would bear his name, it is unlikely that there was any possibility of a significant change in the situation. But the protest did cause a delay. Borica was compelled to defend his actions and argued in rebuttal that the mission had sufficient land for its declining Indian population. He also suggested that the Villa would be able to purchase whatever surplus the mission produced.[47] Thus, it wasn't until December, 1800 that the missionary objections were disposed of and in March of 1801 the cost of the project was given final approval by the *Junta Superior de Real Hacienda.*[48]

Nevertheless, despite these hindrances, the preliminaries for settlement were underway by mid-May, 1797. Córdoba was again directed to "make a plat of the town, including the Church, government buildings and hospital and draw up an estimate of expenses, distinguishing between the costs of the three public buildings and the house of each settler."[49] The latter item was included in the government accounting as a result of the initiative of either Viceroy Branciforte or Governor Borica; it

[44]*Ibid.*
[45]*Ibid.*
[46]*Ibid.*
[47]Borica to Branciforte, Monterey, February 6, 1798, cited in Bancroft, *California*, I, p. 572.
[48]Fiscal to Viceroy Félix Berenguer de Marquina, Mexico, December 11, 1800, cited in Guest, p. 43.
[49]Borica to Córdoba, Monterey, May 15, 1797, CA, *Provincial State Papers. Indices,* pp. 258–261.

is not absolutely clear which deserves credit for the idea.[50] In 1795 the Viceroy had emphasized that the Spanish soldier is at once "a courier, cowhand, mason, shepherd, laborer, serving so that he barely has the time to get the necessary amount of sleep. It is necessary to relieve him of these various tasks without more cost to the Royal Treasury."[51] Eighteen months later Borica noted that nearly two decades had elapsed since the founding of San Jose and fifteen years since that of Los Angeles, yet "their settlers live in tule huts since they are not able to attend to their construction without abandoning the sowings with which they earn their livelihood."[52] Therefore, he ordered that "houses of adobe, roofed with tile, and with shuttered windows are to be built for each settler at royal expense, not to exceed 200 pesos."[53]

Modest progress at Branciforte was apparent by August of 1797. Córdoba reported that the pueblo lands had been surveyed, some houses had been built and that a well had been dug for irrigation.[54] He also furnished the Viceroy with an estimate of the cost of the town which amounted to 23,405 pesos.[55] However, further work was suspended in October pending the appeal of the missionaries. Although the appropriation was finally approved in March, 1801, inflation, Spain's crippled and war-pressed economy, and other factors which were indicative of incompetent direction and the town's unsatisfactory progress eventually caused the appropriation of funds for Branciforte to halt entirely.[56]

---

[50]Guest attributes to Borica not only the departure from the usual practice for the construction of houses, but also the idea that minor criminals and landless vecinos from Los Angeles and San Jose be sent to the new town. (Guest, pp. 35–36). However, the former point was touched on by Viceroy Branciforte at an earlier date, i.e. November, 1795 vs. August, 1796. In light of the great personal interest in the matter assumed by the Viceroy, it is he who merits the distinction.

[51]Branciforte, "Informe . . .," op. cit., p. 399.

[52]Borica to Córdoba, op. cit.

[53]Ibid. Accordingly, Borica instructed Lt. Gabriel Moraga:

> In order that the [temporary] buildings progress rapidly, have the soldiers in your company assist, and have them build near them accommodations for 15 or 20 families, even if it is one dwelling. Thus, they may be sheltered from bad weather until more convenient dwellings are ready. . . . You are to carry out well the orders which have been decreed for the founding and promotion of the villa de Branciforte. The houses which have been mentioned in this order are such that should be used temporarily. . . . Those that are built on the plaza of the villa may also be used temporarily but are to be constructed for permanent use, one house for each settler.

(Borica to Moraga, Monterey, May 26, 1797, CA, Santa Cruz Archives, pp. 67–68).

[54]Córdoba to Borica, Mission Santa Cruz, August 12, 1797, CA, Provincial State Papers, X, p. 150. It is odd that the adjacent river was not utilized for that purpose.

[55]Bancroft, California, I, p. 570.

[56]Marquina to Gov. José de Arrillaga, Mexico, June 3, 1801, cited in ibid., II, p. 155,

The first group of civilian settlers and the Catalonian regiment arrived in California on May 12, 1797 and after an inexplicable delay which consumed the productive months of spring, summer and early autumn, they were transported to Branciforte in November.[57] The long journey had left most of them in a sorry condition, raggedly clothed, and many showed the effects of syphilis.[58] By January, 1798 they had finished their first sowing of twenty *fanegas* of wheat and had commenced the enclosure of their *suertes*.[59] However, they did not "sow or plant any other kind of grain or vegetables," Borica complained, "because of their want of experience and energy."[60] Borica cautioned *comisionado* Gabriel Moraga, who had nurtured the struggling San Jose settlement two decades earlier, "It is very necessary that you treat them with prudence and make them learn how to work and rid themselves of their natural laziness. You are authorized to punish those who make suspicious excuses not to work or who do not apply themselves to it."[61] The results of the harvest confirmed the government's fears. Moraga was warned, "considering the character of the colonists, you must make sure lest there should not be enough to maintain them."[62] However, the government's patience was by then in short supply and within five years of its establishment, it was apparently resolved to fiscally abandon the Branciforte settlement. Census data indicates that the Catalonian Volunteers were reassigned by 1803 and their continuing status as land grantees was doubtful after 1801 despite the fact that they were primarily responsible for whatever progress the town had made thus far. Even though the wartime reassignment of the Volunteers effectively sealed the town's fate, their departure was rationalized in a rather curious manner. Moraga was informed:

> There might arrive . . . an order to form them again into a company and call them to duty and they will have to go . . . Moreover, they have their pay to live on and in addition are also furnished with clothing [whereas] the colonists . . . have only the produce of their crops to live off for the year.[63]

Fiscal to Marquina, Mexico, December 9, 1802, cited in Guest, p. 44; Marquina to Arrillaga, Mexico, July 21, 1803, cited in Bancroft, *California*, II, p. 155.

[57] Branciforte to Borica, Orizaba, November 28, 1797, CA, *Provincial State Papers*, VIII, p. 464.

[58] Engelhardt, II, p. 519.

[59] About 45 bushels.

[60] Borica to Moraga, Monterey, January 27, 1798, CA, *Santa Cruz Archives*, p. 71.

[61] *Ibid.*

[62] Hermenegildo Sal to Moraga, Monterey, October 16, 1799, quoted in Williams, p. 23.

[63] Raimundo Carrillo to Moraga, Monterey, April 9, 1801, CA, *Santa Cruz Archives*, pp. 18-19.

As if to validate the government's hindsight, Governor José de Arrillaga dispatched José de la Guerra to report on the condition of Branciforte in 1803. His account, writes Guest, is "a sad commentary on the town itself, and on the competence of the men who established it."[64] The houses were poorly constructed and haphazardly arranged; of a total of twenty-five, only one was of adobe. Furthermore, all the suitable agricultural land was on the mission side of the river, while the Villa had all the best grazing land. The site was not only poorly chosen for those necessities, but the town itself was ill-situated atop a small hill.[65] As for the settlers, their counter-productivity was such that Guerra remarked that their absence "for a couple of centuries at a distance of a million leagues" could be none other than beneficial.[66] Although Branciforte's population rose to 101 at the end of 1803, that figure was the highwater mark for its early years.[67]

Thus, within less than a decade of the Villa's establishment, events there had given the government good reason to be distressed. In 1805 it was reported that the relatively "felicitious circumstances" which accompanied the progress of San Jose and Los Angeles were absent at Branciforte. Instead,

> There is nothing conspicuous in this establishment with respect to the others that is conveyed by the literal meaning of its title; since its founding a few years after the Mission of Santa Cruz . . . the Mission has already occupied the largest and best lands of said location, for that which remains for the villa . . . is not capable of sustaining the *vecinos* in its district.[68]

A year later, Governor Arrillaga related that although Branciforte had been founded with a complement of nine settlers, excluding the Catalonian Volunteers, it now had but five, only one of whom was married, but even that to little avail since his wife was in Mexico. At that date, the decimated town possessed only seven small houses of mud and timber, all badly roofed with tule.[69]

The instructions given by Governor Pablo Vicente de Sola to the Branciforte *comisionado* in 1816 reflect the government's continuing but ineffectual concern for the town's development. The document's first article pertained to maintaining "peace and good harmony,"

---

[64]Guest, pp. 44–45.
[65]José de la Guerra to Arrillaga, Monterey, June 3, 1803, cited in Guest, p. 45.
[66]Same to same, quoted in Bancroft, *California*, II, p. 155.
[67]Ignacio Vallejo, Branciforte, December 23, 1803, CA, *Provincial State Papers*, VIII, p. 90.
[68]Conde del Valle de Orizaba, Mexico, December 20, 1805, *ibid.*, XII, pp. 15–16.
[69]Arrillaga to Viceroy José de Iturrigaray, Monterey, July 18, 1806, CA, *Provincial Records*, IV, pp. 340–341.

vigilance against immoral activities, and to the dubiously regimented "performance of public and individual labors at the accustomed hours."[70] The next two sections were concerned with religious duties during Lent as well as regular attendance at mass; offenses were punishable by three days in the stocks. Contact with the mission Indians across the river was prohibited so as to avoid "illicit abuses." The balance of the instructions was devoted to matters of population and agricultural production. New *vecinos* were encouraged to settle at Branciforte but the governor's permission was required. And, predictably, "one of the major attentions of the *comisionado* must be to eliminate idleness on the part of each and every *vecino*."[71] By 1818 Branciforte's population had stabilized at fifty-three inhabitants who were housed in a dozen or so dwellings.[72] However, in 1826 Branciforte was the only California pueblo which lacked an *ayuntamiento*. Governor José María de Echeandía wrote that "the *vecinos* of Branciforte belong in the jurisdiction of San Francisco since they are in such short number they will not be able to conduct municipal elections."[73] Yet, although the Governor did not cite any statistics, in 1828 there were thirty-two *vecinos* and a total population of 153.[74]

The impact made by Branciforte on its first foreign visitor speaks ill of its founders' judgment. In 1827, Edmond Le Netrel, a member of the Duhaut-Cilly expedition, saw fit to write only of the Santa Cruz mission, making no mention of the adjacent civil settlement. He observed that "the aspect of the Mission . . . is extremely agreeable, the immense quantity of fir trees which covers the coast, and the beautiful cultivated plains which extend to the edge of the sea presents a charming view."[75] From this account it seems as if the Villa had never existed. Yet, by 1831 its population had increased so that during the following four years it was allowed to elect its own *ayuntamiento*. But, in December, 1835, Branciforte was returned to an outside jurisdiction, this time to Monterey.[76]

[70]Sola to Branciforte *comisionado*, Monterey, May 23, 1816, CA, *Santa Cruz Archives*, pp. 59–61.
[71]*Ibid.*
[72]Sola to Viceroy Juan Ruiz de Apodaca, Monterey, April 3, 1818, CA, *Provincial Records*, IV, p. 439.
[73]Echeandía, San Diego, December 4, 1826, CA, *Departmental State Papers. Benicia. Military*, I, p. 175.
[74]Jose Canuto Boronada, Branciforte, n.d., 1828, CA, *Departmental State Papers*, I, pp. 247–248, 251–252.
[75]Edmond Le Netrel, "Voyage Autour du Monde pendant les Années 1826, 1827, 1828, 1829," *Nouvelles Annales des Voyages*, XLV (January–March, 1830), p. 150.
[76]CA, *Departmental State Papers*, II, pp. 130–131; *State Papers. Missions*, II, p. 8; Gov.

Following the secularization of Mission Santa Cruz, the Villa and ex-mission were joined together in a separate parish which was to be known as the Pueblo de Figueroa.[77] The pueblo was one of the chief beneficiaries of the spectacular growth of San Francisco in the years which followed. The lush coniferous forests of the Santa Cruz mountains provided the raw materials for the buildings which would soon begin their resolute march across San Francisco's sandy valleys and windswept hills. The mountains additionally sheltered many foreign mariners who had chosen Monterey to be the last port of their seafaring lives.[78] In 1835 this sylvan population was sufficiently large to support a distillery operated by Messrs. Job Dye and Ambrose Tomlinson in the vicinity of Felton.[79] By virtue of the vigorous logging industry, the population in the area had risen to 300 though perhaps Simpson was a bit naive when he wrote, "being the least populous, it is also the least profligate of the three pueblos."[80]

The appearance of the Pueblo must have been quite pleasant, although its physical arrangement hardly conformed to a formal aesthetic. Duflot de Mofras wrote, "The houses are scattered on an immense lawn shaded by groves of pines, and seven rivulets."[81] By 1845, the town was known solely as Santa Cruz, "Pueblo de Figueroa" having fallen into disuse. The population numbered 470 of which about a sixth were foreigners and a fourth were Indians. Logging continued as the chief economic endeavor, Bancroft observing that "the Branciforteños strove to maintain their reputation for disorderly conduct with marked success."[82] A year later, Revere noted:

> The population is small and composed partly of Americans; but the inhabitants have improved their time, and the place presents a busy aspect. The people

---

José Castro to Branciforte *alcalde*, Monterey, December 28, 1835, CA, *State Papers. Missions and Colonization*, II, p. 285; Bancroft, *California*, III, pp. 696–697.

[77] Ignacio del Valle to Gov. Jose Figueroa, Pueblo de Figueroa, January 25, 1834, CA, *State Papers. Missions*, I, p. 246.

[78] William Buckle, an Englishman, was the nominal founder of this community, having jumped ship at Monterey in 1822 (Sherwood D. Burgess, "Lumbering in Hispanic California," *California Historical Society Quarterly*, XLI [September, 1962], p. 239).

[79] *Ibid.*, p. 240.

[80] *Ibid.*, p. 239; Sir George Simpson, *Narrative of a Journey Round the World During the Years 1841 and 1842* (2 vols; London, 1847), I, p. 364. However, Duflot de Mofras was a better judge of men. Of the settlers, he wrote, "Some are occupied with commerce and agriculture; but the greatest number devote themselves to chopping wood or working in sawmills. These Americans are known to be *fort turbulents*." (Eugène Duflot de Mofras, *Exploration du Territoire de l'Oregon, des Californies et de la Mer Vermeille* [2 vols; Paris, 1844], I, p. 409).

[81] *Ibid.*, p. 410.

[82] Bancroft, *California*, IV, p. 664.

here are chiefly engaged in the lumber trade, excellent saw-mills having been erected . . . which are constantly in operation, all the lumber they can produce selling readily at high prices.[83]

As for the old settlement of Branciforte, it apparently remained an identifiable entity until 1907. A special election in that year ended its status as a township and officially joined it to Santa Cruz.[84] Prior to that time, a patent for 319 acres, comprising Branciforte, had been issued in 1864 by the United States government to Judge Augustine W. Blair to be held in trust for its inhabitants. Blair then ordered the county surveyor to make a full and accurate survey, designating the names of those who owned buildings and property.[85] This was a most approbrious end for what had been envisioned as the premier town of California, albeit in name only. The *Recopilación* proved to be no better an agent of town planning than the competence of those responsible for the town allowed it to be; even in retrospect it is almost inconceivable how they failed to capitalize on the experiences gained at San Jose and Los Angeles. Ironically, the Villa "with the glorious name of Branciforte" ignominiously ended its days as a ward of the courts.

San Jose State University   DANIEL GARR
San Jose, California

---

[83] Joseph Warren Revere, *A Tour of Duty in California* (New York & Boston, 1849).

[84] Edward Martin, *History of Santa Cruz County, California* (Los Angeles, 1911), p. 15

[85] *Ibid.* Martin's citation of 1868 is in error. A survey of Branciforte had been conducted by Alexander McPherson in September, 1864.

Cultural Tension:
The Origins of American
Santa Barbara

BY JAMES C. WILLIAMS

Spain's settlement of California as a northern buffer zone for her empire to the south began in the 1760s. Within a decade outposts had been established in northern and southern California. By 1782 Captain José Francisco de Ortega established the Santa Barbara Presidio, the last of four such Spanish outposts in California, and found the several thousand Chumash Indians in the channel area peaceful. Four years later Father Fermín Francisco Lasuén dedicated the tenth of twenty-three California missions in Santa Barbara. Some 200 soldiers, missionaries, servants and families populated the area in 1797, and an Indian pueblo adjoining the mission was completed in 1808.'

The first two decades of Santa Barbara's history were dominated by the conquistadores and missionaries. Local authority was vested in the presidio commandante from 1782 until 1826, and the bulk of activity centered on the mission, which would ultimately baptize 4,771 Indians. Santa Barbara and California alike remained isolated outposts of the Spanish-American empire, hardly noticing the change of government in Mexico which came with revolution in 1810.

In 1813 the Mexican government repealed the anti-foreign trade law which had previously helped to isolate California. Trade in hides and tallow brought foreign visitors, ranchos were established under generous land grants, and a pueblo came into existence outside the presidio walls. In December, 1826, an *ayuntamiento* (city council) with two *regidores* (councilmen) and an *alcalde* (mayor) was organized for the fledgling pueblo. Perhaps 400 persons lived in the pueblo-presidio area by 1830, ten of these being foreigners. Within ten years the hide and tallow export amounted to some $25,000, and sea-otter hunters opened headquarters in Santa Barbara. Life in the pueblo was leisurely, perhaps even monotonous tranquillity.[2]

Santa Barbara's role in California politics during the 1830s and 1840s reflected the community character. The 1826 arrival of California's first Mexican governor, José María Echeandía, marked the beginning of the province's domination by "politicos." The day of the padres and conquistadores was gone. Yet, with the exception of some minor support, California political radicals had little impact in Santa Barbara. The community took no part in the move against Governor Manuel Victoria in 1831; and, when radicals throughout the state held back support from California's Bishop Garcia Diego and the church, Santa Barbara residents continued to pay tithes, perhaps because the bishop resided at Mission Santa Barbara and because of their general conservatism. Even in the dispute between northern and southern California from 1835 through 1845 over the location of the capitol, Santa Barbara remained outside the squabble. "Often caught in a cross-fire," suggests one historian, "she remained indifferent and confused."[3]

Santa Barbara's role in American occupation and annexation of California was minor. One historian suggests that, although descriptions of the community written by its American residents constructed a pastoral picture of "two dimensional characters moving about a pleasant landscape, 'without any apparent object' in life," perhaps convincing American readers that California desperately wanted annexation, no one was very concerned about it. The prospect of annexation did not bother the local citizens, and Santa Barbara señoras seemed to express the feeling that Yankee rule could come painlessly and "put an end to all the political confusion."[4]

The events suggest only token opposition to American occupation. In August, 1846, Commodore Robert Stockton occupied Santa Barbara and left a garrison of eleven soldiers. Two months later they were driven out by local *Californios*. Loss of life is not mentioned in the record. In December Colonel John Frémont retook the community with a force of 450 men. He arrived via San Marcos Pass, avoiding an alleged ambush set for Gaviota Pass, and found no resistance. American occupation was final, and it was secured by a detachment of New York Volunteers in the first months of 1847.[5]

The Santa Barbarans began to adjust to the new state of affairs. They consolidated their local power and sent the three most politically astute *Californio* delegates to the 1849 Constitutional Convention in Monterey — José A. Carrillo, Pablo de la Guerra and José María Covarrubias. While they failed to gain more seats in the new legislature for ranching counties and failed to get Santa Barbara named as the state capitol, the three delegates had their successes. They were responsible for getting tax assessment placed at the local government level and for requiring that all laws be printed in both English and Spanish.[6]

As the 1850s unfolded, the *Californios* continued to hold political control of their community. Pablo de la Guerra served as the area's state senator and Antonio María de la Guerra and José María Covarrubias served in the state assembly. One authority suggests that Hispanic influence was no stronger in the state than in Santa Barbara, "a stance that truly reflected the rancheros' economic and numerical strength."[7] But American annexation of California very soon brought profound changes to the face and character of Santa Barbara.

A clash of Hispanic and Anglo-American cultures marked the first two decades of American Santa Barbara. Steady population growth, social and political tension, a shifting economic base and natural disaster characterized the period. By 1870 the economic, social and political power of the native Spanish-speaking or *Californio* population was almost entirely dissipated, and a mixture of European and American immigrants guided the life of the town.

When Santa Barbara was officially recognized as an American town on April 9, 1850, its appearance was largely unchanged from the description given twenty years earlier by Alfred Robinson. The adobes were scattered at random around the old presidio, and no street plan as we know it was in evidence. Characteristic of European villages, the construction of buildings was noticeably more important than a street system, and buildings were placed where they were most convenient for the residents.[8]

The town's main street, the Camino Real, later officially named Estado and then changed through usage and American influence to State Street, was a crooked trail (see Figure 1). It wandered from perhaps as far uptown as Nicholas Den's house down past Lewis Burton's house, then by the imposing two-story De la Guerra home and on to the beach. From the De la Guerra adobe to the ocean stood progressively fewer structures. The Camino Real passed among the Alvarado, Cota, Alvarez, and Leiba adobes to the west and those of Pedro Carrillo and others on the east and then, for almost one quarter of a mile the trail crossed open land to another well spaced cluster of structures. Passing the western side of Francisco de la Guerra's house, it ran between the home of Guadalupe Ortega Chapman which was further east and the houses of María Cordero and the Pablo Vasquez family on the west. The last adobe on the way to the beach was the residence of Charles Brown, a twenty-five year old Prussian sea-otter hunter who had arrived in Santa Barbara six years before.[9]

Life varied little on the lower portion of Camino Real in 1850. Animals probably grazed in the fields separating the lower houses from town, and a vineyard had been planted to the west of the main street. The many children of the Vasquez, Chapman and De la Guerra families tended the hogs, chickens and cows and no doubt played in the ditches which served as fences before the Anglo-American habit of erecting wooden barriers took hold. In 1847 the New York Volunteers reputedly laid out a baseball diamond on Camino Real near the Thompson property, but excitement of this alleged sort was unusual. A new adobe was constructed in 1852 diagonally across from Charles Brown's house. About 25 by 10 feet in size, it was a thatched tule roofed structure on the land of Gaspar Oreña built by Pablo Franco and his son-in-law, Vasquez. Oreña, a well-to-do ranchero and billiard hall owner, permitted Vasquez and Franco to dig adobe on the property and sell the bricks they made. The two lived and worked there for some time, but by the 1860s the house was abandoned and crumbling.[10]

Business, social and political life in Santa Barbara was found north of the Carrillo and Alvarez adobes. Lewis Burton's home and store was the post office and principle retail center, and

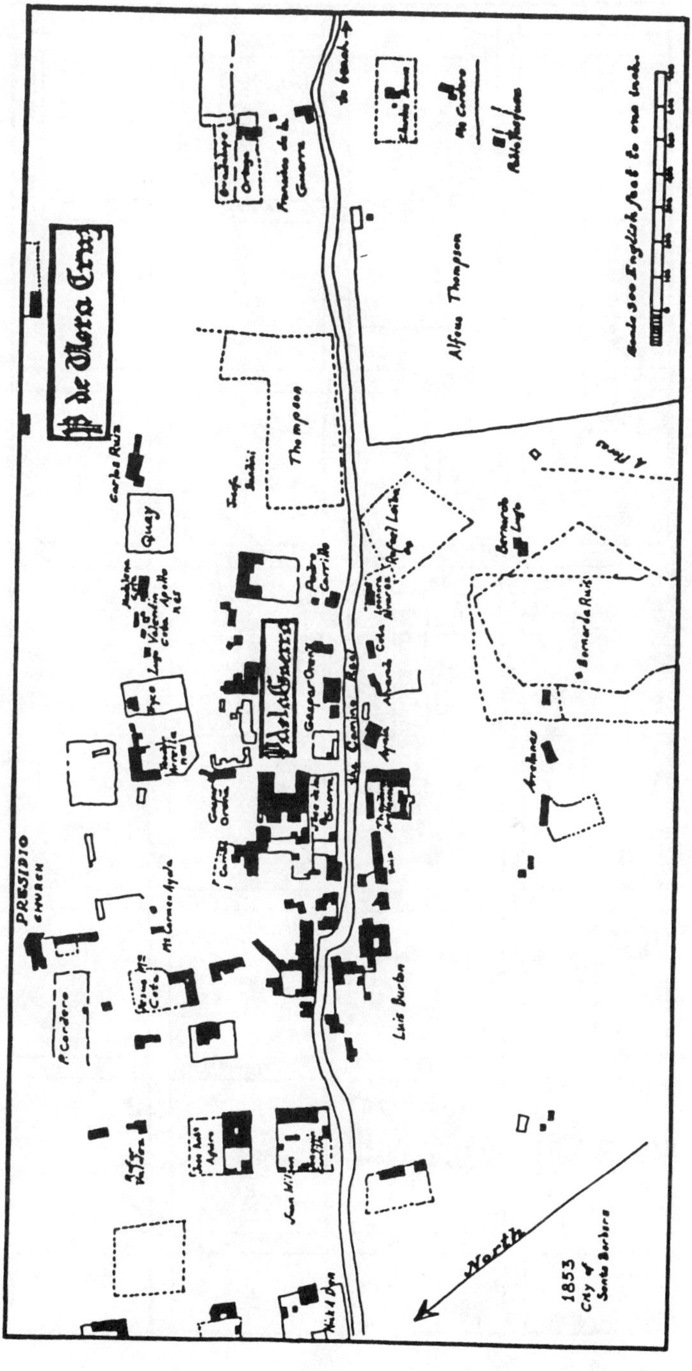

de Mesa Cruz

PRESIDIO CHURCH

Carlos Ruiz
Quay
Thompson
Presidio de la Guerra
Alfonso Thompson
Scale 300 English feet to one inch.

North

1853
City of
Santa Barbara

Figure 1

[353]

329

1853 City of Santa Barbara
Scale 300 English feet to one inch.
Gutierrez Street
Haley Street
Cota Street
Ortega Street
De la Guerra Street
Canon Perdido Street
Carrillo Street
Figueroa Street
Anacapa Street
Santa Barbara Street
Estado Street
Chapala Street
Quay
Alfons Thompson
Thompson
Luis Burton
Presidio Church
248
249
250
251
228
229
230
231
209
210
211
212
191
192
193
194
173
174
175
176
156
157
158
159
140
141
142
143

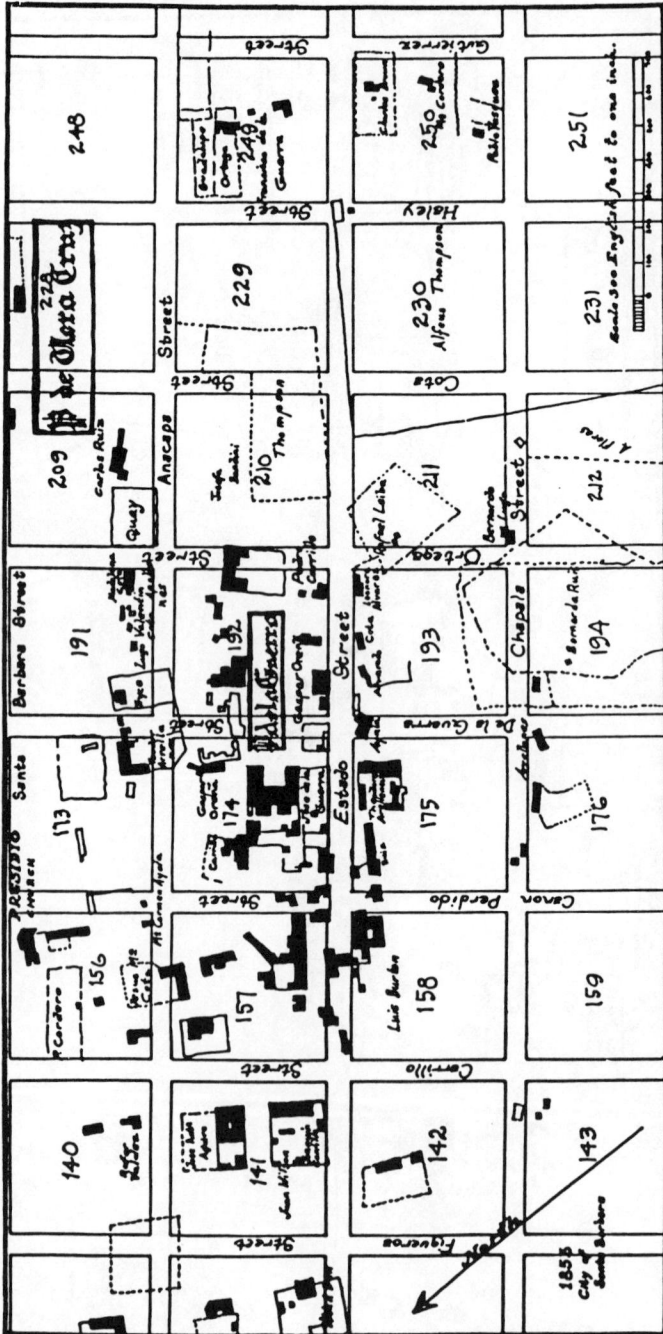

Figure 2

Oreña's billiard hall by the Plaza de la Guerra was the next important focal point of town life. Nearby was the two-story St. Charles Hotel, the major resting spot for travelers. Aware of the traffic at these establishments, one of the first ordinances passed by the Common Council required copies of all city ordinances and business notices be posted at Burton's store and Oreña's hall. Another ordinance further marked the center of town, directing that residents in the area later bounded by Santa Barbara, Ortega, Chapala and Figueroa streets hang a lantern by their doorways each evening from dark until ten o'clock (see Figure 2). While always near the town's center, the city hall floated from one rented structure to another, first to the late James Scott's house and later to Francisco Cavalleri's. By 1860 it occupied the house of José Dolores Garcia but moved in April to that of John Murray. The County Court House and jail were more permanently located in 1853 at the adobe of Magdalena Cota.''

The discovery of gold in northern California had a significant impact upon Santa Barbara. In 1846 cattle sold for about $4 a head in California, but the price soared to $500 a head in Sacramento in 1849. While Santa Barbara cattle did not command that much return, the demand for them substantially increased the prosperity of the community. Alfonso Den is said to have reminisced in the early 1900s that gold nuggets were so plentiful the children used them as playthings. While this was probably a romantic memory, Den's father among others became a wealthy ranchero in the 1840s and 1850s. The new cattle wealth, the area's own 1855 gold discovery near the Santa Ynez mission and Santa Barbara's strategic location along the ocean as a watering stop for the passengers of coastal vessels, brought an influx of visitors, many of whom remained permanently.'²

In 1850 the total population of the Santa Barbara Military and Census District, which included San Buenaventura to the south and the Santa Ynez valley to the east, was approximately 1500. Within ten years some 3500 persons lived in the same area, the Santa Barbara township alone housing 2342 people. A rough estimate suggests that one-fourth of the increase in the Santa Barbara township was caused by an immigration that was primarily male and single. The ratio of men to women among the immigrants was seven to one in 1850 and still five to one in 1860.

Furthermore, the bulk of this population was young, between the ages of twenty and forty.[13]

The large population of single young men in the newly prosperous community led to gambling, liquor sales and prostitution. Since reliable data is virtually nonexistent, one cannot determine if such activities increased during the 1850s and were a prime community issue. However, at least one case alleging prostitution was heard in the Court of Sessions at the end of the decade.[14] The Santa Barbara *Gazette* called for a stiff vagrancy law on June 14, 1855, branding "the idlers of a community for those who constitute the criminals." By 1861 visitor William Brewer noted that Santa Barbara was "so notorious a place for horse stealing and robbery that we have kept guard since we have been here."[15] The early ordinances of the Common Council suggest an effort to control the excesses of the younger men, concerning themselves with drunk and disorderly activity, the discharging of firearms and slaughtering of animals at night and the driving of animals through the streets. In 1855 an ordinance against carrying deadly weapons was passed.[16]

The only ordinance whose passage was actively opposed by members of the community pertained to the issuing of various business licenses. While all manner of licenses were to be issued, including ones for retail merchandising and billiard parlors, the retail liquor license, which cost $10 per month for a minimum of three months, was most opposed. After it passed the Council in November, 1850, a petition against it was presented within a month. In a seven month period, during 1851, licenses just for retail liquor sales were issued to twenty persons. Seven were renewed once, and two of them twice, during the same period. Opposition to the law, however, never ceased. In 1855 Francisco Cavalleri appeared in the Court of Sessions, indicted for running a gambling establishment without a license. Thomas Moore, Gaspar Oreña, Samuel Quay and D. P. Steadman faced similar violations of the liquor license ordinance in the same year.[17]

The changing character of life in Santa Barbara which accompanied the immigration of non-Hispanic peoples and their social order brought severe tension. Some historians have avoided the struggle between differing ethnic groups by suggesting that, while the cultures of the American farmers and the *Californios*

[356]

differed, the two groups shared fundamental kinship in their belief in the pre-eminent importance of home and family, agriculture as a way of life, love of outdoor activity, hospitality and neighborly contacts, [and] community life centered on the church, Catholic or Protestant."[18] Before 1850 immigrants tended to adopt the Hispanic life style, but the blending of cultures after mid-century was not so simply accomplished. In spite of marriages between immigrant men and *Californio* women and some shared concepts of life, the Hispanic culture was placed on the defensive.

Life in pre-American Santa Barbara had relied on a deferential social system. The powerful De la Guerra, Carrillo, and Ortega families were not in control of community life simply because of election to office or successful entrepreneurship, although these considerations were important. Rather their influence stemmed from their position as senior citizens who had extensive land holdings and possessed family lineage of importance in the community. The alcalde was almost always drawn from these families, and their word was more often than not taken as law. The various ordinances of the Common Council, almost all introduced by Anglo-Americans, were new to the *Californios*. The protest against a licensing law and the later tendency to ignore it reflected the conflict of the old and new orders. It is likely also that José Ramón de la Guerra's mid-1860 indictment for issuing unauthorized licenses in his capacity as sheriff was the result of an extension of the earlier conflict.[19]

The deferential system can be nowhere better seen at work than in the verbal banishment from the community of four *Californios* given in 1859 by Pablo de la Guerra. The incident, which followed the alleged hanging of a *Californio* and his son by Anglo-Americans, an evenly split Grand Jury unable to decide upon indictment and the calling in of the United States Army from Fort Tejon to help prevent full-scale violence between the *Californios* and newcomers, was the *Californio* way to prevent unwanted bloodshed. The Anglo-Americans knew the strength of De la Guerra's influence, for they had asked him to banish the four men. The *Californios* accepted unquestioningly their elder's order. Indeed, it was apparently questioned only by Major James Henry Carleton of the 1st Dragoons: "Perhaps it would be difficult to say who should be most censured: — the Americans for requiring their banishment, or the Californians who quietly acceded to it."[20]

The immigrants brought with them not only a new legal and political system but a preference for rational organization. The early survey and mapping of city lands imposed rigidity upon a previously fluid landscape and contributed further to the growing community tension. The inaccuracy of the survey, completed by Captain Salisbury Haley in April, 1851, served to extend conflicts over land titles well into the American period of Santa Barbara's history, but its earliest impact was on the lands held by older residents of the town. The rigid grid system left many homes in the middle of streets and a greater number of property lines crossing or intruding on public domain. No longer were streets secondary to structures (see Figure 2).[21]

Prior to the survey the Common Council had recorded occupied lots and so validated the claims. In doing so, however, the Council reserved the right to "reasume [sic] at any time the possession" of land through which a street ran in any survey completed before January 1, 1852. Residents whose property was found to rest in the city streets had to seek temporary permission to remain there. Protest was inevitable. The first came in March, 1852, in the petition of Octaviano Gutierrez to the Common Council to annul the survey, but his petition was tabled indefinitely. Francisco Cavalleri also protested, refusing to sign a document guaranteeing the city's right to eminent domain. Others acquiesced. As late as 1859 Francisco Leiba and María del Carman Ayala renewed title to their homes on the condition of removal at city request.[22]

Problems determining ownership and location of lots led the Council to have City Surveyor Vitus Wackenreuder map the town in 1853. The Haley survey as illustrated on Wackenreuder's first and second maps was declared official on June 1, 1855. The District Court ruled against the survey in 1867, prompting a new one and further litigation, but ultimately in 1877 the California Supreme Court upheld Haley's work as shown on the maps.[23]

Although early immigrants acted as a buffer between the *Californios* and post-1850 immigrants, the general attitude of the newcomers toward the *Californios* was one of superiority. The citizenship of prominent Hispanic community members was challenged in election disputes during the 1860s, and the absentee voting rights of the *Californio* "Native Cavalry" was overturned by County Judge F. J. Maguire in a heated 1865 election challenge between Anglo-Americans.[24] The Santa Barbara *Gazette* was consistently critical of the lack of public improvements fostered by the community's leadership and of *Californio* county officers. It also opposed the local school teacher because of his alleged ignorance of English. After publishing the *Gazette* for a year, the editor dropped the paper's Spanish page with the excuse that the "upper classes" were using English and the Spanish page was a "disagreeable burden" to him. In May, 1856, the *Gazette* questioned whether the building of a new Catholic Church and conversion of the old one into a nunnery might not be a return to medieval life. The *Californios* retaliated by securing passage of state legislation which allowed local government legal notices to be posted rather than published. The loss of income the paper thereafter suffered forced its demise. Major Carleton probably best expressed what many new immigrants felt. The Spanish were "ignorant of our language and . . . Judicial system," he wrote. "Their weakness is not the wont of mental inferiority but rather of training and education." The Anglo-Americans, he observed, were unwilling to "concede to Californians the same civil rights which they claim for themselves."[25]

The tension between the *Californios* and immigrants, who were arriving in increasing numbers after 1850, had a profound influence on the physical development of Santa Barbara. One early historian accurately notes that "most of the lots of land in the central portion of the city were granted during the period from 1846 to 1850" and recorded with the Common Council in 1851.[26] By mid-decade State Street north of Ortega was well occupied, both by residences of earlier townspeople and the principal early business establishments. Only a couple of new shops were opened after 1855. North of Burton's store and Pacific Express Company office, which blocked State Street above Canon Perdido, was C. R. V. Lee's law office in the house of Fontain and Warren Tarr, builders. South, at Canon Perdido, was David B. Streeter's barber shop. It was soon purchased by his brother, William, who offered dental and surgical work in addition to a shave and haircut. The St. Charles Hotel was still

[359]

the town's hotel, and in the summer of 1856 John C. Kays opened a new store in its vicinity. At the approximate location of State and De la Guerra's northeast corner sat the " 'Drug-store,' 'Pharmecie' and 'Boticia' de Santa Barbara." A converted ship's deck house which had been purchased for $125 and dragged from West Beach in 1854, it was owned by Benigno Gutierrez and Matthew H. Biggs. Diagonally across the intersection, F. J. Maguire competed with Burton's store and acted as agent for Wells Fargo and Company Express. Next to Maguire was the house of Dona Joaquina Alvarado, in which L. A. Wood opened a saddle, bridle and harness business in 1857.[27]

A crucial transition in the community's history was being entered in these years. In 1850 there were very few non-Spanish surname Santa Barbarans, but by 1870 there were twice as many non-Spanish as there were Hispanic residents in the town. The *Californios* were primarily a pastoral and agricultural people, and they yielded to the newcomers domination of the professional, proprietorial and skilled segments of the local economy. Nevertheless, while many non-Hispanics had offices and businesses in the area of the original presidio pueblo above Ortega Street, now called *El Pueblo Viejo*, the *Californios* continued to hold title to most of the land and occupy most of the residential dwellings. Albert Camarrillo suggests that by the 1870s there had actually developed a *Californio* and Mexican *barrio*, adjacent to and east of State between De la Guerra and Carrillo streets. Along that portion of State were the saloons of the *barrio*, for the Spanish-speaking population rarely socialized beyond the area. Thus, the newcomers gradually turned to the building of new establishments on the relatively empty lower State Street.[28]

At approximately the same time that Wackenreuder began to map the city in the early 1850s, Isaac Sparks built a house just below that of Charles Brown on the west side of State Street. This was the first sign of development south of Ortega, since the small adobe had earlier been built on Oreña's lot. Further north, in the middle of the block bounded by Ortega, Cota, Anacapa and State, the Thompson family erected a dwelling and began cultivating the surrounding land. But the area was not to become residential. Shortly after mid-decade, A. J. Williams, opposite Sparks' house on State, advertised his services

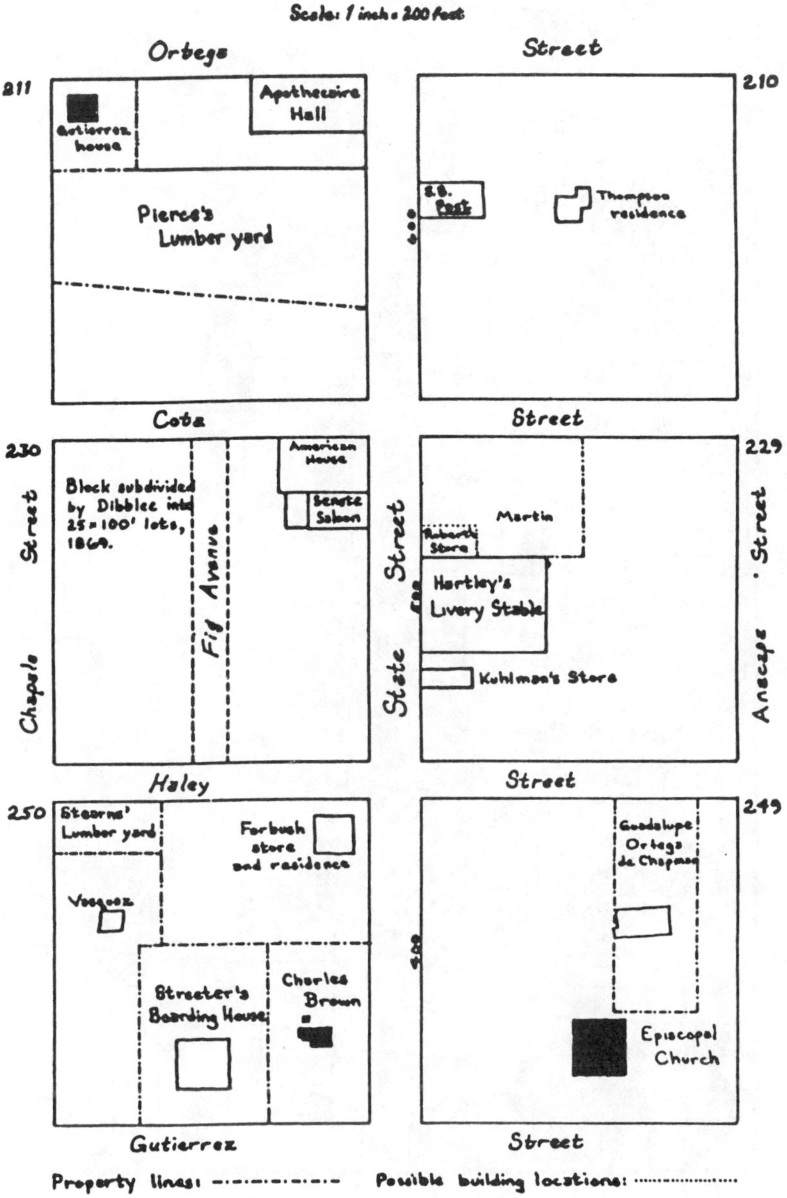
Scale: 1 inch = 200 feet
Ortega
Street
211
Gutierrez house
Apothecaire Hall
210
S.B. Post
Thompson residence
Pierce's Lumber yard
Cota
Street
230
229
American House
Senate Saloon
Block subdivided by Dibblee into 25 × 100' lots, 1869.
Fig Avenue
Martin
Roberts Store
Hartley's Livery Stable
Kuhlman's Store
Chapala Street
State Street
Anacapa Street
Haley
Street
250
249
Stearns' Lumber yard
Forbush store and residence
Vasquez
Streeter's Boarding House
Charles Brown
Guadalupe Ortega de Chapman
Episcopal Church
Gutierrez
Street
Property lines:
Possible building locations:

Figure 3

Perdido Street
Cañon
De La Guerra St.
Anacapa
Ortega
Street
Chapala
State
Street
Street
Cota
Street
Street
Haley Street

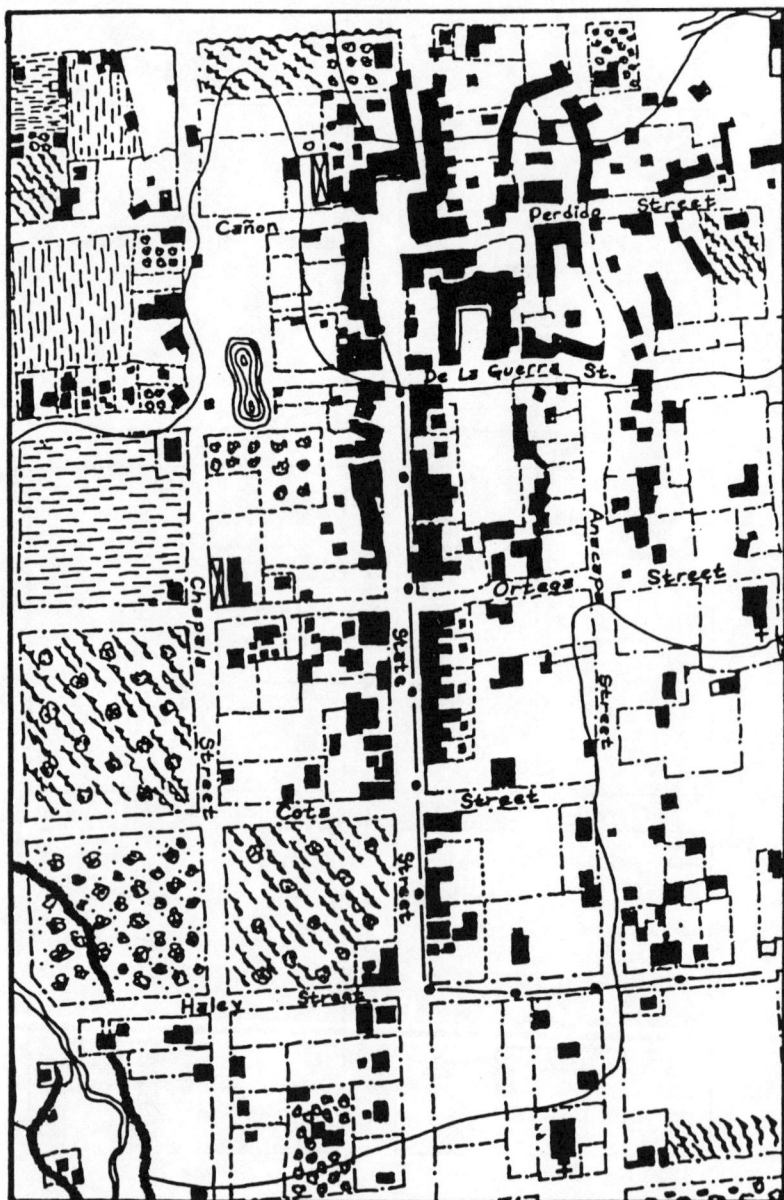

Figure 4

as a painter, glazier and paper hanger. Near Thompson, on the southwest corner of Ortega and State, the Gutierrez drugstore occupied a new brick building in 1856. At its old location in *El Pueblo Viejo* a new warehouse was planned, which would "be an ornament to that part of the city."[29] Most important however, William D. Hobson's new, two-story American House hotel was open for business at the southwest corner of State and Cota in January, 1856. Propitiously named, it became the center of gravity about which a new American and European immigrant business district would form during the next fifteen years.[30]

Between 1856 and 1860 there was increasing activity in the new district. In 1857 the city granted to Lewis Burton and Samuel B. Brinkerhoff, the community's first physician, the block upon which the American House stood and a part of the next block south. In the same year Carlotte de Martin was granted lots on the southeast and northeast corners of State and Cota, and Charles Pierce received title to part of the block upon which stood the new drugstore. Soon Pierce, a wheelwright from Rhode Island, would open a lumber yard on the block. Across the street, William Hobson and his wife took out a $150 mortgage on a lot facing Ortega, perhaps to begin a home or to make improvements at the American House. In the following year, 1858, a lot was granted to John Murray on the southeast corner of State and Haley, and another lot was granted in the same block to William Marris. Rosewell Forbush, a New York carpenter, gained title in 1859 to the block across State Street where the houses of Brown and Vasquez stood, and soon Forbush constructed a building on the southwest corner of State and Haley. Also in 1859, C. R. V. Lee acquired a lot on the southwest corner of State and Ortega.[31] While three more lots were granted below Ortega in 1860, these were the last until after the Civil War. County surveys also declined in number from six in the area in 1857 and 1859 to two between 1860 and 1865.[32]

The years during which the Civil War raged in the east were important ones for Santa Barbara, even though immigration and development activity slowed throughout the county.[33] There was a surfacing of political tension which showed the cohesiveness of the *Californio* community to be faltering. While important American figures in the community supported the Union and

[363]

newly formed Republican Party, anti-Americanism among the *Californios* led many to sympathize with the South in 1860. A desire to be active in local affairs, however, pulled other *Californios* away from the pro-Confederacy political alignment. As the war progressed, the *Californios* gradually lost political impact, their ranks dividing between those Republicans and Democrats who supported the Union, and the Democrats who held out for the South.³⁴ Juxtaposed with this political incohesiveness were economic depression and natural disaster, which served to accelerate a further decline in the Spanish-surname political and economic power.

The cattle economy of Santa Barbara had prospered until 1860. Coincidentally with the outbreak of the Civil War, however, large herds of cattle were assembled in the Central Valley of California by enterprising immigrants. Nearer the state's mining districts and more populated communities, this newly born cattle industry brought economic depression to Santa Barbara rancheros. In June, 1861, Pedro Carrillo wrote that "everybody in this town is broke. Cattle can be bought at any price, real estate is not worth anything."³⁵

Within months the depression was added to by natural disaster. Violent rainstorms in the winter of 1861-62 caused heavy cattle and property losses. After the summer grasses of 1862 were gone, sustained drought engulfed the county. In an attempt to gain something from their herds in 1864, rancheros auctioned some 50,000 animals for their hides and tallow at 37½ cents a head. Cattle died by the thousands, and "entire branches of the age-old oak trees were cut off and the foliage used for fodder in a useless attempt to save a few . . . animals."³⁶ A relief committee was established, and its secretary, Charles Fernald, wrote Antonio María de la Guerra that at least 400 families in the county were receiving daily food and supplies donated by local merchants and sent from San Francisco. Of the some 200,000 head of cattle in the county in 1863, only about 5,000 were left by 1865. Mortgages secured by cattle were foreclosed, and land sold for as little as ten cents an acre. The *Californio* cattle economy was shattered.³⁷

The end of the Civil War brought a resumption of immigration and physical expansion to a distinctively different Santa

[364]

Barbara. The trend of development south of Ortega Street resumed, and *El Pueblo Viejo* continued to be the *Californio* center of town. Its residents no doubt opened their doors to house Spanish-surname rancheros and ranch workers who were forced to leave their land. Many of the original presidio and pueblo adobes were beginning to crumble. The presidio chapel, which was used for a school house in the 1850s, had been vacated after an earthquake in 1857 and was completely abandoned by 1861. De la Guerra Plaza, which had been fenced in and used for bull fighting, was to be opened for other uses, the sport disappearing with the ranchos. Vestiges of Hispanic Santa Barbara were fast disappearing.[36]

The Council prepared an ordinance in 1861 encouraging residents from Canon Perdido to the beach to plant trees along State Street. Authorization was given in 1862 to level State for vehicular traffic, and a Council proposal was made to "turnpike" approximately one mile of Haley from State to the east, thereby establishing a good route to town for the newly emerging farming region. At the same time, this made Haley and State one of the city's main intersections, further enhancing the importance of the emerging new town center. The Chapala Street Wharf Company was formed in October, 1865, and over the winter it built the town's first wharf. The construction of brick and wooden buildings, some embellished with turrets and other ornaments and others of the classic western false-front style, began replacing the adobes. In the boom year of 1868, Yda Storke reported that 80 new buildings were erected in the county, using $70,700 worth of lumber and 600,000 bricks. By 1870 the population of the Santa Barbara township was 3600, a substantial increase of over 1200 persons since 1860.[39]

The character of lower State Street changed little during the Civil War years. The first overland stagecoaches probably stopped at the American House when service began over a newly completed county road from San Buenaventura in 1861, but it is reputed that the stages did not last long, service being disrupted by the war. The first sign of revival came in 1865. Five years before, Council members Charles Pierce and Cyrus Marshall asked James Crabb to apply to the Common Council for a lot on the 400 block where the Thompson house was located. The land

[365]

was ultimately deeded back to Pierce and Marshall, and the latter set out to make bricks on the property in 1865. For a year Marshall made bricks, firing them in two kilns which he constructed, but the "brickmill" was abandoned in 1866 when the property was sold to J. E. Goux. Although shortlived, the mill was a harbinger of future growth. By 1870-71 lots in the area that had been assessed at $10 in 1860 were valued at several hundred dollars. *El Pueblo Viejo's* six square blocks facing State between Ortega and Carrillo were valued at $96,512 in 1870-71, whereas the six square blocks of the new American-European business district were assessed at $102,960. In a decade this previously unsettled area surpassed the older heart of the community in property value.[40]

The pages of the Santa Barbara *Post,* established in May, 1868, provide a glimpse of the post-Civil War community. The north-south stagecoaches of the Coast Line Stage Company, which had its barns and blacksmith shop behind Burton's old store in *El Pueblo Viejo,* stopped daily at the American House at State and Cota (southwest corner). The prosperous hotel, now under the proprietorship of James Shaw from New Brunswick, served meals at all hours for travelers and provided carriage service to the wharf on the arrival and departure of each ocean steamer. The Senate Saloon adjoined the hotel, run by Edgar Van Valkenburg from New Mexico. There travelers could wash the road dust from dry throats with the "best beverages south of San Jose," play a game of billiards and then adjourn to the hair dressing salon in the rear where probably a hot bath could also be enjoyed. The hotel and saloon provided lodging not only for long distance travelers but for the country's farming population.[41]

Only doors away were the new business district's shops. John A. Kuhlman, recently from Germany, ran a variety store across State Street where one could purchase cutlery, toys, fruits and nuts, maps of the United States and Europe, novels, histories and school books. His location, one block south and a block and a half west of the town's Lincoln School, no doubt helped determine the success of his business. John Roberts' new furniture store was nearby, and George Hartley's livery stable near Kuhlman's offered a full range of transportation services. Further south, Roswell Forbush sold Parson's Patented washing machines

[366]

at the southwest corner of State and Haley, and beside him toward Chapala was John Stearns' new lumber yard. On the other side of the block, facing Gutierrez, William Streeter had a boarding house. Residing there were Foy and Daly, masons who were just completing a fine brick house for druggist Benigno Gutierrez on the southeast corner of Ortega and Chapala. Next to Gutierrez' new home was Pierce's lumber yard, which extended from Chapala to State in the middle of the block. Up State, on the corner, was the Apothecaire Hall, and the offices of many of the town's leading professionals occupied the second floor: Doctor O. H. O'Neill; County Surveyor and real estate agent, W. H. Norway; and lawyers Charles Fernald, Jarret Richards, S. R. I. Sturgeon and W. T. Williams. Finally, across from Pierce's on State Street, E. B. Boust's Santa Barbara *Post* printing office was in the Sebastopol Building (see Figure 3).[42]

The growth of the community was quite in evidence in 1868. In *El Pueblo Viejo*, Louis Raffour, an immigrant from France who would later run both a hotel and French restaurant on the 500 block of State, refurbished the old, two-story adobe St. Charles Hotel, opening its doors on October 17. A Santa Ynez Turnpike Company organized to build a toll road over San Marcos Pass, people talked of building another road all the way to the Tulare County mining district and the Santa Barbara Branch of the Southern Pacific Railroad incorporated. A Methodist church organized itself and, with the Congregational and Episcopal congregations formed the year before, it became the third Protestant church in Santa Barbara. Trinity Episcopal Church met each Sunday morning at 10:30 in the town's brick school house throughout 1868. At year's end, its English pastor, Thomas G. Williams, moved the congregation into a new brick home facing south toward Gutierrez, one half block to the east of State. Two decades before, Francisco de la Guerra's house had stood almost next door to the new church's location. The Republican Party Union Central Committee's grand rally in front of the American House, at Cota and State, on the evening of November 2, 1868, might well have celebrated the post-Civil War rebirth of Santa Barbara.[43]

Immigrants from across the world came to Santa Barbara in the late-1860s, and the new business district became a lively, heterogeneous community center. Almost 40 percent of the city's 3600 residents were born outside California by 1870, and only one-third of the population was Spanish-surnamed. Largely Anglo-American but with an important European element, the immigrant population was less transient than it had been a decade before. A third of the immigrants were female, twice the proportion in 1860, and probably half the male immigrants were married as against perhaps 30 percent in 1860. Many of these newcomers settled or worked in the new district, few if any of that area's residents being California born. Furthermore, many of the European immigrants were business proprietors and skilled craftsmen, who worked in or operated the district's shops. By 1880 two-thirds of the European born head-of-household population of the town lived on those streets intersecting and bounding the district. It was truly a cosmopolitan community.[44]

Along the eastern side of State Street in 1870-71, from Ortega to Cota, were a variety of shops.[45] Asa Adams and his father Eber leased the corner lot from Maria Ayers, opening a butcher shop later to be taken over by William Ealand. Next door a saloon opened, soon to be run by Vackenburg whose Senate Saloon was destroyed by fire during the winter of 1870-71. Druggist Enoch Covert from Pennsylvania had a shop next to the saloon, sharing the building with C. C. Hunt's store, and Henry Grunig from Germany sold furniture on the block. Between 1870-72 Cyrus Marshall made $1850 in improvements on his property, which included his house, Hunt's store and Mrs. Tucker's Woodcock Restaurant. Behind Marshall's house, Israel Miller sold and repaired jewelry, and a bootshop run by W. F. M. Goss was next door. Bootmaker Charles (Christopher) Behrens from Germany also ran a shop as did dressmaker M. A. Hickok, and the office of the Santa Barbara *Post* was there. Across State Street was W. Behrendt's general merchandise store, adjoining the "Botica de Santa Barbara" in the Apothecaire Hall, and Robert Breitzmann opened still another drugstore on the north side of Pierce's lumber yard. South of Pierce, Daniel and Andrew Flaying from Hesse Cassel, Germany ran a large blacksmith establishment. Finally, on the northwest corner of State and Cota, in a building which was reported to be two stories in the 1880s, the German Antonio Frisius ran a wine and liquor store.

Diagonally from Frisius, Albert Boeseke from Prussia had a hardware shop on the property of Conrad Schneider, a brick-mason from Germany. Next, on the east side of State below Cota, Thomas Martin had purchased a lot around 1865, and he was adjoined by Hartley's livery stable to the south. Michael Striedl, a Bavarian shoemaker, had a shop between Hartley and Kuhlman's variety store. The corner lot at State and Haley belonged to W. N. Laske, who had recently taken out a $1500 mortgage on the property, and Levy's fruit and grocery market would soon appear there. Around the corner to the east, on Haley, Eli Rundell, who had come to Santa Barbara as a driver for the Coast Line Stage Company in 1866 and was now the company's local agent, bought a small lot in 1871-72. Finally, Prussian Robert Schmidt and French brewer Michael Wurch ran a brewery at Anacapa and Cota, the northeast corner of the block. Undoubtedly they supplied beer to the local taverns.

The American House still occupied the southwest corner of State and Cota and was somewhat refurbished by Scottish architect Albert S. Cranston in 1870, but the fire which destroyed the adjoining Senate Saloon took the hotel as well.[46] Rebuilding began quickly. Thomas B. Dibblee of the Santa Ynez valley, in partnership with William W. Hollister and Albert Dibblee, had almost $200,000 in land holdings outside the city. In 1869 he had the County Surveyor subdivide the entire block on the west side of State between Cota and Haley and marked out the alley known as Fig Street. In 1870 he sold three 75 x 225 foot lots to Louis Raffour, J. A. Johnson and James Shaw. The latter began construction of the Shaw House hotel, a three-story brick structure valued at $10,000, which was finished on the northwest corner of State and Haley by Autumn, 1871. Johnson built a two-story brick building close to the middle of this block on State, in which he placed the offices and printing apparatus of the Weekly Press. Meanwhile, Raffour left the St. Charles to build a new hotel where the American House had stood. Finished by late-1872, the three-story, brick Occidental Hotel on that site was the largest in town and had a telegraph office, barber salon, billiard hall and Cyrus Shotwell's saloon. Out back were two fine new privies for the comfort of the guests, and soon occupants would have the luxury of gas lights. Running water, however, remained an innovation for the future.[47]

The blocks on both sides of State between Haley and Gutierrez had few businesses in 1870-71. Forbush still ran his shop, selling washing machines, and Stearns' lumber yard competed with that of Pierce. The rest of the western block appears to have been residential. Joseph Meroux, a French stonecutter, bought property facing Chapala and next to Stearns. Adjoining him to the south, James B. Ashley, C. M. Opdyke and S. Alexander purchased lots. William Streetcar's boarding house was still on Gutierrez east of State, and Charles Brown continued to occupy the northwest corner of Gutierrez and State. Across State Street the Episcopal Church held Sunday services and shared the eastern block with apparently vacant property belonging to James and Augustias Ord, the De la Guerra estate, John Murray, the Chapman estate and Dolores Chapman's husband, William Marris.

By the 1870s lower State was Santa Barbara's commercial center, and the most frequented businesses extended not much further than a block north of Ortega. In May, 1870, Ortega Street was cleared of buildings still left in the roadway between State and Anacapa as a result of a citizens' petition to the Common Council, and Chapala was opened at the same time. But the Coast Line Stage Company and Burton's old store continued to block State Street just above Canon Perdido until 1873. The telegraph line ran down State to Haley, where it turned east and out of town. Wooden sidewalks fronted the buildings and lots on State, probably starting at Canon Perdido and running to Gutierrez. A jitney of "passenger express wagon" offered rides over the length of the street for eight cents (see Figure 4).[48]

The two decades since the formation of the Common Council had been turbulent ones. Cultural conflict, intensified by a major shift in the community's economic base and continuous immigration, had resulted in the abandonment of *El Pueblo Viejo* to the earliest settlers and the founding of a new American-European commercial center. Serving the new farms which replaced ranchos around the town, the new center radiated the community pride, optimism, idealism and abiding faith in progress typical or midwestern Main Street America.[49] A new Santa Barbara, as distinct from the Old Pueblo, was fully launched.

NOTES

Acknowledgments. The author wishes to thank Professor Robert L. Kelley, University of California, Santa Barbara, for his helpful advise and thorough reading of the original draft of this paper. A Rockefeller Fellowship in Public Historical Studies at UCSB (1977-78) helped make this work possible.

[1] General historical accounts of Santa Barbara include the Southern California Writers Project, *Santa Barbara: A Guide to the Channel City and Its Environs* (New York: Hastings House, 1941); Laurence D. Hill, *Santa Barbara Tierra Adorada: A Community History* (Los Angeles: Security First National Bank, 1930); and Walker A. Tompkins, *Santa Barbara, Past and Present* (Santa Barbara: Tecolote Books, 1975). For the Spanish and Mexican periods Walter A. Hawley, *The Early Days of Santa Barbara, California* (Santa Barbara: Schauer Printing Studio, 1920) is helpful. Maynard Geiger, O.F.M., *Mission Santa Barbara, 1782-1965* (Santa Barbara: Franciscan Fathers of California, 1965) is a definitive work. Wherever possible data has been corroborated with Hubert Howe Bancroft, *History of California* (San Francisco: History Co. Publishers, 1884-90), vols. I-V.

[2] Richard Henry Dana, Jr., *Two Years Before the Mast: A Personal Narrative* (New York: Modern Library edition, 1964 [1840]), offers scattered first-hand comment on the appearance of Santa Barbara during this period. Perhaps the earliest foreigner who tried to stay in Santa Barbara was Joseph O'Cain. He successfully petitioned the presidio commandante, Goycoechea, in 1795, but he was denied entrance by Governor Borica (Bancroft, *History of California*, I, pp. 536 and 669; and Thomas F. Prendergast, *Forgotten Pioneers: Irish Leaders in Early California* [San Francisco: Trade Pressroom, 1942], pp. 11-12).

[3] Leonard Pitt, *The Decline of the Californios: A Social History of the Spanish-Speaking Californians, 1846-1890* (Berkeley: University of California Press, 1966), p. 7. Bancroft, *History of California*, III, p. 653, suggests Santa Barbara had a "controlling" influence during this period.

[4] Pitt, *Decline of the Californios*, pp. 17 and 23.

[5] Bancroft, *History of California*, V, pp. 316-17, 376 and 630; Hill, *Tierra Adorada*, pp. 35-36.

[6] Pitt, *Decline of the Californios*, pp. 43 and 46.

[7] *Ibid.*, pp. 135-136.

[8] Alfred Robinson, *Life in California* (San Francisco: William Doxey, Publisher, 1891), p. 53. Santa Barbara was not officially incorporated until June 14, 1861. City of Santa Barbara, Common Council, *Minutes*, Book "B," August 3, 1860 - May 27, 1875, pp. 5-8. Daniel J. Garr, "A Frontier Agrarian Settlement: San José de Guadalupe, 1777-1850," *San José Studies*, II (November, 1976), 100, notes that the pueblo of San José was also a "laissez-faire arrangement," similar to other California towns. He cites an 1846 observer of that community as saying: "the streets are irregular, every man having erected his house in a position most convenient to him." Spanish pueblos did initially have a somewhat formal plaza and street plan, but in San José it was not followed. Santa Barbara, however, grew without a plan out of the Presidio de Santa Barbara. The presidio pueblo was well settled by the time it was formally designated as a pueblo in 1826.

[9] *Gaspar Oreña v. Charles E. Huse*, Suit No. 239, District Court, 1st Judicial District, County of Santa Barbara, February 2, 1874, testimony of Gaspar Oreña; U.S., *Manuscript Census Schedule*, Santa Barbara District, 1850; Map of the City of Santa Barbara laid out by Salisbury Haley, April, 1853 [No. 1], drawn by V. Wackenreuder; Map of the City of Santa Barbara, February, 1855, No. 2, as surveyed by V. Wackenreuder; William Henry Ellison, ed., *The Life and Adventures*

of George Nidever (1802-1883) (Berkeley: University of California Press, 1937), n. 147, p. 117.

[10] *Census,* 1850; Walker A. Tompkins, "Santa Barbara Yesterdays," *Santa Barbara News-Press,* October 4, 1959 and April 30, 1961; *Oreña v. Huse,* testimony of Gaspar Oreña and William P. Morris; Exhibit C, *Oreña v. Huse,* "Plat of a part of block no. 268."

[11] City of Santa Barbara, Common Council, *Minutes,* Book "A," November 26, 1850 (Ordinance No. 2), January 10, 1852 and March 5, 1860; City of Santa Barbara, *Book "A" of Grants* [ca. 1850-1870], p. 97; Town of Santa Barbara, *Assessment Roll, 1870-71 and 1872,* p. 40; City of Santa Barbara, *Memorandum Book of the Certificates drawn on the City Treasurer,* 1851-1875; Cameron Rogers, ed., *A County Judge in Arcady: Selected Private Papers of Charles Fernald, Pioneer California Jurist* (Glendale, California: The Arthur H. Clark Co., 1954), p. 99; Map, 1853; Map, 1855; City of Santa Barbara, *Ordinances,* Book No. 2, 1850-1872, pp. 56-57 (English translation of Book No. 1).

[12] Michael James Phillips, *History of Santa Barbara County, California, From its earliest settlement to the present time* (Chicago: S. J. Clarke Publishing Co., 1927), I, p. 69; Bancroft, *History of California,* VI, p. 444. In 1856 a company of 80 French and Mexican travelers bound from the north to Sonora, Mexico, stopped for the night in town (Santa Barbara *Gazette,* May 1, 1856). No doubt many other similar groups passed through the community. Charles Fernald, a prominent lawyer, three-time county judge and mayor of Santa Barbara, stopped to visit a friend on the way from San Francisco to New York in June, 1852, and never left (Rogers, *County Judge,* p. 20). Jesse D. Mason, *History of Santa Barbara County With Illustrated and Biographical Sketches of its Prominent Men and Pioneers* (Oakland, California: Thompson and West, 1883), p. 99, tells of the 1855 discovery of gold by Mariano Lopez.

[13] Data compiled from *Census,* 1850 and U.S., *Manuscript Census Schedules,* Santa Barbara Township. 1860. While about one-fourth of the male immigrants in Santa Barbara married *Californio* women and a still smaller number were husbands of immigrant women, single adult males numbered over 100 in the 1850 census district and over 200 in the 1860 township.

[14] *People v. Joseph N. Nevil and Warren J. Tarr,* Court of Sessions, County of Santa Barbara, November 15, 1860, wherein Francisco Cavalleri accused Nevil and Tarr of enticing his 16 year old daughter, Teresa, into prostitution at Tarr's house.

[15] William H. Brewer, *Up and Down California in 1860-1864,* ed. by Francis P. Farquhar (3rd ed.; Berkeley: University of California Press, 1966), p. 63. The records of the local and district courts do not appear to contain a large number of criminal cases. Rather, indebtedness, land litigation, probate and election issues far outweigh criminal proceedings. In one case, however, E. B. Williams testified that he chose to spend the night at another's home after a card game ended at three o'clock in the morning. He was unwilling to walk home that late at night unarmed (*People v. Augustine Wirt,* Court of Sessions, County of Santa Barbara, February 2, 1855). Pitt, p. 174, suggests the town's felony rate was high, but he gives no evidence.

[16] *Minutes,* Book "A," December 10, 1850 (Ordinance No. 6); July 12, 1851 (Ordinance No. 19); November 1 and December 6, 1851 (Ordinance No. 20); September 13, 1851 (Ordinance No. 21); May 30, 1855.

[17] *Ordinances,* Book No. 2, pp. 1-3; *People v. Francisco Cavalleri,* Court of Sessions, County of Santa Barbara, February 2, 1855; *People v. Thomas W. More,* Court of Sessions, County of Santa Barbara, February 2, 1855; *People v. Gaspar Oreña,* Court of Sessions, County of Santa Barbara, February 10, 1855; and *People v. Samuel Quay and D. P. Steadman,* Court of Sessions, County of Santa Barbara, February 11, 1855. Two similar cases are *County of Santa Barbara v.*

Gregorio Arata, Justice Court, 2nd Township, May 16, 1856; and *County of Santa Barbara v. Vincente Deffeles*, Court of Sessions, March 5, 1859.

[18] Walter C. McKain, Jr. and Sara Miles, "Santa Barbara County Between Two Social Orders," *California Historical Society Quarterly*, XXV (December, 1946), 317-318. Albert Michael Camarillo, "The Making of a Chicano Community: A History of the Chicanos in Santa Barbára, California, 1850-1930" (unpublished Ph.D. dissertation, UCLA, 1975), makes a good effort to place a new perspective on the meeting of the two social orders in Santa Barbara. It should be read in conjunction with Pitt's work, which discusses the issue on the state level as well.

[19] *People v. Jose R. De La Guerra*, County Court, County of Santa Barbara, April 25, 1866 (also 1 Cal. Unrep. 345); and *Minutes*, Book "A," *passim*.

[20] Letter from Carleton to Major W. W. Mackell, Assistant Adjutant General, San Francisco, October 5, 1859, in Rogers, *County Judge*, pp. 113-121.

[21] *Minutes*, Book "A," December 5, 1850; January 27 and 29, March 1, April 5 and 7, 1851. Also *Ordinances*, Book No. 2, pp. 27-28, 31 and 58-59; and *Memorandum Book*, *passim*. The inaccuracy of the Haley survey resulted in blocks being some 30 feet off the 450 foot standard at the edge of town.

[22] *Minutes*, Book "A," November 15, 1851; February 2, March 8 and April 22, 1853; and February 26, 1859. Also *Ordinances*, Book No. 2, pp. 19 and 27-28.

[23] *Minutes*, Book "A," October 23, 1852 and June 1, 1855; *Ordinances*, Book No. 2, pp. 58-59; *Henry Penry v. J. T. Richards, et al.*, 52 C. 496; C. N. Gidney, Benjamin Brooks and Edwin M. Sheridan, *History of Santa Barbara, San Luis Obispo and Ventura Counties, California* (Chicago: The Lewis Publishing Co., 1917), I, pp. 85-86; and Mason, *History of Santa Barbara County*, pp. 190-194. Map No. 1 is basically the one reproduced in Figures 1 and 2, although the outer blocks of town are not shown. Map No. 2 covered only the portion of town shown in Figures 1 and 2, and it included the street grid and better located property.

[24] *People ex rel. C. R. V. Lee v. Gaspar Oreña*, County Court, County of Santa Barbara, September 14, 1861; Letter to Hannah Hobbs from Charles Fernald, November 8, 1861, in Rogers, *County Judge*, pp. 212-213; Mason, *History of Santa Barbara County*, pp. 119-121; *People ex rel. M. M. Kimberly v. Pablo De La Guerra*, 40 C. 311; Santa Barbara County, Board of Supervisors, Minutes, 1865, pp. 56-58; *S. R. I. Sturgeon v. Charles Fernald*, County Court, County of Santa Barbara, November 17, 1865; *Walter Murray v. Patrick W. Murphy*, County Court, County of Santa Barbara, November 17, 1865; *Francis W. Frost v. Juan Arata*, County Court, County of Santa Barbara, November 17, 1865; *Thomas Sprague v. W. H. Norway*, County Court, County of Santa Barbara, November 23, 1865 (also, 31 C. 173 and 20 Cal. Rptr. 204); *Anza Porter v. Jose R. de la Guerra*, County Court, County of Santa Barbara, November 25, 1865; Exhibit A, *Sturgeon v. Fernald*, "Voting Returns for General Election, Nobre 8 de 1865;" Exhibit B, *Sturgeon v. Fernald*, "Voting Returns for Co. C, 1st Battalion Native Cavalry en route to Arizona, certified by A. M. de la Guerra, Captain;" and Exhibit C, *Sturgeon v. Fernald*, "Votes of C. 'C' cast under provisions of 'An Act to provide for the support of the privilege of free suffrage during the continuance of the war.' "

[25] Carleton to Mackall, in Rogers, *County Judge*, pp. 114-115. Also Gidney, Brooks and Sheridan, *History of Santa Barbara*, p. 96; Mason, *History of Santa Barbara County*, pp. 112 and 328; and Pitt, *Decline of the Californios*, p. 226. Walker A. Tompkins, *Santa Barbara, Past and Present* (Santa Barbara: Tecolote Books, 1975), pp. 43-46, refers to problems of "racism" in Santa Barbara during the 1850s and 1860s, but he attributes the anti-Californio feelings to a tiny minority of Americans who originally came to California with the New York Volunteers during the Mexican War. The search, for scapegoats, however, is futile.

[373]

One also wonders if the 1859 attempt of Californios in Santa Barbara and other southern California counties to separate the northern and southern portions of the state was not an effort to dilute American influence at their doorsteps. Californios still had a political majority in the southern counties, and life could have been made unpleasant for the American immigrants had the division been accomplished. See Pitt, *Decline of the Californios*, p. 204; and Robert Glass Cleland, *The Cattle on a Thousand Hills* (San Marino, California: Huntington Library, 1951), pp. 123-125.

[26] Yda (Addis) Storke, *A Memorial and Biographical History of the Counties of Santa Barbara, San Luis Obispo and Ventura, California* (Chicago: Lewis Publishing Co., 1891), p. 63. *Book "A" of Grants* appears to contain the bulk of the affirmations.

[27] *Gazette*, December 27, 1855; May 1, April 10 and June 6, 1856; and April 7, 1857.

[28] Camarillo, "Making of a Chicano Community," p. 118. From pp. 45-77, he discusses the shifting occupational patterns of the Spanish and non-Spanish surname populations during this period. In 1870 some 10.5 percent of the non-Hispanic workers were professional, proprietorial or skilled persons, compared to 3.3 percent of those with Spanish surnames. Camarillo's work and additional analysis of the *Census, 1850; Census, 1860*; and U.S., *Manuscript Census Schedules*, Township No. 2, Santa Barbara Post Office, 1870, provide the data used here. Property ownership, however, is less easily traced, but changes in ownership appear to have usually been accompanied by a property survey. Of 30 transactions identified in the area above Ortega Street, only 30 percent involved non-Spanish surname persons, and only six and a half percent were north of De la Guerra (*Book "A" of Grants*; County of Santa Barbara, *Survey Book No. 1*, 1853-1859, and *Survey Book No. 2*, 1861-1870). This seems to confirm the Anglo-American whom Camarillo cites (p. 69) as saying the new district on lower State was built because the Spanish-speaking in pueblo viejo would not sell. The newcomers therefore moved south on State, "leaving the Mexicans . . . to themselves."

[29] *Gazette*, May 1, 1856. Also *Book "A" of Grants*, p. 59. It is not clear, also, who erected the Thompson house. Alpheus B. Thompson is shown owning the property in various grants made adjacent to it in the 1850s (e.g., grant to Carlotte de Martin, *Book "A" of Grants*, p. 91); yet Dixie Thompson claimed, in connection with a later legal action, to have lived in the house and cultivated the land for several years (*J. E. Coux v. D. W. Thompson*, District Court, 1st Judicial District, County of Santa Barbara, November 12, 1868). The A. B. Thompson papers, Santa Barbara Historical Society, do not shed light on this matter.

[30] *Gazette*, January 3, 1856.

[31] *Book "A" of Grants*, pp. 85, 91, 95, 103, 113 and 124. Mortgage records were obtained courtesy of Santa Barbara Title Company, January, 1977.

[32] *Book "A" of Grants*, pp. 130, 132 and 138 show lots granted to Thomas Dennis on block no. 229 and James M. Crabb and Isaac Sparks on block no. 210. No more grants are shown until 1866. Also see *Survey Book No. 1* and *No. 2*, *passim*.

[33] From 1857 to 1859, 25 private-party surveys were conducted in the City of Santa Barbara, 99 in the Carpenteria-Montecito area and 14 elsewhere in the county for an annual average of 46. Between 1860 and 1865, there were 12 in the town, 35 in the Carpenteria and Montecito area (22 in 1863 alone), and 35 elsewhere for an annual county average of 16. After the war there was a steady growth of survey activity, with a large clustering of 68 surveys in Carpenteria-Montecito in 1868 and 65 in the city in 1869. The yearly average for the county in this period was 60. See *Survey Book No. 1* and *No. 2*, *passim*.

[34] For discussion of the politics of the period see Storke, *Biographical History,* p. 43; Mason, *History of Santa Barbara County,* pp. 117 and 119; William Henry Ellison, ed., "Recollections of Historical Events in California, 1843-1878" [of William A. Streeter], *California Historical Society Quarterly,* XVIII (September, 1939), 255 and 271; Rogers, *County Judge,* p. 41; and Pitt, *Decline of the Californios,* pp. 234-239.

[35] Quoted in Pitt, *Decline of the Californios,* p. 244.

[36] Francis Cooper Kroll, *Memories of Rancho Santa Rosa and Santa Barbara* [Santa Barbara ?, 197-?], p. 67.

[37] Cleland, *Cattle on a Thousand Hills,* pp. 126-139; Pitt, *Decline of the Californios,* pp. 244-247; Bancroft, *History of California,* VI, p. 441; and Rogers, *County Judge,* pp. 233-234.

[38] Mason, *History of Santa Barbara County,* p. 325; Gidney, Brooks and Sheridan, *History of Santa Barbara,* p. 111. Phillips, *History of Santa Barbara,* I, pp. 39-40, says Ignacio Flores, son of the last Spanish commander of the Presidio, told him of crawling as a five-year old through the windows of the abandoned presidio church in 1860 to wreck things and carry off some statues and two violins. Phillips (p. 166) also tells of De la Guerra Plaza being used for bull fighting.

The immigration to Santa Barbara was no doubt prompted by the town's growing reputation as a resort town (Bancroft, *History of California,* VI, p. 522), and by availability of cheap land. A less reported impetus to immigration came with oil discoveries, the first in Ojai, seven miles north of San Buenaventura, in 1861. The visit to Santa Barbara of famed Yale scientist, Benjamin Silliman, Jr., in June, 1864, and his subsequent glowing reports about southern California oil must have attracted immigrants (see Gerald Taylor White, *Scientists in Conflict: The Beginning of the Oil Industry in California* [San Marino, California: Huntington Library, 1968], pp. 8-10, 24-25 and 55-57).

[39] *Census,* 1860; *Minutes,* Book "B," October 21, 1861 and March 24 and 27, 1862, pp. 14, 29-30 and 34; and Storke, *Biographical History,* p. 47. The leveling of State Street was not something done only once. In 1870 the Council authorized the grading of State from Ortega to Haley, the center to be the height of the brick sidewalk by the Gutierrez Drugstore, M. H. Biggs' building (*Ordinances,* Book No. 2, pp. 210-211). Paving would not occur until the 1880s. The Chapala Street Wharf proved inefficient, not extending beyond the kelp line and therefore not available to vessels over 100 tons. The well known Stearns' wharf would replace it in the early 1870s. Finally, it is interesting that lumber sold in the area in 1860 for three cents a foot for pine and three and a half cents a foot for redwood (*J. C. Cissna v. J. H. Hill,* County Court, County of Santa Barbara, April 20, 1861). If the average board foot price may be judged at eight cents in 1868, $70,000 would have purchased a million board feet.

[40] Storke, *Biographical History,* p. 42; Mason, *History of Santa Barbara County,* pp. 109 and 119; Tompkins, *Past and Present,* p. 27; Rogers, *County Judge,* p. 180; *Minutes,* Book "A," January 17 and March 31, 1860; and *Assessment Roll,* pp. 1-50, *passim.* The assessed values given here reflect real and personal property on the blocks. California Supreme Court, J. E. Goux v. D. W. Thompson, *Transcript on Appeal* (Santa Barbara: Santa Barbara Press Print, 1869), pp. 10-28, *passim,* deals with the brickmill. It is worth noting that brick manufacturing was the second most important manufacturing industry in Santa Barbara County in 1870. Three brickmills existed, employing 25 persons. Six wineries, employing 46 persons provided the leading manufacturing industry. See U.S., *Ninth Census: The Statistics of the Wealth and Industry of the United States* (1872), III, p. 640.

[41] Santa Barbara *Post,* July 18 and August 22, 1868; and City of Santa Barbara, *Public Surveys,* Book No. 1 (ca. 1870-1880), p. 9. The registers of the Shaw

[375]

House (August 23-24, 1874) and Morris House (June 15-December 15, 1875) show many guests registered from the surrounding towns; e.g., San Luis Obispo, Ventura, Lompoc, Goleta, Los Prieto, Carpenteria and Santa Paula. While the Shaw House, later named Morris House, did not exist in 1868, guests from these and other local areas undoubtedly stayed at the American House.

[42] *Post*, March 3, July 18, and August 22 and 29, 1868; January 20 and May 12, 1869. Also Gidney, Brooks and Sheridan, *History of Santa Barbara*, pp. 97 and 111; and Mason, *History of Santa Barbara County*, p. 92a.

[43] *Post*, September 5 and October 31, 1868; Gidney, Brooks and Sheridan, *History of Santa Barbara*, pp. 102 and 106; Mason, *History of Santa Barbara County*, pp. 135 and 145-146; and Storke, *Biographical History*, pp. 70-71. Gidney, Brooks and Sheridan (p. 106), say the local organizers of the railroad applied for and received a United States land grant for the purpose of building the spur, but the task was not undertaken and the grant forfeited.

[44] *Census*, 1860 and 1870. The immigrant population in 1870 was approximately 55 percent American; 17 percent English, Canadian, Scotch and Irish; 13 percent Continental European; 10 percent South American and Mexican; and 5 percent Chinese and other. 46 percent of the male population and 26 percent of the female population of Santa Barbara were immigrants. The bulk of the immigrants were adults. The proportion of married is estimated from the difference in numbers of male and female immigrants over the age of twenty plus those immigrant males married to California born women (120 in 1870), rather than by actual census count.

In 1860 the immigrant population was largely composed of single males, perhaps coming to the community from the gold mines. Data of the *Great Register of the County of Santa Barbara*, 1879, shows that of 139 naturalized citizens, 10 were naturalized in Sierra-Nevada counties, 18 in San Francisco and other California towns and 62 in Santa Barbara County. This last figure, when compared to the remaining 39 immigrants naturalized in states other than California (generally in the east, 13 in New York alone), suggest that about half the non-American immigrants came directly from their homelands in Europe to Santa Barbara. The author was able to identify 13 European born shopkeepers and craftsmen in the new district, about 20 percent of the total number of persons identified with the businesses and property between 1868 and 1870, by cross-referencing census data, newspaper ads and property assessment information.

The U.S., *Manuscript Census Schedules*, Santa Barbara City, 1880, was the first to indicate the street on which people were enumerated and presumably lived. Since it did not give specific addresses, saying two-thirds of the European immigrants lived on Anacapa, State, Chapala, Ortega, Cota, Haley and Gutierrez Streets does not mean they all lived within the six-block area of the district. Nonetheless, significant clustering of populations did occur on streets. Considering that Santa Barbara was largely a walking city in 1880, there being only one mule-drawn streetcar line installed in the late-1870s on State Street, most workers would live within a couple of blocks of their place of work. Edgar Van Valkenburg, for example, while not known to be European born, lived on the corner of Haley and Anacapa, a block and a half from his saloon (*Assessment Roll*, p. 154). U.S. Coast Survey, Section X, 1870, T-series 1229a, "Map of the Town of Santa Barbara and Vicinity" and T-1229b and c (1878 up-dates) show building locations which seem to confirm this conclusion.

[45] The description of the lower State area was compiled from data gathered from the *Post*, 1868-69; the Santa Barbara *Weekly Press*, 1871; *Survey Book No. 2*; *Assessment Roll*; mortgage records, Santa Barbara Title Company; and *Census*, 1860 and 1870.

[46] There is some disagreement as to the date of the fire. Mason, *History of Santa Barbara County*, p. 339, says March 6 but gives no year. The *Weekly Press*,

March 11, 1871, makes no mention of a fire the week before, but an article does ask when the town is going to get another hotel besides the St. Charles. This would suggest the American House burned some time before. The fact that Shaw had run the American House and started to build the new Shaw House in 1871, would further suggest an 1870-71 date for the fire.

[47] R. N. Wood, *Guide to Santa Barbara Town and County* (Santa Barbara: Wood and Sefton, Book and Job Printers, 1872), pp. 13-14. In 1875 the Shaw House was renamed the Morris House. Room no. 40 is the highest number shown on the Morris House *Register*, 1874-75, so the Occidental was indeed a large hotel if it had more than 40 rooms. Johnson's building may not have been finished until 1872. An etching (ca. 1880) in Mason, *History of Santa Barbara County*, p. 328a, shows the building with the phrase "erected 1872" engraved on the face of the structure.

[48] In the block above Ortega were four Anglo-run businesses (*Assessment Roll*, pp. 14, 19, 24, 26 and 28). On the opening of streets, see *Ordinances*, Book No. 2, pp. 204-207; City of Santa Barbara, Common Council, "Petition for Opening Ortega St.," April 28, 1870; "Petition for Opening State Street," undated; "Proposal of Rich and Dunshee in the matter of opening State Street," September 16, 1871; "Proposal of Charles E. Huse in the matter of opening State Street," September 17, 1871; "Proposition and Resolution of Mssrs. Flint, Bixby & Co. to open State St.," May 4, 1872; "Petition in regard to paying Flint, Bixby & Co.," December 5, 1871; "Plat of the Survey made for the opening of Canon Perdido Street," September 3, 1875. Also *Public Surveys*, Book No. 1, p. 9; *City of Santa Barbara v. Charles E. Huse and Gaspar Oreña*, 51 C. 217; Wood, *Guide to Santa Barbara*, p. 15; and Coast Survey, T-1229a.

[49] Lewis Atherton, *Main Street on the Middle Border* (Bloomington: Indiana University Press, 1954), p. xiv. Garr, "San José de Guadalupe," p. 102, states "It is clear that San José was not a town of much consequence prior to American rule." This probably was the attitude toward Santa Barbara held by most non-Hispanic immigrants during the 1860s.

The port of Monterey was among those landmarks discerned by Sebastian Vizcaino during his voyage along the coast of California in 1602. It was the subject of much discussion in the following century and a half by virtue of its assumed connection with the elusive Northwest Passage. Hence, Monterey's importance to the Spanish was a matter of long standing, and its settlement was the first objective they pursued after the founding of San Diego.

A land expedition under Gaspar de Portolá left San Diego in July 1769 with the intention of reaching Monterey and establishing a presidio there. They arrived at the shores of Monterey Bay on 1 October, but the port they expected was not recognized even though it lay at their feet. Portolá was convinced they had failed to find Monterey: "What should be the Río Carmelo is only an *arroyo*; what should be a port is only a little *ensenada*; what were great lakes are lagunitas." [1] His doubts were supported by the fact that Vizcaino, and later, Cabrera Bueno, had both recorded the incorrect latitude for the port. Another explanation offered was that over the years the port had gradually been filled with sand. [2] However, the most likely reason for Portolá's befuddlement was that the harbor and anchorage at Monterey fell far short of the popular ideal that had conditioned his expectations. [3]

The search for Monterey was renewed in April 1770, and the destination was reached on May 24. This time there was no mistake; the leaders of the expedition, Portolá, Fr. Juan Crespi, and Lieutenant Pedro Fages, unanimously agreed: "This is the port of Monterey which we seek, just as Vizcaino and Cabrera Bueno describe it." [4] The presidio was established on 3 June 1770, and its beginnings were described by Palou:

Hand was put to building a stockade and inside of it some humble habitations for the royal presidio. . . . For a site a level place was chosen on the shore of an estuary. . . . Engineer Don Miguel Costansó made his measurements . . . and drew the plan of the presidio . . . all the people moving to it. [5]

The plan of the presidio called for a square of about 200 feet by 200 feet with an interior plaza of 160 feet. By November the stockade enclosure was completed and a plan of the layout was sent to the viceroy (figure 63c). A powder magazine was constructed, and the buildings were whitewashed inside and out.[6] The presidio was completed by December 1773, as is indicated by Palou's description:

It has a stockade of wood with four ravelins, and on each of them a bronze cannon. Inside the stockade there is a church of adobe with its flat roof of plaster, and near it a room of the same materials for a dwelling unit for the fathers . . . On the front face there is a dwelling for the captain, also of adobe, with two small rooms . . . There is another room built of adobe which serves as a jail, a granary, quarters for the volunteer soldiers and the leather jackets, and other rooms for the muleteers and servants. All of the latter are made of logs with a flat roof of earth.[7]

At this point in its history, there was little to differentiate Monterey from San Diego, already constructed. However, on 1 January 1774 it was made the seat of the political and military governments of Alta California, and a little more than three years later, the capital of the entire California peninsula was transferred from Loreto, in Baja California, to Monterey.

One of the initial problems encountered at Monterey was that of its site, which, apparently, lacked some key amenities. Richard Morse has written that abandonment or transfer is a characteristic of Spanish colonial settlements. Such drastic acton would sometimes become necessary due to poor site selection, Indian raids, or changes in the patterns of trade.[8] However, considerations of strategy were the criteria for selection of presidial sites rather than the usual standards of water, arable land, and sufficient building materials. Monterey, like San Diego, was to be the victim of an inflexible decision concerning its location. Fernando de Rivera y Moncada, its commandant in 1774, stated that he did not consider the presidio's site to be a convenient one and urged that it be moved to a spot near the Salinas River, four or five leagues distant. Viceroy Bucareli tentatively approved the move, but a royal order from Spain commanded that under no circumstances should the presidio be moved because the port of Monterey must be protected at all costs.[9] However, Geiger has claimed that the plan was not taken seriously and that Bucareli's underlings never saw fit to even mention the matter to him.[10] This claim arises from Serra's remark, "I was told that he [Rivera] was not allowed to leave the port, nor to transfer the presidio elsewhere," although

Serra continues that "it was general gossip that the new Captain was going to move the presidio, as if that had been the main object of his appointment."[11]

But the presidio was to remain, and by March 1776 Monterey was growing at a rate that the garrison's walls could not contain for long. The establishment of the town itself was imminent and would have occurred earlier if the inhabitants had been sufficiently industrious. This is indicated by Fr. Pedro Font's account:

Its buildings form a square, on one side of which is the house of the commander. . . . On the other two sides there are some huts of small houses of the families and people who live there. All are built of logs and mud, with some adobe; and the square or plaza of the presidio, which is not large, is enclosed by a stockade. . . . It is all a very small affair, and for lack of houses the people live in great discomfort. Nor is this for want of materials, for there is lime and timber to spare, but for lack of effort directed to the purpose.[12]

However, Governor Felipe de Neve's arrival in 1777 was responsible for a flurry of activity, and by July 1778 a stone wall 537 yards in circumference, twelve feet high, and four feet thick had been completed.

California's physical and economic isolation was a hindrance to the colony's development, though the material and psychological effects of this situation evidently caused little governmental concern. The Manila Galleon was required to call at Monterey, but the commanders preferred, with rare exceptions, to absorb the financial penalty and make directly for Acapulco. However, the order served little purpose even if obeyed since all trade with the Philippines ship was prohibited. In 1791 Governor Pedro Fages reiterated the earlier directive that forbade commerce with the galleon on the few occasions it anchored at Monterey. He insisted that the colonists were provided with all that was necessary, and he believed that if business was allowed to be transacted with the Manila ship, the soldiers and settlers would barter their clothing and other needed effects for "immoderate luxuries which cannot be sustained."[13] Seven years later, Governor Diego de Borica took exception to this statement, citing the desirability of supplying California with "effects for daily use,"[14] but it would be a matter of decades before this situation was remedied.

Knowledge of Monterey, as of the other California settlements, is augmented substantially by the accounts of
foreign travellers. Lapérouse, in 1786, was the first to visit
Monterey, but his observations were chiefly of a scientific
nature. The first visitor of note in California was George
Vancouver, who was in Monterey for much of December
1792. His description of the presidio is not especially revealing, and he was not impressed by its "lonely uninteresting appearance"; nor was he much taken with its worth
as a fortification. But his comments on its situation vindicate, to a degree, Rivera y Moncada's desire to relocate
the presidio:

The presidio . . . does not appear to be much benefitted by
its vicinity to fresh water since in the dry season it must
be brought from a considerable distance, as the Spaniards
had not been at the pains of sinking wells to insure a
permanent supply. There were many delightful situations
in the immediate neighborhood of the presidio, with great
diversity in the ground . . . and a soil that would amply
reward the labour of the industrious, which our Spanish
friends might with equal ease have sat themselves down;
more comfortable, more convenient, and I should conceive
more salutary than their present residence appeared to
be.[15]

The appearance of the settlement was documented by a
French captain, M. Péron, who attributed the slow progress being made in California to lack of motivation:

The aspect of the town shows ignorance in the arts and a
stationery state of the country. The houses and cabins are
constructed without taste, the furniture coarse, the utensils
imperfect—an absolute lack of the conveniences of life.
. . . Industry is in general the feeble side of Spanish establishments and it is for this that they cost so dear to their
government. The governer . . . avowed only that he had
to regret that he had proposed different methods of ame-
lioration without avail.[16]

The population of Monterey at this time was close to
400;[17] the size of the garrison during the decade never fell
below 50 and was as high as 62.[18] A document of December 1797 indicates that 30 individuals paid tithes, but that
is not necessarily an accurate indication of the number of
households.[19]

The first years of the nineteenth century found the presidio in a deteriorating condition, for it had never been of

sound construction. In March 1801 the main gate was demolished by a storm and the rest of the establishment was tottering on the insufficient foundation built after a fire in 1789.[20] In 1801, 298 pesos, 7 reales, were spent in efforts to repair the chronic damage.[21] It appears that there was pressure at this time applied in Mexico to rebuild the entire presidio; however, no action was taken on this item of pork-barrel appropriation.[22]

From the period of revolutionary turbulence in Mexico, about 1811 to 1820, virtually no information about California remains. There were no official communications, nor did the soldiers receive their pay. The missions produced their usual surplus and disposed of it according to the ethics and acumen of the padre in charge, for the missionaries realized it was the lesser of two evils to support the military force. The soldiers suffered the most as they had nothing to sell; everyone else fared as best they could.[23]

Monterey appears to have been the first presidio in Alta California to have produced urban settlement outside the walls of the fortification. Peter Corney's description in the summer of 1815 indicates that by that time it was becoming a substantial town; it had about fifty houses and the surrounding plain provided a lush carpet for the new dwellings.[24] Under the circumstances, the presidio continued to exist in fair condition. In April 1818 Governor Pablo Vicente de Sola noted that the north and east walls had been rebuilt but that the south side still wanted improvement. Plans were also articulated to bring water to the presidio via an aqueduct from the Carmel River, but there were no resources available for such a project.[25] In November 1818 Monterey was attacked by Hippolyte Bouchard, a pirate bearing letters of marque issued by José de San Martín. He demanded that California surrender and launched his assault upon receipt of a negative answer. Isolated from the mainstream of events in Latin America, the Californians were neither impressed by the tenets of revolution nor by credentials issued by a great revolutionary, and they refused to respond. However, no significant damage occurred, and the situation was back to normal within five months.[26] At the time of Duhaut-Cilly's visit in March, 1827, Monterey had grown to somewhat less than 500 in population; Robinson's estimate of about 1,000

359

two years later appears to be an exaggeration.[27] The Frenchman's account of Monterey indicates that growth around the presidio was continuing and that its position as capital of California, despite a brief San Diego interregnum in the 1820s, had become further enhanced by attracting foreign, chiefly Anglo, commercial activity:

To the right of the Presidio, on a small verdant plain, one sees, scattered here and there, about forty houses of quite an attractive appearance, uniformly roofed with tile and with whitewashed exteriors. There, with about as many cabins with thatched roofs, is all which consists of the capital of Upper California.[28]

He was misinformed, however, in his assumption that all the houses dated from a period after 1821, the era of Mexican independence.[29] But he did notice that many of the houses belonged to foreigners; a census taken in 1829 indicated that there were forty-four *estranjeros* in the Monterey area.[30]

The transition from military to civil government at Monterey was accomplished quietly and with little fanfare; there was none of the acrimony that was to accompany the *coup* at San Diego. There the establishment of a purely civilian form of government was precipitated in 1833 by a near-rebellion against the regime of Santiago Arguello, commandant of the presidial company. Arguello was frequently at odds with the townspeople, whose final recourse was a petition to Governor José Figueroa on 22 February 1833. It addressed itself to the termination of military control and the formation of an *ayuntamiento*:

It is sad to know that in all the pueblos of the Republic the Citizens are judged by those whom they themselves elect for this purpose, and that in this port alone one has to submit himself, his fate, fortune and perhaps existence, to the caprice of a military judge, who being able to misuse his power, it is always easy for him to evade any complaint which they might want to make of his conduct . . . and there is no other formula than the imperious words of I command it.[31]

Figueroa upheld the petition and ruled that under Mexican law, San Diego was entitled to an *ayuntamiento*; on 4 May 1834 he recommended that the town be designated a pueblo. Three months later he authorized the election of one *alcalde*, two *regidores* (four were requested in the petition), and one *síndico procurador*.[32] The organization of the pueblo was formally begun on 21 December 1834, and the *ayuntamiento* assumed its powers on New Year's Day 1835.[33]

The institutional cause for this inevitable civil versus military friction lies in the fact that the Spaniards considered a presidio a permanent installation. Its strategic importance was a constant factor, although, in the case of San Diego, this was not necessarily so. Davis wrote, "The location of the presidio was chosen from a military point of view, to protect the citizens of this miniature city from the ferocious and savage Indians of those days."[34] The *Recopilación* made no provision for the transition to a civil form of government at the presidios, nor did Spanish legislation of the eighteenth century provide relevant statutes in that direction.

At Monterey in 1820 an order was issued to form an *ayuntamiento*, but the circumstances surrounding it are not clear; Bancroft suggested that the action was "for purposes largely experimental."[35] *Alcaldes* were in office in 1823 and 1826, but there is no further information concerning the functioning of the government. The *ayuntamiento* appears to have assumed its full responsibilities following an election in December 1826.[36] The first of its documented acts was a series of municipal ordinances promulgated in December 1828.[37] Public morality seems to have been its chief concern. Three of the legislation's fifteen articles were devoted to matters of temperance and two were concerned with the use of firearms; also noted were the problems of excessive card playing, theft of horses, panhandling, idleness, and vagabondage. Curfews and business hours were specified, and pawnshops were condemned as usurious. Monterey's population of 502 in 1830 represented a slow but steady growth; more than 100 of that number was assigned to the presidio.[38]

A second series of ordinances was promulgated in 1833 by Marcelino Escobar, constitutional *alcalde*. However, these were directed at environmental considerations. The owner of hogs that were caught running in the streets would be fined twelve reales for a first offense. Settlers would have to clean in front of their houses at least twice weekly, and the garbage was to be used as landfill for holes caused by erosion and the manufacturing of adobes;

further, bricks were to be made in restricted areas or on one's own property. Another article warned against cutting trees on public land for personal gain.[39]

A steady stream of foreign visitors passed through Monterey after the mid-1830s. Their descriptions reflect their varying degrees of empathy or, more usually, antipathy for Spanish California. But despite their prejudices, a picture of Monterey emerges from which conclusions can be drawn. Richard Henry Dana's account of his travels along the California coast is the best-known description of Hispanic California available to the general public. He visited only the four presidial towns and was led to believe erroneously that "every town has a presidio in its centre; or rather, every presidio has a town built around it.[40] His description of the Monterey presidio in January 1835 indicated that it was "entirely open and unfortified. There were several officers with long titles, and about eighty soldiers, but they were poorly paid, fed, clothed, and disciplined."[41] As for the town itself, Dana was perhaps the only writer to prefer it to Santa Barbara, its younger and more elegant sister:

The town lay directly before us, making a very pretty appearance; its houses being plastered, which gives a much better effect than those of Santa Barbara, which are of a mud-color. The red tiles, too, on the roofs, contrasted well with the white plastered sides and with the extreme greenness of the lawn upon which the houses—about an hundred in number—were dotted about here and there, irregularly. There are in this place, and in every other town I saw in California, no streets, or fences . . . so that the houses are placed at random upon the green, which, as they are of one story and of the cottage form, gives them a pretty effect.[42]

A year later, Faxon Atherton counted but twenty or thirty houses. He observed that Monterey, once again capital of California after a year's hiatus, had "no streets, no hotels . . . and the ground [was] covered with the bones of cattle and the air almost filled with carrion crows and vultures."[43] Ruschenberger's population estimate of about 500 in 1836 is more in line with Dana's observations and presents a more accurate description of the size of the town than Atherton's.[44] Petit-Thouars also noticed that the houses "were scattered here and there, without order," and did not perceive "the slightest trace of culture." He

estimated its population to be no more than 200.[45] Francis
Simpkinson, a seaman of H.M.S. *Sulphur,* commented,

> The town, though it looks rather neat and comfortable
> from the anchorage, is a miserable spot when one enters
> it. The few houses there are scattered over the plain with-
> out the least order or regularity, and carcasses of bullocks
> and horses give the same character of indolence to the
> place as San Francisco.[46]

With the exception of Dana, these sophisticated and
well-traveled men expressed prejudices that reflected their
intolerance and lack of understanding of a latino culture.
Atherton was particularly eager in all his descriptions of
California to vent his contempt on what he saw. Of Monterey he wrote, "We . . . took a stroll about the town if
twenty or thirty houses can be called such."[47] That Monterey was a territorial capital seemed ludicrous to Petit-
Thouars and Simpkinson. The latter wrote, "On the whole
the place did not impress a very grand idea of the capital
of a beautiful country like California."[48] The Frenchman's
idea of a center of polity could not be reconciled with
what he found at Monterey. The houses composed "by
virtue of their agglomeration . . . that which is called the
city of Monterey, doubtless in deference to its seat of
government." He continued, "It serves no purpose to add
that there is no other monument than the church of the
Presidio."[49]

By 1840 Monterey's population had risen to about 700,
and it is possible that a certain amount of attention had
been paid to the city's physical plan.[50] This is indicated by
Duflot de Mofras's description of the town in 1841:[51]

> The city is composed today on two parallel streets and of
> several groups of houses dispersed on the plain. Almost all
> the houses are built with bricks dried in the sun . . . with
> roofing, floors and balconies of wood; some are quite nice.
> Since they all have a garden and a large yard, the town
> occupies a vast area, and from a distance one is deceived
> by its importance; but the population is only six hundred,
> mostly foreigners. All the houses have their main facade
> turned towards the southeast in order to avoid the dam-
> ages of the north-west wind which blows for half the year.
> Seen from the sea, the situation of Monterey is truly ad-
> mirable; there is no position more picturesque and more
> favorable for the establishment of a great city.[52]

However, he remarked that "there is at Monterey no building worthy of attention." The presidio had been demolished, but the *castillo* had three serviceable cannons, "which had been cast in Manila or Lima in the seventeenth century"; the presidial force numbered about sixty.[53] Sir George Simpson of the Hudson's Bay Company dispelled all illusions about planning and street arrangement that Duflot had suggested:

The town . . . is a mere collection of buildings, scattered as loosely on the surface as if they were so many bullocks at pasture; so that the most expert surveyor could not possibly classify them into crooked streets. What a curious dictionary of circumlocutions a Monterey Directory would be.[54]

He also observed that

the habitations have a cheerless aspect, in consequence of the paucity of windows, which are almost unattainable luxuries. Glass is rendered ruinously dear by the exhorbitant duties . . . After all, perhaps the Californians do not feel the privation of light to be an evil. . . . It cannot, by any possibility interfere with the occupations of those who do nothing.[55]

The activities of US Consul Thomas O. Larkin were in large part responsible for a mild business boom in Monterey. In 1841 he successfully agitated for the construction of a wharf, and although he contributed much of his own funds to the project, he was never reimbursed. Larkin was also the prime mover behind the reconstruction of the customs house, "which promises to be a small range of decent offices; for though it has been building for five years, is not yet finished," as Simpson had observed.[56] The wharf and customs house provided the necessary atmosphere to foster a modicum of commerce. We are certain that Larkin did not neglect his own interests. After the wharf was completed, he acquired a number of nearby lots, on which he built stores that were offered for rent.[57] After the arrival of the US fleet in 1846, Larkin invested in a parcel opposite the customs house, which later became one of Monterey's most important business blocks.[58] Laplace's estimate of the population in 1842 was 1,500, a rather exaggerated figure, but he observed that many of the town's leading citizens were American and British merchants, an occupation that Monterey residents had thereto-fore monopolized. The town boasted two newspapers, one in English and one in Spanish, which underscored the binational character of the California capital. Lafond was impressed by "the newly-constructed buildings which give this town an air of youth and freshness, which charms and seduces as much as the amiable hospitality of its inhabit-ants.[59] Even Hastings was struck by the size and vigor of Monterey (figure 62):

Including those within its suburbs, it contains about one hundred buildings. . . . There are many more foreigners at this place, than at any other town in the country. They . . . are chiefly Americans. This town is situated upon one of the most beautiful sites for a town, or even for a city, that I have ever beheld . . . This is, in all respects, a most delightful and favorable site, for a great commercial em-porium, as which it is undoubtedly destinated ultimately to be occupied.[60]

The original presidio had almost entirely disappeared by 1844; a dozen artillerymen and three or four guns in working order were all that remained of the fortification and its garrison.[61] By 1845 Mexico was bracing for war with the United States, leaving the California government weaker and more chaotic than usual. In July 1845 Juan Alvarado issued a proclamation declaring that Monterey had been lacking in civilian authority for a substantial period of time.[62] One *alcalde* owed the municipal treasury thirteen dollars, while another had left town when his resignation was refused. A Captain Torre was appointed to act temporarily, but many would not recognize his authority.[63]

The character of Monterey appeared to have undergone a change by mid-1846 when the Americans seized Cali-fornia. Walpole wrote, "Many of the more respectable inhabitants had left on its occupation by its new masters; but others, and they not a few, were very glad of it, for the Mexican rule had become intolerable."[64] In addition, the commercial axis of California had shifted to Yerba Buena, the rapidly growing settlement on the eastern shore of the San Francisco peninsula. Outwardly, at least, Mon-terey remained as it had been. Larkin reflected, "Monterey is about the same. It will not increase fast. It will, I think, be a good, moral, gentle town for California. . . . Yerba Buena and other places in and about San Francisco will be the busy, bustling, uproar of places."[65] In January 1847 General William T. Sherman wrote, "Everything on shore looked right and beautiful . . .; the few adobe houses, with red-tiled roofs and whitened walls, contrasted well with the dark pine trees behind. . . . Nothing could be more peaceful in its looks than Monterey."[66] Furthermore, he continued, "not a single modern wagon or cart was to be had in Monterey, nothing but the old Mexican cart with wooden wheels, drawn by two or three pairs of oxen, yoked by the horns."[67]

As for Monterey's town plan, Duflot's observation of two parallel streets was not substantiated by any other account. Juan Bandini wrote that "there is a small promenade near the dock," but that is hardly the *plaza mayor* specified by the *Recopilación*.[68] With reference to the chaotic physical development of the town, he noted that "although quite a few large houses have been constructed, these buildings have all been situated without hope of forming a street, since there has been no method for the builder other than whim."[69] A somewhat more understated comment was forwarded by Larkin, who reported in 1843, "The streets are not very straight and about twenty-one yards wide."[70]

The first effort to impose an uncluttered pattern on the Monterey street system was made on 1 March 1847, by William Robert Garner, an Englishman, and Walter Colton, who in 1846 had become the town's first American *alcalde*. Garner wrote,

Some attempts were made to-day to regulate the streets in the town of Monterey. This is a difficult matter, as each person has built his house on the spot and in the form he thought proper, without any attention to regularity. . . . however, after some considerable difficulty, we succeeded in laying off two handsome streets, both of which will form a front line extending in a North and South direction. One of these streets is nine hundred yards long, and the other eleven hundred yards from one extremity to the other.[71]

The area between the two streets was divided into building lots, and their spirited sale furnished "sufficient proof that Monterey is destined to increase rapidly in population, and consequently in improvement and wealth."[72] Accordingly, the demand for land "had increased beyond credulity." He observed in a letter dated 5 March 1847 that in Monterey "so great had been the demand of late, that it was found necessary to set aside sufficient land for a jail, a market place, a burial place, and a public square." [73] This could be read as a sweeping indictment of, and explanation for, the chaotic physical development present in California's towns. It is, no doubt, an accurate report since Craig asserts that Garner's letters "are the most authoritative and complete description of the customs and life of the Californians . . . . to reach the general American public before the Gold Rush." [74] On the other hand, it is reasonable to suggest that the requisite land for these uses may have been so designated long before, however informally. But only at that particular time did it become necessary to identify those sites clearly in response to pressures exerted by private individuals. Visual evidence supports this interpretation, for the required open space is readily apparent in contemporary views of the town. However, Garner's comments emphasize the fragile basis of the Hispanic urban pattern in all the California settlements.

It was finally decided that a comprehensive and orderly blueprint for growth and the alignment of existing structures had to be put into operation. On 27 August 1849 the *ayuntamiento* enacted the following regulations: First, a plan of the town was to be drawn with the boundaries of existing houses and walls in one color; house lots that had been granted but not developed, in a second color; and streets, alleys and plazas, in a third color. Second, the person commissioned to draw the plan would be compensated with grants of house lots if there were, as was likely, insufficient funds in the municipal treasury. Third, if there were lands that had been granted where streets, alleys, or plazas were designated, and if there were no foundations or houses on them, the *ayuntamiento* would name three individuals to determine fair compensation for the obstructing territory. Fourth, if developed lands were in conflict with the arrangement of public walkways, the owners of those properties would be compensated according to the same procedure. And last, no one would be permitted to build foundations or erect fences on land without the council's permission. [75]

This was the first indication of any plan since the presidio was constructed in 1770. Although the town of Monterey began after effective Spanish rule in Mexico had terminated, it is curious that no plan for its development was formulated by the Mexican authorities. Were any plans for new towns drawn up in Mexico during the post colonial era? In California, such actions did occur with reference to activities associated with the founding and growth of Sonoma. Perhaps planning is a function of a government with sufficient scope, resources, and authority, which was not the case in California until the American conquest.[76] Monterey was perhaps the only colonial Hispanic capital without a plan.

If urban chaos was to govern Monterey's physical development, then much the same would be said for Santa Barbara, its sister presidio 200 miles to the south. An early historian of Santa Barbara County has told us that

as the settlement grew stronger, houses were built outside of the inclosure, and the walls were suffered to go down, and in places were removed to make room for buildings. The courts of the Noriega and Carillo houses were laid out partly outside and partly within the presidio walls.[77]

The lack of a plan in those days was noticeable to all. Juan Bandini wrote that in 1847 "in town were lately built houses of some taste, all scattered about without order and according to the caprice of the owner."[78] Another writer was of the opinion that "the town was laid out by means of a huge blunderbuss loaded with adobe houses." And a third thought Santa Barbara "resembled a family of pigs of all ages around the maternal swine"[79] (figure 64).

The first remedy for this chaotic situation was proposed in 1851 when Salisbury Haley was commissioned to conduct a survey; the town was to be arranged in the familiar grid pattern with blocks 150 yards square.[80] Each street was to be sixty feet wide, and the two major thoroughfares, eighty feet wide; however, the blocks that emerged had unequal dimensions. Haley's surveying chain contained rawhide thongs that stretched in damp weather and contracted in the sun so that when the blocks were subdivided, property owners found that their land extended well into the street or into adjoining lots.[81] The survey, however, maintained the implicit pattern stamped on the town by the old presidio. The streets were slanted at an angle of 48°30′ west, which was in close conformance to the *Recopilación*, which specified that the corners of the plaza should be oriented toward the four points of the compass so that the streets would not be exposed to the inconvenience of the four winds, a scheme already followed at Monterey. That is, the streets were to bisect the four quadrants of the compass.[82] In order to avoid further urban chaos, the town council passed an ordinance in July 1852 requiring that

each person who has the intention of building a house on unoccupied land must obtain from the *Comisionado* a certificate which indicates that the house will not obstruct the lands and thoroughfares of the city. . . . Whether the owner of land wishes to construct a house or houses . . . [he] must first advise the *Comisionado* who will inform the Municipal Council.[83]

Another ordinance of similar vintage provided that those who held land "during a period of twenty years without receiving a title for same may do so without any additional costs other than the gratuities of executing such a document."[84]

Fortunately, such procedures were not made any more urgent by the crush of events. The pressures of population and the demand for land remained external to Santa Barbara. Rather, it was Los Angeles that had to grapple with these problems as the state's southern locus of urbanization. Instead, Santa Barbara remained one of the final outposts of California's pastoral era, when a steamship would call twice a month with a surf-soaked sack of mail.

Monterey, too, quietly found itself removed from the mainstream of events. During the Gold Rush, it was virtually abandoned. Even though there was a state constitutional convention in session in Monterey in October 1849, Bayard Taylor found it deserted: "Few people were stirring in the streets, business seemed dull and stagnant; and after hunting half an hour for a hotel, I learned there was none."[85] In April 1852 Bartlett reported, "Many of its houses are now deserted, or in a dilapidated state, and the grass may be seen growing in the streets."[86] What was to be Monterey's fate? San Diego, mired in arid isolation, helplessly waited for the railroad to bridge the continent. Taylor reflected that the growth of San Francisco and the depopulation following the gold hysteria were not to be cause for uneasiness. Monterey may have been dull, but "it [was] . . . in the sense that Nice and Pisa are dull

cities."[87] Bartlett predicted that "Monterey will become
the residence of gentlemen of fortune on account of its
more genial climate and its distance from the noise and
bustle of a great city. It will be to San Francisco what
Newport is now to New York."[88]

What can be concluded about Monterey and its modest
niche within the Hispanic urban tradition? First, as ob-
servers have noted from the days of Bartlett to the present
era when the whole of Monterey's environs are an affluent
riviera, the Spanish were expert judges of terrain. They
knew where to begin their settlements. If these were not
nurtured, it was for reasons of resources and the constraints of an unwieldy, vast, and declining empire. These
factors were particularly relevant in California, 1,500
miles distant from Mexico City. Spain's colonial possessions were a vast incubator of colonizers who, though not
always steeped in the juridicial tradition of codified legislation, were imbued with the ability to recognize terrain
with urban pretensions. If they could not provide site selection criteria per the *Recopilación's libro, título,* and *ley,*
they could at least recognize where possibilities were most
promising.

Second, while abandonment and transfer of a settlement
is a traditional adjustment within Spanish settlement practices, the presidio, in its strategic role, was not afforded
the flexibility of other urban institutions. The mission
could be moved if its terrain or surrounding population
proved too hostile. The pueblo was frequently subject to
recalibration; flooding, attacks, or natural disasters were
an expected component of its pedigree. But the presidio,
in its noncompromising physical location, had to endure.
If a location is of great strategic value, then it is a military
problem and there is no need to consider issues such as
changes in urban form or political authority due to civilian
succession. Such issues are built into the situation.

For example, urban settlements, the *Recopilación* cau-
tions, should not be situated in maritime locations where
the tumult and temptation of the port of call runs contrary
to the presumed industriousness of urban life. But in California inland waterways are not a characteristic of the
landscape, especially on the central and southern coasts,
where most colonization took place. The *Recopilación*
strongly recommends river locations for urban settlements

since they favor transportation, lack the diversions of seaports, and often have access to a fertile hinterland. With this major option lacking, population centers in California would have to be located in a maritime situation. As a result, many travelers never ventured inland. The two pueblos, San José and Los Angeles, languished in the bountiful amenities of their isolation, forgotten and removed outposts of California Pastorale.

If the *Recopilación* did not create civilian settlements from military forts, provincial governors could. And once this occurred, the presidios were quick to assert their control over the problems of municipal management; Monterey, for example, gave prompt attention to morality and environmental considerations. Although this intensity was not sustained, by 1847 planning and land titles were foremost in the town's attention. This was necessary because, as Juan Bandini recalled for San Diego,

as it was not customary at that time for [Governor] José María Echeandía to give [written] titles,[89] nor until now was the plan of the town determined (today it has been made and the town has taken its proper form), it was necessary for me to obtain the documents which authorized the legitimacy of my possessions[90] to the effect that a square of one hundred *varas* on each side was conceded to José Antonio Estudillo and myself divided between both of us.[91]

Two conclusions may be arrived at based upon the information in Bandini's account. First, the presidio and then pueblo of San Diego grew up quite haphazardly. There was no plan or systematic procedure for development until after the American conquest. The *Recopilación* was, if you will, *hors de combat* in this instance. Yet there was at least one copy of it in California during the Spanish period, as a letter of Junípero Serra indicates, and a minimal degree of familiarity with it on the part of lower-echelon officials is not an unreasonable assumption.[92] On the other hand, it did not contain legislation pertinent to the development of presidial towns. The most plausible and simple explanation that can be offered is that there was no competent authority present to exercise control over all but the most rudimentary matters on a day-to-day basis. Uniform and consistently applied principles of town planning were at best a remote possibility on a frontier such as California.

371

As an American observer wrote in 1841, "Although I was prepared for anarchy and confusion, I was surprised when I found a total absence of all government in California, and even its forms and ceremonies thrown aside."[93] Accordingly, the absence of a plan for San Deigo was noted by its many foreign visitors. Second, the lack of authority did not preclude the existence of individual written titles; it was not merely the custom of convenience that dictated that "grants of that class were made verbally."[94] The *Recopilación* specifies that grants of house lots and other lands be entered in the "libro de Cabildo," sometimes referred to as the "libro de Población," and that it was to serve as the permanent record of title.[95] If such a record was not maintained, then it could be said that an anarchic situation prevailed in California. However, a verbal title does not exlude the existence of a written entry, however insufficient it may have been in the eyes of some Anglo lawyers. It is doubtful that any of these *libros* still survive.

Though lacking the orthodox accoutrements of strong central control and a standardized adherence to the model colonial plan, Monterey demonstrates that it is within the tradition of Spanish colonization. Indeed, three and a half centuries after its colonization, this remote outpost has maintained a semblance of its heritage, albeit one rooted in ephemeral custom rather than rigorous adherence to laws long submerged by revolution, miscegenation, and immeasurable distance.

1 Gaspar de Portolá, "Diario del Viaje á la California," quoted in Hubert Howe Bancroft, *History of California* (7 vols; San Francisco, 1884–1890), I, p. 151.

2 Junípero Serra to Francisco Palou, San Diego, February 10, 1770, Serra, *Writings*, ed. Antonine Tibesar, O.F.M. (4 vols; Washington, D.C., 1955–1966), I, p. 159.

3 Bancroft, I, pp. 153–155.

4 *Ibid.*, p. 169.

5 Francisco Palou, *Noticias de la Nueva California*, ed. & trans. Herbert E. Bolton (4 vols; New York, 1966), II, pp. 292–293.

6 James Culleton, *Indians and Pioneers of Old Monterey* (Fresno, 1950), pp. 44–45.

7 Palou to Viceroy Antonio María de Bucareli, Monterey, December 10, 1773, Palou, III, p. 229.

8 Richard Morse, "Latin American cities: Aspects of Function and Structure," *Comparative Studies in Society and History*, IV (July, 1962), pp. 473–493.

9 Bancroft, I, p. 309.

10 Maynard J. Geiger, O.F.M., *The Life and Times of Fray Junipero Serra* (2 vols; Washington, D.C., 1959), I, p. 443.

11 Serra to Bucareli, Monterey, September 9, 1774, Serra, II, p. 175.

12 Pedro Font, *Diary of an Expedition to Monterey by Way of the Colorado River, 1775–1776*, ed. & trans. Herbert E. Bolton (Berkeley, 1933), pp. 289–290.

13 Fages, Monterey, February 26, 1791, CA, *Provincial State Papers*, VI, pp. 159–160. Henceforth, *Provincial State Papers, Provincial Records, Departmental State Papers,* and *State Papers* refer to California (CA).

14 Borica to Viceroy Miguel de Azanza, Monterey, October 25, 1798, *Provincial Records*, III, p. 428.

15 George Vancouver, *Voyage of Discovery to the North Pacific Ocean and Round the World* (3 vols; London, 1798), II, p. 43.

16 M. Péron, "Monterey in 1796," trans. Henry R. Wagner, *California Historical Society Quarterly*, I (October, 1922), p. 176. The authenticity of the account as a first-hand narrative has been questioned, but it is nonetheless sufficiently accurate in its content to warrant inclusion here.

17 Bancroft, I, p. 677.

18 *Ibid.*, p. 467.

19 *Provincial State Papers*. Presidios, pp. 174–175.

20 Raymundo Carrillo, "Los Edificios de Monterey," Monterey, December 31, 1800, *Provincial State Papers. Benicia. Military*, II, pp. 126–127.

21 *Provincial State Papers*, XI, pp. 194, 172.

22 Bancroft, II, p. 143.

23 *Ibid.*, p. 196.

24 Peter Corney, *Early Voyages in the North Pacific, 1813–1818* (Fairfield, Wash., 1965), pp. 129-130.

25 *Provincial Records*, IV, p. 429. José de Jesus Vallejo, *Reminiscencias Historicas de California* (Bancroft Library MS, 1874), p. 77.

26 Bancroft, II, p. 234.

27 Alfred Robinson, *Life in California* (Oakland, 1947), p. 9.

28 Auguste Duhaut-Cilly, *Voyage Autour du Monde* (2 vols; Paris, 1834–1835), I, pp. 362–363.

29 The account of Duflot de
Mofras, published about a decade
later, appears to have drawn
upon Duhaut-Cilly's dating of the
emergence of the town of Monterey: "It was only in 1821 that the
town which has been given the
pompous title of capital city
began to form. The first house
was built by an English merchant
named [William] Hartnell"
(Eugene Duflot de Mofras, *Exploration du Territoire de l'Orégon,
des Californies, et de la Mer Vermeille* [2 vols; Paris, 1844], I, p.
403).

30 *Departmental State Papers,* I,
p. 292.

31 Quoted in Richard F. Pourade,
The History of San Diego (5 vols;
San Diego: 1960–1965, III, p. 14.

32 William Heath Davis, *Seventy-
five Years in California,* (San
Francisco, 1929), p. 258.

33 *Departmental State Papers.
Los Angeles,* IV, p. 620. The
Recopilación provides for a maxi-
mum of 12 *regidores* in principal
cities and 6 in the others
(IV:10:2, II, p. 33). No more
than 2 *alcaldes* are permitted
(IV:10:1, *ibid*). The *sindico procurador* is specified in IV:11:1 (II,
p. 37).

34 Pourade, III, pp. 14–15.

35 Bancroft, II, p. 611.

36 *Idem.*

37 Monterey *Ayuntamiento,*
Monterey, December 6, 1828,
Departmental State Papers, I, pp.
239–242.

38 Mariano Soberanes, Monterey,
July 12, 1830, *State Papers. Missions,* II, p. 7. Bancroft, II, p.
609.

39 Marcelino Escobar, Monterey,
January 6, 1833, *Departmental
State Papers. Monterey,* pp. 61–
65; *Departmental State Papers,* II.
pp. 159–161.

41 *Idem.*

42 *Ibid.,* p. 72.

43 Faxon Dean Atherton, *California Diary,* ed. Doyce B. Nunis,
Jr. (San Francisco & Los Angeles,
1964), pp. 3–4.

44 Ruschenberger was a surgeon
assigned to the United States war-
ship, "Peacock." William S. W.
Ruschenberger, *A Narrative of a
Voyage round the World during
the Years 1835, 36 and 37* (2
vols; London, 1838), II, pp. 400–
404.

45 Abel du Petit-Thouars, *Voyage
autour du Monde* (10 vols; Paris,
1840–1844), II, pp. 84, 110.

46 Richard A. Pierce and John H.
Winslow, eds., *H.M.S. Sulphur at
California, 1837 and 1839* (San
Francisco, 1969), p. 28.

47 Atherton, p. 3.

48 Pierce, p. 28.

49 Petit-Thouars, II, p. 64.

50 Bancroft, III, p. 667.

51 Californian opinions of M.
Duflot were of great variance.
Alvarado found him to be "a
young man of great literary reputation, of spirited character, and
of generous inclinations," while
at the same time having "very
false ideas about our character"
(Juan B. Alvarado, *Historia de
California* [5 vols; Bancroft
Library MS, 876], IV, p. 175).
On the other hand, Dona Teresa
(de la Guerra) Hartnell, wife of
the English merchant to whom
Duflot had referred, had more
strenuous objections to the
Frenchman:

While at my table he found fault
with every one of our dishes,
however, he did full justice to the
wine. . . . Unfortunately in his
sleeping room I had deposited a
barrel of the choicest wine which
my father had sent me from Santa
Barbara to be given to the priests.
. . . Next morning at breakfast

my guest, not making an appearance, I detailed a servant to call him; but Mr. Mofras not giving any answer to call him; I ordered the door to be broken; and there stretched upon the floor my Frenchman lay dead drunk, bedding in a filthy state and many gallons of wine missing from the barrel.

(Quoted in Susanna Bryant Dakin, *The Lives of William Hartnell* [Stanford, 1949], p. 257.)

52 Duflot de Mofras, I, pp. 403–404. The large yards, or corrals, were a custom derived from the *Recopilación*; similarly, the orientation of the houses are a logical component of legislation dictating the corners of a town plaza face the cardinal points of the compass (*Recopilación de leyes de los Reynos de las Indias*, 4th ed. [3 vols; Madrid, 1791], IV:7:17, II, p. 23; IV:7:9, II, p. 21).

53 Duflot de Mofras, I, pp. 405, 325.

54 Sir George Simpson, *Narrative of a Journey Round the World During the Years 1841 and 1842* (2 vols; London, 1847), I, p. 344.

55 *Ibid.*, p. 345.

56 *Ibid.*, p. 346.

57 Reuben L. Underhill, *From Cowhides to Golden Fleece: A Narrative of California, 1832–1858* (Stanford, 1939), pp. 56–57.

58 *Ibid.*, p. 126.

59 Victor Laplace, *Campagne de Circumnavigation de la Fregate L'Artémise pendant les Années 1837, 1838, 1839 et 1840* (6 vols; Paris, 1841–1854); Gabriel Lafond, *Voyages autour du Monde* (2 vols; Paris, 1843), I, p. 208.

60 Lansford W. Hastings, *The Emigrants' Guide to Oregon and California* (Cincinnati, 1845), p. 108.

61 Bancroft, IV, p. 656.

62 *Ibid.*, p. 654.

63 *Idem.*

64 Frederick Walpole, *Four Years in the Pacific . . . from 1844 to 1848* (2 vols; London, 1849), II, p. 205.

65 Thomas O. Larkin to Samuel J. Hastings, Monterey, November 16(?), 1846, Thomas O. Larkin, *The Larkin Papers*, ed. George P. Hammond (10 vols; Berkeley & Los Angeles, 1951–1964), V, p. 279.

66 William Tecumseh Sherman, *Recollections of California, 1846–1861* (Oakland, 1945), pp. 9–10.

67 *Ibid.*

68 Juan Bandini, *Historia de la Alta California, 1769–1845* (Bancroft Library MS, 1874), p. 64. *Recopilacion*, IV:7:9, II, p. 21.

69 *Ibid.*, pp. 64–65.

70 Larkin to Andrew Johnstone, Monterey, June 3, 1843, Larkin, II, p. 19.

71 William Robert Garner, *Letters from California, 1846–1847*, ed. Donald Munro Craig (Berkeley, Los Angeles & London, 1970), pp. 193–194. The streets in question are Alvarado and Castro (later Tyler). The visual effect recalls Duflot de Mofras' apparently incorrect description of 1841.

72 *Ibid.*, p. 194.

73 *Ibid.*, pp. 198–199.

74 *Ibid.*, pp. 1–2.

75 Ignacio Esquer and Ambrosio Gomez, Monterey, August 27, 1849, *Unbound Documents*, pp. 181-182.

76 See Woodrow J. Hansen, *The Search for Authority in California* (Oakland, 1960).

77 Quoted in Jesse D. Mason, *History of Santa Barbara and Ventura Counties, California* (Oakland, 1883), p. 53.

78 Juan Bandini, *Historia de la Alta California, 1769–1845* (Bancroft Library MS, 1874), p. 46.

79 Both quoted in Mason, p. 53.

80 The order reads: "It is authorized that the land surveyor of the city require all owners of houselots situated within the limits of the survey of the City; and that Salisbury Haley mark off the boundary lines of each houselot in order to facilitate the conclusion of the Map of the City" (*Santa Barbara Archivo*, p. 103).

81 Yda A. Storke, *A Memorial and Biographical History of the Counties of Santa Barbara, San Luis Obispo and Ventura, California* (Chicago, 1891), p. 63.

82 *Recopilación de leyes de los Reynos de las Indias*, 4th ed. (3 vols; Madrid, 1791), IV:7:9, II, p. 21.

83 *Santa Barbara Archivo*, pp. 87–88.

84 *Ibid.*, pp. 99–100.

85 Bayard Taylor, *Eldorado, or Adventures in the Path of Empire* (2 vols; New York, 1850), I, p. 133.

86 John Russell Bartlett, *Personal Narrative of Explorations and Incidents in Texas, New Mexico, California, Sonora, and Chihuahua* (2 vols; New York, 1854), II, p. 72.

87 Taylor, I, p. 137.

88 Bartlett, II, pp. 74–75.

89 The first actual written title granted by an *alcalde* was said to have been issued to Tomasa Alvarado in 1838. (Bancroft, III, p. 612).

90 From 1850 to 1854 the United States Land Commission challenged both individual claims of land as well as the town's claim to its area of four square leagues. In December of 1849 the San Diego *ayuntamiento* resolved that "all titles of house lots which are now in the archives of this court of those which may hereafter be presented with *good evidence of their legality* are and shall be admitted by the council as proof of good faith and right of property" (*Documentos para la Historia de California, 1826–1850: Originales y copiados de los Archivos del Condado de San Diego*, pp. 465–466). An act in 1851 provided that the existence of a town on July 7, 1846, should be regarded as *prima facie* evidence of a land grant. San Diego obtained confirmation for its pueblo lands as a result of an official survey by Capt. Henry Delano Fitch in 1845. Santiago Arguëllo testified that the boundaries of the survey "were designated by myself previous to the survey. I have known them since the year 1818" (quoted in Pourade, III, p. 15). The survey was approved in substance in 1870 and a patent was issued in 1874 (Bancroft, IV, p. 567).

91 Juan Bandini, San Diego, January 30, 1850, *Documentos para la Historia de California, 1826–1850: Originales y copiados de los Archivos del Condado de San Diego*, p. 52.

92 Serra to Rafael Verger, Monterey, August 15, 1774, Serra, *Writings*, ed. Antonine Tibesar, O.F.M. (4 vols; Washington, D.C., 1955–1966), III, p. 353.

93 Charles Wilkes, *Narrative of the United States Exploring Expedition during the Years 1838, 1839, 1840, 1841, 1842* (5 vols; Philadelphia, 1845), V, p. 152.

94 *Documentos para la Historia de California . . .*, p. 8.

95 *Recopilación*, IV:12:8, II, p. 41.

The building of Santa Fe, three quarters of a century after the refounding of Mexico City, reveals an amalgamation of Indian and Spanish ideas.[1] The physical form of the city reflects this crucial synthesis between native and imported building customs. The site of Santa Fe, for instance, had been occupied by the Analco pueblo[2] which in turn preserved the site of the Kuapoge pueblo of the early prehistoric period.[3] Still surviving in colonial times near Santa Fe was the Indian pueblo of Quemado, later known as Aqua Fria.[4] Thus, Spanish urban settlements in New Mexico were generally located where preconquest Indian pueblo settlements had been.

The Indian settlements had consisted of groups of cellular, communal houses of stone or adobe (mud brick), made by the repeated linear addition of new rooms, utilizing walls running parallel or perpendicular to one another, and facing onto linear open spaces or courtyards (figures 22 and 23). This system of building was partly determined by the ecology of the region (figure 19) and partly by needs of defense.[5] The area was called New Mexico because the pueblos looked like Aztec dwellings in Mexico.[6] Rows of pueblo houses had two or more storeys. The lower, being used for storage, was completely enclosed and reached by trapdoors. The upper had corridors and balconies of wood, facing in toward the "plaza" and thus forming a sort of citadel.[7]

Just as the Spaniards were willing to learn from the great cities of Mesoamerica, so too at the modest settlements of New Mexico they adopted Indian structures and forms.

Spanish conquerors were little concerned with the climate and soil of New Mexico . . . because neither differed in any remarkable way from that of New Spain. . . . They . . . did not find the country barren. . . . In contrast to the Latins, Anglo-American explorers and surveyors moved into the Southwest from the humid East. (They characterized the region as "barren and uninteresting in the extreme" or "sickening-colored.")[8]

Finding the climate and terrain "normal" and the population "civilized" to the extent that they lived in permanent settlements, the Spanish were ready to come to terms with their new environment and neighbors. These continuing adjustments in some sense parallel the "feedback" system that generated the Laws of the Indies: The Indians accepted the outside influences of these new settlers where these did not affect traditional building forms, and in turn the Spaniards accepted the Indians' age-old communal dwelling, so quickly and easily constructed. Compromise between the Indian town and the needs of Europeans for their particular types of structures became the usual pattern.[9] Indian and Spanish structures alike were "built of mud like Timbuctoo."[10] Common use of materials and common forms meant easy architectural interchangeability between the two cultures.

Like the other Spanish towns of the New World, Santa Fe was established by fiat of a distant government, one highly centralized in theory but with its impact lessened by both distance and the settler's rights of petition, initiative, protest, and delay.[11] For all that the Laws of the Indies might say about the details of land settlement, their administration, at least along the Gulf and in the Southwest, appeared to be tempered with a measure of the freedom that has been characteristic of all frontiers at the edge of permanent settlement."[12] With this degree of freedom possible, then, it is all the more impressive that Santa Fe remains the ultimate expression of the city planning ordinances of the Laws of the Indies on the soil of the United States. Probably this is because of the city's isolation and poverty, which made speculative development and rapid change a minor part of the city's history. "Sluggish fashions and technical conservatism usually characterize the frontier society and peripheral area; in these terms, New Mexico was the provincial outpost in a state of chemical purity."[13] The early seventeenth-century foundation of Santa Fe was the logical outcome of a deliberate policy of pushing the frontier northward, which had been going on in Mexico throughout the previous ninety years. At first, for about forty years, this had been achieved by the sword, but results were unsatisfactory and the cost was high. By 1584, a new procedure had suggested itself, as we see in this letter written by the bishop of Guadalajara to the archbishop of Mexico:

By what I have seen with my own eyes and what I have learned from persons of long experience in this realm of New Galicia (especially from Rodrigo del Rio De Loza, general of the warfare), I would suggest that the king

1. The war as now conducted is very costly and difficult. Although the presidios and soldiers give some protection, they really serve to prolong the war because of the harm they do the natives, capturing their women and children. Thus more nations than ever are now hostile, including many who were formerly at peace and baptized. This past summer all the Indians of Nieves, Rio Grande, the mill of Alonzo Lopez, and of many *estancias* rose up to fight under five or six important chiefs, almost all of them Christian. This uprising was centered at the Pico de Teyre district of Mazapil, but was fortunately stopped, in Christian manner, by Rodrigo del Rio.

2. It is said that these Indians can be subjugated little by little by force of arms; but it is not so, because the costs of such war would end by driving Spaniards out of the land because of heavy taxation. Furthermore, for each nation thus conquered, others nearby, seeing what the Spaniards do and thus fearing them, become hostile and fight, and the process is endless.

3. Cheapest, best, and most Christian remedy is to found six or seven settlements (at Las Charcas, at a point between Mazapil and Saltillo, in the Valley of Las Parras, in the Laguna Grande district, in the Tepeque area, and the mines of Indé), each one of which shall contain two or three Franciscans. At each place there should be erected some modest houses and a church, and the friars should be provisioned for a few years at His Majesty's expense. To protect friars and inhabitants, up to eight soldiers should be stationed in each new settlement, with salary from the crown but receiving orders from the Franciscans. These soldiers would be for defense only, and thus prohibited from making *entradas* without permission of the friars. So that their salary should be small, those soldiers should be married men and be granted the ordinary lands for settlers. To each new settlement should be sent some Mexicans, or Tlaxcalans, or other sedentary Indians, well Christianized, so that they can serve as *fiscales,* song leaders (*cantores*), and in other religious capacities, as well as settlers. Their example, plus the friars' persuasion, will attract the nomads to peaceful settlement. This has been proved on other parts of the frontier. The expense of this will not be great or continuing, such as is the case in the upkeep of the soldiery now. The monasteries can be built for 2,000 pesos each, and the upkeep for two friars in each, with all religious equipment, should be less than 800 pesos; to this should be added 900 pesos for two soldiers (who can be

taken from present presidios and companies, and picked from among married men who would be very desirous of such service). Nor would there be difficulty in getting Indian settlers, excusing them from tribute for ten or twelve years and granting other privileges and aid.

For efficiency all this could and should be entrusted to General Rodrigo del Rio de Loza. He is anxious that this plan be carried out, and he is the only one to whom it should be entrusted. This would not mean immediate suspension of warfare, but within a few years the expense of soldiery could be greatly reduced; and part of this cost could then go into the more desirable activity as above outlined.[14]

By 1609–1610 this procedure had been operating for about twenty years, so that even the details of the beginning of Santa Fe had been worked out at other sites: entrusting the task of conversion to Franciscans, protecting them by a few soldiers, providing supplies for the first few years, and sending a group of already pacified Indians to serve as contacts with and examples for those to be pacified. By this method, it usually took about ten years to pacify a new group of nomadic Indians and turn them into sedentary farmers and dutiful vassals of king and church.[15] Since a great deal of sentimental history has been written deploring the total effect of the Spaniards upon the Indians, it is well to pause here and reflect that so few Spaniards and their civilized Indian partners had so profound an effect upon the tribes they were seeking to domesticate, in large part because they really did have a way of life to offer that the Indians could easily perceive as superior to what they had been living.[16]

The church took a strong interest in urbanization as a corollary of conversion. To show the dominance and prestige of the new religion, Indian sites were frequently reused, as the former Moorish sites in Spain had been reused in the previous century.[17] During the seventeenth and eighteenth centuries, then, control of the Indians in New Mexico rested with the missions.[18] The first mission at the Puarray pueblo was founded in 1581, and by the time Santa Fe was established in 1610,[19] there were already 8,000 Christian converts in the region.[20] This achievement was the result of the work of eight missionary priests.[21] Since San Miguel, the oldest church still in use here, was begun between 1605 and 1608 by Don Juan de Onate,

Bancroft may be right in asserting that all 8,000 converts were at Santa Fe, and we may even infer that the existence of so large a group of converts was a strong motivation for the founding of the new town.[22]

As mission territory, without an indigenous Christian tradition, Santa Fe was placed in the care of Franciscans. The Province of the Holy Gospel of Franciscan Observants of New Spain (headquartered in Mexico City) had in its charge several divisions called *custodies*; the Custody of the Conversion of St. Paul had two branches, a smaller one at El Paso and a larger one in the interior of the Kingdom of New Mexico.[23] Santa Fe remained part of this custody for 177 years, until 1776.[24] Senior religious officer of New Mexico was a *custos* (guardian); there was no bishop until after 1832, and no seminary.[25]

The New Mexican branch of the custody came to include three Spanish villas (towns) and twenty-two Indian *pueblos* (villages), lying along the Rio del Norte. Santa Fe lay farthest from the river, eight leagues away on a branch stream. The whole group lay within forty leagues of each other.[26] In the immediate vicinity of Santa Fe, nine priests cared for eight pueblos and the Villa de la Canada as well as Santa Fe, some 7,480 souls altogether, by the time Dominguez wrote in the late eighteenth century.[27]

The separate settlements of Spaniards in their villas had less influence on the Indians than did the missions, partly because the towns were far fewer, irregularly distributed, and slow to grow. On the other hand, they were centers for the Spanish way of life. In fact, to the invading Anglos of the nineteenth century and their scholarly successors of the twentieth century, there was little to distinguish Mexican and Indian settlements, since both were so different from the Anglo. To cite just one instance, since the Spanish settlement regularly used a grid street pattern, it has been assumed without verification that any regular pattern observable in an Indian settlement must be the result of contact with the Spaniards. On the contrary, excavations have shown the regularity to be an indigenous feature dating to the twelfth and thirteenth centuries, if not earlier[28] (see again figures 1–4).

The site of Santa Fe has been successively an Indian Pueblo before 1609, capital of a province of New Spain 1609–1680, headquarters of rebellious Indians 1680–

1692, capital again of a Spanish province, after 1821 capital of a Mexican province, then center of an American territory from 1846, and finally capital of a US state since 1912.[29] The city under Spanish rule was the seat of political and military authority. As such, it represented the far-off governments of Mexico City (700 leagues, or more than 1,000 miles away) and of even farther Seville—even if it represented them only faintly.[30]

La Villa Real de la Santa Fe was organized during the winter of 1609–10 by Don Pedro de Peralta.[31] From the tradition and law embodied in the 1573 ordinances, Don Pedro could receive instructions about locating his site, founding and laying out his city, and setting up both a government and an economic system.

First, the governor of New Spain would have conferred with him, offering him "honors and advantages," and sending all the paperwork required by Ordinance 2 into the Council of the Indies at Seville. From knowledge gained in earlier exploration, the governor would have assigned him a territory. Then, after an overland trek from Mexico, de Peralta would have "made the selection of the site where the town is to be built" (ordinance 111).

Santa Fe is located at the foot of a *sierra* (mountain range) which rises to the east, later to be called Sangre de Cristo,[32] and on a small river called also Santa Fe (figure 25). These ideas about location conform to ordinance 123 which draws on Alberti, who in turn drew on Vitruvius; by 1573, when the city planning ordinances were codified, the Spaniards had had enough experience in founding cities in the New World to know of the validity of Vitruvius and Alberti's prescriptions. The little river ran across the site, conveniently demarcating the city proper from the settlement for captive Indians whom the Spaniards brought with them. The Spanish settlement lay to the north.

De Peralta then proceeded to lay out the town according to ordinances 110, "dividing it into squares, streets, and building lots, using cord and ruler, beginning with the main square from which streets are to run." The early presidio here answered the demand of ordinance 133 for a "defense or barrier." Don Pedro would also have paid special heed to ordinances 21, 22, 23, 32, and 109. (Trent claims that detailed plans for Santa Fe were sent from Spain,[33] but I have found no evidence of this.)

Thus, the sequence of urban development seems to have been the following:

1. Obtain license to found a town.
2. Recruit settlers, lay in supplies, and so forth.
3. Travel to the site.
4. Arrive at area to be settled.
5. Select precise site.
6. Hold ceremonies of taking possession.
7. Lay out fortified settlement, build it, inhabit it.
8. Lay out fields, plant crops.
9. Build an irrigation system.
10. Subjugate and convert the Indians.
11. Lay out plaza and street of the town.
12. Mark out house lots and build separate houses.

Once the settlement was established, further activities would be

13. Attract more settlers from Mexico.
14. Build large church to replace chapel of original fortress.
15. Lay out subsidiary plazas, streets, and house lots.
16. Build additional churches, monastaries, government buildings, shops, houses.
17. Send reports, illustrated with maps and plans, to Mexico City and Seville.

Spaces of the earliest Santa Fe have survived better than the buildings that edged them, for the settlement suffered some destruction in the Indian uprising of 1680. Considerable building and rebuilding took place after Santa Fe was resettled,[34] but we have no plans from the seventeenth century, and none from the first three quarters of the eighteenth. The earliest plan (figure 25) is from 1766–1768 and was drawn by José de Urrutia.[35]

One reason the river is such a prominent feature on Urrutia's map may be that in October 1767, at the end of the August–October rainy season, there was a great flood in which the river changed its bed and threatened public buildings. By November 7 the water had receded sufficiently that all the city could be called out to work to restore the river to its usual bed.[36] Provision of an irrigation system had been one of the first concerns of de Peralta and his settlers, a system still functioning in the middle of the nineteenth century when Davis described it:[37] There was a major ditch (the *acequia madre*) three to five yards wide and two to six feet deep running on each side of the river. (figure 32) From them, smaller cross ditches led to smaller still, all entering the various plots of land at their highest points. Flow gates were used to control the water. The land was divided into small beds sixty by forty feet, with mounded edges. Since one man could control the flow of water into five acres in one day, most holdings were five acres, though some were ten. Davis commented that territorial law recognized water as a public necessity "like roads in the East." He reported that fifteen to twenty men were hired to repair the system annually, but because of the danger of flash floods, all would rush to repair and prevent damage in the case of a bad storm.

Eventually the river was embanked against flooding, as it ran through Santa Fe. Once established, probably early in the eighteenth century, this irrigation system was used to grow crops of wheat, maize, legumes, green vegetables, melons, and apricots. The water also operated three mills.[38]

As basic as water supply was the defense of the new settlement. An enclosed quadrangle pattern is found generally in Spanish America (figure 63) since defense was a common problem (ordinance 128). The plan of the "presidio" of Santa Fe in 1791 is of the usual pattern; what is today the governor's palace is in the lower right corner of figure 63a. A settlement would outgrow these constraints as soon as it could, since to be "restricted as in a presidio" was something to complain of,[39] but in areas with warlike Indians, there would be continued advantages in having such a refuge. In fact, as late as 1812, Pino describes small semimilitary settlements that were dotted around New Mexico, 102 of them, and were called *plazas* from their form of a rectangle 200 by 500 *varas*, with bastions[40]— just the form of the original presidios of Santa Fe, Santa Barbara, and so on.

A wall that ran northward from the plaza at Santa Fe was described by Pino as "an obstacle to the beauty of the city because it is becoming more dilapidated every day."[41] Since it disintegrated soon after the American occupation, the wall was sold (for materials?), and new private houses were put up in the area. This demise was regretted by some, as the wall had formerly been well kept and "famous for its length and good proportions."[41] This wall probably formed one of the long sides of the original presidio.

384

Inspection of the early maps of Santa Fe shows that the initial enclosed rectangle was soon amplified by a more open and expansive arrangement, so that the governor's palace, instead of turning inward, opened out onto what became the main plaza of the city. The fortified rectangle was originally nearly 400 feet wide, with the palace occupying half of the southern side. The east and west sides were twice as long, some 800 feet. Located within the perimeter were the barracks, chapel, offices, magazines (storage rooms), and prison of the colony, as mandated by ordinances 121, 124, and 126. From existing plans, however, the dimensions were about 350 by 500 feet; the fort may have been rebuilt to smaller size after the 1680 uprising.

When the Governor's Palace was reoriented to the plaza outside the fortification, the builders of the town were responding to ordinance 112. Plaza size was regulated by ordinance 113. The original plan for the city of Santa Fe called for a large central plaza, much larger than the one that has survived, as shown in the 1766–1768 map (figure 25). By 1800 the main plaza was significantly smaller than it had been, probably because of the usual process of encroachment[42] (figure 28).

All the business of the little settlement of Santa Fe took place at the Plaza Mayor (the usual title for such a square)—commerce, politics, marketing, religious processions, and entertainment (figure 31). At the end of the day, the people would gather here to promenade, see, and be seen. From the plaza, the regular caravans departed for Mexico City or Los Angeles, carrying blankets and buffalo skins, and to the plaza they returned three years later, bearing "ecclestiastical equipment, general supplies, missionaries, and an occasional new governor"[43] (figure 30). Even though this was the center of provincial government, few special buildings were put up here to accommodate these needs. Poverty is reflected at Santa Fe and elsewhere in the slow accumulation of community buildings such as town halls, slaughter houses, jails, and hospitals. Besides poverty, the inefficiency of town government contributed to these delays.[44]

The ordinances called for porticoes around the plaza and along the main streets. At Santa Fe, only along the governor's Palace have the usual colonnades survived to our own time. Quite possibly they once bordered the entire plaza as ordinance 115 dictated (figures 29 and 30). Early photographs show the porticoes that edged the plaza at Santa Fe and formed covered sidewalks along the streets at the center of town. Though these were crudely executed with logs, they were reminiscent of the classical porticoes of the plazas of Spanish cities. Some towns in Spain still today have colonnades made of logs, so in this respect Santa Fe was an image of "home" (figure 6).

In Renaissance urbanism and architectural symbolism, the porticoes signified a civic or public space. Consequently, porticoes would be found at the plaza and along the main streets, whereas residential streets would present blank, planar walls to the passerby (figure 29). In Venice, for example, loggias were added to the Piazza San Marco as a Renaissance (and therefore classical) remodeling of the medieval space. So too, here in a most primitive outpost of Spain in the New World, porticoes of logs arranged around the main plaza of the settlement spoke to inhabitant and visitor alike of that venerable urban tradition, and gave a sense of place as well as a practical focus for many functions in all weathers.

Around the plaza were grouped major buildings (figures 28 and 30). To the north lay the palace and a similarly sized building that together formed the southern edge of the military parade ground farther north, which had formerly been the enclosed courtyard of the presidio. The palace was used for the offices of the governor and for the legislature. Along the east and west sides of the plaza were originally houses, most notable of which was the *ayuntamiento* (city council chamber). By the 1840s most of the structures fronting the plaza had shops in them.[45] Commerce in Spanish towns was at first considered a necessary evil, taking up very little space, and that in modest and often temporary facilities. Later, commerce began to invade the major public spaces, such as the main plaza at Santa Fe and along the main streets.[46]

The south side of the plaza was the location of the military chapel, called Our Lady of Light (*Castrense*); at some time an Oratory of the Holy Trinity stood on the west side of the plaza. The area of the plaza was two to three acres.[47] At the center of the plaza, Governor Don Antonio Narvona (also called Narbona) had built in

1825–1827 an adobe base three *varas* high on which stood a rock sundial.[48] In 1844 a bullring was set up in the plaza.

Elias Brevoort, who came to Santa Fe in 1850, reported that the plaza was used then as a corral: "Nothing there but a great space, people encamped and wagons all about the square. The market consisted of people seated on the northwest corner of the plaza with baskets; later buildings were provided for them on the Rio Chiquito. After the arrival of the California troops and at the close of the rebellion under General Carleton's military adminstration, trees were planted and the plaza and other places improved."[49] It was Major John Ayers who began in 1866 to plant trees in the plaza.[50] At that time there were "many places suitable for parks and already planted with many cottonwood trees."[51] The Plaza Mayor was "improved" in the last half of the nineteenth century with a picket fence and a wooden bandstand adorned with gingerbread carvings—replacing the bullring.[52]

Those whom Brevoort saw selling their wares at the northwest corner of the plaza were taking advantage of the traffic going and coming from the Governor's Palace nearby, utilizing the portico of the palace itself as their marketplace. Davis reports that they sold vegetables, meat, and fruit there, while the hay and grass market was in a narrow street at the southwest corner of the plaza. The plaza was the center, then, of the business life of the town, and was also used for cockfights, especially on Sundays.[53]

Although the pattern for the streets was planned at the beginning, the streets themselves remained unpaved for a long time, and were still unpaved when Davis visited in 1846.[54] The plaza was in a very real sense the thoroughfare of the city. Other streets began at the plaza, and were not as regular here as in other Spanish settlements, as inspection of the plans shows (figure 26). Streets were eight *varas* (twenty-two feet) wide. Only near the plaza were the houses compactly sited and fronted with porticoes, "rough but ornamental and convenient," as Davis describes them.[55] The main street, today called San Francisco Street because it leads to the Cathedral of St. Francis, had porticoes on its south side (figure 29).

In Spanish colonial settlements, the important buildings usually face the plaza—"the buildings of the church and royal house and for city use"—as prescribed by ordinance 126. In spite of the prohition against individual lots lining the plaza, at Santa Fe and later at Los Angeles, homes of important persons also faced onto the plaza. We can imagine the little buildings placed at first in a regular pattern around the plaza, helping to form the boundary of the defensible area, and later straggling away from the center in a more haphazard manner, so that they could be described by Dominguez as separate sets of buildings, like homesteads.[56]

Other details of the layout of Santa Fe correspond to other ordinances, such as ordinance 129, which specified the layout of town commons. The commons at Santa Fe stretched to the north, beyond the presidio grounds; at some periods, the boundaries between them were not clear. The 1846 "Military Map" of the city shows this area being used to grow corn (figure 26).

Although in some settlements the church or cathedral also faces the main plaza, at Santa Fe the laws are followed literally and the main church is located off the east side of the plaza; by ordinance 124, it "shall not be placed on the square but at a distance and shall be separated from any other building." An early description mentions two plazas (as suggested in ordinance 118), the second apparently the small square in front of the principal church. By the 1740s, a house was obstructing the entrance to the church, so the governor bought the house and removed it.[57]

The church at Santa Fe served as the administrative focus of a missionary program that by 1630 had sent twenty-five missions to ninety pueblos of 60,000 Indians, as mandated by ordinances 17, 27, 136, 140, and 141–148, "to bring on to our obedience all the natives of the province" (138). At Santa Fe, the church of San Miguel and its *barrio* on the south bank of the river formed the kind of separate Indian town specified by ordinance 148. At first, the Indians would have been Tlascans or other pacified tribes brought from Mexico to serve as examples to the local Indians. Although local legend holds that San Miguel is the oldest church in the United States,[58] excavation has not been able to substantiate this. The records say that by 1630 a church was completed at Santa Fe to serve the garrison and settlers, some 250 Spaniards.[59] This may refer to San Miguel, but more likely to the predecessor of the Church of St. Francis. The latter was built beginning in 1714, on the site of a pre-Revolt church destroyed in 1680. Although rebuilt again in the nineteenth century as the cathedral, its Conquistadora Chapel, sacristy, and sanctuary behind the rear cathedral wall are all eighteenth century. The church of San Francisco stood in its own block, with a garden and spring (which was shared with the other settlers) to the south of the convent. It was probably the spring that determined the location of the religious complex. A cemetary was located within the wall, next to the church (figure 27).

A third church was the Confraternity and Chapel of Our Lady of Light, already mentioned as fronting on the plaza. This chapel housed a religious society for soldiers, founded in 1760. Its building was completed in 1761 with a week of festivities including masses in the mornings and comedies in the afternoons. The structure seems to have utilized a preexisting building, for excavation shows the probable date of the foundations as 1710. The governor, Don Francisco Marin del Valle, provided the construction funds out of his own purse. He built a cross-shaped building 100 feet long and nearly as wide, with two plain towers with bells, a little taller than the roof. The altar stood at the south end, and the choir at the north was reached by a ladder. The roof was supported by large unpainted pine beams braced by brackets at the wall, and a tin chandelier hung at the crossing. In spite of a distinguished membership of military leaders and the affluent (ordinance 99, "illustrious men of known ancestry"), the society was effectively dead by 1781.[60]

Besides these public religious buildings, there were private chapels at people's homes. Since the clergy levied double the usual fee for a marriage if it were not performed in the principal church, it seems evident that rich and important people liked to be married in their private chapels, a practice that the church tried to discourage by the "fine."[61] Eventually Santa Fe had five churches and two public oratories.[62]

In the seventeenth and eighteenth centuries, erecting churches in any Spanish town was a function of wealth, not of congregational pressure for more space. Churches and priests were supported usually by endowments from the rich or tithes from the congregation, except in mission areas where their support was a government function, at least until the waning days of the Spanish Empire. At Santa Fe, in spite of the fact that the area was in mission status for nearly 200 years, the church was supported by tithes.[63] By contrast, the Spanish crown took advantages of the religious zeal of the Franciscans and had them support the colonization of California from their Pious Fund, so that less capital was required from the royal treasury. (This is discussed more fully in the last part of the book.)

The domestic as well as the monumental buildings of the settlement were the concern of the ordinances (for example, ordinances 128, 132, and 134). Not only are the settlers to "establish their houses and to build them with good foundations and walls" (132) but are "so far as possible to have the buildings all of one type for the sake of the beauty of the town" (134). The architecture was extremely simple, using adobe brick and some stone, with room sizes based on lengths of available logs for ceiling beams. Rooms were grouped around a patio, which might or might not have a portico. Flat roofs were common and contours soft because of the use of adobe plastered over for protection against weather. The architecture was a mixture of Spanish and Indian ideas, suitable to a mixed population and to the climate.[64] Adobe is easy to use, not requiring the sophisticated techniques of masonry (figure 33).

For Anglo visitors or settlers after the 1830s, this architecture did not speak of "home," and they tended to dislike it. For one who reported that the private buildings were low, comfortable, and clean,[65] several said that the unadorned earth houses "lacked everything"[66] and that the blank facades of the houses made the town seem "almost deserted" and gave it a disagreeable aspect.[67] "It has more the appearance of a colony of brick-kilns than a collection of human habitations," wrote Davis when he first arrived, and he commented on the dirty streets and the fact that all building was the same mud color. Not content to comment, he went on to find out why the houses were as they were: The houses of adobe have walls thicker than stone or brick would be, he reports, and are therefore cooler in summer and warmer in winter. The adobe bricks were six times the size of an English brick; originally made by the resident himself, by the 1840s they cost $8–10 per thousand delivered. They were laid in the same mud, and plastered. Because of the local weather, this proved to be a very permanent construction system. The thick walls also supported the heavy roof, which had wooden sleepers (beams) holding wooden boards, and was topped by a layer of mud "to make it waterproof." A low parapet surrounded the roof, and the occasional rain water was carried off by wooden spouts and deposited into the street. The residents inspected the roof after every rain, and if it leaked, they added more dirt. With such a system, it is obvious that houses of only one storey would be the rule, and at the time of Davis's stay, there were only two two-storey houses, neither built by Mexicans (figure 34).

The usual form of the house was of a hollow square, with rooms opening by their doors onto the patio via a covered portico that ran all around the court. The interior of the house was finished with a gypsum whitewash (called *vezo* by Davis, but more correctly *yeso*), but since this comes off on one's clothes, the rooms were lined with calico to the height of four feet, adding a touch of bright color to the interiors. Twice a year the houses were renovated by putting a new *yeso* surface on the walls—the women did this using a fleece or their hands—and a new mud surface on the floor. Wooden floors were rare, but sometimes a carpet of local manufacture called *gerga* (again, this is Davis's term; we would say *jerga*) was used. Ceilings were never plastered, but finished either with exposed beams that (in the houses of the rich) were carved and painted or, in the main room, arranged in herringbone pattern of small round sticks painted red, blue, or green placed between the beams. Another choice was to stretch bleached muslin along the ceiling. Heat was provided in the main room by a fireplace in the corner, with a small horseshore-shaped opening eigtheen to twenty-four inches high and wider at the bottom. The plan of the fireplace was also horseshoe shaped, and there was a raised hearth. Logs were placed upright at the back, and this arrangement was an efficient heat source. Furniture was simple—folded mattresses covered with blankets and placed around the edges of the room, in the Moorish fashion. These would be unrolled at night, and the sitting room became a bedroom. Few houses had bedsteads; a low wooden frame was sometimes used. Trunks and chests held clothes. The

391

rich would have pine chests and settees. Sometimes guests would be received and entertained on a blanket spread out in the center of the floor. In the kitchen, earthen vessels were used to cook in, though there was no stove that Davis recognized as such.[68] Glass being unavailable, paper was used to cover windows or make blinds.[69]

But a city does not consist only of houses. Public buildings were mandated by ordinance 121, both royal and civic and religious structures. Though larger than the other structures of the town, and containing the first library to be found in the region, the Governor's Palace was made of the same materials and in the same style as the rest of the town. It may have been the special concern of the architect(s) mentioned in ordinance 135. In a symbolic gesture of conquest, the palace was erected in 1610 on the site of the former Indian pueblo.[70] In the 1680 uprising, it was partially destroyed, so that it had to be rebuilt in 1697. An account of 1731 described the new palace as built by Governor Bustamante at his own expense; this probably means that he removed the old roof and tops of walls and renewed them.[71] By 1832 the building was already in bad repair,[72] but the indefatigable Davis inspected it thoroughly in the 1840s and tells us that the structure is 350 feet long or so—"others say 400 feet"—and 20 to 75 feet wide. A portico 15 feet deep ran along the whole plaza length, with a small projection at each end. The projection at the east was being used as a post office; at one time it had been a chapel for the governor, and at least one governor is buried under its floor. The west bastion was at the time used as the jail. The building was "in the style of the 1650s".[73]

When the parish church was built, by 1717, the east and west towers that had flanked the palace were torn down to straighten the plaza. The east one had extended well out into what became the plaza area, as a bastion, as is shown in the 1791 plan (figure 63a). The one at the west had been the military magazine before it became the jail (*calabozo*), and by the 1840s was partly ruined.

Within the presidio were official reception rooms and offices, military barracks, stables, the arsenal, servants' quarters, and a central patio of ten acres, which was used as a vegetable garden. Water was supplied by springs to the east. Among the suites of rooms opening onto the portico was the Office of the Secretary of the Territory, in whose inner room the archives, by then nearly 300 years old, were stored. The executive office had bleached muslin tacked up as a ceiling and a calico dado, which also was to be found in the legislature's room, "lest they carry away any whitewash on their clothes, a thing they have no right to do in their capacity as law-makers." Also here in the palace was the library of the territory, fifteen feet square and filled with books, mostly law books, court reports, codes and congressional documents.[74] The palace was restored in 1909–1913.[75]

The palace was the special concern of William G. Ritch, who wrote of it in his *History of New Mexico* (1884)[76]

No, that is the only palace in the United States. In Mexican matters every capital town must have its palace on the plaza, and if it was only a 7 × 9 hut it was all the same a palace. [This one] is more like a rope walk than anything else—it is nevertheless a palace and must be preserved.

Just as Alberti could say, "The house is a little city, the city a great house," so too it was easy for Ritch to follow his remarks on the governor's palace immediately with an observation on the city: "Santa Fe is a great historical capital or place, the greatest in the United States, and should be kept so by every means possible, by preserving all that there is and adding as much as possible. The history of old Santa Fe is the history of the Southwest." As a historian, Ritch felt keenly the loss of the archives of the city and territory that had been burned with the church vestments in the plaza during the Indian uprising of 1680. Another nineteenth-century chronicler, M. S. Watts, reported that

the archives, when I first came there, were just in boxes in the Governor's room in the palace: ordinary dry goods 10-bushel boxes without any arrangement. Some Archives were sold as waste paper in 1866 or so by Governor Pile but about 25% of these were recovered, and by 1878 were placed in the Library, with the land grant papers going to the surveyor general's office in old Santa Fe in 1858. Some of the Archives were taken during the Indian uprising to the county of Rio Arriva and concealed, so that not all were burned.[77]

In addition to the archives of the territory and the law books in the palace library, there was another archive at the Church of St. Francis, called the Library of the Custody. In 1788 it was inventoried as having 384 items, a growth from the earlier count of 256. Its contents were baptismal records, burial and marriage records, patents, and inventories of missions and convents.[78] These records were probably housed at the church or in one of the buildings of its compound. The census of 1860 shows fifteen public and two church libraries in New Mexico, with a total of nearly 11,000 volumes.[79]

Another room of the palace deserves mention, though it was kept as purposely empty as the library was full. This was the Office of Indian Affairs, which was kept as an open space for the Indians to sit in when they came to do official business.[80]

Also part of this complex was the 100-foot-long structure used in the 1840s as the courthouse. It had formerly been the storehouse of the quartermaster. The one-storey building was 25 feet wide. In the 60-foot courtroom, square pillars down the middle helped to support the usual earth roof.[81] This part of the old presidio faced on the street that ran from the northeast corner of the plaza, for Davis says that the US, District, and Supreme Courts faced on this street.[82]

By the 1850s, Santa Fe was equipped with the following buildings:[83]

1 hotel,
1 printing office,
25 stores,
3 shoemakers,
1 apothecary,
1 bakery,
2 blacksmiths.

It also had a public primary school which paid its teacher 500 pesos a year, the highest teacher's salary in New Mexico.[84] This growth in public and quasi-public buildings was due to growth in both population and trade. Let us examine first the history of population at Santa Fe and then turn to trade.

We do not know exactly how many Spaniards came with de Peralta to found Santa Fe, but by 1633 there were 50, a large proportion of the 200 in the province.[85] Most of these were soldiers, needed to protect the priests and civil authorities, and to terrorize and "reduce" the Indians—which meant forcing them to live a settled life according to the Spanish pattern. In 1639 more than 50 persons were making a living growing wheat and maize by irrigation, for the Convent of St. Francis.[86] During the entire seventeenth century, the Spanish presence at Santa Fe relied paradoxically on the presence of Indians from Mexico, and later in the century on other nonlocal Indian servants. Ordinances 136 and 138 required that "persons designated for this purpose" shall try to win the friendship of the Indians who are to be converted, and bring them into obedience to the king of Spain. One assumes that the example of converted, peaceful Indians who had already been through the process was considered salutary. It was also convenient to have their services.

Spanish policy toward the Indians was most carefully conceived and self-consistent. Basic to the Spanish approach was the conviction that they were generously sharing with the natives their culture and civilization—both "totally lacking" in Indian life. The Spaniards did not understand that they were attempting to replace one group of cultural traits with another. To them, civilization was synomous with the Castilian language, adobe and stone houses, trousers, a political organization with the king of Spain at its center, and Roman Catholicism. Later, during the briefer Mexican rule, the cultural package consisted of the Mexican dialect of Castilian, rectangular houses, trousers, individual land holding, representative government and citizenship rights, and elementary schools without religion. Then, in the 1840s, civilization meant North American civilization—Indians were to be sequestered on reservations and Mexicans ignored as much as possible. The North American cultural package was signaled by the American dialect of English, American agricultural technology, elementary schools with religion, and the Protestant religion. Today we would probably specify the criteria of our culture as literacy, specialization of labor leading to different social roles, individual rights (citizenship), and freedom of choice.[87]

The Mexican Indians who lived in Santa Fe were called *genizaro* (a word derived from *janissary*); some were captive, others free, but all were living in the Spanish fashion.[88] As time went on, the term *genizaro* came to be used in New Mexico for all non-Pueblo Indians.

395

In spite of having brought pacified Indians with them to serve as good examples, the Spaniards ran into trouble with the indigenous population before the seventeenth century was over. Resentful of the denigration of their religion and the disruption of their culture, the Indians organized a revolt and massacred all the isolated Spaniards at the various mesas, driving the larger groups out of the territory to refuge at El Paso. Some of those killed were missionaries, some were retired soldiers. These had formed small farming villages, marrying and otherwise interacting with the Indians. The two groups mutually borrowed crafts, cuisine, agricultural methods, language, and healing methods.[89] It is difficult now to estimate the numbers involved in these outlying villages, but at Santa Fe, Benavide reports that 250 Spaniards and 700 Indians were living there before the revolt, and that the parish church was nearly completed.[90]

After the Indian uprising and mutual slaughter of 1680, the site of Santa Fe was recolonized in 1692 by Don Diego de Vargas and 800 settlers,[91] "without a blow, by words of pardon and peace."[92] When reestablished, the settlement had 127 Spanish families with a few Indians and two priests. The Indians seem to have been 40 families of *genizaro*.

By 1706 there were 100 soldiers with their wives and children at the presidio of Santa Fe, according to the declaration of Fr. Juan Alvarez, who also mentions "settlers" without giving a number. In charge of these people were the governor and a priest who is described as "poorly supplied with vestments, bells, etc."[93] A little later, by 1744, the number of Spanish families was still at 127, and they earned a living raising wheat, sheep, and cattle, and weaving blankets and hosiery.[94]

A census was taken in 1776. It showed 1 governor and family (6 persons), 229 Spanish families (1167 persons), and 42 families of *genizaros* (164 persons).[95] By the 1790s Santa Fe had a population of 2,000 or a little more and was one of four towns this size in the Rio Grande Valley.[96] Yet its population is supposed to have been 3,741 in 1805, growing to 6,000 by 1821, while New Mexico's grew from 19,000 to 30,000 in the same period.[97] Of these, 9,000–10,000 were supposed to be Indian.[98]

Mexican independence came in 1821, formally celebrated at Santa Fe on 6 January 1822—"Never did Santa
Fe behold such a splendid display"—but at first there was
little actual change for New Mexico or for this city.[99] At
Santa Fe the effect eventually was to make possible direct
trade with the United States.[100] In 1824 the presidio company was supposed to have 119 soldiers, and a budget of
$35,488, but since the budget existed only on paper, one
wonders about the soldiers. In 1827 Col. Narvona took
the first official census, finding that New Mexico had a
population of 41,458, mostly living along the Rio del
Norte within a distance of sixty to eighty leagues.[101] The
population at Santa Fe was 5,275 in 1831.[102] A second
census was taken in 1838 by Gov. Don Manuel Armijo.[103]

Head of the government of the area from 1823 to 1846
while it was under Mexican rule was a *jefe político* who
lived at Santa Fe. The area was a Mexican province to
1824, then temporarily a state with two other territories,
then a territory; in 1836 it became a department, remaining so until the American take over in 1846. All branches
of the government were controlled by the governor.[104]

As late as 1859, when the area had passed to US control,
the population at Santa Fe was only 4,846,[105] while New
Mexico had 61,547, of whom 25,089 were listed as illiterate. Davis says he thinks at least half were illiterate, as
only 460 were in school, and almost no women could read
and write.[106] The population did not grow in the 1850s
but by 1880 it was 6,635, and by 1889 it was 8,000.[107]

For many years Santa Fe was the only city and cultural
center in New Mexico. The territory was never an economically successful colony because there was almost no
mineral wealth in the area and little agriculture. Santa Fe
was thus an artificial city in the sense that it was only a
center of government and missionary effort and had no
viable economic base.[108]

In 1827 Narvona's census reported that people made
their livings in agriculture and stock raising (sheep and
goats), trade, buffalo hunting, and some mining.[109]

As long as Santa Fe was only a distant and tenuous
dependent of Mexico City, the vast distances and hostile
territory were bound to inhibit trade. A caravan of up to
500 persons would leave annually from Santa Fe for Mex-

ico City, but return was expected only in three years. The caravans at this time consisted of burros since there were no roads and the terrain was rough. Each would carry up to 300 pounds. Up to 1000 burros might form one train.[110] These traders would have to pay as much as a 100-percent tax on their goods at the Customs House located on the east side of the Plaza Mayor. The reason for the size of the tax was that under the Spanish economic system, there were no taxes on land, but there were of course some expenses of government that had to be met.

Biggest items of the trade were cotton goods, especially American made, which would be traded for local blankets. To sell these goods brought in from Mexico City and from the Gulf of Mexico, the New Mexican traders would scatter throughout the territory in October to attend as many fairs as possible.[111]

During the years 1775–1776, there were several attempts to find an overland route to California from Santa Fe, especially a safe one to Monterey.[112] These efforts were eventually successful, for Davis tells us, "Since the settlement of California, a considerable trade in sheep has sprung up between the two countries. Large flocks have been annually driven across the deserts from New Mexico, and which have commanded in California a price that renumerates the owners for the risk, trouble, and expense of driving them thither." Sheep that cost $2–3 in New Mexico brought $6–8 in San Francisco.[113]

But by virtue of its location, Santa Fe came to the attention of the vigorous American culture that had rolled over Spanish St. Louis and was on its way west. As early as 1812, Robert McKnight and a party of nine or ten reached Santa Fe over the plains, attempting to trade. Their goods, however, were confiscated, and the party were arrested and held in Mexico for ten years. In 1815, Auguste F. Chouteau and Julius de Mun came to New Mexico from Missouri and were well received for a while, but in 1817 their goods were confiscated and they were arrested.[114]

Once rule had shifted from Spain to Mexico, there was a loosening of this protectionist policy, so that by the 1830s there were many visitors and American merchants at Santa Fe.[115] Some Americans decided to stay over the winter in the area and hunt beaver, returning with the

skins and not money as the skins were not taxed.[116] As
early as 1821 or 1822, a regular caravan left Independence,
Missouri, for Santa Fe each year, composed of as many as
90 to 100 wagons, for protection against wild Indians.
They would arrive in July and sell the goods wholesale at
prices 80 to 100 percent over St. Louis or Philadelphia
prices—which was considered a great bargain. The cara-
vaneers would leave again in August[117] (figure 30). By
1849 caravans of 20 to 40 wagons were arriving "continually," at least in May, according to the report of William
R. Goulding, who accompanied the Knickerbocker Exploring Co. in that year.[118] By the 1850s trade along the
Santa Fe Trail amounted to $1 million per year,[119] a flood
that would greatly dilute the Spanish component of life at
Santa Fe.

Founded a scant 100 years after the discovery and occupation of Darien in the Isthmus of Panama, Santa Fe
marked the culmination of northward expansion of the
Spanish into hostile territory.[120] Though the Indians were
considered at first to be "so barbaric as to be not even
worth exploiting",[121] the ideas of God and Empire proved
strong enough to maintain the settlement and give it a
form that typified Spanish urbanism in the New World, a
form that persists in the central part of the city to this day.
At Santa Fe as elsewhere in Spanish America, Italian Renaissance ideas of city layout, expressed as early as 1554
in the rebuilt urban fabric of Mexico City, were imposed
upon an "Indian civic armature which was found to be
highly suitable," and in fact more easily adaptable to these
ideals than contemporary European models.[122]

The fact that Santa Fe was peripheral to the Spanish
(later Mexican) territory gave it more freedom than other
more centrally located sites. When American culture over-
ran it, Santa Fe was again peripheral and so developed its
own unique blend of Spanish and American cultures.

Santa Fe, for instance, was the first place where persons
of Anglo-American and Mexican-Spanish culture sat together on law courts and in the legislature, as Davis, who
was the US attorney in Santa Fe reported.[123] While they
were trying the cases or making the laws, their Indian
counterparts were waiting in that bare room of the governor's palace to be noticed. Indian culture has continued

to be a largely unacknowledged substratum of Spanish city life in the New World. A paradigm of the city form mandated by the Laws of the Indies,[124] Santa Fe is also to some extent an embodiment of the compromises between Renaissance and Indian ideas of urban form, generated by the particular conditions of colonization in the New World.

19 Native American planning for solar heating. Part of the perceivable regularity of Indian settlements in the Southwest may be due to traditional manipulation of solar heating. Since this region is sparsely wooded, with forests often at great distance from inhabited pueblos, every possible conservation of human energy and of wood for fires is essential. The orderly spacing of these row houses maximized exposure to the winter sun. (Reprinted, by permission, from R. Knowles, *Energy and Form*, Cambridge, Mass.: MIT Press, 1978, figure 28)

K
K
K
0'
50'
250'

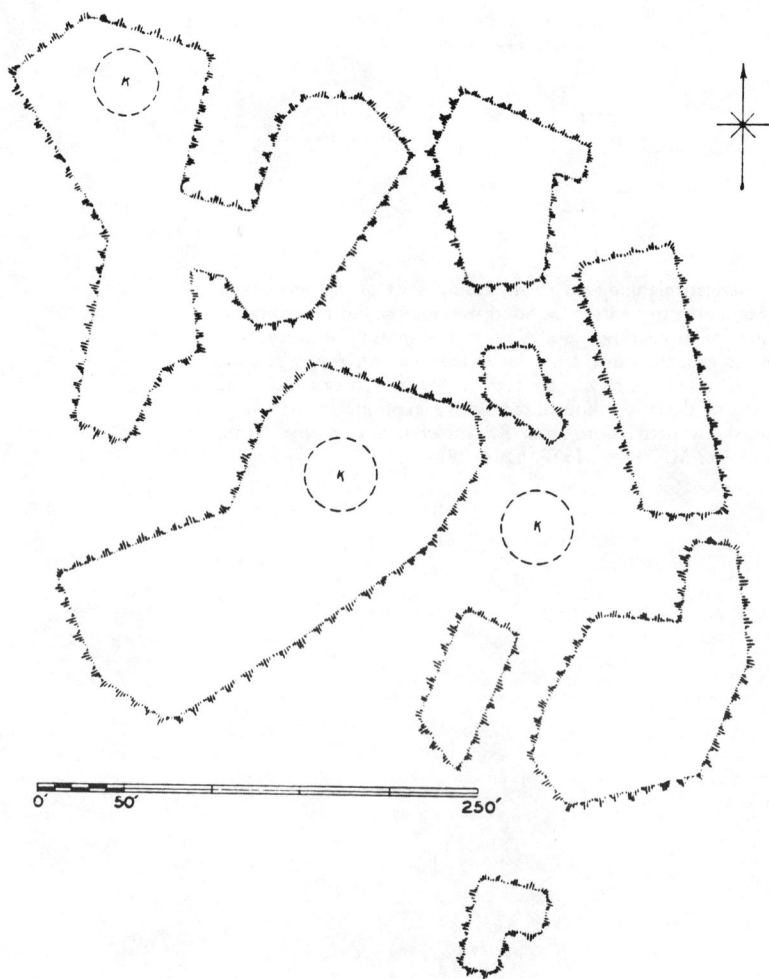

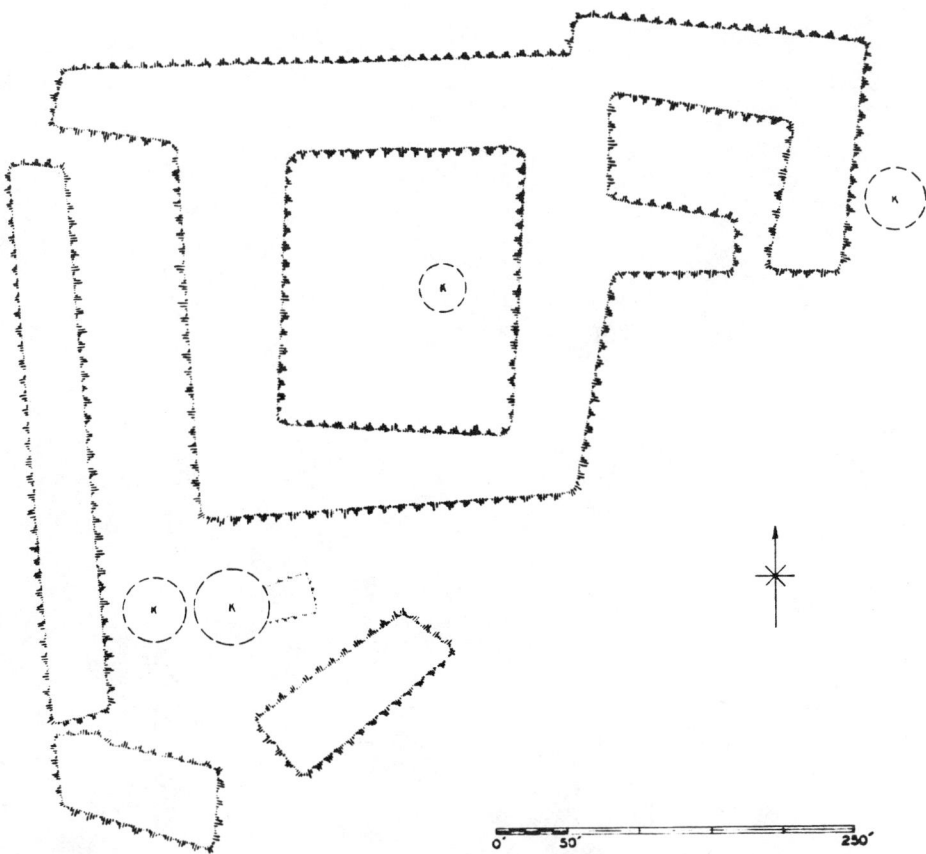

20,21 Regular and irregular Indian settlement patterns from before the Spanish rule in New Mexico. Although some precontact Indian sites were irregularly arranged, others, like the site on the right from north central New Mexico, show not only a regular pattern but also arrangement around open courtyards. This pattern is not, then, the product of interaction with the Spanish conquerors, but rather an indigenous cultural feature that could be easily assimilated by the invaders since it matched their own native settlement patterns. At left, the irregular layout of a prehistoric site at the juncture of the Rito de la Olia and the Rio Grande del Rancho, about seven miles south of Taos, from the thirteenth century. At right, a prehistoric site on the west bank of Ojo Caliente Creek, north central New Mexico from the fourteenth century. (Reprinted by permission from Stanley A. Stubbs, *Bird's-Eye View of the Pueblos,* Norman University of Oklahoma Press, 1950, figures 1, 2)

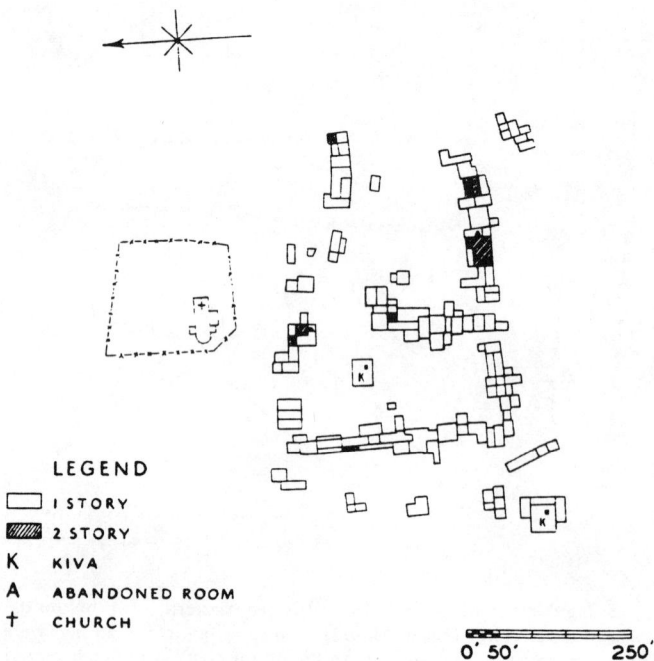

LEGEND

▢ 1 STORY
▨ 2 STORY
K KIVA
A ABANDONED ROOM
✝ CHURCH

0' 50'   250'

22 Plan of Santa Clara Pueblo, New Mexico. Shows the pre-Conquest pattern of dwellings with party walls, arranged around two courtyards. This pattern has persisted in spite of the additions of a church and of a few outlying dwellings. (Reprinted, by permission, from S. A. Stubbs, *Bird's-Eye View of the Pueblos*, Norman: University of Oklahoma Press, 1950)

23 Aerial view of Isleta Pueblo, New Mexico. In 1680, 2000 people lived here; by 1963 the population had recovered to 1974 persons after an earlier decline. In this photograph, newer construction follows the roads at upper right, while the traditional plaza-centered, fairly regular settlement is at lower left. Scholars are agreed that Hopi culture is unusually tenacious in retention of traditional forms, and this includes settlement patterns. (By permission from *Population, Contact, and Climate in the New Mexican Pueblos*, by Ezra B. W. Zubrow, Anthoropological Papers of the University of Arizona, 24, Tucson: U. of Arizona Press, copyright 1974, figure 9, p. 33)

404

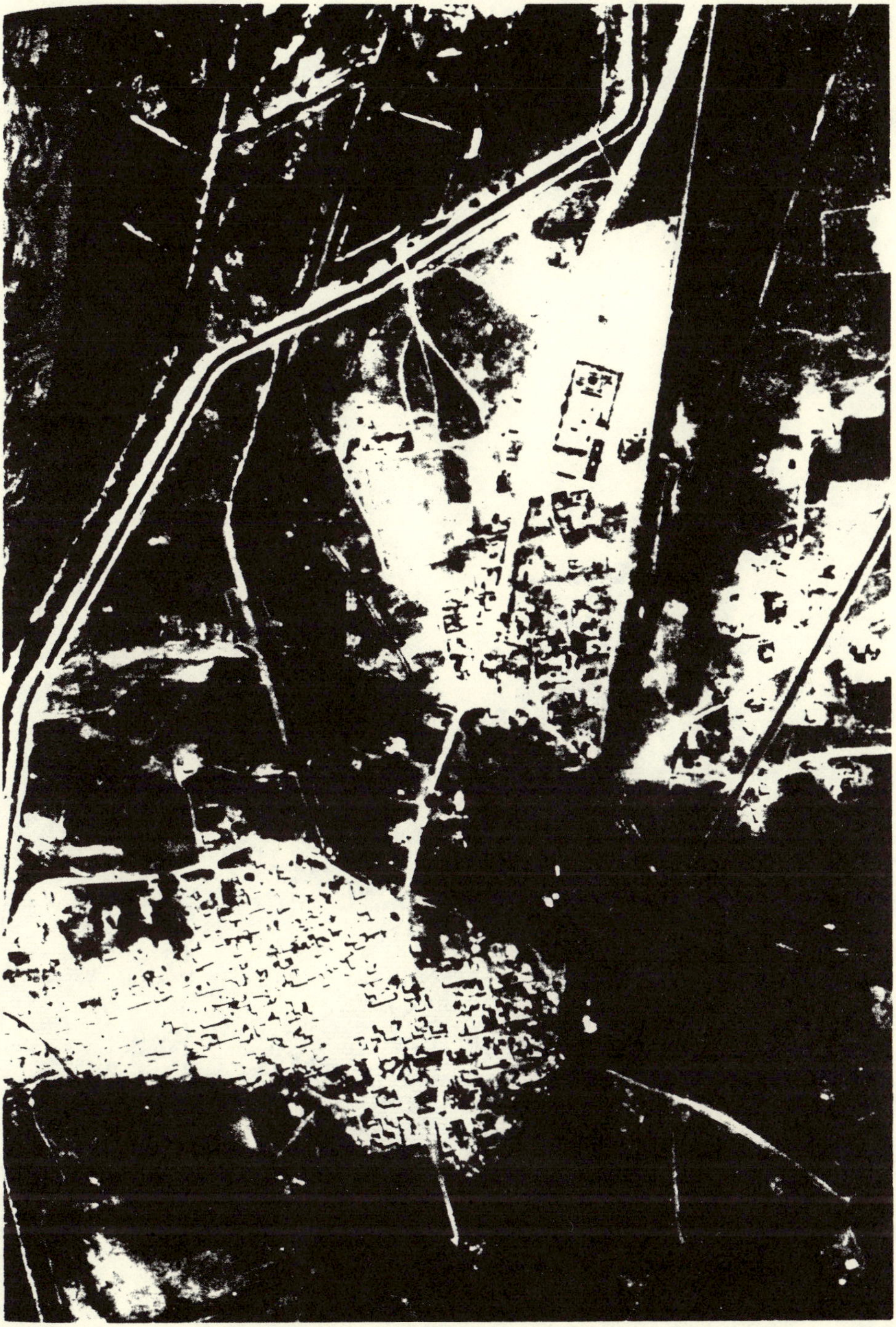

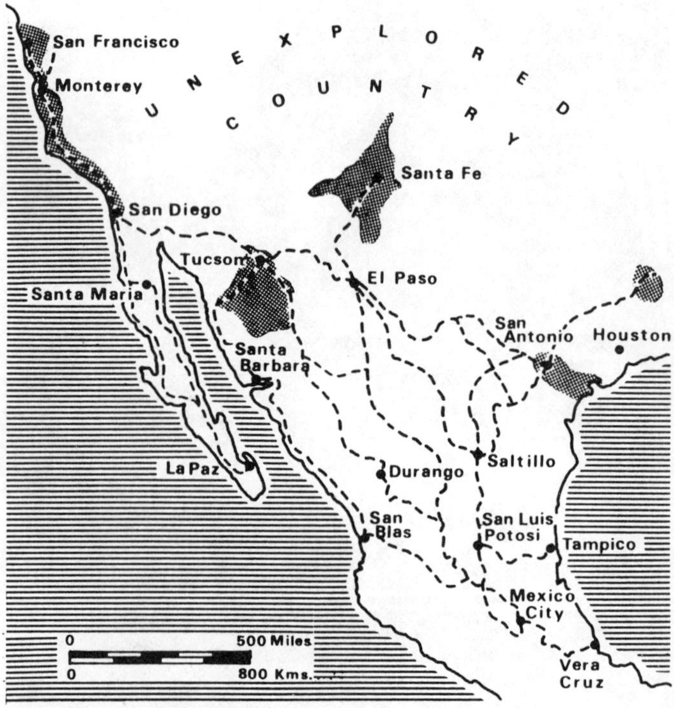
San Francisco
Monterey
UNEXPLORED
COUNTRY
Santa Fe
San Diego
Tucson
El Paso
Santa Maria
San Antonio
Houston
Santa Barbara
Saltillo
La Paz
Durango
San Blas
San Luis Potosi
Tampico
Mexico City
Vera Cruz
0
500 Miles
0
800 Kms.

24 Trails from Mexico into the Southwest. Trails from Mexico City northward into our provincial area are shown in dashed lines, and the mission fields as grey areas. The distance from Mexico City to Santa Fe was about 1,000 miles, much of it through the driest desert. Climatically and topographically the area shown here forms a single region with some internal variation, at least as far north as Santa Fe. The indigenous population, extending the similarity with conditions in Mexico, included tribes like the Hopi, who had already been living in settled villages, and the peaceful California Indians, who took readily to domestication at the missions, but also some warlike groups such as the Apache, who were nomadic and intractable. (Plan originally published in C. Hollenbeck, *Spanish Missions of the Old Southwest*, New York: Doubleday, Page & Co., 1926, figure 1; redrawn by John Harvey for our articles "The Laws of the Indies Revisited", *Town Planning Review*, vol. 48 #4, Oct. 1977, reprinted by permission)

ACEQUIA PARA REGADIO
Camino de la cañada
RIO DE SANTA FEE
camino del Alamo
Acequia Para regadio
Camino de Galisteo
Camino de Pecos
Camino de
PLANO
Explicacion
Yglesia y Convento de S Francisco

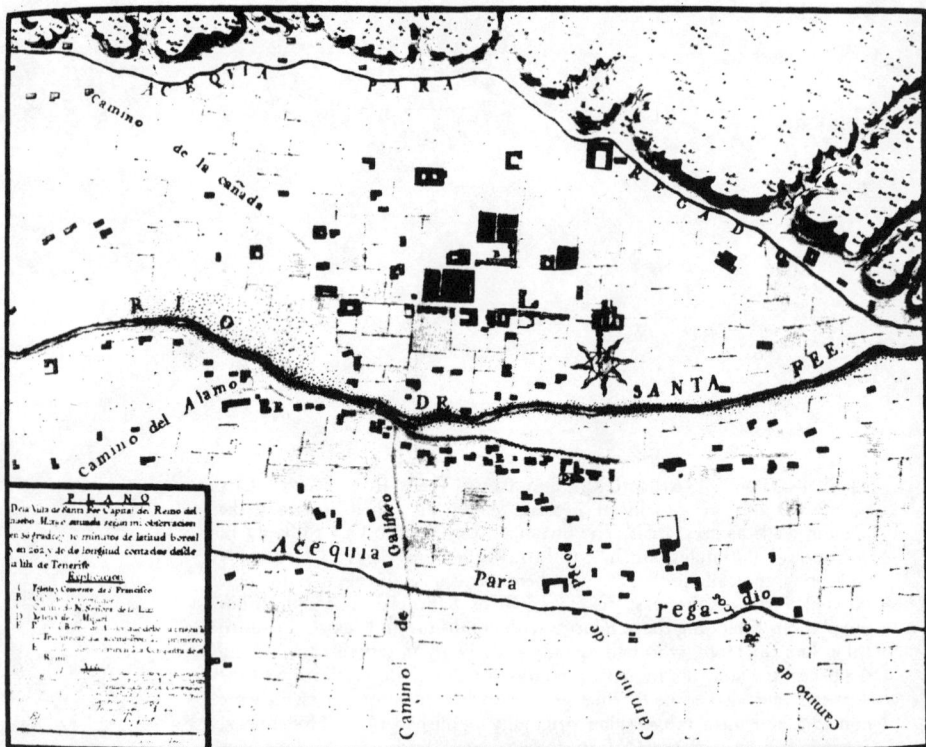

25 Urrutia's map of Santa Fe. This is the earliest known. Its Spanish caption has been translated by Adams and Chavez in their *The Missions of New Mexico, 1776. A Description by Fray Francisco Atanasio Dominquez with Other Contemporary Documents*: "Plan of the Villa of Santa Fe, Capital of the Kingdom of New Mexico, situated according to my observation at 36 degrees and 10 minutes north latitude and 262° and 40′ longitude, reckoned from the Island of Tenerife. Legend: A. Church and Convent of St. Francis. B. House of the Governor. C. Chapel of Our Lady of Light. D. Church of St. Michael. E. Pueblo or Suburb of Analco which owes its origin to the Tlascans who accompanied the first Spaniards who entered in the Conquest of this Kingdom. Note: To the east of the Villa, about a league distant, there is a chain of very high forested mountains which reach so far from south to north that its limits are unknown even to the Comanches, who came from the north, ever along the base of said sierra during their entire migration, which they say was very long. All the buildings of this place are of adobes. Scale of two hundred toises. Joseph de Urrutia."

Comments: The church and convent of St. Francis (A) are the present cathedral, several times rebuilt on this site, originally headquarters of the Franciscan missionaries to New Mexico. The house of the governor, today the Governor's Palace (B) was begun in 1610 as the major structure of the early presidio, rebuilt in 1692 and thereafter; it faces the main plaza of the city. The Chapel of our Lady of Light (C), called Military Chapel on other maps, is a structure of the eighteenth century and later, originally built as a religious confraternity for the officers stationed here. The Church of St. Michael (San Miguel; D), on the other hand, was always for the Indians and claims to be the oldest church in continuous use in the United States; it is supposed to date from before the foundation of Santa Fe by five or six years. This church stood at one end of the separate Pueblo of Analco (E), where the captive Indians whom the Spaniards brought with them from Mexico lived; legend has it that they were Tlascans—no other proof has been found. At the center of the map lies the Rio de Santa Fee, given prominence here probably because of a great flood that occurred in 1767. Lying to the north and south of it, and roughly parallel to it, are the irrigation ditches called "Acequia para regadio." To the west and south of the built-up area are the fields, laid out orthogonally, and among them the routes to other settlements are indicated by their names: Camino de la Canada, Camino del Alamo, Camino de Galifteo, and Camino de Pecos. The town lies at the foot of a sierra shown here as a series of bluffs to the north and northeast. Even in this plan the difference in scale between the Spanish area north of the river and the Indian area to the south is evident, a difference encouraged by the Laws of the Indies. (Courtesy of the British Library, by whose permission this map is printed from the original)

26 Map of Santa Fe in 1846 by Emory and Gilmer. The so-called Military Map, drawn incident to occupation of the city by American forces. Note that they use both Spanish and English to label the map. Among the interesting features: The Chapel and Park of the Rosary at upper left is one of several new religious buildings since Urrutia's days. The sierra appears at upper right, and the channel of the irrigation system seems to lead into the top of the corn fields at center, directly west from the sierra. What had been the enclosure of the presidio is still partially enclosed by buildings but apparently used for agriculture and not military exercises, for it is labeled Corn Fields. The Governor's Palace shows as a dark rectangle below this, facing onto the plaza with its clearly demarcated colonnades. Opposite the palace stands the military chapel. To the east, the Church of San Francisco has an enclosed courtyard in front, marked by a cross. At the center of the city runs the Rio de Santa Fe, with the Chapel of Guadalupe at the west end of the built-up area. Major roads lead off to the northwest, southwest, and southeast, with the Church of San Miguel at the intersection of one of these and the only long east-west street parallel to the river and south of it. This street has houses along both sides, presumably of the original captive Indian families and later comers. At bottom right one segment of the irrigation canal is shown. (Courtesy of the National Archives: Record Group 77: Fortification File, Dr. 142)

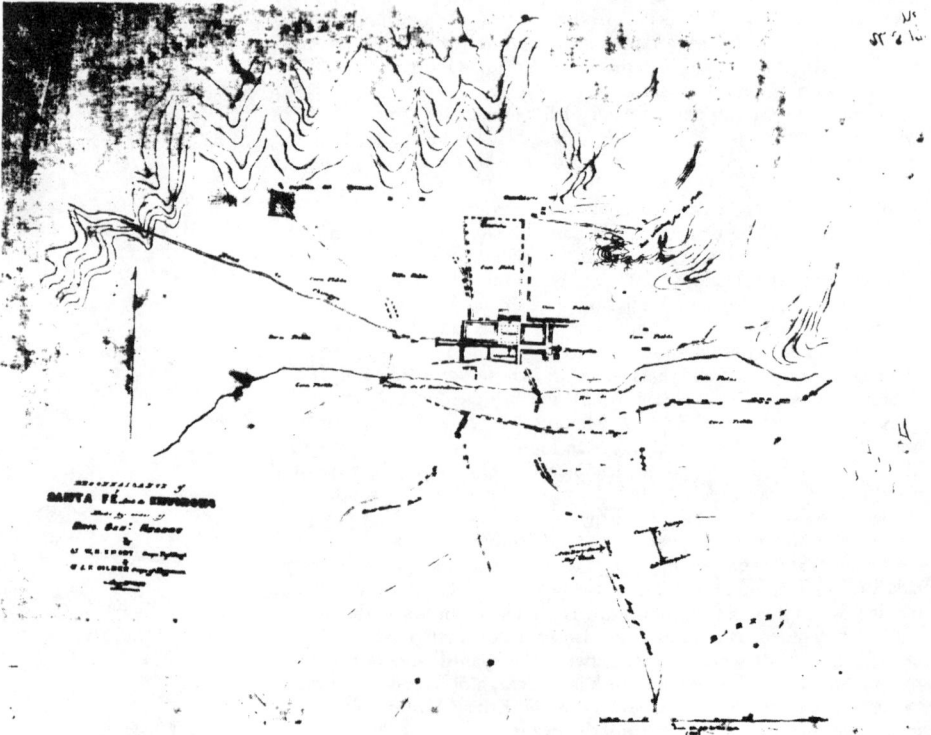

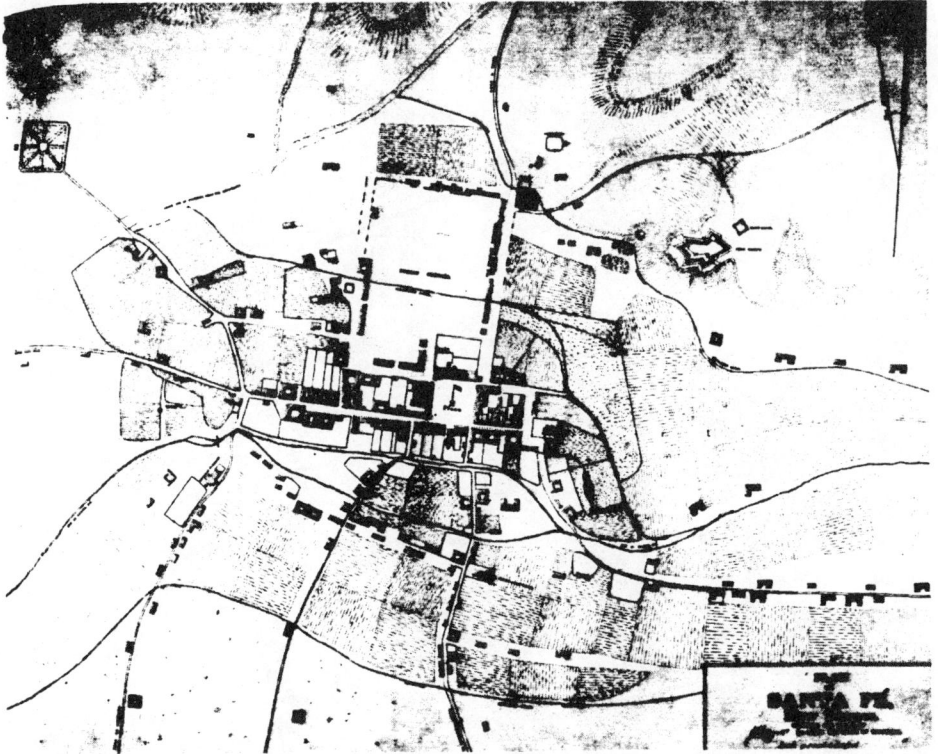

27 A more polished map of Santa Fe, also 1846, by Gilmer. Figure 26 seems to be an early version of this plan by Lt. Gilman, also probably 1846. The church of the Rosary and its formal park are at upper left, while the newly built Fort Marcy stands on the bluff at upper right; this fort was erected at the time of the American occupation, but used only briefly before being allowed to crumble away. The irrigation canals have their direction of flow shown by arrows. The Rio do Santa Fe is blue, as is the water from the spring near the Church of San Francisco. All these water channels flow to the west, where they join the (dry) river bed shown at upper left. One channel flows through the public grounds, the former presidio enclosure, formed by the old military barracks, the hospital, and the Governor's Palace. Colonnades shown as dots edge the plaza, the main streets, the conventual buildings at the Church of San Francisco, and a quasi-governmental building at the end of the street that runs westward from in front of the Palace. Diagonally across the street from the latter, a building has encroached into the north-south street. Many of the houses are arranged around courtyards; others, especially in the Indian village south of the river, are U-shaped. The street leading to San Miguel in an east-west direction is shown to terminate at the church, which, like the cathedral, is set off in its own walled plaza. Fields close to the settlement are shaped as fairly regular quadrilaterals. Roads leading out of Santa Fe usually have their places of destination marked on them; the one to the south "to Independence Mo." is the terminus of the Santa Fe Trail. (Courtesy of the National Archives: Record Group 77: Fortification File, Dr. 142; brought to my attention by John Reps)

411

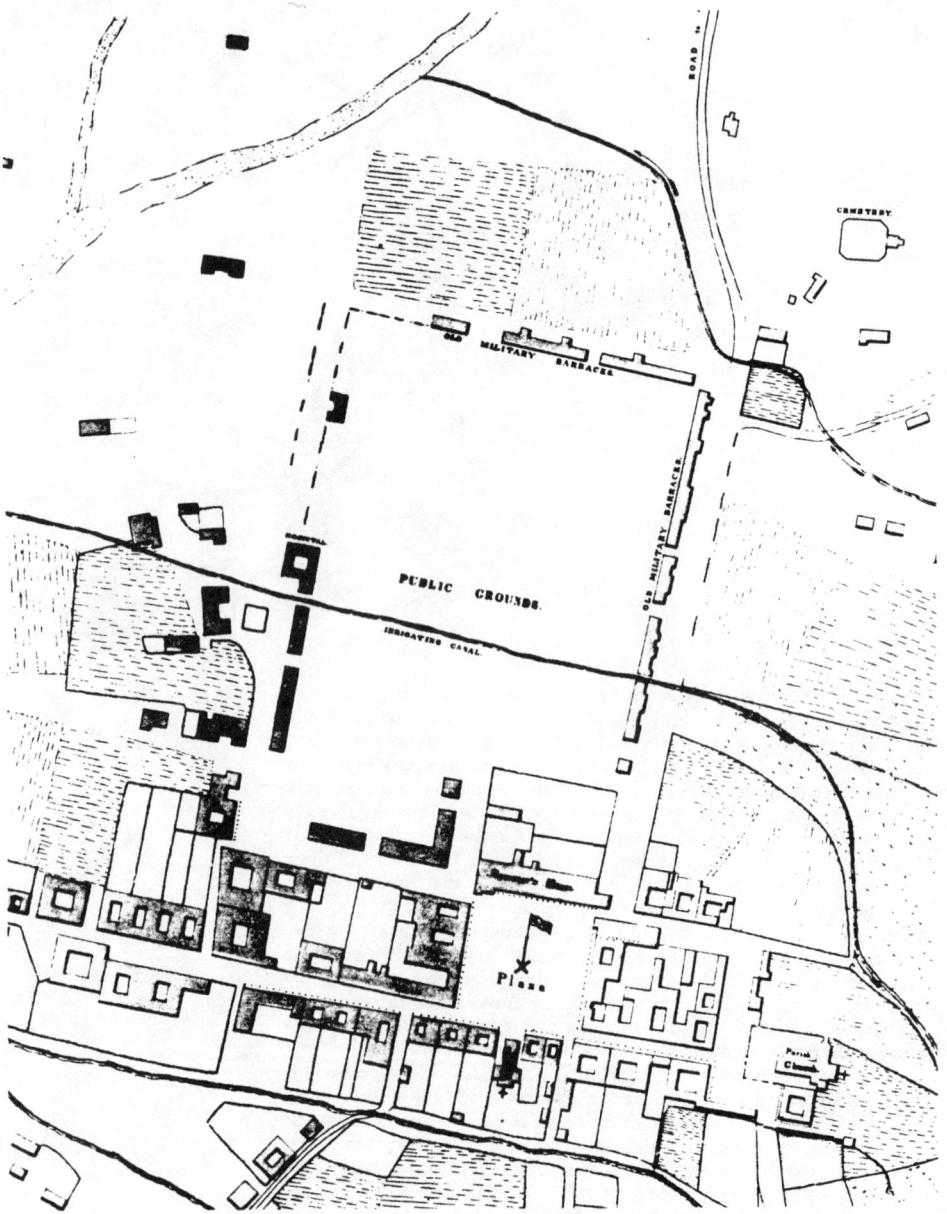

CEMETERY.

ROAD "

MILITARY BARRACKS

OLD MILITARY BARRACKS

PUBLIC GROUNDS.

IRRIGATING CANAL

Plaza

Parish Church

28 Detail of figure 27, showing the central business district of Santa Fe. The quintessential Spanish colonial city center is here dominated by an outsized American flag, which may also be seen in the view of Santa Fe in 1848 (figure 34). From the columns to the structures behind them, roofs would have spanned to protect pedestrians from sun and occasional rain. By the 1840s, most of these structures were occupied by stores, while the informal market was still held in the plaza. Besides the Governor's Palace, which was the administrative and legislative center of the territory, other government functions such as court (northeast corner) and customs house (east side) faced onto the plaza. Here the caravans to Mexico City, Los Angeles, or Independence were assembled, and here the promenade at the end of the day took place. The colonnaded street to the right led to the cathedral; one side of this street was residential, and therefore not colonnaded (see figure 29).

29 View along San Francisco Street, Santa Fe, from the plaza to the cathedral. Though made a cathedral, with a bishop, only in the 1830s, this church was from its founding in the seventeenth century the center of the missionary effort in New Mexico. Often rebuilt, only a few rooms are even as old as the eighteenth century. A low wall encloses the open space in front of, and beside, the church. This street leads directly to the gate in that wall from the plaza, seat of secular power. Houses to the north of the street face directly onto the street, a custom of the Greco-Roman world passed on to the Spanish by their Moorish conquerors. Here, however, the south side of the street had porticoes; we see the roofs of those in the foreground, and the columns themselves of the buildings nearer the church. (Courtesy of the Museum of New Mexico, Santa Fe)

30 Caravan on San Francisco Street just south of the plaza. The westward extension of San Francisco Street, as it edges the plaza, is shown here, with the cathedral in the distance. The military chapel is just off the picture to the right. A caravan, probably from Missouri because of the oxen, which were not used in trips to either Mexico City or Los Angeles, rests in the street. One corner of the plaza appears at left. The crude quality of the log porticoes is evident, as is the renovation of the plaza with trees and a picket fence, both added after the American occupation. (Courtesy of the Museum of New Mexico, Santa Fe)

fu cafa .

Despues, de auer comprado, y fu

31 Scene from the market at Tenochtitlan/Mexico City (previously published with Bernal's article on Tenochtitlan in *Cities of Destiny*). In every Spanish colonial city, Indian vendors sold their wares in the plazas. Here at Santa Fe, these were stationed along the north side of the plaza, and even in the porches of the Governor's Palace. (Courtesy of the Bibliotica Mediceo-Laurenziana; from the Codex Fiorentino)

32 Drawing of a reconstruction of the great irrigation ditch of Santa Fe. The irrigation system, which was the first communal building activity at Los Angeles, was at Santa Fe the means of existence in the desert. It began from the spring near the Church of San Francisco, which was probably located there to utilize the spring; very early the waters were led to the presidio; eventually a whole series of major and minor channels made a network through the fields and houses. This recent drawing shows one such channel at Santa Fe. (Courtesy of the City Planning Dept., Santa Fe; Kate Krasin, artist)

417

33 Earliest surviving house at Santa Fe. Houses at Santa Fe were from the beginning made of easily available local materials: stone, adobe mud, wooden roof beams. The oldest house now standing there is the Juan Rodriguez House, from 1844 and later; though relatively late, it is in the same style as those earlier ones that have disappeared. The same kind of house would have stood at Los Angeles, but not at St. Louis, where the early French influence and the dampness of the climate made adobe both unfashionable and impractical. (Courtesy of the City Planning Dept.. Santa Fe)

34 View of Santa Fe in 1848. The artist placed himself south of the city, between two of the major roads, along which traffic is moving. The wide spacing of the houses, seen here, is still common in desert areas. At center is the huge American flag in the plaza, echoed by another at Fort Marcy on the hill to the right. Between them a tiny cross marks the Church of San Francisco. At the top of the plaza lie the old barracks, which form the northern edge of the old presidio. The regularity of city blocks near the plaza is noteable. (Courtesy of the Map Collection at the Library of Congress; brought to our attention by John Reps)

NOTES

1 Mexico City was refounded 1541; Santa Fe was founded 1609.

2 E. R. Forrest, *Pueblos and Missions of the Old Southwest* (Cleveland: 1929), p. 41; hereafter cited as Forrest.

3 J. G. Meem, *Old Santa Fe Today* (Albuquerque: n.d.), preface.

4 A. Dominquez, *The Missions of New Mexico, 1776*, trans. and annotated E. B. Adams and A. Chavez (Albuquerque: 1956), p. 41, n. 69; hereafter cited as Dominquez.

5 Ralph K. Knowles, *Energy and Form* (Cambridge, Mass.: 1978), fig. 28; George Kubler, *The Religious Architecture of New Mexico*, 4th ed. (Albuquerque: 1972), p. 15; hereafter cited as Kubler, 1972.

6 Herbert E. Bolton, *The Spanish Borderlands: A Chronology of Old Florida and the Southwest* (New Haven: 1921), p. 165; hereafter cited as Bolton, 1921.

7 Don Pedro Bautista Pino, the *Exposición*, 1812, quoted in Lic. Antonio Barreiro, the *Ojeada*, 1832, p. 29, and in Don José Agustin de Escudero's additions, p. 32; all are in *Three New Mexico Chronicles*, trans. and annotated by H. Bailey Carroll and J. Villasana Haggard (Albuquerque, 1942); hereafter each reference will be by author and page only. For further information on the arrangement of pueblos, see S. A. Stubbs, *Bird's-Eye View of the Pueblos* (Norman, OK: 1950) and Ezra B. W. Zubrow, *Population, Contact, and Climate in the New Mexico Pueblos*, Anthropological Papers of the University of Arizona, No. 24, both amply illustrated.

8 Ye-Fu Tuan, *Topophilia* (Englewood Cliffs, NJ: 1974), p. 66 quoting J. R. Bartlett of the United States and Mexico Boundary Commission and Lt. J. H. Simpson.

9 Kubler, 1972, pp. 15–17.

10 William Heath Davis, *El Gringo, or New Mexico and Her People* (Santa Fe: 1938), p. 39; hereafter cited as Davis.

11 Herbert E. Bolton, *Texas in the Middle 18th Century: Studies in Spanish Colonial History* (Berkeley: 1915), pp. 9–10; hereafter cited as Bolton, 1915.

12 Violich, F., "Evolution of the Spanish City: Issues Basic to Planning Today," *Journal of the American Institute of Planners*, vol. 28, No. 3 (August 1962), p. 171.

13 Kubler, 1972, p. 131.

14 As quoted in Philip Wayne Powell, *Soldiers, Indians and Silver* (Berkeley and Los Angeles: 1952).

15 *Ibid.*, p. 213.

16 L. B. Simpson, *The Encomienda in New Spain* (Berkeley: 1929), *passim*.

17 Kubler, 1948, p. 64.

18 Bolton, 1921, pp. 164–166, 190.

19 Most authors, e.g., Sanford Trent, *Architecture of the Southwest* (New York: 1950), p. 90, give 1610 as the date, but Herbert E. Bolton and T. M. Marshall, *The Colonization of North America* (New York: 1930), p. 72, prefer 1609.

20 Forrest, p. 17.

21 *Ibid.*, p. 41.

22 Hubert Howe Bancroft, *History of Arizona and New Mexico 1530–1888* (1889; reprint ed. Albuquerque: 1962); hereafter cited as Bancroft, 1889.

23 Dominguez, p. xv.

24 *Ibid.*, p. 6.

25 *Ibid.*, p. xviii; Pino, pp. 50, 55.

26 Dominguez, p. 6

27 *Ibid.*, p. 127. In Bancroft, 1889, p. 176, there is a good map of the locations of pueblos in the region of Sante Fe.

28 E. H. Spicer, *Cycles of Conquest* (Tucson: 1962), pp. 298–300; Stubbs, p. 14.

29 Reps, 1965, p. 43; Violich, 1962, p. 43.

30 Dominguez, p. 12

31 The phrase "de San Francisco" seems to have been added to the name of the city no earlier than the nineteenth century, referring to the saint after whom the principal church was named, the great patron of the Franciscan missionaries. Dominguez, p. 13, no. 3.

32 Dominguez, p. 12.

33 Trent, p. 91.

34 Bancroft, 1889, p. 203, says the site was retaken by the Spanish on December 16, 1692, but other authors disagree.

35 I have used Dominguez's translation of the caption of this map.

36 Bancroft, 1889, p. 259. n. 13.

37 Davis, pp. 67–69.

38 Dominguez, p. 40.

39 Possibly this complaint was a pun on the meaning of *presidio* as prison. Petition of Fray Francisco de Ayeta, May 10, 1679, as quoted in Hackett (see note 86).

40 Pino, p. 27.

41 *Ibid.*, pp. 80, 84–85, 186, n. 25.

42 Violich, 1962, p. 43.

43 Trent, p. 94.

44 Beyer, p. 55.

45 Davis, p. 41.

46 Beyer, p. 51.

47 Pino, p. 85; Dominguez, p. 40; Davis, pp. 39, 41.

48 Pino, p. 85.

49 Elias Brevoort, "Santa Fe Trail 1884," Manuscript, P-E8, Bancroft Library, University of California, Berkeley.

50 Bancroft, 1889, p. 791, n. 7.

51 Pino, pp. 85–86.

52 Davis, p. 44.

53 Davis, pp. 46–47.

54 *Ibid.*, p. 39.

55 *Ibid.*, p. 41.

56 Dominguez, p. 39.

57 Meem, preface.

58 Forrest, p. 41, claims that San Miguel was built 1605–1608 by Don Juan Oñate.

59 Bancroft, 1889, p. 162.

60 Davis, p. 49; Dominguez, pp. 32–33, 246, n. 52.

61 Dominguez, p. 244.

62 Pino, p. 85.

63 *Idem*.

64 Trent, p. 91; Violich, 1962, pp. 195–197.

65 Pino, pp. 85–86.

66 Dominguez, p. 39.

67 Pino, p. 85.

68 Davis, pp. 40–41, 50–53, 100.

69 Dominguez, p. 278, quoting a letter to Provincial Fray Isidro Murillo, of June 10, 1776.

70 Hugh Morrison, *Early American Architecture* (Oxford: 1952), p. 183. Pino, p. 187, n. 260 (by editors).

71 Dominguez, p. 22.

72 Pino. n. 260.

73 Davis, p. 44, where he does not, however, say that a governor was buried under the floor; unfortunately I have lost the source of this notion.

74 *Ibid.*, pp. 44–45.

75 Trent, p. 91; Pino, n. 260. See also P. A. F. Walter, "El Palacio Real" in *Old Santa Fe*, pp. 333–334.

76 William G. Ritch, "History of New Mexico 1884," unpaginated manuscript, Bancroft Library, University of California, Berkeley.

77 J. Watts, "Santa Fe Affairs," Manuscript, Bancroft Library, University of California, Berkeley, p. 10.

78 Doninguez, pp. 22ff.

79 Bancroft, 1889, p. 641.

80 Davis, pp. 46–47.

81 *Ibid.*, p. 43.

82 *Ibid.*, p. 41.

83 *Ibid.*, p. 42.

84 Pino, p. 96.

85 Davis, p. 39.

86 C. W. Hackett, *Historical Documents Relating to New Mexico Nueva Vizcaya and Approaches Thereto, to 1773* (Washington, D.C.: 1923), pp. 108, 119.

87 Spicer, pp. 5, 7.

88 Dominguez, p. 42, n. 72; Spicer, p. 300.

89 Spicer, P. 300.

90 Bancroft, 1889, p. 163, n. 43; Bolton and Marshall, p. 243, where the figure is 750 Indians. Hackett, pp. 108–119, says Santa Fe had 50 of the 200 Spaniards and Mestizos in the province in 1638; these supported themselves by growing wheat and maize by irrigation.

91 Rexford Newcomb, *Spanish-Colonial Architecture in the United States* (New York: 1937), p. 30.

92 Bancroft, 1889, pp. 197–198; Hackett, however, on pp. 108, 299, quotes Fr. Miguel de Monchero, writing in 1744, as giving the date 1682.

93 Hackett, p. 373.

94 *Ibid.*, p. 24.

95 Dominguez, pp. 42–43. These population figures do not correlate well with Zubrow, *Population, Contact, and Climate in the New Mexican Pueblos*, who gives, in figure 4, a population for the pueblos in 1800 of about 10,000 with the total New Mexico population as about 25,000 for that year.

96 Spicer, p. 100.

97 Bancroft, 1889, pp. 299–300.

98 *Ibid.*, pp. 311–313.

99 *Ibid.*, p. 309.

100 *Ibid.*, p. 299.

101 *Ibid.*, pp. 311, 313.

102 Pino, p. 84.

103 *Ibid.*, pp. 88–89.

104 Bancroft, 1889, pp. 310–311.

105 *Compendium of the 7th United States Census*, p. 381.

106 Davis, p. 64.

107 *Ibid.*, p. 39; Bancroft, 1889, p. 790.

108 Trent, pp. 94–95.

109 Pino, pp. 89–90.

110 Davis, pp. 76–77. Caravans with wagons drawn by oxen became typical of the Santa Fe Trail to Missouri as it developed into a real road.

111 Pino, pp. 109, 119, 120.

112 Dominguez, p. xv.

113 Davis, p. 75.

114 Bancroft, 1889, p. 297.

115 Eleanor Lawrence, "Mexican Trade between Santa Fe and Los Angeles, 1830–1848," *California Historical Quarterly* (1931), pp. 27–39.

116 Pino, p. 108.

117 *Ibid.*, p. 106.

118 Quoted in Oliver LaFarge, *Santa Fe* (Norman, OK: 1970), p. viii.

119 Davis, introduction by Fergusson.

120 Bolton and Marshall, p. 73.

121 *Ibid.*, p. 235.

122 Kubler, 1972, p. 102.

123 Davis, introduction by Fegusson.

124 Kubler, 1972, p. 18.

.III.

Spanish Towns of the Texas Frontier

THE first Spanish settlements in Texas were closely related to colonization efforts in New Mexico. The supply and communications line to that northern outpost of empire followed the route used by Oñate, crossing the Rio Grande at what came to be called El Paso del Norte, now Ciudad Juarez, Mexico. There in December, 1659, Father García de San Francisco de Zúñiga established the first of several missions, naming it Nuestra Señora de Guadalupe de El Paso. The Pueblo Revolt of 1680 in New Mexico and the mass evacuation of settlers from that region substantially increased the population on the right bank of the Rio Grande. A town, *presidio*, and several Indian settlements were founded in the vicinity to accommodate and protect the refugees from New Mexico. By the end of the seventeenth century the area included six missions, four *pueblos* of Spaniards, and the *presidio* of El Paso. Two missions could be found on the north side of the river below what is now El Paso, Texas: Nuestra Señora de la Concepción de Socorro and Corpus Christi de la Isleta del Sur.[1]

The major thrust of Spanish colonization into Texas, however, did not occur here but well to the south and east. Motivations for settlement in that more distant region were mixed. Religious officials wanted to found missions where their obligations to Christianize the Indians might be fulfilled. Individuals and officers of the Crown alike were intrigued by rumors of great and wealthy kingdoms beyond the unknown lands to the northeast of Mexico. Perhaps most important of all, the area lay between the Spanish colonial domain and the territory claimed by or potentially open to occupation by other European powers.

The bewildering sequence of settlement founding, movement, abandonment, and re-establishment of missions, *presidios*, and civil communities in Texas resulted mainly from Spanish reaction to French colonization activities. Herbert Bolton's thesis that the Spanish borderlands were a defensive frontier, expanding and contracting in a series of protective moves when threatened by other nations, is nowhere better sustained than in Texas.[2] Like a chess player, the Spanish crown advanced and withdrew its missions, *presidios*, and *pueblos* as if they were bishops, castles, and pawns threatening to check or stalemate the opposition on a great, continental playing board. The end game was not to be reached for many decades, and then not until both of the original opponents had surrendered their places to others.

At the beginning, however, France made the first move in 1682 with La Salle's bold sortie down the Mississippi to its mouth, where he named the region Louisiana and claimed the land for the French king he so honored. The next year La Salle returned to France to report this event. There also was the former Spanish governor of New Mexico, Diego Dionisio de Peñalosa, who had defected to France and was urging the establishment of a French base on the western side of the Gulf of Mexico. La Salle received authorization to begin a settlement near the mouth of the Mississippi and set out in 1684 with four ships and a party of 300 colonists.

Whether through design or a navigator's error, La Salle and his group landed at Matagorda Bay, more than two-thirds of the distance beyond the Mississippi toward what is now the Mexican boundary on the Gulf. One ship had already been captured by pirates, another was wrecked attempting a landing, and a third sailed for France shortly after discharging its cargo of supplies and passengers.

La Salle supervised the construction of Fort St. Louis at the head of Lavaca Bay and then set out westward. He reached the lower Pecos River, nearly 300 miles from his base, before returning to find that disease had severely reduced the strength of the garrison and that its members were at the point of mutiny. The wreck of the remaining ship during a storm eliminated any further thoughts of exploration, conquest, or permanent colonization. The murder of La Salle in 1687 by some of his own men on the party's desperate march to the Mississippi and, eventually, Canada, brought the venture to a tragic end.[3]

Spain could not be sure, however, that Louis XIV did not intend to pursue an expansionist policy. Intelligence reports as early as 1678 informed them of Peñalosa's attempts to promote French settlement on the western Gulf, and in 1689, two years after La Salle's death, a Spanish exploring party led by Alonso de León reached Fort St. Louis. León's report confirmed the stories of the French expedition. It also contained recommendations for founding a line of *presidios* and several missions in Texas to establish Spanish control of the frontier. These suggestions reached the viceroy at the same time as rumors of further French colonization attempts. León received orders to return to the area, and in 1690 he and Father Damian Massanet founded the mission of San Francisco de los Tejas about seven miles west of the Neches River near the modern town of Weches. This location was less than a hundred miles from the border of what was to become the state of Louisiana.[4] The first Spanish settlement in East Texas thus lay well over three hundred miles from the nearest Spanish source of supply or military power.

León reported his accomplishments to the viceroy, including further information learned from the Indians about French activity to the east.

He pointed out that *presidios* and civil settlements would be needed to control the region of East Texas and to serve as supply points on the long route from Mexico. Father Massanet's suggestions to the viceroy differed somewhat. He advocated founding seven more missions and at least one civil settlement. The latter he proposed to be located with one of the missions on the Guadalupe River roughly halfway between his new mission among the Tejas Indians and the Mexican frontier. He opposed the creation of a *presidio* in the Tejas area, believing that the Indians were peaceful and that the soldiers of such a garrison might molest them and interfere with the work of the missionaries. It was this recommendation that the viceroy decided to follow, although he elected to postpone any attempt at civil settlement on the Guadalupe until receiving approval from Spain.[5]

A second mission founded five miles east of Mission San Francisco by Father Jesús María in the fall of 1691, and named Santisimo Nombre de María, was destroyed a few months later by a flood on the Neches River. This disaster was followed by others. The natives proved unwilling converts, an epidemic swept the area killing many of the Indians and at least one of the missionaries. A crop failure caused by the flood and a subsequent drought caused great hardships. Authorities in Mexico failed to provide expected supplies. In the face of increasing Indian intractability Father Massanet changed his previous position and requested the viceroy either to establish a *presidio* or to allow the missionaries to withdraw. Before a party of soldiers could be sent to escort the priests to safety, the Indians began to harrass the mission. On the night of October 25, 1693, Mission San Francisco was put to the torch by Father Massanet, who then fled with his followers to the southwest on the long march to Mexico. The first and brief period of Spanish settlement in East Texas thus ended in complete failure.[6]

Concern for French influence in the lower Mississippi Valley and along the coast of the Gulf of Mexico led to the Spanish settlement of Pensacola in November, 1698. The move proved to have been made just barely in time, for two months later Pierre, Sieur d'Iberville, arrived with a fleet of five vessels obviously intending to settle at the same place. After a polite but strained exchange of messages the French fleet sailed westward to Biloxi Bay to establish a fort. In 1701 Iberville returned, and a year later, on Mobile Bay, constructed Fort Louis, in whose shadow he laid out a little town.[7]

This time there could be no doubt of French intentions to establish control of the mouth of the Mississippi. To nervous officials in Mexico and in Spain itself it seemed more than likely this rival power would seek to expand westward into Texas as well. Their apprehensions appeared to be confirmed in 1713 when Louis Juchereau de St. Denis planted the trading post of Natchitoches on the Red River in what is now western Louisiana. St. Denis then had the temerity to appear the next year at the Rio Grande *presidio* of San Juan Bautista proposing the opening of trade between Louisiana and Mexico.[8]

The ponderous colonial bureaucracy surrounding the viceroy eventually produced a response to this flood of unwelcome news. On April 24, 1716, a column of 25 soldiers, 40 men, women, and children, 8 Franciscan priests, and 3 lay brothers crossed the Rio Grande to begin the re-occupation of Texas.[9] Their orders called for the establishment of several missions and a military outpost. By the end of the following year six missions and a *presidio* in various stages of construction testified to the will and energy of this group. The *presidio* founded by the military leader, Domingo Ramón, was named Nuestra Señora de los Dolores de los Tejas and occupied a site about thirty miles east of the Neches River near the present town of Douglas.[10] On the east bank of the Neches a site was found for the first mission, which took its name in part from the abandoned settlement dating from 1690: San Francisco de los Neches. Nearer the *presidio* and located between the Neches and the Sabine Rivers were four other missions: Nuestra Señora de la Purísima Concepción, San José de los Nazones, Nuestra Señora de Guadalupe de los Nacogdoches, and Nuestra Señora de los Dolores de los Ais. East of the Sabine and midway to Red River—only a few miles from the French inland post of Natchitoches—stood a sixth mission, San Miguel de los Adaes.[11]

Founding missions and a *presidio* was one thing; keeping them supplied, and the missions protected from both Indians and the French, was another. Ramón and the missionaries wrote the viceroy asking for additional soldiers and for items that could be used as gifts to the Indians, who were already receiving such favors from the French in what was to become a competition between the two powers to secure native cooperation.

The new viceroy, the Marqués de Valero, received an offer from Father Antonio de Sanbuenaventura y Olivares to locate a mission on the San Antonio River. Father Olivares suggested that a few soldiers would also be needed, and that some farmers and craftsmen at the site would be helpful as well. The viceroy's advisers urged him to accept this offer but proposed also that a *presidio* be founded with the mission on the San Antonio River and that a second stronghold be established on the coast at Espíritu Santo (Matagorda) Bay. Accepting the advice,

Valero named Martín de Alarcón to carry out this plan to create an intermediate base between Mexico and the East Texas settlements.[12]

While Alarcón received his appointment as captain-general and governor of Texas in December, 1716, it was not until April, 1718, that he set out on his expedition. The viceroy had instructed him to recruit 50 married soldiers, a carpenter, mason, blacksmith, and a weaver and with livestock and supplies to proceed to the San Antonio River. With Father Olivares, Alarcón was to found one or two missions and assign ten soldiers as a mission guard. Two towns were eventually to be settled in the region through which the San Antonio, Guadalupe, and Colorado rivers flowed, but for the time being only one was to be established near the missions on the San Antonio. He was then to proceed to East Texas.[13]

Impatient with the time taken by Alarcón in preparing for the expedition, Olivares was not on the best of terms with the governor, but with his missionaries he met Alarcón on May 1 at the San Antonio River, and the two men immediately selected a site for the mission a short distance from the west bank of the river at the San Pedro Springs. Five days later, as Alarcón's chaplain records, "the governor, in the name of his Majesty, took possession of the place called San Antonio, . . . and it was given the name of villa de Bejar." Apparently neither the town nor the *presidio* was surveyed at this time, since the account states only that "this site is henceforth destined for the civil settlement and the soldiers who are to guard it."[14]

Even the site of the mission, San Antonio de Valero, on the banks of San Pedro Creek was not firmly fixed, since it was shortly to be moved twice before a permanent location was found.

Alarcón then departed for East Texas. He found conditions far from promising. Ramón and some of his men had been ill, several of the soldiers had deserted, the missionaries found the Indians as reluctant as ever to live under mission supervision, and there were rumors that the French post at Natchitoches was to be strengthened. Ramón had moved the *presidio* closer to the mission of San Francisco de los Texas, thus abandoning whatever work had previously been accomplished in erecting suitable fortifications on the original site. All this Alarcón reported to his superiors on his return to Mexico in January, 1719.[15]

The precariousness of the Spanish position was demonstrated in June, 1719, when eight French soldiers appeared at the mission of San Miguel de los Adaes and captured the single soldier stationed there and a lay brother who was in charge in the absence of the mission priest. The war between France and Spain, begun in January of that year and

including a French attack on Spanish Pensacola in mid-May, had come
to Texas. The episode has a comic opera air. Officials in Spain had apparently neglected to inform the viceroy of the war. The only effective
defenders at San Miguel proved to be a flock of chickens. Frightened by
the strangers, they clucked and flapped their wings in flight. This startled the French captain's horse, who reared and threw his rider. In the
confusion the lay brother escaped to Mission Dolores spreading the
alarm and the story that 100 French soldiers were marching to Natchitoches and that the Spanish were to be driven out of Texas.

Ramón led a retreat to Mission San Francisco on the Neches River.
Although two missionaries returned to Mission Concepción for a time,
by the middle of July all the Spaniards had withdrawn still further to a
camp on the Trinity River. When no reinforcements arrived by the beginning of fall the entire party began the long march westward to
the new mission of San Antonio de Valero, which they reached by
December.[16]

In Mexico City the viceroy, the Marqués de Valero, already had
begun plans for strengthening Texas. News of the abandonment of the
East Texas missions and *presidio* provided added motivation. He appointed an experienced soldier, the wealthy José Virto de Vera, Marqués de Aguayo, to assemble an army, secure Matagorda Bay by the
construction of a *presidio*, restore the missions in East Texas, and build a
second *presidio* on the frontier between Texas and Louisiana.[17]

Aguayo ultimately succeeded in raising a force of 500 men; 6 cannon;
800 mules loaded with arms, clothing, and food; 4,000 horses; 600 head
of cattle; and 900 sheep. All this took time, and it was not until the
spring of 1721 that this impressive array of men, supplies, and livestock
arrived at the San Antonio River. Aguayo had previously reinforced
that settlement with a detachment of 84 soldiers in 1719 and in late 1720
or early 1721 a still larger force of 116 men.[18]

By that time a second mission had been established by the missionaries who had evacuated their establishments in East Texas. This
had been accomplished with the permission of Aguayo in 1720, and its
name, San José y San Miguel de Aguayo, was selected in his honor.
Captain Juan Valdez and Father Antonio Margil chose a site three
leagues, or roughly 7½ miles south of mission San Antonio de Valero
on the east bank of the San Antonio River. In the presence of the Indians Captain Valdez turned the land over to the Franciscans. Plans
were made for the *plaza mayor*, a public square more than 300 feet
square, streets of uniform width on which the Indians were to build
their houses, and for a church, hospital, jail, and cemetery.[19]

From San Antonio Aguayo dispatched a force of 40 men under Captain José Domingo Ramón to take possession of Espíritu Santo (Matagorda) Bay, which the Spanish feared might be occupied by the French. Ramón reported his unopposed occupation of the area early in April, 1721. A month later Aguayo began his march to the east. Movement of such a force proved slow and difficult; it took 16 days to cross the Trinity River, and not until the end of July did the column reach the site of the first mission of San Francisco de los Tejas abandoned in 1693.[20]

Aguayo proceeded slowly to the west bank of the Neches River and made camp near the site of Ramón's temporary *presidio* of 1716. There he received a visit from Louis St. Denis, then commander of the French fort at Natchitoches. St. Denis informed Aguayo that France and Spain had negotiated a truce, but Aguayo responded that while he would not initiate any hostilities he was determined to carry out his orders to re-establish the missions and erect *presidios*. By the end of August this had been accomplished, although Aguayo shifted the sites for two of the missions.[21]

We can only assume that each mission took the usual form of an enclosed square or *plaza* on which fronted the church and other buildings. No plans or other graphic evidence of their form seem to have survived. For the *presidios*, however, our information includes precise drawings of their layout. First to receive attention was the *presidio* de Los Dolores de los Tejas, which was ordered rebuilt on its old site a mile and a quarter from Mission Concepción on August 15.[22]

Aguayo described this event in a later report sent to the king: "Having re-established five missions, building anew the churches and living quarters of the padres, I built in the center of them a presidio for their protection (drawing plans for the fortification to meet the needs of the twenty-five men designated as its garrison)."[23] Figure 3.1 reproduces its plan as published in Mexico City a year later. The site was on a hill overlooking a branch of the Angelina River. It took the form of a square stockade 60 *varas* (about 165 feet) on each side, with two projecting bulwarks at opposite corners. Four short, diagonal streets led from the square parade ground to the bulwarks and the other two corners of the fortification. A single gate at the northeastern corner opened to a street separating the stockade from the barracks, officers' quarters, storehouses, and magazine.

The second *presidio* erected by Aguayo was far more impressive. On the road to Natchitoches, only about 18 miles from the French fort, and a short distance beyond the easternmost mission, Morfi tells us "the marquis established the presidio, the foundations of which gave considerable trouble, it being necessary to dig them with bars in the solid rock."[24]

The plan of this fort appears in Figure 3.2, following the description provided by Father Juan Antonio Peña, the chaplain of the expedition: "On the top of . . . [an] elevation, which commanded the whole plain his lordship laid out and began at once to build the fortification. He gave it the form of a hexagon, making each side about fifty-five yards long. He left three bastions unconstructed and made the other three smaller than he had planned. These he placed at the alternate corners so that each should protect two sides of the fort."[25]

Aguayo designed the Presidio of Nuestra Señora del Pilar for a garrison of 100 men. Thirty-one had brought their families with them, and Aguayo intended, as Morfi observes, that "these, and such others as might come later, should gradually form a settlement, without causing new expense to the royal treasury." They were to have ample protection. The stockade constructed of pointed logs was eight feet high, the bastions were "protected by earthworks," which were to "be replaced by stone defenses." In each bastion Aguayo installed "two small cannon mounted in such a manner as to protect two curtains."[26]

Los Adaes *presidio* became the capital of Spanish Texas from which 13 colonial governors administered the province until 1773. Although no *pueblo* or *villa* was ever formally established as a civil settlement, the community functioned as a trading point, market town, and supply base as well as a fortress. A few earthen mounds on the site about two miles northeast of Robeline, Louisiana, are the only remains of Aguayo's accomplishment in asserting Spanish hegemony over the region.

Aguayo founded two other *presidios* before his work was done and he returned to Mexico to receive from the king the rank of field marshal as a reward for his accomplishments. Reaching San Antonio in January, 1722, after terrible hardships, he determined to relocate that *presidio* on a new site between San Pedro Creek and the west bank of the San Antonio River. Morfi tells us that "the ground being thickly covered by trees, he had it cleared and the necessary timber for the church, storehouse, and soldiers' quarters fashioned." Then, "after a considerable number of mud bricks had been made, he outlined a square seventy-three varas [200 feet] on each side, and had four bastions built, one on each corner."[27] Figure 3.3 shows Aguayo's design for this fort, with a gate at the south opposite the military chapel. Three rows of buildings, the outermost forming the curtain walls, surrounded the

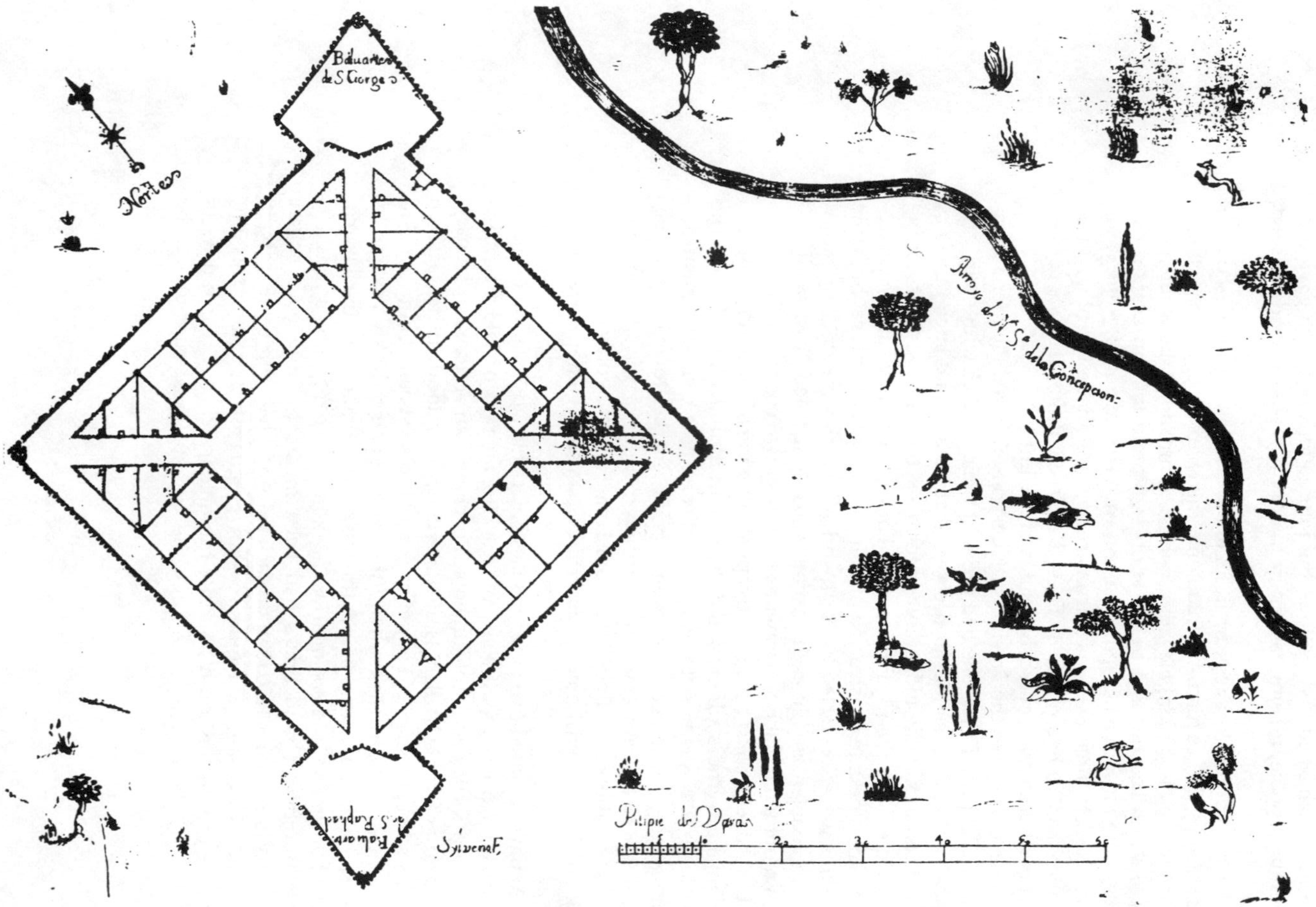

Figure 3.1 Plan of the Presidio of Los Dolores de Los Tejas in East Texas: 1722

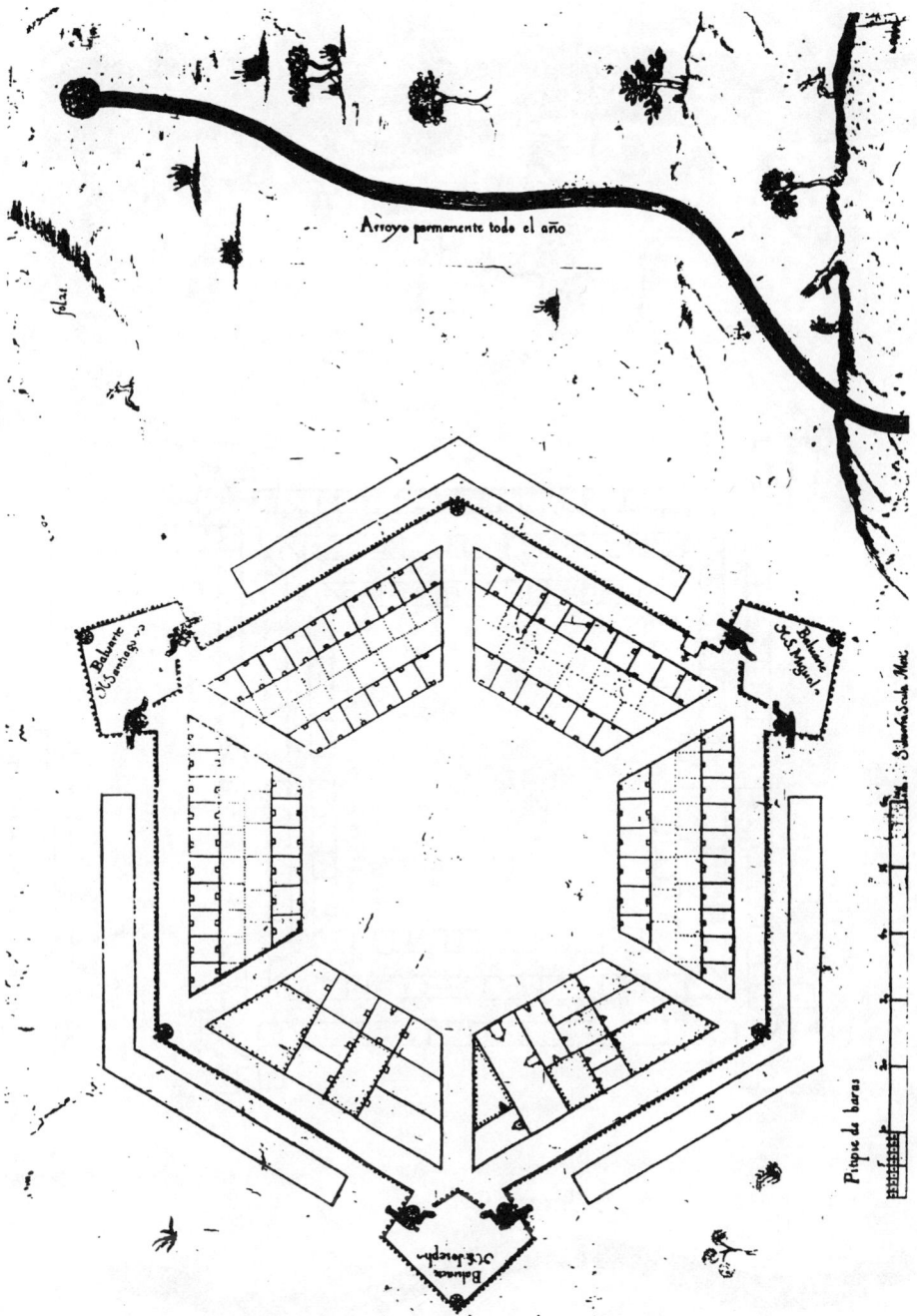

Within the figure:

Arroyo permanente todo el año

Baluarte N.S. Santiago

Baluarte N.S. Miguel

Baluarte N.S. Joseph

Petipie de baras

Figure 3.2 Plan of the Presidio of Los Adaes, Robeline, Louisiana: 1722

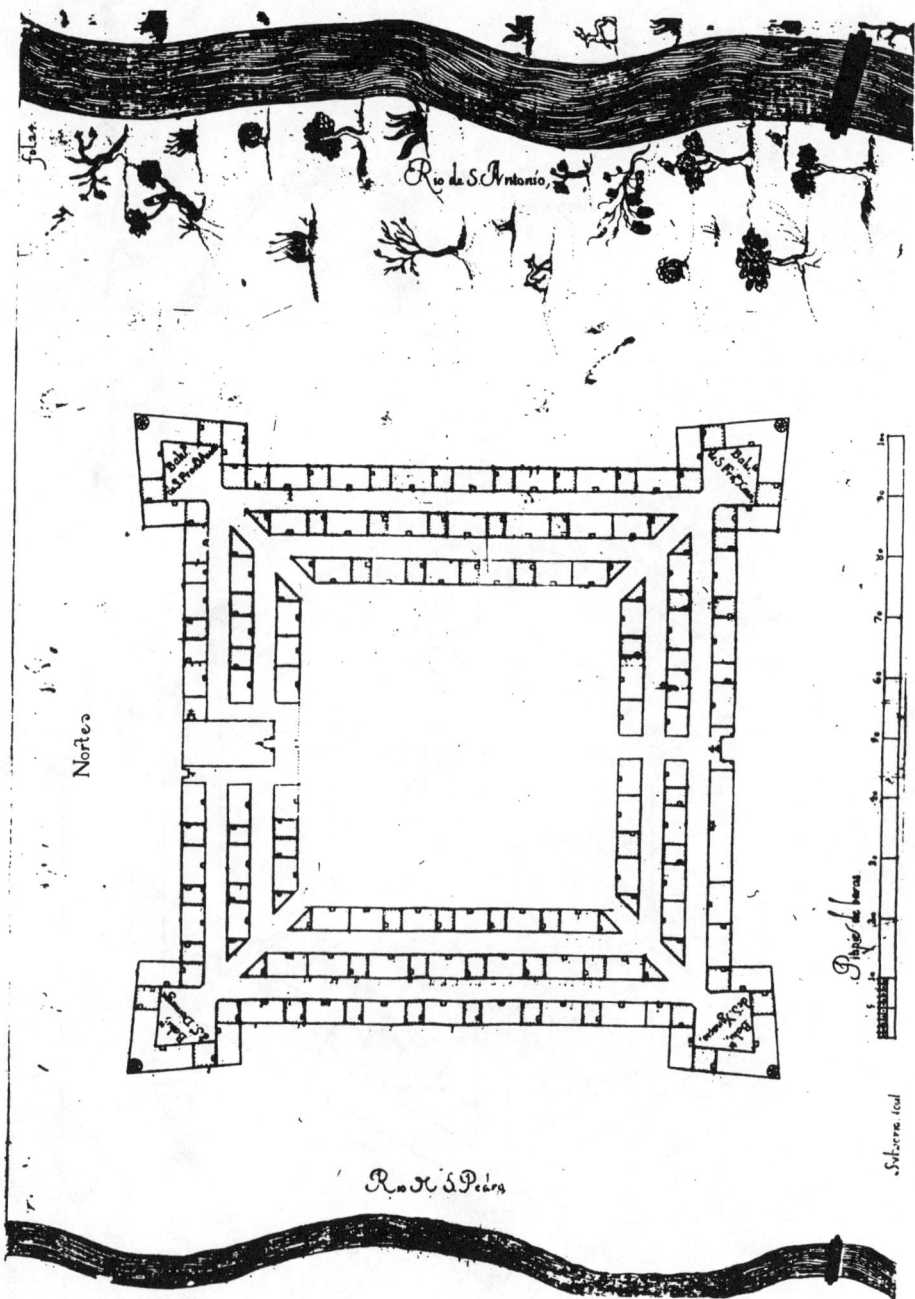

Figure 3.3 Plan of the Presidio of San Antonio de Bejar, San Antonio, Texas: 1722

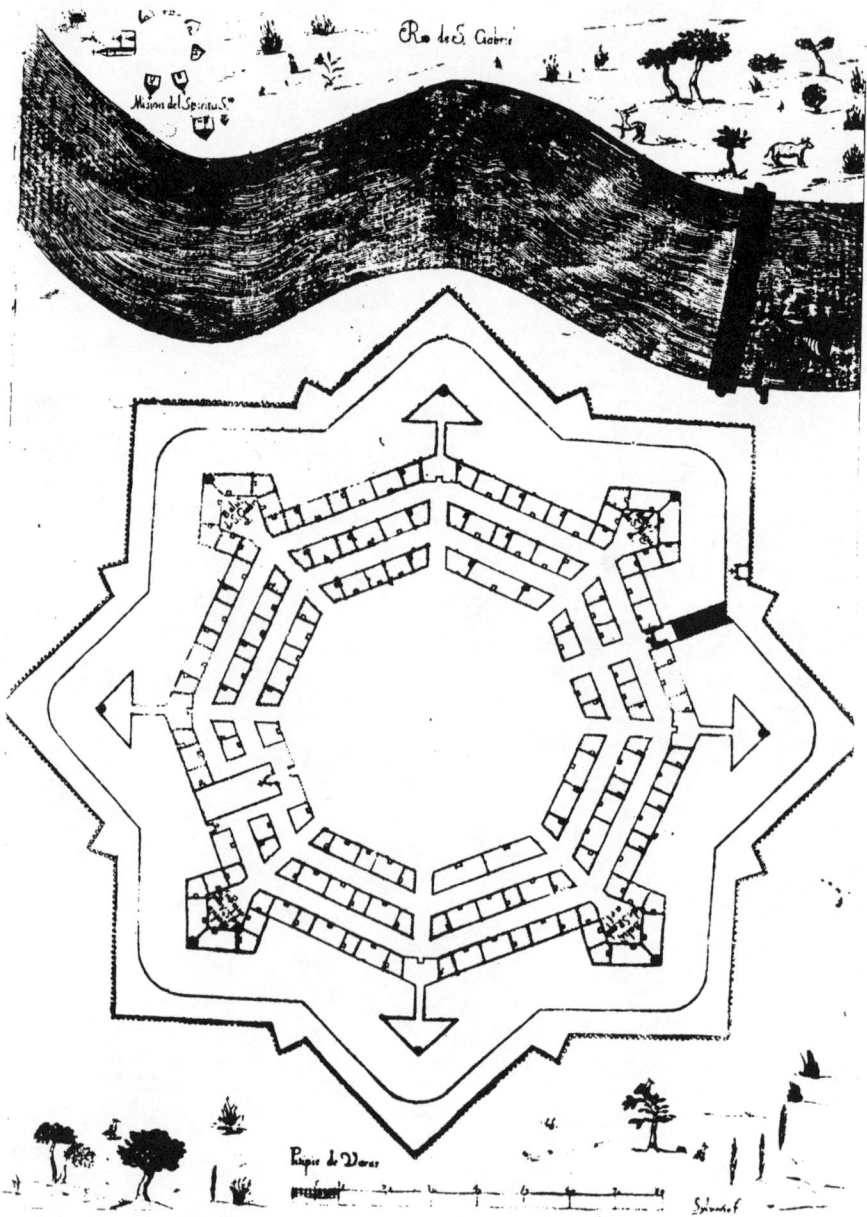

Figure 3.4   Plan of the Presidio of Loreto en la Bahia del Espiritu Santo, Matagorda Bay, Texas: 1722

square parade ground, with short diagonal streets leading from it to the bulwarks at the four corners. Probably the outer walls were of adobe. Although in the course of construction rain ruined 30,000 adobe bricks, the governor "immediately ordered twenty-five thousand more made," paying "out of his own pocket" the "forty laborers" set to work on this project.[28]

At San Antonio Aguayo also founded a third mission, the short-lived San Francisco Xavier de Nájera. The chosen location lay about two and a half miles south of the Mission San Antonio de Valero, which by that time had been moved to a second site on the east bank of the San Antonio River, and which in 1727 was to be shifted "two gun shots" to the south to its present site.[29] Within a few years the new mission failed for lack of funds, and the Indians came under the jurisdiction of Mission San Antonio de Valero.[30]

Aguayo then set out for the Gulf coast to lay out the most elaborate of the four *presidios* he founded. Again, we turn to Morfi for some details of its location and design: "The second day after Easter, April 6, the lines for the fort were laid down on the same spot where La Salle had constructed his. While excavating the foundations, nails, firelocks, and fragments of guns were found, and the place where the artillery had been buried and the powder burned was discovered. The foundations for the new structure were dug in fifteen days. These formed an octagon, with a moat all around and four bastions, to which was added a tower. Each curtain was forty-five varas [124 feet] in length."[31]

The plan of this imposing fortification as published later that year is reproduced in Figure 3.4. Aguayo selected an equally impressive name: Presidio de Nuestra Señora de Loreto en la Bahía del Espíritu Santo. La Bahía is the mercifully shortened title by which it was known, both at this site and at its other two locations.

Aguayo clearly intended this spot to be a major colonial settlement. He established a garrison there of 90 soldiers, and across the Garcitas Creek he founded still another mission known as Nuestra Señora del Espíritu Santo de Zúniga. Its location can be seen in the upper left corner of the *presidio* plan. Further, on his return to Mexico, Aguayo recommended to the king that 400 families—half from the Canary Islands or Cuba and an equal number of native Mexicans—be sent immediately to settle at La Bahía, San Antonio, and in East Texas. Unless this was done, he asserted, "it will be most difficult if not impossible, for that province to be self-supporting."[32] He found a sympathetic reader, for the king issued a *cédula* on May 10, 1723, ordering the transfer of 200 families from the Canary Islands for that purpose. Although this was not carried out, a second order issued February 14, 1729, increased the number to 400 families.[33] It was a partial execution of this royal decree that led to the formal establishment of the first civil settlement in Texas at San Antonio.[34]

Aguayo's settlement pattern of missions and *presidios* soon underwent substantial modifications. At La Bahía lax military discipline, Indian hostilities, and crop failures led Governor Pérez de Almazán to relocate both the fort and the mission in 1726. The spot selected lay on the Guadalupe River about 50 miles northwest of the end of Matagorda Bay.[35]

More drastic changes soon occurred. Viceroy Juan de Acuña, Marqués de Casafuerte, concerned over the mounting costs of maintaining the *presidios* on the northern frontier, appointed General Pedro de Rivera in 1724 to inspect the entire region and report on what adjustments might be made. Rivera's tour required three and a half years. After leaving Texas he submitted his report to Casafuerte in 1728. The report recommended reduction of the garrisons at Los Adaes, La Bahía, and San Antonio, and the abandonment of Los Dolores de los Tejas.[36]

Casafuerte implemented these recommendations the following year. His order closing the *presidio* of los Tejas, issued in April, 1729, caused consternation in the missions located between the Neches and Sabine rivers because this would deprive them of protection from Indian attacks and make maintenance of mission discipline virtually impossible. Protests from mission authorities were to no avail, but a request to relocate missions Concepción, San Francisco, and San José on the Colorado River, well to the west of their existing locations, received approval. By mid-1730 this had been accomplished, but a year later all three were withdrawn further westward to the San Antonio River near the existing *presidio* and mission settlements.[37] Fourteen years of patient, if largely ineffective work was thus abandoned.

Although Rivera severely criticized Aguayo's earlier accomplishments, the two men agreed on one matter—the absolute necessity of attracting civilian settlers to Texas. Rivera earlier had "pointed out how important it was to settle twenty-five families in the . . . presidio of San Antonio" in a communication to Viceroy Casafuerte. In his report of 1728 this point came up again: "I now repeat this recommendation, supporting my statement with the reason that moved me to insist upon the plan. The location being so fertile and pleasant, as I have described it, it is particularly suited for the settlement of twenty-five families, who would fully protect the land and induce others to imitate them in settling such other sites as many seem convenient."[38]

Rivera's proposal was merely the latest of many similar plans that had been advanced over the years for civil settlement in Texas.[39] And although they were accepted, it required three years to put them into effect. Casafuerte first learned of Spain's approval of the policy when at the end of 1729 he received word that families from the Canary Islands would be sent to Veracruz by way of Havana and that they were to be escorted to La Bahía, San Antonio, and Los Adaes.

The viceroy turned to Rivera for advice, and on January 16, 1730, the general submitted a long report suggesting possible settlement locations. When news came that the Canary Islanders had landed at Havana, Rivera proposed moving them to San Antonio. Casafuerte's other advisers concurred. The viceroy then asked Aguayo for suggestions concerning the exact location at San Antonio most appropriate for a municipality.[40]

Aguayo replied in a long communication accompanied by the map reproduced in Figure 3.5. For a man with Aguayo's military experience and firsthand familiarity with the area, this map is a curious piece of work. It contains many errors, and even the compass directions are incorrect since north is to the left rather than as shown on the drawing. The loop in the San Antonio River opposite Mission San Antonio de Valero is shown extending to the west rather than eastward. The *presidio* had been located by Aguayo almost directly west of the loop between the river and San Pedro Creek, and, by 1730 when Aguayo prepared this sketch from memory, Mission San José had been moved from the location shown to the other side of the river. The other principal element, identified as Villa de San Antonio de Casafuerte, represented Aguayo's proposal to locate the civil settlement on the eastern bank of the San Antonio River. When Rivera examined this map he pointed out its flaws and proposed that the new town should be located "a musket shot" west of the *presidio* on a low, flat hill that he had earlier earmarked as a desirable spot for a town.[41]

Casafuerte accepted this recommendation as well as Rivera's other suggestion, made earlier, that it would be better to people Texas with settlers from Mexico than from Spain or the Canary Islands. The viceroy accordingly wrote the king advising him to discontinue recruitment of additional families. It is difficult to understand the motives for this action. Its effect was to stop what promised to be a successful attempt at providing perhaps two thousand settlers so badly needed for the underpopulated province. Fifteen of the promised 400 additional families were detained in Cuba, and only a little group of less than 60 persons from the Canary Islands were brought from Cuba to Mexico and then escorted to San Antonio.[42]

The long march began on November 15, 1730, and it was not until March 9 of the next year that the settlers reached their destination.

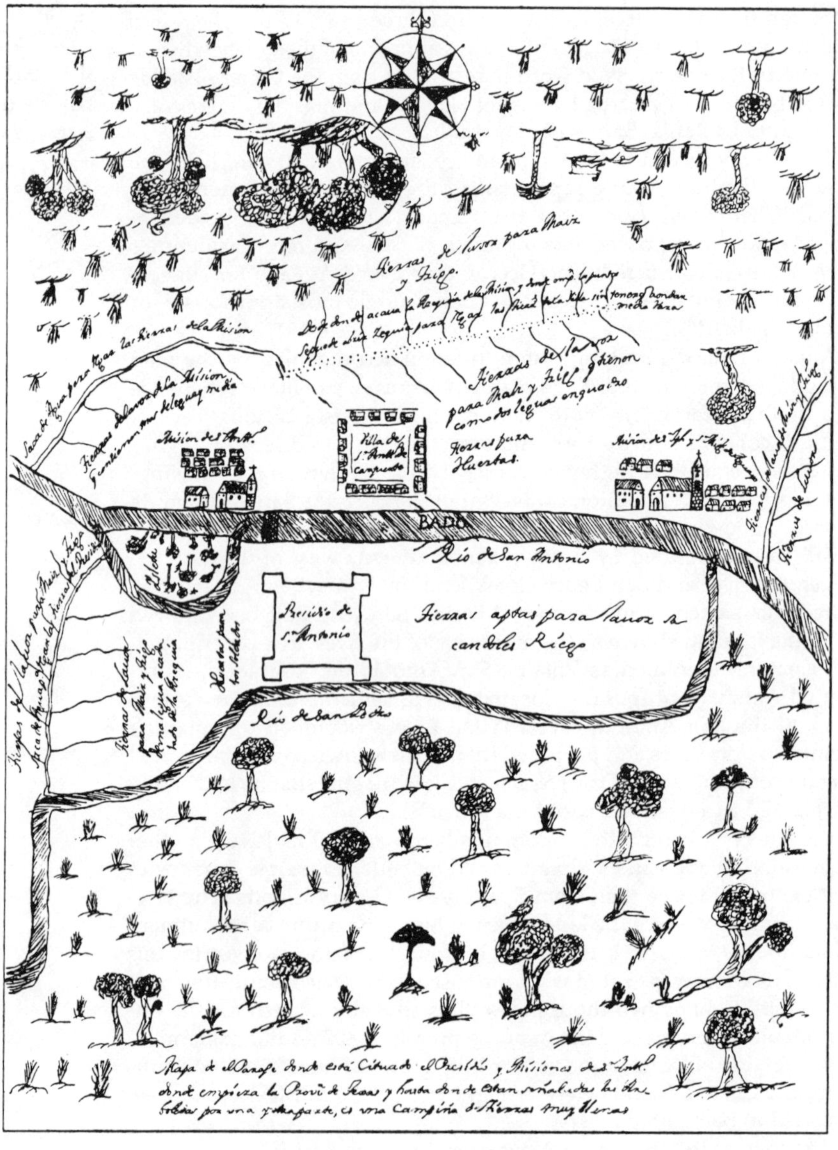

Figure 3.5 Map of San Antonio, Texas and Vicinity: 1730

Viceroy Casafuerte had issued long and highly detailed orders covering all aspects of the project, listing the supplies to be furnished the party, directing them to be given temporary lodging in the *presidio* until they could construct their own accommodations.

Most important for our inquiry were the instructions issued to the governor or, in his absence, the captain of the *presidio* for the selection of the site and planning of the town. The location west of the *presidio* recommended by Rivera was to be used. On this spot the official in charge was ordered to "survey the land, lay off the streets, the town blocks, the main plaza, and the site for the church, the priest's house, the public hall, and the other buildings shown in the map which is sent with these instructions."[43]

The map referred to appears in Figure 3.6. The instructions that it accompanied required that all land grants be made in accordance with the Laws of the Indies, and it is evident that the laws also governed most features of the proposed town plan. The orientation of the streets so that the corners of the rectangular blocks faced the cardinal points of the compass were as specified in the laws. So, too, was the dimension of the plaza, which, if the bordering streets were included, measured exactly 400 by 600 Spanish feet mentioned in the laws as appropriate for "a well proportioned medium size plaza." The plan also showed an arcade (*portales*) around the plaza as called for in the laws.

The drawing prescribed a uniform street width of 40 feet (about 37 English feet, the Spanish "pie" or foot being approximately 11.1 inches). Blocks of three different dimensions were to be used. The two largest blocks, each 320 feet square, faced the ends of the plaza. That at the northeast was intended for the church, and the one opposite for the "Royal Palace" or government building. Four smaller blocks, 240 feet square, also faced the plaza, one of which was to be occupied by the grain market. Additional blocks of this size and others 240 by 320 feet were to be laid out, and one block given to each family.

The instructions specified that the surveyor should then lay out the commons, the pasture lands, and the farm tracts. The entire unit would consist of a series of great squares. The inner square for the town itself was to have the church door as its center and to measure 2186 *varas* (about 6,000 feet) on each side (1093 *varas* in each direction from the church). The surveyor was to mark this boundary between the town and the commons with a plowed furrow "in order that willows and other trees may be planted to mark out the four sides of the area of the inner town. They will serve not only to beautify it, but as soon as they grow to the height of a man their branches will furnish shade to the

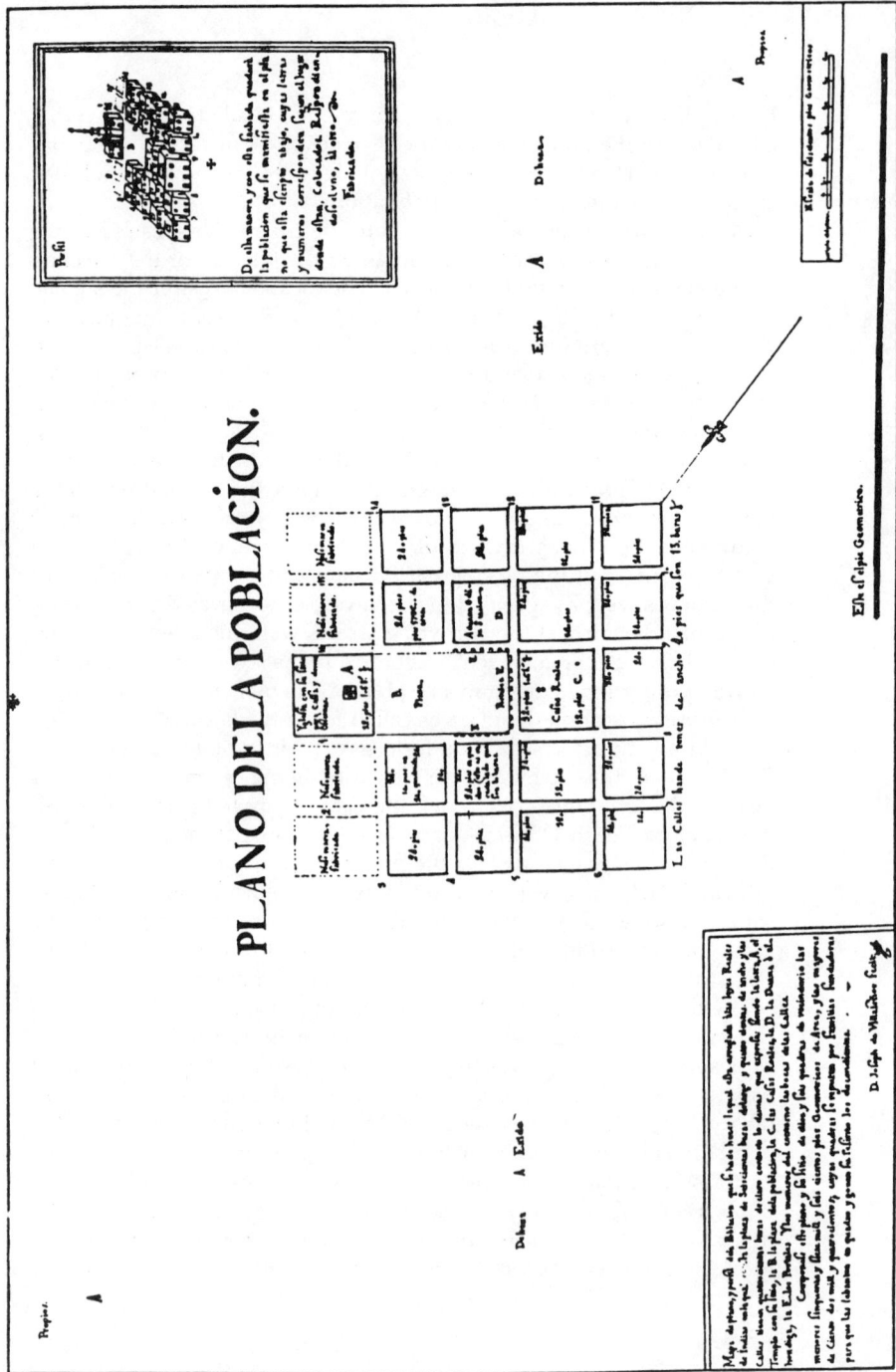

Figure 3.6 Plan of San Antonio. Texas: 1730

444

settlers." The outer boundary of the commons was to lie 1,093 *varas* beyond this point on each side. The sides of the square for the pasture lands were to be surveyed parallel to these lines 2,186 *varas* farther away, and the farm fields were to occupy the area an equal distance beyond. The entire urban-rural unit would thus have an area of just under 12 square miles, the outer boundaries being a square slightly under 3½ miles on each side.[44]

It should have been obvious to the viceroy and his advisers that, if the town lands had been surveyed in this manner, their boundaries would have encroached on the domain of Mission San Antonio de Valero as well as on the site of the *presidio*. This issue became more of a problem when Captain Juan Antonio Pérez de Almazán, the commander of the *presidio*, decided that the site designated for the town west of the fort was unsuitable because the lands could not easily be irrigated. He selected as a substitute location the land immediately to the east of the *presidio* and including the area within the eastward loop of the San Antonio River.

The common, pasture, and farm lands could not be located as prescribed in the instructions, and these outlying portions of the settlement were surveyed instead in a roughly triangular pattern with the approximately north-south alignment of the San Antonio River as the base. The specified distances between the boundaries of the town, the commons, the pastures, and the farms were increased, however, to provide the same area of land for each purpose as described in the instructions.[45]

Almazán also found it necessary to modify substantially the design of the town itself when on July 2, 1731, he assembled the settlers for this purpose. The plan sent from Mexico showed the church facing southwest from one end of the elongated plaza. The captain felt the best site for this structure was immediately to the east of the *presidio*, and therefore the plaza could not extend westward without encroaching on the fortifications. His solution was to turn the church in the other direction so that its entrance was on the east side, lay out the plaza in this direction and place the church almost adjacent to the *presidio*.

In the report describing what he accomplished Almazán stated that he laid out a plaza 200 by 133⅓ *varas* (555 by 370 feet) east of the church, two blocks facing the plaza on both it north and south sides, and three streets leading to the plaza on those two sides. The northeastern block was set aside for the *aduana* or grain market. Other blocks were then surveyed 80 *varas* or 222 feet on each side, with all the streets made 13⅓ *varas* or 37 feet wide. Opposite the church, occupying the entire block at its western and shorter side, he provided a site for the *casa real* or government house.[46]

It is not entirely clear if Almazán used an east-west orientation or the northeast-southwest axis for the plaza prescribed by his instructions. His statement seems to indicate the latter, but this appears at variance with all subsequent maps, plans, and surveys of the town. The only detailed eighteenth-century plan of the new *villa* reveals other departures from the captain's instructions and his report of how he planned San Antonio.

This is reproduced in Figure 3.7, a manuscript map drawn about 1777. The drawing reverses conventional orientation, for north is at the bottom, and the church thus faces east to the plaza. Here the plaza appears as a square, about 80 *varas* or 222 feet on each side including the boundary streets. The streets scale approximately 10 *varas* in width, or less than 28 feet. Most of the blocks appear to be about 60 *varas* square, or 166½ feet on each side. The smaller blocks around the edges of the town are shown one-half or one-fourth this size. If this drawing is an accurate representation of the town at the time it was made, one possible explanation for these discrepancies is that major changes and adjustments to the town plan were carried out some time between 1731 and 1777. The only other possibility is that it represents a proposed replanning of the community.

Some weight is given to this latter view by the description written by Morfi, probably late in 1777, to whose manuscript *History of Texas* this map is attached: "On the west bank of the San Antonio river . . . is situated the villa of San Fernando and the presidio of San Antonio de Béxar, with no other division between them than the parochial church. . . . The town consists of fifty-nine houses of stone and mud and seventy-nine of wood, but all poorly built, without any preconceived plan, so that the whole resembles more a poor village than a villa, capital of so pleasing a province. . . . The streets are tortuous and are filled with mud the minute it rains."[47] Certainly this scornful description and the neat regularity of the drawing do not correspond.

A second map of the area that was eventually to become the city of San Antonio is reproduced in Figure 3.8, a general survey of the *presidio* and *villa* on the west bank of the San Antonio River opposite Mission San Antonio de Valero east of the loop in the river. It also shows the other four missions, two on each side of the river, south of the first three establishments. The parochial church can just be discerned standing in the center of what appears to be a large quadrangle. This was in reality divided into two plazas, that of the *presidio* on the lower or west-

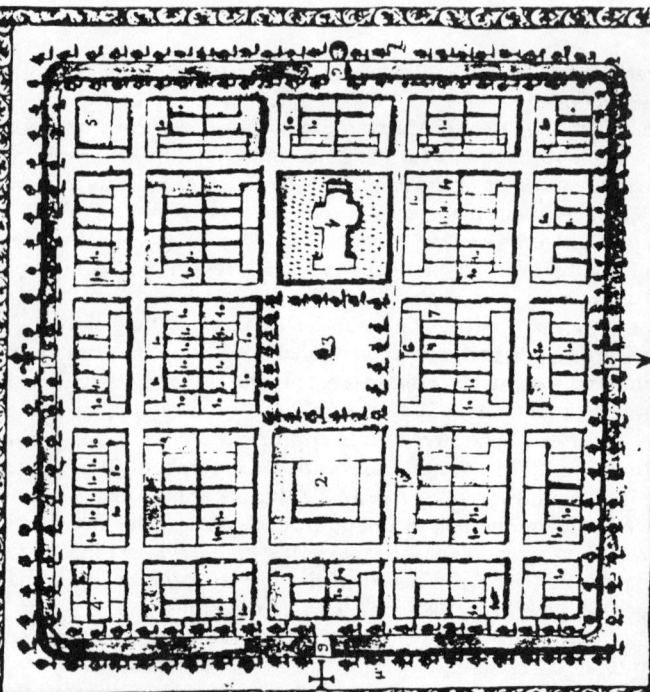

Figure 3.7 Plan of San Antonio, Texas: ca. 1777

448

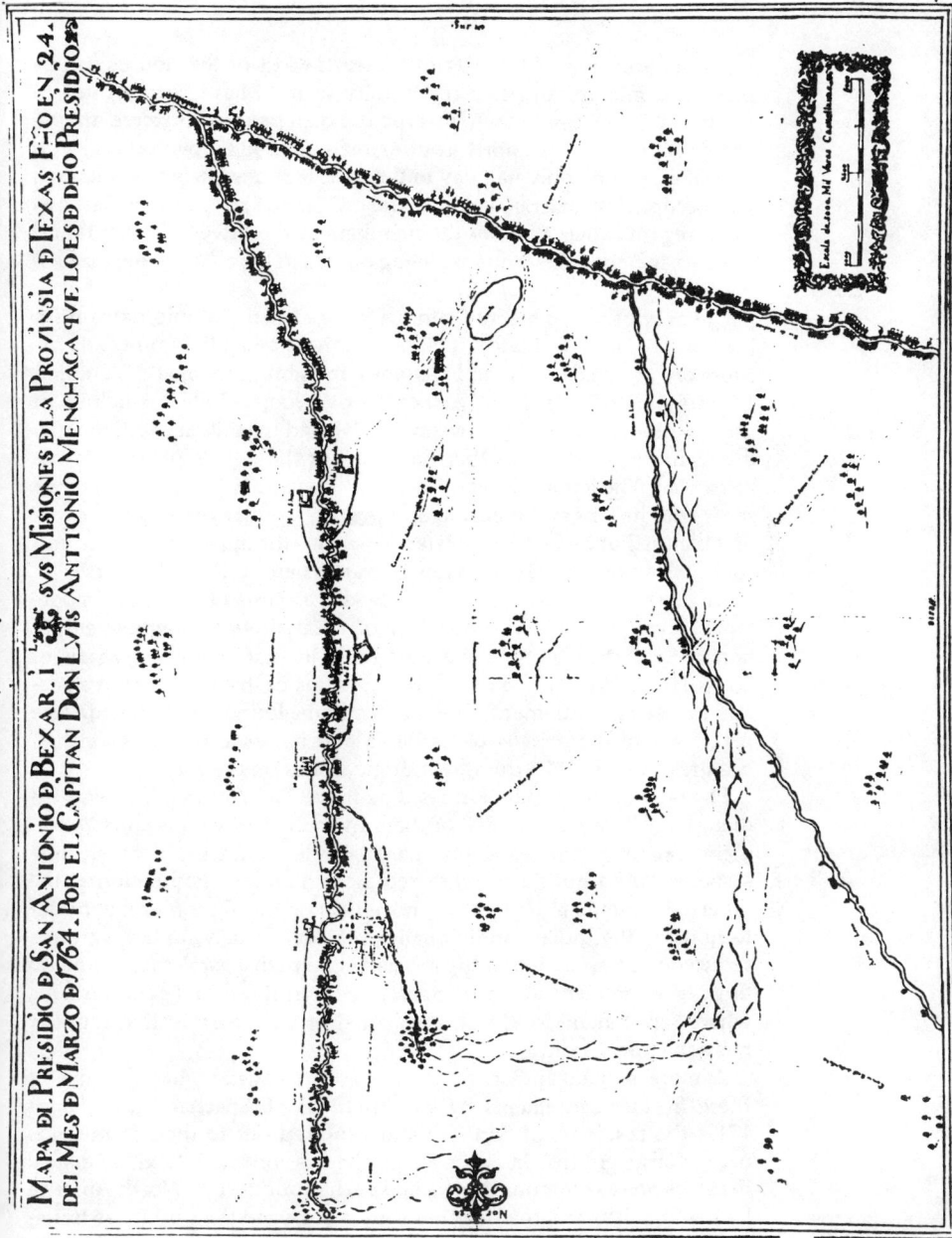

Figure 3.8
Map of
San Antonio,
Texas and
Vicinity: 1764

ern side, and that of the *villa* to the east. Most of the houses in this combined military and civil community seem to have been located to the north of the *presidio*, where structures can be seen clustered among three roughly parallel, north-south streets crossed by two others, with a third extending only halfway to the east. It seems likely that this area was occupied by married soldiers and civilians attracted to the San Antonio region rather than by the members of the fifteen Canary Island families and their descendants living on lots in the *villa* planned by Almazán.

The only other eighteenth-century map of San Antonio dates from 1767. Reproduced in Plate 4, it shows in more detail the immediate vicinity of the *presidio*, *villa*, and the oldest mission—incorrectly identified as "Mission de San Joseph" east of the river loop. While it is helpful in showing the relationship between the civil and the military settlements, this map introduces a further doubt about the details of the original town plan. The letter "D" identifies the "Plaza de la Villa," but here we see it with its longer dimension on the north-south axis! Whatever was first planned or had occurred later, however, the approximate size and shape of the two plazas shown here was to persist in future years.

Small as it was, San Antonio enjoyed the status of the most important settlement in the vast province of Texas. It was an almost empty honor, for there existed few competitors. In East Texas the *presidio* of Los Adaes and the three remaining missions of the area formed a second nucleus of settlement. The third could be found on the Guadalupe River, where the *presidio* of La Bahía and its associated mission had been relocated in 1726 from their original sites on the coast.

The bulk of the population residing in the San Antonio area was Indian. In 1740 more than 800 of them lived in the five missions.[48] Soldiers and their families, the Canary Islanders, and the Spanish missionaries could not have numbered more than 200. Population at the other settlements must have been well below this figure. Frequent defections by the Indians individually and, occasionally, in large groups reduced the population in the missions and native *pueblos* from time to time. This problem was particularly acute in the East Texas missions where few Indians could be persuaded or coerced into living under mission supervision.

A more serious Indian problem was the constant harrassment of these frontier settlements by various tribes of Apaches. In the mid-1740s the residents of San Antonio ventured out to their farm fields only in large groups. Indian raids on the mission lands to kill and steal livestock were common. Horses had been introduced to North America by the Spanish, and the Apaches soon recognized their utility as trans-

portation for war parties that could strike swiftly and withdraw to
safety. Guns provided by both the Spanish and the French made the
Indians an even greater menace.[49] Punitive forays by Spanish soldiers
brought temporary relief, but Indian hostility remained a constant
threat.

Attempts to pacify the Indians through missionary activity in the region north of the San Antonio met with little success. On the San
Xavier River (now the San Gabriel) missionaries of the College of Santa
Cruz established a provisional mission in 1746. Late in the next year
they succeeded in obtaining approval from the viceroy to found three
missions under the protection of a detachment of soldiers: San Francisco Xavier de Horcasitas, San Ildefonso, and Nuestra Señora de la
Candelaria. The missionaries also advocated the establishment of a civil
settlement, but this was never approved. In 1751 the *presidio* of San
Francisco Xavier was formally established in the area with a garrison of
50 soldiers. This venture proved short-lived. Indian attacks and hostilities between the missionaries and the *presidio* commander caused the
abandonment of the site and a temporary relocation of mission activities to the San Marcos River in 1755. Two years later the soldiers and
missionaries were withdrawn from this location as well.[50]

While the San Xavier settlements passed through their brief and
bleak existence on the edge of the northern frontier, a whole series of
new missions and civil settlements was being successfully planted
along the valley of the lower Rio Grande under the skillful direction of
José de Escandón. In 1746 Viceroy Revilla Gigedo directed him to explore the hitherto unsettled region from Tampico, Mexico, to the mouth
of the San Antonio River, an area to become known as Nuevo Santander.[51] His exhaustive tour of inspection of the new colony was followed
by a detailed report containing a series of recommendations.

Escandón proposed to take 500 families from the settled parts of
Mexico and to settle them in 14 new towns. A number of missions
would also be established. His plan called for two of these towns to be
located north of the Rio Grande: the Villa de Vedoya composed of 50
families and located on the lower Nueces near what is now Corpus
Christi; and the Villa de Balmaceda with 25 families on the lower San
Antonio River to the site of which would be moved the *presidio* and mission of La Bahía. Shortage of funds and the hostility of Indians at the
Nueces River site prevented Escandón from carrying out these proposals except for the transfer of the two La Bahía settlements. In all other
respects his colonization efforts that began in December, 1748, succeeded admirably. Seven years after he had prepared the map in Figure
3.9 to accompany his report he stated that he had founded 1 city,

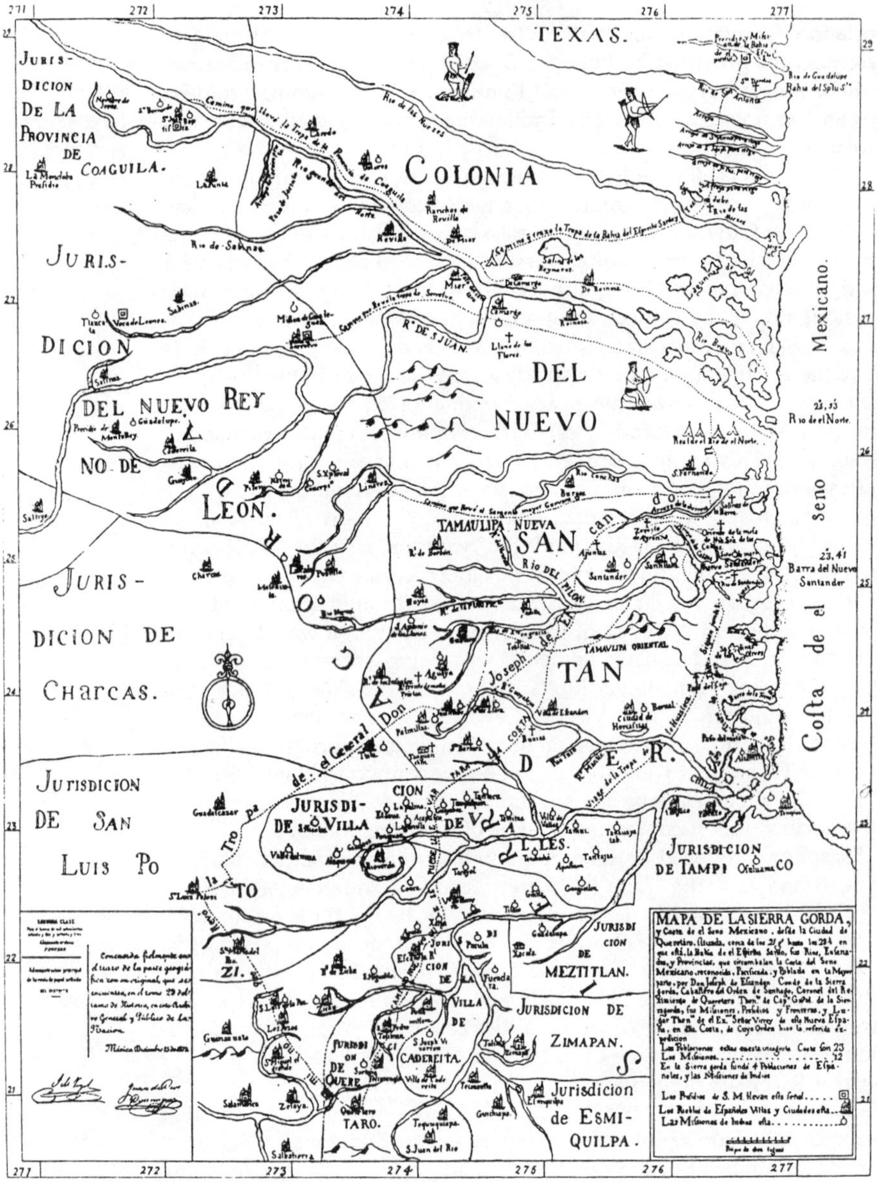

Figure 3.9 Map of the Northeastern Part of Mexico and the Adjoining Area in Texas: 1755

17 *villas*, 3 military settlements, 2 mining camps, and 15 missions. Settlers flocked to join the expedition. Nearly 700 families and 750 soldiers moved northward in a huge column. On Christmas Day, 1748, Escandón laid out his first *villa*, Santa María de Llera, for 67 families. At suitable intervals and on favorable sites, other towns were surveyed on the march to the Rio Grande during the spring of 1749. Along the south bank of that river Escandón planned the *villas* of Reynosa and Camargo. A year later an aide planned Revilla (now Guerrero) further upstream.

The plan of Reynosa as drawn at the time of its founding is reproduced in Figure 3.10. Virtually identical designs were used for at least 14 other towns founded by Escandón or at his orders.[52] If his proposals for towns on the lower Nueces and San Antonio rivers had materialized, they doubtless would have taken this form. At Reynosa, as at most of his towns, Escandón planned a square plaza 124 *varas* (345 feet) on each side. The eight streets entering its corners were 12 *varas* (33⅓ feet) wide. Their extension to the limits of the town created blocks of two sizes. Those fronting the plaza measured 100 by 200 *varas* (278 by 556 feet). The four corner blocks were twice this size. All lots measured 20 by 100 *varas* (55½ by 278 feet).[53]

It is possible that an identical or similar plan was used in 1755 when Tomás Sánchez, after securing approval from Escandón, settled with a few families north of the Rio Grande, where he had previously pastured his cattle. Escandón designated this as the *villa* de Laredo, and later that year he reported that 13 families with a population of 62 persons were living at this location in Texas. Escandón authorized this settlement only after directing Sánchez first to examine the site on the Nueces River that he had originally proposed for a town. The Laredo grant was made after Sánchez reported the Nueces River location to be unfavorable. Although Laredo may have consisted mainly of a series of farms, it seems likely that Escandón would have insisted on some kind of town survey.

This is strongly implied in a report submitted by Tienda de Cuervo in 1757 following his tour of inspection of Nuevo Santander. In describing conditions at Laredo he used the designation of "town" or "town of Laredo" at least six times. It then consisted of 11 families with 85 persons.[54] The only graphic record of Laredo during this period is so small in scale that it is difficult to judge if the buildings in the little settlement followed some kind of formal town design. This is reproduced in Figure 3.11, a small section of an enormous map of the new province drawn in

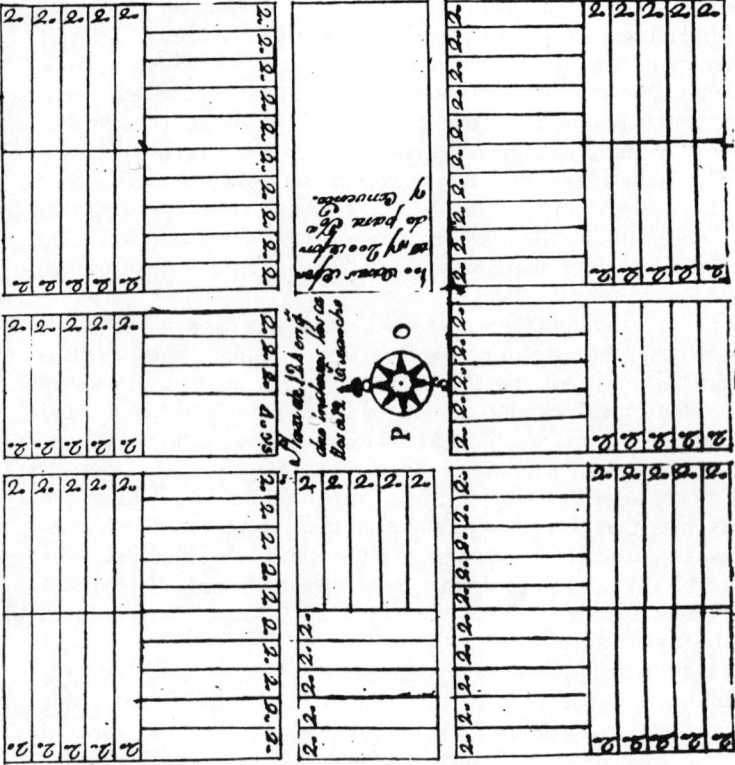

Figure 3.10 Plan of Reynosa, Tamaulipas, Mexico: 1751

1758. At the left appears a sketch of the Rancho de Dolores, ten leagues down the Rio Grande. This, too, Escandón had founded at the time he established Laredo. The drawing indicates that Dolores then had 30 houses and 111 inhabitants. Laredo consisted of only 12 houses and 84 persons, although it continued to bear the more exalted title of *pueblo*.

Laredo may have been given a more precise layout in 1767 when a royal commission arrived in the province to confirm land ownership of individual settlers who until that time held their property only under provisional title. New surveys of the towns were carried out, streets were reduced in width from 12 to 10 *varas*, and sites for public buildings facing the plaza were designated. Laredo, the first settlement visited by the commission, probably was thus surveyed either on a new plan or one that followed the street, block, and lot lines made in 1755.[55]

Escandón's original settlement program included moving the mission and *presidio* at La Bahía and combining them with a civil settlement. He was able to accomplish only the first part of this project when in 1749 he transferred the existing settlements westward to the San Antonio River near the present town of Goliad. Nearby, a second mission, Nuestra Señora del Rosario, was begun 5 years later.[56] Within a few months after the new site was selected the *presidio* consisted of a single barrack 20 feet wide and 70 feet long, a stable, 40 temporary houses for the soldiers and their families, and a more substantial structure for the captain.[57] Twelve years later it was described as being laid out in a square 76 *varas* (210 feet) on each side, stockaded on the north, and with the chapel, guardhouse, barracks, captain's quarters, and several houses nearly completing the enclosure.[58]

The only drawing of the *presidio* of La Bahía on this, its third site is reproduced in Figure 3.12, another of the valuable graphic records of Spanish colonial settlements prepared by Joseph de Urrutia in 1767. The main elements previously described can be clearly seen, and it is obvious from the number of soldiers' houses (identified with the letter "D") that the post had a substantial civil population living in or near the rectangular garrison. Slightly more than a decade later Morfi put the population at "515 persons, including all ages and both sexes and counting the members of the garrison stationed there as well."[59]

One other major Spanish colonization project in the eighteenth century began in 1757 when Colonel Diego Ortiz Parilla led a column of 61 soldiers and missionaries 130 miles northwest of San Antonio with orders to establish a *presidio* and two missions. This action culminated years of discussion about further efforts to pacify the Apaches and secure the outer frontier of Texas. On the north bank of the San Sabá

River, Parilla laid out the Presidio de San Luis de las Amarillas. A few miles downstream on the south side of the river the Franciscans began construction of mission Santa Cruz de San Sabá.[60]

By the spring of 1758 more than 300 persons were living in the *presidio*, of which 237 were women and children. The mission compound, on the other hand, was nearly deserted, since the Apaches stubbornly refused to live under religious supervision in an Indian *pueblo*. In March a series of attacks—not by the Apaches but by their more warlike neighbors to the north, the Comanches—culminated in the destruction of the mission and the massacre of its inhabitants.[61]

A campaign of reprisal against the Indians led by Parilla in 1759 ended in failure. In 1762 missionary activity was transferred to the upper Nueces at a site some 85 miles south of San Sabá and about the same distance west of San Antonio where two missions were founded.[62] The San Sabá *presidio*, however, was allowed to remain, and its new commander, Felipe de Rábago y Terán, began to strengthen it on his arrival in 1760. A year later he reported to the viceroy that he had replaced the rotted stockade, built a stone blockhouse, and dug a moat around the perimeter.[63]

Rábago may have exaggerated the improvements he accomplished, for when the Marqués de Rubí visited the *presidio* in July 1767 on his long tour of inspection of the Spanish northern frontier, he found the fort poorly located and inadequately designed. In a secret message to the viceroy he stated that it was beyond a doubt the worst *presidio* he had seen.[64]

Rubí had not yet visited the Texas *presidios* of San Antonio, Los Adaes, and La Bahía, and it may be that he was totally unprepared for the rather primitive military installations on the borderlands frontier. The plan of the *presidio* of San Sabá drawn at the time of Rubí's inspection and reproduced in Figure 3.13 suggests that, whatever its faults, it was better designed to withstand attack than any of the others in Texas. The northwest corner contained the commander's quarters, chapel, and guardhouse located near the circular tower protecting the principal gate. A smaller tower rose from the southeast corner. Two outlying walls provided access to the river, and the large parade ground was completely enclosed by barracks forming the defensive wall. An elevation of the north side of the fort from the interior can be seen at the top of the drawing.[65]

Renewed Indian attacks and an epidemic in 1768 led Rábago to abandon the fort, and although it was subsequently reoccupied for a time under a new commander, by the summer of 1770 the *presidio* of San

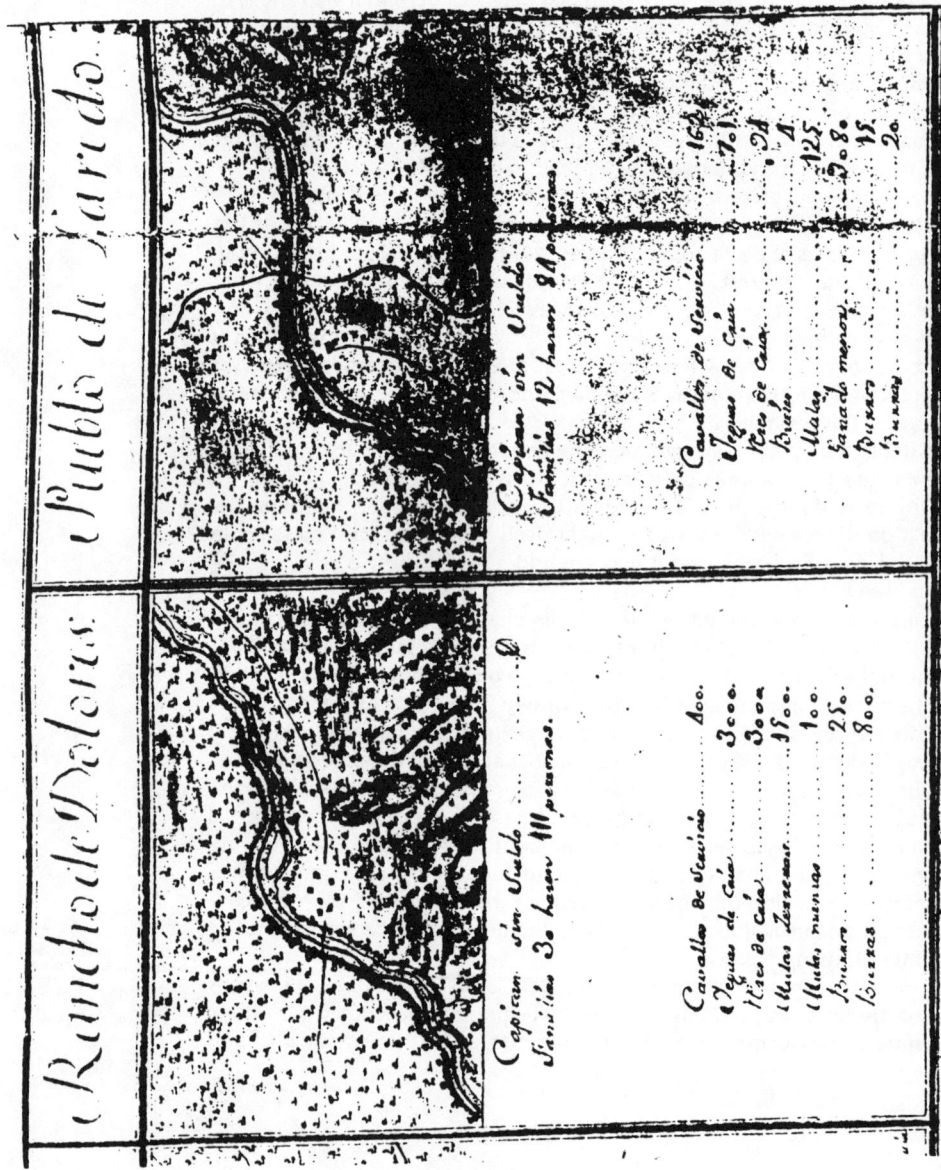

Figure 3.11
Plans of Dolores at
Laredo, Texas 17?

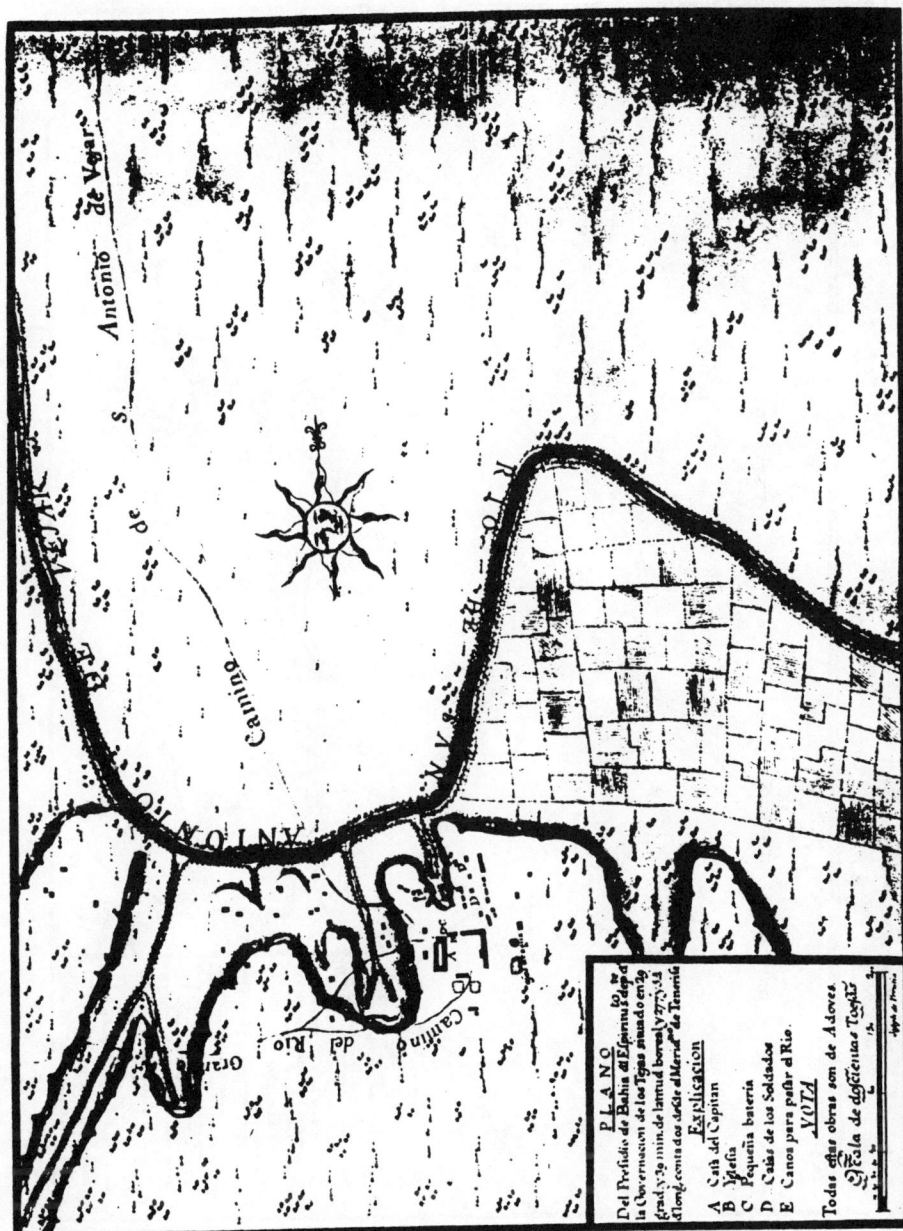

Figure 3.12 Plan of the Presidio of Bahia del Espiritu Santo near Goliad, Texas: 1767

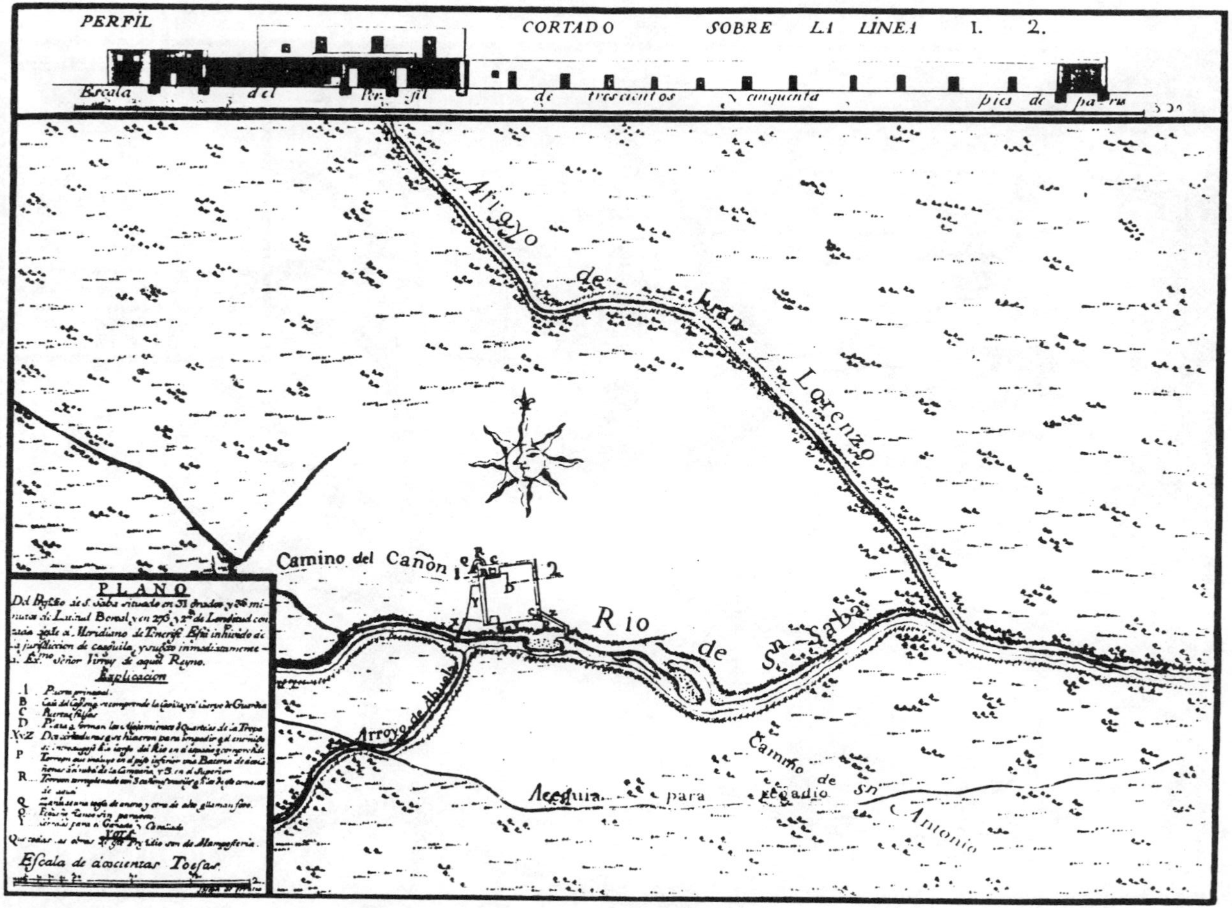
PERFIL
CORTADO SOBRE LA LINEA 1. 2.
Escala del Perfil de trescientos y cinquenta pies de parís
Arroyo de San Lorenzo
Camino del Cañon
Rio de Sn Saba
Arroyo de
Acequia para regadio
Camino de Sn Antonio
PLANO
Explicacion
Escala de docientas Toesas

Figure 3.13 Plan of the Presidio of San Sabá near Menard, Texas: 1767

Sabá lay deserted. Visited over the years by occasional explorers and passed in 1849 by wagon trains bound for the California gold fields, the old *presidio* finally became the temporary home of pioneers moving into this part of Texas in the 1860s. After the town of Menard was platted in 1864, a mile downstream and across the river, stones quarried for the fort were hauled away and used in the construction of a courthouse, jail, and school.[66] Today the fort has been partly restored on its original foundations and stands in the Texas State San Sabá Historic Park as a mute reminder of a colonization effort that failed more than two centuries ago.[67]

The withdrawal from San Sabá marked the beginning of a general retrenchment of Spanish colonial activities in Texas and the Southwest—a period that was to witness in California the last northward thrust of a dying empire. The Marqués de Rubí concluded his tour of inspection in 1768 with a lengthy report and a series of recommendations on how the military defenses of the borderlands should be organized. In 1772 King Charles III incorporated them in his Royal Regulations for Presidios, which reduced the number of forts along the frontier and required the relocation of many others. The decree established a cordon of military posts in an east-west line from Altar, near the Gulf of California, to La Bahía. Except for this latter *presidio* the only other fort within what is now the United States was Tucson. San Antonio and Santa Fe lay well to the north of the presidial cordon. In these two places and at a few other points military posts were to be retained, but the effect of the king's decree was to signal a drastic consolidation of resources and a falling back to the Rio Grande as the real frontier of New Spain.[68]

Rubí seriously considered proposing the abandonment of San Antonio with its five missions, *villa*, and *presidio* but reluctantly concluded that too much money and effort had been expended on these settlements to justify such drastic action.[69] That is precisely what he did recommend, however, for the *presidio* of Los Adaes and the missions in East Texas. There were few logical arguments against such a move. Mission activity there had proved an almost total failure. At the time of Rubí's visit in 1767 not a single Indian was converted to Christianity or even under instruction. Only thirty Spanish families lived in the vicinity of the *presidio*, and the importance of this as a military post had been almost totally eliminated when Louisiana passed to Spanish control in 1762.[70]

The Baron de Ripperdá, governor of Texas in 1773, journeyed to Los Adaes that spring to carry out the new policy. Determined to waste no time, he ordered the evacuation of all residents within five days. On June 25 most of the angry and resentful settlers began the long march to San Antonio, where they had been promised land. Some refused to obey orders and vanished before the march began. Others dropped out on the way. Most of the defectors gathered at El Lobanillo, the ranch of Antonio Gil Ybarbo, who vigorously opposed the policy of evacuation.

At San Antonio the evacuees petitioned to be allowed to return to East Texas, and with the support of Ripperdá their case was put before the viceroy by Ybarbo. Surprisingly, Viceroy Antonio María Bucareli y Ursua granted their request, and although this was later partially rescinded, the matter was eventually left in Ripperdá's hands with the understanding that no settlement would be made within 100 leagues (250 miles) of Natchitoches, the French outpost in western Louisiana. The initial approval had included a stipulation that the settlement would be made in accordance with the Laws of the Indies, and although no plan of the settlement has apparently survived it was under these regulations that Nuestra Señora del Pilar de Bucareli temporarily joined the small number of Spanish civil communities in Texas.[71]

On the west bank of the Trinity River, where the road to Los Adaes crossed the stream, Ybarbo in the fall of 1774 staked out a plaza. Doubtless the streets and house lots were also planned at this time according to the provisions of the laws. The first chapel was replaced two years later by a more substantial church 25 varas (70 feet) long. A little more than a year after its founding Ripperdá reported that the town consisted of a number of huts, 20 houses of hewn timber, and a guardhouse. Two years later he found more than 50 houses in the town, and a number of farms and corrals in the vicinity. Adding to its growth were the persons who had refused to leave East Texas some years earlier and who now moved to the new and apparently permanent town. A census in 1777 revealed the population to consist of 125 men, 87 women, 128 children, and 5 slaves.

Bucareli's life proved short. Comanche raids in 1778 terrorized the settlers. Requests for an armed guard of soldiers were refused. Ybarbo, without authorization from the governor, began to move the settlers eastward toward their former homes where they proposed to settle in the area occupied by friendly Indians. A flood in February, 1779, following a disastrous fire the previous month convinced those remaining that they, too, should join their friends in yet another search for a permanent home.

Sometime in March or April, Ybarbo led his followers to the now deserted mission of Nuestra Señora de Guadalupe de los Nacogdoches near the Angelina River. Although re-settlement in this region was clearly in violation of the Royal Decree in 1772 and the subsequent orders to evacuate East Texas, this re-occupation of the region was eventually approved, and Ybarbo in October 1779 received a commission as captain of the militia and lieutenant governor of the *pueblo* of Nacogdoches.[72]

In view of Ybarbo's previous action in planning Bucareli according to the Laws of the Indies it seems likely that he also surveyed the new site in much the same manner. One of the early plats of Nacogdoches dates from a much later period—1846—and is reproduced in Figure 3.14. The "public square" probably was the plaza of 1779. Eight streets leading from its four corners provided the basis for the familiar gridiron pattern of streets, blocks, and lots where the settlers began to erect their dwellings. The large Washington Square and the site of Nacogdoches University represents a later addition to the town begun in 1845.

Four years later, in 1783, a census of Texas showed that the population of Nacogdoches had reached 349. At that time there were 1,248 persons residing at the San Antonio *presidio* and *villa*. At the *presidio* of La Bahía there were 454 persons, most of whom must have been civilians or the families of soldiers stationed at the fort.[73] When Francisco Xavier Fragoso passed through Nacogdoches on September 23, 1788, he noted that the town consisted of 80 or 90 houses, although he placed the population at only around 250 persons.[74] By 1803 when the population of San Antonio was estimated at 2,500, Nacogdoches was said to have 770 residents. It had then outstripped La Bahía, whose population was thought to be 618.[75]

These three settlements and the surviving missions represented all that the Spanish had been able to accomplish in more than a century of colonizing activities. In the waning years of the empire new efforts were to be made, stimulated by fear of American penetration following the Louisiana Purchase in 1803. A series of proposals for new civil settlements was made by officials and advisers. Perhaps the most elaborate was put forward in 1805 by Governor Manuel Antonio Cordero, who outlined a program of founding towns according to the Laws of the Indies on the Brazos, Trinity, Colorado, San Marcos, and Guadalupe rivers to form a string of settlements along the road from San Antonio to Nacogdoches.[76]

Only two new towns were begun as a result of this proposal. The settlers for the Villa de Salcedo set out from San Antonio in December, 1805, bound for a location on the east bank of the Trinity River opposite the abandoned town of Bucareli. On January 23 the first house lot was conveyed to one José Luis Durán. The town probably was laid out according to the Laws of the Indies, for detailed instructions to this effect had been given to the settlers. The first residents were joined by others from Louisiana, and in the fall of 1809 the population was 101.[77]

News of the new community of Salcedo reached Louisiana and resulted in a flood of applications from residents for permission to settle in Texas, some of them including proposals for founding other new towns. Spanish officials viewed these requests with some suspicion, believing that opening Texas to settlement in this way would only weaken their already tenuous control over the region. Instead, Governor Cordero recruited 16 families from Nuevo Santander in December, 1807, and had them escorted to the San Marcos River, where the Villa de San Marcos de Neve was laid out. Although no plat of the town exists, this also probably followed the Laws of the Indies pattern.

San Marcos enjoyed only a brief existence. A flood in the summer of 1808 caused much destruction, the hardships of frontier life proved too much for many of the settlers, and the Indians continually raided the tiny community. In 1812 the place was abandoned.[78] Trinidad de Salcedo lasted perhaps a year longer, but by 1813 it too stood deserted.[79]

In 1810, a few years after the founding of these short-lived communities, another new town was planned on the southern border of Texas some 30 miles above Laredo. The governor of Coahuila, Antonio Cordero y Bustamente, ordered the commander of the nearest *presidio* in Mexico to establish the *villa* of Palafox on the left bank of the Rio Grande. One Manuel Garza owned the chosen site, and Juan José Díaz, commander of the Presidio del Rio Grande, found it necessary to condemn the land in order to secure proper title. Garza received another large tract in the vicinity as payment.

The plan reproduced in Figure 3.15 shows the design for the town surveyed under Díaz' direction: a square plaza 100 *varas* (277½ feet) on each side, excluding the 13-*vara* (36 feet) streets entering the plaza at each corner. It seems likely that this drawing was intended only to indicate the size and shape of the plaza and the location of the earliest buildings erected facing it, for one of the few surviving records of the town reveals that as early as 1814 there were 36 heads of households residing in the community, while an official census two years later recorded the population as 277 persons.[80]

It proved easier to settle Palafox than to maintain its existence. A series of Comanche raids in 1818 caused its abandonment for 8 years. Although many of the original settlers returned in 1826 to re-occupy the town and resume their farming and ranching activities, they once again

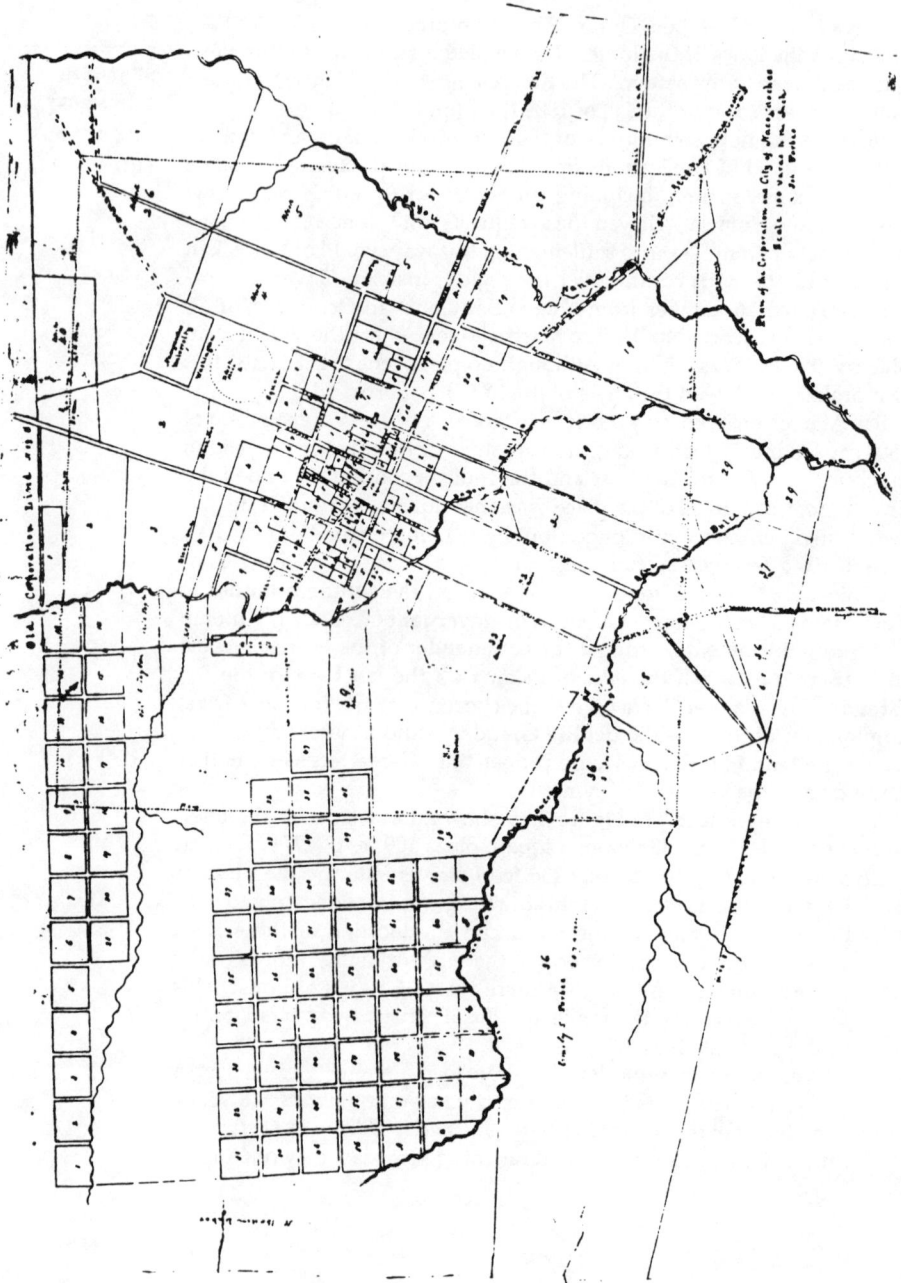

Figure 3.14   Plan of Nacogdoches, Texas: 1846

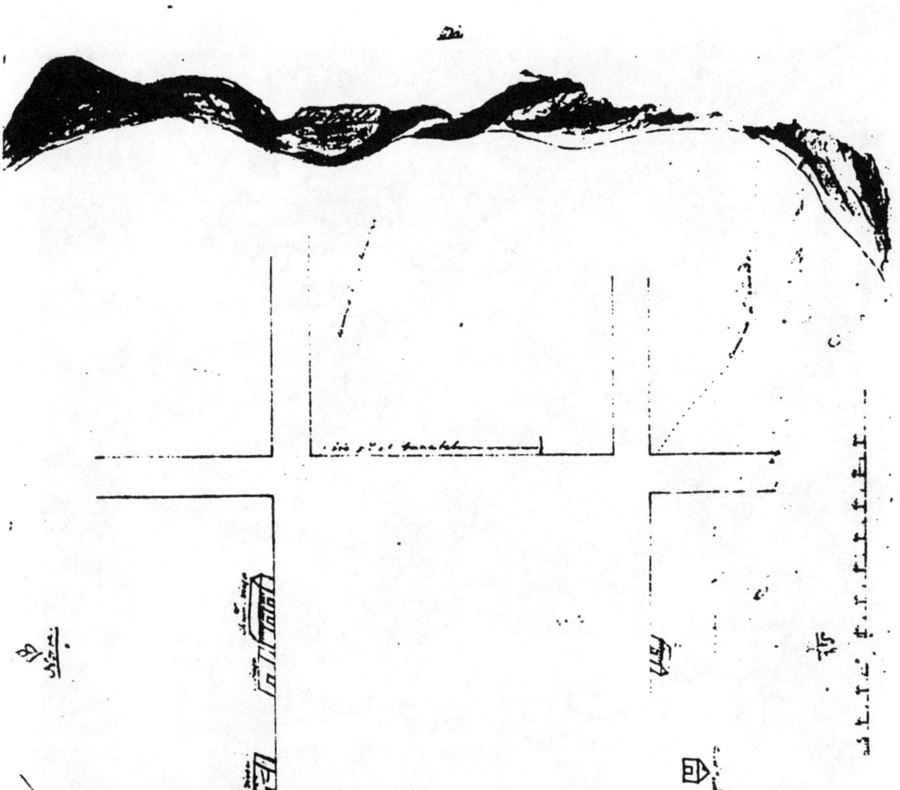

Figure 3.15   Plan of Palafox, Texas: 1824

Figure 3.16 View of Champ d'Asile, Texas: 1830

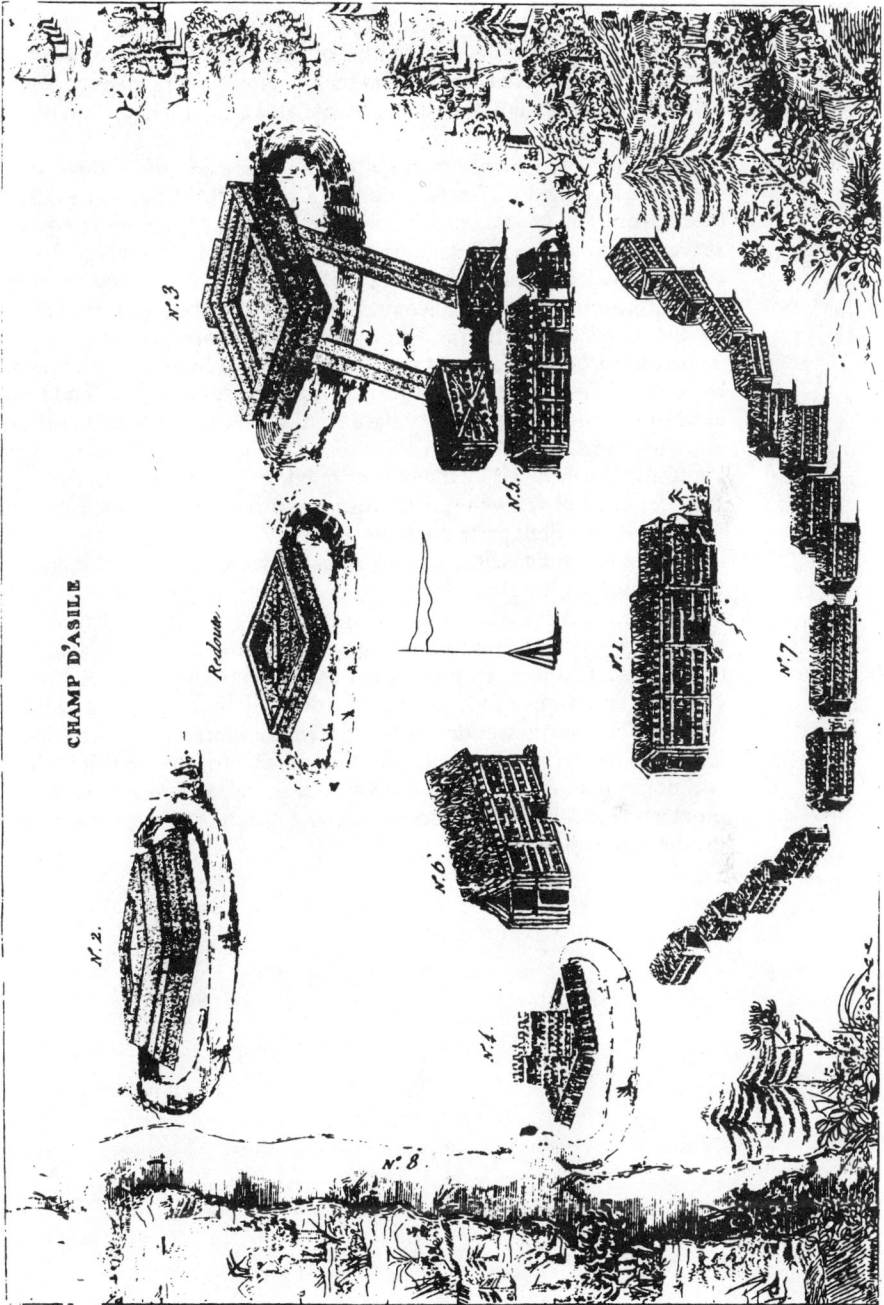

Figure 3.17 View of Champ d'Asile, Texas: 1819

469

found it necessary to evacuate their homes when the Indians soon renewed their attacks. Before the end of the decade the little *villa* had been sacked and destroyed, and no further attempt was made to establish an urban community in this desolate and uninviting portion of the Rio Grande valley.

One other town passed through a brief existence before the end of the Spanish period in Texas. This was Champ d'Asile or Aigleville, a bizarre community with an unusual plan and one begun under equally strange circumstances. In January, 1818, a group of French Napoleonic exiles landed on Galveston Island. There they were joined by their leader, General Charles Lallemand, who, with other former officers, led the party 50 miles up the Trinity River. The general announced that it was his purpose to found a peaceful agricultural community where all land would be held in common. It is more likely that he intended to establish some kind of military base from which exiled French officers and their families could gradually expand their holdings in territory so ineffectively controlled by the now crumbling Spanish empire. Perhaps they dreamed of an even greater future—of an empire of their own in America with a Bonaparte on its throne.[81]

It was a romantic vision; equally so is the view reproduced in Figure 3.16 purporting to show the progress of construction. In the background one can see a massive fort, one of several such structures described by a young Frenchman who participated in the project: "We constructed two earthen forts, each 640 feet around, with eight-foot parapets and twelve-foot ditches surrounded by cut logs, a square, wooden fort twenty feet on a side, and another fort which was not finished, a small wooden redoubt, another called a traverse, a third which was not completed; a covered runway, a hospital, a store, a bakery, and nineteen wooden cabins to serve as living quarters, one of which was for the commander-in-chief, etc."[82]

These buildings appear in the curious view of Champ d'Asile reproduced in Figure 3.17. It was published in France the year after the project began as an illustration in a book describing the colony. It was already out of date. The Spanish had learned of the French invasion and had begun to mobilize, food ran short at the new town, promised supplies never arrived, and by the end of the summer the entire company retired to Galveston Island.[83]

Texas did not seem to be a region in which towns and cities could thrive. Certainly Spanish colonial policy had produced little in the way of urban life. Civil settlements and presidial towns were few in number and small in size. Secularization of the missions in the latter part of the eighteenth century proved as disastrous for the Indian neophytes in Texas as it was to be in California some decades later.[84] Although some of the mission lands, such as those at La Bahía, were to be incorporated into later towns, the Texas mission system itself did not result in the creation of permanent towns for Indians as contemplated by Spanish law and practice.

It was, therefore, a largely pastoral Texas over which an independent Mexico assumed jurisdiction when that new nation began its existence in 1821. Mexican colonization policies adopted after that year changed this situation swiftly and irrevocably. In deciding to open the Texas borders to settlement from abroad the Mexican government achieved in a few years what Spain had labored unsuccessfully to accomplish for more than a century.

This decision, however, brought to Texas a predominantly English-speaking population with cultural and political backgrounds quite different from those who previously had inhabited the land. The clash of these two cultures as it affected the planning of towns will be examined in a later chapter after an exploration of Spanish and Mexican colonial planning accomplishments in Arizona and California.

Titles in the Series

1. The Idea of Spanish Borderlands
   Edited by David J. Weber
2. Native American Demography
   Edited by Clark Spencer Larsen
3. Ethnology of the Alta California Indians
   I: Precontact
   Edited by Lowell John Bean and Sylvia Brakke Vane
4. Ethnology of the Alta California Indians
   II: Postcontact
   Edited by Lowell John Bean and Sylvia Brakke Vane
5. Ethnology of the Baja California Indians
   Edited by W. Michael Mathes
6. Ethnology of Northwest Mexico
   Edited by Randall H. McGuire
7. Ethnology of the Texas Indians
   Edited by Thomas R. Hester
8. Ethnology of the Indians of Spanish Florida
   Edited by David Hurst Thomas
9. The Native American and Spanish Colonial Experience in the Greater Southwest
   I: Introduction to the Documentary Records
   Edited by David H. Snow
10. The Native American and Spanish Colonial Experience in the Greater Southwest
    II: Introduction to Research
    Edited by David H. Snow

11. The Hernando de Soto Expedition
Edited by Jerald T. Milanich
12. Earliest Hispanic-Native American Interactions in the American Southeast
Edited by Jerald T. Milanich
13. Hispanic-Native American Interactions in the Caribbean
Edited by William F. Keegan
14. Documentary Evidence for the Spanish Missions of Alta California
Edited by Julia G. Costello
15. The Archaeology of Alta California
Edited by Leo R. Barker and Julia G. Costello
16. The Spanish Missions of Baja California
Edited by Robert H. Jackson
17. The Spanish Missions of New Mexico
I: Before 1680
Edited by John L. Kessell
18. The Spanish Missions of New Mexico
II: After 1680
Edited by John L. Kessell and Rick Hendricks
19. The Jesuit Missions of Northern Mexico
Edited by Charles W. Polzer, Thomas H. Naylor, Thomas E. Sheridan, and Diana W. Hadley
20. The Franciscan Missions of Northern Mexico
Edited by Thomas E. Sheridan, Charles W. Polzer, Thomas H. Naylor, and Diana W. Hadley
21. Archaeology of the Spanish Missions of Texas
Edited by Anne A Fox
22. Documentary Evidence for the Spanish Missions of Texas
Edited by Arthur R. Góme
23. The Missions of Spanish Florida
Edited by David Hurst Thomas
24. Pedro Menéndez de Avilés
Edited by Eugene Lyon
25. America's Ancient City
Spanish St. Augustine: 1565–1763
Edited by Kathleen A. Deagan
26. Native American Perspectives on the Hispanic Colonization of Alta California
Edited by Edward Castillo
27. Hispanic Urban Planning in North America
Edited by Daniel J. Garr